A MODERN ENGLISH GRAMMAR

by the same author

A MODERN ENGLISH GRAMMAR ON HISTORICAL PRINCIPLES
IN SEVEN PARTS

LANGUAGE : ITS NATURE, DEVELOPMENT AND ORIGIN

HOW TO TEACH A FOREIGN LANGUAGE

CHAPTERS ON ENGLISH

AN INTERNATIONAL LANGUAGE

NOVIAL LEXIKE

THE PHILOSOPHY OF GRAMMAR

MANKIND, NATION AND INDIVIDUAL

LINGUISTICA

THE SYSTEM OF GRAMMAR

ANALYTIC SYNTAX

GROWTH AND STRUCTURE OF THE ENGLISH LANGUAGE

A MODERN ENGLISH GRAMMAR

ON HISTORICAL PRINCIPLES

OTTO JESPERSEN

Part VI
MORPHOLOGY

GEORGE ALLEN & UNWIN LTD
LONDON

EJNAR MUNKSGAARD
COPENHAGEN

REPRINTED IN GREAT BRITAIN 1954

PRINTED IN GREAT BRITAIN

BY BRADFORD & DICKENS
DRAYTON HOUSE
LONDON, W.C.1

Preface

I lectured on English Morphology in 1925, just before I resigned my professorship in the University of Copenhagen. Those lectures, based as they were on many years' collection of material, were not at that time written out for publication and lay for some time quietly in my drawers. But when, some years later, the directors of the Carlsberg Foundation—that unique institution, the mainstay of scientific work in Danmark —generously granted me a yearly sum with which to pay assistants in my scientific labours, I engaged three young philologists to work out with me this part of my Modern English Grammar, Paul Christophersen, M. A. (now Ph. D.), Niels Haislund, M. A., and Knud Schibsbye, M. A. (now Ph. D.). I assigned one part of my book to each of them, gave them my instructions, and handed over to them my first draft, so far as that was written, as well as my thousands of slips and notes. Mr. Schibsbye (denoted in what follows with his initials KS) worked with me for a short time only. Mr. Christophersen (PC) worked with very great ability on his part of the book until in 1939 he went to England, from where he has not been able to return after what happened to our country on April the 9th, 1940. This left me with only Mr. Haislund (NH) to finish the book, and he has thus done the lion's share of the whole. I want on this occasion publicly to express my great gratitude to all my three co-adjutors, without whose valuable assistance this part of my life's work would never have seen the light of day. But I owe a special debt of thankfulness to Niels Haislund, who has not only with the greatest diligence and conscientiousness worked out the great part allotted to him—for much of which I had done less preparatory work than for the rest, so that he had to do independent research work, but who has also assisted me in various other ways, making fair copies of my own contributions and finally reading the proofs with extreme care and thus contributing very considerably to the correctness of this book.

I give here a list showing what parts of the volume have been written by each of us. Some parts are based on papers I have myself published, viz. 9.7 (*housekeep*) in EStn 70, 1935; 12.1 ff (voiced and voiceless) in *Linguistica* 379 ff, 1933; 15.1 (*-ster*) in *Modern Language Review* 1927 (here reduced from eight to two pages), 17 (group-genitive) in *Progress in Language* 1894 (here with a number of new quotations), and 20.5 (verbs in *-en*) in *Acta Linguistica* 1939 (here shortened); 26.1 ff (negative prefixes *un-* and *in-*) in *Negation* 1917.

Chapter	
I	OJ '39
II	NH/OJ
III	OJ/NH/OJ
IV	PC/OJ
V	PC/OJ
5.7	(PC)/OJ
VI	OJ & PC/OJ
6.1	OJ '25
VII	PC/OJ
7.4-6	OJ(PC) '37
VIII	OJ/PC/OJ
8.9	OJ
IX	PC/OJ
9.7₁	OJ '35
X	OJ
XI-XII	PC/OJ
XIII-XV	NH/OJ
15.1	OJ '27/'41
XVI	OJ '25/KS
16.8	OJ '25
16.9	OJ '25 & '41
XVII	OJ 1894/KS/OJ '37
17.9	OJ 1894/'37

The manuscripts of these collaborators have been revised by me at different times, sometimes immediately after they were written, sometimes much later, and not seldom more than once.

In consequence of the manuscripts having in some instances passed to and fro between others and myself it would now be difficult for me to decide which particulars are due to me and which to my co-workers. But anyhow the full responsibility for any shortcomings rests with me exclusively.

My alterations have in some cases been very slight, in others much more thorough; but my chief endeavour has throughout been to cut down all prolixity and to remove what seemed superfluous so as not to make the volume too bulky. If I had not, the volume might easily have been bigger than it is by half its size. At the last moment I decided to leave out here what had been written on -er and -est in the comparative and superlative and to remove it to vol VII. All the same I am afraid that many readers will find the volume too big as it is and will wonder why I have included so many very rare words, even nonce-words. This, of course, would have been useless if the book had been a prescriptive, normative grammar, but in a historical grammar not meant for beginners such things will have their importance as showing the possibilities and tendencies of the language.

Some unevenness in the treatment has been unavoidable on account of the work being distributed among so many hands, which might, perhaps, have been better coordinated. In some cases my young friends have contributed quotations from their own collections and have not always used the same editions of standard authors as I have myself, but this inconvenience has not been deemed very important.

It is a worse drawback that the nature of linguistic phenomena often leads to the possibility of placing one and the same phenomenon in different chapters and thus assigning it to different writers; this has in some cases led to repetitions which it is hoped that the benevolent user will excuse, as well as to many cross-references to other chapters and to previous volumes.

When writing the first four volumes of my Grammar I was in constant touch with friends in England, most of them competent scholars, whom I was able to consult on knotty points. If it had been possible I should very often have done the same with regard to this volume, but to my great regret the unfortunate happenings to my country during this miserable war have prevented me from asking the advice of native Englishmen. A few pages, however, were revised by the then lecturer in the University of Copenhagen, Mr. A. F. Colburn, before he was forced to leave Denmark. Something is rotten in the state of the world. May Heaven direct it!

Volume VII, the final part of the Syntax, of which a few chapters have already been written, will bring this work to a close.

Finally I must repeat my sincere thanks to the directors of the Carlsberg Foundation for their very generous subvention, which has made it possible to write and to print this volume.

Lundehave, Helsingør (Elsinore), in February 1942.

Otto Jespersen.

Contents

Chapter I

Introduction

General Plan

1.1. I have dealt with the division of grammar into Morphology and Syntax in various places, chiefly in PG p. 37 ff., but also in *The System of Grammar* (in Linguistica p. 304 ff., also separately) and *Analytic Syntax*. Though I do not in every respect follow the system sketched in PG, I still adhere to its fundamental idea, namely the possibility and necessity of viewing things grammatical from two opposed angles, from without (forms) and from within (notions). The former part of grammar (O→I) I term *Morphology*, the latter (I→O) *Syntax*. The former represents the point of view of the hearer, who perceives the form (sound or string of sounds) and has to interpret it; the latter is the point of view of the speaker, who wants to express his thoughts and therefore has to 'clothe' them in certain forms. The same grammatical facts may be, and have to be, viewed from both points of view, but the classification and arrangement must be totally different according as the facts are seen from without or from within.

In Morphology the first thing to be considered is the form, and second to that comes the use made of it, in Syntax the order is exactly the reverse, but it is essential that in both parts of the grammar form *and* use should be mentioned in every case.

1.2. To take an obvious example. In Morphology we deal with the *s*-ending in its triple sub-forms in the spoken language [z, s, iz] and then say that it denotes

(1) the plural of a substantive—as in *kings*—, (2) the genitive singular—as in *king's*—, (3) the genitive plural —as in *kings'*, cp. *dukes | duke's | dukes', princes | prince's | princes'*—and (4) the third person singular of verbs—as in *sings*, cp. *sinks, kisses*. One and the same form may in some cases be a plural of a substantive and the third person of a verb: *rings*. But such forms as the plurals *men, oxen, sheep*, and the third person singular *can* belong to totally different chapters of Morphology.

In Syntax, on the other hand, *kings, men, oxen, sheep*, etc., are classed together, and the various uses of the substantival plural—no matter how formed—are dealt with (as seen in our volume II) more in detail than in Morphology, where the bare indication 'plural of substantive' is sufficient. In another chapter of our Syntax (in vol VII) the uses of the genitive are dealt with, etc.

The relation between *send* : *sent* and *descend* : *descent* is formally identical, but the sound *d* : *t* changes one word from the verbal base to a preterit or participle, and another from the verbal base to a nexus substantive, and while in Morphology it forms two subdivisions of the same 'consonantal change', in Syntax we find it in two widely separated chapters.

As one and the same grammatical thing has to be considered from the two angles, only more succinctly from one than from the other, it will in some cases be more or less arbitrary where to place the fuller and where to place the less full treatment.

1.3. Perfect consistency is very difficult to achieve. It would lead, for instance, to such consequences as placing the vowel-change in *abide* (vb) and *abode* (sb) at the same place as that in *ride* (inf) and *rode* (prt), or *food* (sb) and *feed* (vb) together with *foot* (sg) and *feet* (pl)—and this has also been done below in this volume of Morphology. But the curious interplay of

form and sense leads naturally to some inconsistencies
which may puzzle the reader here and there. In vol V
12.2 and 12.3 it has been found practical to deal with
the use of the forms *dare | dares, need | needs* in the
3rd person sg together with the use of the bare infinitive and *to*. But below, under the ending *-s* in the
present, will be found a cross-reference to the treatment
in vol V.

The most important deviation from the general plan
will be found below in chapters 2—5, in which for
practical reasons I have placed together the various
formal changes found in the flexion of the verbs. In
ordinary grammars these are treated as part of Accidence. Their most natural place would have been in the
beginning of vol IV (Time and Tense), and this arrangement has also been followed in the corresponding part
of *Essentials of Eng. Grammar* Ch. 23. The ending *-st*
in the second person has thus been separated from
-(e)st in the superlative, etc., and *-s* in the third person
from *-s* in sbs, etc. In this way *-s* and *-th* have come
together. But I call attention to the fact that I have
thus been led to the treatment under *-st* of some phenomena which from the syntactical point of view belong
under the chapter on the use of the subjunctive and
will be referred to again under that heading in vol VII.

Koziol

1.4. When two-thirds of this volume had been
written and were nearly ready to be printed, a book
appeared that covered a great part of the same ground,
Herbert Koziol, *Handbuch der englischen Wortbildungs-
lehre* (Heidelberg 1937). It will not be found inappro-
priate that I present here a comparison of the two
books so as to bring into view the chief differences
between them: it is not meant as a criticism of Koziol's
very able and extremely useful work.

(1) Koziol takes into consideration the whole extent of the English language from the oldest times, while this volume in accordance with the plan of the preceding volumes deals with the modern period only, though, as it is "on historical principles", with occasional glances at the earlier periods. I lay also more stress than Koziol on what are really in Present English living, i. e. productive, formations.

(2) Koziol's book deals with word-formation only and thus follows the traditional division of grammar, in which this part is strictly separated from the theory of flexions, generally termed accidence (formenlehre). I do not recognize this distinction as fundamental and therefore include here flexions; where they use the same or similar formal means as word-formation I treat both together.

(3) The arrangement in this volume is (with the exception mentioned in 1.3) strictly according to forms: what is identical in form is treated together, while Koziol often separates it according to its place in the traditional scheme of word-classes, placing e. g. substantives in -*an* in §§ 439—440 and adjectives with the same ending in §§ 544—548. His subdivisions are often of a purely semantic nature, for instance, diminutives, names of persons, of things, and abstracts, dealing, e. g., with words in -*ness* in § 466 (concrete) and § 479 (abstract),—but the same division would apply to other derivatives as well, where Koziol does not mention it. Koziol throughout keeps apart native and foreign formatives, which cannot always be thus sharply separated.

(4) Koziol's book is in so far old-fashioned as it really speaks of the written language, i. e. letters, only, with very little regard to the actual sounds, which to me, as a matter of course, are of fundamental importance. The phonetic difference between *create* and *creation, creature*, between *Gladstone* and *Gladstonian*, to take only two

examples, is nowhere hinted at in his treatment. Nor is there any mention of such an important thing in word-formation as the stress-shifting in *record* sb and vb.

(5) Koziol's book is based chiefly, though not exclusively, on previous treatments of each subject; in his notes he cites not a few monographs that were inaccessible to me. On the other hand I have relied mainly on the material collected independently through a long life's occupation with English language and literature supplemented in part by my young coadjutors themselves. This book therefore gives a great many more quotations from the actual use in English and American writers, and besides being fuller has on the whole a much more personal character than Koziol's. In this way I think I have been able to clear up many points left unexplained by my predecessors. Here also the arrangement according to purely formal criteria has been of assistance. I may perhaps mention the chapters on -*en* as particularly illustrative because they bring together things that previously were torn apart; one point only: Koziol's remark (§ 626) that adjective-forms may be "used as verbs" even where verbs with -*en* are already in existence really turns the historical facts upside down.

1.5. This volume naturally falls into five parts:

Part I. Verbal flexions, Chs. 2—5.

Part II. The naked word (i. e. the kernel without any formative either before or after), Chs. 6—12.

Part III. Endings (i. e. the kernel with formatives added after it), Chs. 13—25).

Part IV. Prefixes (i. e. the kernel with something placed before it), Chs. 26—28).

Part V. Shortenings (i. e. the kernel minus something, Ch. 29.

Chapter II

Personal Endings in Verbs

Second Person Singular

2.1. In OE the earliest form was *-s* (*bindes, dēmes*, cf.
Goth. *bindis, dōmeis*). The later *-st* is no doubt due to
the frequent use of combinations of verb and the
pronoun *þū* : *-s þ-* > *-s t-*, thus *bindes þū* > *bindestū*,
later interpreted as *bindest* (*þ*)*ū*; the *-st* form then was
transferred to *þū bindest*, etc.

This explanation is found, though expressed with
some doubt, in Kluge PGr[2] 1067, as also in Kaluza,
but neither in Sievers nor Sweet. The same explanation is given of *-st* in German (Early OHG has *-s*), e. g.
in Paul Gramm 2.192.—Wright OEGr 247 supplements
the explanation with analogy from forms like *wāst,*
þearft, scealt, etc.

Note. Why *-s* in the 2. pers. sg and not *-z*, as was to be
expected according to Verner's law? (Cf ON *-r* < *-z*). This is
explained by the assimilation to the frequently following pron.
tū < *þū;* thus Wilmanns 2 p. 6, Streitberg Urg. 320: unter
mitwirkung der häufig gebrachten athematischen einsilbigen
formen. Cf Loewe 147 f., Wright OEGr 247.

-(e)st occurred in OE, only in pres ind: *bindest* or
bintst, lufast, and in prt ind of weak verbs: *lufodest;*
but not in pres subj: *binde, lufie*, prt ind of strong
verbs: *bunde* [properly from the subj], prt subj: *bunde,*
lufode.

In Late OE *-st* was extended to the prt subj of weak
verbs: *lufodest* (Sweet NEG § 1189; seemingly not
mentioned in other OE grammars).

2.2. ME has *-est* corresponding to OE *-est, -ast, -st*.

In Juliana there is a clear distinction between weak
verbs with *-st* and strong verbs without *-st*.

AR has -s in 108 hwat tu þouhtes & souhtes þo þu
uorsoke thene world.

And Orrm Dedication l. 11 icc hafe don swasumm
þu badd... þu þohhtesst.

Ch has several examples of strong verbs without -st:
B 848 thow sawe (ind) | B 3641 thou gaf | R 7453 whan
thou him saugh | R 7519 thou spake | H 294 thou
songe whylom.

Even in Malory: 111 thow took, but 113 sawest
thou. Here also 141 where thou was.

In Southern OE -e- was more or less regularly syncopated, as in *bintst* < *bindest*, etc., but preserved in
Anglian, see Sievers-Cook § 358.2 (p. 260 f.).

In ME -e- was generally preserved, thus in the present
and the prt of weak verbs Ch A 1142 *woldést* | A 1602
and 1603 *sholdést* | A 2377 *fortunést* | A 2387 *haddést* |
B 106 *blamést* | B 639 *savédést*, etc., but in accordance
with OE *darst* | *seyst* | *mayst*, etc.

2.3₁. The general loss in Early ModE of weak *e* in
the endings also affected -e- in -est, which was dropped
in speech except after sibilants [s z ʃ ʒ]. "But in the
higher language the full endings -est, -eth, -ed were
freely used after all consonants indifferently, especially
in poetry, for the sake of the metre" (Sweet), a statement which also holds good of later language.

In ElE syncopated forms are extremely frequent. In
verse drama and poetry the elision of *e* of course may
generally be ascertained from rhythm and rime. Further,
the elision is often indicated by an apostrophe, or the
e is simply left out. But in prose, in cases where *e* is
printed, of course nothing can be decided.

Marlowe has many forms with syncope. But T 2193
diest two syllables.

From ElE I have noted the following forms of the
strong preterit, all with syncope:

Marlowe F [Tucker Brooke's ed.] 208 knewst | Arden
IV. 3. 58 cam'st | IV. 4. 91 drewst | ib V. 5.8 knewest |

Sh Ado I. 1. 313 beganst | BJo P III. 4. 413 stunkst | Ford 128 cam'st.

Sh has e. g. *got'st* (3 times) and *took'st* (twice).

Ford seems to have syncopated forms only. Thus also Mi PL 1.19 *know'st* | 180 *seest* | 2.696 *reckon'st* | 697 *breath'st*, etc. Even such harsh forms as 5.38 *sleep'st* | 5.175 *meet'st* | 12.610 Whence thou *returnst*, and whither *wentst*, I know.

2.3₂. But from the latter part of the 18th c. poets frequently use forms with *e* pronounced, thus Blake, but also e. g. *deal'st*, | *Pray'st* | 203, 220 *know'st*, etc.

Wordsw prefers syncopated forms, even such as 121 *greet'st* | 224 *worshipp'st*, though forms with *e* occur. Thus also Scott Lady of the Lake in which I have noticed no forms with *e*.

From Shelley I have 41 *feel'st* | 106 *speakest* (1 syllable) | 250 *Leap'st*, whereas forms with *e* abound.

The preterit of weak (and originally regular) verbs in ModE has practically always syncope:

Lyly C 287 wentst | Spenser FQ 5.11.16 sauedst | Mi SA 781 show'dst | ib 1135 Feign'dst | ib 1188 stripp'dst (but PL 4.724 madést) | Cowper 34 madest (1 syllable) | Blake P 5 pitchedst | Lamb E 1.12 enteredst | Scott Lady of the Lake 4.10 saidst | Browning said'st | Arnold 289 shared'st | ib 267 lov'dst. But perfect consistency is rare.

2.3₃. The preterit of *do* is nearly always syncopated: Roister 73, 81 dydst | 85 didst. Sh has Hml IV. 7.58 Thus diddest thou—to be read as two syllables, though Q₂ has Thus didst.

Thus also the preterit of *have* : *hadst*, though Spenser has FQ 1.2.18 haddést. The syncope must here be old, as Ch has nadstow (A 3780, 4088).

Syncope of the preterit of *shall* is frequent in Early ModE. But *couldést, shouldést, wouldést* may be found in poets from the 18th and 19th centuries (Blake, Scott, etc.).

Present tense of *dare* and *may* always one syllable (spelt darst, dar'st, darest; maist, mayst, may'st, etc.).

From OE times the present tense of *say* has been a monosyllable. Browning has *sayést* at least once (1.568).

In the second person present of *do* which in OE was a monosyllable, a differentiation similar to that of *doth* and *doeth* (see 3.7) seems to be developing, *dost* being used as an auxiliary and *doest* as an independent verb.

2.4. Heavy groups like *-stst* are often alleviated. As early as OE we have the haplological *bierst* for *bierstst* from *berstan* (Sweet AS Reader lxi, cf Sievers² § 359 note 2). Similar forms are frequent in ME and in ElE, though the spellings are generally normalized in modern editions of the latter. Examples:

Sh Cor III. 2.128 Do as thou list || LLL V. 2.208 requests | Meas II. 2.20 exists | Lear IV. 6.166 lusts || Sonn 19 fleets | Meas II. 2.116 splits | Hml. I. 4.53 revisits || Marlowe T 4120 respects | Sh Merch IV. 1.22 exact'st F; Qq exacts | Cy III. 3.103 refts.

After *-ed* the heavy combination of consonants is also often avoided: Caxton R 110 forsest [for forcedest] and deceyuedest | Marlowe E 1545 watcht...and headed. Especially characteristic is Sh Tp I. 2.333 Thou stroakst me, and made much of me | Tit II. 3.144 suck'st [modern editions suck'dst, as the sense requires the preterit]. Always *thou must* (OE *most*, perfecto-present).

2.5₁. At rather an early stage of ME (especially in Northern ME) the form of the 3rd person comes to be used for that of the 2nd person, both in the present and the preterit. Thus possibly in Ch HF 1908 bringes : tydinges. Further, Towneley 23 thou maide...wroght ...myght | 26 thou was | 34 and 177 shall thou | 177 thou shedys...thou shall...thou has done | 178 thou dyd | Gammer 126 thou met (ind) | 117 if thou had kept (but 118 if thou hadst tarried...thou wouldst).

Forms in *-s* from the third person singular occur as

early as ElE; in some cases they may be considered
phonetic weakenings of *-st:*

Arden I. 138 thou that comes | I. 305 what makes
thou | III. 5.74 thou has | III. 5.125 Why speakes
thou not? Sh Sonn 8 chide thee, who confounds [riming
with *sounds*] In singlenesse the parts | Sterne M 1.29
and when thou viewest him in that light too, and
reckons up his friends and musters up with them the
many recruits.

2.5₂. After *thou* was supplanted by *you* as the general
pronoun of address (see vol VII Cases in Pronouns),
the *-est* form has been kept alive in literature. The
artificialiality of *thou* explains the fact that poets not
infrequently forget to add the ending, especially if
several words are found between *thou* and the verb:

By Ch 1.22 There thou, too, Vathek! England's
wealthiest son, Once form'd thy Paradise | 4.83 Thou,
who didst...ere thou wouldst...thou, who with thy
frown Annihilated senates...thou didst... | 4.132 And
thou, who never yet of human wrong Left the unbalanced
scale...Thou who didst call... | Shelley PU 1.770 till
thou, O King of sadness, Turned by thy smile the
worst I saw to recollected gladness | Shelley 670 Thou
lovest—but ne'er knew love's sad satiety | Burns 438
thou sat...thou drank...thou wad be found.

In Tennyson's Northern Farmer the *s* of the third
person singular has been extended to all forms of the
present of most verbs, thus also the second person, e. g.
229 tha knaws | 231 Doesn't thou | thou's an ass | thou's
beän talkin' | thou's sweet upo' parson's lass.

Quakers (Friends) use *thee* (formerly also *thou*, see
vol VII, Amr Speech IV. 359—363) as their only pronoun of address, and then generally with the form of
the 3rd person of the verb, though forms like *art, shalt,
hast* may occur rather frequently:

Fox 2.145 what thou said | 2.183 thou knows | 2.184
thou considers | 2.195 thou quotes | 2.196 and 230

thou says | 2.247 thou never gave him. But ib 2.183
and 196 hast thou | 2.200 thou wouldst | 2.229 thou
hast | 2.230 thou shalt.

On contracted forms of the 2nd person, such as *th'art, thou'тt*
for *thou art, thou wert, thou'lt* for *thou wilt, thou'dst* for *thou
wouldst, thou'st* or *th'ast* for *thou hast*, etc. see vol VII, Case
in Pronouns.

2.61. The *-st* originally belonged to the indicative
only, but in Late OE it was used in the preterit, where
we should expect a subjunctive, e. g. Apoll. 20 gif ðu
me lufodest þu hit besorgodest | Wulfstan 259 sceoldest |
feddest | gecyddest | sceoldest | 260 sealdest (but in
the present gif þu wene ... hæbbe ... sy... mæge).

These forms witness to a conflict between the feeling
for the subjunctive and that for the pronoun *thou* and
the ending *-st* as belonging together, in which the
latter gained the upper hand.

In the present, too, *-st* has encroached on the territory
of the subjunctive, because authors have felt that *thou*
always required *-st*. That these *-st*-forms should really
be considered as subjunctives is clear from the not
infrequent occurrence of the form *be'st*.

Note. It is a remarkable fact that all the examples of indicative
used after (*an*) *if*, etc. for subjunctive quoted by Franz[3] 527
§ 644a except one are in sentences with *thou*.

Examples with *-st:*
Sh As I. 1.153 if thou dost ... or if hee doe not |
Ado I. 1.287 if euer thou doost fall from this faith,
thou wilt proue a notable argument | ib I. 1.310 If
thou dost loue faire Hero, cherish it | ib V. 1.79 If thou
kilst me, boy, thou shalt kill a man | Lr I. 4.5, ib II.
2.5, II. 2.26 | Mcb V. 5.41 | AV Job 33.32 If thou hast
any thing to say | ib 35.6 If thou sinnest | but ib 35.7
If thou be righteous | ib 38.4 if thou hast understanding |
Ford 102 if thou dost— | Wordsw 180 if thou goest,

1 follow | Scott Lady of the Lake 2.14 if thou join'st
a suitor's claim.

2.6₂. Examples with ordinary subjunctive and *-st*
form close together:

Lyly E 59 If thou hast belyed women, he will iudge
thee vnkinde: if thou haue reuealed the troth, he must
needes thinke thee vnconstant | Sh Sonn 3 Whose
fresh repaire if now thou not renewest ... But if thou
liue | Hml I. 1.128 If thou hast ... If there be any
good thing ... if thou art ... Or, if thou hast (cf As
I. 2.155) | AV Gen 4.7 If thou doe well, shalt thou not
be accepted? and if thou doest not well, sinne lieth at
the doore | AV Prov 6.1 if thou be surety for thy friend,
if thou hast stricken thy hand with a stranger (also ib
Lev 25.14, Tobit 4.8, Matth 5.23).

Examples of *be'st:*

Marlowe F 381 whether thou beest with me, or no |
Sh As I. 3.46 Within these ten daies if that thou beest
found ... Thou diest for it | Alls II. 3.107 if thou be'st
not an asse, I am a youth of fourteene | Lr I. 4.23,
Mcb V. 7.15 | Scott Iv 33 help me an thou beest a man |
Shelley Prom II. 3.12 And if thou beest The shadow
of some spirit lovelier still (thus in Shelley's MS according to Locock; in all editions corrected to *be*).

2.7₁. In some verbs, especially the perfecto-presents,
we find *-t* instead of *-st*, thus *art*, OE *eart*, *shalt*, OE
scealt (dial. also *shat*, e. g. Fielding), OE *þearft*, *wāst*
obsolete, *wilt*, OE *wilt*, ME also *wolt*, in ElE rarely
woo't, e. g. Sh Hml V. 1.298 woo't weepe? woo't fight?
woo't faste? woo't tear thyself? | Ant IV. 2.7, IV. 15.59,
see further Franz[3] 174 (§ 176),

May in the 2nd pers. sg was OE *meaht*, *miht*, preserved
till the ME period; but in the 14th cent. the analogical
form *maist*, *mayst* arose, from the 15th cent. also *mayest*;
pronounced [meist] more often than [meiist].

Other perfecto-presents had *-st* already in OE: *canst*,
dearst 'darest', *manst*, *monst* 'intendest', *ahst* 'hast'.

2.7₂. In the second person of the past tense of *be* the OE form was (*þu*) *wære* both in the ind and subj; it is still found sometimes in the 16th c. as *thou were* (Sir Thomas Elyot, Roister, Puttenham, see Fitzedward Hall, Mod. E. 79), but the ordinary ModE forms are the analogical *wert* and *wast*.

I have noted *wert* (as ind) in the following authors: Lyly (C 317), Marlowe (J 1235, E 984), Sh (R2 III. 2.73 hearing thou wert dead | Tit I. 1.339 when wer't thou wont to walke alone | Sonn 20.9, 82.1, etc.), Dekker (S 8, etc.), Eastw (485), Massinger, Mi (PL 3.9 before the heavens thou wert | ib 8.623 pure thou wert created), Otway (221, 265, etc.), Congreve (179), Defoe (R 108), Wordsworth (135 thou art the same That wert a promise to me ere my birth), Coleridge (32), Byron (408, 411, 723), Shelley (669 Bird thou never *wert*, also 42, 43, 62, 86, 118, 141, 572, 809, etc.; never *wast*), Scott (Iv 139, 238, 244, 376), Lamb, Carlyle (always), Kingsley, Tennyson (34 Where wert thou, 35, 265 thou wert strong as thou wert true), Hazlitt, Swinburne, Hewlett.

The frequency of *wast* is due, not only to "the influence of Tindale and the Bible" (NED), but also to the clearness of the form, *wert* being suggestive of the subjunctive. This was expressly stated by Robert Browning (see Mrs. Orr's Handbook, p. 14): "I make use of 'wast' for the second person of the perfect-indicative, and 'wert' for the present-potential, simply to be understood; as I should hardly be if I substituted the latter for the former . . . 'Where wert thou, brother, those three days, had He not raised thee?' means one thing, and 'Where wast thou when He did so?' means another."

Thou wast is found, among others, in Marlowe (T 3895, E 984 and J 864), Sh (H4B V. 5.65, Mcb V. 7.11 Thou was't borne of woman, etc.), AV (many examples), Dekker (F 2077), Mi (S 239, 784, and often), Bunyan,

Butler, Defoe, Keats, Byron, Quincey, Arnold (often), Rossetti, Swinburne, Hawthorne.

Examples of *wert* in the subj are frequent, see for instance Marlowe T 1218 As if thou wert the Empresse of the world | Sh Tit I. 1.206 would thou wert shipp'd to hell | AV Rev 3.15 I would thou wert cold.

2.8. The frequent combination *-st + þu > -st tu* or *te > -st*, in which [ə] was lost in the 15th cent., leads to the frequent omission of *thou* after the *-st*, which in itself is a clear indication of the 2nd person: Sh LLL I. 1.180 What would'st? | Rehearsal 67 what dost talk of meaning for? | Congreve 227 dost hear, boy? | Shaw StJ 28 Why dost let him? ... Art afraid? | 29 What else art fit for? | 31 Wilt be a poor little Judas ... ?, etc.

Chapter III

Personal Endings in Verbs Continued
Third Person Singular

3.1. The third person singular in the present indicative of all verbs except the well-known 'small' verbs has the same three varieties of *s*-ending as the genitive and plural of substantives: [he] *loves, likes, kisses* [lʌvz, laiks, kisiz].

The vowel is shortened and altered in *says* [sez]— but *gainsays* [geinseiz]—and *does* [dʌz], thus also in compounds: *outdoes, overdoes; ve* [v] is elided in *has* [hæz, həz].

Some other sound-changes see 16.1₂, 16.8₉.

[z] is left out in the colloquial negative forms *don't* for *does not*, *ain't* for *is not* (see vol V 23.2, where also other similar forms are mentioned).

Do instead of *does* is found in some writers' renderings of vulgar speech, e. g. Di Do 332 that don't look well; do it, Polly? | Meredith H 53 "But what do it matter, sir?" urged

the postillion | Shaw 1.58 it do look so silly;—but is this really
genuine, apart from *don't*, on which see vol V 23.2 and apart
from some dialects, cf 3.3?

On *dares* and *needs* see vol V 12.2 and 12.3.

3.2. This verbal *s*-ending has in Standard English
ousted *th* [þ], and its history cannot be treated except
in close connexion with that ending.

In OE *-th* (*þ*) was used in the ending of the third
person singular and in all persons in the plural of the
present indicative, but the vowel before it varied, so
that we have e. g.

Infinitive	3rd Singular	Plural
sprecan	spricþ	sprecaþ
bindan	bindeþ, bint	bindaþ
nerian	nereþ	neriaþ
lufian	lufaþ	lufiaþ.

But in the Northumbrian dialect of the tenth cent.
s was substituted for *þ* (sg *bindes*, pl *bindas*), and as
all unstressed vowels were soon after levelled, the two
forms became identical (*bindes*). As in the same dialect
the second person singular too ended in *s* (as against
the *-st* of the South), all persons sounded alike except
the first singular. But the development was not to
stop there. In OE a difference is made in the plural,
according as the verb precedes *we* or *ge* or not (*binde
we, binde ge*, but *we bindaþ, ge bindaþ*). This is the
germ of the more radical difference now carried through
consistently in the Scottish dialect, where the *s* is only
added when the vb is not accompanied with its proper
pronoun, but in that case it is used in all persons.
Murray D 212 gives the following sentences among
others:

aa *cum* fyrst—yt's mey at *cums* fyrst.

wey *gang* theare—huz tweae quheyles *gangs* theare.

they *cum* an' teake them—the burds *cums* an' pæcks
them.

3.3. In other parts of the country the development was different. In the Midland dialect the *-en* of the subjunctive and of the preterit was transferred to the present of the indicative, so that we have the following forms in the standard language:

14th century	16th century
I falle	I fall
he falleth	he fall(e)th
we fallen (falle)	we fall.

In the South of England, finally, the *th* was preserved in the plural, and was even extended to the first person singular. Old people in the hilly parts of Somersetshire and Devonshire still say not only [i woˑkþ] 'he walks', but also [ðei zeþ, ai zeþ] 'they say, I say'. In most cases, however, *do* is used, which is made [də] without any *th* through the whole singular as well as plural (Elworthy, *Grammar of the Dialect of West Somerset* 191 ff.).

3.4. But the northern *s*'es spread and became universal in Standard English. H. C. Wyld, *A History of Mod. Colloquial English*[2] p. 332 ff. gives a careful analysis of the occurrence of *th*- and *s*-forms in a number of ME texts; but he is wrong in thinking that *s* is found once only in Chaucer; as a matter of fact it is found three times: Duchesse 73 and HF 426 telles : elles | Duchesse 257 falles : halles. In the Reves Tale the *s*-forms are used to characterize the North of England dialect of the two students (*gas* for Chaucer's ordinary *gooth*, etc.). As a result of his research Wyld thinks that *s* did not wander south through purely 'regional' influences, for it is wanting in some texts in which we should have expected it if geography had been the deciding factor. On the other hand, poets begin to use *s* for the sake of rhythm and because these forms increased the number of available rimes considerably. Still Wyld thinks it hard to believe that what was destined to become the only form in the colloquial language should have come into that form of English primarily from poetry. "It is more likely that the use of the -s forms in poetry is quite independent of their introduction into colloquial English." But surely poets would not have thought of introducing these forms if they had not been supported, to some extent at any rate, by occurrence in ordinary conversation. Wyld thinks it possible that the extremely common auxiliary *is* may have provided the model for the *s*-forms. This, of course, is possible, but if that had been the decisive factor one would have expected the parallel auxiliaries *have* and *do* to have been the first to accept the *s*-forms; now as a matter of fact *hath* and *doth* were in common use long after *s* had prevailed in other verbs. On the whole Wyld has not really arrived at a clear-cut positive theory of the reason why *s* has prevailed.

3.5. To understand this I think we must go back to OE: why did *s* become so frequent instead of *þ* in late Old Northumbrian? It cannot, as stated by Sievers and others, be a purely phonetic change, parallel to other sound-laws. Then we should expect a transition of *þ* to *s* in other places of the sound-system as well. As this is not the case, the change is not an instance of the ordinary 'blind sound-laws', but is a purely morphological change. But a transfer from the 2nd person sg, not only to the much more common 3rd person sg, but to the plural as well (Luick § 698) is no satisfactory explanation. In my view we have here an instance of 'Efficiency': *s* was in these frequent forms substituted for *þ* because it was more easily articulated in all kinds of combinations. If we look through the consonants found as the most important elements of flexions in a great many languages we shall see that *t, d, n, s, r* occur much more frequently than any other consonant: they have been instinctively preferred for that use on account of the ease with which they are joined to other sounds; now, as a matter of fact, *þ* represents, even to those familiar with the sound from their childhood, greater difficulty in immediate close connexion with other consonants than *s*. In ON, too, *þ* was discarded in the personal endings of the verb. If this is the reason we understand how *s* came to be in these forms substituted for *th* more or less sporadically and spontaneously in various parts of England in the ME period; it must have originated in colloquial speech, whence it was used here and there by some poets, while other writers in their style stuck to the traditional *th* (*-eth*, *-ith*, *-yth*), thus Caxton and prose writers until the 16th century. The alleviation produced by *s* instead of *þ* is in some way similar to the smoothing found in the forms *binde we*, *binde ge* mentioned above: these, too, cannot be accounted for by means of blind phonetic law.

3.6. We shall now (as in GS § 212 ff.) deal with the fortunes of the two endings in later centuries.

In poetry *s* was used in rimes by Wyatt and Surrey (Holmqvist, Hist. of the Engl. Pres. Inflections, 1922, p. 161 ff.). In Marlowe *s* is by far the commoner ending, except after hissing consonants (*passeth*, *opposeth*, *pitcheth*, *presageth*, etc., T 68, 845, 1415, 1622). Spenser prefers *s* in poetry. In the first four cantos of FQ I have counted 94 *s*'es as against 24 *th*'s (besides 8 *has*, 18 *hath*, 15 *does*, and 31 *doth*). But in his prose *th* predominates even much more than *s* does in his poetry. In the introductory letter to Sir Walter Raleigh there is only one *s* (*it needs*), but many *th*'s; and in his book on 'the Present State of Ireland' all the third persons singular end in *th*, except a small number of phrases (*me seems*, several times, but *it seemeth; what boots it; how comes it*, and perhaps a few more) that seem to be characteristic of a more colloquial tone than the rest of the book. Shakespeare's practice is not easy to ascertain. In a great many passages the folio of 1623

has *th* where the earlier quartos have *s*. In the prose
parts of his dramas *s* prevails (Franz[3] 151: In Ado
(Q 1600) *th* is not found at all in the prose parts and
only twice in the poetical parts; Wiv., which is chiefly
in prose, has only one *-th*), and the rule may be laid
down that *th* belongs more to the solemn or dignified
speeches than to everyday talk, although this is by
no means carried through everywhere. In Mcb I. 7.29
ff. Lady Macbeth is more matter-of-fact than her husband: Lady: He *has* almost supt ... Macb.: *Hath* he
ask'd for me? Lady: Know you not he *ha's*. Macb.: ...
He *hath* honour'd me of late ... ; but when his more
solemn mood seizes her, she too puts on the buskin:
Was the hope drunke, Wherein you drest your selfe?
Hath it slept since?.—Where Mercutio mocks Romeo's
love-sickness (II. 1.15), he has the line: He *heareth* not,
he *stirreth* not, he *moveth* not, but in his famous description of Queen Mab (I. 4.53 ff.) he has 18 verbs in *s*
and only 2 in *th*, *hath* and *driveth*, of which the latter
is used for the sake of the metre. (Cf also Helen T.
Miller, *Hath*, *has doth*, *does* in Sh., Philological Quarterly,
Oct. 1930, 373 ff.).

Contemporary prose, at any rate in its higher forms,
has generally *th;* the *s*-ending is not at all found in the
AV, nor in Bacon A (though in Bacon E there are
some *s*'es). The conclusion with regard to Elizabethan
usage as a whole seems to be that the form in *s* was
a colloquialism and as such was allowed in poetry and
especially in the drama. This *s* must, however, be
considered a licence wherever it occurs in the higher
literature of that period. But in the first half of the
17th c. *-s* must have been the ending universally used
in ordinary conversation, and we have evidence that
it was even usual to read *s* where the book had *th*, for
Richard Hodges (1643) gives in his list of words pronounced alike though spelt differently among others
boughs boweth bowze; clause claweth claws; courses cours-

eth corpses; choose cheweth (see Ellis EEP IV. 1018),
and in 1649 he says 'howsoever wee write them thus,
leadeth it, maketh it, noteth it, we say *lead's it, make's it,
note's it.* The only exceptions seem to have been *hath*
and *doth,* where the frequency of occurrence protected
the old forms from being modified analogically (this
applies, partially at least, to *saith* as well), so that they
were prevalent till about the middle of the 18th c.
Milton, with the exceptions just mentioned, always
writes *s* in his prose as well as in his poetry, and so
does Pope. No difference was then felt to be necessary
between even the most elevated poetry and ordinary
conversation in that respect. But it is well worth noting
that Swift in the introduction to his 'Polite Conversation', where he affects a quasi-scientific tone, writes
hath and *doth,* while in the conversations themselves
has and *does* are the forms constantly used. In the
Journal to Stella all verbs have *s,* except *hath,* which
is, however, less frequent than *has.*

At church, however, people went on hearing the *th-*
forms, although even there the *s*'es began to creep in,
see Spect 217 (no. 147) a set of readers [of prayers at
church] who affect, forsooth, a certain gentleman-like
familiarity of tone, and mend the language as they
go on, crying instead of pardoneth and absolveth,
pardons and absolves. And it must certainly be ascribed
to influence from biblical language that the *th*-forms
again began to be used by poets towards the end of the
18th c.; at first apparently this was done rather sparingly,
but 19th c. poets employ *th* to a greater extent. This
revival of the old form affords the advantage from the
poet's point of view of adding at discretion a syllable,
as in Wordsw P 13.276

 In gratitude to God, Who *feeds* our hearts
 For his own service; *knoweth, loveth* us,
or in Byron Heaven and Earth I sc. 2
 Whate'er she *loveth,* so she *loves* thee not,

What can it profit thee?

Sometimes the *th*-form comes more handy for the rime (as when *saith* rimes with *death*), and sometimes the following sound may have induced a poet to prefer one or the other ending, as in Byron DJ 11.69

.......Coleridge *hath* the sway

And Wordsworth *has* supporters, two or three,

but in a great many cases individual fancy only decides which form is chosen. In prose, too, the *th*-form begins to make its re-appearance in the 19th c., not only in biblical quotations, etc., but often with the sole view of imparting a more solemn tone to the style, as in Thackeray's 'Not always *doth* the writer know whither the divine Muse *leadeth* him.' Some recent novelists affect this archaic trick *usque ad nauseam*.

3.7. The 19th c. has even gone so far as to create a double-form in one verb, making a distinction between *doth* [dʌþ] as an auxiliary vb and *doeth* [du·iþ] as an independent one. The early printers used the two forms indiscriminately, or rather preferred *doth* where *doeth* would make the line appear too closely packed, and *doeth* where there was room enough. Thus in AV we find Luke 12.34 a henne *doeth* gather her brood under her wings | Matth 7.21 he *doth* the will of my father,— where recent use would have reversed the order of the forms, but in Matth 7.24 whosoever heareth these sayings of mine, and *doeth* them—the old printer happens to be in accordance with the rule of our own days. When the *th*-form was really living, *doeth* was certainly always pronounced in one syllable (thus in Sh). I give a few examples of the modern differentiation; Lowell 1.129 She doeth little kindnesses ... Her life doth rightly harmonize ... And yet doth ever flow aright | Haggard S 199 [both forms in the same sentence] Man doeth this and doeth that, but he knows not to what ends his sense doth prompt him; cf also Tennyson 115 He that only rules by terror, Doeth grievous wrong.

3.8. The final result is a curious alternate play in the 3rd person in which an *s* is required in most sentences, its place indicating the difference between sg and pl:

The king comes

The kings come.

Cf from a comic paper: the proverb 'He laughs best who laughs last' improved upon by saying 'he laughs best whose laugh lasts, or whose laughs last.'

The non-occurrence of -*s* in the 3rd pers. sg in *shall*, *will*, *may*, *can* is explained historically by these vbs being old perfecto-presentia; *must* has later from a preterit come to be used as a present. To these *need* has to a great extent been assimilated, hence *he need do it*, *he needn't do it*, while on the other hand *dare*, which from of old had never -*s*, has now to some extent been treated as a full vb and has taken -*s*: *he dares do it*; see for details vol V. 12.2.

On *wills* as a full vb see vol IV. 15.1.

The old *wot* 'know', OE perfecto-pres. *wāt*, is completely obsolete, but when revived is occasionally provided with -*s*: Lamb E 1.163 he wots not of the license.

3.9. In speech of a colloquial type, verging more or less on vulgarity, -*s* forms of the first person may be found from ME to the present day; Towneley 178 I am best of you all, and euer has been | Rehearsal 53 I makes 'em both speak fresh | Farquhar B 327 Then I, sir, tips me the verger with half-a-crown | Defoe R 245 I takes my Man Friday with me | id M 176 immediately I takes one of them ... and away comes I with the two children | (ib 207, 220), 224 so I left the footman, and puts myself in a rank with this young lady | 230 Come away then says I, and takes him with me | Fielding 3.43 [vg] I'll warrant I gives you enough on't | pretty often in Fielding TJ | Goldsm 648 I likes | Franklin 151 [vg] I am very poor, and I sweeps before gentlefolkses doors, and hopes they will give me something.

Dickens's Sam Weller uses -*s* in all verbal forms of the present tense (see Storm EPh 804 f).

The -*s* form is especially frequent in the inserted sentence *says I* or *thinks I;* thus Spect 808 | Defoe R, Pl, M very frequent (but always *I say*) | Goldsm 169 I must confess, says I, a curiosity ... (and ib 175) | Franklin 40 and 159 | Austen S 253 "Lord!" says I, "is Mrs. D. ill?" | Di P 126 [Sam Weller:] so long life to the Pickvicks, says I! | id D 126 And what do you mean to do, says I, wistfully | Thack S 95 A great dinner-party, thinks I to myself (and 118) | ib 107 and 110 says I | Hardy F 118 I say, says I, we get a fine day | ib 221 why, thinks I, I'll go.

Chapter IV

Tense-Formation in the Verbs

4.1₁. As already remarked in the Introduction, I have here for practical reasons collected together things which according to my usual plan would have found their place in separate chapters, *lived* under the ending -*d*, *kept* under the ending -*t* with change in the kernel, *cut* under unchanged kernel, *sit* under change of kernel without any ending, etc.

On no other point, perhaps, has the old English grammatical system been revolutionized to the same extent as in the formation of the tenses of the verbs. The old principal divisions of verbs into three classes, strong, reduplicating, and weak, have no sense if we consider the flexions as found in actual usage, and new divisions must be substituted for them. It will be well in this place to throw a glance at the chief elements of this historical development, leaving all details to the separate treatment of each verb in particular.

4.1₂. In OE the so-called *strong verbs* were character-
ized by changes in their vowels, due to apophony
('gradation', ablaut), which in the main goes back to
primitive Aryan and may be to a great extent explained
by old accentual rules. The following classes are generally distinguished in OE; in each we give one typical
example:

I   inf *wrītan*—prt sg *wrāt*—prt pl *writon*—ptc *writen;*
II   inf *bēodan*—prt sg *bēad*—prt pl *budon*—ptc *boden;*
III inf *bindan*—prt sg *band*—prt pl *bundon*—ptc *bunden;*
IV   inf *beran*—prt sg *bœr*—prt pl *bǣron*—ptc *boren;*
V   inf *sittan*—prt sg *sœt*—prt pl *sǣton*—ptc *seten;*
VI   inf *scacan*—prt sg *scōc*—prt pl *scōcon*—ptc *scacen.*

Note: the abbreviation ptc is here short for second
ptc ('passive' or 'perfect' participle).

In course of time several intricate phonetic and analogical changes took place to modify this scheme.
Thus in III the short *i* and *u* were lengthened before
-nd (cf vol I. 4.221), and these long vowels were later
diphthongized (I. 8.21), which led to the modern forms
bind [baind] and *bound* [baund]. This is in accordance
with the ordinary laws of sound-change; similarly,
ModE *write* [rait]—*wrote* [rout] are the normal representatives of OE *wrītan*—*wrāt*. On the other hand, the
influence of analogy is responsible for the loss of the
distinction between prt sg and prt pl (discarded everywhere except in *was*—*were*), by which process the four
principal parts of the verb were reduced to three.
Moreover, in many cases the parts were further reduced
to two as the prt and ptc became levelled under one
form (see e. g. *sit*—*sat*). The members of the various
classes have not all had the same development; partial
and total transitions from one class to another occur.
In this way the old system has been broken up; nothing
is left in ModE except scattered clusters of words
which still cling together. We shall now give the above

examples in their ModE forms (for *bēodan*, which has
not been preserved, we substitute *frēosan* 'freeze'):

I   *write—wrote—written;*
II   *freeze—froze—frozen;*
III   *bind—bound—bound;*
IV   *bear—bore—born;*
V   *sit—sat—sat;*
VI   *shake—shook—shaken.*

The grouping in six classes is no longer typical of ModE.
Had we chosen a different set of examples, we might
have arrived at a totally different scheme from the
above. Compare e. g. *bite, shine* (I), *choose, shoot* (II),
begin (III), *give, get, see* (V).

In some OE verbs the stem-consonant was modified
in prt pl and ptc owing to an original (Aryan and
primitive Gothonic) shifting of the accent ('Verner's
Law'). The original voiceless *s* has been voiced, and
the original *z* has become *r;* e. g.

inf *frēosan*—prt sg *frēus*—prt pl *fruron* ptc *froren.*
Very few traces of this change are found in ModE:
frore 'frozen, frosty' (see 5.3₇), *lorn* (from *lose;* see 4.5₂;
also *forlorn*); the only remnant of this shift in everyday
use is *was—were.* Further we have *sodden* from *seethe,*
see 5.3₇.

4.1₃. To the second class of OE verbs, the so-called
reduplicating verbs, belong verbs which originally had
preterits like Gothic *haíhait, laílōt* from *haitan* 'call' and
lētan 'let'. In OE, traces of this system had been preserved in the Anglian dialect and in poetry (e. g. *heht*
'called' by the side of *het*), but on the whole the reduplication disappeared in the prehistoric period of
the language. The prt of these verbs in OE was distinguished from the prs merely by a change of vowel,
as in

inf *feallan*—prt sg *fēoll*—prt pl *fēollon*—ptc *feallen.*

Here, too, later sound shifts have often obliterated the OE features. ModE in this case has

fall—fell—fallen.

4.1₄. The third main division of OE verbs, *weak verbs*, had only three principal parts: present, preterit, and participle; no vowel-change distinguished prt sg and prt pl. The preterit and participle were formed with the help of an ending -*d(e)*, which became -*t(e)* after voiceless consonants:

deman—demde—gedemed;
lufian—lufode—gelufod;
cyssan—cyste—gecyssed.

As may be seen from the examples, a group of verbs had no medial vowel in the preterit, e. g. *demde* and *cyste* as opposed to *lufode*. This difference was levelled in ME, when *e* in the ending -*ed* became silent everywhere except in special cases. The corresponding difference in spelling has in most cases also been abolished, but curiously enough through the introduction of an *e* everywhere, even where it was never pronounced; see 4.2₃. One more levelling took place during the development to ModE: the merging of prt and ptc in one form, usually ending in -*ed:*

deem—deemed;
love—loved;
kiss—kissed.

The stem-vowel of the weak verb is generally the same throughout; one class of OE verbs, however, had mutation in the inf and prs, but not in the prt and ptc, e. g.

sellan—sealde—geseald.

If the stem ended in -*c*, -*nc*, or -*ng*, it underwent some further changes:

sēcan—sōhte—gesōht;
þencan—þōhte—geþōht;
bringan—brōhte—gebrōht.

These peculiarities are still traceable in the ModE forms:

sell—sold—sold;
seek—sought—sought;
think—thought—thought;
bring—brought—brought.

Consonant-groups arising from the addition of flex-ional endings often caused shortening of the vowel in ME (cf vol I 4.31 ff). The difference in quantity later became also a difference in quality, the result being such ModE flexions as

keep—kept (OE *cēpan, cēpte*);
hear—heard (OE, Angl. *hēran, hērde*).

If the stem ended in *-d* or *-t*, the *-dd-* and *-tt-* were simplified to *d* and *t* after the loss of final *-e* in ME. The ending thus became fused with the stem:

bleed—bled (OE *blēdan, blēdde*);
meet—met (OE *mētan, mētte*).

Many verbs originally not belonging to this group have later been attracted into it, such as *kneel* (orig. regular) and *creep* (orig. str.). To this type of flexion may now also be reckoned *flee—fled | shoe—shod | say—said.*

Words ending in *-d* or *-t* but having a short vowel in the present, became invariable as a result of the loss of final *-e:*

rid—rid—rid (OE *hreddan,* the vowel due to influ-ence from ON *ryðja*);
set—set—set (OE *settan*).
shut—shut—shut (OE *scyttan*).

Sometimes the vowel of the present stem was originally long, but was shortened by analogy with prt and ptc:

spread [spred]—*spread*—*spread* (OE *sprǣdan*); cf vol
I 8.412.

Even verbs originally strong or reduplicative, or of
foreign origin, have been drawn into this group: *bid,
burst, slit; let, shed; cost.*

The weak type of flexion was already in OE times
by far the most important and has since grown in
importance. For many centuries the strong class has
been suffering a steady loss in favour of the weak
conjugation, e. g. *laugh, starve, walk, wash.* Practically
all new verbs enter the weak class; only in a few cases
have weak or foreign words been drawn into the strong
class, esp. *ring, string, chide, hide, stick, wear; dig,
strive.* For details see below under each verb.

In consequence of all these changes the modern
flexional system is totally incongruous with OE. A
classification on historical lines is therefore hardly
advisable. Altogether, a grouping is rather difficult,
owing to the often large number of parallel forms of
each verb. The best way of systematizing ModE verbs
seems to be the division into two main classes, regular
and irregular, the latter falling into several subclasses.

Regular Verbs

4.2₁. These have no change in the kernel itself. The
prt and ptc are formed by the addition of written *-ed*,
which has three phonetic forms according to the final
sound of the base:

[id] after [d] and [t]: *ended, rested;*
[d] after voiced sounds other than [d]: *gathered, called,
    screwed, managed;*
[t] after voiceless sounds other than [t]: *locked,
    hopped, kissed, coughed, wished.*

The sound [k] is often left out in familiar speech
between another consonant and [t]: *thanked* [þæŋ(k)t];
asked is frequently [aˑst].

Note: The historical development of *-ed* is parallel to that
of the plural ending *-(e)s*, where *e* was dropped in late ME
except after a consonant of the same type as the one in the
ending itself, i. e. a sibilant (see vol I 6.16 ff). Similarly, the
ending *-ed* has retained its syllabic value after *t* and *d*, while
in other cases *e* is dropped. Where *e* is silent now, the *d* of the
ending is unvoiced after voiceless consonants: OE *lōcode* >
looked [lukt]. Cf also 4.2₃.

4.2₂. Contrary to the above rules the old full pronunciation [id] is often retained in archaic language. In
poetry the old form comes in useful when an extra
syllable is required: Keats 207 to keep Their clenchëd
teeth still clench'd.—In ordinary prose a few participles
are pronounced with [id] especially when they are used
as adjuncts: a *learned* professor (4.3₁) | his *beloved* wife |
blessed innocence. It is interesting to note the parallelism
with the rules for the retention of *-en* in participles
(see 5.7), where there is a strong inclination to
keep the *en* in adjunctal position before a substantive.
Rhythm is no doubt in part responsible for this. In
purely verbal constructions the contracted pronuncia-
tion is used, e. g. *he was beloved* [biˈlʌvd] *by all* | Sh
Shrew IV. 5.18 Then God be blest, it is the blessed sun.
We say *a man aged* [eidʒd] *fifty*, but *an aged* [eidʒid]
man; always *middle-aged* [-eidʒd]. *Sacred* [seikrid] is no
longer felt as a participle.

The full pronunciation is also generally preserved in
derivative adverbs and substantives: *fixedly* [fiksidli],
fixedness [fiksidnis], *perplexedly, perplexedness; impliedly,
unfeignedly, markedly, confessedly, assuredly*, etc. Sometimes there is vacillation: *ashamedly* [əˈʃeimidli, əˈʃeimdli]
confusedly, preparedly. Only *d* is sounded in *tiredly*
(*-ness*), *good-naturedly, hurriedly, determinedly, astonish-
edly, embarrassedly*, and several other words. Note here,
too, the parallelism with the *en*-ending in participles
(*brokenly*, etc.): [id] forms a connecting link (syllable)
between stem and ending, but it is not required when
the stem itself ends in an unstressed syllable.

The archaic 2nd pers sg prt ending -*edst* is now
usually pronounced [-idst], cf above 2.3₂.

Spelling

4.2₃. In ElE and later the dropping of *e* ind -*ed* was
often indicated by spellings like *bless'd* and *rain'd*,
sometimes even without the apostrophe. But usage was
not consistent; Milton hesitates between *seemed*, *seem'd*,
and *seemd*. The *e* was commonly reintroduced in the
18th century and is now universally employed except
in poetry, where '*d* is still sometimes used to distinguish
it from the full pronunciation [id] mentioned above. On
Keats's usage see Buxton Forman's edition vol I p.
VIII ff. After voiceless consonants older English also
often used the phonetically correct form *t*: *plac't*, *ban-
isht* (Mi). In some of these verbs the *t* goes back to OE:
cyste, etc. (see 4.1₄), while in other cases it is due to
the loss of medial *e* in ME: OE *lōcode* > early ModE
lookt, now *looked*. Forms like *storm-tost* may still be met
with by the side of *tossed* (see Fowler MEU), but the
general rule in PE is to write -*ed* everywhere:

$$
\left.\begin{array}{l}
\text{MnE } kissed \\
\text{— } looked \\
\text{— } deemed \\
\text{— } loved
\end{array}\right\} < \left\{\begin{array}{l}
\text{OE } cyste \\
\text{— } l\bar{o}code \\
\text{— } d\bar{e}mde \\
\text{— } lufode
\end{array}\right.
$$

Exceptions are the cases in which [t] is used after a
voiced consonant, see 4.3₂, 4.5, 4.6. A distinction is gen-
erally made between *past* (it is past noon | he hurried
past | the past year) and *passed* (pure ptc): see vol IV
3.7. Spelling reformers, among whom Tennyson must
be reckoned, have often extended the use of *t* instead
of -*ed* to other cases. A few other orthographical peculiarities in received PE are:

(1) Verbs ending in silent -*e* or in -*ee* [i·] add only -*d*:
love—loved, *free—freed*, *guarantee—guaranteed*.

(2) Final -*y* after a consonant becomes *i* before -*ed:*
reply—replied, but: *play—played*. Yet we write *laid*
(but *belayed*) and *paid; staid* is now an adjective, while
stayed is a form of the vb *stay*. On *said* see 4.7.

(3) A final consonant after a short stressed vowel is
doubled before -*ed: drop—dropped, beg—begged*. Yet
l after a short vowel is always doubled in British (but
not in American) orthography: *travel—travelled* (one
exception: *paralleled*, see Fowler MEU); *c* is generally
made into *ck* to indicate the pronunciation [k]: *mimicked,
bivouacked;* and *p* is doubled after an unstressed vowel
in a few words: *worshipped, kidnapped*, and *handicapped*.
With *s* and *t*, too, there is some tendency to double
the consonant after an unstressed vowel: *nonplussed,
bias(s)ed, focus(s)ed, benefit(t)ed;* cf Fowler MEU. Verbs
ending in -*ar, -er, -ir, -ur* (where *r* has disappeared in
StE pronunciation after modifying the preceding vowel:
see vol I 13.21 ff) make -*arred, -erred*, etc.: *starred—stared
| preferred—interfered | stirred—tired | blurred—lured*.

In one case the infinitive has been formed by subtraction
of -*t* from the Lat. ptc stem: *mix* from Lat. *mixtus* > earlier
English *mixt*, now written *mixed*. The infinitive *mix* was extremely rare before Sh's time. It is now perfectly regular.

Irregular Verbs. Class 1

4.3₁. First we take those in which the kernel is kept
unchanged, and in which the irregularity consists only
in the addition of *t* after a voiced sound, a nasal or *l*.—
burn — burnt. OE had a strong vb (III) *beornan, byrnan*
intr., and a weak vb *bærnan* transitive. In ME the two
ran together. The present form probably owes its *u* to
the influence of the lip-consonant *b*. The form *burned* is
'slightly archaic and somewhat more formal in effect;
it occurs more frequently as pa. t., or in combination
with the auxiliary *have* than as pple adj.' (NED). ‖
kempt is a ptc of the obs. vb *kemb* (= *comb*, which is
regular); it is chiefly used in combinations such as

unkempt, ill-kempt. || *learn—learnt.* Alternative prt &
ptc form: *learned* [lə·nd]; cf the adj *learned* [lə·nid]
mentioned above (4.2₂). || *pen* 'enclose'—*pent*; esp. *pent
up.* Colloquially only the regular form: they penned
me in | I was penned in. There is another vb *pen* 'write',
from the sb; this is regular. || *wont* [wount] 'used,
accustomed (to)' is a ptc of the obs. vb *won* 'dwell, be
accustomed'. It is now mostly used predicatively after
is, was, etc.; as an adjunct the expanded form *wonted*
is employed: "he acted with his wonted courtesy".
There is also a rare vb *wont* either from *wont* ptc or a
back-formation from *wonted* (see NED).

Wells N 449 has the rare form *earnt* as ptc of *earn.*—
The form *joint* (from the Fr ptc) looks like a parallel
formation to the above; it is now a pure adj (joint
author | Haggard S 3 during our joint lives), while
joined is used in verbal constructions.

In *-l* we have *dwell—dwelt.* The present sense 'tarry,
remain in a place' is probably due to Scandinavian
influence. || *smell—smelt* (rarely *smelled*). || *spell—spelt*
(or *spelled*). || *spill—spilt* (or *spilled*); see also *spoil.*
|| *spoil—spoilt* (or *spoiled*). OF < Lat. *spoliare.* Its sense-
history is mixed up with that of *spill;* it appears
that *spoil* took over the meaning 'destroy', after *spill*
had acquired its present sense 'waste liquid' (see
NED). In the now archaic sense 'plunder' *spoil* is always
regular.

The *t*-forms in all these verbs are much more common
in speaking than in writing. Even people who write
learned, spelled, etc., often pronounce [lə·nt, spelt].
Americans, in contrast to British people, generally
prefer the regular forms in pronunciation as well as in
spelling.

Strictly, *used to* [ju·stu, ju·stə] also belongs here; see vol
IV 1.91: the [t] is due to assimilation to the following *t* in *to.*

On *-ed* and *-t* see Fowler MEU 594 f.

4.3₂. This is in our survey of forms the first group
of verbs ending in voiced consonants which add *t* in
the prt and ptc. In other groups we have also vowel
change: *deal—dealt* (see 4.5), and *bring—brought* (see
4.9), while still others change final *d* into *t: bend—
bent* (see 4.6). Why do we have *t* in these cases? Apart
from the verbs in group 7 (*bring—brought*, etc., which
from a modern point of view are quite irregular), the
t is of later date than OE. The explanation given by
Morsbach and many other scholars is that the phenomenon is due to the analogy of *keep—kept* and similar
words, which owe their *t* to the voiceless final consonant of the stem. But why is the influence of analogy
felt only in these comparatively few cases? Why do
we not say *pelt* (from *peel*) and *semt* (from *seem*), etc.?
It is remarkable that the type of preterit in question
in most cases has the vowel [e], frequently corresponding
to a present tense with [iˑ]; other vowels such as [i]
end [əˑ] are rare. In the *send—sent* group OE sup-
pressed the *d* of the stem before the ending: *sendan,
sende, gesend(ed)*. I have often thought that the ME
innovation *sent(e)* may originally have stood for *sendd*
with a long, emphatic *d* to distinguish it from the prs
form. This explanation, however, does not account for
felt, meant, left, etc.

There is a remarkably full treatment of "Origin and
Extension of the Voiceless Preterit and the Past Participle Inflections of the English Irregular Weak Verb
Conjugation" by Albert H. Marckwardt in Essays and
Studies in English and Comparative Literature by
Members of the English Department of the Univ. of
Michigan (Ann Arbor 1935). He traces the beginning
of these *t*-forms back to the eleventh century and then
follows their chronological and geographical spreading
from century to century up to the year 1400, thus just
the period when the subject-matter of my own work
begins. There is accordingly no occasion here to deal

with details in Marckwardt's exposition, but only to
mention that according to him the first germ of these
t-forms lay in stems in *-nd*, *-ld* and *-rd*. The third person
sg of the present of such a verb as OE *sendan* was
often shortened into *sent* from *sendeþ*. On the analogy
of such very frequently occurring syncopated presents
the *t* was transferred to the prt and ptc. It must be
admitted that this assumption is more convincing than
the analogy adduced by previous scholars, but it is
rather difficult to explain why the *t*-forms spread, e. g.,
to such verbs as *leave* : *left*. From the point of view
of Modern English Grammar, however, we must be
content to leave this question open: we must take
forms as we find them in the period with which we are
concerned.

Irregular Verbs. Class 2

4.41. Some verbs ending in *d* or *t* are unchanged in
prt and ptc. For a historical explanation see above 4.1$_4$.
dread. The verb is regular in PE, but the old unchanged
ptc has been kept as an adj = 'dreadful, fearsome':
the last dread moment. || *rid*. In England the regular
form *ridded* is common in the prt, but rarer as a ptc,
especially in the passive construction where *rid* prevails:
"I cannot get rid of my cold", "I thought myself well
rid of him". || *shed*: the old meaning 'separate' is pre-
served in *watershed*. || *shred*. The regular prt and ptc
shredded is now generally preferred. || *spread*. || *wed*. In
England the unchanged prt & ptc is now rare. As an
adjunct *wedded* is universal: *wedded life*. Cf Fowler's
complaint (MEU) that newspaper headlines are bringing
the short ptc into use: SUICIDE OF WED PAIR

On the use of *need* as a preterit see vol IV 1.71

Bet (Perh. from OF). Also regular; in England both
forms are in use. Fowler MEU: *bet* is preferred with

reference to a definite transaction: "he bet me £5 I
could not", while *betted* is used when the sense is more
general: "they betted a good deal in those days". ||
burst. OE *berstan;* the *u* in the ModE form may be due
either to the lip-consonant *b* (cf *burn* above) or to the
OE prt pl *burston.* There is a coll. or vg form *bust*,
which is inflected regularly: Huxley L 2.115 I should
have "busted up" | Lewis B 17 a busted bookkeeper.
On the old ptc *bursten* see 5.7₅ || *cast* (from ON). Regular
forms were formerly in use. Both *broadcast* and *broad-
casted* are used in the prt, in the ptc generally only *broadcast.* Similarly, *forecasted* is found by the side of *forecast*
(from the sb). || *cost* (from OF). || *cut.* || *hit* (from Scand.)
|| *hurt* (from OF). || *knit.* Also regular; the short form is a
favourite in figurative use: "she knit(ted) her brows",
but usually: "she (had) knitted a pair of socks". || *let.*
A ptc *letten* is still heard in north-country dialects. The
obs. vb *let* 'hinder' made *let* or *letted* in prt & ptc. || *must.*
This verb has no inf and no ptc; the form is an old
preterit (OE *mōste,* prs *mōt*), extended through imagin-
ative use to the present: see vol IV 1.61 ff. || *ought.* OE
āhte, prt of the perfecto-present vb *āgan* 'possess'.
Like *must,* the original prt form has come to be used
as a present tense as well (see vol IV 9.55-6). *Ought* is
now entirely dissociated from the normal descendent of
OE *āgan,* ModE *owe,* which is inflected regularly. *Ought*
has neither inf nor ptc (cf however vol IV 9.83). ||
put. || *quit* (from OF). *Quitted* is the ordinary prt &
ptc in England. || *roast* (from OF). Generally regular,
but an old unchanged ptc is in limited use as a pure
adj: "I like roast beef ', but: "I prefer my meat roasted".
|| *set.* || *shut.* || *slit.* || *split.* || *sweat.* Now more often reg-
ular in British English (Maugham Pl 4.260 I've just
sweated my guts out). As a causative, *sweated* is usual
in both countries, thus always in the sense of paying
workers badly. On the ptc *sweaten* see 5.7₅. || *thrust*
(from ON). || *wet.* The unchanged form is now rarely

met with in England; Bennett has it: HL 359 the rain
wet them.

The unchanged forms *rid, wed, bet, quit, sweat, wet*
are used more frequently in America than in England.

A special case of invariableness is presented by the
vb *damn*. When used in swearing the ptc is often
damn, especially as a subjunct: Kaye Smith HA 17
you're damn cynical | Bennett LM 48 I don't want to
go, but I damn well have to | Norris P 96 the damn
fool.—In the sense 'condemned' the form is always
damned.

4.4₂. The influence of analogy has increased the
number of invariable verbs. Especially verbs ending in
-*t* tend in this direction. The tendency perhaps cul-
minated in early ModE, when several words now regular
had unchanged forms, sometimes side by side with
forms in -*ed:*

fast. Sh Cymb IV. 2.347 I fast and pray'd for their
intelligence. || *fret.* More U 75 fret prt. || *lift* (from ON).
AV John 8.7 hee lift vp himselfe | ib 8.10 when Iesus
had lift vp himselfe (in AV also regular forms) | Mi
PL 1. 193 With Head up-lift above the wave | Bunyan
P 19 lift ptc. || *start.* AV Tobit 2.4 I start [prt] vp. ||
waft. Sh Merch. V. 1.11 Stood Dido .. and waft her
Loue To come again to Carthage | John II. 1.73 a
brauer choice of dauntlesse spirits Then now the English
bottomes haue waft o're.

4.4₃. It was thus not at all unusual in earlier English
for a ptc in -*t* to be = the inf. The analogy of these
cases was extended even to a series of words of Romanic
origin, namely such as go back to Latin passive participles, e. g. *complete, content, select,* and *separate.* These
words were originally adopted as participles but later
came to be used also as infinitives; in older English
they were frequently used in both functions (as well as
in the preterit), often with an alternative ptc in -*ed;*
cf Franz § 159 and Abbott § 342. A contributory cause

of their use as verbal stems may have been such Latin
agent-nouns as *corruptor* and *editor;* as *-or* is identical
in sound with *-er* in agent-nouns, the infinitives *corrupt*
and *edit* may have been arrived at merely through
subtraction of the ending *-or*, cf my article in EStn
70, pp. 121—2. Finally, the fact that we have very
often an adj = a vb, e. g. *dry, empty*, etc. (see 6.9),
may also have contributed to the creation of infs out
of these old ptcs (adjectives).

In PE the forms in question have as pure ptcs been
replaced by forms in *-ed;* they are used only as verbal
stems and as adjectives: *to separate, a separate room* (note
the difference in sound [-eit, -it], vol I 5.74 | *to complete,
a complete set*. Indeed, it has now become the recognized
method of anglicizing Latin verbs, to use the Lat.
past ptc as the stem of the English verb; cf Ole Reuter,
Engl. Verbs from Lat. and Fr. Past Participles (Soc.
Scient. Fennica, Helsingfors 1934) and Koziol in Anglia
65.58 ff. By this process, the ending *-ate* has developed
into a common suffix for verbs adopted from Latin
or French (see under that suffix). The difference in
sense between adjs and the corresponding ptcs in *-ed*
is, of course, often slight: OHenry C 120 well content
to serve a country that was contented with so little
service (as an adjunct only *contented*). Short forms are
sometimes used archaically in place of *ed*-forms (Wordsw
P 5.230 This verse is dedicate to Nature's self | Wells
TM 46 the big building was situate on the slope of a
broad river valley); but in pure verbal function the
short form is no longer possible, as in More U 235
whom no lawier has instruct with deceit | Sh Mcb
III. 6.38 And this report Hath so exasperate their
King, that ...

4.4₄. In this connexion we might also mention the
inverse process, the introduction in the inf of a *t* originally belonging to the ptc. This is the probable origin
of the following two verbs:

graft: earlier *graff* (< OF *grafe*). The ptc *graft* was mistakenly interpreted as the unchanged ptc of an inf *graft.* Sh has both *graff* and *graft;* the latter is now the only form in use; it is inflected regularly. || *hoist:* originally *hoise* (perhaps < Middle Dutch *hyssen*). From the regular ptc *hoist* a new inf *hoist* sprang into use. Sh has both forms; now only *hoist* as a regular vb. The old ptc occurs in the well-known Shakespearean phrase "hoist with his own petard" (Hml III. 4.207).

Irregular Verbs. Class 3

4.51. *t* is added, and the vowel of the base is changed. *deal* [di·l]—*dealt* [delt]. || *feel—felt.* || *kneel—knelt* (rarely *kneeled*). Sh has only *-ed; knelt* is from the '19th c. and of southern origin' (NED). || *dream—dreamt* [dremt] (or *dreamed*). The modern meaning was taken over from Scand. || *lean—leant* [lent] (or *leaned*); it is the colloquial form in British English, though Walker 1791 stamps it as vg.—*Leant* and *leaned* used side by side: Walpole OL 214 She *leant* over the bed .. Agatha .. *leaned* over her | ib 221 Agatha *leant* over the bed .. She *leaned* right over the bed. Cf Fowler's remarks MEU 594-5. || *mean—meant.* || *creep—crept.* || *keep—kept.* || *leap—leapt* [lept] (or *leaped*). Cf By DJ 2.58 leap'd : stepp'd. || *sleep—slept.* || *sweep—swept.* || *weep—wept.*

In U. S. the regular forms *dreamed, leaned, leaped* are used more frequently than in England.

Many of the above words, once strong or reduplicative, preserve their old flexion in dialects. Thus, OE reduplicating prts like *hlēop, swēop, wēop,* and *slēp,* became, through shortening in ME, *lĕp, swĕp, wĕp, slĕp,* forms that are still used in British and American dialects, both as prts and ptcs; cf group 6 (*bleed—bled.*) Still other words have been attracted, in dialect, into this group: *creep—crep* | *keep—kep* | *reap—rep* (regular in StE).

4.5₂. Some stems ending in *v* or *s* [z] besides vowel-change undergo unvoicing of the final consonant:

cleave—cleft 'split'. OE *clēofan* (strong II). By the side of the new-formed prt & ptc *cleft*, the strong forms *clove—cloven* have been preserved (see 5.3₆). A regular form *cleaved* is also in use.—There is another vb *cleave* 'adhere' from OE *cleofian*. This obsolete vb is generally inflected regularly (*cleaved*) but with an occasional prt *clave*, perhaps borrowed from another OE vb *clīfan* (strong I, now extinct). *Clave*, which is now archaic, is chiefly used in set phrases like: Caine E 401 her tongue clave to the roof of her mouth. Also: Lewis MA 115 they clave faithfully to the inquiry. Shelley uses *clove* for *clave* or *cleaved*, in: 115 a human thing which to my bosom clove. || *leave—left*. || *(be)reave—(be)-reft* (or *bereaved*). Generally regular in reference to the loss of relatives, etc., esp. when used as an adjunct; otherwise *bereft* is the more common form: Death bereaved (bereft) him of his best friend | the bereaved family || the blow bereft him of consciousness | a life bereft of joy.

lose—lost. OE *(for)lēosan* (strong II) 'destroy' and *losian* 'get lost'. In ME the two verbs were merged. *Lesen*, the normal descendant of OE *lēosan*, is found as late as Sh and the AV; the present form *lose* is very difficult to explain, it is possibly due to association with the adj *loose*. The prt & ptc is now *lost*, but the old ptc *lorn* is used as an archaic adj: "a lone, lorn woman", also in *forlorn* 'abandoned, wretched'.

Irregular Verbs. Class 4

4.6. *t* is added, and *d* disappears before it:

bend—bent. The ptc *bended* is used especially in the phrase "on bended knees". || *blend—blent* (or *blended*). *Blent* is now archaic or poetic: pity and anger blent. || *lend—lent*. The excrescent *d* was added to the present tense form, perhaps after the analogy of the other verbs

in this group. || *rend—rent.* || *send—sent.* || *shend—shent*
'disgrace, put to shame'. Now dial. or arch. || *spend—*
spent. || *wend—went* (*wended*). OE *wendan* 'turn (tr)'.
Went is now exclusively used as prt of *go* (see 5.6),
while the archaic vb *wend* has developed a regular
form: he wended his way | Carlyle S 65 the Postwagen ..
wended through the village. || *geld—gelt* (from ON). The
form *gelt* is rare; Sh has it by the side of the regular
form: Merch V. 144 Would he were gelt | R2 II. 1.238
Bereft and gelded of his patrimonie. || *build—built.* A
regular form was formerly frequent: Marlowe H 1.225
a stately builded ship | Sh: *built* and *builded* (see Sh-
lex) | Defoe R 100 to have builded a boat. The form
is still occasionally met with, especially in American,
but also in British English: Hardy L 78 as fair a place
of hopes as was ever builded | Raleigh S 39 the un-
builded city of their dreams || Lewis MS 372 had builded.
|| *gild—gilt* (or *gilded*). In pure verbal function now
only *gilded; gilt* is a pure adj = 'covered with gold'
("a gilt bracelet"), while *gilded* as an adjunct has more
dignified associations and is often figurative: *the Gilded
Chamber* = the House of Lords, *the gilded youth* = the
young men of fashion. || *gird—girt* (or *girded*), now gen-
erally regular.

Irregular Verbs. Class 5

4.7. *d* is added, and the vowel of the base is changed:
say [sei] (but *says* [sez])—*said* [sed]. OE *secgan,
sægde, gesægd. Secgan* would have become ModE [sedʒ],
but in ME the *cg*-forms were replaced by new formations from *segest, segeþ;* cf *buy* and *lie.* The shortened
ptc with [e] was probably at first used in unstressed
position (cf vol. I 11.35). *Gainsaid* (from *gainsay*) is more
often pronounced [geinseid] than [geinsed]; always [gein-
seiz]. || *flee—fled.* OE *flēon* 'flee' and *flēogan* 'fly' (both
of the 2nd strong class) differed only in the inf and
were frequently confused already in OE, and the con-

fusion has persisted to the present day. On *fly—flew—flown* see 5.4₁. *Fled* as a prt & ptc may be an analogical formation (cf *shoe—shod* below). In PE, *flee* is felt as archaic and is generally replaced by *fly* in talk and ordinary prose. *Flew* and *flown*, however, are not usually substituted for *fled*. Consequently, the normal ModE flexions are: *fly* 'move through air'—*flew—flown* | *fly* 'escape'—*fled—fled*. This scheme, of course, is not always closely adhered to, especially in older literature. While *fly* for *flee* is common in Shakespeare (see Sh-lex; *flee* occurs only once, LLL III. 66, in rime!), *fled*, on the other hand, is used twice apparently in the meaning of *flew* and *flown:* H4B I. 1.123 Arrowes fled not swifter toward their ayme | Ven 947 Ioues golden arrow at him should have fled.—*Flew* seems to stand for *fled* in Goldsmith 583 (Des. Vill. 94) And, as a hare whom hounds and horns pursue Pants to the place from whence at first he flew.—It is sometimes said that the avoidance of the form *flee* is due to the unpleasant homophony with *flea*. || *shoe* [ʃuˑ]—*shod* [ʃɔd]. || *hear* [hiə]—*heard* [həˑd]. The vowel of the prt & ptc was shortened in ME (vol I 4.31 ff); *er* was preserved from becoming *ar* by the analogy of the present stem (I 6.46). In vulgar speech a regular form [hiəd], usually written *heerd*, is common, e. g. Di Do 12 Polly heerd it; it is mentioned by Walker 1791 (§ 236). || *sell—sold*. || *tell—told*.

Irregular Verbs. Class 6

4.81. *d* is added, and the final consonant of the base is omitted:

have—had. OE *habban, hæfde, gehæfd;* in ME, *v* (OE written *f*) was gradually extended to the forms that had had *bb*. The present vowel [æ] is from the ME unstressed form; *behave* [biˈheiv] represents the stressed form (see vol I 4.432, cf on *ha'n't* vol V 23.1₇). In the prt & ptc *v* was lost in ME through assimilation with

the following *d* (I 2.532). || *make—made; k* was dropped
before *d* in unstressed position (vol I 2.325).

4.8₂. The vowel, too, is changed in a few verbs:
clothe—clad (or *clothed*). Shortening in ME before -*dd*-
(< *ðd*) in the prt & ptc. Cf vol I 3.31. The form *clothed*
is always possible, *clad* is a little archaic and can only
be used accompanied by some sort of specification:
lightly clad | clad in blue.

4.8₃. *will—would* [wud]. || *shall—should* [ʃud]. || *can—
could* [kud].—*Will, shall,* and *can* have no inf and no
ptc in ModE (cf vol IV 1.4). *Can* and *shall* belong to
the perfecto-present (preterit-present) verbs. The OE
ptc *cūþ* survives in the adj *uncouth* orig. 'unknown',
now 'strange, odd', but the prt of *can* became *coude*
in ME, and later, in early ModE, *could* on the analogy
of *would* and *should*. The *l* in the three forms was dropped
in unstressed position (vol I 10.453), and later the weak
forms came to be used even in accented position and
new weak-stressed forms arose [wəd, d, əd, ʃəd, kəd]. The
ME variant form *wol* of *will* survives in *won't* [wount],
vol I 10.33 and V 23.1₇. On *sha'n't* see vol I 10.452
and V 23.1₈, on *can't* V 23.1₈.

There is another vb *will*, which goes back to OE
willian (from *will* sb) and is inflected regularly: see
IV. 15.1.

Irregular Verbs. Class 7

4.9₁. *t* is added after further change of the base:
bring—brought [brɔ·t]. || *think—thought* [pɔ·t]. OE had
two distinct verbs: *þencan* (prt *þōhte*) 'think' and *þyncan*
(prt *þūhte*) 'seem'. The latter was impersonal: *me þyncþ*
('it seems to me') meant very much the same as *ic
þence* ('I think'). In ME the two ran together by purely
phonetic changes, see vol I 3.111 and I 3.113. The
preterits were levelled under *þōhte*. In consequence of
this fusion the impersonal construction practically disappeared, though a remnant is found in *methinks* (prt

methought). ‖ *seek—sought* [so·t]. ‖ *beseech—besought*
[bi|so·t]. From the same OE source as *seek*, with a
prefix added in ME. (*Be*)*seech* is the normal southern
English descendant of OE *sēcan;* the different final
consonant in *seek* may be due either to dialectal influence or to the analogy of OE *sēcst, sēcþ* (2nd & 3rd
pers. sg), which were pronounced with [k]. ‖ *reach—*
raught (*reached*). *Raught* is now extinct, but Sh has it:
Ant IV. 9.30 and Keats 1.99: with wings outraught. ‖
teach—taught [to·t]. The original meaning was 'show',
but in ME the word gradually ousted *leren* (< OE
lǣran) 'teach'. ‖ *catch—caught*. ME *cacchen* from OF
(Picard.) *cachier* (< Low Lat *captiare*); this is a dialectal
variant of OF *chacier* (mod. *chasser*, which in English
became *chase*). While *chase* has the general meaning of
'pursue', *catch* has acquired a special meaning: 'overtake,
seize'. The preterit *caught* is an analogical formation
modelled on the synonym (now lost) ME *lacchen*, prt
laughte, ModE *latch*). The regular form *catched* was
formerly not infrequent. As a prt Sh has it only once
(Cor I. 3.68) against several instances of *caught;* the
ptc *catched* is recorded three times in Sh-lex by the
side of *caught* (six times), apparently without any distinction, though the two are pitted against each other
in: LLL V. 2.69 None are so surely caught when they
are catch'd. Milton has *catcht* ptc once (PL 10.544),
but *caught* seven times. *Catched* remained in literary
use throughout the 18th century, but in PE it is dialectal
or vulgar: Ridge S 85 I mustn't be catched alone with
a young man. ‖ *stretch—straight*. The OE past ptc became ME *straught* or *streight* according to dialectal
development. The former is now extinct, the latter
survives as a pure adj *straight*. It is now entirely dissociated from the verb, which is regular. ‖ *buy—bought*
[bo·t]. OE *bycgan, bohte;* the *cg*-forms disappeared in
ME: see *say* and *lie*. On the ptc *boughten* used in U.S.,
see 5.7₅. ‖ *work—wrought* (or *worked*). *Wrought* from

worhte shows metathesis of the *r* (see vol I 2.824). *Worked* is now the usual form; *wrought* is chiefly used as an adjunct: wrought iron, overwrought nerves. Also in certain other expressions: this wrought wonders | she wrought upon his feelings.

4.9₂. *May—might; maught* is a dialectal form of the prt in frequent literary use in the 16th and 17th centuries (see NED); no ptc or inf. The verb in ModE has come to express not ability, but possibility or permission. ‖ *dare—durst* (or *dared*). *Durst* is now obsolete; the verb is most often regular (he dares | he (had) dared), thus always in the sense of 'challenge'. On *dare* as a prt see vol IV 1.8; on *had dared* ib 10.8(9); on the use with inf vol V 12.2. ‖ *wot—wist*. OE *wāt, wiste* 'know'. The verb is obs. and occurs only in scattered phrases: *wot* is used in *God wot*, the inf *wit* is found in *to wit* 'namely', and the ptc survives in the adverb *unwittingly*. The old prt was still in use in early ModE (e. g. AV Mark 9.6 he wist not what to say), now only in very archaic style.

Chapter V

Tense-Formation in the Verbs. Continued

Irregular Verbs. Class 8

No addition but vowel-change.

5.1₁. Apart from the originally weak verbs of the *bleed—bled* type (see 4.1₄, 5.1₂), this group of verbs has chiefly been created through the levelling of the difference between strong preterits and participles. In a number of verbs the prt has influenced, and assimilated to itself, the form of the ptc: *abide—abode—abode* | *shine—shone—shone*. This tendency was even more strongly felt in former times: ptcs like *drove, wrote, chose, broke, spoke* occur in Sh by the side of *driven,*

written, chosen, broken, spoken. Vulgar speech has kept
some of these forms, e. g. *took* for *taken.* On the whole
question of the loss or retention of *-n* in the ptc, see
5.7.

A levelling influence in the opposite direction, from
ptc to prt, may also be instanced. Thus, in early ModE
there was a great deal of fluctuation between *a* and *u*
in the preterit of some words (e. g. *cling, sing*). The OE
3rd class of strong verbs had an alternation between
a in the sg and *u* in the pl, but the *u*-forms in question
were used also with sg subjects, and vice versa. It is
probable that the *u* was chiefly due to the influence
of the ptc. In PE some of the words have generalized
the *u* (e. g. *cling*), while others preserve the old scheme
i—a—u (e. g. *sing*). Other examples of prts with ptc-
vowels are: *bit, bore, stole.* In vulgar speech the levelling
influence of the ptc is even stronger: *n*-forms like *seen*
and *done* frequently serve as prts. This phenomenon is
particularly common in U.S. (see Mencken's list of
verbs).

As the whole group presents a highly variegated
aspect, the following arrangement in sub-groups is
only tentative, both vowels and consonants having
been taken into account.

5.1₂. *Bleed—bled.* || *breed—bred.* || *feed—fed.* || *lead—led.*
|| *plead—ple(a)d* [pled]. OF *plaidier.* In England the
short prt & ptc is now obs. except in dialects, but
Americans still use it frequently: Lewis EG 274 pled
[prt] | Bromfield GW 66 I've pled with him. || *read—
read* [red]. || *speed—sped.* In older English also regular:
Sh H4B IV. 3.38 I haue speeded hither with the very
extremest ynch of possibilitie. In ModE the vb is regular
when = 'regulate (or increase) the speed of' esp. with
up, as in: we speeded up the work as much as we could. ||
meet—met.

To this type of flexion also belonged, in early ModE,
the verbs *greet* and *heat,* which now follow the regular

conjugation. The prt & ptc *het* survives in vulgar speech
and in dialects. The dialectal & vulgar conjugation
leap—lep is probably of a different historical origin
(see 4.5₁).

5.1₃. *Slide—slid.* The prt owes its vowel to the old
ptc *slidden*, which is now rare.

The type of conjugation represented by *slide* was
much more common in former times: *ride—rid | stride—
strid | bite—bit | write—writ | rise—riz.* All of these
belonged to class I of strong verbs in OE; see now
class 10. On the once weak *chide* and *hide* see 5.3₂.

light—lit (or *lighted*) 'kindle'. The old prt *lihte*, if
regularly developed, would have given ModE [lait]; *lit*
must be due to analogy with the vbs mentioned above
Elphinston 1765: 'very familiar, or rather low'. In the
sense 'set fire to' both *lit* and *lighted* are common,
though as an adjunct the latter is the usual form: he
lighted (lit) a candle | the candle was lighted (lit) | a
lighted candle | Barrie MO 38 once the lights of a
little town are lit. . looked at the lighted windows.
But *lit* is used as an adjunct in compounds: Kipling
L 201 moonlit streets | Stevenson D 97 the lamplit city.
Cf Mannin CI 109 An unlit lamp bears no resemblance
to a lighted one. In a figurative sense *lit* is preferred:
Harraden D 99 his grim face lit up | Hardy W 37 the
radiance lit her pale cheek. On the rare ptc *litten* see
-en 5.7.—There is another vb *light* 'descend' (fig.)
< OE *lihtan* from the adj *liht* > *light* 'not heavy', inflected
with *lighted* or *lit* as prt & ptc: Di DC 52 I sought Mr.
Murdstone's eye as it lighted on mine | Brontë V 123
I lit upon a crape-like material. In the literal sense of
'descend' (e. g. from a carriage) *alight* is used, generally inflected regularly, though *alit* is found in poetry:
By 440 And once so near me he alit.

5.1₄. *Abide—abode* (or *abided*). In the archaic meaning 'dwell' *abode* is still the usual prt & ptc, otherwise
abided is more usual: Norris P 43 she had not abided

by her decision. The old ptc *abidden* is archaic: Scott
Iv 346 the priest hath abidden by the wine-pot a thought
too late.—The vb *bide* (OE *bīdan*) is now little used
outside the phrase "bide one's time", where it is generally regular: Barrie T 417 I bided my time, as the
tragedians say | Ridge L 243 [she] bided her time
patiently. Sh has a prt *bid* by analogy with *slide—slid*,
etc.: R3 IV. 4.304 Endur'd of her, for whom you bid
like sorrow. ‖ *glide—glode*. The strong inflexion was
superseded by the form *glided* in early ModE. Sh has
glided once (H6B III. 2.260 That slyly glyded towards
your Maiestie), but no instances of *glode*. The strong
form was used archaically down to the 19th century:
Shelley 95 as o'er Heaven it [the sun] glode | Tennyson
535 [Sun-star of morning-tide] ... Glode over earth.

5.1₅. *Stand—stood*; the old ptc *standen* is now lost and
replaced by the prt form *stood*. Thus also *understood;*
a ptc *understanded* was common in the 16th century
and is still sometimes used as a quotation from the
Thirty-Nine Articles: Ru F 69 not understanded of
the people. Cf Stoffel S 168-9. ‖ *hold—held*. The modern
prt *held* goes back to an early shortening of OE *hēold*, and
this form was extended to the ptc. The regular ModE
continuation would have been [hi·ld]; this is found once
in Sh as a ptc: Sonn. 2.4 held (: *field*), and a shortened
form *hild* (: *kill'd*, *fulfill'd*) occurs in Lucr 1257. The
old ptc *holden* is used once by Sh: H6B II. 4.71 I summon
your Grace to his Maiesties Parliament holden at Bury.
Even at that time the form appears to have been
obsolescent and used only in official phraseology, where
it has kept its place to the present day: "a meeting
holden on such and such a date". In the AV it is the
usual form, though *held* is used once: Rom. 7.6 wherein
we were held.—*Behold* is inflected like the simple verb.
The old ptc *beholden* is kept in the special sense 'obliged'.

5.1₆. *Sit—sat*. Both prt & ptc are now *sat* from the
OE prt sg form. There is also a form with long vowel

sate [seit] (cf Beaumont 2.411 late : sate | Wordsw
363-4 sate : translate), which is now archaic. Al.
Schmidt's Sh-lex gives only *sat*, but *sate* occurs three
times: Tw II. 4.117, Mids II. 1.66, H5 II. 2.4. Certain
authors seem to make a distinction between *sate* and
sat, using the latter only in *sat down:* Spect no. 34 I last
night sate very late in company with this select body
of friends | ib 57 We were no sooner sat down | Ru P
2.65 sat down .. they sate laughing and chattering.
Yet Goldsmith V 1.149, 2.5 & 180 writes "sate down",
but ib 1.157 he sat with the family | ib 2.223 my two
little ones sat upon each knee. Among 19th century
writers Shelley has *sat* prt 12 times, but *sate* much
more often, also as ptc. Thackeray has most often
sate, both as prt & ptc, yet not infrequently *sat*. Tennyson, according to Baker's Concordance, has *sate* only
once, but *sat* very often. The old ptc in *-en* has disappeared from StE; remnants are found in early ModE:
Deloney 10 they had not sitten long. || *spit—spat*. The
verb is a mixture of two originally distinct words: OE
spittan, spitte and *spǣtan, spǣtte*. These would regularly
have given ModE *spit—spit* and *spete—spat* (*spet*). The
prt *spit* occurs in older literature, e. g. in Sh & AV,
and it is still the usual colloquial form for prt & ptc
in U.S. In British English its place has been taken by
spat, whose present tense form *spete* is now extinct. The
form *spet* was in use in early ModE: Sh Merch I. 3.113 prs |
Deloney 39 haue spet.—The entirely unrelated vb *spit*
'pierce with a spit or sword' is of course regular. ||
shoot—shot. OE *scēotan* (str. II). The form *shoot* arose
through shifting of the stress in the diphthong *ēo* from
the first to the second element, the unstressed *e* being
absorbed into the palatal consonant: | ʃeˑot > ʃoˑt |;
cf vol I 3.602. ME also had a form with unshifted
stress: *shete* (e. g. in Chaucer, now extinct). Similarly,
the prt *shot* probably goes back to OE *scēat*, which
first underwent stress-shifting and later shortening. On
the ptc *shotten* see 5.7₅.

get—got. OE *ȝietan* only in compounds (*be-, on-, for-*). Scandinavian influence is responsible for the use of the uncompounded form and for the initial stopped consonant *g*. The conjugation in ME came under the influence of class IV: *geten, gat, gotten*. The prt *got* with the vowel taken from the ptc is met with in the 16th century, and in the 17th century this became the usual form. *Gat* occurs once in Sh: Per. I. 2.6 (riming with *at*); otherwise *got* is used. *Gat* is now only found in archaic and poetic language. On the ptc with or without *-en* in Sh, Sc and U.S. see vol IV 4.4(6). In StE, *gotten* is now archaic (though kept in the phrase "ill-gotten gains"), but it is found in dialects: Phillpotts M 29 I've gotten a fat old volume somewhere (SW dial.). Also in Irish and Scotch: Moore L 146 we have gotten the after-glow | Scott Iv 343 those of the castle, who had gotten to horse | Cronin H 150 this young pup .. had .. gotten away with it. Cf also *beget* and *forget* (5.7₅). ‖ *fight—fought* [fɔ·t]. A prt *fit* & ptc *fit(ten)*, formed on the analogy of *bite—bit—bit(ten)*, are in vg and dialectal use (NED). Elphinston 1765 calls the form *fit* 'very familiar, or rather low'. On the ptc *foughten* see 5.7₅. ‖ *freight—fraught*. The latter form originated in ptc of the invariable vb *fraught*, which is now extinct and replaced by *freight* (both vbs prob. fr. Dutch). *Freight* is usually regular; *fraught* is now only used in the phrase "fraught with (danger, fate, etc.)". Galsworthy's usage is unusual in: F 71 Stanley's car, fraught with Felix and a note from Clara. ‖ *distract*. The adj *distraught* 'bewildered, agitated' is now to some extent associated with the regular vb *distract*.

5.1₇. *Cling—clung.* The prt *clang*, recorded by the NED till the 15th century, is now dialectal. ‖ *fling—flung* (from ON). The word was originally weak but was made strong in English by analogy with the other words in *-ing*. The prt *flang* occurred in StE till the

17th century and is still found in dialects. || *sling—slung* (from ON), originally weak. A prt *slang* occurs in the AV: 1 Sam. 17.49 Dauid .. tooke thence a stone, and slang it. It is now dialectal. || *slink—slunk. Slank* prt is archaic: Allen W 158 he slank noiselessly from the room. || *sting—stung*. || *string—strung*, formed in ME from the sb and made strong by analogy. A regular form in -*ed* is used as a pure adj 'provided with strings': *stringed instruments*, but: *highly strung nerves. Hamstrung* and *hamstringed* are both in use. || *swing—swung*. The form *swang* is now obs or dialectal. || *wring—wrung*.

spin—spun. Span prt is obsolescent though recorded in the NED down to the 19th century; Sh has only *spun*. || *win—won* [wʌn]. *Wan* was the usual prt down to the 16th century.

hang—hung. OE had a reduplicative transitive vb *hōn, heng, hangen* and a weak intransitive vb *hangian*. In ME a new inf *hangen* took the place of *hōn* in the South of England, by which process the two vbs partially coalesced and were consequently generally confused, the weak forms being used transitively and vice versa, e. g. Ch D 760 his wyves three Hanged hem-self. In northern English, *hōn* was replaced by ON *hengja*, which was adopted as *heng* or *hing*, and this new verb, which was originally weak, was later remodelled on the analogy of the *cling—clung* type. StE now uses the southern inf *hang* with the northern form *hung* as prt & ptc. The weak form *hanged* was common in the older language (it is universally used in all Bible-versions subsequent to Tindale), but was gradually superseded by *hung* in the general sense, trans. and intr., *hanged* being now as a rule restricted to the meaning 'killed by hanging'. Even in this sense, however, *hung* is common; in vg American, according to Mencken AL, "the literary *hanged* is never heard", and even in British literature numerous examples of *hung* for *hanged* occur: Southey L 60 he ought to be hung,

drawn, and quartered | Hunt A 70 every bad boy
was to be hung | Shelley L 497 a beam, on which prison-
ers were hung in secret | Thackeray N 769 I have not
the least objection in life to a rogue being hung | Di
OT 20 | Galsworthy T 65 I couldn't face letting an
innocent man be hung for me | Masefield S 224 the
ground about the hung man. Cf also McCarthy King
230 I haven't *hanged* a man for a week | ib 232 as if
every man in the world had been *hung* | Benson D 2.270
murderer .. be *hanged* | ib 315 going to be *hung* |
Crofts St 53 he was to be *hung* | ib 197 he was ..
hanged.

shine—shone [ʃɔn]. Regular forms might formerly be
met with: Marlowe H 103 shin'd (: mind) | Pope Man 4.281
shin'd (: mankind). As a causative verb = 'polish
(boots, etc.)', it is generally regular: "he shined my
boots till they fairly shone". Yet: Gaye Vivandière 126
he was cursing his servant heartily for not having
shone his boots up properly.

5.1₈. *Bind—bound.* On the old ptc in -*en* see 5.7₅. ||
find—found. || *grind—ground.* || *wind—wound.* OE *wind-
an* (strong III). The meaning of the OE vb was 'twist,
coil'; at a later date a new vb *wind* 'blow' was formed
from the sb *wind*, which at that time was pronounced
[waind]. This verb was probably at first regular (e. g.
Sh Ado I. 1.243 I will haue a rechate winded in my
fore head), but when later the sb came to be pronounced
[wind], the two (sb and vb) were no longer felt as belonging together, and the vb was associated with the
old strong verb *wind* 'twist' and consequently assumed
strong forms. At the present day both *wound* and *winded*
[waindid] are in use as prt & ptc of *wind* in the sense
'blow, sound (a horn, etc.)'. There is another vb *wind*
[wind] 'get wind of; exhaust the wind of; let recover
wind', which is always regular: the hounds winded the
fox | to get winded by running.

5.1₉. *Climb—clomb* [kloum] or *climbed. Clomb* is poetic

or dialectal: Shelley 101 the sun clomb Heaven's eastern
steep | Wordsw P 6.212 having clomb. A form *clum(b)*
is common in vg Amr: Norris B 225 Billy .. clum up
in that bally pulpit.

strike—struck. The normal descendant of OE *strāc*
(prt sg) is *stroke*, which was displaced in the 17th century by the present-day form (a form *strook* was also
in use for a period; it is found as late as Shelley 107).
As there may have existed an inf *strick*, it seems pròb-
able that *struck* owes its origin to analogy with *stick—
stuck* (see below). The old ptc is now always used
figuratively; it survives chiefly in particular archaic
phrases such as *stricken* ('affected') *with disease* | *stricken*
('advanced') *in years* | *a stricken field* 'a pitched battle',
and in compounds, often side by side with *struck:
horror-stricken, panic-stricken, heart-stricken, conscience-
stricken*. Very often it is a matter of personal taste
whether *struck* or *stricken* is preferred in a compound,
the latter being more literary; in some cases one of the
forms is generally preferred: *awestruck, stage-struck*. In
pure verbal use *stricken* survives in U.S. in the sense
'deleted, struck out': they moved that the clause be
stricken out. See also 5.7₆. Other archaic ptc forms are:
Marlowe H 1.121 strooken | Mi PL 9.1064 struck'n mute.

stick—stuck. Two vbs fused, OE *stician* and ME
steken; stuck arose in early ModE, probably under the
influence of *sting—stung*. ‖ *dig—dug*. The verb (from
OF) was at first weak, but developed a prt & ptc *dug*
after the analogy of other words with the shift *i—u*.
The form *digged*, which is the only one used in Sh and
AV, is now rare; the two forms are used side by side
in: Stevenson MP 89 The earth, that he had digged so
much in his life, was dug out by another for himself.

heave—hove (or *heaved*). In early ME the *bb* of the
OE present stem was supplanted by *v* from the inflected
forms. The ModE prt *hove* is due to influence from
class IV. The verb is more often regular, but the strong

flexion is used in nautical phrases: the ship hove in
sight, hove alongside, hove out of harbour | Byron
DJ 3.20 He left his ship to be hove down next day. ‖
stave—stove (or *staved*). The verb was formed in the
ModE period from the sb *stave* 'piece of a cask'. Its
strong inflexion is due to analogy and is chiefly nautical,
usually comb. w. *in:* the fore compartment was stove
in at the collision | Wells Blw 105 I had some ribs
stove in ‖ he staved off bankruptcy for a while.

Irregular Verbs. Class 9

No addition; vowel-difference between prs and prt,
and between prt and ptc:

5.21. *Swim—swam—swum.* A prt *swum* from the OE
prt pl form, or from the ptc is sometimes met with,
especially in older literature; on the other hand, a ptc
swam also occurs. Sh's usage wavers; both *a* and *u*-
forms are used in prt as well as in ptc: Tp III. 2.16
swam prt | As IV. 1.38 swam ptc ‖ Gent I. 1.26 swom
prt sg | Tp II. 2.133 swom ptc. Even at a much later
date deviations from the vowel-scheme *i—a—u* occur:
Brontë V 8 swum prt | id P 208 swam ptc | Dreiser
AT 2.174 to have swam (but ib 193 swum). According
to Mencken AL, vg Amr has *swim—swum—swam.* ‖
begin—began—begun. The same fluctuation as in the
case of *swim:* Bunyan P 1 I begun, 3 he began, 34 I
have began | Defoe R 104 & 252 I begun, 105 & 351
I began, 150 I should have began. Though there can
be no doubt what is the usual flexion in 19th and 20th
century English, deviations occur: By L 194 I begun |
Keats 4.199 *et al.* I have began | Black F 1.237 began
[prt] .. begun [prt] | Masefield E 62 I begun. Vg Amr
has *begin—begun—began* (Mencken AL). ‖ *ring—rang—
rung;* orig. weak but made strong by analogy. A prt
rung was formerly not infrequent and is still sometimes
used: Sh Meas IV. 2.78 the Curphew rung | Mi PL 3.347

Heav'n rung With Jubilee | By DJ 7.49 The whole
camp rung with joy | Scott Iv 227 the hall rung with
acclamations | Norris P 90 I rung 'em up. Mencken
gives *ring—rung—rang* for U.S. || *sing—sang—sung*. Sh
has *sang* prt only once: Sonn. 73.4 (in rime!), otherwise
sung. The latter form was the usual prt form for several
centuries, but is now rare. Instances occur, for example,
in Walton, Milton, Defoe, Fielding, Goldsmith, Boswell,
Scott, Byron, Shelley, Tennyson, Thackeray, Emily
Brontë, Meredith, Wilde, and Hugh Walpole. Several
of these authors also use *sang*. Mencken AL gives
sing—sung—sang. || *spring—sprang—sprung*. Besides
the more common prt *sprang*, an alternative form
sprung occurs, e. g. in Sh (Err I. 1.6, H4B 1.1 III, etc.,
cf Ven 1168 A purple floure sproong vp), Cowper,
Byron, Shelley, Macaulay, Charlotte Brontë, and
Compton Mackenzie. Vg Amr, according to Mencken
AL has *spring—sprung—sprang*.

5.2₂. *Drink—drank—drunk.* A prt *drunk* is instanced
from the 16th to the 19th century: Sh Alls II. 3.106
thy father drunke wine | Di P 617 Mr. Pell sighed . .
and the rum having by that time arrived, drunk it up.
On the other hand, a ptc *drank* has been in frequent
use for several centuries, possibly to avoid association
with *drunk* 'intoxicated'. It is now getting rare, but
instances occur in all the best-known authors from
Bunyan (P 231 I have drank) down to our time: Scott
Iv 172 he had drank | By DJ 11.75 having voted,
dined, drank, gamed, and whored | Shelley 55 had
drank | Keats 4.54 the quantity of wine that would
be drank | Di P 308 . . who had eaten and drank very
heartily | id OT 189 I've eat and drank | Trollope A 61
having first drank the brandy | Kingsley Y 88 they
had drank | Graves Goodbye 78 I had drank a lot of
cherry-whisky. Mencken AL gives *drink—drunk, drank
—drank.*—The full ptc form *drunken* is rare and archaic
in pure verbal function: Wells OH 555 They had all

drunken from the same cup. It is mostly used as an adj in adjunctal position see 5.7₆. ‖ *shrink—shrank— shrunk*. There is an alternative prt form *shrunk*, used since late ME; it was the usual prt form in the 18th century, but is now archaic: Sh Hml I. 2.219 it shrunke in hast away | Cowper L 2.406 I shrunk from the precipice | Di P 523 Mrs. Cluppins shrunk within herself.— The old ptc *shrunken* (not in Sh) is archaic in pure verbal function: Wells F 59 cities have shrunken. It is now chiefly used as an adj (5.7₆). ‖ *sink—sank—sunk*. OE *sincan* (str. III). A prt *sunk* in use from the 16th century: Spencer FQ II. 1.46 thrise she sunke againe | AV 1 Sam. 17.49 the stone sunke into his forehead (but *sanke:* Ex. 15.10) | Di P 207 he sunk to sleep again. —The form is now rare. On the other hand, a ptc *sank* is occasionally met with: By DJ 3.89 has sank (: rank). Mencken AL has *sink—sunk—sank*.—The old ptc *sunken* is now rare except as a pure adj: Hawth Sn 14 the sun had sunken so nearly to the edge of the world | Wells OH 562 this had not sunken very deeply into the imagination ‖ Galsworthy FM 95 He is still unshaven, a little sunken in the face. Cf 5.7₆. ‖ *stink—stank—stunk*. The alternative prt *stunk* is not uncommon; its use goes back to the 16th century. The AV has: Ex. 7.21 the riuer stunke (but *stanke:* Ex. 7.14 *et al.*). From modern slang: Benson DB 143 smoking .. How did you know? .. Because I stunk you when you came back.

5.2₃. *Run—ran—run*. Besides the older form *rinnan* (str. III) OE had *irnan* (or *iernan, yrnan, eornan*) with metathesis of the *r*. It is probable that the ME form *rinne(n)* was partly of Scandinavian origin (ON *rinna*). The ModE present stem *run* is hard to explain; the *u* may have been introduced from the ptc. A prt *run* is found, by the side of the more common *ran*, in a great many writers from the 16th to the 19th century: Sh (Mcb II. 3.117 Th' expedition of my violent Loue

Out-run the pawser, Reason), Bunyan, Defoe, Swift,
Fielding, and Goldsmith. The form is used to characterize dialectal speech in: GE M 1.10 That niver run i'
my family | Synge 1.16 Then I run and I run. A ptc
ran is also occasionally met with: Massinger N III.
2.65 I have ran | Bunyan P 67 thou hast ran away.
Mencken AL gives *run—run—ran.* || *come—came—come.*
The ModE prt *came* goes back to late ME *cām*, earlier
căm, which is a new formation, probably on the analogy
of *niman, nam* (now extinct). The old prt *come* died
out in the literary language about 1600; Sh has it
once: H4A II. 4.201 and then come in the other. Vg
Amr has *come—come—come* (or *came*): see Mencken
AL. A vulgar and dialectal prt & ptc *comed* has been
in use for some time, earlier in the ptc than in the
prt (see NED).—The compound *become* is conjugated
like the simple verb (Sh has *misbecomed* once: LLL V.
2.778), but *welcome* (< OE sb *wilcuma* 'welcome guest')
is always regular.

Irregular Verbs. Class 10

5.3₁. No addition in the prt, but *-n* in the ptc; vowel-
difference between prs & prt, and often between prt
& ptc.

Drive—drove—driven. The form *drove* was once commonly extended to the ptc; this is now vulgar: Shaw
J 256 he has just drove up to the door [said by a servant].
Driv (prt & ptc) is still heard in popular American. An
alternative prt *drave*, the northern descendant of OE
drāf, is occasionally encountered in older literature: Sh
Troil III. 3.190 And draue great Mars to faction |
AV Josh 24.18 The Lord draue out from before vs all
the people. || *shrive—shrove—shriven.* The verb is now
archaic. Regular forms are also met with: Sh Rom
II. 4.194 be shriu'd and married. || *strive—strove—striven*
(from OF), in ME made strong by analogy. A ptc

strove is occasionally used, e. g. by Sh (only once: H8
II. 4.30) and Scott. Regular forms were fairly common
in literature down to the 19th century, e. g. Ridge
S 47 a high goal to be strived for. They still occur in
U.S. || *thrive—throve—thriven* (from ON). In early ModE
the verb was frequently inflected regularly; Sh and
Pope have only weak forms; Defoe R 2.92 thriv'd,
but R 136 throve. The regular flexion is now rare in
England (GE A 235 they thrived), whereas Americans
still use it commonly.

(a)rise— (a)rose—(a)risen. A prt & ptc *riz* (variously
spelt) was in use for a period in ModE (see NED).
Arose is used as a ptc for example by Sh (Err V. 1.388),
who, on the other hand, has only *risen* as ptc of *rise*. ||
ride—rode—ridden. A form *rid* (prt & ptc) was in use
as far down as the 19th century: By DJ 13.23 Henry
rid Well, like most Englishmen | Austen S 268 he had
rid into the country. Sh uses *rode* as a ptc: H5 IV. 3.2
The King himselfe is rode to view their Battaile. Cf
5.7₅. || *smite—smote—smitten.* The flexion *smite—smit—
smit* is archaic. Altogether the verb is now hardly colloquial, except *smitten* = 'in love'. *Smote* as a ptc
occurs in Sh LLL IV. 3.28 their fresh rayse haue smot
| By 440 I could have smote | Cronin H 273 they had
smote him. || *stride—strode—stridden.* The ptc *stridden*
is hardly used any longer, a weak form *strided* being
generally substituted. An alternative ptc form is *strid*,
which was also in use as a prt for a period. Stevenson
has a ptc *strode:* T 58 the captain, who had so often
strode along the beach. Like the simple verb, *bestride*
shows much vacillation; Sh has *bestrid* prt & ptc: Ant
V. 2.82 His legges bestrid the Ocean | R2 V.5.7 9 That
horse, that thou so often hast bestrid. || *write—wrote—
written.* A prt & ptc *writ* was once in common use by
the side of *wrote* and *written*. *Wrote* prt is rare in Sh,
who generally has *writ*. As a ptc the form is found, for
instance, in Milton's famous line: Presbyter is but Old

Priest writ Large. In StE, *writ* is now archaic, but it
is used in dialects: Hardy W 165 you've not writ a
line. *Wrote* as a ptc is found in older literature alongside
of *writ(ten)*; Sh has it a few times, other examples are:
Swift J 465 has wrote a book | Boswell 1.318 I have
wrote them down—have written only half lines. I have
written a hundred lines in a day.

5.3₂. *Chide—chid—chidden, chid.* OE weak *cīdan, cidde*
regularly became ModE *chide—chid.* In early ModE
the verb became mixed up with originally strong verbs
like *ride*, etc. In consequence of this fusion the forms
chode and *chidden* arose, the latter of which is still in
common use. *Chode* prt is found in AV Gen. 31.36 &
Nu. 20.3, but has now disappeared. In the ptc Sh has
chid and *chidden*, but always the *n*-form before a substantive, and this state of affairs has remained to the
present day. Regular forms are now also in use: Barrie
T 237 she chided him merrily for being forgetful |
Brontë W 33 she got chided. || *hide—hid—hidden.* OE
weak *hȳdan, hȳdde.* Like *chide*, this verb came under
the influence of strong verbs and developed a ptc in
-en in the 16th century; Sh uses *hidden* only as an adjunct, but the AV makes no such distinction between
hid and *hidden.* The ptc is now usually *hidden*, thus
always in adjunctal use: Collins W 75 the same hidden
source. In the predicative and in pure verbal use, the
short form is now felt as old-fashioned; it is perhaps
a little more common after *lie* than after *be:* Macaulay
H 1.165 ingratitude may lie hid under the obsequious
demeanour of courtiers | Collins W 71 some undis-
coverable danger lying hid from us all | MacCarthy
2.442 the worshippers in the Catholic faith had long to
lie hid in caves | Rose Macaulay P 17 so much of it as lay
hid in the rocky Cornish caves. || *bite—bit—bitten.* The
old prt sg *bote* (OE *bāt*) died out in southern English
in the 16th century and was replaced by *bit* with its
vowel from the old prt pl or from the ptc: AV Am.

6.19 a serpent bit him. The ptc is now usually *bitten;*
the form *bit* was formerly not uncommon, e. g. Swift
J 490 you will think it to be mine, and be bit ['mistaken'].
Cf Thack E 2.150 Miss Beatrix at first was quite *bit*
(as the phrase of that day was). In PE the form is only
used in the phrase "the biter bit"; otherwise it is dialectal or vulgar: Wells L 146 One 'ud think something
had bit him.

5.3₃. *Bear—bore—born(e).* There is an older prt form
bare from OE *bær* (prt sg) with vowel-lengthening in
ME by analogy with the other forms of the verb. In
late ME this became the usual form in the plural as
well, but in early ModE *bare* was superseded by *bore*
with *o* from the ptc. Sh has both *bare* (3 times) and
bore (many times), the AV only the former, Pope only
the latter. A ptc *bore* was in use till the 18th century,
when it was abandoned, except in vg language: Di F
405 to be bore in mind. The *n*-form has two spellings:
born and *borne;* the latter is used in all senses except
that of birth, but even in that sense *borne* is used in
the active ("she has borne five children") and if *by*
follows ("borne in a stable by the Virgin Mary"); but:
"he was born blind; born in a stable; all children born
to them; the first-born son; he was born in 1899". This
distinction, of course, is purely artificial; it dates from
the latter half of the 18th century (see NED). ‖ *swear—
swore—sworn.* The prt *swore* may owe its vowel [ɔ·]
to the analogy of *bore* or to the influence of the *r* (cf
I 13.351 ff). A prt *sware* (cf *bare*) was in wide-spread
use for a period in early ModE; it is rare in Sh, but
it is the only form used in the AV. It still sometimes
occurs in poetic and archaic language. A ptc *swore*
was once in literary use (e. g. Fielding 3.446 he had
heartily swore), but is now confined to dialectal and
vulgar speech: GE M. 1.97 to sit by and hear me swore
at. ‖ *tear—tore—torn.* The prt *tare* was superseded about
1600 by *tore* with *o* from the ptc; the old form is still

found in AV, but Sh has *tore*. As a ptc, *tore* was used
for several centuries (e. g. Swift J 370 I have .. tore
it); it is still used in dialects and popular Amr: Lewis
MS 136 to see the town .. being tore down. || *wear—
wore—worn*. OE *werian*, a weak verb which in ME was
made strong by the analogy of *bear*. The strong prt
was at first *ware* (thus in Caxton), but this form later
gave place to *wore*. Sh has *wore* everywhere except in
Tit. I. 1.6 (Qq *ware* but the Ff *wore*); AV has *ware* in
Luke 8.27. The form may still be met with in poetry: Tennyson 446 That ware their ladies' colours on the casque.
A ptc *wore* occurs in vg language: Di F 401 was wore.

5.3₄. *Tread—trod—trodden*. (V). Caxton has *trade*
prt; the *o*-forms in prt & ptc are due to association
with *bear*, etc., where the *o* of the ptc was extended
to the prt. In early ModE long and short forms existed
side by side in inf, prt, and ptc, e. g. Sh Tp II. 2.73
trod prt | AV Luke 12.1 trode prt. Long prt forms may
still be met with in 19th century poetic language and
in modern dialects: By DJ 6.111 trode (: show'd) |
Tennyson 29 trode (: glow'd) | Hawth S 87 | Brontë V 53.
Besides *trodden* there is also a less usual ptc *trod:*
Coleridge B 26 the greater part have been trod under
foot | Mary Shelley F 38 I have retrod the steps of
knowledge. Sh has both forms, the short one in active
and passive verbal constructions, the long one in the
passive and in adjunctal use (see Sh-lex). || *forget—
forgot—forgotten*. Its history is the same as that of
get (5.1₆), with the exception that the long ptc *forgotten*
has remained in StE and is now the more common
form. *Forgot* as a ptc was extremely common in older
literature, often used side by side with the longer form,
which appears to have been universal in adjunctal posi-
tion (e. g. in Sh): Swift J 471 & 487 I have forgot |
ib 80 lest R. should have forgotten | Goldsm V 2.180
I have not forgot you | ib 2.143 .. seem to have for-
gotten me | Cowper L 1.370 to be forgot | ib 1.170 to

have forgotten. The short form was still in ordinary use in the beginning of the 19th century: Austen S 321 have you forgot what passed? | By L 4 what I have almost entirely forgot | Macaulay L 1.124 [letter 1821] my remarks, which I have quite forgot. Outside archaic style, the form is now vg or dialectal: Bennett ECh 7 Master's forgot his key | Hardy L 77 By Jerry, I'd forgot it.—The flexion of *beget* is on the whole the same as that of *forget*, but the old prt *begat* has remained in archaistic use by the side of *begot:* Wells Ma 2.225 the powers that begat us | Phillpotts K 137 it begat fresh and gathering gloom.

5.3₅. *Break—broke—broken.* Already in OE the verb developed a ptc *brocen.* The *o* of this form was later extended to the prt. The AV has only *brake* in the prt, but in Sh this form is rarer than *broke;* it is not in Mi at all, and in later use is archaistic. Pope has only *broke,* but 19th century poets use *brake* occasionally (e. g. Shelley and Tennyson). In the 17th and 18th centuries *broke* was common as a ptc alongside of *broken;* Sh has both forms, but as adjunct always *broken:* Troil III 1.52 here is good broken musicke.—You haue broke it. This usage continued, but with decreasing frequency, in the 19th c.: Austen S 290 I have broke it to her | Scott OM 57 had broke out | Quincey 91 St. George's Channel had broke loose | Thack P 222 my mamma's anguish would have broke out next term. Nowadays *broke* ptc is a colloquial term for 'out of money, bankrupt': Kipling L 266 I am about as completely broke as a man need be | Shaw 1.172 He's stony broke | Galsw Sw 44 'go broke'. The form survives as a true ptc in vg Amr: '*Broke* is always used in the passive. One hears "I was broke" but never "I was broken"' (Mencken AL).

speak—spoke—spoken. The *r* of OE *sprecan* was dropped as early as the 10th century (cf vol I 2.823). The vowel *o* in the prt & ptc is due to the analogy of class IV (cf *break*). The older prt *spake* persisted for a long time, and *spoke* did not become the usual form till after 1600. Sh has both forms, AV only *spake*. In the ptc the shortened form *spoke* was probably never as common as *spoken* (Sh has both), but occurred fairly often down to the beginning of the 19th century: Austen P 25 being spoke to | Keats 4.59 I have spoke to Haydon. It is now obsolete.—*Bespoke* as the ptc of *bespeak* lingers only in adjunctal use ("bespoke goods" in contrast with *ready-made*, "a bespoke bootmaker"), otherwise *bespoken*, but GE S 143 He's bespoke her for the next dance.

wake—woke—woken (*woke*). These are the strong forms of the verb, but a weak prt & ptc *waked* is also in common use. Originally two distinct verbs, OE **wacan* (strong) 'arise, be born' and *wacian* (weak) 'be awake, watch' ran together in ME and developed a causative meaning as well = 'rouse from sleep'. OE had also a weak vb *wæcn(i)an*, which became ModE *waken*, at first only intransitive. Finally, there is a whole corresponding set of forms with the prefix *a* (OE *ā, on*). ModE thus has four synonymous verbs: *wake, awake, waken, awaken*, the last two of which are always regular, while the first two have also strong forms. The forms *woke* and *woken* are probably due to the analogy of *broke—broken*, etc. The *n*-less ptc (*a*)*woke* has remained in ordinary use. A direct descendant of the OE ptc *awacen* is preserved in *awake*, which is no longer felt as a ptc, but associated with the common type of formation, *a* + the base of a verb, e. g. *asleep*.

The four verbs are in PE to a wide extent used indiscriminately. Cp. Benson A 307 there began to wake in her that new sense that almost always wakens in those .. | Bennett P 139 Paul did not waken .. to waken him .. You told me to wake you at six. And Paul woke | ib 205 a servant awoke him | ib 231 he had been asleep and had awakened | Bromfield GW 40 he always wakened quickly and sharply | ib 133 he awakened quickly.—All four verbs are intransitive ('become awake') as well as transitive ('cause to become awake'). *Wake* formerly had also a static sense 'remain awake', which is now archaic except in a few phrases: "in his waking hours", "waking or sleeping", "waking dreams". The other static sense of *wake* 'hold wake over (dead person)' is also rare. In the inchoative senses *up* is often added: "wake up there!", "this woke him up". *Waken* is = *wake up*, but conveys 'less of abruptness' (Conc. Oxf. Dict.). There is perhaps some tendency to prefer the vbs in -*n* in the passive ("he was (a)wakened by the noise"), but it is not carried through: Rose Macaulay O 14 she was woken by infants clamouring for breakfast | AHuxley PCP 278 Walter would be woken from his dream | Galsworthy F 39 be waked up. In a figurative sense *awake* and *awaken* are often preferred ("he awoke to what it all meant", "this had awakened his sense of honour"); yet: Parker R 37 something had waked in the odd soul of B | Masefield M 233 the sight woke in him a blind pity || Norris O 380 the heart of the man had not yet wakened | Carpenter P 57 wakening vengeful feelings in his bosom.

A few remarks are necessary about the inflected forms of (*a*)*wake*. As mentioned above, both strong and weak forms are in use. In early ModE the weak flexion appears to have been generally preferred; Sh has no strong forms. According to the NED, there has been a tendency in later times to restrict the strong forms to the original intransitive sense, but this has never been fully carried out. As a matter of fact, strong forms are very often used transitively: London M 408 the gong woke him | Butler ER 318 I woke with a loud cry that woke my dog also | Locke A 287 he woke me up | Bennett P 205 a servant awoke him || Merrick MG 94 you've woke him up | Deeping RR 392 Sorry I've woken you up | Gissing H 31 I like to be awoke by the

cock crowing.—All the available forms, however, are
not equally frequent. The ptc *woken*, for example, is
avoided by many speakers, and the shortened ptc *woke*
is not so common as the regular form *waked*. On the
other hand, in the prt the strong form *woke* seems to
be the prevailing form. In the parallel vb *awake* we
find similar tendencies. The strong prt *awoke* predominates, but *awaked* is used in the ptc alongside of
awoke, the *n*-form being now obsolescent. The commonly
used forms may be thus tabulated:

wake—woke (waked)—waked (woke),
awake—awoke—awaked (awoke).

Actual usage is so uncertain, that no quite definite
rules can be laid down.

5.3₆. *Steal—stole—stolen.* The old prt *stale* has been
replaced by *stole* with its vowel from the ptc; *stale* is
found in AV by the side of *stole*. The ptc is now always
stolen, but a shortened form *stole* was in occasional
use down to the 19th century: By L 7 had I stole.
Now only vg: Shaw C 222 has stole my coat. ‖ *weave—*
wove—woven. The prt & ptc have assumed the vowel *o*
after *speak*, *break*, etc. Weak forms began to appear
in ME and were fairly frequent in the 16th century,
thus often in Sh. Now rare. There is a shortened ptc
wove (Mi PL 9.839 Adam had wove .. a garland |
Sterne M 1.111 the web she had wove), now chiefly
used in trade terms such as "wove paper", "hard-
wove fabrics": Di P 567 extra superfine wire-wove
penitence. ‖ *cleave—clove—cloven.* 'split'. The prt *clove*
may be an analogical formation (cf *weave*), or it may
be a modified form of OE *clēaf* (cf vol I 3.603). There
was formerly also a prt *clave* (e. g. AV Gen. 22.3 Abraham
.. claue the wood), perhaps due to a confusion with
the homophonous vb *cleave* 'adhere' (see 4.5₂). Besides
the forms here mentioned two other flexions of *cleave*
'split' are in use: *cleave—cleft* and *cleave—cleaved*. The
ptc *cloven* is now chiefly used as an adjunct, as in:

a cloven hoof (Brontë V 399 | Thack H 86 he showed his cloven foot; yet always: "a cleft palate", "in a cleft stick", i. e. a tight place), but one also sometimes finds it in verbal function: Parker R 51 he had irresistibly cloven his way to their judgment | Locke S 290 [he would] have cloven the blasphemer from skull to chine.

5.3₇. *Freeze—froze—frozen.* The old consonant-change (due to Verner's Law, cf 4.1₂) has disappeared. The old ptc is seen in the archaic adj *frore:* Shelley 133 in the frore and foggy air. The prt *froze* owes its vowel to the ptc. A shortened ptc *froze* occurs in Sh (never adjunctally) and is still found in dialects and vg speech: Ridge G 15 you get almost froze. || *seethe—sod—sodden.* The consonant-change is due to Verner's Law (cf 4.1₂). The original prt (OE *sēað*) disappeared in ME and was replaced by *sod* from the ptc. The vowel in *sod(den)* has undergone a shortening parallel to that in *trod(den)*. In the ptc Sh has both *sod* and *sodden*, but as an adjunct generally the latter form. In PE, *seethe* is regular; *sod* is obsolete (AV Gen. 25.29 And Iacob sod pottage), and *sodden* is a pure adj meaning 'soaked through', employed without any feeling of its relation to *seethe*.

choose—chose—chosen. The vowel of the present stem is due to a shifting of the stress in the original diphthong *ēo;* cf *shoot* (5.1₆) and vol I 3.602. Similarly, the prt *chose* is a descendant, through stress-shifting, of OE *cēas.* The OE ptc *coren* (Verner's Law! cf 4.1₂) was re-formed in ME as *chosen*, after the present stem. A present stem *chuse* of dubious origin (see NED) was in use for a period in ModE alongside of *choose*, but went out of use in the 19th century. A shortened ptc *chose* was frequent till the 18th century. Sh has *chose* and *chosen*, but only the latter as an adjunct. Gay BP 109 Hath chose me; a late example is Churchill C 313 Meant to have it all chose.

5.3₈. *Forsake—forsook—forsaken.* There is an archaic ptc form *forsook* from the prt: Sh and Mi have *forsook*

and *forsaken* as ptc, AV only the latter. Sh Oth IV.
2.125 Hath she forsooke so many Noble Matches |
Mrs Browning 287 memories unforsook. || *shake—shook—
shaken*. The form *shook* was once in ordinary use as a
ptc (e. g. in Sh by the side of *shaken*), while AV has
only *shaken; shook* as a ptc occurs as far down as the
19th c.: Thack N 457 Her attendant may have shook
her fist behind her | Stevenson T 38 the house must
have shook with it. It is now dialectal or vg. Weak
forms sprang up in ME and were frequent in early
ModE: More U 71 he shaked his heade. Sh has *shaked*
beside the more usual *shook* and *shaken,* and so has the
AV: Ps 109.25 they shaked their heads (but Acts 13.31
shooke). The form is now extinct in Standard English. ||
take—took—taken (from ON). In the ptc the contracted
form *ta'en* (cf *made:* see vol I 2.325) now belongs to
poetry, but seems to have been once more commonly
used, e. g. in Sh. *Took* as a ptc was in literary use, by
the side of *taken* (which is the only form in AV), down
to the 19th century: Sh Ant IV 6.2 Our will is Antony
be tooke aliue | Keats 4.171 if I had stayed .. and
took tea || By DJ 13.85 neither eyes nor ears For com-
moners had ever them mistook | Hazlitt A 84 I have
mistook my person. The form is now vg: Ridge S 64
Who's took my money?

5.3₉. *Blow—blew—blown.* OE redupl. *blāwan* 'blow (of
wind)' and redupl. *blōwan* 'bloom' ran together in form
in ME; in the latter sense the verb is now rare and
poetic. Weak forms occurred in former times (Sh H5
III. 2.96 I would haue blowed vp the Towne | Defoe
P 71 they blowed up a watchman with gunpowder |
id R 77 it had blow'd hard) and are still heard in popular
Amr and in British dialects; even StE uses only *blowed*
in the meaning 'cursed': "I'll be blowed if I do". ||
crow—crew—crown. A weak form *crowed* is also in use;
in the ptc it is the prevailing form, *crown* being now
only dialectal; in the prt, *crew* is the usual form when

talking of a cock, while of persons (in the sense 'exulted, triumphed') *crowed* is used (NED). ‖ *grow—grew—grown.* The weak form *growed* is dialectal and vg: GE M 1.16 folks as are growed up. ‖ *know—knew—known; knowed* in dialectal and vg use: GE 1.16 she knowed it all beforehand | Shaw P 226 You an me knaowed it too. ‖ *throw—threw—thrown. Throwed* is heard in dialects and vg: Hardy L 201 She's throwed up the sperrits | Wells Kipps 130 "You ain't thrown up your place?"..."I 'ave," he said; "I've throwed it up."

5.4₁. *Fly—flew—flown. Flew* cannot be from OE *flēah* or *flugon,* but must be an analogical formation (cp. *blew—blown*). The verb has been mixed up with *flee— fled* (see 4.7). ‖ *draw—drew—drawn.* ME prt *drough* (*drow*) was displaced by *drew* after the analogy of the other *ew*-verbs. Weak forms are common in dialect and illiterate speech: Kipling L 230 the young woman that used to come to your rooms to be drawed. ‖ *slay—slew—slain.* The present stem was re-formed in ME after the ptc (Caxton B 43 has *slee < slēan*), and the prt was made *slew* by analogy. ‖ *lie—lay—lain.* The present stem was re-formed in ME with a single consonant instead of *cg,* as in OE *licgan* from the 2nd and 3rd pers. sg of the present: *ligest, ligeþ* (cf *say*). A ptc *lien,* formed after the inf, was common in late ME and early ModE; Sh has both forms, and so has the AV: John 11.17 hee had lien in the graue foure dayes already | ib 20.12 Where the body of Iesus had layen. Confusion with the weak vb *lay* is found now and again, especially in vg speech, where *laid* often takes the place of *lay* and *lain: lay down* and *laid down* were easily confused, see vol III 16.7₄ (Byron!).

5.4₂. *Bid—bad(e)—bid(den).* OE *biddan, bæd, bǣdon, beden* (str. V) 'pray, ask' and *bēodan* (II) 'command; offer' were confused in ME. The PE forms are all from the former verb (the ptc has become *bidden* after the inf), but the sense is to a large extent that of the latter (cf NED). In the prt the spelling *bade* is probably more common than *bad*, but even when written *bade* the word is often pronounced [bæd]. The prt form is occasionally extended to the ptc: Di N 535 | Browning 1.289 | Trollope B 299 | Churchill C 411 she would not have bade Bob write to his father | Crofts in BDS 367 all his instincts had bade him beware of this Snaith.—On the other hand, a prt *bid* from the ptc is frequently met with, often side by side with *bad(e):* Fielding 4.134 he bid me consider (ib 8 he bad me enquire) | Goldsm V 2.167 he bid the postillion stop (ib 138 he bade us take comfort) | Brontë W 123 he bid me tell .. (ib 62 bade us go) | Stevenson K 20 he bade me go in .. I did as he bid | Walpole ST 102 he bid us good-day | Christie LE 43 he bid us farewell. *Bid* prt also in Bunyan, Spectator, Swift, Defoe, Scott, Ruskin, Stevenson, etc.— In the sense 'offer (a price) for something' (at an auction) the verb is invariable (cf *rid:* 4.4₁): he bid five shillings | King O 23 Fifty dollars is bid. Apart from this sense, the long form of the ptc (*bidden*) is generally preferred, thus Bacon A 28.18, Thack N 21.25, MacCarthy 2.393, Bennett H 66, etc. But *bid* ptc is found in Swift (often), Fielding, Byron, Kinglake, Trollope, Ruskin, Morris, etc. —In Sh, however, *bidden* is only found once (Ado III. 3.32 Verges!), while *bid* is common. The short ptc *bid* is still found in phrases like Stevenson D 66 to do as I was bid (but Haggard S 271 as I was bidden).—*Forbid* on the whole follows the flexion of the simple verb: *forbid—forbad(e)—forbidden*. In the ptc Sh has *forbid* more often than *forbidden* (see Sh-lex); the short form was still common in the 18th century (Fielding 4.132 he had forbid him to think any more of me) but is now obsolete. In the prt the rarer form *forbid* was used by Defoe, Fielding and Franklin.—Prt *outbid* GE M 2.176.

give—gave—given. The present initial consonant [g] is due to Scandinavian influence. A present stem with

long [i·] was formerly in existence (cf vol I 4.214): Sh
H8 Prol. 7 giue (: beleue). Sh's use of *gave* as ptc (only
once, Ven. 571) survives in vg speech.—*Forgive* is in-
flected like *give*. || *fall—fell—fallen*. OE redupl. *feallan*.
Sh sometimes has *fell* as ptc: Lr IV 6.54 the altitude
Which thou hast perpendicularly fell. This usage
survives in illiterate speech: Di DC 543 I'd fell. On the
ptc *downfall* see 5.7₉.

eat—ate, eat—eaten. The OE prt sg form had an
anomalous long vowel: *ǣt*. The normal ModE continuation [i·t] is found in dialects. In early ModE, *eat* was
the more common prt form (Sh and Mi have only *eat*),
but then this spelling may have represented a long
or a short vowel. Milton has *eat* riming with *feat:*
L'Allegro 102. *Ate* is the only form in AV. Since the
beginning of the 19th century *ate* has been the usual
spelling for the prt, but the corresponding pronunciation
[eit] is rare in British English, where [et] is generally
used for both *ate* and *eat* (prt). Americans commonly
spell *ate* and pronounce [eit]. The ptc *eaten* [i·tn] is
normal, but a shortened form *eat* was formerly common:
Marlowe F (1616) 1584 till he had eate vp all my loade
of hay | Sh: *eat* and *eaten* (Sh-lex) | Southey L 94 Tom
has actually eat some land-crabs | Tennyson 55 Have
eat our substance. The form is now restricted to archaic and illiterate usage. The same is true of *ate* as
a ptc, which was once in frequent use: Austen E 18
the wedding-cake was all ate up (but ib 19 the cake
was eaten) | Lamb R 53 meals ate and walks taken
together | Shelley 110 the flames had ate the other |
Masefield C 96 [vg] you'd only get et.

see—saw—seen. ModE *seen* cannot represent the OE
ptcs *sewen* (*sawen*) or *segen*, but must be from the adj
gesēne (W. Sax. *gesiene*) 'visible', which already in late
Northumbrian came to be used as a ptc. A prt *see*
is instanced in literature from the 16th century onwards,
but now belongs only to uneducated speech: Sh H4B

III. 2.33 [Shallow] I see him break Skogan's head at the court-gate, when 'a was a crack not thus high [thus in the Qq, but the Ff have *saw*] | Dekker Sh II. 5.34 The strangest hunting that euer I see | Defoe R 278 I thought he had kill'd them all; for I see them all fall of a heap into the boat | Di Do 221 I never see it .. I never touched the Testament | Ade A 10 He was the best I ever see.—In vulgar speech *seen* is sometimes used as a pure prt, sometimes it stands for a perfect tense phrase with *have* (*'ve*) omitted: Defoe G 140 But I seen a bookseller's shop before now.—The weak form *seed* is also confined to dialects and vg speech: Sheridan 38 I never seed such a gemman | Shaw C 192 Ive seed for myself.

5.4₃. Two other verbs are best treated here: *do—did— done.* OE *dōn, dyde, gedōn.* In vg speech *done* is widely used as a past tense form: "I done my bit". On the other hand, Amr popular language sometimes employs *did* as a ptc (see Mencken).

beat—beat—beat(en). But for the ptc, which usually ends in *-en*, the verb would now belong to the invariable verbs (4.4). The shortened ptc was formerly more common; cf By DJ 7.42 their enemy is beat, (Or *beaten*, if you insist on grammar..). *Beat* is still used colloquially in the sense 'surpassed': Shaw C 192 he has never been beat yet | Worth S 295 you're beat. But always *-en* in adjunctal position: "the beaten cricket team". The short ptc is the only form used in *dead-beat* 'tired out'.— The normal descendant of the OE prt *bēot* would be *beet*, but this form became obsolete in the 16th century under the influence of the prs tense and the ptc. A prt & ptc *bet*, on the analogy of *meet—met*, was once in frequent use: Gammer 145 Bet [prt] me | Roister 28 bet [prt] | Gammer 142 bet [ptc]. The form is still used in dialects and in vg speech: Shaw C 25 Sam bet Ebony in twenty minutes.

Irregular Verbs. Class 11

(Mixed Verbs)

5.5₁. Several verbs by the side of regularly inflected forms in *-ed* have also *n*-participles, sometimes with vowel-change. Some of these participles are remainders of earlier strong flexion, others are new formations by analogy with old strong verbs. The *n*-forms are used preferably as adjuncts before substantives. ‖ *Hew—hewed—hewed, hewn.* The weak forms date from the 14th century. The *n*-ptc is probably still more common, thus always in adjunctal position: rough-hewn stone. ‖ *strew—strewed—strewed, strewn.* There is an archaic variant *strow* (cf I 3.603) correspondingly inflected. The *n*-form is preferably used as an adjunct. ‖ *mow—mowed—mowed, mown.* In adjunctal position only the *n*-form: new-mown hay. ‖ *show—showed—showed, shown.* The diphthong *ea* underwent stress-shifting in ME (see I 3.602); the unshifted form is extinct in pronunciation, though the spelling *shew* is still often used. The ptc in *-ed* (Caxton R 51 shewd | Marlowe F 1268 & 3479 shewed | Fielding 4.528 shewed) is now rare. ‖ *sow—sowed—sowed, sown* 'scatter seed on the ground'. The *n*-ptc is the more common. ‖ *sew—sewed—sewed, sewn* 'fasten with a needle and thread'. ME had *sewe* and *sowe* (cf vol I 3.603); ModE uses the spelling of one form and the pronunciation of the other [sou]. The *n*-form of the ptc is said to be more frequent with women than with men. ‖ *gnaw—gnawed—gnawed, gnawn.* Sh has *gnawed* prt, *gnawn* ptc. The latter form is now archaic. ‖ *saw—sawed—sawed, sawn.* The ptc *sawed* is rarely used.

5.5₂. *help—helped—helped, holpen.* Sh has often *holp* as prt & ptc, but not *holpen* ptc; the latter form is found in the AV and is still, though extremely seldom, used in archaic style, mainly as a biblical reminiscence: Morris E 110 live unholpen. ‖ *lade—laded—laded, laden.*

The meaning 'draw water' must be kept apart, as the verb is always regular in this sense. In its other senses the verb usually makes *laden* in the ptc. In most of these senses, however, the vb *load* (from *load* sb) is substituted, *lade* being generally restricted to the loading of ships. The ptc *laden* has a wider application; it is still common in compounds ("heavy-laden buses", "a hay-laden cart", but usually: "a cart loaded with hay"; see Fowler MEU) and in figurative use: a soul laden with sin (sorrow, etc.).—A ptc *loaden*, formed on the analogy of *laden*, was in use from the 16th to the 18th century: Marlowe T 78 loden with | id J 80 loaden with | Defoe R 278 the musket which was yet loaden | Swift 3.192 my stoop was so deep loaden. || *shear— sheared—sheared, shorn.* The strong prt *shore* is found by the side of the new form *sheared* in early ModE: Sh Oth V. 2.206 pure greefe Shore his old thred in twaine | Spenser FQ II 6.31 And thereof nigh one quarter sheard away. *Shore* prt is now archaic. In the ptc, *shorn* remains in fairly frequent use in England, while in America it is restricted to poetical usage. A ptc *shore* was formerly in use, e. g. in Sh Mids V. 1.331 (in rime!). || *swell—swelled—swelled, swollen.* The ptc *swollen* is not so widely used in America as in England, where it is still common, perhaps the more common form, not only in adjunctal but also in verbal function. Note the difference between "swollen head" (from physical causes) and "swelled head" ('conceit'): Bennett P 197 he arrived home swollen. Now it happened that Eve also, by reason of her triumph in regard to the house in Manchester Square, had swelled head.

5.5₃. *Rive—rived—rived, riven* (from ON). The ptc is generally *riven:* Bennett C 1.290 the riven trunk of a man dying. || *carve.* The old ptc *corven* went out of use in early ModE; a ptc *carven* with its vowel from the inf 'occurs in 16th c., but its present use is a 19th c. revival, orig. poetical, but now frequent in rhetorical

prose' (NED): Keats 188 carven imageries | Wilde H 47
carven niches | Kipling B 179 upon the carven door ||
Masefield S 3 Lopez had caused a rhyme to be carven
over the door. || *fold*. The verb is now generally regular,
but the old ptc is occasionally met with: Kipling P 116
the same folden piece of parchment. || *grave*. The strong
prt died out in the 15th century, but the ptc remained;
Sh has it by the side of *graved*. Its use is now limited
to a few archaic-sounding phrases: Ru Sel 2.444 every
graven stone | Swinburne T 69 graven gold | Haggard S 7
graven on the memory. || *melt*. In verbal function the
old ptc *molten* is archaic; as a pure adj it is still in literary
use: like molten glass | Hawth T 55 & 61 molten gold |
Ru C 6 molten iron. || *pave* (from OF). The usual ptc is
paved, but in the 16th century an *n*-form arose on the
analogy of *shaven*, and this form is still sometimes met
with, chiefly as an adjunct: Shelley 466 she pebble-
paven shore | Bennett W 1.193 the gentle paven slopes. ||
prove (from OF). The word is as a rule regular, but a
ptc *proven* occurs; this form may be really a participle
of the now obs vb *preve* formed on the analogy of
cleave—cloven, weave—woven, but later associated with
the vb *prove*. It may also be due to influence from Sc,
where, as mentioned in 5.5$_4$, *n*-participles are frequent,
The form was once more commonly employed, but is
now chiefly used in legal phraseology, especially in
not proven from Sc law: Brontë V 383 he had proven
his fidelity (ib 417 it is proved now) | Tennyson 548
nothing worthy proving can be proven, Nor yet dis-
proven | Sinclair R 278 to have proven our thesis |
Bellamy L 44 men of proven abilities | Kipling K 287
upon a proven charge of murder. NED and Jones know
only the pronunciation [pru·vn], but Harrap's Dict. has
[not prouvn] in Sc law. || *shape*. The strong ptc was
still in free use in the AV: Ps 51.5 I was shapen in
iniquitie. It is now chiefly employed in *misshapen;* else-
where its use is archaic: GE M 1.261 an unshapen fear |

Lang T 135 his shapen fate. || *shave.* In pure verbal
function the *en*-form seems to have been obs. since early
ModE: Sh has *shaved* as ptc, but *shaven* as an adj.
The following quotations will illustrate present usage:
Sayers NT 23 Does your Lordship desire to be shaved?
.. Descending, clean and shaven, to the dining-room |
Macdonell E 43 He was clean-shaven, or rather the last
time he had been shaved he had been clean-shaven | Free-
man Th 383 he is rather short, fair, thin, and clean-shaven |
ib 386 My friend was tall and thin, dark, and clean-shaved |
Galsw D 223 clean-shaved||*wash.* The old ptc has remained
as an archaism in adjunctal use: Kipling DW 317 This fat-
ted, clipped, and washen land | Housman J 118 all the
washen beggars || AV Mark 7.2 with unwashen hands |
Kipling K 342 of singular, though unwashen, beauty |
Walpole F 4 unwashen faces. || *wax.* The old ptc is
kept alive as a conscious archaism: Swinburne A 99 [I] am
waxen red | Tarkington Penrod 88 Mr. Williams, waxen
clean. || *writhe.* The vb early became weak, but the
strong ptc *writhen*, with its variant *wreathen*, remained
in use for a time as pure adjectives; thus in the AV:
Ex. 28.24 two wreathen chaines of gold. *Wreathen* is
now obs. (Tennyson has it: 134 the mist-wreathen
isle), and *writhen* is archaic: Rossetti 153 her writhen
limbs | Hewlett Q 472 her face all writhen with grief |
Shaw D 258 her mouth writhen and piteous.

The following extremely rare forms are perhaps
chiefly dialectal: Marlowe F (1616) 1583 I am a *cursen*
man; this form I have met nowhere else; it is not in
the NED. *Bereaven* is occasionally met with (see NED);
but its use in Buchanan J 26 (to stand bereaven Of
that) must no doubt be put down as a Scotticism. The
same author has *clothen* (J 91 & 96), which is not in
the NED as a ptc. *Approven*, the latest NED example
of which dates from 1637, is found in Buchanan J 96 |
Lang T 114 Arthur is approven king.

5.5₄. There seems to be some tendency to use *n*-ptc's

instead of regular ones more extensively in poetry than
in prose, partly owing to their old-fashioned ring, partly,
perhaps, under dialectal influence: *n*-ptcs are more
common in northern English and Scottish than in the
StE; Elphinston (1765) 1.261 declares that '*carven,
proven, shaven, shapen, baken, wasten, spitten; holpen,
stricken, foughten, bounden,* etc., are grown entirely
obsolete', and yet several of these forms survive in
poetic and archaic language, used not as true participles
in verbal function, but as adjuncts before substantives.
In the following pages a list will be given of verbs
otherwise regular but with *n*-forms used as adjuncts.
On the whole question of adjunctal use of *n*-participles
see 5.7$_2$.

It is noticeable that *n*-ptcs occur with particular
frequency after the voiced fricatives [v, ð, z].

5.6. Two verbs with participles in -*n* form their preterits from a different root altogether:

go—went—gone. The old prt *eode* has not survived,
though it was still occasionally used in early ModE, spelt
yede. The form *went* has been borrowed from the vb
wend (see 4.6), OE *wendan.* It was at one time used
also as a ptc (e. g. Swift (p. ?) the dangers I had
underwent), but this usage is now restricted to vg and
dialectal speech: Austen S 272 the troubles we had
went through | Hay B 67 I would ha' went in | Phill-
potts M 56 I'd have went | Payne Alab. I would 'a'
went. The ptc *gone* [gon] has suffered shortening (see
vol I 10.81). A different form of the ptc (from the
southern dialects) with unshortened vowel and loss of
final -*n* is seen in the adv *ago* (orig. = 'passed', cf vol
V 6.8$_3$); formerly also *agone,* which is now archaic or
poetic.

be (am, is, are)—was, were—been. The verb is made up
of three distinct roots, which are seen in: (1) *be,* (2) *is,*
(3) *was.* Their distribution in OE was different from
now: no. 2 was used only in the prs ind and subj (*eom,*

eart, is, etc.), while no. 1 was a complete prs stem (ind, subj, imp, inf, present ptc), and no. 3 was used chiefly in the prt, but had also inf, imp, and prs ptc. Though the three roots to some extent overlapped, the parallel forms sometimes had slightly different meanings; thus in the prs ind, *bēo, bis, biþ,* etc., often had a future sense in contradistinction to *eom, eart, is.* In PE the parallel forms have been done away with (note the archaic prs ind pl form *be* from OE *bēoþ,* preserved in the one phrase "the powers that be"; cf Stoffel S 168): no. 1 is used to form inf and ptc's (*be, being, been*), no. 2 is used in the prs ind (*am, is, are*), and no. 3 in the prt (*was, were*).

Root 3 in OE was a verb of the 5th strong conjugation-class: *wesan, wæs, wǣron,* past ptc missing. The consonant-difference *s—r* is due to Verner's Law (cf 4.1₂). Now in this one case the prt forms have not been levelled; ModE still has *was* and *were.* In accordance with the OE rules the forms with long vowel were employed in the whole of the prt subj and in the ind pl and the 2nd person sg. Apart from uneducated speech ModE still has: *I was, you were, he was; we (you, they) were.* The subj is now getting rare, *if he was* being generally substituted for *if he were;* a few isolated phrases survive, such as *if I were you, as it were.* Cf vol IV ch. 10.—In older literary English *was* was often used with *you* in addressing one person only: Fielding T 4.272 [Mr. Alworthy:] And was you in company with this lawyer? In present-day vg speech *was* tends to become the universal form even in the plural.

Participles in *n*

5.7₁. Originally, the second participle of all strong and reduplicative verbs ended in *-n.* While in the infinitive the final *n* has disappeared, the participle has in many cases preserved its *n,* probably from the inflected forms, ME *-(e)ne,* used after the definite article and in the plural. In older English there was a good

deal of vacillation on this point, which in some cases
has remained to the present day. In PE some verbs
have -*n* while others have not, and a number of verbs
have double forms, with and without -*n*. All this gives one
the impression of complete lawlessness; cf Murray D 201:
'No rule can be given for the dropping or retention of
-*en* in the Book-English'. As will appear from the
following pages, it is after all possible to establish a
certain order in this chaos. The reason why no rules
have hitherto been found is that this point has never
received isolated treatment; the verbs have either been
arranged in the usual paradigmatic order, or each verb
has been treated separately.

Note: Since ME times the *n*-ptc has been a favourite in the
northern English and Scottish dialects, where *n* is employed
to a much wider extent than in StE. Thus, the *n*-ending is
very often appended to originally weak participles e. g. *hearn*
(*heern*), *putten*, *setten*, *shutten*. The form *proven* (see 5.5₃) may
be due to this tendency.

5.7₂. In surveying the whole field of forms in use in
StE one is at once struck by the frequency with which
the *n*-forms are used as adjuncts before sbs. There is
a tendency to drop the *n* in absolutely final position,
e. g. *he was drunk*, but to keep it in the middle of a
syntactic (and phonetic) group to form a sort of connecting link or 'buffer-syllable', e. g. *a drunken sailor;*
cf also Fijn van Draat, *Rhythm in English Prose*, Anglia
36 (1912) pp. 25—36. Even verbs that have been drawn
into the weak class have sometimes kept the *n*-form,
and originally weak verbs have occasionally developed
one, for use as an adjunct; se 5.5, 5.5₄. Owing to the
same principle, when an adverb is formed from a ptc
which has two forms, with and without *n*, it is always
the *n*-form that is used: *brokenly* (Sh), *forbiddenly*
(Sh), *hiddenly* (NED: from 1580), *forsakenly* (NED:
from 1591), *mistakenly*. Cf advs in -*edly* 4.2₂. Similar
tendencies may be observed elsewhere in English mor-

phology, e. g. *maid: maiden aunt* | *old: olden days*, etc.;
see vol I 2.427 f. and 20.4₄, 20.5₆, cf *l* 22.3₅. Consequently,
there is never vacillation in the ptc of a verb whose stem
ends in a vowel, because in this case the *n* cannot form a
separate syllable; here it is always kept (unless replaced
by a regular *ed*-form). On the other hand, we have
never *n* when the stem ends in a nasal consonant, because a syllabic [n] is never in English found after
[m, n, ŋ]. The only cases that really concern us here are
those in which *n* when kept adds an extra syllable to the
participle. Where *n* is lost in these cases it is very often
because it is made uniform with the prt (e. g. *held,
stood, struck;* cf Chs IV and V), or else the verb is intransitive and the ptc is therefore rarely used as an adjunct
(e. g. *slunk, stunk, sat*). We shall now go through the
various classes of words arranged according to the final
sound. For examples of the use of the forms mentioned
below, see also each verb in Chs IV and V.

5.7₃. The stem ends in a vowel: always *-n*, e. g.
been, seen, done, gone (cf the adv *ago* from the southern
dialects; se 5.6), *drawn, lain, slain, blown, flown, grown,
known, thrown.*

Several of these forms were not originally monosyllabic, but at the silencing of *e* in the ending *-en* (cf
vol I 6.16 ff), the *n* became part of the preceding syllable.
In early ModE, post-vocalic *r* had still some of its old
consonantal value left; hence formerly vacillation in
the following words, which now always have *-n: born,
shorn, sworn, torn, worn;* see 5.3₃. On *lorn* see 4.5₂.

A series of verbs, some of them old strong verbs,
others originally weak, have *n*-forms beside regular
forms in *-ed;* the *n*-forms are chiefly used as adjuncts
(cf esp. 5.5): *gnawn, sawn, hewn, strewn, mown, shown,
sown, shorn.*

5.7₄. The stem ends in a nasal consonant [m, n, ŋ]:
never *-n*, e. g.

come (Bacon sometimes has *comen*, see Bøgholm 133), *swum, clomb.*

begun, run, shone, spun, won.

clung, flung, hung, rung, sung, sprung, stung, strung, swung.

Here belongs also *numb* 'deprived of sensation' < OE *numen*, ptc of *niman* 'take'. On the spelling with *b* see vol I 7.51; Sh (fol.) has *numme* (H6A II. 5.13).

5.7₅. *p* (no instances of *b*):

shapen, rare for *shaped;* see 5.5₃.

holpen, now practically extinct, replaced by *helped;* see 5.5₂.

t and *d:*

beaten, now more common than *beat*, thus always in adjunctal position; see 5.4₃. ‖ *bitten; bit* ptc is now rare; see 5.3₂. ‖ *boughten.* The normal ptc is *bought* (< OE *geboht*); the NED records *boughten* from 1793 (Coleridge) and explains it as due to the analogy of *foughten* (see below). It is common in popular American, but only as an adjunct: boughten bread ('not home-made'). ‖ *bursten.* The old ptc was in occasional use till the 18th century; now archaic: Morris E 115 a huge half-bursten sack. ‖ *eaten; eat* ptc is archaic or vg; see 5.4₂.

forgotten is now the usual ptc of *forget*, while the uncompounded verb generally makes *got* ptc in British English. The reason may be that *forgotten* is more often used in adjunctal position; the form *gotten* is still kept in a few phrases where it functions as an adjunct, e. g. ill-gotten gains; on *got* and *gotten* in U.S. see vol IV 4.4(6).

foughten. The usual participle of *fight* is now *fought; foughten* is preserved in archaic language, esp. in "foughten field" = battle-field: Sh H5 IV. 6.18 in this glorious and well-foughten field [elsewhere in Sh *fought*] | Tennyson 200 the foughten field | Stevenson U 51 the unfoughten field.—In pure verbal function the form is very rare: Scott Iv 421 the field must be foughten in our presence.

litten, ptc of *light*, is rare; it is an analogical formation to *bitten:* Poe S 260 the red-litten windows | Kipling J 2.183 the star-litten sky. || *molten* competes with *melted* in adjunctal position; see 5.5₃. || *shotten* is preserved in the archaic phrase "a shotten herring" = a thin, emaciated person (orig. a herring that has shot, i. e. ejected, its spawn). || *smitten*, also *smote;* see 5.3₁.—

sweaten. The form is unetymological, the verb being originally weak; it is found in Sh Mcb IV. 1.65 [witch:] grease that's sweaten From the murderer's gibbet (: eaten). In later use it is pseudo-arch. (NED): By 4. 256 I have toil'd and till'd and sweaten in the ground.

On *written* and *writ* see 5.3₁.

bidden. This is now the usual form except in the special sense 'offer a price' (see 5.4₂), but *bid* was formerly common.—Now only *forbidden* ptc, probably because of its frequent use as an adjunct: forbidden fruit, degrees, etc. || *chidden*, since early ModE the only possible form in adjunctal use, see 5.3₂. || *folden* is still sometimes found in archaic language, see 5.5₃. || *hidden;* this unoriginal form is becoming the universal one, see 5.3₂. || *holden;* since the 16th century *held* has been the usual form, *holden* being used only in formal language and in *beholden* 'obliged'; see 5.1₅. || *laden* and *loaden;* see 5.5₂. || *ridden;* this is the old form, which has now ousted the newcomers *rid* and *rode;* see 5.3₁. The word *bedridden* is from the OE sb *bedrida* ('bed-rider'); in ME the form was reduced to *bedrid*, which was misinterpreted as a ptc, and *-en* was added (see NED); cf such ptcs as *hag-ridden* and *priest-ridden*. Sh and Milton have only *bedrid*, but this form is now archaic: Mrs Browning A 119 the bedrid wretch. || *slidden*, rare for *slid* ptc. || *sodden* and *sod*, see 5.3₇. || *stridden*, generally replaced by *strided*. || *trodden*, see 5.3₄.

Generally no *en* after *-nd: found, ground, wound.*

Yet besides *bound* we also find *bounden:* Sh John III.
3.29 I am much bounden to your Majesty ('obliged') |
Poe 344 a bounden slave. Now only in the phrase
"bounden duty".

5.7₆. *k* and *g:*

drunken. According to Fowler MEU the PE rule is
that in adjunctal position only *drunken* is possible,
whether expressing a permanent quality 'given to drink'
or a temporary state 'intoxicated', while in the predicative a distinction is made between *drunken* 'given to
drink' and *drunk* 'intoxicated': he was drunken and
dissolute | he was drunk yesterday. Quotations: Ward
R 1.35 leaseholders, less drunken, perhaps, and better
educated | Di Pw 1.274 he's drunk—he's a drunken
plebeian | id T 2.15 I was more drunk than—than
usual | McKenna M 283 a drunken man should never
be so drunk as not to know that he was drunk.—This
rule was not strictly observed in former times; Sh has
drunken = 'intoxicated' in the predicative: Ven 984
who is but drunken | Ant V. 2.219 Antony shall be
brought drunken forth; and this usage is found as late
as London M 37 he had been made drunken by a woman's
face. In pure verbal function the *en*-form is archaic:
Hewlett F 46 have you well-eaten and drunken? |
Masefield C 312 She had drunken some drug. In the
following quotation Thackeray perhaps uses the *en*-
form to avoid confusion with *drunk* 'intoxicated': N 20
Wherefore should the butler brew strong ale to be
drunken three years hence.

shrunken. This form has been rare for several centuries;
Sh has only *shrunk.* In PE, *shrunken* is seldom used in
pure verbal function (cf 5.2₂), but it is common as a
pure adj = 'thin, lean', both in the predicative and,
especially, in adjunctal position (in both cases *shrunk*
is also possible; cf Fowler MEU): Shelley 157 shrunken
ashes | Thack S 128 girls wither into shrunken decay |
Bennett RS 194 The doctor saw a shrunken woman ..

Mr. E was worse than shrunken—he was emaciated |
Wells TB 2.145 he looked shrunken | Galsw F 380 her
cheeks were shrunken, shadowy. | Stevenson B 111 a
shrunken company.

sunken. Sh has *sunk* as a true ptc, but *sunken* as an
adjunct. In PE the *en*-form is common both in adjunctal
position and in the predicative: Hart BT 255 the roses
grow in a sunken garden | Benson N 75 his eyes were
red and sunken. *Sunk* as an adjunct is chiefly used of
what has been sunk by human agency (Fowler MEU):
sunk carving, a sunk panel.

broken and *broke; spoken* and *spoke, bespoken* and
bespoke; see 5.3₅. || *woken* and *woke;* see 5.3₅.

forsaken, shaken, taken, see 5.3₈.

stricken. The normal ptc of *strike* is now *struck;*
stricken is always figurative in sense (e. g. Bennett
RS 232 He was a stricken man); it is rather old-fashioned
and more literary than *struck* (Gissing B 359 Christian
was stricken dumb), cf 5.1₉.

stuck and *dug,* both of them new forms to originally
weak verbs, seem never to have had *-en* added.

5.7₇. v (no instances of *f*):

driven; earlier also *driv* and *drove,* see 5.3₁. || *given,* cf
5.4₂. || *shriven,* also regular: 5.3₁. || *striven.* Regular
forms may also be encountered; see 5.3₁. || *thriven.*
Earlier also inflected regularly, e. g. in Sh, and still
often in U.S., see 5.3₁. || *cloven* is used chiefly as an
adjunct, but also sometimes in verbal function, see
5.3₆. || *woven, wove* now only in some trade phrases,
see 5.3₆.

Competing not with simple *n*-less forms, but with
regular forms in *-ed* (cf 5.5₃), we have:

carven, (en)graven in archaic style, generally as an
adjunct, *paven, proven,* chiefly in the phrase "not
proven", *riven, shaven,* mostly preceded by a subjunct:
clean-shaven, closely shaven, but never used in compound
tenses; see 5.5₃.

[ð] (no instances of [þ]):

clothen, not in NED as a ptc, but found in Buchanan J 91 & 96. It is probably a Scotticism, cf 5.5₃. || *writhen*, *wreathen* used chiefly as an adjunct, see 5.5₃.

5.7₈. [s], [z], and [ʃ] (no cases of [ʒ]):

cursen, very rare (not in NED); and *waxen*, now only in very archaic style, see 5.5₃.

chosen and *chose; frozen* and *froze*, see 5.3₇. || (*a*)*risen;* both (*a*)*rose* and (*a*)*riz* were formerly in use, see 5.3₁. || *washen*, used archaically as an adjunct, see 5.5₃.

5.7₉. *l:*

fallen. Sh uses *downfall* twice (Mcb IV. 3.4 bestride our downfall birthdome | H4A I. 3.135 the downfall Mortimer); this may really be the sb used as an adjunct. On the ptc *fell*, taken from the prt, see 5.4₂. || *stolen.* A form *stole* was once in use, now only vg, see 5.3₆. || *swollen;* also *swelled*, see 5.5₂.

On stems in *r* see 5.7₃.

Chapter VI

The Naked Word

6.1₁. The naked word, i. e. the kernel without any internal change and without the addition of any formative, is used in sbs as the common case in the sg (see Syntax, vol VII, sub Case), and as the common case in the pl in some words (see vol II ch. 3 and the Case-chapter in vol VII); in adjs as adjunct (cf i. a. vol II chs 6, 14, 15), as principal (ib ch. 11), as predicative (cf vol III chs 17, 18), and as tertiary in some cases, see vol VII), in advs as tertiary, in some cases also as preposition and conjunction, in vbs (the 'base') as the present tense of the indicative (except in the 3rd person in most vbs), as the present tense of the subjunctive, as an imperative (cf vol V ch. 24), and as an infinitive (ib chs 10—20).

On vbs in compounds cf below 9.3.

On vbs derived from sbs and adjs (without any
change and on sbs derived from vbs without any change
see chs VI and VII below.

Word-Classes

6.1₂. One of the most characteristic traits of ModE
is the formal identity of a great many words belonging
to different word-classes; this constitutes one kind of
grammatical homonymy (cf *Efficiency in Linguistic
Changes* ch. 5). This phenomenon is found in many
fields, as seen for instance in the following list of
typical examples, in which (2) denotes that the same
form has two different values (cf 7.4). Adverbs, prepositions, and conjunctions might have been classed
together as particles (without regimen, with nominal
regimen and with a clause as regimen, cf PhilGr 87ff.).
Substantives used as adjuncts (cf vol II ch. 13) are
here reckoned as adjectives.

+ means that the form is used, and 0 that it is not
used in that function.

	sb	adj	adv	prep	conj	vb
like	+	+	+	+	+	+
fire	+	+	0	0	0	+
smoke	+(2)	+	0	0	0	+
swell	+	+	0	0	0	+
copyright ..	+	+	0	0	0	+
squat	+	+	+	0	0	+
squint	+	+	+	0	0	+
mock	+	+	0	0	0	+
scratch	+	+	+	0	0	+
home	+	+	+	0	0	+
back	+	+	+	0	0	+
round	+	+	+	+	0	+
many	+	+	0	0	0	0
down	+(2)	+	+	+	0	+
after	0	+	+	+	+	0
hold(-)up ..	+	+	0	0	0	+

The development of such identical forms must be reckoned one of the chief merits of the language, for this 'noiseless' machinery facilitates the acquirement and use of the language enormously and outweighs many times the extremely few instances in practical life in which ambiguity can arise. A few examples of possible misunderstandings (Huxley's "between these two lies") are mentioned Lingst 402. But in at least 999 out of 1000 sentences the context shows unmistakably whether a word is to be taken as a sb or a vb, etc. See, e. g., *water works wonders* | the inspector of the *water works wonders* how it came about | the *painter views* art from a different angle | the *painters view* art from a different angle | the *painter's view* of art | *will change* of *air cure love*? (5 ambiguous words!) | the *devil's look's like fire* | the *devil looks like fire* | *devils like fire* | they *fire like devils*, etc.

The phenomenon here dealt with is often termed conversion (sbs converted into vbs, and vice versa); it would be better to speak of verbs formed from sbs with a suffix zero, to use a now fashionable term. Instead of saying that a sb is made into a vb, or a vb into a sb, we should rather say a verb made from a sb, or a sb made from a vb, without any change. Anyhow it is ridiculous to say, as is sometimes done, that English no longer distinguishes between the parts of speech, between noun and vb, etc. As a matter of fact English distinguishes between the sb and the vb *love*, because the former has the pl *loves*, and the latter, besides the 3rd person sg *he loves*, has the form in *-d* as preterit and as participle, and the form *-ing* as participle and gerund. English has not, as is said by some writers, returned to a 'barbaric' or 'primitive' or to the 'early Indo-European' standpoint[1]: no one knows if our Aryan

[1] I find this view as late as Sept. 1940 expressed in IF 57. 291: Ein engl. wort kann ohne veränderung .. sogar die verschiedensten wortarten bezeichnen. Es ist damit ... der frühindogermanische zustand wiederhergestellt.

languages ever passed through a stage in which there
was no formal distinction between noun and verb: the
oldest accessible languages go straight against such an
assertion. So do most, or at any rate a great many, of
those languages that are spoken by the most primitive
or barbaric tribes. To my mind it is rather to the credit
of a highly civilized people that it has done away with
many cumbersome traits of primitive languages without
losing the capacity for expressing the finest shades of
thought in the most unmistakable way.

Verbs from Substantives

6.2. In OE there were a certain number of verbs and
nouns (sb or adj) of the same 'root', but distinguished
by the endings. Thus 'I love' through the three persons
sg ran *lufie lufast lufaþ,* pl *lufiaþ;* the infinitive was
lufian, the subjunctive *lufie,* pl *lufien,* and the imperative
was *lufa,* pl *lufiaþ.* The sb 'love' on the other hand was
lufu, in the other cases *lufe,* pl *lufa* or *lufe, lufum,*
lufena or *lufa.* The two word-classes are thus still kept
apart by the endings, the form *lufa* alone being ambigu-
ous. Let us take another example: the verb 'sleep' was
slǣpan, pres *slǣpe slǣpest slǣp(e)þ, slǣpaþ,* subj *slǣpe,*
slǣpen, imp *slǣp, slǣpaþ,* while the sb had the forms
slǣp (Goth. *slēps*), *slǣpe,* and *slǣpes* in the sg and
slǣpas, slǣpum, slǣpa in the pl. Thus the forms *slǣp*
and *slǣpe* may be both noun and verb, the other forms
are distinct. In the subsequent centuries, we witness a
gradual simplification with mutual approximation of the
verbal and nominal forms. The following is a very
brief sketch of this development. The *-m* was changed
into *-n;* all the vowels of the weak syllables were levelled to one uniform *e* [ə]; the pl forms of the vbs in
-þ (which as early as in OE were not used immediately
before a pronoun: *slǣpe we*) gave way to forms in *-n;*

the gen pl in -*ena*, though kept comparatively long in
the South of England, ultimately disappeared, forms in
-*s* becoming the only gen and pl forms. As a late ME
type we can thus give: sb sg *luve* (written *love*) *luves*,
pl *luves;* vb inf *luven*—ind *luve luvest luveth*, *luven*—
subj *luve, luven*—imp *luve* (*luveth*). Similarly with the
other example: sb sg *slep, slepes*, pl *slepes;* vb inf.
slepen—ind *slepe slepest slepeth, slepen*—subj *slepe,
slepen*—imp *slep* (*slepeth*). In Chaucer, the plural of
the imperative is about to disappear, and we soon get
sg = pl. The two classes of words thus have approached
very much. Furthermore, towards the end of the ME
period *thou* already begins to be less used, and the
polite *ye, you*, which becomes more and more universal,
claims no distinctive ending in the verb. In the 15th c.,
the *e* and -*n* of the endings, ceased to be sounded.
Somewhat later the *s*-ending in the third person sg
came in from the North and finally ousted the -*th* (see
above ch. 3). These changes brought about the modern
scheme:

noun: *love loves—sleep sleeps*

verb : *love loves—sleep sleeps,*

where we have perfect formal identity of the two parts
of speech, only with the curious cross-relation that *s*
is the ending of the pl in the nouns and of the sg (third
person) in the verbs—an accident which might almost
be taken as a device for getting an *s* into most sentences
in the present tense (*the lover loves; the lovers love*) and
for showing by the place of the *s* which of the two
numbers is intended.

To appraise how far this phenomenon: noun (sb or
adj) = verb is carried out in ModE, we have to distinguish, from a historical point of view, between several
classes:

6.3. (1) Words found in the language since the OE
period and undergoing, just like *love* and *sleep*, the

regular development into the modern identity of form.
To these must also be reckoned words adopted at an
early date from Old Norse. In several cases the development described above may have been helped on by
Old Norse influence. Thus the sb *fast* (found in Orrm,
probably from ON *fasta*) supplants the OE sb *fœsten*,
which is preserved in dial. *fasten(s) een, fasten Tuesday;*
the last instance of the use of the word outside compounds is from Cursor Mundi (1300). The OE verb
fœstan becomes ME *feste(n)* and *faste(n)* and ModE *fast*.

anger ME sb *anger* (c. 1250) < ON *angr*—ME vb
anngrenn (Orrm) < ON *angra* (or formed in ME from
the sb).

answer OE sb *andswaru*—OE vb *andswarian* (also
andswerian, andsworian); on stress see vol I 5.71.

bed OE sb *bedd*—OE vb *beddian* 'make a bed', later
with other significations, too: Sh Alls II. 3.187 I will
not bed her | Barrie M 121 Birse had twice or thrice
to bed with me ('put up for the night'), see NED.

blossom OE sb *blōstm*—OE vb *blōstmian*.

book OE sb *bōc*—OE vb *bōcian* 'to grant by charter,
furnish with books'; in the sense 'to enter in a book'
(AR) the vb may be a new formation.

busy OE adj *bysig*—OE vb *bysgian*.

care OE sb *caru*—OE vb *carian*.

dew OE sb *deaw*—ME vb *dœwwenn* (Orrm).

din OE sb *dyne*—OE vb *dynnan, dynian*.

drink OE sb *drinc*—OE vb *drincan;* 'the normal mod.
form of the sb would be southern *drinch* ..., northern
drink; the latter has become the standard form, prob.
under the influence of the verb' (NED).

dry OE adj *drȳge*—OE vb *drȳg(e)an*.

ebb OE sb *ebba*—OE vb *ebbian*.

edge OE sb *ecg*—ME vb (variously spelt).

empty OE adj *ǣmetig*—a vb without prefix *ge-*, as in
OE, from the 16th c.

end OE sb *ende*—OE vb *endian*.

fathom OE sb *fæþm*—OE vb *fæþmian.*

fear OE sb *fǣr*—OE vb *fǣran* 'to terrify'; in other senses from ab. 1400.

fight OE sbs *feohte* f. & *(ge)feoht* n.—OE vb *feohtan.*

fire OE sb *fȳr*—in most senses the verb is apparently created afresh in ME.

fish OE sb *fisc*—OE vb *fiscian.*

free OE adj *frēo(h)*—OE vb *frēog(e)an, frēon.*

harm OE sb *hearm*—OE vb *hearmian.*

heap OE sb *hēap*—OE vb *hēapian.*

heat OE sb *hǣte* 'heat, inflammation', *hǣto* 'heat'—OE vb *hǣtan;* both sb and vb are derived by mutation from the adj *hāt.*

help OE sb *help* mf., *helpe* f.—OE vb *helpan (strong* vb).

hire OE sb *hȳr* 'hire, wages'—OE vb *hȳrian, hȳran.*

hold OE sb *hald, heald* 'protector; protection'; 'in other senses the word is only ME or later' (NED), Sh R2 III. 4.83 hold = custody (cf *stronghold*)—OE vb *haldan, healdan.*

hope late OE sb *hopa* (earlier *to-hopa*)—OE vb *hopian;* on the etymology see my book *Language* 309.

lie ('falsehood') OE sb *lyge*—OE vb *lēogan;* the two vowels fall together in ModE, see vol I 3.123.

light OE sb and adj *leoht*—OE vb *leohtan = liehtan* 'shine, give light', *leohtian* 'become light, dawn', etc.

love OE sb *lufu*—OE vb *lufian.*

man OE sb *mann*—OE vb *mannian* 'to garrison' (Sweet), the earliest instance in the NED is from 1122.

mark OE sb *mearc*—OE vb *mearcian.*

mind OE sb *gemynd* 'memory; solicitude'—OE vb *(ge)myndgian.*

name OE sb *nama*—OE vb *(ge)namian.*

need OE sb *nīed* (and other forms)—OE vb *nīedan, nēadian.*

own OE adj *āgen* (also sb 'property')—OE vb *āgnian.*

plough OE sb *plōh*—the vb only from 15th c.

rest OE sb *rest*—OE vb *restan.*

right OE adj (& sb) *riht*—OE vb *rihtan.*

shame OE sb *sc(e)amu*—OE vb *sc(e)amian* 'be a-shamed'.

ship OE sb *scip*—OE vb *scipian.*

shoe OE sb *scōh*—OE vb *scōg(e)an, scō(i)an.*

sin OE sb *synn*—OE vb *syngian.*

sleep OE sb *slǣp*—OE vb *slǣpan.*

smoke OE sb *smoca*—OE vb *smocian.*

sorrow OE sb *sorh*—OE vb *sorgian.*

spell OE sb *spell*—OE vb *spellian.*

spring OE sb *spring*—OE vb *springan.*

step OE sb *stæpe, stepe*—OE vb *stæppan, steppan;* 'The mod. form of the sb is influenced by the verb' (NED).

thank(s) OE sb *þanc* 'thought; expression of gratitude' —OE vb *þancian.*

thunder OE sb *þunor*—OE vb *þunrian.*

timber OE sb *timber*—OE vb *timbr(i)an.*

time OE sb *tīma*—OE *getīmian* 'happen, befall'; the other senses of the vb date from ME or ModE.

token OE sb *tācen*—OE vb *tāc(e)nian.*

wash OE sb *wæsc* (many modern applications derived from the verb)—OE vb *wæscan, wascan.*

water OE sb *wæter*—OE vb *wæt(e)rian.*

weed OE sb *wēod*—OE vb *wēodian.*

whirl ON sb *hvirfill*—ON vb *hvirfla.*

whistle OE sb *hwistle*—OE vb *hwis(t)lian.*

will OE sb *willa*—OE vb *willian* (ModE "he wills, he willed").

wound OE sb (& adj) *wund*—OE vb *wundian.*

wonder OE sb *wundor*—OE vb *wundrian.*

work OE sb *weorc*—OE vb *wyrcan;* 'The normal representative of OE *wyrcan* would be *worch*' (NED); ModE *work* is due mainly to the sb. (NED).

yoke OE sb *geoc*—OE vb *geocian.*

The list does not pretend to be exhaustive.

Many vbs from adjs are mentioned below 20.5,

where their displacement by formations in *-en* is dealt
with.

6.4. (2) Words adopted from French, but where a
French sb and vb fell together.

As to the French loan-words, it should be noticed that it is
not the infinitive but the stem as found in the present participle
that has served as basis for the English form. This is shown
most clearly in the case of the French verbs in *-ir*, which in
English end in *-ish: finish, punish*, see 19.5. Where the French
infinitive has been imported it is generally as a sb: *dinner* <
dîner, but *dine* vb | *rejoinder* < *rejoindre*, but *rejoin* vb |
attainder < *attaindre* | *remainder* | *tender* (from which is
formed a new verb).

The date given after each word in the following list
represents the first occurrence in English noted in the
NED.

accord OF sb 1297—vb 1123 | *account* sb 1260—vb
1303 | *arch* sb 1297—vb 1400 | *arm(s)* sb 1297—vb 1205 |
array sb 1300—vb 1297 | *bar* sb 1175—vb 1300 | *blame*
sb 1230—vb 1200 | *cause* sb 1225—vb 1340 | *centre* sb
1374—vb 1610 | *change* sb 1225—vb 1230 | *charge* sb
1225—vb 1297 | *chase* sb 1297—vb 1300 | *check* OF sb
1314—vb 1384; 'From its use in chess the word has
been widely transferred in French and English. In the
sense-extension the sb and vb have acted and reacted
on each other' (NED) | *claim* sb 1300—vb 1300 | *coin*
sb 1362—vb 1330 | *comfort* sb 1225—vb 1290 | *combat*
sb 1567—vb 1564 | *copy* sb 1330—vb 1387 | *cost* sb
1297—vb 1320 | *couch* sb 1340—vb 1330 | *counsel* sb 1295
—vb 1290 | *count* sb 1325—vb 1325 | *cover* vb (found
1300) from OF *cuvrir*; the sb is mainly from the vb |
cry sb 1275—vb 1225 | *dance* sb 1300—vb 1300 | *despair* sb
1325—vb 1340 | *doubt* sb 1225—vb 1225 | *escape* sb (1300)
from the vb | *flame* sb 1340—vb 1377 | *form* sb 1225—
vb 1297 | *guard* sb 1426—vb 1500 | *injury* F sb 1382—
vb 1484 | *lodge* sb 1290—vb 1225 | *merit* sb 1225—vb
1484 | *offer* sb 1433—in the religious sense 'to offer a

sacrifice' the vb is found even in OE, in the prevailing
sense in ModE 'to present or tender something for
acceptance' not till 1375 | *order* sb 1225—vb 1240 |
people sb 1292—vb 1489 | *plant* sb—OE vb *plantian;*
'The sense-development agrees in the main with that
of F. *planter* (12th c.)' (NED) | *reign* sb 1272—vb 1297 |
ruin sb 1374—vb 1581 | *touch* sb 1297—vb 1297 |
triumph sb 1374—vb 1483 | *trouble* sb 1230—vb 1225 |
turn Anglo-F sb **torn* 1250—OE had *tyrnan* and *turnian*
(from Lat), the word was perhaps reinforced in ME by
OF *torner, turner* (NED) | *vow* sb 1290—vb 1300.

There is an Uppsala dissertation Studies in Denominative Verbs in English (1911), by Bladin. See also
Koziol p. 201 ff.

6.5. The following is a list of verbs not found in Old
English, but corresponding to, and probably formed
from, OE nouns (sbs or adjs) or nouns adopted from
Old Norse. The fact that we do not know any OE
ancestor, however, is no final proof that the verb was
formed from the noun at a later period, so some of the
words in this list may really belong to those given in
6.3. To each verb is added the date of the earliest
occurrence recorded in the NED.

anchor—vb (ancren AR) | *ape*—vb ape 1632 | *awe* sb age
c. 1250 (< ON agi, which supplanted OE ege)—vb 1303 |
badge sb 1350—vb 1380 | *birth* sb probably from ON
*byrþ(i)r—vb intr. rare 1865; tr.: Whitman L 295 a
happy painless mother birth'd a perfect child | *bloom*
sb c. 1200 (< ON blōm)—vb 1200 (Orrm) | *clean*—vb
1450 | *cook*—vb 1380 | *finger*—vb 1483 (verbid in *-ing*
1450) | *horse*—vb before 1100 | *husband*—vb 1545 (verbid
in *-ing* 1420) | *night*—vb (now rare or obsolete) 1303 |
race ON rās—vb 1757 (*ing*-form earlier) | *riddle*—vb
1571 | *slack*—vb 1530 'in some senses taking the place
of the earlier *slake* v.' (NED) | *wheel*—vb 1225 | *while*—
vb 1606 | *worship*—vb 1200.

6.6. I give a similar list of verbs which were probably

derived from substantives adopted from French in the ME period, but some of them may have existed in Old French and thus belong to the list given in 6.4.

act—vb 1475; is the verb *act* a back-formation from *actor*? | *age*—vb 1398 | *camouflage* sb 1917—vb 1917; but Fr. vb *camoufler* | *capture*—vb 1795 | *chance*—vb 1393 | *cross*—vb 1340 | *dart*—vb 1374 (cf F *darder* from 15th c.) | *face*—vb 1440 | *faint*—vb 1350 | *flower*—vb 1225 (OF *florir* > *flourish*, see vol I 2.743) | *image*—vb 1440, cf *imagine* | *intelligence*—vb 1593 (now obsolete) | *interest*—vb 1610 'an alteration of the earlier *interess* v., after *interest* sb' (NED) | *level*—vb 1440 | *notice*—vb 1450 in the now obsolete sense 'to notify', the other senses much later | *pity*—vb 1515 | *progress*—vb 1590 | *sabotage* sb 1910—vb 1918, but Fr. vb *saboter* | *service*—vb 1893 | *sugar*—vb 1412.

6.7₁. It is difficult to give a general definition of the sense-relation between substantives and de-substantival verbs. The verb may designate any action or state that bears a relation to the substantive in question.

One and the same verb may very often mean two or more different things, the context only showing what is meant in each particular case. Thus the vb in *stone a man* means 'kill by throwing stones', but in *stone cherries* 'remove the stones from'. *To powder* has the sense of 'sprinkling or covering with powder', but *to dust* generally means 'to free from dust', though in *dust a cake with sugar* it has the directly opposite sense. *Father a child* means 'be or become the father of a child', but *knight someone* is 'make him a knight'.

In the following pages we shall look a little more closely at some of the most frequent senses found in de-substantival verbs. Cf also vol III 16.6. My treatment does not claim to be exhaustive.

6.7₂. Substantives indicating a *place* or the like may be used to form verbs with the sense of 'putting in that place':

Locative

Bed 'put to bed' (arch): fig.: bed stones in mortar, etc. | *book* 'enter in a book' | *bottle* beer | *can* (meat, etc., chiefly U. S.) | *church* 'bring (a woman) to church after childbirth' | Sh R2 V. 1.23 *cloister* thee in some religious house | *cupboard:* Sh Cor I. 1.103 the belly .. still cubbording the viand | *corner* 'place in a corner, drive into a corner, put in an awkward position' | *floor* 'strike down to the floor' | *focus:* Kipling L 136 it would let you focus things at their proper worth | *island* 'isolate': Waugh W 169 Julia islanded him from the rest | *jug* 'put in prison (jug)' | Bridges E 1 Demeter *nurseried* his wheat | *pillory*, also fig. | *pocket* | Hughes T 2.31 you'll be *quod'ed* ['put in prison (quod)'] | *sidetrack*, also fig. (chiefly U. S.) | Norris P 13 the war *skied* the prices of all food-stuffs | Amr NP Cleveland was *slated* to speak at the meeting | *tree* 'force (an animal, fig.: a person) up a tree' | Sh Ant IV. 14.72 Would'st thou be *window'd* in great Rome.

6.7₃. De-substantival verbs frequently come to mean 'provide with or furnish with sth, put on a garment, etc.'. This process may have been furthered by the use of the adjective-ending *-ed* (see 24.1). Thus, from the sb *wing* is formed an adj *winged* ('having wings') which is easily apprehended as the past participle ('furnished with wings') of a vb *wing*. Still, in many cases there exists no other form than the *ed*-form: Galsw EC 78 Men, silk-hatted or plus-foured | in his stockinged feet | a knock-kneed person, etc.

Arm 'furnish, equip with arms' | Philips L 98 I wonder whether I ought not to *diet* you, feed you with plain meats, and leave out the sauce | *dress* | *flesh* (a dog) 'give it flesh to incite it', hence figuratively 'incite': Sh Alls IV. 3.19 this night he fleshes his will in the spoyle of her honour | *gassed* in the War | Carlyle S 83 hoodwink and *handcuff* him | ib 34 not only dressed, but *harnessed* and draperied | Stevenson B 6 every man that we can *horse* | Ridge G 103 she wrote the

bill and took it to Miss Connor to *initial* | *pension* off |
Anstey V 198 .. insisted upon *pomatuming* his hair |
ring (a bull); rare: Sh John III. 4.31 I will .. ring these
fingers with thy houshold wormes | Thack V 214 George
had *shawled* his wife [rare] | Di N 472 I'll *summons*
you for having a broken winder [= window] | Chesterton
F 287 you'll have to *subpoena* me | Harraden S 86 she
did not care for flowers to be *wired* | Hammett Th 87
a line had been *x'd* and *m'd* out here [in a typewritten
letter]. ? means not place?

6.7₄. The vb means to deprive of that which the sb
indicates:

Bone 'pull out the bones of' | *brain* 'knock out the
brains of': Phillpotts M 385 the idea of E. waiting to
brain her | Black Ph 368 black cock and grey hen
dusting themselves in the road | *pinion* 'cut off the
pinions of, bind the arms of' | *skin* | *stem* 'remove the
stem(s) of': | *stone*, see above | *sweat* 'remove sweat from
(a horse) by scraping' | *weed* (a garden).

6.7₅. From the names of implements (in a widened
sense) are derived a great many verbs that denote the
action for which the implements are meant (cf *cable*,
nail, *screw*, *wire*).

Axe 'cut down (expenses)' | *bomb* | Di D 85 he was
caned every day, except on holiday Monday when he
was only *ruler'd* on both hands | *chain* | *chalk* | *cork*
'blacken with burnt cork': Jerrold C 49 ... who corked
whiskers on my dear aunt's picture | Herrick M 82 a
conspiracy to *dynamite* the city | *hammer* | *hook* 'catch
with a hook, steal' | *key* up 'brace up' | *knife* | Doyle
M 15 I can see him now *levering* himself up from his
lowly seat | *ransom* 'redeem by payment of ransom,
etc.' | *sandbag* 'protect with sandbags, knock down
with a s.' | *sandpaper* 'polish with sandpaper' | Wells
Cl 483 Then we will *taxi* to Hyde Park Corner | *torpedo* |
Carlyle H 31 men who as it were *toyed* with the matter |
Maxwell WF 98 shoes that had not been well-*treed* |

wire 'telegraph' | *x-ray* 'treat with x-rays' | Wells Br
174 they will *Zeppelin* the fleet.

Cf combinations with *it* 6.8₇.

Names of drinks may be regarded as implements in
a widened sense: *liquor* 'consume strong drinks' | Di
N 480 you could come and *tea* with me | dine and *wine*
with some one | Hughes T 2.99 Will you come and
wine with me next Thursday?

But we never have verbs in that way from names of
food: we cannot possibly say to *bread* or to *meat;* cf
however Pinero M 2 grub = 'eat'.

6.7₆. *Parts of the body:* used as a kind of implement:

Arm 'take in one's arms' (once in Sh: Cymb IV. 2.400);
'put one's arm round; offer one's arm to' | *beard* 'oppose,
defy; remove the beard from': Galsw WM 141 oysters
.. Michael bearded them; Bicket swallowed them whole;
—(rare) 'furnish with a beard' | *body:* Sh Mid V. 1.14
imagination bodies forth the forms of things unknown |
brain 'conceive in the brain' (rare): Sh Cymb V. 4.147
such stuffe as madmen Tongue and braine not;—'dash
out the brains of': see 6.7₄ | *breast* 'present the breast
to (the waves, a storm)' | *cheek* 'address with impudence
(cheek)' | *chin* (Amr) 'chatter': Lewis MS 247 dropping
in to chin with Bea and me | *ear* (very rare) 'give ear
to'. In vulgar pronunciation *hear* becomes *'ear,* which
is felt by the common people as formed from the sb
ear. Cf NED: 'in some cases perhaps a misspelling for
hear' | *elbow* (one's way, etc.) | *eye* 'observe, stare at';
(rare) 'appear': Sh Ant I. 1.97 when they [my becom-
ings] do not eye well to you | *face* (often fig.) | *finger* |
fist: Sh Cor IV. 5.131 fisting each other's throat | *foot*
'tread, walk; supply a new foot to (a stocking)': all
three meanings are found in Sh | *front* | *hand* | *head*
esp. 'act as the head of, appear at the head of' | *jaw* 'lect-
ure, scold, speak' | *knee* 'kneel' (Sh) | *limb:* Mi PL 6.352
they limb themselves | *lip* 'kiss' (Sh) | *nose* 'smell,
scent; speak through the nose; pry; oppose in an in-

solent manner (obs.)'; in Sh only = 'smell': Hml IV.
3.38 you shall nose him as you go vp the staires | *paw*
'touch with the paw; handle awkwardly' | *shin:* Vachell H
283 you shin down the tree | *shoulder* (arms, etc) | *stomach*
(an affront, etc.) | *thumb:* Hemingway Sun Also R 116
I thumbed my nose | *toe:* Maynard Smith F 238 how
did you resist the temptation to toe him out of the
door? | *tongue* 'speak, utter': see Sh-example under
"braine".

On combinations with *it*, see 6.8₇.

Cognate with the above category are:

sense: Hewlett Q 181 it needed not so quick an eye
to sense the brewing of a storm | *wing:* Lawrence L 153
as he would watch a wild goose he had shot. Was it
winged, or dead?

6.7₇. Another minor group is formed by words denoting periods of time, weather, etc. Derivatives from
these generally mean 'spend the time indicated by the
substantive': *honey-moon* | Beaconsfield L 462 We shall
certainly *winter* in Rome | Waugh W 273 Wouldn't it
be a good idea if they *week-ended* there? || Herrick M 4
it began to *mist* pretty hard | Curme S 8 it *frosted*
heavily last night.

6.7₈. Not infrequently, a de-substantival verb is
used about an action or state that resembles the thing
in shape:

Cave in 'yield' | *elbow* 'make an 'elbow' in one's path,
go out of the direct way' (NED) | *honeycomb* 'riddle,
undermine' | *mushroom* 'take (or cause to take) the
shape of a mushroom' (esp. of bullets) | *sandwich* 'insert
between two others' | Doyle S 1.230 their conversation
. . . suddenly *tailing* off into silences (cf *queue* up) |
spread-eagle 'stretch out in the form of a spread eagle' |
telescope: the train was telescoped; also intr.: the train
telescoped.

Similar sense-relations are found in Archer Am 48 her

silvering or silver hair | Wells Cl 254 Dickon's pink skin *freckles* at a mere glimpse of the sun.

In some cases there is no resemblance to the thing itself but to that which is done with or by the thing:

Shaw 1.53 Blanche's face *clouds* | Russell FO 494 Admiral Fisher advised that the German Navy should be *"Copenhagened"*, i. e. sunk without previous warning, as the Danish Fleet had been sunk by us a century earlier.

6.7₉. Verbs derived from the names of animals to denote the action characteristic of the animal in question, are not so frequent:

Buck up 'cheer up' | Twain H 1.126 I *crawfished* as fast as I could | *dog* 'follow closely' | *fox* 'behave craftily'| Robinson Mind in the Making 88 it seems to be pretty well established that the monkey learns by *monkeying*, but that he rarely or never appears to *ape* | Galsw WM 81 In Piccadilly he *moused* along on the Park side | Galsw WM 113 he *peacocked* about his ancestry | *rat* 'desert a cause, become a blackleg' (Galsw P 3.15) | *skylark* | *wolf.—Ferret* (out) does not belong here because it means 'to hunt with ferrets', whence figuratively 'to make a persevering search'.

Where there is a special name for the young of an animal, this is often made into a vb meaning 'to bring forth young': *cub* | *foal* | *lamb*.

In stock exchange slang, the sbs *bear* and *bull* have a special sense; hence the vbs: *bear* | *bull*.

Names of persons may produce vbs meaning 'make, be, become, or do the thing characteristic of'. Some of them, such as *father*, have several significations:

Baby 'treat as a baby' | Collingwood R 286 Thor, *berserking* among Rime-giants | *boss* 'be the manager (boss) of' | *child* 'bring forth, bear a child' (obs. at the beginning of 17th c., the NED has an isolated example from 1808, apparently a new formation) | *chum* 'share rooms (with); be intimate' | Harris Shaw 30 Shaw used

the circus-tents of publicity to *clown* his way to this
notoriety | Dreiser AT 1.338 a mental and physical
animation which quite matched and *companioned* her
own | Meredith H 273 She's been *countessed* [= made a
countess] | Pinero M 45 *devilled* oysters; also = 'work
as a lawyer's (etc.) devil' | *dwarf* 'make small' | *father*
'be, become, or acknowledge oneself, father to'; also in
the phrase 'father sth upon one' | Twain M 214 promis-
ing to *fool* his possibilities away early | *gossip* 'be god-
father or godmother to' (Sh Alls I. 1.189); now usually
'talk idly' | Pope 165 two fair daughters *heir'd* his
state and throne | *jew* 'cheat' | *knight* | Galsw EC 955
what a place to wander about in, *lovering* | *martyr*
'put to death as a martyr' | Ridge G 165 soothing
her and *mothering* her | Carlyle S 71 quite *orphaned*
and alone | Gaye Vivandière 272 she *pickpocketed* for
a change | *slave* | *squire* 'escort, accompany': Congreve
218 who squires me to the exchange | Sh Cor IV. 4.15
who *twin*, as 'twere, in loue Vnseparable [= are like
twins] | *volunteer* information | *widow* 'make a widow'
(Sh Cor V. 6.153); 'survive as a widow': Sh Ant I.
2.27 let me widow them all | Shaw TT 228 I was not
born for *wifing* and mothering | Sh Alls III. 2.53 the
first face .. can *woman* mee vntoo't.

On phrases with *it*, see 6.8₇.

Verbs formed from names of persons occupied in a
certain way are comparatively rare because many of
these substantives are in their turn derived from verbs
by means of *-er* or *-or:* cf, however, *cook*, *nurse*, and:

Galsw WM 119 a man .. who's done most of the
agenting for the German business | *beggar* 'reduce to
poverty' (NED: 1528-1864); 'go beyond, outshine': to
beggar description | *butcher* | *captain* (a football team,
etc.) | Hay B 15 I don't like figures well enough to
clerk [= become a clerk] | *doctor* (up) 'treat medically' |
McKenna Sh 225 a small army of inspectors *generalled*
by a parcel of boys in a Government office, takes a

man and *nursemaids* him | Di D 372 I've *laundressed*
other young men besides yourself | Caine P 237 you
have gone away to *recruit* [= enlist as a soldier] |
shepherd | *soldier* | *star* 'appear as a star actor' | Carlyle
S 37 this same fact of there being Tailors and *Tailored* |
Sh R2 IV. 1.166 Giue sorrow leaue a while to *tutore*
me To this submission | Benson D 2.84 she *valeted*
him | Ronald Knox in BDS 80 Not till he came in to be
vetted for his insurance.

In this connexion we might also mention verbs from
words denoting a mass of persons: *people* usually
'to populate, fill with people'; rare (not in the NED):
Ruskin U 158 [the labourer] will people down to the
same point of misery at which you found him | A.
Huxley Crome Yellow 79 diseases have *unpeopled* half
the globe | *mob:* Hughes T 2.29 the boys would mob you.

A few formations are due to proper names: *boycott* |
burke 'suppress' (Burke executed 1829 for smothering
people) | *jobe* (< Job) obs. = 'rebuke in a long and
tedious harangue', hence *jobation* which is still used |
lynch | Macdonell E 229 one can't *Shylock* the poor
devils.

In the following examples the development appears
to have been: proper name > common name > vb:
jack (up) 'lift with a jack' | *meander* | *pander* | *silhouette.*

6.81. Verbs are, of course, rarely formed from action-
nouns which have themselves been derived from a verb.
When it does happen, the new verb generally has a
special application:

Allowance: Di N 406 to allowance him. To do what?
To put him upon a fixed allowance | Meredith R 119 I am
allowanced two glasses before dinner || *Dinner:* Burns
264 I dinner'd wi' a Lord | Carlyle R 2.143 noisy Liver-
pool, with its dinnerings, wine-drinkings, and dull even-
ing parties || *Drift*, different in sense from the vb *drive* ||
Sight 'get sight of; take observation of a star; adjust
the sights of a gun, etc.'

But where there does not exist any verb on
English soil, or where the sb and vb have become
isolated from each other either in form or in meaning,
a vb may be formed = the sb.

Action 'bring a legal action against' | *caution* | *com-
mission* | *condition* | *function* (cf F *fonctionner*) | *mention*
(cf F *mentionner*) | *motion* | *partition* (off) | *pension*
(off) | *petition* | *proportion* | *requisition* | *sanction* |
station | *suspicion* (Twain H 1.131).

Capture | *feature* | *pleasure:* Mrs Browning A 123 It
pleasures him to stop for buttercups.—*Pillage* has now
supplanted the earlier vb *pill* (found in Sh).—Norris S
52 he *gestured* with one hand.

6.8₂. Sometimes a vb is not formed direct from a
corresponding sb but only through a detour. The endings
-er and *-ing* were at first nominal suffixes (cf modern
hatter, Londoner; shirting, sacking). They are now
chiefly used as de-verbative formatives, but the fact
that it is impossible to tell from such a derivative itself whether it is from a vb or a sb may lead to new
vbs being formed by subtraction of the ending of a
nominal formation ("back-formation"). Thus *nut* ('gather
nuts') is not direct from the sb *nut* but from the phrase
"go (a) nutting", and the vb *bird's-nest*, according to
the NED, is 'inferred from the gerund *bird's-nesting*,
which was much earlier in use'. Though many verbs
have been formed in this roundabout way, we cannot
always conclude from the existence of a form in *-ing* or
-er that there must also be a corresponding verb.

Further examples: *dairying* is found as early as 1649,
but the rare verb *dairy* not until 1780 | *caucusing* is
recorded from 1788, to *caucus* 1850. No vbs are recorded
in the NED to *sempstering* and *trickstering*, and though
we can use the phrase "in my schoolmastering days",
we cannot say "to schoolmaster".

On the detour through adjs in *-ed* see below under
that suffix.—Cf also the type *house-keep*, below 9.7₁.

6.8₃. With regard to form, we must notice:

(1) In the majority of cases the vb is taken from the singular of the sb. An exception is the vb *dice*.

(2) Verbs are freely formed from compounds: Mrs Browning A 40 *bee-bonneted* | Shaw D 14 his face looks machine-made and *beeswaxed* | *belly-ache* (U. S.) 'complain' | Golding SD 23 Sometimes they whistled and *cat-called* at the very sight of her | Di N 457 she wouldn't *charcoal* herself to death with him | Kipling S 155 F. made us *cock-fight* | Di P 401 Mr. Bantam *corkscrewed* his way through the crowd | Deeping RR 149 Ruth *day-dreamed* | a *dog('s)-eared* page | Dane FB 9 the same spirit that *fig-leafs* Apollo and measures the Milo Venus for a pair of stays | Tracy P 31 he's *finger-printing* 'em | Young, Custody Children 204 don't let us stand here and *fish-wife* each other [= scold like fishwives] | Zangwill G 227 the steps being scrubbed and *hearth-stoned* | Defoe M 94 I must *housewife* the money | Locke W 247 he asked her if she *hunger-struck* | Mannin W 132 she will draw his head down to her breast and *little-boy* him | Christie 3A 23 Her .. mouth *lip-sticked* to a curve | Rose Macaulay P 133 Gideon had murdered (or anyhow *man-slaughtered*) Oliver | White N 134 if you could *Mind Cure* by mere force of will | Tracy P 139 I *nose-dived* for the floor [in flying] | Galsw WM 113 he *peacocked* about his ancestry | to *pigeon-hole* sth | *pipe-clay* (shoes, etc.) | NP 1911 on your arrival you *postcard* your friends | Amr NP 1912 the bill was *railroaded* through the New York Senate [= put through rapidly] | Barnes Y 195 she wasn't going to be railroaded into marriage | *sand-bag* | *sand-paper* | *short-circuit* 'cause a short-circuit in' | Caine C 136 the shouts and laughter of people *snowballing* in the streets | Montague Rough Just 203 "That's right"—he *stage-whispered* | Shaw F 46 there is no question of the *steam-rollering* of little States | *stone-wall* 'block balls persistently (in cricket)' | Doyle B 238 I *tiptoed* down the path

| Keats 2.42 Pal'd in and *vineyarded* from beggar-spies |
water-mark | Wells N 431 she *week-ended* with them.

Among the words mentioned in previous paragraphs
are: *honeycomb* | *honeymoon* | *machine-gun* | *side-track* |
x-ray.

In the above group, the basis of the new verbs was
a combination of two sbs; it may also be an adj + a sb:

Kipling DW 224 he just *bad-worded* 007 [a locomotive]
| to *blackball* a person | he was *blackholed* for twelve
hours (NED) | Galsw P 9.47 Who *black-legged*? | Amr
NP 1904 dressmakers *blacklist* slow-paying women |
Bennett HL 112 the Daily Telegraph .. was *blue
pencilled* | *cold-shoulder* a person | *dry-nurse* a child |
fair-copy sth | Swift J 398 I will not meddle with the
spectator, let him *fair-sex* it to the world's end | Holmes
A 25 *French-polished* by society and travel | Lewis MA
62 I figured out you were going to *high-hat* me | Marshall
Sorry Sch 97 I *high-kicked* with the rest | Ade A 22 so
I *hot-foots* up to the dance | Tennyson 213 So she *low-
toned* [= read in a low tone] | Lewis MS 11 she *one-
stepped* demurely | Amr NP 1923 they invaded a public
meeting .. *rotten-egged* and then assaulted the speakers |
Ru 1.389 Do not *rough-cast* your walls with falsehood |
London V 40 they only *rough-house* | id M 281 enable
me to *short-cut* my way to truth .. you certainly *short-
cut* with a vengeance | Galsw F 325 with whom it would
be quite impossible to gossip or *small-talk* | Lewis MA
286 I can't go out and *soft-soap* the people | *spread-
eagle* sby (sth) | Ade A 10 would n't that *upper-cut* you?

The adj in these compounds may easily come to look
like an adverb prefixed to the verb. In a phrase like:
Roister 56 Then did ye wrong copy it [the letter], it
is impossible to tell whether 'wrong' is an adverb or
the first member of a composite verb (< adj+sb).

A little apart stands: Thack V 157 the girls *Christian-
named* each other at once.

Compounds of the above-mentioned type are especi-

ally common with *new* as the first member: it is often
written as a word by itself but is in reality part of the
vb; cf vol II 15.3.

Caxton R 62 *newe* shood | BJo 3.205 to *new-paint*
his pole | Dryden 5. 336 Then she *new-names* her jewels |
Sterne 110 he would *new fore-front* his house | Austen
M 51 had I a place to *new-fashion* | Di P 127 If the
Buffs proposed to *new skylight* the market-place |
Hughes T 2.244 bringing his old coat to be *new sleeved* |
Caine M 82 Black Tom was there, *new thatching* the
back of the house.

In a few cases, where the phrase is of Romanic
origin, we have the inverse order: sb + adj > vb: Caine
M 77 we generally *court-martial* him | Galsw WM 182
His reflections *sum-totalled* in a decision to talk it over
with M.

We have also derivative vbs of a still more complicated
character: Di Do 271 to *soap-and-water* | id P 416 the
manner in which she *hooks-and-eyes* that infernal ..
gown of hers behind | Southey L 48 I am .. *pen-and-
inking* for supplies. But to 'penny-a-lining poets'
(Symonds, Sh's Predecessors 248) there is probably no
infinitive or finite form, see the next paragraphs.

Substantive (< vb + object) > vb: Gaye Vivandière
272 she *pickpocketed* for a change | *snapshot*.

New-formed vbs are usually weakly inflected. Mencken
Am L³ 288 wonders at the weak vb *joyride*, because he believes
it to have been formed by putting the sb *joy* and the vb *ride*
together. As a matter of fact, however, it has been formed
direct from the sb *joyride*, which explains its weak conjugation.
The vb *hamstring* may be either weak or strong, 'hunger-
strike' is strong in: Locke W 247 he asked her if she hunger-
struck.

On the type *house-keep* see 9.7₁.

6.8₄. The ease with which the English language coins
"nonce-words" is especially seen in the frequent formation of a verb from a sb, an adj, an adv, or indeed any

kind of word or phrase, without any formal alteration.
In many cases the urge to use such a term is so great
and universally felt that the word is coined independently by several speakers at different times, and the word
will then have to be reckoned among the common
stock of words in the language. In other cases the term
is so bold, being produced by the requirements of an
individual speaker on the spur of the moment, that it
can never be counted more than a momentary out-
growth of the state of language in which the type
"sb = vb" has become fixed.

"Nonce-words" are found early, even before the loss
of the endings that distinguish verbs from substantives,
but then only rarely: AR 420 uorte *ureonden* ou (= to
gain friends for you). They become very common from
the 15th century: Malory (see Baldwin § 23) 282 thou
couragest me | ib 405 they *peaced* them self, etc. They
abound in Sh (see among others Abbott § 290; Theo-
bald, Sh Restored 7-17). Here only some few examples
collected from my own reading: Cymb V. 4.147 such
stuffe, as Madmen tongue, and *braine* not (*brain* as a
verb usually = dash out the brains of) | *disease:* Cor
I. 3.117 (= 'make uneasy', Sh-lex.) | ib V. 3.11 This
old man lou'd me aboue the measure of a father; nay,
godded me indeed (= deified, idolized) | ib III. 2.132 I'll
mountebank their loues | *surety* (= 'to be evidence for,
to bail', Sh-lex.): Cor III. 1.178 wee'l surety him | Alls
V. 3.2 he shall surety me.

6.8₅. A special class of "nonce-words" is often used
in retorts. In anger one simply seizes one word or
phrase in what was said by the other party, and repeats
it as a verb in a scornful tone of voice.

Sh Wiv IV. 2.193 Come, Mother Prat . . —I'll *prat*
her | Dekker Satirom. (NED) I cannot, my mad cum-
rade . . Sir V: Cumrade? By Iesu, call me cumrade
againe and Ile *cumrade* ye about the sinnes and should-
ers | Massinger N III. 2.260 . . the rost turned powder —

I shall *powder* you | Sheridan 83 Trinkets! a bauble for
Lydia! .. So this was the history of his trinkets! I'll
bauble him! | Macaulay B 10 "I was explaining the
Golden Bull to his Royal Highness". "I'll *Golden Bull*
you, you rascal!" roared the Majesty of Prussia | Trol-
lope B 163 Mr. Slope, indeed! I'll *Slope* him | ib 108
Lame, said Mrs. Proudie. I'd *lame* her if she belonged
to me | Hope Ch 112 The man is thinking of nothing
but Nihilists and what not. I'd *Nihilist* him! | Kipling
S 157 you call yourself a beastly poet. I'll *poet* you |
id L 37 You're in luck .. Huh! call it luck! .. I'll *luck*
them later on | Shaw J 219 God forgive you.—You
Gawd forgive me again and I'll *Gawd forgive you* one
on the jaw thatll stop you praying for a week.

In the following quotation it is a vb that is taken
up and flung back with scarcely any meaning at all:
Salt Joy 139 Now, don't get so excited. You know it's
bad for you.—I'll *excite* you one of these days if I have
any more of your impudence.

We also, though not so frequently, witness the change
of a vb into a sb (quotation-sb): Mackenzie C 93 I'll
kill myself if I don't.—I'll give you "kill yourself",
cried Mrs. R.

When the word taken up for retort is, or resembles,
an agent-noun, the ending is often removed ("back-
formation"): Sh H4A II. 2.97 you are Grand Iurers,
are ye? Wee'l *iure* ye ifaith | Marlowe F (1616) 383
Belcher? and Belcher come here, I'le *belch* him: I am
not afraid of a deuill | Shaw J 142 You will be killed:
he is a prize-fighter.—I'll *prize-fight* him.

Another type of retort consists in using the same
word twice, first as a verb and then as the object:
Gammer 145 Sweare me no swearing | Sh R2 II. 3.87
My gracious Vnckle.—Tut, tut, Grace me no Grace,
nor Vnckle me no Vnckle [the last two words not in the
folio] | Ro III. 5.153 Thanke me no thankings, nor
proud me no prouds | Massinger N I. 3.39 you lose the

cause.—Cause me no causes | Scott A 1.169 "I heartily
wish I could, but—" "Nay, but me no buts—I have
set my heart upon it." | Tennyson 392 "Advance and
take thy prize, The diamond;" but he answered, "Diamond me no diamonds! For God's love, a little air!
Prize me no prizes, for my prize is death."—See also
Bartlett, *Familiar Quotations.*

6.8₆. Outside retorts proper, "nonce-words" are
common in the sense of calling somebody something:
Scott A 2.300 She began to read, "Dear Sir". "He
dears me too, you see". | Zangwill G 54 "Darling,"
he cried in amaze. "I told you not to *"darling"* me." |
Hewlett Q 117 I do not choose to be *mistressed* by a
maid of honour || Thack V 371 they *my-loved* and *my-
deared* each other | Hewlett Q 313 she neither *sir'd*
nor *my-lorded* him | Tennyson L 2.254 If you call me
Mr. Tennyson any longer, I think that I must *Your-
grace* you till the end of the chapter | Shaw D 3 Dr
Ridgeon has been made a knight. Mind you dont go
Dr Ridgeoning him in them letters.

Thack H 34 Don't *Milly* me! | Smedley F 88 we
don't *Mr.* each other here | Meredith H 7 he began *mar-
quising* Mel || Trollope D 71 He had *my-Lorded* his
young friend at first | Di Sk 145 I've been *Lord Peter'd*
by. .

Nonce-words of the above-mentioned type are also
formed from pronouns, adverbs, etc.:

Hewlett F 104 to be *thee'd* and *thou'd* by this lady |
Thack N 699 is there a bishop that has not *amen'd*
the humbug | Hankin 3.21 Really, Lady Remenham . .
—Tut, tut, sir. Don't *"really"* me || BJo P V. 81 Pish.
Ha, ha.—Dost thou *pish* me? | Thack N 816 the boys
invariably *hurrayed* him | Ridge G 278 it was worth
while at times to *shoo* him away (now a regular vb).

The vb may be intransitive, meaning to exclaim what
is indicated by the basal expression: Plunket Greene
E 348 "Poor Robin." "What are you two girls *poor*

Robining about?" | Galsw SP 49 You and I will fight
for a decent life for everybody. No *hands-upping* about
that! || Southey L 361 They could fight, though they
could not *parlez-vous*.

In this way the ordinary vbs *ha(w) haw, hum and
haw, tut—tut*, etc., have been formed. "Shilly-shally"
(< shall I? shall I?) belongs here etymologically though
the origin is no longer felt by the ordinary speaker.

A curious kind of such vbs is exemplified in: Bennett
Cd 84 He was not an hour in the tour, and yet was
already *hanging* expense! What he says is: "Hang
expense!" but instead of the whole phrase only "hang"
is taken over as a verb, and "expense" is incorporated
as the object of the nonce-verb. Similarly: Thack N 47
I *confounded* Brett's man | Locke GP 213 Don't you
understand, I must perfect my metal?—She *bothered*
his old metal | to *speed* the parting guest (= to say
"God speed" to). The subject "God" may also be
expressed, in which case it forms part of the verb:
Keats 5.183 These laughers .. who would have *God-
bless'd* me from you for ever (not in NED) | Locke
HB 266 Baltazar gripped him by the hand and *God-
blessed* him | Drinkwater Linc. 11 I've seen your hus-
band .. *god-darning* some rascal.

In the following example, too, only the first word of
the quotation is made into a verb: Bennett Helen 121
"But, uncle—" "It's no good *butting uncle*."

6.8₇. When from a sb is formed a vb which from
its signification must be intransitive, there is a strong
tendency to add *it* as a kind of "empty" object. Many
of these formations are nonce-words and phrases.

From words designating persons and animals, etc.,
meaning 'to play the—': *cat* it (up a water-pipe) | Sh
Mcb II. 3.19 Ile *deuill-porter* it no further | Cor II. 3.128
rather than *fool* it so | Bridges E 8·Not long shall that
poor girl of Crete *God* it in my despite | *hare* it 'run
away' | Sterne M 1.42 she could not *heroine* it into so

violent and hazardous an extreme | *lord* it | Dryden
5. 345 Well, I must *man* it out | Mencken AL 561
man-and-womaning it 'in love' | Sh Wint IV. 4.460
I'll *queen* it no inch farther, etc., see Sh-lex 600b |
Cor V. 3.48 my true lippe hath *virgin'd* it ere since.

From names of inanimate things, meaning 'to use'
them: Jerome T 27 we would sleep out on fine nights;
and *hotel* it, and *inn* it, and *pub* it when it was wet |
common phrase: shall we *cab* it or *bus* it? || *foot* it | *hoof*
it | *leg* it. The sense-development is obscure in: *hook* it
'make off' (Trollope D 3.166, Philips L 124).

A little hard to classify are: BJo 3.188 How the slave
does *Latin* it | Kipling B 26 An' you're sent to *penny-
fights* and *Aldershot* it.

From adjectives we have: *brave* it | Moore EW 132
a nice one indeed to *high-and-mighty* it over her | *rough*
it.

Perhaps on the analogy of *foot it* and *leg it* we have
also: *walk* it (Di P 119, Haggard S 269).

6.9₁. Verbs derived from *adjectives* generally denote
a change: become or make someone (something) what
is expressed by the adj; cf also vol III 16.5:

Phillpotts M 392 he *calmed* down a little | *clean* |
clear | Shaw 1.29 I have *dirtied* my hands | *double* |
dry | *English* 'render English' | Masefield C 265 The
world had *gentled* him by some such blow as had crushed
her | Wells H 96 hard work .. *greyed* his hair | Kaye-
Smith GA 17 I've never *hotted* the tea-pot | Herrick
M 57 he .. bullied me, *jollied* me, as his mood happened
to be | Linklater J 153 he who *lightlied* commerce must
suffer appropriate pains | *loose* | *near* 'approach' | *negative*
| Merrick MG 3 She *queers* the best line I've ever got
in the piece | *ready* (racing slang) 'prevent a horse
from winning in order to get a better handicap later' |
Holmes A 32 I *rough* out my thoughts in talk as an
artist models in clay | Galsw F 221 He'll *savage* some-
thing over this | *shoal* | Hewlett Q 137 he always *shrilled*

his *s*'s | *shy* 'start in alarm' (especially of horses) |
Meredith E 220 the lustre of the maid *sicklied* the poor
widow | Caine E 514 the train *slowed* down | *steady*
'make steady' | London M 389 her body *tensed* angrily |
Beaconsfield L 471 It was August, and town was
thinning fast | *true* up a machine | *wanton* 'be wanton':
Greene F 8.57 | Macaulay B 262 the gay spirit of France
wantoned in a thousand forms | *wet* 'make wet' | *wireless*
'send a wireless telegram' | *wise* up (U. S.) 'get or put
wise'.

Two verbs which are no longer felt as derivatives, are
probably formed from old past participles: *faint* (vb
from 1350), formed direct from the English adj (p. p.)
feint, which is found from 1300 | *swoon* < ME *iswowen* <
OE *geswōgen*, p. p. of *swōgan* 'to choke'. The NED
regards the latter as a back-formation from *swogening*,
swowening, the ME verbal sb.

To *worst* is apparently from the superlative but may
be an expanded form of the comparative, see I 7.64.
On the analogy of 'worst' is formed the vb to *best*
'get the better of'. The earliest example in NED 1863,
but in dialects found earlier, e. g. in Scott Iv 152 when
he discovered the leader so hard bested. Apart from
these two, no superlatives have become verbs.

On verbs formed from comparatives, and on obsolete
forms replaced by vbs in -*en* see under that suffix below
20.5₄₋₅.

6.9₂. From an adverb denoting a place or a direction
a verb may be formed to designate a movement to
that place or in that direction:

Di D 293 Then I *aways* to him, and I says | id F 278
lest Boots should have occasion to mount and *away* |
Stevenson T 252 They might *round* upon us in a twinkle
of an eye | Smollett: we ought to *down* on our knees
and bless God | Browning 2.504 Unless you *down* with
cash, perhaps! | Ridge L 58 If it happens again, I shall
simply *on* with my hat and .. | Shaw M xxv a stage

villain who smothers babies and *offs* with people's
heads || By DJ 12.63 [she] keeps you *on and off-ing*
On a lee-shore | Mrs Carlyle 2.275 Mr. C always *hithers
and thithers* in a very interminable way before he can
make up his mind | NP 1934 the vast area over which
troops were *to-ing and fro-ing*.

The verb thus formed may also be transitive:

Sh Alls I. 3.48 to *inne* the crop | *down* tools (Maugham
Pl 4.172) = go on strike | Norris O 332 Everybody is
trying to down me | Collier E 428 I would not like to
see the old man downed.

In a few cases vbs from sbs have passed through the
use as an adv: Kipling B 228 the good souls flocked like
homeing doves | Archer A 13 my companion and I
express our baggage to our hotel [= send it by the
American Express; different from the old vb *express*
one's meaning, sympathy, etc.].

6.9₃. The formation of verbs from adverbs is especially
common with "out" and "up":

Out: Di Do 174 it's better I should out and say my
boy's gone wrong | Phillpotts M 160 the poison had
to out | Kipling B 7 1 outs into the street an' to myself
sez I || By L 184 I could not out with the truth | Di
F 479 Then why don't you out with your reason for.. |
Huxley L 1.112 the only chance is to out with it |
Stevenson T 241 I'm still your cap'n, mind—till you
outs with your grievances | Shaw D 257 you have views
of your own and are not afraid to out with them ||
Galsw FM 273 girls who get outed .. no girl gets "outed"
as you call it, unless she is predisposed that way.

Goldsm V 1.174 let him up with it [a song] boldly.
Or as a transitive vb: Stevenson T 182 they had nothing nearer their hearts than to up anchor and away to
sea. But by far the most common construction is for
up to be followed by "and" + a verb. They may be
combined in three different ways: (1) quite formlessly:
"I up and ran"; (2) *up* as an infinitive: "Why don't

you up and run?"; (3) *up* as a finite verb with flexional
endings: "He ups and runs".

(1) Kipling B 7 The publican 'e up and sez | Di F
99 me and Mrs. Boffin up and faced the old man · |
Longfellow 14 then up and spake an old sailor | Norris
P 186 she up and died | Gibson Diplom. Diary 230 I
up and ran | Phillpotts M 183 if anybody had told me,
I'd have up and answered | Amr NP 1925 from the
up and coming Arkansas town of Stuttgart.

(2) Browning 1.263 Then we would up and pace |
Kipling B 17 I'll up an' tend to my true love | Masefield
E 7 I'll up and say the fault was mine | Wells Ma 1.92
Why don't you up and marry Mr. Magnet? || Kipling
Sev. S 173 I'm going to up and see her | Shaw D 194
ladies that would fairly provoke you to up and cheek
them | Wells Cl 692 exhorting the "white" peoples to
up and have a fearful lot of children.

(3) Browning 2.70 Guido ups and cries | Arden Green
Hat 208 I upped and said he could go | Macdonald
Maze 225 she could have upped with the quartz.

Up may occasionally be found without a verb immediately following: Doyle G 61 But no, she up again
as light as a piece of fluff, and we all drew up our stools.

Somewhat different constructions: Henley & Steven-
son Plays 23 I had to up and after him | Doyle S 3.70
with that he ups and he outs.

Chapter VII

The Naked Word Continued

Substantives from Verbs without Change

7.1₁. The peculiar freedom with which substantives
are made from verbs in English without change of
form, is another consequence of the coincidence in form
dealt with above 6.1₂. Accordingly we see an ever

increasing number of these formations from about
1500. I shall give some examples in alphabetical order,
adding the date of the earliest quotation for the vb and
the noun in the NED.

Of course, we are not here talking of the usage common
to many languages by which a verbal form, or any other word,
is taken as a "quotation-substantive": Sh Meas II. 2.32 I am
at warre twixt will, and will not; cf vol II. 8.2.

approach vb 1305, sb 1489 | *beat* vb OE, sb 1615 |
bend vb OE, sb 1529 | *bid* vb OE, sb 1788 | *blemish*
vb 1325, sb 1526 | *blow* vb OE, sb 1660 (= 'a blowing,
a blast'; the sense 'a stroke' is earlier: 1460) | *blush* vb
1325, sb 1340 | *bow* vb OE, sb 1656 (= 'inclination of
head or body') | *build* vb OE *byldan, sb 1667 (= 'style
of construction'; the sense 'building' is earlier: 1325) |
burn vb OE, sb 1563 | *bustle* vb 1563, sb 1622 | *call*
vb OE, sb 1306 | *cast* vb 1270, sb 1300 | *catch* vb 1205,
sb 1430 | *climb* vb OE, sb 1577 | *command* vb 1300, sb
(probably from the English vb) 1552 | *concern* vb 1450,
sb 1589; the use of *concern* for *concernment* was censured
1655 by Dorothy Osborne (see NED); Sh has the vb,
not the sb | *crave* vb OE, sb 1830 (= 'craving'; not
in general use, NED) | *crowd* vb OE, sb 1567 | *cry* vb
(= 'shed tears') 1532; sb (= 'a fit of weeping'): NED
gives 1852 as the first date, but the word is found in
Austen S 191 she had better have her cry out at once |
cut vb 1275, sb 1530 | *dawn* vb 1499, sb 1599 | *dig* vb
1320; sb (= 'a tool, a mattock') 1674, (= 'a thrust or
poke with the elbow') 1819, (= 'an act of digging')
1887 | *dip* vb OE, sb 1599 | *dislike* vb 1555, sb 1577 |
dismay vb 1297, sb 1590 | *dispute* vb 1290, sb 1594 |
dissent vb 1425, sb 1585 | *distemper* vb in various mean-
ings 1340, 1400, sb 1555, 1632 | *dive* vb OE, sb 1700 |
divide vb 1374, sb 1642 | *drain* vb OE, sb 1552 | *dread*
vb 1175, sb 1200 | *dress* (= 'attire') vb 1440, sb 1606 |
drive vb OE, sb 1697, the sense 'carriage road' 1816 |

embrace vb 1386, sb 1592 | *fawn* vb OE, sb 1590 | *fetch* vb OE, sb 1530 | *find* vb OE, sb (= 'an act or instance of finding') 1825, (= 'that which is found') 1847 | *flutter* vb OE, sb 1641 | *fold* vb OE, sb 1250 (OE had *fyld* sb) | *frown* vb 1386, sb 1581 | *gather* vb OE, sb 1555 | *gaze* vb 1386, sb 1542 | *glance* vb 1450, sb 1503 | *go* vb OE, sb 1727 (in most senses not till 19th c.) | *hang* vb OE, sb 1797 | *harass* vb 1618, sb 1667 | *hatch* vb 1250, sb 1597 | *haul* vb 1557, sb 1670 | *haunt* vb 1230, sb 1330 | *hear-say* vb OE, sb 1532 | *hunt* vb OE, sb 1375 | *incline* vb 1300, sb 1600 (= 'mental tendency', only in Watson), (= 'slope') 1846 | *insult* vb 1570, sb 1603 (not in Sh) | *invite* vb 1533, sb 1659 | *keep* vb OE, sb 1250 (= 'attention, notice'; other senses later) | *kill* vb 1205, sb (= 'the act of killing') 1852, (= 'a killed animal') 1878 | *laugh* vb OE, sb 1690 | *lead* vb OE, sb 1300 | *lean* vb OE, sb (= 'the act or condition of leaning') 1776 | *lend* vb OE lǣnan, sb 1575 (Sc & north. dial.) | *lift* vb 1300, sb 1470 | *look* vb OE, sb 1200 | *meet* vb OE, sb 1831 | *mistake* vb 1330, sb 1638 | *nap* vb OE, sb 14th c. | *pinch* vb 1340, sb 1489 | *ramble* vb 1620, sb 1654 | *ransack* vb 1250, sb 1589 | *reach* vb OE, sb 1548 | *rebuke* vb 1325, sb 1430 | *reply* vb 1385, sb 1560 | *run* vb OE, sb 1450 | *say* vb OE, sb 1571 | *search* vb 1330, sb 1400 | *seethe* vb OE, sb 1816 | *split* vb 1590, sb 1597 | *stare* vb OE, sb 1480 (the sense 'power of seeing' is found in the 14th c.) | *strain* vb 1340, sb 1432 (= 'a strainer'; other senses later) | *slumber* vb 1220, sb 1386 | *smile* vb 1300, sb 1562 | *thaw* vb OE, sb 1412 | *tread* vb OE, sb 1225 | *visit* vb 1225, sb 1621 (Sh has only *visitation*) | *walk* vb OE, sb 1386 | *whisper* vb OE, sb 1596 | *wish* vb OE, sb 1300 | *worry* vb OE, sb 1804.

7.1₂. In some cases the sb is not derived directly from the verb, but an older sb has been made to agree in sense and form with the vb.

compare vb 1375; sb adopted from F *compair* 'com-

peer', 'afterwards conformed to *compare* v.' (NED) |
advance vb 1230; sb 1668 'partly a.Fr. avance .. partly
subst. use of Eng. vb.' (NED) | *come* vb OE; the OE
sb *cyme* would have given ModE *kim*, 'but in early
ME. the sb was assimilated to the vb' (NED). Björkman, Loan-Words 11 holds that the sb was borrowed
from Scandinavian | *fill* vb OE; the OE sb *fyllo* 'has,
from similarity of sound, always been associated with
the vb *fill*' (NED). Some of the modern senses are
derived direct from the vb | *swell* vb OE; sb 1225
(= 'a morbid swelling'; in this sense probably representing OE *geswell;* the other senses (not till 1606) are from
the vb) | *want*, both the vb and the sb are from ON,
but 'in later usage, the sb is often a direct derivative
from the vb.' (NED) | *write* vb OE; sb 1303 (chiefly
Sc), a variant of *writ* or directly from the vb, cf NED.

It is sometimes doubtful whether we have a derivative
from the vb or a sense-development of the sb:

trumpet = 'trumpeter' possibly from F *le trompette*
or simply the name of the instrument for the man
who employs it | *whip* = 'one who wields a whip',
1775 (NED); *whip* in parliamentary use (originally
whipper-in) from 1853 | Cp. with these the word *shot*
("he is a good shot, I am no shot"), which can only
be from the sb.

A few similar sbs have now become obsolete:

accuse = 'accusation': Sh H6B III. 1.160. Cf excuse |
amaze = 'amazement': formerly not infrequent, now
chiefly poetical | *choose* as a sb (1375-1620) ousted by
choice | *dispose:* sb (from 1590) | *exclaim* = 'exclamation',
from 1489 | *like* sb (from 1425) is now rare except in
"likes and dislikes" | *mock* sb (from 1440) | *manage* as
a sb meaning 'manège' or 'management' (thus often in
Sh) | *prepare* = 'the act of preparing', from 1535 |
remain sb from 1456. Sh has "make remain" (Cor I.
4.62). Now only in the pl | *suppose* sb from 1566, e. g.
Sh Tit I. 1.44. 'Now always referring to a supposition

expressed or expressible by means of the vb 'suppose' '
(NED).

7.1₃. Occasionally, we find sbs (= vbs) denoting
agents. Cf the OE ending *-a: melda* corresponding to
meldian, slaga to *slean,* and *swica* to *swician, swican.*
In the ordinary course of development, *-a* became *-e* [ə]
and finally disappeared in late ME.

Ally, from 1375 | *blab:* Congreve 281 I am no blab |
bootblack, also *shoeblack,* but not *black* by itself | *catch*
'sth that catches' | *cheat* 'swindler' (in Sh 'deceit') |
cut: "they are cuts" = they cut each other | *drudge* |
flirt, 1732: a man, 1748: a woman | the *haves* and the
have-nots (common; occasionally NP 1937 the "have-
gots" against the "have-nots") | *help* 'helper, domestic
servant' | *lie* 'liar' (Payne Al) | *romp* 'child or woman
fond of romping' | *scold* 'scolding woman' | *sham,*
both of persons and things | *sneak* | *spy* | *surround*
'that which surrounds (a carpet)', also Galsw Sw 262
his face, in its surround of grey beard and hair | *tease*
(e. g. Galsw F Ch 62) | *tramp* | *trot* 'toddling child'.

Many compounds (*pickpocket, gadabout,* etc.) are
agent-nouns, see vol II 8.6 and below 7.3₁.

7.1₄. It is rarer to meet with sbs (= vbs) that denote
the result or object of the action designated by the vb:

Bite | *catch* 'thing or person caught or worth catch-
ing' | *find* 'sth found' | *hit* 'success': Di N 299 The new
piece being a decided hit | *godsend* orig. 'sth sent by
God' | *spit* 'saliva' | *spread* orig. 'what is spread (on
the table)', hence 'a copious meal' | *take* 'the amount
of fish or game caught; the takings at a theatre; one
scene of a film', also GE A 82 the woman as marries
him 'ull have a good take | *telegraph* 'telegram' (rare
or vg) Zangwill G 102 I'll send you a telegraph.

As for compounds (*frame-up, write-up,* etc.), see
7.3. *Hearsay* and *make-believe* are now common as a
sb, *hearsay* also as an adjunct (hearsay evidence);
occasionally *make belief* is found (Lawrence Sons & L

77); cf Di OT 70 making belief that he was staring ...
into shop-windows — and vol II 8.66.

7.2₁. The most usual meaning of sbs derived from
and identical in form with a vb is the action or an
isolated instance of the action. This is particularly frequent in such everyday combinations as those illustrated
in the following paragraphs after *have* and similar 'light'
verbs. They are in accordance with the general tendency
of ModE to place an insignificant verb, to which the
marks of person and tense are attached, before the
really important idea— of combinations with *do, can,*
etc., he *has* written, etc., cf vol V 25.6 and especially
25.9. Such constructions also offer an easy means of
adding some descriptive trait in the form of an adjunct:
we had *a delightful bathe, a quiet smoke,* etc. They thus
in some way form a parallel to those with a 'cognate
object': *fight the good fight,* etc., cf PG **137** f. and vol
III 12.3. By extension we have, e.g. "Did you enjoy
your bathe?"

7.2₂. Examples with *have:*
Austen S 191 she had better have her *cry* out at
once | Ridge L 150 I do like to have a good *cry* [at a
theatre] | Benson D 2.115 I have a bad *lie* [in golf] |
Ridge L 87 I want a rest and a *read* | Wilde W 26 I
really must have a good *stare* at her | Durand Story of
Phil. 390 a much better fellow he would be if he had
a good *swear* now and again | Hardy L 188 he was
having 'a good *think*' | Hammett Th 128 I'm going
over and have a *try* at her | have a *care,* a *look (peep)*
at, a *chat, wash, shave, swim;* a *drink,* a *smoke.* Cf below
12.3₁ have a *bathe.*

7.2₃. With other vbs than *have,* but still in more or
less stock expressions: Galsw EC 444 none of them will
submit to dictation, a *dare,* or let the others down |
Lewis MS 214 How about taking a *sneak?* | Di N 182
having taken a very long *stare* at Mr. Gregsbury |
take a *toss* 'be thrown from horseback, etc.' | take *care*

| take a *drive, ride, walk, rest* || make a *bolt, plunge* |
Walpole W 417 she thought she must make one more
try | he made his *bow* to the hostess || AHuxley PCP
117 'we must do a *creep*,' she said. 'Furtive's the word.' |
do a *bunk* 'run away' || get a *move* on || give a *glance,
look, kick, .push, shock, sigh, hint.*

7.2₄. With *give* the construction is almost as frequent
as with *have*. The phrase often denotes an involuntary
reaction: give a *sigh*, a *groan*, a *laugh*, a *shout* | Walpole
OL 105 she gave a little *shiver*.—But also: Di L 595
It rather did give me a shiver up the back | Maxwell
G 223 She had given him a bad *scare* | give sth a *pull*,
a *push* | give him the *slip* | give a *guess* | give a person
a *miss* | NJacob G 103 Give us a *ring* the day before
[= call on the telephone] || Galsw WM 65 (vg) They'll
give you a good *recommend*.

7.2₅. Finally, we might mention the use of the sb
(= vb) with the definite article in such phrases as:
to give someone the *chuck* | to give each other the
cut (Thack S 11) | to give someone the *slip* (Sterne
M 1.30) | give (get) the *push* (slang) | have the *pull* of |
have (get) the *bulge* on (slang). Also in: to put someone
to the *blush*, to the *test*.

By extension of the above usage, we get freer con-
structions like: to get a *remove* | he has not got his
remove 'promotion to a higher form at school' | King
O 281 to receive their final *acclaim* | Austen M 308
explaining away that *shake* of the head || it was a near
guess, a close *shave* || Zangwill G 178 there was a *quiver*
about the mouth.

Sbs (= vbs) are also frequent after prepositions:
Hope R 28 with a great *heave* of my body I flung them
from me | Stevenson K 291 he fell into a still deeper
muse | Brontë P 8 After a long and hard *stare* at me |
Doyle S 6.177 after a long *wait* we were at last admitted |
Kingsley H 172 with a sudden *writhe* and shriek she
sank to the ground | get into a *jam*, a *scrape*.

7.2₆. Sbs formed from vbs in the above-mentioned way may be put in the plural just like other sbs: Kipling J 2.109 I have three *bites* for each flea upon me | Sheriff F 58 things that you could not guess if you had a thousand *tries.*—A few words are only found in the plural: *eats* ('eatables', U. S. slang) | for *keeps* (another U. S. term). In this connexion we may also mention the *creeps* ("that gives me the creeps") | the *fidgets* | the *giggles,* etc.

7.2₇. In not a few instances, sbs formed from vbs without change of form compete with sbs formed by means of derivative endings, especially Latin formatives. There is often a difference in sense, the rôle of the shorter word being generally to denote a single occurrence.

abound, abundance, 'abound' is rare: GE A 437 I have all things and abound at Snowfield | *acclaim, acclamation,* the former poetical and rare: MacCarthy 2.591 public acclaim | *amends* (rarely *amend*), *amendment,* the former = 'compensation', the latter = 'improvement, alteration', esp. in the text of a bill | *combine, combination,* 'combine' is chiefly a commercial term | *command, commandment,* a 'commandment' is a divine 'command' | *differ, difference,* the former vg or popular: Shaw J 220 theyll find the differ | *divide, division,* the former generally means 'watershed', but we also find: Hope Z 81 a divide of the road | *exhaust, exhaustion,* 'exhaust' is solely technical | *exhibit, exhibition,* an 'exhibit' is a thing exhibited at an 'exhibition' | *invite, invitation,* the former colloquial: Pinero Q 56 I've got an invite down to Richmond | *know, knowledge,* the former dialectal except in the phrase "in the know", see 7.5₅ | *laugh, laughter,* the latter is a mass-word, while 'laugh' denotes a single burst of laughter: someone gave a loud laugh, or an individual quality: a harsh, ugly laugh | *move, movement, motion* the three are clearly differentiated | *repeat, repetition,* 'repeat' denotes particularly 'a passage of music meant to be repeated', but is often in colloquial parlance = 'repetition' | *repute, reputation* the difference, if any, is slight; the former is more literary | *resolve, resolution* the former stresses the single occurrence: Caine S 1.195 there was a dauntless spirit of resolution in the eyes of the younger man. His resolve was taken | *think, thought,* a 'think' is a single spell of thinking, during which many thoughts may pass the mind | *try, trial:* Galsw T 49 After the trial he would have another try to get them both away.

7.2₈. We also very often witness a competition between the sb (= vb) and the *ing*-form, the two being more or less differentiated in sense. To the general remarks in vol V 8.1₄ f. we may add some special instances: *bid, bidding,* the former only of the offer of a price at an auction or the like | *cover, covering* in a material sense, a 'cover' is a single piece of 'covering' | *find, finding,* the former a single thing found, the latter e. g. the finding of a judge | *paint, painting,* the former the material, the latter the action or the result of it | *say, saying,* 'say' only in a few locutions: have a say in the matter, etc. Cp. *saw* (< OE *sagu*) 'proverbial saying, maxim' | *shoot, shooting,* 'shoot' especially of a young branch or a shooting party.

Sometimes the substantive (= vb) seems to encroach upon the domain of the *ing* form: Mi PL VII .. With admiration and deep *muse* | Lamb E 1.24 the cattle, .. were at *feed* round us | Quincey XVI I have spent six months upon the *re-cast* of this one small volume | McCarthy 2.579 the purchase and the *keep* of fat women | Herrick M 157 if he had any *dare* in him.

7.3₁. Sbs formed without any derivative ending from vbs may also be formed from verbal phrases. First we have sbs of the type *pickpocket.* For these, which always denote an agent, we may refer to the full treatment in vol II 8.61 ff , besides the literature quoted

there see also Petersen IF 34.278 ff; Bøgholm EStn
44.93 ff; Uhrström, Pickpocket, Turnkey, Wrap-rascal,
and Similar Formations in English, Stockholm 1918;
Langenfelt, Select Studies, p. 82 ff. Compare also Will-
manns, Deutsche Gramm. II § 304, and Grimm, Deutsche Gramm. II. 961 ff.

The order of the members is the inverse in the follow-
ing compounds: *heart-break* (Sh Wiv V. 3.11) | James
S 61 Oh, the *headshake* she gave me! | *leg-pull* | a *nose-
dive* (Rose Macaulay P 241). These cannot be explained
as ordinary verbal sbs. In fact, only to the last of the
four words given above has the NED recorded a vb
nose-dive, which is perhaps from the sb *nose-dive*. There
is no vb *leg-pull*, but the sbs *leg-puller* and *leg-pulling*
may lead to the back-formation a *leg-pull*. Or the
compounds may have been formed direct from the
simple sbs *break, shake, pull* by the prefixing of another
noun.

7.3₂. Next we have sbs formed from vbs+an adv.
These in the first place are agent-nouns, thus in the
popular type *go-between* (II 8.67), to which new words
are constantly being added: Bennett LR 162 the class
of half-unreliable *dash-abouts* | Allingham P 175 some
lie-about's [= some tramp's], cf ib. 177 My experience
of lie-abouts, as your friend Mr. Bowditch so neatly
describes them | *roustabout* (U.S.) 'wharf-labourer' |
stowaway | *suck-up* (schoolboy slang) 'toady' || *hang-over*
'something remaining, esp. the unpleasant effects of
drinking' | *hold-back* 'hindrance' | *pull-down* 'wire in an
organ that pulls down a valve' | *runabout* 'light motor-
car' | *take-up* 'device in a sewing-machine for taking
up the thread'.

Such sbs may be used as adjuncts: *stand-up* collar |
stay-in strikes, *stay-in* tactics.

7.3₃. Similar formations also denote the object or
result of the action: *frame-up* (U. S. slang) | *hand-out*
(U. S.) 'food handed out to a beggar at the door' |

lay-out | *pull-on* (*-over*) | *rake-off* (U. S.) 'share of profits' |
shakedown 'makeshift bed' | *slip-on* (*-over*) | *step-in* |
turnover 'kind of pie; amount of money turned over in
business' | *write-up* 'elaborate account' || *Sit-upons*
(pop.: 'trousers').

7.3₄. The general rule, however, is that sbs formed
from vbs+advs denote the action itself: Galsw Sw 68
she's having a *lie-off* | Deeping 3R 295 Then I had a
tidy-up and a good breakfast || Galsw EC 43 make a
get-away || id Ca 736 they ought to give that byre a
good *clean-up* | King O 38 until I get a chance to get
down and give him a good *go-over* | Collins M 205 The
Monday gave him a good *shake up* | give him the *go-by* ||
Sackville-West E 109 It was the last *flare-up* of her
passing youth | Maugham Pl 4.250 Wasn't it an awful
let-down when you came back?

Other examples of substantives of this class fre-
quently met with: *break-down* (*-off*, *-up*) | *clean-out*
(*-up*) | *comb-out* 'search' | *come-back* (*-down*) | *hold-up* |
knock-about (*-out*, *-under*, *-up*) | *lay-off* 'temporary dis-
missal of workmen' | *let-off* (*-up* 'cessation, pause') |
line-up | *lock-out* | *look-in* (*-out*, *-over*, *-round*) | *pull-
up* 'sudden stop' | *round-up* | *send-off* | *set-back* (*-down*,
-in, *-out*, *-to*) | *shake-out* | *show-down* | *stand-easy* |
(*standstill*) | *take-in* (*-off*) | *tidy-up* | *toss-up* | *try-on*
(*-out*) | *walk-over* | *whip-round* 'appeal circulated for
contributions' || *say-so* (now dial. and U. S.): on her
say-so (Cole Corpse 150), I'll take his say-so, to have
the say-so || to play *touch-last*.

7.3₅. Many words are hard to classify: Linklater J
66 you're a *throwback* to your very-great-grandfather |
it is a *toss-up* whether he will come or not | *wash-out*
'failure'. The manner, rather than the result, is designated by *get-up*, *make-up*, and *set-up*.

Finally, in a class apart come *pull-up* and *speak-
easy*, which denote the place of the action.

A more complicated kind of deverbative noun is

from two combined .vbs: *touch-and-go* (from 1655) |
give-and-take (1769) | *come-and-go* (only instance re-
corded in NED suppl.: 1924) | *cut-and-come-again* 1738.

As an adjunct: a *rough-and-tumble* fight.

As mentioned in vol II 8.61, when compounds of the
pick-pocket type began to make their appearance in
the 14th century they seem to have been modelled on
the similar French formation consisting of an imperi-
tive+an object. U. Lindelöf, in his painstaking book
(which appeared after this chapter of my book had
been written) *English Verb-Adverb Groups Converted into
Nouns* (Helsingfors 1937), considers this to have been
also the origin of the *go-between* type (vb+adv > noun
with a personal sense, usually an agent-noun). Lindelöf's
material shows the personal formations to have been
very numerous up to 1700, after which date they
suddenly declined, whilst 'abstracts' (mostly pure action-
nouns) have been steadily increasing all the time: they
constitute 34 per cent. of the words recorded before
1600, but 63 per cent. of those after 1900. This increase
is undoubtedly due to the ease with which, in present-
day English, the simple verb-stem can be converted
into a nexus-substantive (noun of action), but more
rarely into an agent-noun. Of the total number of
examples collected by Lindelöf, only 17 per cent. made
their first appearance before 1800, while more than two
thirds have not been recorded till after 1850. Cf below
9.4₃. See also Koziol § 127.

7.3₆. Adjunctal use of the simple verbal stem is rare.
A peculiar example is Gibbs BR 288 To-day is one of
my *think* days. See on *mock* and *sham* (from vb+object)
vol II 14.78 and add Graves IC 129 with *mock-serious*
insistence | Galsw EC 812 this *mock-pretty* state |
mock-heroic poems.

Adjuncts formed on the patterns 'verbal stem+
adverb' and 'verbal stem+object' are extremely frequent, cf vol II 14.71. Here only a few additional

examples of the former type: Lowndes Ivy 19 the
simple *pull-on* brown hat | Hammett Th 52 Most of
the *follow-up* stories on the murder of Julia Wolf were
rather vague | Maugham Pl 2.311 I'm going to stand
myself a *slap-up* dinner at the Ritz | a *stay-in* strike |
a *lock-up* house | *tip-up* seats | *run-on* lines (perhaps
ptc.) | NP 1906 The .. Company's new liner has a *send-off*
trip round the Isle of Wight.

Predicatively: Maugham Alt 1389 The secretary was
not exactly *come-hither* | Sayers NT 146 His wife ..
plump where he was spare, *bounce-about* where he was
stately.

Of a different type from those mentioned above are
hear-say and *make-believe*. On their use as adjuncts, see
vol II 14.73.

7.37. The simple verbal stem may be used as a
tertiary, chiefly with more or less echoic words. King
O 200 my carefully built hypothesis would have
gone *smash* | Maugham Pl 2.111 I may as well tell
you the whole truth *bang* out | the ball went *smack*
through the window | hit him *slap* on the nose.

Slapbang and *slapdash* may be both adjuncts and
tertiaries. The exact relation between the component
parts is hard to analyze.

Oscillation

7.41. We sometimes find a curious oscillation between
sb and vb. *Smoke* is first a sb (the smoke from the
chimney), then a vb (the chimney smokes, he smokes
a pipe); then a new sb is formed from the verb in the
last sense (let us have a smoke).

This type *sb*>*vb*>*sb* is common. Other examples are:
argument: sb 'reason advanced for sth' > vb 'exchange arguments' > sb 'an exchange of arguments'
i. e. 'a debate' | *bolt:* sb 'arrow' > vb 'move as fast
as a bolt, run away quickly' > sb 'a rapid run, escape' |

brush: sb 'implement' > vb 'use that implement' >
sb 'the act of using it': let me give your hat a brush
(up) | *cable:* sb 'metallic wire' > vb 'telegraph' > sb
'telegram'. Cp. *wire* | *canvas(s):* sb 'kind of cloth' >
vb 'toss in a canvas sheet' (obs.), 'solicit votes' > sb
'canvassing for votes' | *cheek:* see under *jaw* | *club:* sb
'thick stick' > vb 'use a club, club together' > sb 'associa-
tion'. This development is not quite certain | *corner:*
sb in usual sense > vb 'drive into a corner' > sb ("a
corner in wheat") | *dart:* sb 'weapon' > vb 'throw
(a dart), move rapidly (like a dart)' > sb 'sudden
movement' | *deal:* sb 'amount' (OE dǣl = 'part') >
vb 'distribute' > sb 'distribution of cards to players',
note Roosevelt's New Deal | *feather:* sb > vb 'feather
an oar' > sb 'the act of feathering an oar' | *gossip:*
sb 'godfather, intimate friend, idle talker' > vb 'talk
idly' > sb 'idle talk' | *help:* sb 'assistance' > vb 'help
(oneself at table)' > sb 'a helping' (coll. & vg.) | *jaw:*
sb in usual sense > vb 'use the jaw in talking, scold'
> sb 'a talk, a scolding'. Cp. *cheek* and *lip,* where we
have the same development | *lip:* see under *jaw* | *nark*
(from Romany *nak* nose): sb 'nose' > vb 'watch, look
after'; intr. 'act as an informer' > sb 'a police spy' |
nose: sb > vb 'poke one's nose into, pry into' >
sb: Sherriff F 45 there are few things more attractive
than a leisurely nose round somebody else's house |
ooze: sb 'juice, sap' (obs.), 'infusion of oak-bark' >
vb 'pass slowly through the pores of a body' > sb 'the
act of oozing, exudation' | *order:* sb 'rank, class' > vb
'arrange in order, govern, command' > sb 'the action
or an act of ordering' | *paddle:* sb 'kind of oar' > vb
'use a paddle'; tr. 'move (a canoe) in that way' > sb
'act or spell of paddling' | *phone:* sb short for *telephone*
> vb 'use a telephone'; tr. and intr. > sb: Crofts St
238 we had a 'phone from Inspector Marshall | *sail:*
sb 'a piece of canvas' > vb > sb 'a sailing excursion' |
taper: sb 'slender candle growing gradually thinner

towards one end' > vb 'be, make, or become shaped
like a taper' > sb: Hardy F 378 the two sides approach-
ing each other in a gradual taper | *value:* sb 'worth'
> vb 'attach value to, prize' > sb 'high esteem, re-
spect': Shelley L 417 My value, my affection for you,
have sustained no diminution | *wire:* see under *cable.*

7.4₂. The following are dubious:

chime probably: sb 'that which produces the sound
of a chime' (NED senses 1-3) > vb 'produce that
sound' > sb 'the sound' (NED senses 4-6) | *outlaw:*
sb 'a person placed outside the law' > vb 'make somebody an outlaw' > sb 'the being an outlaw, outlawry':
Hawth S 223 the whole seven years of outlaw and
ignominy.

7.4₃. Adjectives form the starting-point:

faint: adj (from OF, orig. 'feigned') 'sluggish, timid,
weak' > vb 'become weak, swoon' > sb 'a fainting
fit' | *slight:* adj 'inconsiderable' > vb 'regard as in-
considerable, disregard' > sb 'the act of slighting'.

Probably also:

blind: adj > vb 'make blind' > sb 'anything which
obstructs the light or sight, a screen, etc.' | *shy:* adj
> vb 'be shy (of horses); fling, throw' > sb 'a throw'.
Or do the two senses of the verb really represent two
different words?

Compare also: Di F 428 to have a *warm* in the sun |
Wells Inv 3 give them a good *dry* in the kitchen | Spect
111 a man gives a *loose* to every passion.

7.4₄. The starting-point is a vb:

frame: vb 'form' > sb 'a fabric, a border for a picture,
etc.' > vb 'set in a frame' | *sweat:* vb > sb > vb
'remove sweat from (horses)' | *wake:* vb intr. 'be awake'
> sb 'vigil beside a corpse' > vb tr. 'hold a wake over
(a corpse)'.

Perhaps also:

fun: vb 'cheat, hoax' (from 1685) > sb 'cheat or

trick' (1700, now obs.), 'diversion' > (1727) vb 'make
fun, joke' (1833, verbal sb *funning* 1728).

7.4₅. It is sometimes doubtful whether the noun or
the vb is the starting point; cf Bladin, Denom. Verbs
32 ff. We may mention:

Dun: The probable development has been: sb ('one
who duns') > vb ('to act as a dun') > sb ('an act of
dunning') | *Roll:* sb ('cylinder') > vb > sb ('act of
rolling')? | *Skill* sb & vb (archaic; intr. 'to matter, be
of importance', tr. 'to understand, know (how to do
sth)'). The intr. sense of the vb seems to be direct
from ON *skilja* 'to divide, distinguish'. In English *it
skills not* comes to mean 'it makes no difference, it
does not matter'. The tr. sense must be influenced by
the English sb *skill* | *Squat* vb, sb, & adj. Presumable
development: vb (tr. & intr.) > sb ('she sits at squat',
Dryden) > adj. In Mi PL IV. 800 (him there they
found Squat like a Toad) and other quotations *squat*
may be an infinitive rather than an adj or an adv.
See also NED *bait* sb and vb.

Hero-worship as used by Carlyle is a compound of
the sb *worship*, which is from the verb; but a new vb
may be formed from the compound sb: Mannin RS 61
He *hero-worshipped* Teddy.

In some contexts it cannot be decided whether a
word is a vb or a sb, see, for instance, Sh R2 V. 2.80
Peace, foolish woman.—I will not *peace*. Thus often
after *do:* Sh John V. 2.46 this dew that silverly doth
progress on thy cheeks.

7.5₁. An important consequence of the falling together of the noun and the verbal stem is the growing
frequency of formations like *aswoon*. This particular
instance is found as early as Chaucer; *a-* represents *on*
(cf vol I 2.424) and *swoon* is originally the sb; Gower
has *on swowne* (cf however the doubt in NED). In
some cases it is impossible to decide whether the word

after *a-* was originally a sb or a vb, but in recent centuries the linguistic feeling has certainly been in favour
of taking it as a vb, and thus a great number of new
combinations have arisen where there was no sb in
existence. They may for all intents and purposes be
regarded as a new type of present participles, but
their use is often more literary than colloquial.

All these and other combinations with *a-* are dealt with
in two papers by Carl Palmgren, "A Chronological List of
E. Formations of the Type *alive, aloud, aglow*" and "The
history of E. Words formed by the Prefix *a- < on (in)*", Norrköping 1923 and 1924. As P. remarks: "From a NE. point
of view words like *asleep* and *awake* are, of course, formally
on a level. Historically, on the other hand, they belong to
different types, the former containing the subst. *sleep*, the
latter being identical with the past part. of the verb *awake*...
afresh, anew, going back to earlier *of fresh, of new*..." These
latter do not concern us here.—Dyboski, Tennysons Sprache
und Stil, 1907, p. 429, has a list of the formations found in T.

Nowadays such words may be formed practically
from any intransitive vb which is monosyllabic or else
disyllabic ending in unstressed *-le, -er,* or *-en,* provided
the new word does not coincide with an already existing word (*abound, across, amount,* etc.). Neither can
they be formed from verbs beginning with a vowel
(*ask, ooze,* etc.).

Afloat was used as early as 1023 (NED). A few in-
stances found in ModE date from ME: *aswoon* (above) |
aweep, Ch T 2.408 a-wepe | *a-work:* Sh H4B IV.3. 123
that sets it a-worke | The 16th century has given us
ajar and *asleep.* From the two following centuries
date the earliest examples of *adrift, aflame* (Locke W
280 he waited, his soul aflame), *agape* (Scott Iv 478
the guests, still agape with astonishment | Wells Am
48 I found myself agape), *asquat* (Zangwill G 36),
astart, aswim. During the last century a very great

number have arisen, among which may be mentioned
abob (Mackenzie C 377), *aboil* (Barrie Adm. C 86),
acrack (Elizabeth Exp 88), *acurl* (Dreiser F 171), *aflow*,
agasp, *aglare*, *aglow* (Ward El 339, Locke W 338),
aprick (Dane FB 369 her ears a-prick at every sound),
a-sprawl (Wells Ma 207 the lynx ... its clumsy paws
a-sprawl), *a-sweat* (Kaye Smith GA 107), *aswirl* (Wells
TB 2.253), *awash* (Galsw SS 42). I have given very
few of my numerous modern quotations.

7.5₂. A few more may be given of formations from
disyllabic verbs:

Benson A 199 the birds were *a-chuckle* in the bushes |
Browning 1.518 the slave that holds John Baptist's
head *a-dangle* by the hair | Wells H 401 the ornamental
water *aripple* with ducks and swans | Childers R 327
standing *astraddle* on both seats | Crockett in NP 1897
dark locks all *a-tangle* about her brow | Locke W 255
the reckless folly of it all had kept his veins *a-tingle*
(and ib 275) | Wells Ma 2.232 she was all *atremble* |
Bennett W 1.199 *a-twinkle* || Mackenzie S 1.375 the
dusky room *a-flicker* with sad firelight | Hewlett Q 36
her face *aflower* in the close coif | Zangwill G 51 every
nerve *a-quiver* (frequent in Wells e. g. T 54, 117, Ma 1.172)
| Dreiser F 178 Binns was all aquiver on the instant ||
Rose Macaulay T 278 with ivory teeth *a-glisten*.

7.5₃. Naturally, we have also cases where *a* (< *on*)
is prefixed to a sb or an adj without there being any
corresponding vb: *acold* | *acrook* (both of them ME) ||
anigh (1773). Like many of the formations from vbs,
they are preferably used, and even coined, by poets:
adeep and *adusk* are due to Mrs Browning, *adust* to GE.
Other formations dating from last century are: *adead* |
ajoint | *awing*.

In some instances where there does not appear
originally to have been a vb, a vb was formed at an
early date by a kind of back-formation: *slant* 1521,

squint 1599, *peak* 1626, which shows the formation to have been felt as deverbative as early as the 16th century.

7.5₄. As an example of the above-mentioned phenomenon must also be classed *athirst* though the word is from OE *ofþyrst*.

Awake and *alight* ('lighted (up)') are not parallel to the examples given above because they are originally past participles.—*Alive* (OE *on life*) is outside this class of formations because of its diphthong, the vb having a short [i].

7.5₅. In the type represented by *on the go* we have a kind of gerunds like those in *-ing: on the go = a-going*. They are now freely formed from nearly all verbs, but have a certain colloquial or vulgar flavour. Many of them represent the only possible application of the verbal noun in question: *on the listen | on the marry*. Apart from these phrases, we could hardly use the sbs *listen* and *marry*. Even where a freer use of the verbal noun does exist, this is generally of much later origin and has a different sense: *on the mend* (NED: from 1802) as opposed to *a mend* (from 1888).

Further examples: *on the boil* | Austen M 167 there were girls enough *on the catch* for them | Wells A 119 going nowhere, like a cabman *on the crawl* | Montgomery Misunderstood T 96 H. was *on the fidget* all day | Trelawny R 99 Byron's spirit was always *on the fret and fume* to be doing something new | Galsw P 12.33 I want to enjoy things, and you can't do that when everybody is *on the hate* | *on the increase* | Priestley AP 363 the telephone is ringing every few minutes and you are for ever *on the jump* | *on the make* | *on the mend* | Wells A 305 land legislation will keep the ... squatter *on the move* | *on the prowl* | Myers M 35 I came in here *on the run* | Shaw Ms 38 shes an old woman .. Cant enjoy things: not real things. Always *on the shrink* | Stevenson T 214 I waited, every nerve *upon the stretch* |

on the tramp | Locke St 67 Tongues were set *on the wag* | *on the wane*.

Other prepositions than *on* are not so frequent in these phrases. *In* seems to have been common in earlier literature: Sh Mids V. 258 he [the man representing the moon] is *in the wane* | Shelley Witch 47.1 when the weary moon was *in the wane*. It is still in use before 'know' and 'swim': Barrie T 308 those *in the know* still call them the Tommies | *in the swim*.—*At* and *to* are used with 'boil'.

Another similar type of phrase is exemplified in: Rose Macaulay P 120 I was all of a didder | Masterman WL 20 I am all of a fluster | Galsw FCh 60 she was all of a flutter | Di F 569 why are you all of a shake? | Cole Corpse 241 I'm all of a swear with it still | GE A 432 she's all of a tremble.—Also with *in:* Di P 536 I'm all in a tremble. The colloquial or vg colouring of such phrases is not so pronounced when an adj is inserted: Austen E 167 I was in such a tremble | Hewlett Q 86 the Queen had been in a hard stare the while.— With *aswoon, aflame* (see above 7.5₁) compare Thack N 245 all the windows in a blaze | Zangwill G 54 'Darling!' he cried in amaze.

Supplementary Remarks

7.6₁. By contamination of the sb and the vb we find instead of "let go a thing" the curious expression *let go of a thing*, which is found in the best-known modern authors: Dickens, Wilkie Collins, Swinburne, Hewlett, Kipling, Hope, Caine, Haggard, London, Ridge, Priestley, etc. Also, though not so frequent: Thack H 56 *leave go* my hand | id V 418 he leaves go of his hat to use his telescope.

7.6₂. The verb *matter* 'signify, be of importance' probably owes its existence to the substantive being mistaken for a verb. Many phrases lend themselves to

misunderstanding. In: Thack P 3.363 Well, an hour
sooner or later, what matter? *matter* must of course be
a sb, but the slightly altered phrase: "What matter!
Two hours sooner or later!" might in former times be
taken as a question with *matter* as the vb. "What
matter is it?" and "what matters it?", were hardly
distinguishable from each other when spoken. "It is ('s)
not much matter", and "it does not much matter"
may in rapid pronunciation be nearly alike, cf GE M
1.52 What's it matter,—where, *'s* no doubt represents
does.

Examples: Congreve 271 what matter is it who holds
it? | Thack P 3.3 But what matters [sic] a few failings? ||
Sterne 12 it is not much matter what I say | Black
P 325 It does not much matter.

Some instances are dubious: Bunyan P 39 what's
matter which way we get in? (vb)—but id P
206 For what matter how we live (sb). And how
to analyze: Defoe R 2.10 it is not one farthing matter
to the rest?

7.6₃. Similarly with the formerly synonymous *force*.
From phrases like "what force" and "no force" the
sb came to be apprehended as a vb 'to signify, matter'.
This usage is now quite obsolete (see NED).

7.6₄. The origin of the vb *chance*, too, must probably
be ascribed to the sb. See Sh-lex, Abbott § 37 Franz
§ 437. According to Abbott, a stage in the development
has been the adverbial use of *chance*, possibly due to
the phrase *by chance*. It is impossible to tell whether
chance is meant as a vb or an adv in: H4B II. 1.12
It may chance cost some of us our lives. Cp. Troil
I. 1.28 you may chance burn your lips (where the
folios have: *to* burn). "How chance" was formerly used
in questions where we should now expect "how chances
it that . . ?" The phrase is exceedingly frequent in Sh,
and we also find: Marlowe E 569 I, but how chance
this was not done before? | BJo 1.99 how chance that

you were of Cob's? | Swift J 61 How chance you did
not see that? As *chance* is not inflected ("how chances"
is found once in Sh: Hml II. 2.43), it cannot be regarded
fully as a vb, but the word-order shows that the idea
of *chance* as a verb must have been at the back of the
writer's mind.

The development of *fortune* from sb to vb seems to
furnish an exact parallel to *chance*, cf Marlowe E 1422
Well, and how fortunes that he came not?

7.6₅. The command *face about!* (or *about face!*) with
the sb *face* is easily apprehended as an imperative,
which leads to the use of a vb: *he faced about* 'turned
round'; also transitively: *he faced his men about*. The
command is made a sb in Hammett Th 136 you make
another *about-face*.

Bladin 23-24 mentions some other vbs that may have
been originally sbs used in commands, e. g. *fire!*

7.6₆. On the other hand, we also have instances of
the conversion of a verb in the imperative (or the
subjunctive,—an exclamation at any rate) into a
substantive. The imperative *damn (you)*! has given us
the substantive *damn* in phrases like: I don't care a
damn | they don't matter a damn || Locke GP 232
What does she care? Not a little twopenny-halfpenny
damn.—Similarly with other words: Harris Shaw 97
the British proletarians did not care a *dump* about
Home Rule | Mackenzie C 179 Not one of them matters
the tiniest *dash* | I don't care a *curse* | a *hang* | a *hoot* |
a *whoop*.

A verbal origin must also be ascribed to *collect* 'be
paid by the receiver': London M 344 he sent the message
collect.—Originally an imperative: collect!

Cf from German G. Hermann Nacht 159 ehe Amelie
kehrt machte.

Non-verbal commands or requests as a kind of quotation
sbs: Slow and steady wins the race [from 'slow and steady!'] |

Galsw Sw 45 but steady does it | Morgan S 517 To talk after
lights-out was among their happiest domestic vices.

7.6₇. *Thank* in *thank God* (*Heavens, goodness*) is probably of substantival origin. OE had *Gode þonc* 'thanks
(be) to God'. Cf F *grâce à Dieu.* After the loss of the
case-ending *thank God* was felt as a vb+an object.
Cp. *thank you* abbreviated from *I thank you.* In former
times analogical constructions were used: Beaumont
253 They have had better yet, thank your sweet squire
here!

7.6₈. *Witness* in *witness Heaven* and similar phrases
(also *as witness* ..) is taken in NED as a sb, while
Curme CG 261 takes it to be the subjunctive of the
vb. NED takes *witness* in *call to witness* as a sb, but it
is clearly taken as a vb in Di N 405 I call Mr. Nickleby
to witness the course I intend to pursue with you.—
Pray don't call me to witness anything.

Chapter VIII

Compounds

Introductory

8.1₁. A compound may perhaps be provisionally defined as a combination of two or more words so as to
function as one word, as a unit.

According to Brugmann, *Das Wesen der sogenannten
Wortzusammensetzung*, Berichte d. sächs. Ges. d. Wiss.
phil. hist. Kl. 52 (1900) p. 359ff., the chief characteristic
of a compound is "isolation", i. e. a difference in sense
from that held by a free combination of the same
elements. This view has sometimes been criticized, e. g.
by Paul IF 14.251ff. At any rate, in a morphological
treatment of compounds a definition based entirely on
meaning seems insufficient. It would be better if we had
a formal, external criterion.

In many languages we have one in flexion; OE *heahfœder* is shown to be a compound by having *heah-fœder* in the accusative, too, while an adjectival phrase would make *heahne fœder;* cf G gen. *des rotweines* as against *des roten weines*, Dan. pl *stormagter* as against *store magter*, etc. But in ModE this criterion fails us: *blackbird* and *black bird* are inflected alike.

Bloomfield, *Language* (New York 1933 and London 1935) 227ff., maintains that it is a mistake to use the meaning as a criterion, because 'we cannot gauge meanings accurately enough; moreover, many a phrase is as specialized in meaning as any compound'. Stress, according to him, is the best criterion; 'wherever we hear lesser or least stress upon a word which would always show stress in a phrase, we describe it as a compound-member: *ice-cream* ['ais-ˌkriˑm] is a compound, but *ice cream* ['ais ˈkriˑm] is a phrase, although there is no denotative difference of meaning'. Now, although level-stress composition is a fairly recent development in English (cf vol I 5.33), the number of such combinations is considerable, and seemingly on the increase. If, therefore, we stuck to the criterion of stress, we should have to refuse the name of compound to a large group of two-linked phrases that are generally called so, such as *headmaster* or *stone wall*.

8.1₂. There are also certain drawbacks attaching to the criterion of stress. First of all, it is very often extremely difficult to ascertain with certainty whether a collocation has level or unity-stress. As a matter of fact, pronunciation varies a great deal on this point from individual to individual; thus *overload* (sb), *subcommittee*, and *non-conductor* are stated to have level stress in Sweet NEG §§ 914 & 919, while in Dan. Jones's Pronouncing Dictionary (4th ed. London 1937) they are stressed on the first element. Moreover, 'level stress' really means unstable stress, the particular stressing used in a definite situation being determined either by value (¹plum-₁pudding as contrasted with ¹rice-₁pudding) or by sentence-rhythm.

Furthermore, the prefixes un- (negative) and mis- are often as strongly stressed as the following element; are they, then independent words? It is obvious that stress alone is not a sufficient reason for recognizing an element of speech as a separate word.

Sometimes two sbs may be combined both with level and with unity-stress, but with a difference in significa- tion (cf vol I 5.35): a ¹glass-case (to keep glass in), but a ¹glass ¹case (made of glass) | a ¹bookcase (with shelves for books), but a ¹book ¹case 'case or cover for holding a single volume' | a ¹headstone 'upright stone at the head of a grave', a ¹head ¹stone 'chief stone in a founda- tion, corner-stone'. All this goes against excluding level-stress phrases from compounds.

8.1₃. The difficulty attaching to compounds is in no way cleared up by PE orthography. Regarding this point prevailing usage is little short of chaotic. There are three possible ways of writing a combination of two words: as two independent words, or joined by a hyphen, or run together in one word, and, as a matter of fact, one and the same combination is often found spelt in all three ways by different writers or even by the same writer at different moments. Compare also: Aumonier OB 13 It was their *bedroom*, and their *sitting- room*, their *eating room*, Irene's *workroom*, and on unique occasions—everybody's *bathroom*.—All these combina- tions have unity-stress on the first element. Fowler in MEU advocates the use of hyphens for one-accent combinations (*red-coat*, *sea-god*), while one is left free to choose either of the remaining forms for level-stress phrases: *head master* or *headmaster*. It appears a little strange to unite in one word elements which are in fact less closely joined than those designated by a hyphen: *headmaster* v. *red-coat*. But quite apart from this, it must be admitted that Fowler's rules only represent a desideratum; they are never closely adhered to.

As formal criteria thus fail us in English, we must fall back on semantics, and we may perhaps say that we have a compound if the meaning of the whole cannot be logically deduced from the meaning of the elements separately, see e. g. *bedroom, -clothes, -post, -time*.

8.1₄. Why do we use compounds at all, instead of free syntactic combinations of the same elements? The merit of compounds lies in their conciseness, as compared with paraphrases following the usual syntactic rules; thus, a *railway-company* is a 'company running a railway', and a *schoolboy* is a 'boy going to school'. Compounds express a relation between two objects or notions, but say nothing of the way in which the relation is to be understood. That must be inferred from the context or otherwise. Theoretically, this leaves room for a large number of different interpretations of one and the same compound, but in practice ambiguity is as a rule avoided. Many compounds have become traditional names for one definite thing, thus giving up their other potential meanings (this is what is meant by "isolation", which, as we saw, Brugmann took to be the criterion of a compound): a *goldfish* looks like gold, a *gold-digger* digs for gold, while a *gold-smith* works in gold; *home-sickness* is caused by absence from home, but *sea-sickness* by the motion of the sea. A change of the relation expressed in whichever one of the above compounds is no longer feasible; *goldsmith* could not possibly be used of a smith with a gold-like appearance, and neither could *sea-sickness* be used, except punningly, of a sailor's longing for the sea. Only in recently formed or rare compounds can there be any doubt, but the context will nearly always guide one to a correct understanding.

On account of all this it is difficult to find a satisfactory classification of all the logical relations that may

be encountered in compounds. In many cases the
relation is hard to define accurately. Noreen, *Vårt
Språk* V. 190 ff, attempts a classification under different "status" of the chief relations in which ideas can
stand to one another, and this system has with various
modifications been applied to English by Nils Bergsten
(*A Study on Compound Substantives in English*, Uppsala
1911 p. 137 ff), but he himself admits that 'the relation
between the members of a compound cannot always be
assigned to a specified category'. The analysis of the
possible sense-relations can never be exhaustive.

Naturally, the illustrations given in the following
pages will be mostly of compounds that have become
established in the vocabulary of the English language,
but wherever possible attention will be called to the
types of compounds which are still productive.

8.1₅. It is often maintained that English has lost the
power of forming compounds found in the other Gothonic languages, and even in OE. Thus it is said that
numerous German compounds must be rendered in
English by an adjective plus a substantive or some
similar phrase: *textkritik* 'textual criticism', *zukunfts-
musik* 'music of the future', *weltmann* 'man of the
world', etc.

Some of these instances, however, show nothing but
the arbitrariness found in all departments of all languages: some combinations are avoided without any reason
being demonstrable; *future* cannot be used in a compound *future music* because it would be taken as an
adjective: *welt* in *weltmann* means 'fashionable society',
cp. F *homme du monde* (not *de monde*), and in other
combinations *world* enters freely as first part of a compound: *world dominion, event, peace, politics, renown,*
etc. *Text-criticism* may be avoided on account of the
special meaning given to such a compound as *text-book*.

It seems more to the point to adduce a great many

OE compounds used where ModE has more or less learned word-units (see examples in GS § 42 ff.): *godspellere* : evangelist, *handpreost* : chaplain, *scincrœft* : magic, *leorningcniht* : disciple, *efnniht* : equinox, *lœcecrœft* : medicine, etc. In the old times the English had the healthy habit of using the resources of their own language to the fullest extent possible, whereas after the Norman Conquest, and especially after the revival of learning, English developed a linguistic omnivorousness that made it fashionable to introduce a great many words from French or Latin (cf GS § 151 ff.). But while many old compounds were thus disused, this does not mean that the language lost its power of making new ones. New compounds have at all times been formed, and are constantly being formed whenever the necessity arises—very often without the user being conscious of the fact that he is framing a new combination.

Good illustrations are found in the new words that were coined when the immigrants in Australia found themselves confronted with an entirely new flora and fauna, and formed such words as *friar-bird, frogsmouth, ground-lark, long-fin, sugar-grass, ironheart, thousand-jacket*, etc. (GS § 160 from E. E. Morris, *Austral English*).

In the ordinary everyday language new compounds are frequently formed, but there are limits to this power, though it is difficult to say for certain which groups are admissible and which are not. There seems to be least difficulty with regard to designations for concrete, material things, such as *food-card, book-token, cycle-shed, cocktail-shaker*, etc. Indeed, new compounds are often formed on the spur of the moment: Shaw 2.142 I'm only a beer teetotaller, not a champagne teetotaller | Cambridge Trifles 17 I was enthusiastically received by the landlady and by the whole of the land-family | ib 21 landlady .. landlord .. and two landchildren. In this connexion one might also mention such picturesque American slang-words as *road-louse*, *loan-shark*, and *lounge-lizard*.

Where immaterial notions are concerned, there is often a certain aversion to compounds; thus a term like Carlyle's *mischief-joy* is felt by most people as foreign to the genius of the language. But why do not *language-difficulty*, *minority-question*, *birth-rate*, *joy-ride*, *road-sense*, *college education*, and many others, grate on the ear? No definite and exhaustive rules seem possible; sometimes an already existing compound serves as a model. It seems to be always possible to form compounds containing a name of action with its object prefixed: *birth-control*, *frontier-revision*, *car-construction*.

As examples of recent linguistic terminology I adduce a few compounds taken from Grattan & Gurrey's *Our Living Language*, none of which are to be found in the NED: *number-noun*, *case-phrase*, *sentence-row*, *relation-word*, *word-link*, *sentence-link*, *paragraph-link*. In poetry, too, there seems to be unlimited possibilities of word-composition; cf *apple-arbiter*, *tree-tower*, *mind-mist* (Tennyson; see Dyboski) and *storm-star*, *name-fellow*, *guerdon-gift* (Swinburne; see Serner, *Lang. of Sw.'s Lyrics and Epics*, Lund-thesis 1910).

8.1₆. With regard to compounds we find two opposite tendencies. One is to strengthen the feeling of their composite nature by making each element more and more independent. This is particularly strong in English, where it leads to the frequency of level stress and to the development of a series of formal characteristics (see vol II 13.21) by which the first element of a compound is made into a separate adjunctal word approaching the status of an adjective, e. g. coordination with adjs: his personal and *party* interests | a *Yorkshire* young lady; the use of *one:* five gold watches and a *silver* one; the use of adverbs: a purely *family* gathering; isolation: any position, whether *State* or national. The symbol for dissolved compounds is 2(-)1, AnalSynt 6.8. But it is impossible to draw a fixed line between them and ordinary compounds, and some dissolved or dissolvable compounds are included in the following lists.

8.1₇. The second tendency is to strengthen the unity of a compound which is thereby made into a fixed unit with obliteration of its composite character.

The elements of a composite word may in the course of time undergo more or less radical phonetic changes (cf vol I 4.34 ff), which may make them quite unrecognizable. Examples abound: *lammas* (< OE *hlāf-mæsse* 'loaf-mass'), *goshawk* (< OE *gōshafoc* 'goosehawk'), *cupboard* [kʌbəd], *blackguard* [blæga·d], and the nautical terms *channel* (< *chainwale*), *gunnel* (< *gunwale*), *boatswain* [bousn], *forecastle* [fouksl], *topsail* [topsl], etc. Sometimes a word dies out in free use, while it is continued as one of the elements of a compound, e. g. *lady* from OE *hlǣfdige*, lit. 'loaf-kneader', or the particular sense involved may die out, as in *gospel* from OE *gōdspell* 'good message' (*spell* no longer means a message or story). Such words, as well as *lord* (OE *hlāford* < *hlāf-weard* 'loaf-ward'), *doff* (< *do off*), etc., might be termed ex-compounds, cf Erich Klein, *Die verdunkelten Wortzusammensetzungen im Neuenglischen* (diss.), Königsberg 1911.

There are various degrees of obscuration. Take the names of the days of the week. Though the all-but universal pronunciation of *Sunday*, etc., is [-di], and though the first element in *Monday*, *Tuesday*, etc., is not at all understood, the words are more or less vaguely felt as compounds of *day*, and the sound [-dei] may occasionally be heard, e. g. when *Sunday* is contrasted with *weekday;* cf also the pronunciation [ˈ(h)witsndei] alongside of [(h)witˈsʌndi].

Very often a reaction sets in, and compounds are revived or renovated from a feeling of the composing elements. An extreme example is OE *huswīf*, which as

a unit has become *hussif, hussy* [hʌzi] in various significations (needle-case, bad woman), see vol I 4.38, 6.52,
7.32, but the compound is re-formed as *housewife*.
Several other examples (*grindstone, goshawk,* etc.) are
found passim in vol I. In many cases, especially in
recent times, spelling-pronunciation has been at work,
as when *waistcoat*, which 40 years ago was universally
pronounced [weskət], now more and more commonly
is pronounced [weis(t)kout], cf also *boatswain* [bout-
swein] instead of [bousn], etc. In many cases the obscuration of the sound has not been accompanied by
an obscuration of the composition, e. g. *-man* [-mən] in
postman, statesman, etc., which are still felt as belonging
to *man*.

Substantive-Compounds

8.2₁. The present section will deal only with pure
substantive-compounds (sb+sb); other compounds containing sbs are treated in Ch. IX. The chief types to be
dealt with in this section are (formulas as in *Analytic
Syntax*):

(1) AB means B modified by A: *gas-light* is a kind
of *light* (final-determinative compounds). Formula 2-1.

(2) AB means A modified by B: *tiptoe* = 'tip of the
toe' (initial-determinative compounds). Formula 1-2.

(3) AB means A plus B: *Schleswig-Holstein* consists
of two districts, Schleswig and Holstein (copulative
compounds). Formula 1-&°-1.

(4) AB means: at the same time A and B, the two
combined in one individual: *maid-servant, servant-girl*
(appositional compounds). Formula 1-1.

(5) Bahuvrihi-compounds, e. g. *red-coat*, which is
not a kind of coat, but a person wearing a red coat.
Formula 2(21)1°.

(6) Type *son-in-law*. Formula 1-2(p 1).

Compare the classification in Koziol's Wortbildungs-

lehre § 87 ff, which appeared after this part had been
written.

8.2₂. Compounds of the first type, in which the second
element is determined by the first, are extremely frequent and may even be considered the normal ones,
to the extent that frequently the whole meaning is
changed if we invert the word-order: *a garden flower* is
a kind of flower, but *a flower garden* a kind of garden;
cf also *racehorse* and *horse-race; a book-case* and *a case
book*. The general formula is 2-1; some special formulas
indicated below.

As already mentioned (8.1₄), the number of possible
logical relations between the two elements is endless.
The following grouping, therefore, does not pretend to
any degree of exhaustiveness, but is meant merely to
illustrate the manifoldness of the relations.

If the second element is an action- or agent-noun,
the first part of the compound may indicate the subject
of the action: *sunrise, sunset, daybreak, nightfall, earth-
quake, landslip*. Symbol 2(S)-Y or 2(S)-X. Or the
object: *sun-worship, self-esteem (-contempt, -control),
childbirth, dog-show, handshake, manslaughter, life-insurance, wool-gathering, haymaking; body-guard, shoe-
maker, dog-fancier, bricklayer, grave-digger, innkeeper,
nutcracker, typewriter; bell-foundry*. Symbol 2(O) Y or
2(O)-X.

Even where there is no verb directly associated with
the last element, the relation may be a sort of objective
one: *iron-merchant, book-trade, goldsmith, cheesemonger,
wheelwright*. In the last two examples the second element is now rarely used except as part of a compound.

The first element indicates the place in which the
second is (takes place, etc.): *garden-party, tombstone,
headache, rope-dancer, grasshopper, airship, air-mail*.

Or the place from or to which: *land-breeze, side-
glance, playgoer*.

The first-word denotes the time when what is ex-

pressed by the second element happens (appears, etc.):
*nightmare, night-train, night-club, evening-star, day-dream,
day-boy, wedding-breakfast*.

Or the time how long: *day-fly, all-night restaurant,
life annuity* [different from *life-insurance*!], *life member*.

The first element indicates what the second is meant
for: *flagstaff, grass-plot, beehive, keyhole, bird-cage,
wineglass, cigar-case, clothes-brush, bedroom, warehouse,
ice-boat, horse-cloth, hand-cuffs, gunpowder, minute-hand,
workhouse, eating-house, dining-room, landing-place,
Salvation Army*.

The relation is a little different in: *prize-fighter:* 2-Y.

Football as a name for the ball itself belongs here,
while as a name for the game it must be classed in the
following group.

The first element denotes a tool, instrument, or the
like, by means of which the second is brought about:
gunshot, sabre-cut, footstep, handwriting, book-learning.

The first element denotes something contained in,
and thus characterizing, the second: *stone-fruit, feather-
bed, sand-paper, mountain-range, newspaper*.

The first-word denotes something which the second
element resembles: *needle-fish, goldfish, silver-fox, bell-
flower*.

Perhaps some sort of similarity is also expressed in
phrases with *head* and *chief* = 'principal, leading, most
important': *headmaster, chief inspector*. These have
usually level stress and may be reckoned among appositional compounds, group 4, formula 1-1

The first element denotes the material out of which
the second is made. These have nearly always level
stress: *gold ring, stone wall*, etc. Exceptions are: *oatmeal,
ironware*, and *railway* (if this word belongs here).

There is still a large residue of compounds which
do not fit in anywhere. Thus, how is one to classify:
*sunflower, sun-dial, weathercock, rainbow, life-boat, life-
blood, fountain-pen, godfather, lawsuit, conscience money,*

almshouse, and many others? Though the meaning in each case is clear, the relation between the elements is not as simple as in the preceding groups.

This type of composition has thus proved extremely fertile: new compounds can be formed when needed. Among recent formations may be mentioned the numerous new terms beginning with *air* (*air-base*, *aircraft*, *airfleet*, *air-force*, *air-line*, *air-liner*, *air-mail*, *air-pilot*, *air-port*, *air-raid*, etc.) as well as *poison-gas*, *tear-gas*, *gas-mask*, *gas-shell*, and other pieces of evidence of human wickedness.

8.2₃. Final-determinative compounds often compete with prepositional phrases. We have both *battle-field* and *field of battle*. *Point of view* is the old idiomatic phrase, but *viewpoint* (originally U. S.) is getting increasingly common. In other cases there is a clear difference of sense between the two expressions. A long series of compounds denote bottles, boxes, or similar receptacles, while in each case the corresponding prepositional phrase denotes the receptacle plus its contents, sometimes the latter alone: a *beer-bottle* is so called whether it is empty or not, but a *bottle of beer* means primarily the (amount of) beer contained in a bottle, formula 2^q 1 (p 1); similarly: *wineglass—glass of wine, cigar-box—box of cigars.—Weekday* means any day of the week other than Sunday, but in *the days of the week* Sunday, too, is included.

Another rival of the type of compound under discussion is genitival composition, which is treated in more detail in another connexion (16.9).

8.3. Compounds of the second type (1-2—the first part determined by the second) are frequent in some other languages, e. g. Gaelic *Macdonald = Donaldson*, Semitic *Hannibal* = gift of Baal = Greek *Theodoros*, Provençal *dilus, dimars* = F *lundi, mardi*, F *hôtel-Dieu*, *Montmartre*, *rue Rivoli*, etc., It. *capostazione*, *capo-lavoro*, *capotavola*. Cf also Danish *Nykøbing-Falster*,

Nykøbing-Mors, the German compounds taken over as
Hesse-Darmstadt, *Hesse-Nassau*.

In English this class is rare and to a great extent
due to foreign influence. The chief representatives are:

Tiptoe (on tiptoe = on the tips of the toes), possibly
from some combination like *on tipped toes*, where *tipped*
= 'formed as a tip', or probably on account of the
favourite vowel-play as in *tick-tock*, etc. Chaucer has:
B 4497 stonden on his tiptoon. Cf *finger-tip* with a
different order, which is occasionally found with *toe:*
Rogers Wine of Fury 144 Naritza [a dancer], resting
on toe-tip.

Midday = the middle of the day; similarly: *midnight*, *mid-ocean*, etc., but *mid* is here probably an
adjective (cf II 12.55), and the compounds thus fall
under the class treated in 9.1.

Noonday (AV Job 5.14 in the noone day) is a strange
formation, as there is no corresponding noon of the
night; neither is it possible in the same way to say
'morning-day'. The form probably arose through con-
tamination of *noon* and *midday*.

Gold leaf means gold beaten into a thin leaf, Dan.
bladguld, G. *blattgold*. This cannot be explained as an
ordinary final-determinative = 'a leaf made of gold',
as it is a mass-word: never *a* gold leaf or gold leaves,
cf Strachey EV 218 the Celestial King .. swallowed
gold leaf until he ascended to Heaven.

Headborough originally denoted the head of a tithing,
later a petty constable. The term is now used only
historically.

Gum is used as first-word in a number of compounds,
chiefly of a technical kind: *gum dragon*, *gum juniper*,
gum senegal. Bergsten p. 59 suggests that the order
may have been influenced by groups like *gum elastic*
and *gum arabic* with the French position of the adjective.

We also suspect French influence in a series of compounds with *herb* (e. g. *herb Paris*, *herb Robert*) and in

apple-John, a kind of apple named after St. John's Day, when it is ripe: Sh H4B II. 4.5 A dish of Apple-Iohns.

Finally, English has this type of compound, more or less obscured, in some loan-words: *cauliflower*, cf F *chou-fleur* | *cornucopia*, orig. Lat. *cornu copiae* | *porcupine*, ME *porkepin* from OF *porc espin* (Mod.F *porcépic*) | *hippopotamus* | *saltpeter*, Lat. *sal petrae* | *chlorophyl* (cp. German *blattgrün*, which is final-determinative) | *court-baron* 'a court in which the baron exercised his private jurisdiction' (now only hist.).

In dialects the preposition is sometimes omitted in formations like *son-in-law* (cf. 8.7), thus producing initial-determinative compounds; see vol II 2.54.

A vast number of composite place-names in Northern England, Scotland, Wales, and Ireland are constructed as initial-determinatives: *Kirkpatrick*, *Kilkenny*, etc. They are either of direct Celtic origin or formed of English elements on the Celtic model. Cf Ekwall, *Scandinavians and Celts in the North West of England* (Lund University Årsskrift 1918), who terms them *inversion-compounds*.

8.4. Type three (copulative compounds—formula 1-&°-1) is very sparsely represented in English, the only true instances being names of countries and districts: *Austria-Hungary*, *Alsace-Lorraine*, *Schleswig-Holstein*.

8.5. The exact delimitation of type four (appositional compounds, formula 1-1) is a little doubtful. In the first place, even if the members may be said to be in apposition to each other and thus far equal ('equipollent'), one of them will often be apprehended as superior in relation to the other. Thus, a *boy-king* is perhaps not to be understood as 'a human being who is at the same time a boy and a king'; the phrase may be explained as 'a boy who is also a king' (initial-determinative!) or, more probably, as 'a king who is also (only) a boy (yet)' (final-determinative!). In many cases, as a matter of fact, the order of the elements is vacillating.

These phrases as a rule have level stress. Yet, the
first-words in these phrases are not on a level with
adjectives (for instance, we can hardly say "a young
actor, almost a boy one").

With the exception of *subject-matter, pathway,* and
court-yard all the examples I have been able to collect
are of living beings, mostly persons. A large group is
made up of those in which the first element determines
the sex or age of the second: *man-servant, maid-servant,
woman writer, lady doctor, girl friend, boy friend, infant
prodigy; cock-pheasant, hen-pheasant, buck-rabbit, doe-
rabbit, dog-wolf, bitch-wolf.*

A little different, because the first element is a name,
are: *billy-goat, nanny-goat, jenny-ass, tomboy.*

In a few terms the element denoting sex is put last:
roebuck, servant-girl, washerwoman. These phrases have
unity-stress on the first element, in contrast to most
of those with the inverted order of the elements.

The first element denotes various kinds of rank:
*pupil teacher, gentleman farmer, master builder, journey-
man tailor, deputy governor; queen bee, queen mother,
queen dowager; prince consort, prince regent.*

Also with the inverted order: *dowager duchess.*

In this group we might perhaps also class *man-god*
'a god who is at the same time a man', but what about
sun-god?

Equality of rank is designated by the first element in:
fellow-creature, fellow-citizen; brother officer, brother student.

The first element is a proper name, the second a
common-name designation for the same thing: *the
Browning family, the Brontë sisters, the Savoy Hotel,
the Times newspaper, the Rodney cutter.*

A special group is made up of compound titles and
the like: *lord lieutenant, Lord Chancellor, Knights Temp-
lars, lieutenant general, major general.* In the last two
examples *general* may be an adj (cf vol II 2.37).

A few terms are hard to classify: *boa constrictor,*

pussy-cat, man-jack: Meredith H 494 every man Jack
of us.

8.6. The fifth type of compounds is, by a name taken
over from the ancient Indian grammarians, termed
bahuvrihi. A modern English example is *red-coat* as
used of a British soldier, orig. a soldier wearing a red
coat. These formations go back to Indo-European times,
cf e. g. Pollak IF 30.55 and Petersen ib 34.254 ff. In
spite of Sweet, NEG § 1545 they are chiefly used as
sbs, not as adjs. The formula is 2(21)1° denoting a
secondary consisting of adj+sb belonging to a latent
primary.

They must be classed simply as instances of the
stylistic trick called *pars pro toto,* which is found with
compounds as well as simple words (cf *buttons* 'liveried
page': vol II 5.723 and below 8.9₂), and also with free
syntactic constructions: "faint heart never won fair
lady". Bahuvrihi-compounds nearly always denote living beings (or personified inanimate things), the final
member being generally the name of some part of the
body or dress. They are frequently used as (nick)names:
Bluebeard, Edmund Ironside, like other (nick)names indicating a single conspicuous characteristic of the person or thing to be named.

Bahuvrihi-compounds exhibit on the whole the same
features as ordinary final-determinative compounds (cf
8.2₂). Compounds of two sbs are comparatively rare,
though they do occur: *feather-brain, blockhead, hunch-
back, pot-belly, butter-fingers;* cf Bergsten 160—1. In OE
they were still rarer (see Storch, *Ags. Nominal-composita,*
Jena-diss. 1886, p. 50); examples from Beowulf: *hring-
mǣl* 'adorned with rings', *stȳlecg* 'steel-edged (sword)'.

Adjective+substantive compounds, on the other
hand, have been common in all periods of the language:
OE *fāmigheals* 'foamy-necked' | *heardecg* 'hard-edged' |
gyldenfeax 'golden-haired' etc. ModE *blue jacket* |
blue-stocking | *bald-head* | *madcap* | *pale-face* | Bennett

ECh 24 you silly old *long-face* | Galsw Tat 166 a good-
looking old *grey-beard*.

In most bahuvrihi-compounds the last member is in
the singular, and the pl of the whole compound is
then formed in the usual way: *pale-faces* | *grey-beards* |
Gibbs BR 323 those old *bald-heads* | Galsw IC 128 a
forlorn hope of *blue-bloods*.

An exception is formed by compounds in which the
first element is a numeral (cf vol II 5.722): a *five-leaf* |
a *five-finger* | a *nine-bark* 'Amr shrub having several
layers of bark' | a *four-way(s)* 'place where four roads
meet'.

We also use the sg in *blue-stocking* and *tenderfoot*.

Sometimes, however, the last member is, logically
correct, in the pl even when the whole compound denotes
something singular (cf vol II 5.721, see also Appendix):
Sh Oth I. 1.66 does the *thick-lips* owe | Thack S 16
Louis XIV, his old *squaretoes* of a contemporary |
Caine M 192 an old *sly-boots* | Shaw TT 257 You are a
dear delightful bighearted wrongheaded half-educated
crazy-boots | a *lazy-bones* | a *light-skirts* | a *butter-fingers* |
a *sobersides*.

The use of bahuvrihi in adjunctal function is not
common in ModE, a derivative adj in *-ed* being generally substituted. Examples: Sh Shr II. 2.10 a *mad-
brain* rudesby | Page J 259 the *gapped-tooth* official |
a *barefoot* child | a *fourpost* bed. Cf vol II 8.93.

In a few cases a bahuvrihi-compound is used as
subjunct or quasi-predicative: Galsw FS 642 she had
come down *hot-foot* on hearing the news (cf below sub
-ed 24.1$_{11}$) | Dickinson S 122 we can't ride horses *bareback*.

8.7. As a sixth type we have compounds in which two
elements are joined by means of a preposition. These
are in so far parallel to group two as the main element
is placed first (initial-determinative); formula 1-2(pl).
Their genitive-inflexion is with group-genitive: *son-in-*

law's, while in the pl *s* generally added after the first
element: *sons-in-law*, see vol II 2.53.

Examples with *of*: *mother-of-pearl* | *bill-of-fare* |
Jack-o'-lantern | *will-o'-the-wisp* | *cat-o'-nine-tails* | *man-
of-war* | *man-of-the-world* | *maid-of-all-work* | *Jack-of-
all-trades*.

With *in*: *father- (mother-, sister-,* etc.) *in-law* | *com-
mander-in-chief* | *lady-in-waiting* | *Jack-in-office* | *Jack-
in-the-box* | *Jack-in-the-green*.

Other prepositions are rarer: *man-at-arms* | Franklin
216 it is the aim and *reason-for-being* of officials [from
F *raison d'être*].

In a few combinations the first element is not a sb:
good-for-nothing | *light-of-love* | *four-in-hand*, see vol II
2.55, but the whole must be reckoned a sb.

With these compounds may be ranged groups like
a *coach-and-six*, a *whisky-and-soda*, etc. (For further
examples see vol II 2.57; cf II 8.26) and finally phrases
used as quotation-substantives, as in Shaw D 197 she
would go from her home without *with-your-leave* or
by-your-leave (cf II 8.2).

8.8₁. After considering compounds as wholes we shall
now take up the question what can be the first element
of a compound and what its form can be.

In sbs as first part the all-but universal rule is
that this has the uninflected stem-form. This may be
considered a continuation of the old Aryan practice.
With the disappearance in English of most weak vowels
the old stem-vowels retained in some OE compounds
as in winemæg, dur*u*weard have of course also been
dropped. There is likewise no trace left of such genitive-
endings as that in OE *sunnandæg*, which has become
Sunday. As mentioned in vol II 7.11 ModE *book-reading*
may be equally well a continuation of OE *bōcarœding*
and *bōcrœding*, which are both found.

In a few ModE compounds an extra vowel is added to the first element: *handiwork, handicraft, workaday. Handiwork* goes back to OE *handgeweorc;* the *i* has later been carried over, analogically, to *handicraft. Workaday* is explained by the NED as due to ON *virkr dagr* > ME *werkedai;* the reason for the retention of the vowel is perhaps to be sought in the isolation of sense in contrast to the regular form *work-day;* Hope C 248 ordinary work-a-day eyes.

The use of a genitive in -*s* as the first part of a compound will be dealt with in the chapter on the *s*-ending, below 16.9.

8.8₂. Sometimes two modes of composition compete, the first part being in the stem form or in the genitive. The genitive is the more common with designations for living beings, especially persons, and particularly so where the relation between the elements is a sort of possessive one. In these cases, according to Bergsten 118, the genitive has spread at the expense of the simple way of compounding. Compare: *a chambermaid* : *a lady's maid | a schoolboy* : *a baker's boy | a night-gown* : *a lawyer's gown.*

Usage is far from settled, however, on this point. I shall give some examples of stem composition with appellations for human beings as first-words: Di N 248 in his bachelor days | Thack P 11, 330 a bachelor life | GE S 182 it occurred to Silas's dull bachelor mind | Stevenson JHF 15 came home to his bachelor house | Shaw M 170 in comfortable bachelor lodgings | ib 157 this is only a bachelor allowance | Stevenson T 257 soiled sailor clothes | Doyle F 169 in rule sailor dress | Ward D 3.140 he bore his country-gentleman life patiently | ib 1.226 made an impression on her school-girl mind | Holmes A 236 in small school-girl letters | Thack V 236 in his big school-boy handwriting | Shaw C 23 a large schoolboy hand | Benson D 134 you do great important man things, and I do silly little woman things.

By way of contrast compare the following examples: Sh As III. 2.11 And how like you this shepherds life? | Austen M 219 from being the mere gentleman's residence, it becomes the residence of a man of education, taste .. | Thack V 299 that snug and complete bachelor's residence | Thack P 1.5 written in a great floundering boy's hand | Ward R 2.177 that independent exciting student's life.

Compare also: Mrs. Browning A 156 our woman-hands | ib 236 'tis our woman's trade To suffer torment for another's ease.

The genitive is never possible in appositional compounds (*a woman writer* | *a lady friend;* cp. *a ladies' friend*) or where the first-word is the object of the second (cf 8.2₂): *a woman-hater*. The same applies to animal names: Ru Sel 1.256 Daniel in the lions' den .. a lion hunt.

8.8₃. As the stem is generally used as the first element of compounds, and as the stem is equal to the singular, the prevalent rule is for the sg to be used even where the idea is pl, e. g. *cigar-box*, *feather-bed*, *a five-pound note*, etc. On this rule as well as the exceptions to it we may refer to the detailed account in vol II ch. 7.

We say *goods-train* to avoid misunderstanding. In the following nonce-formation the *s* could of course hardly be left out without detriment to the meaning: Shaw P 3 they conceive goodness simply as self-denial. This conception is easily extended to others-denial.

That there is a growing tendency in PE to use the pl if the conception is pl, is beyond question, but usage is far from being settled. Apart from the cases where no singular form exists or where it has a different sense, pl composition is chiefly met with: (1) when the compound denotes something special and unique, especially when it is the official name of something, (2) when the first element consists of a whole phrase. The two conditions are often combined: *the Aliens*

Act | *the Contagious Diseases Act* | *the Natural Sciences Tripos at Cambridge* | *the Hotels and Restaurants Association.*

String-Compounds

8.91. The first element of a compound can itself be a compound: Quincey 165 on moonlight nights, formula 2(2-1)-1 | Maxwell BY 33 Ursula stood there ... her legs well apart in the boy-girl attitude of modern fashion.

Or it may be an adj+sb: Dead-letter office, formula 2(21)-1 | first-class passenger | a first-rate dinner | a commonplace remark | everyday life | long-distance telephone | the dirty-clothes basket | a public schoolboy | a high churchman; cf vol II 12.32, where many examples, especially in 322 | Thack V 468 an East Indiaman.

A three-storey house, formula $2(2^q1)$-1 | a ten-pound note, etc.

Formations of this type may be formed for the nonce: Hope D 6 Give him Saturday evening lectures, or what? Oh, every evening lectures, and most-morning walks | Mackenzie C 19 when it was wet .. This isn't a new bonnet morning, she used to say.

A more complicated example is Shaw 1.3 with undignified medical-student manners, formula 2 2(21)-1 | an all-night restaurant. Cf vol II 12.322 ff.

Sometimes a further qualification is added. In the sentence (Vachell H 258) "a small girl with only threepence a week pocket-money", we may parse *pocket-money* as being in apposition to *threepence,* to which *a week* is added; but in the following quotations a whole combination parallel to *threepence a week* and containing like that an indication of time is made the first part of a compound:

Di N 91 she has stopped his halfpenny a week pocket-money, formula $1^2(2^q13)$-1(2-1) | Walpole Cp 91 he

gave his twopence a week pocket-money to his school-
fellows | Tennyson L 2.231 I take my ten miles a day
walks | Wells T 1 the nine-pence-an-hour computers |
Caine E 70 paying a penny a week subscription to the
great association | Beswick OD 47 Snelling drove a
good car, an expensive car for a £ 1,500 a year man |
Stevenson MB 139 Do you want a thousand a year,
a two hundred a year, or a ten thousand a year live-
lihood? Cf vol II 7.13.

The first element may consist of sb+preposition+
its regimen (cf 8.7): BJo A 4.358 your innes of court-
man | Zangwill G 393 I'm no breach-of-promise lady |
a penny-in-the-slot machine || a house-to-house call |
Kipling L 18 the hand-to-hand nature of the battle.—
Many more examples in vol II 14.53 ff.

A few examples of compounds of more than three
links; Old time steamboats, formula 2(21)-1(2-1) |
Thack V 270 the great Southdown female family
carriage | Twain M 203 the Walter Scott Middle-Age
sham civilisation | NP 1908 How to cure winter weather
skin troubles | Wells N 214 War Office barrack archi-
tecture | a New Year Eve fancy dress ball; the formula
for the last one is 2(2(21)-1)-1(2(2-1)-1).

8.9₂. From examples like the above the step is easy
to those in which a whole phrase, not a compound, is
used as first element. Thus, the first element may consist of two sbs joined by means of *and:*

Thack N 449 she did not make her calculations in
this *debtor and creditor* fashion | a *cat and dog* life [stressed
on *dog:* vol I 5.3₁2, formula 2(1&1)-1] | Herrick M 136
there was a *cat-and-dog* time after that | a cock and
bull story | Brontë P 1 I never experienced anything
of the *Pylades and Orestes* sentiment for you | Meredith
R 107 the fantom, now *blood and flesh* reality | Philips
L 98 a *flesh and blood* confederate | Caine C 17 their
happy *boy and girl* days together | Ruskin C 3 their
street and house foulness | Dickinson S 95 on the one

hand simplicity and size; on the other a *hole-and-corner*
variety | Swinburne L 271 the *tooth-and-nail* system |
Jennings Tennyson 49 he tells a good story of the
Carlyle and Tennyson friendship | ib 51 she married a
dog-and-horse man | Maxwell S 293 the big map turned
in her hands as she followed those thin *north and south*
lines | Ade A 101 one o' them *bride-and-groom* pictures |
Merriman S 19 a prosperous *hot-sausage-and-mashed-
potato* shop | Bennett ECh 228 he was on *chocolate and
Christian name* terms with Betty. Further examples in
vol II 14.51.

Also with other words than sbs: *deaf-and-dumb* school |
Hardy W 84 a row of those *two-and-two* brick residences.

Clipped Compounds

8.9₃. A contrast to string compounds is formed by
those instances in which the first part of a compound
is made an independent sb. This subject was treated
in vol II 8.9 with many examples like *copper* = copper
coin or copper cauldron, *return* = return ticket, etc.
Some additional examples may find their place here:
canary = canary bird | *chamber* = chamber pot (in
the nursery) | *char* = charwoman (not NED); Ertz
Mme Claire 260 There's a Cornish char here some-
where. I'll tell her) | *Cuba* = Cuba cigar (Di P 325 a
fragrant odour of full-flavoured Cubas) | *excursion* =
excursion train (Priestley G 306) | *foot-and-mouth* =
foot and mouth disease (Rhode Murd. Praed 180) |
head = headache (Brett Young OC 207 Aunt Cathie
was on or over one of her "heads" | *hunter* = hunter
watch (Galsw FS 515, Priestley A 22) | *oil* = oil painting
(Walpole ST 209 a print or an oil or a water-colour) |
patent = patent leather shoe (Bentley T 95 the only
patents in the row) | *sailor* = sailor hat (OHenry B 94
swinging her straw sailor in her hands) | *saloon* =
saloon car | *stag* = stag party or dance (only for men,
common U.S.) | *Steinway* = Steinway piano | *taxi* =
taxi(meter) cab | *top* = top boot (Di P 100) | *Van Dyke* =

Van Dyke beard (Cather PH 13 an oval chin over which
he wore a close-trimmed Van Dyke; similarly his grey
Dundrearys, Galsw FCH 92) | *water colour*, see above *oil*.

Cp also *a sixpenny* = sixpenny paper; *ninepenny* =
9d seat (Priestley G 308), etc., vol II 8.93.

In some cases, when the meaning of a clipped compound would not be immediately intelligible, a syllable
without any definite meaning is added, particularly in
slang, *-y* (13.4), *-o* (13.8₁), or *-er* (14.2₈).

8.9₄. Sometimes one element of what should be a
string-compound is left out: *twelfth(night)cake* (e. g. Di N
783, id X 35), *waste-(paper-)basket* (common in U.S., does
not seem to be used in England), *news(paper)boy, news-
vendor*.

Additional examples of clippings in 29.2.

Chapter IX

Compounds Concluded

Adjective + Substantive

9.1₁. The first part of a compound is very often an
adj; there is no fixed rule for the spelling: *blackbird,
blackboard, blackmail, bluebell, bluebottle, Broadway,
easy-chair, freeman, free-mason, gentleman, grandfather,
halfpenny, highway, holiday, hothouse, nobleman, public-
house, public school, quicksilver, shorthand, short cut,
smallpox, small-talk, strong-box, wildfire*.

Note the phonetic change in *halfpenny* [heip(ə)ni] and
holiday [hɔlidi], and in the second part of the words
in *-man* [-mən].

A few OE examples: *heahfœder* 'patriarch', *efnnight*
lit. 'even-night', i. e. equinox, *freoman* 'free man',
frumbearn 'first-born child'.

Though the adjs in these examples stand in the
ordinary relation of adjuncts to their sbs, there is a
marked isolation of sense, as expressed in the unity-

stress on the first element. Cf Fox 2.58 "Why don't
the noblemen live on their Irish estates?" asked some
one. "Because they are not noble men," was his [Dr.
Ball's] reply.

Groups of sb and postposed adj (vol II 15.4), *body-
politic*, etc., may to some extent be considered compounds (initial-determinatives, cf above group 2 (8.3).—
Cf also compounds with *-ful*, below 23.2).

9.1₂. In other cases the relation between an adj and
a sb united in a compound is not as simple as that.
A *sick-room* means a room for sick people, and a *poor-
box* a box in which contributions for the relief of the
poor are placed. *Sick* and *poor* in these cases mean
'sick people' and 'poor people'; it is only indirectly
that they are used as first-words. An evidence of this
relation is seen in the old form *poor's box* (found e. g.
in Goldsm.). See the full treatment in vol II 12.4. In
AnalSy 6.1 *sweet-shop, greenhouse, madhouse, lunatic
asylum* are analyzed 2-1, while in 6.6 *blackbird*, etc.,
are transcribed $2 + 1$, cf the comments ib 31.8.

Pronoun + Substantive

9.2. The first part of a compound may be a personal
pronoun, used to denote sex: *he-rabbit, she-cat*, etc.
They have as a rule level-stress. We sometimes meet
with extended uses of this sex-mark which have more
of the character of nonce-formations: Tennyson 168
he longed .. for she-society | ib 183 the head and
heart of all our fair she-world | Wilkins P 61 her she-
houshold [= brothel].—Note the recent Amr *he-man* =
'virile man'.

A compound of numeral + sb is *four-ale* 'ale sold at
fourpence a quart'.

But the obsolete *se(ve)nnight* contains an adjunctal use of
the numeral; *fortnight* is not now felt as containing *fourteen*.
A *ninepin* is a back-formation from the pl. *Four-wheeler,
three-decker, nine-ender* are not compounds of the numeral,
but derivatives with *-er* from adjunctal combinations, 14.3₃.

Verb + Substantive

9.3₁. The sb is the subject of the vb in *cry-baby:*
Kennedy CN 68 She often cries. She's a regular cry-baby | Dreiser AT 135 Sparser was more manly, not so much of a cry-baby.

The sb is the object: *drawbridge, show-bread, throw-stick, treadmill, tread-wheel.* (On *pickpocket,* etc., see 7,3₁).

The sb is the instrument by means of which the action is carried out: *grindstone, whetstone, bakehouse, bakestone, go cart, wash-basin, wash-board, wash-house, wash-stand. Slapstick,* orig. the wand used by the harlequin in a pantomime, is now chiefly used fig. to define knockabout farce: Harris Shaw 25 the portrait .. there shall be no slapstick, no caricature.

More difficult to define are such compounds as *go-fever* 'longing to travel': Kipling L 121 he has the beginnings of the go-fever upon him | ib 135 the go-fever, which is more real than many doctors' diseases.—Or *hang-choice* 'choice between two evils': Scott A 2.139 It would be hang-choice between the poet and psalmist. —Is the relation objective in *keep-sake?*

9.3₂. In many compounds of this type we meet with the difficulty of deciding whether the first-word is a sb or a vb: *pay-day, wash-day, work-day; guess-work; show-man; search-warrant; plaything.*

In AnalSy 18.6 compounds like *a sit-down supper, go-ahead nations, stay-at-home people* are analyzed as containing infinitives, but why inf rather than the bare verb-stem or base?

A rival of this type is *ing*-composition; compare: *draw-well, drawing-pin | bakestone, baking-powder | go-cart, going-wheel | wash-board, washing-machine | playground, playing-field,* etc. Cf vol V 8.6. *Ing*-form compounds are on the whole more common than base-form ones; sometimes the two are used side by side: *swimming-suit, swim-suit.* Cf on compounds with gerunds vol V 8.6.

Particle + Substantive

9.4₁. Compounds of prepositions and their regimen are not very numerous, see vol II 8.71-2. *Afternoon*, the oldest example of the formation, dates back at least to the 15th century and is perhaps due to Fr. *après-midi*. Some such compounds are used as adjuncts only, II 14.61 ff.

Analysis p-1 (AnalSy 6.4).

9.4₂. The first part of a compound may be a particle (adverb):

Out = 'situated some way off, etc.': *outhouse, out-field, out-patient, outpost, out-relief* | = 'external': *out-line, outside* | *In* = 'internal': *inside* | *Up* = 'going upwards': *up train, up stroke* | *Down* = 'going down (or connected with downward movement)': *down shaft, down train, down platform, down side* | *Over* = 'upper, outer, extra, in excess': *overcoat, overlord, overdose, over-draft, overtime, overweight* | *Under* = 'situated beneath, subordinate': *under-agent, under-clothes, undercurrent, under-dog, under-king, under-plot, under-secretary, under-tenant, understone, underwood, underworld.*

Further:

after = 'happening afterwards': *afterglow, after-grass, aftertaste, afterthought* | *off* in various senses: *off-licence, off-print* | *between*, prob. only in *between-maid* (more usually *tweeny*) 'servant who assists two others' | *fore-head* is no longer felt as a compound; the usual pro-nunciation is ['fɔred, -id].

These are different from *afternoon*, etc., see 9.4₁. But it may be questioned whether we should here talk of compounds or simply of adjuncts, cf vol II 14.95. Analytic Synt 6.4: *afterthought* 2(3)-1.

9.4₃. In the type *outbreak* we have a particle+a sb, which is identical in form with the corresponding vb. The order of the elements is the same as the old order, in which an adverb preceded infinitives and participles. But as compound verbs with this order are now found

in comparatively rare instances (see below 9.7₂) the
sbs here considered cannot be taken as simple substantivations of such vbs, but form a type apart. Sbs
like *outcome, upkeep,* and *uptake,* which came into use
during the 19th century, seem to have come in from
Scotch dialects. There is a certain amount of over-
lapping among the sense-categories here established.

Denoting agent: *offshoot | offspring | offal* (now no
longer felt as a compound) | *upshoot | upstart,* and
perhaps also: *downpour | income | outcome,* which may
also be classed in the following groups.

Object or result: *inlet* 'sth let in' | *outcast | output*
(the stem of these three words may be the ptc.) ||
outfit | Wells F 39 the *uprush* of it all.

Place: *inlet* 'creek' | *intake | outfall | outlet.*

Action: *downfall | downrush* (Wells T 3) | *inrush |
offset | onset | outbreak | outburst | outcry | outlook |
outset | upkeep | uplift | uprise* (chiefly poetical: Shelley
119) | *uprush | uptake* (chiefly in: slow (etc.) in the
uptake).

Formula 3-1, often 3-Y.

The old rule was for the sb to take the stress on the
first part; the different distribution of the stress often
heard in *upset* and *uprise* is probably due to the influence of the still existing vbs.

With agent-nouns, *onlooker* and *outfitter* represent
the old mode of composition, but whenever a new
composite agent-noun is to be formed, it is on the
model of *hanger-on, passer-by, diner-out,* etc.

Look-out, turn-out, etc. are substantivations of phrases
(vb+adv).

Substantive + Adjective (Participle)

9.5₁. After considering those kinds of composition the
final result of which is a sb, we shall now deal with
those which result in one of the other word-classes,
first adjectives.

For practical reasons adjective is here taken as in-
cluding the two participles. The result of the compound is an adj. The possible logical relations between
the two parts are manifold; we shall here mention a
few of them.

The first element is the subject of the action expressed in the second participle: Kingsley H 327 reassert
their *God-given* rights | this *god-forsaken* country |
Wells V 41 We live under *man-made* institutions | id
E 9 this *foreigner-invented, foreigner-built, foreigner-
steered* thing | Whittier 434 the *Indian-haunted* region |
Hardy W 11 the *self-invited* comer.—So also: *weather-
beaten, frost-bitten, sun-struck, wind-dried, sea-girt.* Formula $2(S^a)-Y^b$.

The first element is the object of the action implied
in a first participle: *heart-rending* sobs | *soul-destroying*
monotony | a *God-fearing* man | *daylight-saving* time.—
OE has *mægen-āgende* 'having strength' and *æsc-berende*
'spear-bearing'.—Formula O-Y.

Self must be reckoned a sb in compounds like *self-
absorbed, self-assertive, self-centred, self-conscious, self-
complacent, self-imposed, self-denying, self-determined,
self-reliant, self-sacrificing, self-satisfied.*

The first element indicates the place of an action,
etc.: a *sea-faring* nation | *London made* goods | *home-
brewed* ale | Kaye Smith GA 2 He was *town bred*, though
not *town born* | Thack V 327 I'm an honest girl though
workhouse bred | Caine M 49 you that's *college bred* |
Hardy L 28 he was *country-born* | *heart-felt* | *world-wide.*
—More rarely the place to which: Kinglake E 66 the
shore-gone sailors.—Formula 3-Y; *sea-faring nation* of
course 2(3-Y)1, etc.

In *tongue-tied* and *heart-broken* the first-word indicates
the part that is affected by the action expressed in
the second element; one hesitates whether to class
these combinations as objective or as local. In the

related compounds *heart-sick*, *headstrong*, *foot-sore*, *top-heavy*, however, only local interpretation is possible. Formulas 3-2 or 3-2(Y), respectively.

The first-word denotes the instrument, etc., by means of which the action (or state) expressed in the second takes place (is brought about). Some of the phrases might also be classed as subjective: *hand-made* | *machine-made* | *moss-clad* | Butler Er 43 *lichen grown* | Galsw WM 26 it's a trifle *flyblown* since the war | Di T 1.123 the *thief-and-rascal-crowded* passages | Locke W 277 the *star-hung* sky | Hawthorne Sn 52 *leaf-strewn* forest-land | Hardy W 123 the empty, *shaving-strewn* rooms || *book-learned* | *seasick* | *lovesick* | *spell-bound* | *snow-blind*.

Formulas as above.

Similarity: *grass-green* means 'green like grass', i. e. having the particular shade of green that grass has, as distinguished e. g. from *sea-green*, *emerald-green*, or *olive-green*. Similarly with other colours: *blood-red*, *snow-white*, *milk-white*, *jet-black*, *coal-black*, *nut-brown*, *pitch-dark*, *sky-blue*, *steel-grey*.—Other qualities than colours: *clay-cold*, *stone-cold*, *stone-dead*, *stone-deaf*, *stone-still*, *bone-dry*, *dirt-cheap*, *cock-sure*, *dog-tired*, *sun-bright*, Carlyle R 2.177 on ice *paper-thin* | NP 1912 a special kind of small ale, *water-thin* | Gissing R 215 voice .. *silver-sweet* | Sh Alls IV. 3.286 *swine-drunke*.

Formula: a snow-white dress 2(3-2)1.

The first member in many cases serves rather as an indication of a high degree than as the basis of a real comparison. This is even more marked in: Mac-Carthy 2.584 the *fire-new* [arch. for 'brand-new'] title of Empress | Wells Br 316 this very new man, *mint new* and clean and clear | *span-new* | *bone-idle*, e. g. Bennett HL 140 and Locke CA 1.

A comparison of another kind is expressed in compounds like *godlike*, *snowlike*, *gentleman-like*, where the

second element governs the first. Cf also *suchlike:*
Austen M 179 such and suchlike were the reasonings of
Sir Thomas.

In this connexion we may mention another series
of compounds in which there is a sort of governance
between the elements: *respectworthy, blameworthy,* etc.;
sea-worthy, airworthy | careful, playful, etc., see suffix
-ful(l) (23.2).

With names of colours new compounds can be formed
freely on the old model; in other cases they are rare:
Chesterton F 28 turning slowly from peacock-green to
peacock-blue | Collier E 27 the women from Eve-old
vanity think the same.—While German has *kugelrund,*
zirkelrund (correspondingly in Dan.), we cannot say
in English *ball-round* and *circle-round,* but shall have
to use *spherical* and *circular; blitzschnell* is *quick as*
lightning, not *lightning-quick.*

Measure or extent. The first-word usually indicates
the limit of the quality expressed in the second element;
brimful (see *-ful* 23.2) | *knee-deep* | Norris S 163 she
swung herself over the side, *hip deep* in the water |
the books stand *two deep* on the shelf | Carlyle FR 316
Three-deep these march | Doyle S 1.96 *shoulder high*
and *waist high* | *lifelong* | *world-wide* | Phillpotts M 15
wife-old [= old enough to take a wife].

In other phrases the first-word serves merely to indicate a high degree: Lewis MA 161 the attic .. it's
jam full already | Masefield C 288 he repeated it till
he had it *letter perfect* | Ridge G 231 I rehearsed with
the book .. the others were *word perfect* | Walpole
F 113 *mother-naked.*

Other relations of an indefinable nature. Many of
these compounds may be paraphrased by means of
prepositional phrases, e. g. *gallows-ripe* 'ripe for the
gallows', *colour-blind* 'blind in regard to colours'. Fur-
ther: *water-, bullet-proof* | Thack V 8 to live *cost free* |
Spencer A 2.437 *rote-learnt* lessons | Phillpotts GR 32

My grandfather was *furniture mad*.—Still stranger are:
Sh Hml V. 1.261 *peaceparted* soules [= (de)parted in
peace] | Sh Meas. I. 2.85 I am *custum-shrunke* [= have
fewer customers].

Pronoun + Adjective (Participle)

9.5₂. It will suffice here merely to mention compounds with *all*.

All is the subject of the action expressed in the
second element: Sh H4A V. 1.16 all-abhorred.—*All* is
the object: *all-sufficing*, *all-seeing*, *all-knowing*. This
type is common in Shakespeare: Meas. II. 4.95 all-
building | Rom. I. 1.139 all-cheering | Lucr. 801 all-
hiding | LLL II. 1.21 all-telling || Sonn. 55.9 all-oblivious.
—*All* = 'completely': *almighty*, *all-bountiful*, *all-
righteous*, *all-sufficient*. Formula 2(3-2).

Adjective + Adjective

9.6₁. In compounds of two adjectives the first generally modifies the second.

Thus in colour-names: light-green | dark-blue |
Bennett A 231 an expanse of grey-green field | Galsw
P 3.21 a brown-grey beard.—Very often the first-word
is made to end in *-ish* or *-y*: *reddish-brown*, *bluish-grey*,
etc. *A blue-green dress* should be analyzed 2(3-2)1, and
not, as in AnalSy, 2(2-2)1.

While *dark-looking*, etc., is 2(P-Y), I should give the
formula for *new-made*, *British-made*, *dear-bought*, *high-
born*, *English-born*, Norris O 320 a ship ... *American
built*—as 2(2-Y), for *dead-tired*, *dead-beat*, *dead-drunk* as
2(3-2) and for *red-hot* and *dead-alive* as 2(2-2). *Clean-
cut* is 2(3-Y[b]).

Copulative compounds of adjs are rare. For German
schwarzweissrot English says *black, white, and red*. We
may class here, however, formations like *the Franco-
Prussian war*, *the Sino-Japanese conflict*. If we reckon
numerals as adjectives, we may also include numbers

like *twenty-three, sixty-four*, etc. All of these phrases generally have level stress. Formula 2(2-&°-2). But an *English-German dictionary* should probably be analyzed 2(2p°2)1, because it is different from a German-English dictionary: from one language to another.

Particle + Adjective (Participle)

9.6₂. With *ever* we have one certain compound: *evergreen;* other phrases such as *everlasting, ever-living* usually have level stress.

Over is used before adjectives, etc., to express the notion of excess, too much (cf 9.4₂): *over-anxious, over-careful, over-confident, over-delicate, over-eager, over-fond, over-happy, over-many, overmuch, over-nice, over-ripe, over-scrupulous, over-sensitive*, etc. These, too, have level stress as a rule.

Under is occasionally prefixed to adjs in the sense 'insufficiently' (cf 9.4₂); with pure adjs this is rare except when opposed to *over:* Vachell H 247 neither *under-* nor *over-confident | under-ripe | under-scrupulous*.

Far is used e. g. in *far-fetched* and *far-reaching*, both generally with level stress.

Poets use compound adjectives much more freely than prose-writers, see S.P.E. tract (no. 49) by Bernard Groom.

We finally have to consider compound verbs.

Substantive + Verb

9.7₁. Compound vbs of the type *housekeep* are not usual in the Gothonic languages, and are felt to some extent as contrary to idiom. On the other hand, compound nouns like *housekeeper* and *housekeeping* are perfectly legitimate, and from these the vb *housekeep* must have been formed by back-formation. In other cases the vb probably originated in a participle; e. g. the regular form *henpecked* may have given rise to the finite vb *henpeck*. The earliest instances of back-formation

that I have come across are *backbite* (1300), *partake*
(16th c.), and *soothsay* and *conycatch* (Sh.). Though
still a stranger to the language, the formation is fairly
well-represented in PE; cf my paper in EStn 70.118 ff.,
the lists of which I reprint here with a few additions.

Backbite, NED 1300—from *backbiter, backbiting* ||
book-hunt, NED Suppl. 1880—from *book-hunter, -hunting*
|| *book-keep*, not NED. Shaw C 20 I could book-keep
by double entry || *boot-leg* 'traffic illicitly in liquors'
NED Suppl || *boot-lick*, NED Suppl. 1845, also Payne
Al 'to seek to ingratiate oneself' || *bottle-wash*, not in NED,
Mason Ch 75 he ... he generally bottle-washed for the
regular conductor || *button-mend*, not NED. Holmes
A 72 see him sheltered, warmed, fed, button-mended,
and all that || *caretake*, NED Suppl. 1893, also Jenkins
B 157 women ... to caretake for him || *cony-catch*,
NED 1592, frequent in Elizabethans || *eavesdrop*, NED
1906, from *eavesdropper, -dropping;* but possibly a
simple formation from the sb *eavesdrop(s)*. Galsw SS
260 in any case I don't expect to be eavesdropped |
Macdonnell E 252 It was surely better to eavesdrop a
passionate proposal of marriage than to interrupt it ||
flag-wag, not NED. NP 1923 the French have got their
victory, as they call it, and will now flag-wag || *fortune-
hunt*, not NED. Byron L 82 I cannot fortune-hunt ||
gate-crash, not NED. Sayers GN 165 because you gate-
crashed the meeting || *globe-trot*, NED Suppl. 1883,
also Bookman Dec. 1908. 124 she globetrotted || *hand-
shake*, NED Suppl. 1898, also Lewis EG 314 as he
handshook his way from store to store || *hay-make*, not
NED. Macdonell E 270 no one hay-makes in May ||
hen-peck (NED) || *horror-strike*, NED 1811. Seeley E
136 the horror-striking stories.—From *horror-stricken,
-struck* || *housebreak*, NED 1820 (Shelley) || *house-hunt*,
NED 1888, also Wells N 276 we'll have to house-hunt;
cf *book-hunt* || *housekeep*, NED 1842, also NP 1925
with no palaces to housekeep for | Kipling L 240 you'd

better come and housekeep for me | Merriman V 114
to housekeep generally ... I could never housekeep ...
a lady who housekeeps for all humanity | Shaw IW
336 I have to be housekept-for, nursed, doctored ... ||
hut-keep, Morris Austr. 'to act as a hut-keeper' || *love-
make*, cannot perhaps be inferred from Walpole DW
245 A man 'ud have a stiff time love-makin' with her
(not quite the same thing as making love to her, as it
implies mutuality) || *man-handle* 'treat roughly', NED
1865. Kipling MOP 198 He's been man-handled ||
merrymake, NED 1714. Maurier T 142 you merrymake
together || *mix-bathe* (not NED) is probably an abbrevi-
ated form of *mixed-bathe* from *mixed bathing:* NP 1906
the girl who marries is the girl who does not smoke,
does not play hockey or bridge, and particularly does
not mix-bathe || *pap-feed*, NED. Carlyle S 58 for a
time suckled and pap-fed thee there || *part(t)ake*, NED ||
rough-ride, NED 1890 || *safeguard*, NED || *sheepsteal*,
NED 1820 (Shelley) || *sight-read*, NED Suppl. 1903 ||
sight-see, NED 1835, 1843; also Elizabeth F 228 She
had come to sight-see || *slave-drive*, not NED. Shaw
J 112 employing him to slave-drive your laborers ||
sleep-walk, not NED. NP 1923 The heroine sleep-
walks || *soothsay*, NED 1606 || *spring-clean*, NED
Suppl. 1930. Earlier ex. NP 1908 He was helping his
wife to "spring clean" || *strap-hang*, NED Suppl. 1917;
also Bennett H 78 you strap-hang on the Subterranean ||
sunbathe, not NED. Shaw TT 73 Lets sunbathe ||
sunburn, NED 1530—chiefly from *sunburnt* || *thought-
read*, NED 1898; also in Wells L 164 Why don't they
thought-read each other? | ib same page: let them
thought-read their daughters || *tongue-tie*, NED 1555—
from *-tied* || *trench-dig*, not NED. Pennell L 49 By this
time the Regiment was ... getting drilled and marched
and trench-dug into shape || *type-write*, NED 1887;
also Shaw 2.88 and 113 | Wells L 169 I could typewrite

if I had a machine || *waylay*, (NED). Maugham MS
146 he waylaid her in the street || *word-paint*, not
NED. NP 1894 to word-paint the wreathing of the mist
and every caprice and humour of the sky.

It will be seen that the sb is most often the notional
object of the vb, yet the compound may be transitive
(*button-mend*); in other cases it indicates the place
(*sunbathe*) or time (*spring-clean*) or instrument (*word-
paint*). The first element may be an adj in a predicative
or similar relation (*merrymake; rough-ride*).

Difficult to analyze are *manhandle* and *dry-cure*. The
explanation of the latter is perhaps the same as for
white-wash and *wet-nurse*, which are formed direct from
the homophonous (compound) sbs and thus are only
indirectly compound vbs.

On *new-paint* etc. see vol II 15.33 and above 9.1_1.

Blindfold is difficult to place; the ME vb was *blind-
fellen* from the adj and *fellen*, but from the 16th c. it
was connected with the vb *fold*.

Water-mark, *dry-nurse*, etc., are not back-formations,
but belong to 6.8_3.

Particle + Verb

9.7₂. The old Gothonic type preposition+vb seen
e. g. in G. *den krieg durchleben*, Dan. *gennemleve krigen*
'live through the war' was still living in OE (*oferstigan*,
æfterspyrigan and others) has nearly disappeared from
ModE, where we have combinations with *over* and
under only.

Over- is used in a series of related senses, often creat-
ing transitive vbs out of intransitive ones:

(1) passing over a boundary or obstacle: *overbrim*,
overcome, *overflow*, *overlap*, *overleap*, *overstep*. Devil
E 528 the old knight Hath over-run his annual revenue.

(2) passing across a surface, etc.: *override*, *overrun*
("the enemy overran the country").

(3) situated above, or covering: *overcloud, overcrust, overlie, overlook* 'have the prospect of', *oversee* 'super-intend'.

(4) prefixed mostly to denominative vbs to express the idea of mastery, superiority: *overtop, overtower, over-master, overrule, overforce, overpower.*

In sense 1 and 2 the mode of composition in question was formerly more common; Sh has it in many cases where we must now use the simple vb followed by *over* as a preposition: H4A I. 3.192 to o're-walke a current | Merch. V. 1.7 ore-trip the dewe. Corresponding to a modern adverbial phrase Sh has *o'erlook* = 'look over, peruse', e. g. Lr. V. 1.50.

Under in a few compounds makes an intransitive vb transitive: *underlie, underrun.*

9.7₃. In all other compound vbs beginning with a particle this must be considered an adv, and as the normal position of an adverbial modification is after the vb, only a few particles are capable of being put first, chiefly *out, over,* and *under,* and only in special significations; note the difference in *take over—overtake, set up—upset.*

Over is found as an adverbial prefix.

(1) expressing 'beyond' in degree or quality, i. e. 'too much': *overdo, overrate, over-estimate, overload;* thus often reflexively with the sense 'damage oneself by doing to excess': *overdrink (overeat, overreach, over-sleep, oversmoke, overwork) oneself.*

(2) implying disturbance of equilibrium: *overbalance, overset, overthrow, overturn.*

(3) Outside these classes: *overhear* 'hear by accident', *overlook* 'fail to notice', *overtake* 'catch up'.

The difference between 9.7₂ and 9.7₃ is brought out in the analysis of two sentences: *he oversteps the boundary* (9.7₂) S V(p*-V) O*—the stars show that *boundary* is at the same time the object of the whole verb and the

regimen of *over*—*he overstates the difference* S V(3-V) O:
over adverbial. Similarly with *under*.

Cf the combination *think over* vol III 13.9₁₁.

Under- is used

(1) denoting the placing of something under some-
thing else: *underlay, underline, undermine, underprop* ||
underhung ptc: Wells N 60 his jaw was underhung.

(2) = 'at a lower rate than': *underbid, underbuy,
undersell.*

(3) = 'insufficiently': *underact* (a play or part),
undercharge (a gun), *under-develop* (a plate or film),
underestimate, undervalue, underman (a ship). Many
such compounds are used mostly as ptcs: *underdone,
underpaid, under-populated, understaffed.*

Up- is used chiefly in *uphold* and *upset,* whose sense
differs entirely from that of *hold up* and *set up;* cf NP
1923 Questions of the competence of the League were
thus far upheld (and so far held-up) without Italy
withdrawing her opinion. *Upbraid* is hardly associated
with *braid* at all. In a purely literal sense *up-* is more or
less archaic: *uplift, uprise, uproot* | Norris O 130 ploughs
up-stirred the land | Bennett SR 105 the flash of desire
upleaping in his heart.

Off- is now only used in a single combination, the
(chiefly U. S.) phrase *offset* = 'counterbalance': Cooley
Human Nature 183 they are aware of this lack of
frankness, and try to offset it by reckless confessions.

Out- is used (1) in its original sense 'towards the
outside, etc.', equivalent to the simple vb followed by
out; this use is now rare or archaic: Shelley Adonais
X. 9 She faded, like a cloud which had outwept its
rain | Thack P 250 he outcried at the enormity of
Pen's transgressions | Bennett ECh 287 Then outbursts
a perfect roar of applause | Galsw TL 33 before his
artistic talent had outcropped.

(2) in the figurative sense of exceeding or surpassing

something or somebody. In this sense *out* is capable of making an intransitive vb transitive; it is prefixed not only to original vbs, but also to denominative vbs very often formed for the nonce: *outbrave* 'defy' | *outbalance* 'weigh down' | *outgo* 'surpass': Marlowe E 1548 as much as thou in rage outwentst the rest | MacCarthy King 191 Can he *out-dance* me, *out-drink* me, *out-courtier* me, *out-soldier* me? And must I now believe that he can *out-love* me? .. The old love may *out-last* the new | Shaw Peace Conf. 15 Germany was *outwitted*, *outprepared*, *outgeneralled*, *outfought*, *outflown*, *outgassed*, *outtanked*, *outraided*, *outbombed* and finally brought to her knees.

Particularly frequent are the many compounds formed on the pattern of Shakespeare's well-known phrase *it out-Herods Herod* (Hml III. 2.16), e. g. Carlyle F 2.89 Fraser's Magazine .. This *out-Blackwoods* Blackwood.

In particle-verb combinations the last element is always stressed (except in adjunctal position, under the influence of rhythm; cf vol I 5.42), but there is a tendency to stress the first element as well, particularly if it is disyllabic as in the case of *over* and *under:* 'over'*value*, 'under'*estimate*. Cf vol I 5.7 and below 11.9.

The inclination to keep the old word-order (particle + vb) is stronger with participles than with finite forms, because of the nominal character of the former. Thus, we say *she stretched out her* arms, but often *with outstretched arms;* and there are no finite forms corresponding to an *outlying village, inborn gentleness, downtrodden peasants*. Similarly: *she lifted up her eyes*, but in choice prose: *with uplifted eyes*. Examples with *under-* have been given above (sense 4). Usage wavers a great deal on this point, however; we can only say *a put-up scheme, cast-off clothes, a broken-down car; lighting-up time*. Cf vol II 14.31 ff.

Outside these groups we find in a few military phrases

the word-order adv+vb: Maxwell G 233 as he brought
his heels together with a click and about-turned to the
Mansions | Shaw TT 68 Meek comes to attention,
salutes, left-turns, and goes out.

Compounds of adverbs+vb like *ill-treat* require no
comments, (Sh has *false-play*).

Chapter X

Reduplicative Compounds

10.1₁. Repetition of the same syllable or syllables
comes natural to all human beings and is found very
often in all languages as a means of strengthening an
utterance. What is repeated may be an ordinary word,
as in the repeated interjections *Come, come!* | *Hear,
hear!* | *Well, well!*.—Further such combinations as *girly-
girly* | *goody-goody* | *pretty-pretty* | *talkee-talkee* or *talky-
talky* (Shaw J 110 all that Irish exaggeration and
talky-talky) | *far far* away | Science moves, but *slowly
slowly* (Tennyson 101) | those *many many* bodies (Sh
Hml III. 3.9)|an *old, old* man (e. g. Di X 46, Shelley
168) | this eternal *cackle, cackle, cackle* about things
in general is only fit for old, *old, old* people (Shaw
Ms 31). Combined with *and: again and again* | for
years and years (= 'many years') | *more and more* |
by *little and little* | he would *dig, and dig* (Di T 1.22) |
when a man *listens and listens* (Stevenson JH 5) || he
sat *as glum as glum* (Galsw F Ch 50), also *as plain
as plain could be* (cf vol III 9.5₃). Cf. also Fijn van
Draat EStn 43.302 and Poutsma in Curme-volume 124.

Note the curious repetition of the base of a verb
with the ending *-ing* added after the last in Di Bleak H.
(Nelson) 354 I went on *prose, prose, prosing* for a length
of time | Lewis MA 58 a dame that keeps *nag-nag-
naggin'* and *jab-jab-jabbin'* at me all day long.

Babies will repeat long strings of identical syllables without attaching any meaning to them, and parents will often assign meaning to them, and thus arises the fertile class of words *papa*, *mama*, etc., see my book *Language*, p. 154 ff. From the nursery we have i. a. *geegee* 'horse', *tata* 'goodbye' (also from that word *bye-bye*). As is well-known, many languages utilize (partial) reduplication for grammatical purposes, e. g. Latin perfects like *cecidi*, *spopondi*.

10.1₂. Reduplicated compounds are very frequent in English as in other languages. They fall into the following groups:

(1) The kernel repeated unchanged; sometimes with an extension of one of the kernels.

(2) The kernel repeated with change of vowel.

(3) The kernel repeated with change of consonant.

Koziol § 641-655. Bibliography ib § 641. E. Eckardt in EStn 72.161 ff. (1938), cf ib 73.158 and 317. Eckardt's lists are much fuller than mine, gathered as they are through a systematic going through the NED (the earliest date of which is given for each word), while my own examples were collected unsystematically in connexion with reading English literature.—Cf also Fijn van Draat, EStn 74.156 ff.

It should be noted how often reduplication in its varied forms is combined with the hypocoristic ending *-y* (*-ie*). Besides the examples found in the following paragraphs see the chapter on this suffix (13.4).

Kernel Repeated Unchanged

10.2₁. This very often expresses repeated sounds, natural or produced by human activity. As the sounds denoted generally have no real similarity to those produced by human speech-organs, they have to be "phonematized", i. e. rendered by sounds forming part of the English sound-system.

Examples, with the instrument, etc., producing the

sound placed in parenthesis: *blang-blang-blang* (ambulance, train; Lewis). *bubble-bubble.* *chip-chip* (axes; Mason) *chuff-chuff* (train, motor-boat; Priestley). *chug-chug* (engine; Tracy; feet of prisoners in mud; Sherwood-Anderson). *chut-chut* (chut-chutted, motor-car; Priestley) *click-click* (needles; Cronin). *clank-clank* (clank-clanking, horses; Carlyle). *clock-clock* (clock-clocking, clock-clocked, hansom-cab; Lawrence). *clop-clop* (hoofs; Galsw; waves against a boat; A Huxley). *clump, clump* (steps; Swinnerton). *clunk-clunk* (oars in rowlocks; Asterisk). *drip-drip* (water; Priestley). *flop, flop* (kettle; Maxwell). *gobble-gobble* (turkey; Kaye-Smith). *hish-hish* (rain; Macdonald). *honk-honk* (motor horn; Gibbs). *jug-jug* (nightingale; Coleridge; motor-cycle; Mason). *lock-lock* (oars; Dreiser). *nick-nick* (needles; Bennett). *pad-pad* (bare feet; Gaye, Farnol). *plod-plod* (horses; Tarkington). *plop-plop* (Hope D 38 Miss Phaeton flicked Rhino, and the groom behind went plop-plop on the seat). *plup-plup* ("plup-plup"-ing, gas bubbles; Arnot Robertson). *pooh-pooh.* *puff-puff* (= 'train'; nursery). *quack-quack* or *quark-quark* (quark-quarking, ducks; Lawrence). *ramp-ramp* (sea; Walpole). *snip-snip* (snip-snipped with his scissors; Dreiser). *tap-tap* (knock at door; Bennett). *thump-thump* (crutch; Collins; feet; Sherwood Anderson). *tick-tick* (clock). *ting-ting* (clock, telephone bell; Bennett). ting-ating-ting (bell; Hawthorne; cf Dan. *dingelingeling*). *tong-tong-tong* (cowbells; Lawrence). *whish-whish* (Graves G 153 I heard one shell whish-whishing towards me).

A somewhat fuller list is given by G. Kirchner in Anglia 65 p. 328 ff.

10.2₂. The same repetition with extension: Ridge G 36 sent him *bumpety-bump* down the stairs | Barrie AdmCr 128 His gay old heart makes him again proclaim that he is a *chickety-chick* | Swinnerton S 8 [typewriter] *Clackety-clackety-clack-clack. Clackety-clack-clackity* | ib 58 The only noise in the office was that of Mercy Simmons's clacking typewriter. They were all so used

to it—to the *clack-clacka-clack-clack-clack* | Rogers Wine
of Fury 163 [railway-train] with the "*clickety-click*" of
the rails sounding in his ears (similarly Daly King
OR 98) | Prokosch A 338 little Chinamen going *cloppety-
clop* in their clogs across the cobble-stones | Galsw Ca
279 There was silence, but for the *slip-slippering* of
the woman's feet behind.

Kernel Repeated with Change of Vowel

10.3₁. In the most frequent type, found in all parts
of the world—in all Gothonic and Romanic languages,
in Greek, Lithuanian, Turkish, Magyar, Bantu, etc.,
see e. g. v. Ginneken, Princ. de linguistique psycholog-
ique 390 ff.—we have in the first member [i] and in
the second [a], in English [æ] or a back-round vowel.
The reason why we find everywhere this and not the
inverse sequence of sounds was already hinted at in
my book Language p. 402 f.: you begin with what is
light and indicates littleness and nearness and end
with the opposite. On the shrill sound [i] as meaning
'small' see my paper in Linguistica 283 ff.; cf also the
contrast between 'near' and 'far' in F. *ci* and *là*, *here*
and *there*, G. *hier* and *da*, *dort*, etc. The duller and
more open sound is also musically best adapted for the
conclusion. The alternation often serves to express the
sound produced by a movement to and fro or the
movement itself as in *zig-zag*, hence vacillation, in-
decision, etc., and contemptible things in general. Cf
also L. Spitzer in KZ 54 p. 213 ff.

A selection of examples with the alternation [i : æ]:
bibble-babble (Sh, etc.). *chiff-chaff* (a bird, also called
chiff-chat or *chik-chak*, the last form in Maugham).
chit-chat. *click-clack* (walking-cane; Allingham). *clinkum-
clankum* (ringing noise; Butler; also in obscene sense,
see Grose). *clish-clash* ('gossip'). *clitter-clatter* ('idle
talk'; Caine). *dilly-dally* ('loiter'; Stevenson). *dimber
damber* ('top man, chief rogue'; cant, Grose). *dingle-*

dangle. driggle-draggle (†). *fid-fad. fiddle-faddle* (with
variations *fiddlededee, fiddle-come-faddle, fiddlecome*). *fix-
fax* (EDD). *flim-flam* (common; also as vb, Cain Postman 109 We've been flim-flammed; variant *flimmery-
flammery;* Allingham). *flip-flap. frish-frash* (Synge 177
a woman pouring any frish-frash from a cup). *gibble-
gabble* ('incomprehensible talk'; Dekker). *jibbering jabber-
ing* (Shaw). *jim jams* ('nervous fit'; D. T.; McKnight
EW 427). *jingle-jangle.* the *Kit-cat* club. *kittle cattle*
(common). *knick-knack* (also spelt *nick-nack*). *mingle-
mangle* (old, cf *mingle-mangleness* in Southey). *mish-
mash. mixty-maxty* or *mixy-maxy. niffnaffy* or *niffy-
naffy* (Dictionaries). *pibble bable* (Sh). *pick-pack. pindy-
pandy* (Dekker). *pinkie-pankie* ('tinkling sound'; Sc.).
pishery-pasherie ('idle talk'; Dekker). Mrs. *Princum-
Prancum* (slang). *prittle-prattle* (Swift, etc.). *ribble-rabble*
(also Sc. *ribblie-rabblie*). *rickety-rackety. riff-raff* (common). *rip-rap* (Sc., in curling; also fig.). *skimble-skamble*
stuffe (Sh, etc.). *snip-snap* (Dekker, etc.). *snipper
snapper* (Marlowe, etc.). *swingledome, swangledome* (Jack
Straw). *tick-tack* (Sh, a game, F. *tric-trac*). *tig-tag* (tig-
taggin'; Cronin). *tittle-tattle* (old, still common; in Sh
tiddle taddle). *triddle-traddle* (Hall Caine). *tringum trangum*
('whim'; Grose). *twittle twattle* (Swift). *whim-wham* (old,
still common; also *whimsy-whamsy*). *whittie-whattie* (Sc.,
Cassell's Dict.). *wig-wag* ('signal by means of flags').
wiggle-waggle. zig-zag.

10.3₂. It will be seen that in some cases one of the
forms exists as an ordinary word, or even both may;
note especially *kittle cattle;* cf also Collins W 328 the
respectable lawyers who scribble-scrabble your deeds
and your wills—but in other cases the components are
in themselves meaningless.

Pishy-pashy (a game) is said to be a corruption of
'Peace and Patience'.

An interesting formation is *shilly-shally,* based on
shill-I shall-I? as in Fielding T 4.337 if I had suffered

her to stand shill I shall I, dilly dally, you might not
have had that honour—with the meaningless *shill;* now
it is used as a regular verb as in Maugham TL 263
He's a weak man and he shilly-shallied | Sayers DC
139 We can't stay shilly-shallying all night.

Cf on the differently formed *willy-nilly* vol V 23.1₁.

10.3₃. The same alternation with extension in one
of the members: *clipperty clapper* (Hall Caine). *pit-a-pat*
(also *pitter-pat*, *pitter-patter*, rarely *pit-patting* (Galsw
Ca 932)). *tippety-tap* (Sayers). a *tit-tattering* noise
(Walpole).

10.3₄. The alternation [i : ɔ] is in a few cases caused
by the existence in ordinary language of words with
these two vowels; *drip-drop, sing-song, slip-slop, tip-top.*

In *wish(y)-wash(y)* it is occasioned by the ordinary
transition of [a, æ] to [ɔ] after [w]; the spelling *a* is
retained; but in *wiffle-woffle(s)* the spelling is *o*.

Criss-cross is said to be from *Christ-cross;* cf however
G. *kribskrabs,* Dan. *krims-krams.*

Other examples of [i : ɔ]: *clip-clop* (of hoofs; Kennedy
R 332). *ding-dong. flick, flock* (laces of boots; Wells H 10).
flipflops (Lewis B 86). *flipperty-flopperty. jiggety-joggety.
jiggy-ioggy* (Dekker). *nid-nod* with variants *niddle-
noddle* and (Carlyle) *niddy-noddy. ping-pong. slippery-
sloppery* (Hall Caine). *tick-tock* (clock). *tisty-tosty* (Hardy).

[i : ʌ] in *shiffle-shuffle.*

10.3₅. Sometimes we have an intercalation of one or
more words between the two members; in some cases
with [æ] before [i]:

Dekker Sh III. 4.89 nor said *bih nor bah* | Wells N
100 *crappled* and sometimes *crippled* ideas | Butler
Er 110 *higgling and haggling* (but Wells H 47 haggles and
higgles; also Quincey 267) | Rossetti 85 *jeer and jar* |
Di T 1.99 *jingle and jangle* | (id Do 33 *petted and patted*) |
Thack N 18 *pribbles and prabbles* | *spick and span,*
rarely *spick-and-spandy* (Galsw T 340, id Sw 127) |
Kemp NineDW 10 hips .. went *swig and swag* | NP

1894 the great law of *swing and swang* | *tit for tat*, orig.
tip for tap | Blackmore LD 58 safer to *tickle* than to
tackle him | Thack N 18 *tittling and tattling* | Hope Z 80
the track *zigged and zagged* || Williams N 96 *jigging
and jogging*.

Cf also Maugham Alt 766 with *gurglings and garglings*.

10.3₆. Sometimes we have three members with three
vowels: *bim-bam-bum, fiss-fass-fuss* (Perrett, Phon.
Theory 52), *flip, flap, flop* (Wells H 11), *snip-snap-
snorum;* cf *dick-duck-drake* with the two ordinary words
duck and *drake*.

There is a childish game of *tit-tat-to* (Tylor A 307),
also *tip-tap-toe;* cf *tattoo*, older form *tap-to.*—A nursery-
rime *Ding, dong, dended*, My tale's ended. London W 22
I'll be *ding-dong-danged* if I do.

Here we may place perhaps *teetotum*, orig. the name
of the letter *t*+Lat. *totum*, but possibly felt as a three-
member compound.

10.3₇. Irregular alternations of a similar type are
seen in: *balow-baloo* (Scotchman speaking; Allen A 181).
gew-gaw. mizmaze (NED). *scrimshankers* (Cronin). *teet-
ertottering* (Tarkington). *tilley-valley* (Scott). *twisty-
twirly* (Ward). *whipper-snapper* (NED ? a jingling
extension of *whip-snapper, a cracker of whips ... on
the model of the earlier *snipper-snapper*). Walpole DW
236 The train went *whir-whack—whack-whir* and the
telegraph wires flew up. *willy-walloo* (OHenry).

10.3₈ Outside these reduplications we have similar changes
of vowels in a certain number of 'roots', often with more or
less pronounced sound-symbolism, especially with the vowel [i]
as indicating smallness (cf Linguistica p. 283 ff. and Language
ch. XX). Here only a few examples. They belong to several
word-classes:

chick—chuck | *chip—chap—chop* | *clink—clank* | *clip—clap* |
didder (more usual: *dither*)—*dodder* | *dribble—drabble* | *drip—
drop* | *gibber—jabber* | *higgle—haggle* | *jig—jog* | *jiggle—joggle* |
jingle—jangle | *lip—lap—lop* | *nib—(k)nob* | *nibble—nobble* |

nip—(*k*)*nap* | *peep* (*pip*)—*pap*—*pop* | *rig*—*rag* | *rip*—*rap* |
sip—*sup*—*sop* | *sleek* (*slick*)—*slack* | *slip*—*slap*—*slop* | *slit*—
slot | *snick*—*snack* | *snip*—*snap* | *squib*—*squab* | *stick*—*stock* |
strip—*strap*—*strop* | *tick*—*tack*—*tuck* | *tickle*—*tackle* | *tip*—*tap*—
top | *tit* (*teat*)—*tot* | *titter*—*totter* | *twiddle*—*twaddle*.

Also without the *i*-grade:

blabber—*blubber* | *clatter*—*clutter* | *slabber*—*slubber*—*slobber* |
spatter—*sputter* | *splatter*—*splutter*.

On combinations like *blare and blore, peak and pine,*
etc., see Wright R 122 f.

Repetition with Change of Initial Consonants

10.41. This produces a riming combination, the second
part of which is felt as a playful appendix to the first.
These formations have as a rule a less serious character
than those in the preceding section; many of them
distinctly belong to the nursery, where it is customary
in speaking to children to vary names and other words
on the pattern of *Georgy-Porgy.* This childish practice
explains the universal tendency to have an initial labial
consonant in the repeated syllables (thus in many
languages, see e. g. Wood IF 22.133, Lewy Zur finnisch-
ugr. wort- und satzverbindung 82 ff., Spitzer in KZ
54.220 f., Wackernagel in IF 56.161 ff. on Winkler's
Aleph-beth regel, etc.). The following pages contain only
a selection of my own independent collections, cf also
Growth and Structure § 244.

Second element begins with *p: blamby-pamby* idiot
(Wells Cl 372). *Charlie-parlie* (Maugham) *clatter-patter*
of the horse (Wells). *Jorjy Porjy* (= George, Shaw
Getting Married 187). *georgy-porgy* (vb 'to pet, to
fondle'). *hanky-panky* ('juggglery', common). John *Heez-
lum Peezlum* (Sc. 'the man in the moon'). *higgledy-
piggledy,* rarer *higglety-pigglety* (Darwin L). *hockery-
pockery, hockery-pokery,* (Sc.) = *hocus pocus. hotch-
potch* (*hotchpot* (from French *hocher* 'shake together' ?
and *pot*) was made *hotch-potch* for the sake of the rime;

then the final *tch* was changed into *dge* (cf *knowledge*
from *knowleche*): *hotchpodge*, and the rime was re-
established: *hodge-podge*). Clever little *liony-piony*! Shaw
A 6. *namby-pamby* ('sentimental', common, from Carey's
satire on the poet Ambrose Philips). *nimini-piminy*
('very small', rarer form: *nimmy-pimmy;* Wells JP 461).
nosy-posy (Maugham Pl 4.241). *numb-plump* (Carlyle
FR 325). Nicolson Byron 24 He [Byron] did not even
appreciate his [Leigh Hunt's] poetry. He would refer
to The Story of Rimini as *"Riminipimini."* *rosey-
posey* (Masefield). *wifey-pifey* (Shaw). *wimmeny-pim-
meny*, cf above. a *wobbly-pobbly* sort of voice (Priestley).

10.4₂. With *w* (thus always if the first word begins
with *p*): *Andy Wandy* (Shaw, Androcles 6 in childish
talk). (*bigwig*). *kiddie-widdie* (Maugham). *kissie-wissie*,
kittlie-wittly (Alford). *nit-wit* ('fool', prob. from G.
ni(ch)t). *kicky-whicky* ('wife, woman'; Sh Alls). *kiddie-
widdies* (Maugham Pl 4.235). *peesy-weesy* (in nursery-
rime 'little finger'). *piggie-wiggie* (Di, etc.). *pinkie-
winkie* (Sc., a barbarous pastime among young children).
popsy-wopsy ('girl'). *pow-wow* (an Algonkin word transformed after this pattern, now chiefly = 'palaver').
a *snuggly-wuggly*, lovey-dovey little chap (Aldous
Huxley). *Sweetie-Weetie* (Shaw). *teeny weeny*. *tirly-whirly*
(Burns in Farmer and Henley). *titter-witter* (Walpole).
tootsy-wootsies ('feet', NED, but used differently in
Lawrence LG 114 Calling me your tootsey-wootsey lady
[in vg song], also Lewis EG 10). *tootsums wootsums*
('feet'; Shaw, A 5 in childish talk). *twisty-wisty* stairs
(Kipling).

With *b*: *argle-bargle, argey-bargey, argy-bargy* ('talk
idly', cf *argument*). *chock-a-block* ('chock-full'). *holus-
bolus* (common). *hubble-bubble* ('hookah'). *hunkum-
bunkum* ('excellent'; Payne Alab.). *hurley-burley* (already
More U 87). *ragbag* (Wells, Shaw). *rumble-bumble* (U. S.,
Mencken). *tootelus bootelus* (U. S., 'imaginary disease').

With *m*: *cagmag* ('offal'). *Clydie-Mydie* (Dreiser AT

2.114; pet-name for *Clyde*). *curmurring* (Burns). *Hogen
Mogen* (a Dutchman, from *Hoogmogendheiden*). *hugger
mugger* (Harpsfield M 84, Sh, common). *tosy-mosy* (Sc.).
tuzzy-muzzy (Grose).

With *f*: *airy-fairy* (common). *grumpy*, *frumpy* (Di).

10.4₃. Outside these groups: *Bizzy Izzy* (kind of
'highball'; Lowndes). *canny-nanny* (kind of bee). *cherry-
derry*. play *chuck-a-luck* (U. S.). *clap-trap* (common).
crackajack or *cracker-jack*. *flibber-jib* or *flibber-gibber*
(Wells); cf Sh *flibbertigibbet*, also *flibberty-gibberting*
(Galsw). *flub-dub-and-guff* (U. S. 'rhetorical embellish-
ment'; Farmer and Henley). *flybie-skybie* ('tomboy',
Lawrence). *fusty-rusty* (Cowper L 1.170). *haggarty-
taggarty* (Barrie). *heeby-jeebies* (= jimjams; NED Suppl.,
also Golding, Hurst, Sayers). *hiddy-giddy* (NED). *highty-
tighty* (Thack) = *hoity-toity*. *hobgoblin*. *hobjob* (NED).
hockerty-crockerty (Sc., 'riding on a person's shoulder's,
with a leg over each'). *hoddy doddy* (term of abuse;
Kemp NineDW 21 and BJo 1.95). *hoochee-couchee*
dances (U. S.). *hoity-doity* ('haughty'; cf above). *honky-
tonky* (Cronin). *hootchy-kootchy* (kind of dance; NED
Suppl., cf above). *Hootsy-Tootsy* (Priestley). *hotsy-
totsy* (Wodehouse). *huftie-tuftie* ('swaggering, gallant';
old, Farmer and Henley). *humperdee clumperdee*
(Roister 36 and NP 1934). *hurdy-gurdy* (musical instrument, cf *hirdy-girdy* 'disorderly noise'). *lardy-dardy*
('affected', also *lah-dee-dah*, *lah-di-dah*). *lovey-dovey*.
molly-dolly (at a fair; Cronin). *mumbo-jumbo*, (cf Cronin
C 12 It's reassuring to meet the dear old *mumbo-
jummery*). *pitter-litter* (Wells). *plug-ugly* (U. S.). *raggle-
taggle* (common). *rantum scantum*. *ran-dan* (bells; Sayers
NT 311; cf *randem-tandem*). *ranty-tanty* (Sc.). *razzle-
dazzle*. *rumble-tumble*. *rum-dumm* liars (Lewis). *ram-stam*,
ram-stram, *ram-tam*, or *stam-ram* (Sc. 'headlong, precipitate'). *rub-a-dub*). *twiddle-diddles* (Grose).

It will be noticed that many combinations occur in
several slightly different forms.

Cf also *cockyolly* bird (nursery, 'dicky-bird'; Galsw).
chickery-pockery (Freeman) = *jiggery-pokery* (Wells).
the *jinglety-jink* o' the chains (Kipling). *topsy-turvy*
(= old *vpsie-turuy;* Greene J4 378)—and further riming
combinations of separate words like *toil and moil.* it
will neither *make nor break me. town and gown, by
hook and by crook, fairly and squarely; sneering and
fleering at him* (Carlyle FR 313 cf GS § 244.

Chapter XI

Change of Vowel without any Addition
of Formative

Plural of Substantives

11.1₁. The plural is formed by mutation of the stem-
vowel in the following ModE substantives (the vowel-
pairs having undergone various changes since OE
times):

[u(·) : i·] (OE ō > ē): *foot, goose, tooth;*

[æ : e] (OE a > e): *man;*

[au : ai] (OE ū > ȳ): *mouse, louse;* note the spelling
with *c: mice, lice.*—On *woman,* see below 11.1₃.

In Alabama, according to Payne 284, the forms
gooses, louses, mouses are found; also *mices, geeses.*

The mutation-plural is lost and *-s* is added instead
in: *book; goat, oak; borough, furrow, nut, stud* (OE studu);
shroud; friend. The same is true of *turf,* though here
the ModE continuation would have been the same for
both OE *turf* and OE *tyrf.*

11.1₂. *Irregularities.* An extra plural ending is added
to a mutation-form:

brethren: OE sg *brōþor,* pl the same or *brōþru;* in
ME the word had three plurals: *brōþeres, brēþer* (on
the analogy of pairs like *gōs, gēs*), and *brēþren* with *-en*
from the weak declension. ModE has preserved *brothers*

and *brethren*. The latter is archaic (biblical) in the ordinary sense; it is generally applied to members of the same society | *kine:* OE sg *cū*, pl. *cȳ;* in ME, the weak *n*-suffix was added. The later plural *cows* has now supplanted *kine*, which is arch. (biblical) or dial. | *breeches:* OE *brēc*, pl. of **brōc;* the old plural *breech* is now used as a sg = 'the rear end of a gun'.

On dialectal [fi·ts, fi·tn; gi·zəz] see EDG § 380, 383.

A plural without vowel-change is formed from words belonging to 11.1₁ above, chiefly to indicate a special sense:

According to the NED, *goose* = 'tailor's smoothing iron' is *gooses* in the plural.—The form is used playfully in another sense in: Swift J 21 next year I hope to eat my Michaelmas goose at my two little gooses' lodgings.

Grouse has been explained by some as a spurious sg to the supposed pl *grice* (thus a kind of "back-mutation"), but this is wrong (see NED).

Compounds.

11.1₃. Like *man* are inflected genuine English compounds. Yet the vowel is weakened to [ə] both in the sg and the pl, which are thus pronounced the same: *Englishman, -men* [iŋgliʃmən]; also: *aldermen, cabmen, footmen, noblemen, postmen.*

A pronunciation of *gentleman* with [e] is used when addressing several people, 'so we can distinguish the common pl [dʒentlmən] from the vocative pl [dʒentlmen]' (Sweet NEG § 1004). The distinction, however, is not recognized by everybody.

Woman (OE *wīfman*), too, is a compound of *man*. The pronunciation is now: sg [wumən], pl [wimin]. The vowel of the first syllable in the sg is due to the influence of the labials *w* and *m*. The [i] has been preserved in the plural owing to the front vowel in the second

syllable. The plural is now spelt *women* with *o* from
the singular. Cf vol I 3.43.

In ME, forms with *i* or *o*, for [u], were used both
in the sg and in the pl: Layamon A (Sp I. 5.359) a
Sexisc wimmon | AR Hwarse wummon liueð oðer mon
bi him one (NED) || Layamon A (Sp I. 5.540) fæirest
wimmonen (gen. pl.) but B (same verse) fairest of al
wommanne. Ch uses both forms in the plural: *wimmen*
(HF 335, 1741, 1747, 1760; L, text A, 478), *woman*
(A 213, 217; L, text B, 484, 488). In the Nut-Brown
Maid *women* pl is only found once, while *wymen* pl is
used six times (Sp III. 10). Malory 150 *woman* sg, ib
128 *wymmen* pl.

Compounds with *woman* are treated like the simple
word: *gentlewoman, countrywoman, horsewoman*, etc.

Though originally a compound, *leman* is now no
longer associated with *man* and therefore, when occasionally used, adds *-s* in the plural: Ch A 903 & 1998, Marlowe E 993, Byron Ch 1.77, Keats 3.21. The dissociation
from *man* is shown by the fact that the word, when
used in ModE, usually means 'mistress'.

11.1₄. Words ending in *-man* but not formed from
the English substantive *man*, add *-s* in the plural.
Thus always: *brahmans, Bochimans* (Carpenter L 116),
Germans, hetmans, Normans, Romans.

By popular etymology, words of this type are sometimes associated with English *man* and consequently
make *-men* in the plural: *Bushmen* (Lang C 54, but
always *-ans* in Westermarck, Hum. Marriage), *drago-
men* (also: *-ans*), *Mussulmen* (rare), *Ottamen* (rare:
Marlowe J 2368). Dryden and Byron jocularly use
Mussulwoman.

Chess-men is interesting: *-men* is originally OF *meyné*
'company', but popular etymology took it to be the
plural form of *man*, and a sg *chess-man* (rare) was
formed.

Words denoting animals or inanimate things do not lend themselves so easily to this misapprehension: *caimans, dolmans, talismans*.

Popular etymology is also responsible for *dormice* (e. g. Shelley 538) and *titmice* as plural forms of *dormouse* (prob. from F *dormouse, dormeuse*) and *titmouse* (< *tit*+OE *māse*, cf Spenser Shep C Nov. 26 titmose).

Though actually a compound with *foot, crowfoot* as a plant-name adds *-s* in the plural (NED, which however has no examples).

Muret-Sanders has *pig-foot* (a kind of fish), pl *-foots* or *-feet;* not in NED.

11.1₅. The change of kernel found in *child—children* goes back to an original difference in vowel-length [i·—i]. See vol I 4.221. *-n* is added to *childre* < OE *cildru*.

Noun Distinguished from Verb by Vowel

11.2₁. A. *Apophony* (*Gradation, Ablaut*). The difference is preserved down to our time in the following words:

abode, abide: ME sb *abode* ['vbl sb of *abide*, with same stem-vowel as the pa.t.' (NED)], OE vb *abīdan; abode* generally = 'place', rarely 'stay': Quincey 165 during my first mournful abode in London.

band (*bond*), *bind:* ME sb *band, bond* (f. Scand.), OE vb *bindan;* new vbs *band* and *bond* and a new sb *bind* have later been formed.

bit, bite: OE had two sbs: (a) *bite* 'act of biting, bite', (b) *bita* 'piece bitten off, morsel, bit'; they both fell together in ME *bite* > ModE *bit*, in various senses. New formations from the sb: *bit* vb 'put the bit into the mouth of a horse; curb', and from the vb: *bite* sb 'act of, or piece detached by, biting; hence something to eat': Galsworthy MP 327 he took a large bite at his sandwich | Priestley G 399 A bit o' supper before we start, and a good bite after we finish.

drove, drive: OE sb *drāf*, vb *drīfan;* of later date are: *drove* vb and *drive* sb.

grip, gripe: OE had *gripe* 'grasp, clutch' and *gripa* 'handful' corresponding to the vb *grīpan*, but as early as ONthmb a vb *grippa* with short vowel is recorded; in the 14th c. we find a new sb *gripe.*

life, live: OE sb *līf*, vb *libban.* On the final consonant, see 12.2₁.

road, ride: OE sb *rād* 'riding; journey on horseback; warlike expedition' (cp. *raid* a northern variant, & *in-road*); vb *rīdan.* New formations: *road* vb 'follow up (a game-bird) by the scent' and *ride* sb.

seat, sit: seat is from ME *sete* (< ON *sǣti*). New formations: *seat* vb 'afford sitting accommodation for', *sit* sb: the sit of a coat, etc.

shot, shoot: OE sb *sc(e)ot*, vb *scēotan.* To these were formed at a later period: *shoot* sb and *shot* vb 'load with shot'. Later still (18th c.) is *shot* sb 'one who shoots': Borden AS 10 Major Daviot is a good shot. Cf *snapshot* sb from vb+obj, hence also *snapshot* vb (Williamson L 4).

song, sing: OE sb *sang, song,* vb *singan.* Usually a difference is made between *song* and *singing*; in quite modern times we have a sb *sing:* let us have a sing.

stench, stink: OE sb *stenc*, vb *stincan.* There is also an OE causative vb *stencan,* continued down to the 19th c., but now rare; since ME there is also a sb *stink;* cf 12.5₁.

stroke, strike: OE sb **strāc*, vb *strīcan.* The sb *strike* is later; *stroke* vb is from OE *strācian.*

writ, write: OE sb *writ*, vb *wrītan.* Of quite recent date is *writ* vb 'serve writs on' (Frankau, Dance 41); a sb *write* is found in compounds: *write-off, write-up* (U. S.).

11.2₂. In some cases previously existing vowel-differences between noun and verb have been levelled as a simple consequence of sound-shiftings:

OE *spryng* and *springan* > *spring;* cf Juliana 50 ān
of þe sprunges [u read y] þat hit mēst of springeþ | OE
weorc and *wyrcan* > ME *wurk* > *work;* cf with regard
to *k* and *ch* 12.5₃ and for the vowel vol I 11.12 | OE
morþor and *myrþran* (cf vol I 11.12) > *murther* >
murder | OE *þurst* and *þyrstan* > *thirst* | OE *lyge* and
lēogan (cf vol I 3.123) > *lie.*

11.2₃. Often a fresh verb formed from the noun
supplants an old verb:

blind: OE adj *blind,* vb *blendan; blend* is recorded
up to 1600 in the NED, the new vb *blind* from 1300 |
lock: OE sb *loc,* vb *lūcan; lock* is now the only form
used for both sb and vb | *snow:* OE sb *snāw,* vb *snīwan*
Ch A 345 "it snewed", now always *snow.*

B. *Mutation,*

11.3₁. The old distinction has in many cases been
obliterated by analogical formations.

(1) *a* > *e*

The difference is still preserved:

sale, sell: OE sb *sala,* vb *sellan;* a new sb *sell* 'dis-
appointment; hoax' | *saw, say:* OE sb *sagu,* vb *secgan.*
Some of the forms in OE had no mutation; ME had
seien and *saien.* Both ME words would give a ModE
pronunciation [sei], but the present spelling points
rather to an unmutated origin. New formation: *say* sb
(have one's say, etc.) | *tale, tell:* OE sb *talu,* vb *tellan;*
tale vb (now rare) comes from OE *talian;* we have a
deverbative sb *tell* (now dial.) 'message, account; talk,
gossip'.

11.3₂. The difference is lost, new verbs having been
formed from the nouns:

comb: OE sb *camb, comb.* The vb *comb* has supplanted
OE *cemban,* ME *kemben;* in ptcs like *unkempt* and
well-kempt it has been preserved down to our time, see
4.3₁ | *hand:* OE vb *gehendan†;* new vb *hand* | *lame:* OE
lemian †; new vb *lame* | *land:* OE *lendan* †, new vb *land* |
name: OE vb *nemnan;* new vb *name* | *salt:* OE vb

sieltan †, new vb *salt | sharp:* OE vb *scierpan* †, ModE *sharp* 'make sharp' only dial., *sharpen* is the usual form of the vb | *swarm:* OE *swierman* †. ModE vb *swarm*. See Palmgren, Eng. Gradation-Nouns 8—9 | *tame:* OE adj *tam* (the vowel lengthened in inflected forms in ME), vb *temian* †; new vb *tame | warm:* OE had (1) *wierman (werman)* tr., (2) *wearmian* intr., of which only the latter could have given early ME *warmen*. As, however, we find *warmen* as a tr. vb as early as 1200 (Orrm), some sort of levelling must have taken place.

To the adjectives *long* and *strong* corresponded the OE vbs *lengan* and *strengan*, ME *lengen* and *strengen* †. New verbs formed from the related substantives *length* and *strength* with the suffix *-en*, see 20.5.

11.3₃. In some cases the levelling process has been the inverse, new substantives having been formed from old verbs and the mutated vowels having thus been carried from vbs to sbs.

step: OE *stæpe* sb would have made ModE *stap; step* sb from the vb (see NED) | *wem* (now arch. or dial.) 'defilement, stain'; OE had *wam* sb, *wemman* vb, but the old sb was lost at an early date, cp. Ch Ros 930 withoute wem.

Finally, we have a few instances of a sb with a mutated vowel being exchanged for the unmutated vowel of the verb.

fall sb cannot come from OE *fiell*, but a sb *feall* is found as early as OE (acc. to Sweet's Dict.) | *hate:* OE had *hete* sb, the sb *hate* dates from the 13th c.

(2) $\bar{a} > \bar{æ}$

11.3₄. The difference still retained:

cloth: OE sb *clāþ*, vb *clǣðan; clad* and *cled* (chiefly participles) are the only extant forms of the vb *clǣðan*, *clothe* (< OE *clāðian*) being now the usual vb | *hot*, *heat:* OE adj *hāt*, vb *hǣtan;* the sb, too, has a mutated vowel: *hǣtu > heat | lave* (now obs. exc. Sc), *leave:* OE sb *lāf* 'remnant', vb *lǣfan | whole, heal:* OE adj *hāl*,

vb *hǣlan*. The OE sb *hǣlu* has given us the now obsolete
heal 'health'. A new vb *hole* was formed from the adj
in ME (Havel. 2039 *holed*, altered by Skeat & Holt-
hausen without reason to *heled*). The EDD has *whole*
vb (Yks, Lin, Cor.).

11.3₅. A previous difference levelled through the
formation of a new vb from the noun:

broad: OE adj *brād*, vb *brǣdan*, ModE *brede*, which
is now dial.; a vb *broad* was in use 1250—1399, now
always *broaden* | *foam:* OE sb *fām*; vb *fǣman* †; new
vb *foam* | *stone:* OE sb *stān;* vb *stǣnan* †, new vb *stone*.

The old difference levelled through the formation of
a new noun from the vb:

bleak: OE adj *blāc*, vb *blǣcan;* the ModE adj is prob.
Norse (cf Björkman, Scand. Loan-W. 41), or may be due
to *blāc* modified by the vowel of the vb. Cp. *blake*, the direct
northern descendant of OE *blāc* | *sweat:* OE sb *swāt*,
vb *swǣtan*. ModE sb *sweat* with vowel from the vb;
the old sb has given the popular *swot* both as a sb
'hard study' or 'a person studying hard', and as a vb.

(3) *e* > *i*

11.3₆. The original vowel-difference has nowhere been
preserved down to ModE. The levelling consists in most
cases in the formation of a new verb.

feather: OE sb *feðer*, vb *gefiðrian;* acc. to the NED,
the vb was assimilated to the sb in form in 14th c.,
cf however Palmgren, Eng. Gradation-Nouns p. 10 |
nest: OE sb *nest*, vb *nistan;* the vb *nest* dates from ME |
rain: OE sb *regn* (*rēn*), vb *rignan* (*rīnan*); the ModE
vb *rain* comes from the rare OE denominative *regnian* |
sail: OE sb *segl*, vb *siglian;* even OE had also *seglan*,
seglian.

(4) *ēa* > *īe*

11.3₇. As this kind of mutation was exclusively WS, the
other dialects having *ē*, it is often difficult to establish
the exact etymology of a modern word with [i·], because this vowel may just as well be a continuation of

WS (unmutated) *ēa* as of Anglian (mutated) *ē*. In pronunciation, the old vowel-difference is now completely lost, but we have traces of it in the spelling.

believe: OE sb *(ge)lēafe,* vb *(ge)līefan.* The vowel of the noun must be from the verb. As for the final consonant, see 12.2₃ | *lather:* OE sb *lēaðor,* vb *līeðran.* The modern vb *lather* from the sb | *team (teem):* OE sb *tēam,* vb *tīeman.* OE *tēam* sb has given us the modern sb, our vb *teem* is from Anglian *tēman; team* vb is a 16th c. formation from the sb.

The vowel of the sb, not the vb, was mutated in OE, but has later been exchanged for the vowel of the vb:

leap: OE sb *hlīep,* vb *hlēapan;* our sb *leap* might come from Anglian *hlēp,* but the spelling points to influence from the vb.

(5) *o, u > y*

11.3₈. Old difference preserved:

drop, drip: OE sb *dropa,* vb *dryppan* (rare: 'the modern vb possibly from Norse'). New formations: *drop* vb and *drip* sb | *full, fill:* OE adj *full,* vb *fyllan.* The OE sb, too, had mutation: *fyllo > fill,* e. g. Ch B 2167 til she have wept her fille | Doyle S 1.31 two fills of shag tobacco | *knot, knit:* OE sb *cnotta,* vb *cnyttan.* Later formations: *knot* vb 'tie in a knot; remove the knots from' and *knit* sb 'knitted texture, style of knitting' | *lust, list:* OE sb *lust,* vb *lystan.* Later formed: *lust* vb 'have a strong desire' and *list* sb 'wish, inclination' | *stunt, stint:* OE adj *stunt* 'stupid', vb *styntan* 'stupefy'; the adj *stunt* is now obs. or dial., the vb *stint* has come to mean 'check, keep on short allowance'; the later formed, partially synonymous, vb *stunt* is mainly used in ptc only.

11.3₉. Old difference lost by the formation of a new vb:

dung: OE sb *dung,* vb *dyngan* †, new vb *dung* | *hunger:* OE sb *hungor,* vb *hyngr(i)an; hunger* vb from ME | *short:* OE adj *sceort,* vb *scyrtan;* new vbs: *short* (obs.) and *shorten* | *storm:* OE sb *storm,* vb *styrman* †, replaced

by *storm* vb | *trust:* ON sb *traust* > ME *trost, trust;*
ON vb *treysta* > ME *traiste* and other forms; *trust*
vb from the sb.

Old difference levelled by the formation of a new
noun:

kiss: OE sb *coss,* vb *cyssan.* The words were kept
apart in early ME, cp. AR 102 *Cus* me mid *cosse* of
þine muðe; in the 14th c. we get vacillation: Ch R 3663
a *cos,* but ib 3746, 3750 a *kis* | Caxton B 39 to haue
a *kysse or cusse* of her mouth | ib 43 a *cusse* .. that
same *kisse* | Prompt. P. 111 *cus,* or *kysse,* osculum,
basium (Mätzn.). In Roister 24 the old form of the sb
is used as an intentional dialectal trait. A new vb
formed from the sb was also in use at a certain time
(Wyclif Gen. 27.27 He .. *cossyde* hym), but has later
disappeared | *trim:* OE adj *trum* †, vb *trymman* > *trim;*
sb and adj *trim* of later date.

Special mention must be given to:

work: OE sb *weorc,* vb *wyrcan,* with gradation and
mutation combined. From both the OE forms we can,
through regular sound-shiftings, arrive at the ModE
vowel; the noun and the vb naturally influenced each
other. Mandv has *werk* sb but *worche* vb. The substitution of *k* for *ch* in the vb (12.5₃) is due to the sb. Palmgren p. 11 considers the vowel of the sb to be taken
from the vb.

OE sb *cyme,* with mutation, † vb *cuman.* ModE sb
come is rare except in compounds like *income, outcome*
(orig. Sc), and *come-and-go.*

(6) $\bar{u} > \bar{y}$

11.4. Original difference preserved:

foul, file: OE adj *fūl,* vb *fȳlan; file* vb is now obs.
and replaced by *defile,* cp. Sh Mcb III. 1.65 For Banquo's
Issue haue I fil'd my Minde. The vb *foul* 'become, or
render, foul' is partly from the OE intr. vb *fūlian,*
partly a new formation from the adj | *town, tine:* OE
sb *tūn,* vb *tȳnan* 'fence, enclose'; *tine* (obs. exc. dial.)

is now totally separated from the sb on account of the new signification of "town".

The former difference lost:

shroud: OE sb *scrūd*, vb *scrȳdan* †; new vb *(en)shroud* | *wish:* OE sb *wūsc* (only in *wūscbearn* 'beloved or adopted child') †, vb *wȳscan; wish* sb from the vb in the ME period.

(7) *ō* > *ē* (*ǣ*), now generally [u·, i·].

11.51. In the first example the vowel has undergone a peculiar change, see vol I 11.64.

blood, bleed: OE sb *blōd*, vb *blēdan.* Of more recent date is *blood* vb 'draw blood from a patient; give a hound its first taste of the blood'; in the first sense it is = *bleed* (which is more common) and the two words are sometimes used indiscriminately by the same author: Fielding T 1.217, 218; 2.187. Another recent formation is *nose-bleed* sb: Norris P 115 I have the nose-bleed | *boot, beet:* OE sb *bōt* 'remedy, compensation, atonement', vb *bētan; boot* sb is now rare exc. in "to boot"; *beet* vb is dial., chiefly used in the phrase "beet the fire". A new vb *boot* sprang up in ME, now only impers., = 'avail, matter' | *brood, breed:* OE sb *brōd*, vb *brēdan.* New formations: *brood* vb '(of hen) sit on eggs, whence fig.' and *breed* sb 'race' | *doom, deem:* OE sb *dōm*, vb *dēman.* The vb *deem* has been supplanted in its juridical sense by F *judge, sentence, condemn;* it is now = 'consider, be of opinion that'. The new vb *doom* is chiefly used in p. p. 'predestined (esp. to destruction or evil)'.

food, feed: OE sb *fōda*, vb *fēdan.* The new formation *food* vb has now gone out of use, but the new-formed sb *feed* is common, esp. in the sense of 'meal': Shaw 2.100 come in and have a good feed | Priestley G 237 a place where they'll give us a decent little feed ... There's no food really here, of course.—Also = 'food': Mitford OV 194 the transition from starvation to good feed | GE A 8 a promise of good feed | Churchill C 466 the feed dealer; and = 'pasture': Stevenson M 6 the feed was better | *smooth, smeethe:* OE adj *smōþ,* vb *smēð-ian;* outside dialects *smeethe* is now replaced by the later vb *smooth,* yet we have: Galsw Frat 273 the late perfume of the lilac came stealing forth into air faintly smeethed with chimney smoke | *tooth, teethe:* OE sb *tōþ,* vb *tēðan;* from late ME dates the vb *tooth* 'supply (a wheel, a rake, etc.) with teeth; become interlocked (of the teeth or cogs on gear-wheels)'. Cf 12.3₂.

11.5₂. Old verb lost, new one formed from noun:

cool: OE adj *cōl,* vb *cēlan; cool* vb 'become, or make, cool' is partly from OE *cōlian* intr. vb, partly a new formation from the adj | *flood:* OE sb *flōd,* vb ME *fleden* 1175—1225); new vb *flood.* | *ooze:* OE sb *wōs,* vb *wēsan;* new verb: *ooze* (ME *wosen).* | *roof:* OE sb *hrōf,* vb *hrēfan;* new verb: *roof.*

The substantive is mutated in OE, but later levelled to the vowel of the verb:

sough: OE sb *swēg,* vb *swōgan;* new sb: ME *swo(u)gh* > ModE *sough* (cf vol I 7.31 & 10.23).

C. *Other vowel changes:*

11.6. Some word-pairs which had originally the same vowel underwent different developments in late OE and ME owing to different syllabic structure. A few of these cases show later levelling, while others have preserved the vowel-difference.

(1) The difference in vowel may be the result of a change of quantity in one of the members of a pair.

The vowels *a, e, o* were lengthened in open syllables in ME. In accordance with this rule, the vowels of many verbs were lengthened while the corresponding nouns retained their short vowels. In spite of later changes, the long and the short vowels have remained apart. The following are the chief vowel-pairs of this kind met with in ModE:

$$(\bar{a}>) \quad \text{æ} \quad \text{—ei} : batch—bake$$
$$\text{ɔ—ei} : watch—wake$$
$$\text{a·—ei} : bath—bathe$$
$$(\breve{e}>) \quad \text{e—i·} : web—weave$$
$$(\breve{o}>) \quad \text{ɔ(·)—ou} : cloth—clothe$$

Many examples of this phenomenon are given in Ch. XII. One further example is: *slack, slake:* OE adj *slæc*, vb *slacian*. The vbs *slack* and *slacken* have sprung up in the ModE period.

On *pass, pace* see vol I 10.67; both forms are used as sb and vb.

In late OE and early ME long vowels were shortened before two or more consonants and, in trisyllabic words, before single consonants. As a result of this change we have:

beacon, beckon: OE sb *bēacn*, vb *bēacnian;* the words are now differentiated in sense, and a new vb *beacon* has been formed | *holy, hallow:* OE adj *hālig*, vb *hālgian;* a new vb *holy* was in use 1578—1622.

On *cloth, clothe:* see above 11.3₄.

In many cases, however, where we should expect a shortening, the long vowel was generalized (see Palmgren p. 5):

bridle: OE sb *brīdel*, vb *brīdlian;* the regular ModE form of the verb would be [bridl], which does not exist | *housel:* OE sb *hūsel*, vb *hūslian* | *token:* OE sb *tācn*, vb *tācnian*.

11.7. (2) Gothonic *a* became *æ* in OE, but remained in closed syllables when followed by a back vowel. To this change we owe the following pairs:

day, dawn: OE sb *dæg*, vb *dagian* > ME sb *day*, vb *daw*, which latter was supplanted by *dawn* (of the same root, prob. from ON) whence a new sb *dawn* | *fain, fawn:* OE had two adjs *fægen* and *fagen* (the suffix of the latter had previously a back vowel), and two vbs *fægenian* and *fagenian*. ModE has *fain* adj, *fain* vb,

and *fawn* vb; the last word is now differentiated in
sense from the two others. A sb *fawn* 'an act of fawning'
is recorded in the NED 1590—1744.

11.8. (3) Mutation in adjectives as opposed to adverbs.
To this group are generally reckoned the three pairs:
OE *swēte—swōt* | OE *smēþe—smōþ* | OE *sēfte—sōfte*. The
distinction, however, was not absolute even in OE,
see NED s. vv. *soot* (adj), *smooth*, and *soft*. It is now
obliterated, the only extant forms (*sweet*, *smooth, soft*)
being adjectives, from which adverbs are formed by
appending *-ly*. *Swot* as an adjective is found in Ch L
(B-text) 118 & 173, and in the form *soot* it continued
down to the 17th century. *Smeeth* is preserved in dialects
and (with shortened vowel) in the name *Smithfield* in
London.

Difference in Stress

11.9. A very important means of differentiating
nouns and verbs—not mentioned in Koziol's Wort-
bildungslehre—is by shifting the stress, nouns having
fore-stress and verbs end-stress. As this has been dealt
with in our vol I 5.7, nothing is called for here except
a few additions and corrections. This section is placed
here because change of stress often involves change of
vowel.

Native words:

ˈ*dislike* sb only in strong contrast to *like*.

outcast should be struck out, but *outflow* added; stress
in many the *out*-words is uncertain or shifting, see
Daniel Jones.

The same is true of words with *over-* and *under-*
instead of *overchange* read *overcharge*.

upcast sb is doubtful, so is *upstart* vb, but *uplift* and
upset have shifting stress according to word-class.

Romanic words:

address sb in England always [əˈdres] as the vb, in U.S.
often [ˈædres].

ally should not be marked as †, for [ˈælai] is still common for the sb; the vb is [əˈlai], but the ptc may be [ˈælaid] when adjunct before a sb.

asphalt sb [ˈæsfælt], vb [æsˈfælt].

bombard sb [ˈbɔmba·d], vb [bɔmˈba·d].

canton sb [ˈkæntən]—vb [kænˈtɔn] or in a different sense [kənˈtu·n].

complex sb and adj [kɔmpleks]—vb rare [kəmˈpleks].

dictate sb [ˈdikteit], vb [dikˈteit].

entail?, generally end-stress in both cases.

invite sb U.S. [ˈinvait]; in England only vb [inˈvait].

prostrate adj [ˈprɔstreit, -rit], vb [prɔˈstreit].

quadrate sb, adj [ˈkwɔdrit, -eit], vb [kwɔˈdreit].

refund sb [ˈri·fʌnd], vb [ˈri(·)ˈfʌnd].

research generally [riˈsə·tʃ] for both sb and vb; but some people note the sb [ˈri·sə·tʃ].

second sb, adj, vb [ˈsekənd], but in military circles vb [siˈkɔnd] some one for promotion.

surmise sb [ˈsə·maiz] or [səˈmaiz], vb generally [səˈmaiz].

suspect sb, adj [ˈsʌspekt], vb [səsˈpekt].

The change in stress is combined with a consonant-change (see 12.4₃) in *refuse* sb [ˈrefju·s], vb [riˈfju·z].

To the words of three or more syllables, in which the vb has a full vowel while the sb and adj have weakened vowels (vol I 5.74), might be added

document sb [ˈdɔkjumənt], vb [ˈdɔkjument]. Some of the vbs in *-ment* have sometimes full stress on the ending, e. g. *ornament*.

In various other instances stress is used to distinguish word-classes (I 5.75). Thus also in

arithmetic sb [əˈriþmetik], adj [æriþˈmetik(əl)].

arsenic sb [ˈa·snik], adj [a·ˈsenik].

instinct sb [ˈinstiŋkt], adj [inˈstiŋkt].

Cf also Dan. Jones sub *gallant* and Fowler MEU p. 385.

Chapter XII

Change of Consonant without any Addition of Formative

Noun distinguished from verb by final consonant.

12.1. A. *Voicing:* noun voiceless, verb voiced.

This difference is found in fricatives only and is due to their being voiced in medial position in OE and ME, but voiceless when final (See also Linguistica, p. 379 ff). Consequently, in the basic form of many nouns in OE, especially those of the old *a*-declension, these consonants were voiceless, while the inflected forms had voicing (we still have: *wolf—wolves*, etc.). Nearly all verbal forms, on the other hand (in weak verbs all, in strong verbs all exc. the imp. sg. and prt. sg), had voiced consonants. In course of time levelling took place, in nouns usually to the voiceless form, though a few words have preserved the old shifting between voiceless consonant in the sg and voiced consonant in the pl, in verbs to the form with voiced consonant. With the loss of -*e* this consonant became final in verbs, too. This distinction between noun and verb has even become so established in the minds of speakers of the language that new verbs have been formed from substantives by voicing the final consonant and new substantives from verbs by the inverse process.

OF had a similar shifting between medial voiced and final unvoiced consonant. As this principle coincided with the English rule, it was kept in words imported into English and has even been productive on English soil. The French shifting was different from the English in that it also comprised stops, but no instances of this are found in words adopted in English: where French has *dart* sb—*darder* vb, English has adopted *dart* and formed a new vb *dart* from it.

In some of the word-pairs given below there is also a difference in stem-vowel, see Ch XI.

12.2₁. (1) *f—v*

There is a curious interrelation between the existence of plurals in [-vz] to singulars in [-f] and that of verbs in [-v] to nouns in [-f]. Both phenomena are restricted to nearly the same set of words.

Native words:

The original difference is preserved up to modern times:

behoof, behove: OE sb *bihōf, vb *bihōfian* (nearly obsolete); Sh has once the sb in *-ue* in an old song, Hml V. 1.71, but otherwise sb in *-f* | *calf, calve:* OE sb *cealf*, vb *cealfian* | *life, live:* OE sb *līf*, vb *libban;* most of the OE forms of the vb had *f* [= v], even in OE they were beginning to supplant the forms with *bb* | *thief, thieve:* OE sb *þēof*, vb *þēofian;* the vb is rare in OE and not recorded in ME, it was revived in the 17th c. | *wife, wive:* OE sb *wīf*, vb *wīfian;* the most common signification of the (now rare) vb is 'take a wife, marry', in the sense 'act as a wife' its role has been taken by a later formed vb *wife:* Shaw TT 228 I was not born for wifing and mothering | (*woof, weave:* OE sb *ōwef*, vb *wefan*).

The old verb is now lost:

deaf: OE adj *dēaf*, vb (a) *dēafian;* the vb is preserved in Sc (Burns, Scott OM 83 dinna deave the gentlewomen wi' your testimony), now only tr.; from 1460 dates a new vb *deaf*, now arch. or dial., *deafen* is from 1597.

The old noun is lost:

delve: OE sb *dœlf* (late OE), vb *delfan;* the sb *delf* is 'now only local' (NED), the sb *delve* 'cavity' dates from 1590; in the sense 'act of delving' from the vb.

12.2₂. The difference is of later date than OE, verbs having been formed from OE substantives in subsequent periods of the language:

chaff, chave: OE sb *ceaf*, ME vb *chave;* the latest quotation for the vb in the NED is from 1726, it is now replaced by *chaff* vb | *half, halve:* OE sb *healf*, ME *halven* | *knife, knive:* (late) OE sb *cnīf*, ModE vb *knive* 1850 = *knife* vb 1865 | *leaf, leave:* OE sb *lēaf* 'leaf on tree, etc.', ME vb *leve*, now usually *leaf* vb | *sheaf, sheave:* OE sb *scēaf*, ModE vb *sheave* 1579 = *sheaf* vb 1506, Sh | *shelf, shelve:* cf OE *scylf* 'rock, crag' & OE *scylfe* 'ledge, floor', *shelve* vb 1591 | *staff, stave:* OE sb *stœf*, ModE vb *stave* 1595; cp. *staff* vb 1859 'provide with a staff of officers, teachers, etc.'. The vb *stave* may to some extent be considered a new formation from the sb sg *stave* (cf 16.2₂) | *stiff, stive:* OE sb *stīf*, ME vb *stiven*, now extinct and replaced by *stiffen* | *wolf, wolve:* OE sb *wulf*, ModE vb *wolve* 'behave like a wolf' 1702, but *wolf* vb 1862 'eat like a wolf'; Maugham Pl 4.95.

In spite of the plural forms *elves* and *loaves*, the corresponding vbs are *elf* (Sh, rare) and *loaf* 1578.

If the plural of a noun ends in *-fs*, a derived verb never has a voiced final consonant: *dwarf* vb 1626, *roof* vb 1475, etc.

12.2₃. A new substantive in *-f* is formed from an OE verb:

belief, believe: OE sb *(ge)lēafa*, vb *(ge)līefan* *(gelēfan)*; the forms with *v* were in use right down to the 16th c., now always *belief*. The sb *make-believe* 'pretence' is a substantivization of the phrase "make believe", but quite naturally the feeling that *-f* belongs to the sb leads some people to the form *make-belief* (quotations in Linguistica 380). The two forms are sometimes used indiscriminately by the same author: Maxwell G 156 He had begun his make-believe | ib 157 She had yielded to the make-belief.

leaf, leave: OE sb *lēaf* 'permission, leave', vb *līefan* *(lēfan)*. The usual ModE sb is *leave; leaf,* which is used

by private soldiers and sailors, is probably a new
formation from the verb.

12.2₄. French Words:

grief, grieve: OF sb *grief, gref* 'burden, encumbrance',
vb *grever* | *mischief, mischieve:* OF sb *meschief,* vb
meschever; the vb is now dial. or arch. | *relief, relieve:*
OF sb *relief,* vb *relever;* a sb *releue* is found in Latimer
(Specimens 2.166), influenced from the vb? Cp. Ch
B 1080 in relief of with stress on *re* | *safe, save:* F
adj *sauf,* vb *sauver;* Sh has *safe* vb 'make safe': Ant
I. 3.55, cp. IV. 6.26. In the 16th c. we also find
save for *safe:* Gammer 119 all is saue (riming to:
haue) | More U 69 for theyre sauegarde | *serf, serve:*
F sb *serf,* vb *servir* | *strife, strive:* OF sb *estrif,* vb *estriver*
| *waif, waive:* OF sb *waif* (later *gaif*), Anglo-F vb
weyver.

A new substantive in *-f* is formed from an old verb:

proof, prove: OF sb *prueve,* vb *prover.* After the loss
of final *-e,* the *-v* of the noun became *f* on the analogy
of the other pairs. Ch has as sb: *proeve, preve* and *preef,
proef, profe;* but as vb: *proeve, preve* | Mandv, as sb:
preef; as vb: *pre(e)ve,, prove.* As late as the 15th c. the
old form was still in use: Fulg 80 *proues* = 'proofs' |
Malory 113 soo he told and made *pryeues* of his dedes.—
A similar fate has overtaken *reproof* (earlier *reprove*),
Wyclif has *repreef.* In a different sense Ch *repreve* and
still *reprieve.*

12.2₅. There is one word of Dutch origin:

reef, reeve: Dutch sb *reef,* vb *reven,* see Bense, Dict.
of Low-Dutch El., p 320. A new vb *reef* has been formed
from the sb.

12.3₁. (2) [þ]—[ð] (only native words)

Original difference preserved:

bath, bathe: OE sb *bæþ,* vb *baþian;* the vowel of the
verb was lengthened in ME, now [beið]. In ModE the
two words have been partially dissociated and thus

have occasioned new formations: from *bath* sb 'a vessel,
etc. for bathing in; a washing in a bath', a vb *bath*
[ba·þ] "bath the baby"; from *bathe* vb a sb *bathe* 'the act
of bathing in the sea, etc.': Tennyson L 2.117 I walked
into the sea and had a very decent bathe. The sb *bathe*
is unknown in U. S., "bath" or "swim" are used in-
stead | *cloth, clothe:* OE sb *clāþ*, vb *clāðian;* on ptc
clad see 4.8₂ | *lo(a)th, loathe:* OE adj *lāþ*, vb *lāðian* |
sooth, soothe: OE adj *sōþ*, vb *sōðian;* the sense-development of the vb has been 'declare to be true > flatter
(a person) by confirming what he says > humour,
calm, soften, etc.'.

Old verb now lost:

wroth: OE adj *wrāþ*, vb *gewrǣðan* (ME *wrethe*).

12.3₂. New verbs formed from old nouns:

breath, breathe: OE sb *brǣþ*, ME vb *brethen; breathed*
is sometimes from the vb and pronounced [bri·ðd]
'uttered in a breath, whispered', sometimes from the
sb [breþt] as a phonetic term, and in compounds, e. g.
in long-breathed | *mouth, mouthe:* OE sb *mūþ*, ME vb
mouthen 'speak, utter', now 'utter in an affected manner',
spelt *mouth* in Sh Meas III 2.195 | *sheath, sheathe:* OE
sb *scǣþ*, ME vb *shethe* | *teeth, teethe:* OE (pl) sb *tēþ*,
late ME vb *teethe.* As the vowel of the vb is mutated,
it is perhaps the descendant of an OE vb *tēðan. There
is also a vb *tooth* [tu·þ] 'furnish with teeth; (of cog-
wheels) interlock'. Cf 11.5₁ | *wreath, wreathe:* OE sb
wrǣþ, ModE vb 1530, cf vol I 6.92.

12.4₁. (3) [s]—[z]

Native words.

Old difference preserved:

brass, braze [bra·s, breiz]: OE sb *brœs*, vb *brasian;* in
addition to the OE sense 'make of, or cover with,
brass' the verb may now also mean 'make hard like
brass', Sh Hml III. 4.37; new formation 1859 *brass* vb
'coat with brass; fig. cover with effrontery', *brass it*

'behave with effrontery' | *grass, graze* [gra·s, greiz]:
OE sb *græs* (or more usual *gœrs*), vb *grasian* 'feed on
grass'; from 1604 also a vb *graze* 'touch a surface
lightly', prob. only a fig. use of the old word. New
formations: *grass* vb 'cover with grass, place on grass,
knock down'; *graze* sb 'pasturage, act of touching
lightly' | *house* [haus, hauz]: OE sb *hūs*, vb *hūsian;*
Smith 1568: *hous* domus. *houz* operire, tegere, domus
dare. The same distinction is usually observed in *warehouse* sb & vb (D. Jones, H. C. Wyld), thus also the
Conc. Oxf. Dict., while the Cent. Dict. and the big
Oxf. Dict. (NED) give [-s] for both sb and vb.

12.4₂. New verbs in [-z] formed from substantives
in [-s]:

glass, glaze [gla·s, gleiz]: OE sb *glœs*, ME vb *glasen*
'furnish (cover) with glass or a glass-like substance'.
New formations: *glass* vb esp. 'reflect, mirror'; *glaze*
sb 'act of glazing, superposed coating' | *louse* [laus,
lauz]: OE sb *lūs*, ME vb *lousen* 'clear of lice; be infested
with lice' (Sh, now rare). Smith 1568: *lous* pediculus.
louz pediculos legere | *mouse* [maus, mauz]: OE sb
mūs, ME vb *mousen* 'hunt for, or catch, mice; prowl
about in search of sth'.

But the vb *race*, formed 1672 from the sb *race* 'swift
course', has retained the voiceless consonant.

The deverbative sb *rise* (from 1400) is now in England always [raiz]; evidence of an earlier pronunciation
[rais] is given by Elphinston, Sheridan, Walker, Stephen
Jones, Fulton, Jameson, and Smart, while Perry, En-
field, and Knowles have [raiz]; cf Ellis Plea f. Phon.
Spell. 1848 p. 175: '*rise* [rais] s., [raiz] v. (this distinction is not usual, both words being pronounced [raiz])'.
The pronunciation [rais] must have been due to analogy
with other word-pairs with [s]—[z]. According to Sapir
(Language 1921,78) many Americans use [s] in the
noun, e. g. "the rise of democracy".

Doubtful cases:

gloss, gloze: sb 1548 'explanatory word, interpretation' was refashioned in the 16th c. after Lat *glossa*. ME had *glose* sb (>ModE *gloze*, now rare) 'gloss, comment, flattery', *glosen* vb (> ModE *gloze*) 'comment upon, interpret, palliate'. New formation: *gloss* vb 'insert glosses in (a text); veil with glosses, explain away'. —These words have been mixed up with another sb *gloss* 'lustre' (from Norse?), whence the vb *gloss* 'put a gloss on, veil in specious language'. The two vbs *gloss* are now hardly distinguishable, cp. two quotations in NED sub both vbs.

noose: origin obscure. Ellis has sb [nu·s], vb [nu·z], dictionaries vacillate, the sb is often given as [nu·z]; D. Jones has *noose* (s. v.) nu·s [nu·z], H. C. Wyld [z, s] for both sb & vb.

12.4₃. Romanic words.

The old difference preserved:

advice, advise: F sb *avis*, vb *aviser* | *close* [klous, klouz]: F adj *clos*, no corresponding vb in OF, OE had a vb *clȳsan* from *clūs(e)* (< late Lat *clusa*); this vb 'came down to 13th c. in form *cluse-n* (ü), and probably *close-n* was at first viewed simply as a frenchified pronunciation of this earlier word' (NED). New formation: *close* [klouz] sb 'conclusion, end', spelt *cloze* in Sh H4A I. 1.13; the existence of this sb seems to have caused some confusion, the two sbs being often mixed up and the pronunciation being given now with [s], now with [z] | *device, devise:* OF sb *devis* (&-*devise* f.), vb *deviser* | *diffuse* [di·fju·s, di·fju·z]: F adj *diffus*, vb *diffuser* | *price, prize:* OF sb *pris* (Lat. *pretium*, now *prix*), vb *prisier*. The sb and vb are now differentiated in sense: sb = 'money for which a thing is bought or sold', vb = 'value highly'; a new sb and vb have been formed to fill the gaps: *price* vb 'note the price of', *prize* sb 'reward'. In this sense Ch had *pris*, with [s] as shown by the rimes A 67, 237. Note that *praise*, sb and vb

with [z] etymologically belongs to these words | *refuse*
['refju·s, ri|'fju·z]: OF sb *refus*, vb *refuser;* the spelling
refuce for the sb is found in Prompt. P. The sb and
vb are now not felt as belonging closely together: the
proper verbal substantive is *refusal*, recorded from
1474 | *use* [ju·s, ju·z]: OF *us*, vb *user*. Smith 1568: *ūz*
uti. *ūs* usus. Note *used to* '(was) accustomed to' [ju·stu],
see vol IV 1.9 with many quotations.—The above
distinction applies also to *abuse* and *misuse*.

The verb now lost:

peace: OF sb *pais;* there was formerly a vb *paisen*
(< OF *paiser*) recorded 1275—1652 in the NED.

12.4₄. New verb in [-z] formed from old noun in [-s]:

grease [gri·s; gri·z]: OF sb *gresse;* the vb (recorded
from 1440) was probably formed on English soil, cf F
graisser which would have given a form in [-s]. Wallis
p. 27 has sb [s], vb [z], but the pronunciation with [s]
in the vb is still often heard.

New noun in [-s] formed from old verb in [-z]:

excuse [iks|'kju·s, iks|'kju·z]: if taken direct from F
excuse, the noun would have had [-z], the unvoicing
(found as early as Cooper 1685) must be due to analogy
with other word-pairs in English.

The original difference levelled through the formation
of a new noun:

carouse: the sb (< F < German *garaus*) originally
with [-s], [-z] must come from the vb | *repose:* the form
of the sb is taken from the vb, F *repos* would have
given [-s].

12.4₅. Doubtful cases:

licence sb, *license* vb: does the difference in spelling
indicate different pronunciations? Now both have [s] |
practice, practise: both words now [præktis]. The etymology is difficult: acc. to the NED, earlier *practic* sb
was supplanted by *practyse, -ize,* from the vb, later
assimilated to words in *-ce* (justice, service, etc.). But
did the pronunciation change with the spelling? The

vb was originally *practize* with stress on the last syllable
and with voiced final consonant, later unvoiced under
the influence of the noun. On the pronunciation see
also Linguistica 363 | *promise:* both sb and vb now [-s].
Smart has sb [s], vb [z], Walker [z] for both | *recompense:*
both sb and vb now [s], but was there formerly a differ-
ence? Cp. Dryden 5.193 recompence sb | ib 5.194
recompense vb | *sacrifice:* the pronunciation with [s] is
now common for both sb and vb, though some dictionaries give [z] for the vb and [s] for the sb (thus
e. g. Smart), and others [z] for both (Walker).

12.5₁. B. *Shifting* [tʃ]—[k]

A series of verbs and nouns differ in this way because
[k] before palatal vowels became [tʃ] in OE. It is usually
the noun that has the palatalized form, sometimes, however the verb. Many of these pairs are not now felt as
closely connected.

Noun [tʃ], verb [k]:

batch [bætʃ], *bake* [beik]: ME sb *bache*, OE vb *bacan*.
New formation: *bake* sb 'biscuit' (Sc); 'act, process, or
result, of baking' | *breach* [briˑtʃ], *break* [breik]: OE sb
bryce, *brice* (> early ME *bruche* > (infl. f. F *brèche*)
ME *breche*), vb *brecan* | *drench* [dren(t)ʃ], *drink* [driŋk]:
OE sb *drenc*, vb *drincan;* OE had two other sbs *drinc*
and *drinca*, which have given the ModE sb *drink*, and
a causative vb *drencan*, whence the ModE vb *drench* |
match [mætʃ], *make* [meik]: OE sb (*ge*)*mæcca*, vb *macian* |
speech [spiˑtʃ], *speak* [spiˑk]: OE sb *spǣc* (earlier *sprǣc*),
vb *specan* (earlier *sprecan* from Lat. *exprœdicare??*).
To the vb *bespeak* there is no sb in [tʃ], we have a late
formation *bespeak* sb a bespeaking, a benefit night' |
stitch [stitʃ], *stick* [stik]: OE sb *stice*, vb *stician*. New
vb *stitch* 'fasten together with stitches' and a new sb
stick 'a single act of sticking' | *stench* [sten(t)ʃ], *stink*
[stiŋk]: OE sb *stenc*, vb *stincan;* OE had also a causative
vb *stencan*, now obs. A sb *stink* has later been formed
from the vb: Swift J 105 this house has a thousand stinks

in it | Coleridge 452 I counted two and seventy stenches. All well defined, and several stinks! | *watch* [wɔtʃ], *wake* [weik]: OE sb *wæcce*, vbs *wacan* & *wacian;* the vb *watch* need not be a later formation from the sb, OE had a pres ptc *wæccende* from **wæccan*.

12.5₂. Old difference lost, new noun formed from verb:

ache: OE sb *œce*, vb *acan*. The two words were kept apart till well into the ModE period. Hart Orthographie (1569): 'We abuse the name of h, calling it ache, which sound serueth very well to expresse a headache, or some bone ache'. Baret Alvearie (1573): 'Ake is the verbe of this substantiue ache, ch. being turned into k'. The Sh-folio of 1623 everywhere writes *ache* for the sb but *ake* for the vb (except in compounds, see below); that the sb was [eitʃ] in Sh is also shown by the fact that the pl form always counts as two syllables (3 instances, see Sh-lex); furthermore, the identity in form of *ache* sb and the letter *h* is a source of numerous puns in Sh and other Elizabethan writers; conversely, *ake* vb rimes to *brake* and *sake* in Sh (Sh-lex).—On the other hand, that *ake* was early in use as a sb is evidenced by Bale Three L 412 toth ake | 534 head ake. In Sh, too, we find *ake* as a sb, but only in compounds: cp. Tro II. 3.20 & V. 1.26 bone-ach | Hml III. 1.62 heart-ake (the same in Q₂, not in Q₁) | Ado III. 2.21 & 25 tooth-ach | ib III. 2.72 & V. 1.36 tooth-ake.—The only pronunciation now used is [eik], cp., however, Thack P 89 Lady Brouncker .. never wanted medicine certainly, for she never had an *h* in her life. The spelling was finally settled as *ache* by Johnson, who mistakenly derived the word from Gr. *akhos*.

New verb formed from noun:

pitch: OE sb *pic*, vb *pician* 'cover with pitch'. The palatalization was regular in the sb in OE, but not in the vb; ME had as vb *pik(k)en* and *pichen*, now only *pitch* under the influence of the noun.

12.5₃. Noun [k], verb [tʃ]:

Old difference preserved:

bleak, bleach: OE adj *blāc*, vb *blǣcan.* As for the vowel, see 11.3₅.

Old difference lost, new substantive formed:

work: OE sb *weorc*, vb *wyrcan;* cf above 11.3₉.

12.6. C. *Other consonant shiftings.*

web, weave: both words had ƀ originally. This sound, when doubled under the influence of a following *j* (as was the case in the sb) became *bb* in OE, later reduced to *b*. In medial position ƀ became *v* in English; cf *live.*

Chapter XIII

Vocalic Endings

13.1. After considering those types of derivation in which the kernel is used in itself unchanged or with internal change (in vowel or consonant) we shall now proceed to those types in which a formative is added either as an inflexional ending or suffix, or as a prefix. In this vast domain we meet with a great number of instances in which such an addition is accompanied by an internal change. This may be due to pre-historic vowel-changes like apophony (ablaut, gradation), or to the later mutation (umlaut), or finally to a great many changes in historical times; the latter were dealt with historically in vol I. It would be impracticable here to give a complete systematic treatment of such changes, but they will be dealt with in connexion with the sound or sounds added before or after the kernel.

Thus, to give a few examples, the difference between *descend* : *descent* | *thrive* : *thrift* | *thief* : *theft* will be treated under the ending *-t*, and similarly

steal : *stealth* | *broad* : *breadth* | *long* : *length* | *wide* : *width*—under *-th*

wise : *wisdom*—under *-dom*
throat : *throttle*—under *-le*
colony : *colonial*—under *-al*
seam : *seamstress*—under *-stress*
dear : *darling*—under *-ling*
Christ : *christen*—under *-en*, and
please : *pleasant* : *pleasure*—under *-ant* and *-ure*, etc.

But as this is a grammar of Modern English, no mention will generally be given of such prehistoric changes by which the same 'root' appears in different forms in instances like *learn* : *lore* | *do* : *deed* | *blithe* : *bliss* | *fleet* : *float* | *rise* : *rear* | *cold* : *cool*, etc.

-y, -ey, -ie [-i]

13.2. This ending is of different origin. It is used
1) as a substantival suffix to form nexus-words,
2) as an adjectival suffix to form adjectives from substantives, adjectives, and verbs, and
3) as a diminutive and hypocoristic suffix added to substantives, and in elliptical forms of substantives and adjectives.

It finally occurs in verbs developed from OE *-ian*-verbs, but in this function it is now obsolete except in dialects, cf NED *-y*, suffix[2].

-y in Substantives

13.2₁. *-y*, from the F participal ending *-é(e)*, from L *-atus*, *-ata*, *-atum*, as in *deputy* (F *député*), *treaty* (F *traité*), *assembly* (OF *asemblée*), has been used to form a few nexus-words only, viz. *enquiry* and *expiry*, and *entreaty*.

In other substantives *-y* represents F *-ie*, from L *-ia* (Gk *-ia*, *-eia*), as in *comedy*, *glory*, *history*, etc. This *-y* has been little used as an independent suffix in English. Early forms are *beggary* and *coopery* (on the analogy

of words in *-ry*); in recent times we have learned words
like *brachycephaly, synchrony,* etc.

But it enters as the final part of a large number of
compound suffixes, such as *-ancy, -cy, -ery, -ry,* and
learned suffixes like *-graphy, -logy, -archy,* etc. Some of
these suffixes will be dealt with separately in following
chapters.

13.2₂. A subdivision of nexus-words in *-y* is formed
by those in *-cy* and *-sy*.

-cy [-si] is from L *-cia, -tia*. In late Lat. and in F
-t- became *-c* . Thus we have a group from med. Lat.
words in *-ia* added to participial stems in *-at-*, such
as *advocacy, prelacy,* or from adjs or sbs in *-ate,* e. g.
*accuracy, curacy, degeneracy, delicacy, diplomacy, im-
mediacy, intimacy, inviolacy* (Meredith E 81), *magistracy,
piracy, privacy*. In some of them we have L words in
-atio. This is also the case with *conspiracy* and *procuracy*.

Lunacy is formed irregularly from *lunatic* on the analogy of the type *diplomacy : diplomatic*.

The ending *-acy* is also found in some loanwords,
where we have no corresponding word in *-ate: fallacy*
(formerly *fallace,* as in Bacon A 43.26 fallaces; from L
fallacia), *abbacy, papacy,* and *supremacy*.

The ending *-ncy* very often corresponds to words in
-ant, -ent, see below 21.6.

From words of this type *-cy* was extended to words
in *-n,* as in *aldermancy, captaincy, chaplaincy, ensigncy*
(Austen P 383 | Thack E 1.274), and even to words in
-t, as in *banktruptcy, baronetcy, idiotcy* (Meredith E 436),
a by-form of *idiocy* (Ruskin Sel 1.4), and *paramountcy*
(NP 1899).

Normalcy is especially U. S.

The variant spelling *-sy* occurs only in loanwords.
In a few cases it represents Gk (L) *-sia,* thus in *apostasy,
idiosyncrasy, leprosy* (?), in others Gk *-sis,* e. g. in *poesy,
hypocrisy,* or Gk *-tis* as in *pleurisy*. In others (*courtesy,
embassy, minstrelsy*) it is of different origin.

Note the difference made between the sb *prophecy* [prɔfisi] and the vb *prophesy* [prɔfisai].

The F spelling is retained in *bourgeoisie*, whence a facetious Am *booboisie*, Mencken AL⁴ 560.

13.2₃. -*cracy* [-krəsi] (-*ocracy* [-lɔkrəsi]), is from F -*cratie*, Med. L. -*cratia*, Gk -*kratia*, and denotes 'power, rule', as in the loanwords Gk *aristocracy*, *democracy*, *plutocracy*, *theocracy*, F *bureaucracy*, later also 'class of rulers'. From such words -*o*- came to be considered as belonging to the suffix, and new derivatives are generally formed by adding -*ocracy*, as in *technocracy*. -*ocracy* is added to native roots in words used in colloquial or newspaper language, all with a pejorative, mocking sense, e. g. *barristerocracy*, *beerocracy*, *blackguardocracy* (Shaw TT 302), *cottonocracy*, *landocracy*, *millionocracy*, *mobocracy*, *snipocracy* (from slang *snip* 'tailor'), *snobocracy*, etc. Why not *gangsterocracy* to describe present conditions? By subtraction -*ocracy* may even be used independently as in 'the bureau-ocracy, shop-ocracy, trade-ocracy, and other -ocracies' (NED: -*o* 3.).

-*y* in Adjectives

13.3₁. -*y* in adjs corresponds to OE -*ig*. Some of the old words are now isolated: *dizzy*, *giddy*, *empty*, *merry*, *pretty*, etc., but others are still felt as derived from sbs: *bloody*, *crafty*, *icy*, *mighty*, *misty*, *speedy*, etc. In ME and ModE innumerable new adjs have been formed on the same pattern: *bushy*, *flowery*, *needy*, *dirty*, *dreamy*, *noisy*, *racy*, *throaty*, etc. "New derivatives tend in a large measure to be colloquial, undignified, or trivial" (NED).

From the large number of words coined after 1800, I shall give a few rarer ones only (in chronological order with first date in NED): *goosey* (1816 Nursery rhyme: goosey, goosey gander), *oniony* (1838; Sherriff), *almondy* (1847; Mannin), *slangy* (1850), *lemony* (1859;

Morley), *churchy* (1864), *hefty* (1867), *jumpy* (1869),
painty (1870; Aumonier), *jowly* (1873; Maugham),
circussy (1876), *Christmassy* (1882; Williamson), *bossy*
(orig. U. S. colloq. 1882; Lawrence), *classy* (1891; Shaw),
pomatumy (1894; Ritchie), *arty* (Galsw Sw 262 a gift
should be nothing arty or elegant; Maugham), *Londony*
(1907; Galsw, Bennett), and *sexy* (1928; Shaw).

To these I may add a few recent formations not recorded in NED: *actressy* (Maugham PV 47), *Bibly*
(Rose Macaulay T 94 old Bibly clergymen), *chickeny*
(Galsw T 79 you were as chickeny as an old hen),
gandery (Caine E 79 screeching like an old gandery
goose), *indoory* (Shaw TT 137 my mother was that
indoory that she grudged having to go out and do her
marketing), *lineny* (Morley Human Being 134 a crisp
lineny smell), *trainy* (Wells H 93 I'm so dirty and
trainy).

13.3₂. We also find a great many slang-words in -*y*,
some of them of obscure origin, others special applications of ordinary -*y*-words, e. g. *balmy* or *barmy* 'mad'
(orig. obsc.), *bluggy* ('a euphemistic twisting of bloody'
(Partridge); Sayers GN 444 a nasty bluggy sight),
cheesy 'stylish', *dippy* 'mad' (RBennett), *dotty* 'silly'
(Shaw TT 145; cf off his dot), *fishy* (common), *loopy*
'silly' (Sayers), *nervy* 'coolly or impudently confident'
(Herrick), *nutty* 'mad' (esp. U. S.), *potty* 'mad' (Mackenzie, Galsw, etc.), *shirty* 'ill-tempered' (Sherriff; cf don't
get your shirt out), *squiffy* 'drunk' (Kipling), and
finally a word derived from a pronoun: *itty* (U. S.
college slang) 'sexually attractive' (Weseen 186).

-*y* may be added to compounds and other types of
word-combinations, e. g. *moon-beamy* (Keats 15), *sun-
beamy* (ib 17), *goose-fleshy* (Walpole), *graveyardy* (Freeman, Walpole), *headachy* (Gissing), *open-airy* (Milne),
other-worldy (Walpole), *seaweedy* (Sayers), *second-classy*
(Herrick), *Exeter Hall-y* (NP 1906), *milk and watery*

(Di), *spick-and-spandy* (Galsw; from *spick and span;
spandy* esp. U. S., see Storm EPh 909), *thunder and
lightiɳy* (Galsw), *end-of-termy* (Walpole).

13.3₃. Special Cases.

Pigmy sb is often used as an adj because of -*y* (given
as an adj Roget 193).

Naughty is now felt as separated from *naught*, cf.
Hood Miss Kilm. She had an idea from the very sound,
That people with naught were naughty.

-*y* takes the place of OE -*e* in *ready*, OE *ræde*, and
murky, OE *murke;* cf also *wary* by the side of obs.
ware (*aware*).

Earthy, recorded in NED from 1398, is often quoted
in the Biblical phrase 'of the earth, earthy' (1 Cor.
15.47). Some expressions formed on the analogy of
this phrase have been collected by Fijn van Draat,
EStn 43.299 ff. I have further noted Butler W 99
everything was of the sea sea-ey (not in NED) | NP
1905 it is a thing of the stage stagy.

Spelling

13.3₄. Cf Fowler MEU -*ey* & -*y* in Adjectives.

After a consonant -*e* is generally dropped before -*y*,
thus in *easy, greasy, hasty, racy, shady*, etc.

Wavering between -*y* and -*ey: chanc(e)y, gam(e)y,
hom(e)y, hors(e)y, mous(e)y, stag(e)y*, etc.

The rare word derived from *hole* is always spelt
holey, so as not to be mistaken for *holy* 'saint'.

After a vowel *e* is preserved: *bluey, gluey*.

And -*ey* is generally added after another vowel than
e: clayey, skyey (Hewlett F 61); but note Chaplin: It
must be nice to act 'cryie' parts.

Note *fiery* from *fire*.

A consonant after a stressed vowel is doubled (cf
vol I 4.94): *catty, chinny, chummy, leggy*.

-*ck*- is written instead of -*cc-: carbolicky, panicky*, etc.

Pronunciation

13.3₅. The suffix is generally added to the radical without any change of pronunciation.

In *worthy* from *worth* [wəˑþ], probably the earliest derivative in *-y* after *th*, we have [ð]. Otherwise we have [þ], thus in *breathy*, *earthy*, *healthy*, *wrathy* [rɔˑþi, U. S. raˑþi], *teethy*, *deathy*, etc.

From *scurf* we have both *scurvy* and the rarer *scurfy* (Lewis MA 7), from *sheaf*, *sheafy;* from *leaf* an older *leavy* (Sh, Milton) and younger *leafy;* both *shelvy* (Sh) and *shelfy* occur.

In *greasy* from *grease* [griˑs] many people distinguish between [griˑsi] 'covered with or containing grease', and [griˑzi] 'slippery', see Dan. Jones. From *louse* we have *lousy* with [z].

Crumby is pronounced [krʌmi], cf the earlier spelling *crummy*.

Adjectives in -y Derived from Adjectives

13.3₆. From late ME it has been possible to add *-y* to adjs, thus generally modifying the sense of the original word much in the same way as *-ish* 'of the nature of' or 'somewhat'.

Examples are: *bleaky*, *bluey*, *greeny* (and other colour adjectives), *lanky*, *paly* (chiefly poet.; Keats Endymion I. 341), *plumpy*, *rummy* (slang), *stouty*, *vasty* (in mod. use only in quoting or imitating Sh).

Some of the early formations are now obsolete, e. g. *cooly*, *hugy* (Marlowe T 1187), *moisty* (Ch, Spenser).

Bonnie (from ME *bon, bonne* < F; now chiefly northern and Sc.) and *haughty* (from *haught* < F *haut*) have supplanted the shorter forms. *Dusky* is commoner than *dusk* adj, which in some senses is obsolete. *Blacky* and *darky* are frequently used as substantives (= 'negro'). So is also *deary;* note the exclamation *Dear, deary me!*

Stilly (chiefly poet.) may have the suffix -*ly* (thus
NED).

The suffix is still productive with adjectives: Galsw
F 105 a goldeny, misty, lovely feeling | Lewis MS 106
her woodeny ... cottage.

Adjectives Derived from Verbs

13.3₇. Common forms obviously derived from verbs
are *catchy, choky, drowsy, quaky, quavery, shivery, slippy,
swimmy* (Galsw WM 176 [after a strong drink] If only
she could go swimmy), *twiddly* (Galsw F 360 in the
twiddly chair), and others.

In many cases it is immaterial whether the *y*-form
is derived from sb or vb: e. g. *bumpy, creepy, dancey,
screwy* 'mad', *shaky, smelly, touchy, trembly,* and *washy*.

Thus also the following rare forms or nonce-words:
bothery (Galsw F 161), *drinky* (Hardy F 335), *preachy*
(Herrick M 254), *shuddery* (Beresford G 364), *slithery*
(Doyle S 6.8).

13.3₈. In a few words -*y* is from F -*if*, -*ive*, see vol
I 2.534. Osborne 54 has *Masty* = *mastiff*, and cf *pursive*
> *pursy* 'short-winded'.

13.3₉. In some cases we have -*sy* instead of simple
-*y*, thus first, when -*y* was added to a pl as in *tricksy*
(Goldsm V 2.112; on the distinction between *tricksy*
and *tricky* see Fowler MEU), *backwoodsy* (Weseen 305),
folksy (Morley Thunder on the Left 225 the long famous
'folksy' hospitality of the Bayview Hotel), *newsy,*
"*out-doorsy*" (NP 1909). Next in other words: *cocksy*
= cocky, *tipsy, weepsy* (Vachell H 135 I felt odd when
you were singing—quite weepsy, you know), and perhaps *flimsy* (from *film*?), and *lazy* (from *lay*? Orig.
laysy).

Diminutives, etc

13.4₁. The origin of -*y*, -*ey*, -*ie* in diminutives, elliptical, and hypocoristic words, is explained at large by

K. F. Sundén in *On the Origin of the Hypocoristic Suffix
-y (-ie, -ey) in English* (in Festskrift tillegnad K. F.
Johansson. Göteborg 1910 p. 131-170). In *Linguistica*
(296-297) I criticized Sundén's explanation as rather
artificial, and especially called attention to the sym-
bolic value in many languages of the vowel *i* to denote
something small, hence often used with a hypocoristic value. And "Why may not the ME. pet-ending -*e*
have passed into -*i* in the same way as ME. *pite* became
pity? The vowel would be especially liable to resist
mutescence if felt to be possessed of signification."

13.4₂. The hypocoristic ending was first used in Sc.
proper names; from these it was soon transferred to
common names, and the suffix then went southwards.
According to Sundén Sc. derivatives of Christian names
with hypocoristic -*y* (-*ie*) are found from the 15th c.
(*Lowrie, Perrie* (< F *Pierre*), *Willi*, etc.).

Later English and Scottish hypocoristic forms of
Christian names are: *Algy* (from Algernon), *Andy*
(Andrew), *Billy* (William), *Bertie* (Albert, Robert,
Bertha), *Bobby* (Robert), *Carrie* (Caroline), *Charlie* (see
below), *Debby* (Debora), *Dicky* (Richard), *Dolly* (Doro-
thy), *Freddy, Georgie, Harry, Henny* (Henrietta), *Jenny*
(Janet, Genevieve), *Jerry* (Jeremiah), *Juley, Kitty*
(Catherine), *Nellie* (or *Nelly*) (Helen, Eleanor), *Reggie*
(Reginald), *Sandy* (Sc.; Alexander), *Susie, Tommy,
Vicky* (*Viccy* or *Vickie*) (Victoria), and *Willy* (esp. Sc.
Willie).

Charlie is generally pronounced [tʃaˑ(ə)li] when =
Charles, but [ʃaˑ(ə)li] when = *Charlotte* (vol I 14.7₄),
but in Di Bleak House ch 15 the two pet-names, there
spelt *Charley*, seem to be confused.

In many cases several possibilities of forming the
hypocoristic form have been utilized, thus we have

Bessy, Betty, (*Betsy,*) *Elsie, Lizzie,* (and *Tetsy*) from
Elizabeth.

Eddie, Neddy, and *Teddy* from *Edward.*
Henny and *Nettie* (Huxley L 1.36 ff.) from *Henrietta.*
Jackie (Sc. *Jockie*) and *Johnny* from *John.*
Jemmy and *Jimmy* (Sc. *Jamie*) from *James.*
Maggie, Margery, Margie, and *Peggy* from *Margaret.*
Molly and *Polly* from *Mary.*

13.4₃. Hypocoristic names in *-y* from surnames are only recorded from the 18th c., thus we have from the Johnson circle *Bozzy* from Boswell, *Goldy* from Goldsmith, and *Sherry* from Sheridan. Later forms are *Boney* from Bonaparte, *Dizzy* from Disraeli, *Gladdy* or *Gladdie* from Gladstone, *Busy* from Bismarck, and *Worthy* from Worthington, cf 29.4₅.

Of course the fact that most of these forms became identical in pronunciation with some well-known adjs was not overlooked by their inventors.

Note these two American forms: *Philly* for *Philadelphia,* and *Prexy Wilson* for *President Wilson.*

13.4₄. A number of the hypocoristic forms of Christian names have been used as common names as well (mainly in colloquial language): *archie* (war slang) 'anti-aircraft gun' (from *Archibald*) | *billy* (Austral.) 'tin can used as kettle' | *bobby* 'policeman' (from the name of Robert Peel; cf *peeler* with the same sense) | *dolly* 'doll, female pet' (1648 Herrick), also name of various appliances | *gillie* (from *Gillian* < *Juliana;* 1529 Skelton) 'giddy young woman, mare' | *jemmy* 'burglar's crowbar' (from *James*) | *jenny* 'spinning jenny', etc. (from *Janet*) | *jerry* 'beer-shop; (slang) chamber-pot' etc. (from *Jeremiah*); (*Jerry,* army-slang for German soldier from *German*) | *jockey* 'professional rider' (from Sc. *Jockey* from *John*) | *johnny* 'fellow' | *nanny* 'nurse' (from *Anna*) | *polly* 'parrot' (from *Mary*).

Some of these names are used to denote gender, cf *billy-goat, nanny-goat, jenny-wren, jenny-ass,* and *tabby-cat.*

13.4s. The earliest hypocoristic derivative in *-y* from a common name is *baby* (1377 Piers Pl.) from *babe;* from the end of the 14th c. the suffix comes to be commonly used in such derivatives, thus *daddy* (and *dad*) first in Chester Plays about 1500, *brownie* 'kind goblin' from 1513, now used for a small camera, *mammy* from 1523 Skelton (NED): Your mammy and dady Brought forth a godely babi!, *laddie* from 1546.

From 17th c.: *granny, missy, deary* (*dearie*), *cocky, hubby* 'husband'.

18th c.: *lassie, lovey, goody goody* (1745 Swift; *goody* 1756), *pappy* (from *papa*), *dovie* (*dovey*), *auntie, birdie*.

Forms coined after 1800: *blokey* (from 1840 Comic English Grammar 226 "Now, then, come along, old Blokey!" From *bloke*, which is only recorded from 1851), *matey, smarty* 'smart fellow', *softy* 'simpleton', *sweety*.

13.4e. From the hypocoristic function in common names *-y, -ie* has come to be used in forming elliptical words, mainly of a slangy character. In some of these the hypocoristic connotation is still preserved.

Examples: *Bolshie* from Bolshevik | *bookie* from bookmaker | *brolly*—umbrella (Kipling S 79, etc.) | *comfy*—comfortable | *conshie*—conscientious objector (to military service during the Great War) | *daffy*—daffodil | *hanky*—handkerchief (nursery) | *looney* or *luny*—lunatic, sb and adj | *middy*—midshipman | *mizzy*—miserable | *navvy*—navigator (for spelling see vol I 4.94) | *nighty, -tie*—night dress (nursery) | *piccy*—piccaninny (Kipling) | *pinny*—pinafore (nursery) | *toady*—toad-eater | *tummy*—stomach (nursery). Cf. 29.1 ff.

Exceptionally *-y* may for semantic reasons be added to the last syllable, as in *tweeny* from between (maid), cf also *baccy* [bæki] from tobacco.

Some of the elliptical words are generally or exclusively used in the plural, thus *civvies*—(officer's) civil clothes | *movies*—moving pictures | *oilies*—oilskin clothes (Freeman Certain Thorndyke 58) | *speakies*

—COD: (slang). Acted plays as opp. movies | *talkies*— talking film(s) | *undies*—under-clothes.

13.4₇. As a diminutive or hypocoristic ending the suffix is regularly spelt *-y* in most words. In others the originally Sc. *-ie* is the established spelling: *auntie, brownie, giftie, laddie, lassie,* and (English formations) *bookie* and *cookie* 'cake'.

In some words both spellings are found.

E from the radical is generally preserved, e. g. *matey, dovey, lovey,* etc.

Most pet names have *-y*, see above. In some *-ie* is the rule: *Annie, Connie, Maggie,* etc. And *-ey* in *Juley* and *Boney.*

But in some words the spelling vacillates: *Charlie* or *Charley, Nelly* or *Nellie, Georgy* or *Georgie, Jacky* or *Jackie, Susy* or *Susie, Willy* or *Willie.*

13.4₈. The popularity of hypochoristic *-y* is seen also in the frequency of its occurrence in a reduplicated form, either unchanged or with more or less fanciful change of sounds. To the examples already given in Ch. X I add here some more.

First of proper names, in talking to children or pet animals:

Shaw A 6 [Androcles talking to the lion:] Yes kissums Andy Wandy | Maugham Pl 4.234 little Judy-pudy | ib. my old Dolly-polly | ib 240 old Charlie-parlie.

Then a larger group of adjectives, first with simple reduplication: *goody goody* 'obtrusively or weakly virtuous' | *knocky-knocky* (Maugham Pl 4.254) | *preachy-preachy* (Moore EW 112 them preachy-preachy Brethren).

Then with rimes and apophony: *airy-fairy* (common) | *fusty musty* (Galsw IC 73) | *hitty-missy* (Am. slang; from 'hit or miss', = 'undependable, uncertain', Weseen 350) | *highty-flighty* (Galsw TL 295, etc.) | *hoity-toity* (both sb, adj, and interj; Shaw GM 312) | *honky-tonky* (= ? Cronin H 537 Is it honky-tonky tricks you've

got up there, Mary? | ib 285 a pair of honky-tonky,
morocco slippers) | *roly-poly* (from *roll* vb; Mitford
OV 52 a roly-poly child) | *swishy-swashy* 'fickle, un-
reliable' (Am. slang, Weseen 407) | *teeny-weeny*
(Maugham Pl 4.234; cf *Linguistica* 286 and 303) |
wiggly-waggly.

13.4₉. Some back-formations originate from words in
-*y: cad* sb, from *caddy* = F *cadet* (GS § 183) | *cose* vb
(Kingsley), from *cosy* adj | *greed* sb (ab. 1600), from
greedy adj | *difficult* adj, from *difficulty* sb; displaces
ab. 1600 the earlier adj *difficile* | *jell* vb, from *jelly* sb |
jeopard vb, from *jeopardy* sb | *laze* vb, from *lazy* adj |
nast vb, U. S., from *nasty* adj | *pet* sb and vb, from
petty = F *petit* (GS § 183) | *pup* sb, from *puppy* sb
(from F *poupée*) | *toad* sb, from OE *tādie* sb.

13.5. A by-form of hypocoristic -*y* is -*sy* [-si], which
may have originated from names like *Bessy, Cissy,
Susie,* etc.

Derivatives from proper names are *Betsy* and *Tetsy*
(Elizabeth), *Magsie* (*Margaret*), *Nancy* (Anna), *Patsy*
(Patrick), and *Topsy* (in Uncle Tom's Cabin).

Common names are *babsy* (baby), *boysie, chapsie,
ducksy, hotsie totsie* 'attractive girl' (from *hot;* Am.
college slang, Weseen 186), *mamsey* or *mumsie* (mama),
mopsy (mop (slang) 'woman'), *tootsies* 'feet' (nursery;
from foot).

-ee.

13.6₁. -*ee* [-ˈiˑ] is a development of the French participial ending -*é(e)*, from L -*atus* (-*ata*), and is first found
in legal terms from French (or Anglo-Latin), such as
appellee, assignee, committee, donee, lessee, presentee, etc.
On the analogy of these, and frequently as parallels to
agent nouns in -*or*, a great many law terms in -*ee* have
been coined on English soil, not only from verbs of
French (Latin) origin, as *bailee, mortgagee, electee, re-
feree* (also non-legal), *nominee* (irreg. from *nominate*),

depositee, promisee (first in Swift), *donatee, payee,*
pledgee, allottee, abandonee. etc., but also from a few
verbs of native origin, e. g. *trustee, drawee,* and *draftee*
(= drawee, U. S.; Mencken AL⁴ 180), *meetee* (Galsw
SS 288 Society lady inviting people 'to meet' prominent
people The "met" or "meetee" ... was the great
Italian violinist), *mergee* (Locke GP 256), *floggee* (Shaw
C xviii flogging may be troublesome to the flogger
and painful to the floggee), *jestee* (Sterne 17 the mort-
gager and mortgagee ... the jester and jestee), *laughee*
(NED only Carlyle), *moneylendee, pickpocketee.*

13.6₂. In Elna Bengtsson, *Studies on Passive Nouns
in English* (Lund 1927), mainly based on NED, *-ee* is
discussed at some length (pp. 79—135), and a distinction is made between

1) Direct Passive Nouns (i. e. names of persons (rarely
things) as direct objects of the verb from which the
noun is derived), and

2) Indirect Passive Nouns (i. e. names of persons (or
things) as indirect objects of the verb, or regimens in
prepositional phrases).

To her examples I may add the following nonce-
words or rare forms from my own collections:

blackmailee (Abyssinia (New Statesman Pamphlet)
1935. 49 to make of the British Empire a sort of inter-
national blackmailee) | *boree* (Butler Er 86 professional
borees) | *directee* (Shaw IW 337) | *murderee* (Huxley
Point Counter Point 209) | *raidee* (Lowndes BD 202
at a gambling hell) | *revengee* (Elizabeth F 285) | *philan-
thropee* (Rose Macaulay K 111) | *sayee* (Butler E 183
it takes two people to say a thing—a sayee as well as
a sayer) | *throwee* (Hunt A 73) | *evacuee* (from the war
1939).

13.6₃. A number of words in *-ee* fall outside these
two semantic groups, thus the following with *-ee* from
F *-é(e)*: *absentee* (Seeley E 69 and common: an absentee
landlord) | *debauchee* (note the pronunciation according

to Jones: [debɔ·ˈtʃi·] or [-ˈʃi·]) | *devotee* (NED) | *fusee* 'kind of match', and *refugee*.

13.6₄. In the following words -*ee* seems to be a by-form of the hypocoristic and diminutive -*y* (see 13.4): *bootee* (Jones: [buˈ·ˈti·] or [ˈbuˈ·ˈti·]), *coatee*, and *shirtee*, in which -*ee* has a diminutive force, and *bargee* (Jones: [baˈ·ˈdʒi·] or [ˈbaˈ·dʒi·]), *coachee* or *coachy* [ˈkoutʃi] (Cowper L 2.38), *goalee* (Sherriff F 72 'goalkeeper'), and *townee* (univ. slang; Sayers Hangman's Holiday 210 nobody says 'undergrads' except townees and journalists), which correspond to the elliptical forms in -*y* (see 13.4₆).

13.6₅. -*ee* in some cases is due to the ending -*ese* in which -*s* was mistaken as the plural ending; such back-formations (*Portugee*, etc.) are mentioned in vol II 5.632. *Yankee* has been explained by H. Logeman as Du. *Jan Kees* 'John Cheese' used as a nickname of the Dutch of New England, with -*s* subtracted as a plural *s*.

Dungaree, grandee, jamboree, Pharisee and *Sadducee* (on the pattern of which Carlyle coined *Benthamee* H 69, or with -*ee* from *devotee*?), *puttee*, and some others are more or less arbitrary English modifications of borrowed words.

In *goatee* [gouˈti·] (but [ˈgouti·] in *goatee beard*) and *settee* -*ee* is of uncertain origin, though *goatee* might belong to the group of elliptical words (short for *goat's beard*).

-ia.

13.7₁. -*ia* [-iə], substantival suffix, is etymologically identical with Latin (and Gk) -*ia* as used in names of countries, e. g. *Russia, Prussia, Algeria*, etc. (also borrowed through French, now in the form -*y*, as in *Italy, Germany, Araby*, poet. for *Arabia*, etc.). On this analogy we have English coinages like *Rhodesia* and some names of fictitious countries or localities like *Utopia, Moronia* 'the world of morons' (Weseen 369), and *suburbia* (NED 1896; 'the suburbs', esp. of London).

The ending is much used in scientific words most of them coined in modern times from Latin or Gk roots, thus in pathology, e. g. *amnesia, anæsthesia, hydrophobia* (and others in -*phobia*) -*mania* (*monomania*), *neuralgia*, etc.; botany e. g. *cineraria, euphorbia*, and many derived from personal names, e. g. *banksia, boswellia, wisteria*, and *woodsia*.

-*ia* can hardly be considered an E suffix, except in -*phobia* as formed from -*phobe* (*Russophobe*, etc.).

On *cafeteria* etc. see 15.7₆.

13.7₂. Some other vocalic endings are found in learned plurals, see vol II 2.6: -*ae, -i, -a*.

-o

13.8₁. -*o* [-ou] has not been treated in NED (with Suppl.). Joyce Ir 82 mentions Anglo-Irish forms like *boy-o, bucko, lad-o*. It is probably from Keltic, where the interjection *ó* is often used enclitically. This may explain some slangy and hypocoristic words in -*o*, thus *like billy-o, lie doggo, gabbo, kiddo*, and some others.

Note also the use of *O* in verse after the rime-word, as in Burns My Nannie O, etc. The *o* in *righto* (right-ho, righty-(h)o, right-o(h)) and *cheerio* (cheero, cheeroh, cheerho) seems naturally explained as a parallel to this use.

In slang *o* is often added immediately to some word, e. g. *floppo* (Weseen: big failure), *all sereno, leggo* (Partridge: to leg it),—but it is especially frequently added to a clipped compound (above 8.9₃), very often in army-slang, thus in *ammo* 'ammunition', *beano* (from *bean-feast*, 'jollification'), *combo* 'combination', *commo* 'communication', *compo* 'compensation', *obbo* 'observation balloon', and *ricco* 'ricochet bullet'. Cp also short forms like *dekko* 'look', and many others, thus many elliptical forms: *compo*(sition), *demo*(crat), *hippo*(po-

tamus), *intro*(duction), *memo*(randum) *photo*(graph) and
others, 29.6₃.

The suffix -*o* must now be considered an independent
suffix of a slangy, often also a hypocoristic, character,
which does not really change the sense of the root-
word itself.

Different from this suffix is the connective -*o*- in loan-words
mainly of Greek and Latin origin, and in English compounds
and derivatives formed on the analogy of these. From loanwords of the type *aristocracy, stenography, philology,* etc., and
compounds with stems like *aero-, astro-, pneumo-, dramatico-,
politico-,* etc., the *o* came to be used in words like *aero-bomb,
mystico-literary* (Graves in Scrutinies (1928) 85), and especially
names of languages and nations, e. g. *Anglo-Saxon, Franco-
British, Dano-Norwegian, Sino-Japanese, Indo-European,* etc.
Further in *speedometer* and in jocular words like *shop-o-cracy,
trade-o-cracy* (cf 13.2₃), *buy-o-logy* (the science of buying!).

Chapter XIV.

The Ordinary -*er*-Ending.

After considering the vocalic endings we next have
to deal with the ending -*er*, which in StE pronunciation
is vocalic too, as final -*r* has become the vowel [ə].

14.1. This ending is first found in comparatives, like
bigger, etc., but this will be treated together with the
superlative ending -*est* and best relegated to the chapter
Comparison in vol VII, Syntax, to which we refer in
this place.

Next in Substantives.

-*er*, -*or*, -*our*.

14.1₁. The suffix -*er* [-ə] is a development of an
ending of agent substantives common to all Gothonic
languages. It has been suggested that the suffix was
borrowed from Latin -*arius*, see H. Möller, *Zur ahd.
allit. poesie* 1888, 142.

The suffix -ere was originally used to form designations for persons from substantives, e. g. OE *bocere*,
Goth. *bokareis*, cf Lat. *librarius*, but in English it became of special importance as a means to form agent-
nouns from verbs, a word like OE *fiscere*, from *fisc*,
being interpreted as formed from *fiscian* vb; similarly
fuglere from *fugol*, cf *fuglian* 'catch birds' (> *fowler*),
hence verbal derivatives already in OE such as *bæcere*
from *bacan* 'bake', ModE *baker*.

14.1₂. This primary -er coalesces with other suffixes,
which in course of time have developed the same pronunciation [-ə] (see e. g. the rimes in Sh (Franz § 43)
senator : *singular* : *publisher*, etc.), and in some cases
also have adopted the spelling -er:

(1) F -er, -ier (from Lat. -(i)arius, thus perhaps
ultimately identical with Gothonic -er), as in *carpenter*
from ONF *carpentier*, *officer* from OF *officier*.

On -eer, -ier, from the same source but stressed, see 15.5₁.

(2) F. -aire (etymologically the same form), in Engl.
generally -ar, as in *vicar* from F. *vicaire*.

On stressed -aire and on -ary, also from Lat. -arius, see
15.4₃ and 15.8.

(3) OF nom. -ere < Lat. -ator, acc. -eór < Lat.
-atorem. In ME this generally gave the form -our,
which was later simplified to -or, or -er, see below.

(4) Latin -or, borrowed direct from Latin, and generally with the spelling -or preserved, or through French,
often with the spelling -our. On *saviour* see 14.5₂.

On the inserted *n* in *message* : *messenger*, *passenger*,
porringer and others see vol I 2.429.

14.1₃. Sometimes there are two formations from the
same root, one formed on English soil direct from the
verb, and one borrowed from Latin, e. g. *composer*
'one who composes (music)', *compositor* 'type-setter'
(Phelps Mod. Novelists 57 Howells was a compositor

before he was a composer), *defender* 'one who defends', *defensor* (rare), a Roman law term, 'counsel for the defence' (Note here a third derivative *defendant* 'a person sued in a court of law'; corresponding to *offend* we have only *offender*), ⎸*executer* (rare) 'one who executes'⎸ *executor* 1) [ig⎸zekjutə] 'one appointed to execute a will', 2) [⎸eksikju·tə] = *executer* (Note also *executioner*).

In some cases -*er* has ousted other endings, e. g. OE -*a*, as OE *hunta*, ME *hunte*, supplanted by the clearer form ME *huntere*, ModE *hunter;* OE *bylda*, ME *bilder*, ModE *builder.*

Compare, further, ME *scriveyn* from OE *escrivain* (ModF *écrivain*) > ME and ModE *scrivener.*

Similarly *parishioner* from F *paroissien*, earlier Eng. *parishen, parishion,* and *practitioner* from F *pra(c)ticien,* earlier *practician,* as if derived from a substantive in -*ition.*

Partner looks as if formed from *part* + a suffix -*ner,* but is a development of ME *parcener,* OF *parçonier,* from *partition*+-*ier.*

Here probably also belong *astronomer* (NED 1366), cf the earlier *astronomien, -an* (from OF), and *astrologer* (NED c 1374 Chaucer), cf *astrologien, -an* (also in Ch from OF); from these -*er* was transferred to later loans of the same type such as *geographer, historiographer,* and others from Lat. -*graphus, philologer, chronologer,* and others from Lat. -*logus* (now generally supplanted by forms in -*ist*). -*grapher* may be considered as an independent suffix that may still be used to coin new words of Gk origin.—*Philosopher,* formerly also *philosophe,* but F had already -*re.*

Spelling

14.1₄. As a consequence of these various origins and the development of the pronunciation of all to [-ə] we find great vacillation in spelling.

Several words now spelt in -*er* and considered as

ordinary -er-derivatives are actually French loanwords
and were formerly spelt -our and -or, e. g. *interpreter*,
receiver; -er was very frequent in the 15th and 16th c.,
but under the influence of Latin the original -or became
prevalent from the 17th c., though -our may be found
as late as the 18th c.

In some words a secondary -or has become the established form, e. g. in *ancestor* ME (= OF) *ancestre, bachelor*
(formerly -er(e)), *castor* (a variant of *caster*), *chancellor*
(ME and AF c(h)anceler), *proprietor* (from 1639; "an-
omalously formed and substituted in 17th c. for the etymological word PROPRIETARY". NED), *sailor* (from
the 16th c.; an altered spelling of *sailer*) 'seaman,
mariner', also in the phrases *a good sailor, a bad sailor;
sailer* of the ship (Franklin 197 it can never be known
whether a new ship will or will not be a good sailer).

The spelling -ar is found in *scholar, bursar* and *templar*
(all of them from F -ier; also in *burglar* (Anglo-Latin
burg(l)ator), *registrar* and *sizar* (formerly also written
sizer). On *beggar* see 14.3₉. The great variety of spellings
may be studied in NED, e. g. sub *bachelor, chancellor,
debtor, survivor,* and *soldier*.

The spelling *visiter* is now rarer than -tor.

Pronunciation

14.1₅. The addition of -er to a root generally causes
no change in the pronunciation of the root. Thus -ng
before the ending preserves the pronunciation [ŋ], e. g.
sing [siŋ]—*singer* [siŋə] (as against *strong* [strɔŋ]—
stronger [strɔŋgə]).

In diphthongs before -er (-or), however, there is a
tendency to elide the last component, e. g. *purveyor*
[pəˈve(i)ə], *surveyor* [səˈve(i)ə] *mower* [mo(u)ə], *sower*
[so(u)ə], *goer* [go(u)ə], etc.

Note *prayer* 'one who prays' [pre(i)ə], but *prayer* 'act
of praying' [prɛˈə]. Coleridge distinguishes between the
two in spelling: Asserting the efficacy of prayer relative-

ly to the pray-er or precant himself (quot. by Brynild-
sen).

Similarly *layer* 'one who lays' [le(i)ə] as in *bricklayer*
[brikle(i)ə], but *layer* 'stratum' [lɛ·ə].

In some cases, especially in law terms. where a contrast to another ending is expressed or implied *-òr* may
be pronounced [-ɔ·(r)] e. g. *donor* [dounə] or [dounɔ·],
lessor [lesɔ·], *vendor* [vendɔ·], as contrasted with *donee,
lessee, vendee* (cf Sweet NEG § 1686). *Committor* [kɔmi-
ˈtɔ·(r)] as a law term, contrasted with *committee* [kɔmi-
ˈti·] (lunatic).

Note also the difference between *settlor* [setˈlɔ·] 'one
who makes a settlement on a person' (Galsw T 142
Bob said that Mr. H. was your settlor) and *settler*
[ˈsetlə] 'one who settles (in a colony, etc.)'.

Registrar is generally pronounced [ˈredʒistra·] (vol I
6.44), or even with end-stress, and *senator* in U. S.
often [ˈsenəˈtɔ·(r)].

Names of Persons

14.2₁. A large number of nouns in *-er* derived from
verbs denote persons following some special trade or
profession, e. g. *baker, brewer, cobbler, composer, drum-
mer* 'player of drum', U. S. 'commercial traveller',
joiner, lecturer, painter, plasterer, player, singer, teacher,
etc. By far the largest number of words in the Dictionary of Occupational Terms issued by the Ministry
of Labour. London 1929 (1927) are *-er*-derivatives from
verbs.

Another large group comprises words denoting persons apt to perform the action implied by the verb
often with an adj implying manner (cf vol II 12.2
shifted subjunct-adjuncts) as in Sidney AP 19 speedy
goers, and strong *abiders, triumphers* in Camps and
Courts | Osborne 198 both sayed you were an arrant
Gadder [what is now called 'gadabout'] | Shaw Getting
Married (T) 260 a *stickler* for morals | Skimpole Shaw

61 a *contemner* of all ideals | Rose Macaulay T 108
Miss Garden was no *giver* of confidences | Bennett Acc
189 I tell you Mrs. Lucas is a *go-er* when she starts |
Morley Human Being 87 women were insincere *drinkers* |
ib 154 The *laughers* are too busy enjoying life's freaks
to sit down with a pen | ib 235 Minnie is no sentimental
praiser of the past | RBennett P 89 If one's only an
unimaginative *plodder*.

A subdivision includes some more or less derogatory
slang words, e. g. *blighter* '(annoying) fellow', *bounder*
'noisily ill-bred person' (Shaw in Henderson Shaw[1] 310
a swaggering impostor of the species for which contemporary slang has invented the term 'bounder'),
clipper 'a swift mover, something excellent; air-liner',
crammer 'coach, private tutor', *rotter* 'worthless fellow',
soaker 'drunkard', *sucker* (esp. U. S.) 'one easily taken
in'.

Very often verbal derivatives in *-er* denote persons
performing an action or being in a certain state at the
moment in question. It is allowable to form new words
of this type from practically any verb, see the following examples: Swift J 179 they have not enough to
satisfy all *expecters* | Austen M 25 odd *comers* and *goers* |
Kingsley H 132 Pambo laid his hand on the *weeper's*
shoulder | Stevenson JHF 91 the tea stood ready to
the *sitter's* elbow | Ward M 312 under the *gazer's* eye |
Hardy U 82 his spectacles flashed in the *passer's* face |
King O 151 his fellow *breakfaster* | Beresford R 41 the
necessity for taking the opinion of a potential *striker*
[= one who might possibly strike].

14.2₂. Compounds of an object and an agent-noun in
-er generally denote a person who follows a certain
occupation or who habitually does something, e. g.
*bookbinder, bookseller, bricklayer, paperhanger, pew-
opener, letter-carrier* (Am.) 'postman', *tavern-keeper* (Am.)
= *innkeeper* | Sidney AP 44 *Play-makers* and *Stage-
keepers* | 47 these *Poet-whyppers* | 48 *Poet-haters* | 49

Fault-finders | 61 *Paper-blurrers* | 68 *Prose-printers* |
Stevenson K 280 *evil-doers* are aye *evil-dreaders* | Graves
G 15 he [Swinburne] was an inveterate *pram-stopper* and
patter and kisser.

Note the following derivatives from compounds of
two verbs: *make-believer* (Maxwell WF 81) and *go-getter*
(orig. U. S., Swinnerton S 217 The go-getter despises
the non-go-getter; but never as much as the non-go-
getter despises the go-getter).

14.2₃. We have the same groups with words in -*or*
denoting persons, thus occupational terms like *actor*,
author, *compositor*, *doctor*, *emperor*, *professor*, *sailor*,
tailor, and others. Many of these have been borrowed
isolatedly from Latin or French, and the verb from
which they are ultimately derived is often unknown
in English, or the connexion between the two words
is no longer felt, hence a use as the following is rare:
Macaulay H 1.174 to grant liberty of worship to the
professors of that religion.

U. S. -*or* or -*tor* is rather popular. Many new words
have been coined, and words used in British English,
too, have been given a special sense, e. g. *auditor* 'listener'
(may also be used, e. g., about children), *avigator*
'aviator' (coined on the analogy of *navigator*), *chiro-
practor* 'one who heals by manipulating the spinal
column', *educator* 'educationalist', *exhibitor* 'owner of
cinema' (now used in Brit., too), *furnitor* 'seller of
furniture', *janitor* 'caretaker, porter', *operator* 'film
photographer', *realtor* 'real estate broker', *solicitor* 'can-
vasser, beggar' (in England 'legal practitioner', cf in
U. S. *solicitor-general* 'second officer of the Department of Justice').

Others in -*or* have a clearly verbal sense, either referring to habitual action or state, such as *creditor*,
debtor, *orator*, *successor*, etc., or referring to one (momentary) action or state, e. g. *conqueror*, *traitor*, *violator*,
visitor, etc.

14.2₄. Some words may belong to more than one of these groups, thus *liar* 1) 'one who habitually tells lies' (Wells Ma 1.179 She faced the disagreeable word; was she a liar? At any rate she told lies), 2) 'one who tells a lie (now)' (You are a liar!) | *listener* 1) 'one who (habitually) listens on the wireless', 2) 'one who is listening', *reader* 1) as an occupational term (lecturer, proofreader, etc.), 2) 'one who habitually reads' (I am not a reader), 3) 'one who is reading the book in question' (Gentle reader!) | *singer* 1) as an occupational term, 2) 'one who is singing for the moment' (Who is the singer?) | *Speaker* 'president of the House of Commons', *speaker* 1) 'one who habitually speaks' (He is an able speaker), 2) 'one who is speaking' | *writer* 1) as an occupational term (author, writer in a lawyer's office), 2) 'one who is writing'.

14.2₅. In some cases *-er* is avoided, (1) because of the existence of another derivative, thus, e. g., *student* instead of the very rare *studyer* (Austen P 55 I did not know before that you were a studyer of character). Similarly *representative, correspondent*. And *connoisseur* is nearly always used for *knower*.

(2) because of the existence of another word, for which the derivative might be mistaken, thus

betting-man is used instead of *better* 'one who bets', because of *better*, the comparative. NED, however, has both *better* and *bettor* | *dyer* 'one dying' is avoided because of *dyer* 'one who dyes' | *letter* 'one who lets', because of *letter* 'written missive'; NED has quotations with *of*: builders and letters of boats, etc. | *prayer* 'one who prays' because of *prayer*, from F *prière*, 'request to God', cf the quot. from Coleridge above: *precant* is obviously a nonce-word, not in NED | *liver* 'one who lives' is not very common because of *liver* 'organ of the body', cf the pun: Is life worth living?—It depends on the liver. I have noted Bunyan P 162 I have

been a good liver | Lamb R 41 she resembled the livers
in the antique world.

Names of Things

14.2₆. Often an -*er*-derivative of a verb is used of
a thing, meaning 'what does', e. g. (1) from vb with
an intransitive sense, *breaker* 'breaking wave' | *cracker*
'thin hard biscuit' (Am. common biscuit) | *gusher* 'oil
fountain' (Am.; Sinclair Oil 25) | *trailer* 'carriage drawn
behind another; short extract from a film' | (2) from vb
with a transitive sense; often of instruments, e. g.
atomizer (Am.) 'scent-spray' | *bracer* 'a drink' | *buzzer*
'buzzing mechanism' | *carrier* 'part of (motor-)bicycle' |
flipper 'limb for swimming', (slang) 'hand' (Galsw WM
35 Give us your flipper) | *fighter* 'fighting aeroplane' |
freshener e. g. a walk (Wells Kipps 90) | *knocker* (of
door) | *lighter* (for lighting cigars) | *propeller* | *silencer*
(in a revolver, hence a revolver provided with such a
device) | *transmitter* 'wireless sender'.

Hunter 'kind of watch' is probably short for *hunter watch*,
see 8.9₃.

In a somewhat different way we have e. g. *kneeler*
'stool on which to kneel' | *taster* 'bit of something to
taste' | various names of garments, e. g. *drawers* |
slipper | *jumper* | *sweater* | *flinger* 'a necklet of fur'.

Slang-words are legion within this group: *banger*
'something big, especially a lie' | *bloomer* 'blunder' |
creepers 'legs' | *gasper* 'cheap cigarette' | (Galsw Sw 140 |
id MW 273, etc.) | *janglers* 'money' | *kickers* 'legs' |
kisser 'mouth' | *peepers* 'eyes' | *pickers* 'fingers' | *shiners*
'money, precious stones' | *smeller, snorer, snorter* 'nose' |
stealers 'fingers' | *stinker* 'cheap cigarette' (Galsw MW
268).

14.2₇. Here, too, we find a great many compounds,
some of them with the first component as object of
the agent-noun, e. g. *bone-shaker* 'oldfashioned bicycle'

(Bennett W 1.192) | *bum-freezer* 'short coat' (Maugham AK 187) | *can-opener* (Am.) = *tin-opener* | *ice-breaker* (ship) | *stem-winder* (watch) | *tooth-picker* (Sh Ado II. 1.274, now generally *tooth-pick*).

14.2₈. A special type of slang-words is formed by supplanting the latter part of a word by *-er*, and generally keeping only the first syllable of the word. Such formations are especially frequent at Oxford, perhaps originated there. Ware (Partridge, Slang 208) terms this *-er* a "suffix applied in every conceivable way to every sort of word." Some of the words are known at Cambridge and in the public schools, too, and a few belong to general slang. A few of them denote persons as well as things.

Cf above 8.9₃ on clipped compounds.

The following examples are mainly taken from Partridge, Slang 208 ff.:

bedder (Oxf. 'bedroom', Cambr. 'bedmaker') | *bed-sitter* 'bed-sitting-room' (now general slang) | *bluer* (Vachell H 101 'blue flannel jacket') | *brekker* 'breakfast' | *footer* 'football' (now general slang) | *fresher* 'freshman' | *lamper* 'lamp-post' (Vachell H 257) | *leccer* 'lecture' | *memugger* 'memorial' (Oxf.) | *rugger* 'Rugby football' and *soccer* 'association football' | *topper* 'top-hat' (common).

Some proper names are also thus treated at Oxford, often completely distorted, e. g. *Bodder* 'Bodleian Library', *Giler* 'St. Giles', *Padder* 'Paddington Station', *Pemmer* 'Pembroke College', *Pragger Wagger* 'Prince of Wales', *Radder* 'Radcliffe Camera', *Ugger* 'the Union'. Cf my *Language* p. 300.

Some of these words have *-ers* (pl or gen?), e. g. *Adders* 'Addison's Walk', *congratters* 'congratulations', *divvers* (orig. *diviners*) 'examination in Divinity', *Quaggers* 'Queen's College', *rollers* 'roll-call'.

And *-er* may even be added to ordinary words, e. g. *canoer* 'canoe', *deaner* 'dean', etc.

Another type of contracted forms are made from compounds generally with a gerund as first component. The -er-derivative then takes the form of a verbal agent-noun, e. g. *diner* and *sleeper* (in railways) | *duster* 'dust-coat' | *rocker* 'rocking-chair' | *sitter* 'sitting room' | *smoker* 'smoking-compartment; meeting with smoking allowed'; cf also *steamer* 'steamship', *liner* 'steamer belonging to a 'line'.'

Words from Substantives, etc

14.3₁. In the case of derivatives in -er from sbs it is difficult to set up semantic groups. In general they denote someone or something that has something to do with the thing denoted by the radical.

We have occupational terms such as *banker* | *colleger* 'one of the 70 boys on the foundation of Eton College' (Ward M 395) | *glover* | *hatter* | *musicker* (U. S.) | *potter* | *roper* | *saddler* | *slater* | *tinner*.

From the synonyms *jail* and *prison* are *jailer* and *prisoner* in opposite senses.

14.3₂. Some words denote inhabitants, or persons belonging in some place, e. g.

Englander (Tennyson in L 1.273 we Englanders) | *New Englander* | *Green Islander* 'person from Ireland' (Chesterton Shaw 28; nonce-word) | *Switzer* (esp. 'body-guard') | *Londoner* | *New Yorker* | the *Scotland Yarders* (Doyle St 51).

Note obs. *Romer* 'pilgrim going to Rome' (OF *romier*), from which, by back-formation the vb *roam*.

On *wisenheimer* see Linguistica 417.

Here perhaps belong *Northwester* (wind), *Southeaster*, etc. Also, though rarer, *norther*, *souther* in a corresponding sense. With a transferred sense we have *sou'wester* 'sailor's waterproof hat'.

Of a similar kind are the following derivatives from adjectives: *Britisher*, *northerner*, *southerner*, *foreigner*, *stranger* (OF *estrangier*), *outsider*.

14.3₃. We have a great many derivatives from adjunct+sb: *bitter-ender* 'one who fights to the bitter end' | *first-nighter* 'one who goes to first nights of plays' | *Free Fooders* (NP 1906) | *Free Trader* | *half-way housers* | *happy-ender* 'who tells a story with a happy ending' | *left-hander* (person) | *Red-flaggers* (Shaw TT 266) | *whole-hogger.*

Here belongs derivation from numerals with sb: *three-decker* | *three-master* | *thirty-pounder* (Fox 2.13 Carlyle is bringing out a thirty-pounder of a book) | *four-poster* (bed) | *four-wheeler* (cab) | *two-seater* (motor-car) | *six-bedder* (room) | *nine-pointer* (stag).

14.3₄. Thus also with some compounded words, e. g. *back-hander* (blow) | *birth-controller* 'supporter of the birth-control movement' | *blackbirder* (Maugham Alt 249 he had once been captain of a schooner engaged in the slave trade, a blackbirder they call it in the Pacific) | *mountain-topper* (climber) | *pea-souper* (dense fog) | *sundowner* (Austral.) 'tramp who times his arrival for the evening; drink at sunset'.

Cf further from groups and phrases: *rank and filer* | *penny-a-liner* (journalist) | *art-for-arter* (AHuxley Barren Leaves 82) | *betwixt-and-betweener* (NP 1925) | *down-and-outer* (Mannin Conf. 163) | *out-and-outer* 'great lie' | *merry-go-rounder* (Di D 96; generally *merry-go-round*).

14.3₅. The suffix *-er* is freely used to make a word from another word-class into a sb. Thus, there are several derivatives from numerals, e. g. *a oner* 'a first-class person, lie, blow, etc.' | *fiver* 'five pound (dollar) note' | *tenner* | *sevener* (NP 1906 the Labour Party ... The Seveners, as they are called, since none of them begin work later than 7 a. m.) | *fifteeners and sixteeners* 'boys of 15 and 16' (Mitford OV 166) | *forty-niner* 'man of '49' (in California).

Similarly from adjs: *a goner* (slang) 'going to die,

ruined, etc.' | *deader* (Benson DB 204 I say, do lobsters really eat deaders) | *greener* (Ridge N 89 in the class for greeners, the youngsters newly arrived).

14.3₆. With derivation from a verb+a tertiary, e. g. *look on*, there are several possibilities:

(1) the tertiary is placed before the *-er*-form, e. g. *onlooker, after-liver* (Sidney AP 43 the after-liuers), *ill-willer* (Webbe 27 which the Poets vsed against their ill wyllers), *well-willer* (Sh Wiv I. 1.72 your well-willers; now *well-wisher*), etc.

(2) the tertiary is placed after the *-er*-form, e. g. *looker-on;* on the plural *lookers-on*, see vol II 2.51. A few examples may be added:

(a) Singular. Gascoigne 65 to euery *commer by* | *diner out* | Lewis MA 253 a sigher and *drawer-out* of her M's and O's | Sh Oth II. 1.248 a *finder out* of occasions | Galsw Ca 208 a *getter-up* of amateur theatricals | Bennett L 206 *layer out* [of a corpse] | Morris E 116 The *pourer forth* of notes | Hunt A 178 to me, Voltaire was *putter down* of a great deal that was wrong | Sherwood Anderson Many Marriages 153 this *raker-up* of forgotten things | Black Ph 240 a sunset is a wonderful *smoother-down* of these artificial features in a landscape.

Note with the comparative: Earle M 22 The elder he growes, hee is a *stayer lower* from God.

(b) Plural. Sidney AP 71 *bringers in* of all ciuilitie | Lond E 87 to haue assercion be [= by] *comers betwene* of your gode desires | Sh Alls I. 2.48 *goers backward* | Maxwell F 43 other *lookers-in* | Mannin W 132 Then porters were ... commanding the *see-ers-off* to stand-away-there | Harpsfield M 41 *setters forth* of the diuorce | Merriman S 129 there is a school of *speakers out* | BJo A 3.28 the *stirrers vp* Of humours in the bloud.

(3) *-er* is very rarely added to the tertiary, e. g. Hawthorne 1.331 *come-outers* | the "*stand-patters*" (U. S.) 'supporters of the party through thick and thin'.

(4) the tertiary is left out, e. g. *caller* from *call on* |

listener from *listen to* or *listen in* | *waiter* from *wait on*.

14.3₇. Often *-er* is used without any definite meaning as a convenient, substantival ending, instead of definite formation (compound), e. g.

facer 'blow in the face; great difficulty' | *toother* 'blow on the teeth' | *header* 'plunge head foremost' | *heller* 'a hell of a fellow' | *lifer* 'prisoner for life' (Di GE 81) | *lunger* (Am.) 'lung patient' | *meetinger* 'chapelgoer' (Hardy F 335) | *Rumper* 'member of the Rump Parliament' (Swift P 22).

In *widower* the ending has come to mean male sex.

14.3₈. On the ways of expressing the relation between the object (direct or indirect) and the verb inherent in an agent-noun (his supporter, his debtor, Am I my brother's keeper?, a respecter of him, a believer in God, etc.), see vol V ch 22 and AnalSynt 21.1.

On shifted subjunct-adjuncts (a late comer, repeated offenders, etc.) see vol II 12.21 f. and AnalSynt 21.1.

But a shifted subjunct-adjunct may be compounded with the agent-noun, e. g. *good-looker* (Sitwell M 176 Rather a "good-looker", too, what?—What a curious expression, Birdie .. One you've picked up out hunting).

If the tertiary is a prepositional phrase the preposition and the article, possessive, etc, are left out, e. g. *sleep-walker* from *walk in one's sleep*, *theatre-goer* from *go to the theatre*.

14.3₉. We have several instances of back-formation in which the ending *-er* has been subtracted. On *housekeep*, etc., see above 9.7. Several vbs originate from sbs in *-er* (*-ar*, *-or*), which were not originally agent-nouns (GS § 184, EStn 70.119). *Butcher* is the F *boucher*, derived from *bouc* 'a buck, goat' with no corresponding vb, but in E it has given rise to the rare vb *butch* and to the sb *a butch-knife*. Similarly *harbinger, hawker, rover, pedlar, butler, scavenger, burglar* call into existence the vbs *harbinge* (Whitman), *hawk, rove, peddle, butle,* *scavenge, burgle.* Similarly from the F *viveur* the curious nonce-word *vive* (Galsw Sw 218 they posed as *viveurs* ... but they didn't vive; they thought too much about how to). The vb *beg* probably in the same way comes from *beggar,* derived from OF *begard,* taken over as *beggar,* or from OF *beg(h)in,* apprehended as a ptc. Cf on vbs like *edit, vivisect,* etc., above 4.4₃.

-erer

14.4. -er-er occurs in a few words: *caterer* (till the beginning of the 17th c. *catour* from OF *acatour* 'buyer'). *Fruiterer, poulterer,* and *sorcerer* are formed from the corresponding sbs in -ery by subtracting -y and adding -er. In *upholsterer* we have two suffixes: *uphold*+-ster +-er; formerly *upholster* was in use as an agent-sb by the side of *upholder;* the vb *upholster* according to NED is a back-formation from *upholsterer* or *upholstery.* From *huckster* (15.1₂) we get the vb *huckster* 'bargain, haggle' and from this a new sb *hucksterer.*

-ier, -yer. -iour, -ior

14.5₁. -ier, -yer [-iə, -jə] (unstressed) seems primarily to originate from ME agent nouns formed from weak verbs in -ien, OE -ian, as in *tiliere* (cf OE *tilia,* like *hunta,* supplanted by *hunter,* see 14.1₅), *lovier* (Ch A 80 a louyere), and others. But in these *i* has now disappeared.

At an early date we find a few loan-words from OF in -ier and -iour, such as *cottier, osier, barrier.* We also find occasional spellings with -ier of such originally F words as ModE *bachelor, chancellor, scholar, singular,* and *familiar.*

Finally, there is a number of analogical derivatives in -ier (-yer) from sbs, some of them, e. g. *bowyer, lawyer,* of early occurrence. Examples are *brazier, clothier* (earlier *clother*), *collier, drovier* (Sh Ado II. 1.201; now *drover*), *glazier, grazier, hosier, sawyer,* and *spurrier.*

-yer is the established spelling after *w* (only).

Unstressed *-ier* (*-yer*) is no more used to form new words.

On stressed *-ier* see 15.5₁.

14.5₂. *-iour, -ior* [-iə] is from F *-our, -or* added to *i-* or *e-*, e. g. *saviour* (OF *sauvëour*, vol I 9.84), on the analogy of which *paviour* was coined. *Behaviour* is from *haviour*, obs. *havour* (cf Redford W 635 *behavoure*), which is an anglicized form of OF *aveir* (ModF *avoir*), like *saviour* developed through *-eour* to *-iour*. *Warrior* is from AF *werreieor, werrieur*, derived from the vb *werreier*.

Chapter XV

Other Endings Containing r

-ster

15.1₁. This ending is generally considered an originally feminine ending which has since been transferred to the male sex, too. In an article first printed in *Mod. Language Review* (April 1927) and reprinted in *Linguistica*, p. 420 ff., I opposed this view and showed that the suffix was really from the very first beginning a two-sex one, and that when we find a sentence like "Scho was the formest webster þat man findes o þat mister", this can no more be adduced as a proof that the word was specially fem. than a modern sentence like "she is a liar" proves that *liar* is now a feminine word. In OE we find *bæcestre, seamystre* and *wæscestre* used of men, but it is true that some (not all) old glossarists use the *-stre*-words preferably as translations of Latin feminines. In later use words with that ending are decidedly two-sex words or even used of men only.

My theory offers a natural explanation of three facts which under the old view must seem very strange indeed. (1) That names in *-ster* are used in speaking of professions that have always been reserved exclusively

for men: *deemster* or *dempster* (from 1300, 'judge', still
in the Isle of Man) and *barrister;* the unusual preservation of the vowel before *st* in this word may be due to
a desire to keep the consonantal quality of *r*, aided
by a vague association with *minister* and *solicitor*.
(2) That such words were used as family names: *Baxter*,
Brewster, *Webster*. (3) That special feminines were
formed by means of the ending *-ess: huckstress, seamstress* or *sempstress, songstress, spinstress:* the ending
-ess is never added except to words denoting men
(*princess*) or at any rate indifferent to sex (*heiress*).

15.1₂. Words in *-ster* are as a rule not formed from
a verbal, but from a nominal stem and in this respect
are different from words in *-er*, compare thus *singer : song-
ster, weaver : webster*. They are to some extent stronger
than the *-er* words and might, as it were, be considered
a kind of superlatives of that ending (cp. *st!*); hence
the depreciatory tone attached to some of them, cf
also 15.1₃.

The most important of the *-ster* words not already
mentioned are *boomster* (recent slang, speculator),
fibster, gamester, gangster (chiefly U. S., from 1896),
huckster, maltster, punster, rhymester, roadster (bicycle),
*tapster, teamster, tipster, tonguester, trickster, whipster,
whitster* (Sh). From adjectives we have *youngster* and
the rarer *oldster*, further *lewdster* (Sh) and *dryster* (U. S.,
lawyer who practises in an unprofessional manner).

Finally we must mention *spinster*, which was formerly
used of a man as well (Sh, Deloney), but when spinning
ceased to be done by men, it came to be used as a kind
of nickname for old maids without any reference to
spinning. The restriction to women is like what has
happened to such words as *leman, milliner* and *witch*.

15.1₃. A tainting of this suffix (see Language 388) is
seen when in U. S. *gangster* has caused a contemptuous
connotation in new-formations like *bankster* 'profiteering

banker', coined 1932, *dopester, funster, mobster, ringster, shyster, speedster* (See Mencken 178).

15.1₄. *-ister* (earlier form *-istre*) as in *alchimister, chorister, palmister* is a loan from OF, where it is supposed to be developed on the analogy of *ministre*. *Sophister* (beside the ordinary form *sophist*) from OF is found in Marlowe A 197 and still used in some Am. universities and in Cambridge to denote a student in his second (junior sophister) or third year (senior sophister).

French Infinitives

15.2. In some sbs *-er* represents the French infinitival ending *-er*. Thus in *dinner* and *supper, attainder, rejoinder* and *remainder*, and some legal terms such as *cesser, demurrer, detainer, merger, oyer* and *terminer, retainer, (legal) tender, trover, user,* and *waiver*.

In these words the *-er* is not now felt as an independent suffix, and the same holds good of the French *-er* in a few verbs such as *(em)broider, (sur)render, saunter* (from *s'auntrer, s'aventurer*), and *tender*. Cf GS § 104.

Echo-Verbs

15.3₁. The ending *-er* is frequently found in words denoting repeated sounds or movements, such as *blubber, chatter* (*blub* and *chat* seem to be shortened forms), *clatter, flicker, flutter, glister, glitter, jabber* and *shiver*.

In some cases such *-er*-vbs are obviously strengthenings of shorter forms, e. g. *dumbfounder*, from *dumbfound* with the same sense (Ward RE 3.109, Rose Macaulay I 16), *patter* 'make a succession of light sounds or steps' from *pat* (but *patter* 'chatter, utter mechanically' is a shortening of *paternoster*), *quaver* from ME *quaven* (or a variant of *quiver*?), *sputter* from ME *spouten* 'spout', *stutter* from ME *stutten*, and *waver* from *wave*.

15.3₂. Often there is an etymological relationship between a monosyllable and the -*er*-form, e. g.
beat : *batter, climb* : *clamber, gleam* : *glimmer, sway* : *swagger* (from obs. or dial. *swag*), *wend* : *wander*.

-ar

15.4₁. This ending is first found very frequently in sbs as a variant spelling for the ordinary -*er*-ending (unstressed [ə]), see 14.1₄.

Next in adjs, where it ultimately originates from L. -*ar(is)*, -*ar(em)*, a by-form of -*al(is)* (see 22.1) used after *l*. Another ModE form is -*ary*, see 15.8₁. In OF -*ar* became -*er*, and the spelling -*er* was the rule in ME and early ModE, e. g. Ch A 215 *famulier*, Sidney AP 22 *populer*, 33 *particuler*, etc.

But later the spelling was adjusted according to Latin usage.

Most words in -*ar* are borrowed from French or Latin, but a few have been coined on English soil from Latin roots, e. g. *muscular, oracular, spectacular, titular*.

15.4₂. Note the shift of stress between radical and derivative, and the preservation of *u* in the penultimate in (some of) the following pairs: ˈ*family* : *fa*ˈ*miliar*, ˈ*oracle* : *o*ˈ*racular*, ˈ*spectacle* : *spec*ˈ*tacular*, ˈ*triangle* : *tri*ˈ*angular*.

Because of special developments of the radical in French or Earlier Eng. there is in some cases a marked difference between the two words, apart from the suffix, e. g. *joke* [dʒouk] : *jocular* [ˈdʒɔkjulə], *muscle* [mʌsl] : *muscular* [ˈmʌskjulə], *people* [pi·pl] : *popular* [ˈpɔpjulə] *rule* [ru·l] : *regular* [ˈregjulə], *table* [teibl] : *tabular* [ˈtæbjulə], *title* [taitl] : *titular* [ˈtitjulə].

In some words there is no *l* immediately before the suffix, e. g. *lunar, vulgar, columnar*. The latter also has a variant form *columnal*.

Some of the words may be used as sbs, too, e. g.

familiar, jugular (= jugular vein), *particular, perpendic-
ular, singular,* and *titular.*

-aire

15.4₃. *-aire* [-ˡɛ·ə] etymologically = L. *-arius, -arium,*
in a few words borrowed in modern times from French,
e. g. *secrétaire, questionnaire,* and *millionaire.* On the
pattern of the latter have been formed *multimillionaire,
milliardaire, billiardaire* (Norris P 124), and Sinclair
Lewis's facetious *ten-thousandaire* (MS 66).

-eer, -ier

15.5₁. Words in *-eer, -ier* (stressed) [-ˡiə] are mostly
originally F words in *-ier* (generally from L *-arius*).
Most of the OF words in *-ier* were adopted in ME with
-er, and the stress was shifted to the first syllable (see
14.1₂), as also in a few in which the *i* was kept (see
14.5₁).

A few words borrowed in ME times kept the final
stress, and so did nearly all the later loans (many
from the 16th and 17th c.). The established spelling
of most of these, and of nearly all words coined on
English soil, is *-eer,* as in *auctioneer, cannoneer, charioteer*
(Keats 46), *gazetteer, jargoneer* (NED from 1913),
mountaineer, muffineer 'small castor for sprinkling salt
or sugar on muffins' (NED 1806), *muleteer* [mju·liˡtiə],
musketeer, pioneer, pistoleer (Carlyle Essays 251),
routineer (Shaw D 54), and *volunteer,* but many of
them preserved the F spelling, e. g. *cavalier* and *chevalier,
cuirassier,* and *financier.*

The recent *motorneer,* is coined on the pattern of
engineer.

Sh in some cases has initial-stressed *-er*-forms instead of *-eer,* e. g. ˡ*enginer,* ˡ*mutiner* (Cor I. 1.244),
and ˡ*pioner.*

15.5₂. From the disparaging sense of such words as *garreteer* 'hack writer', *pamphleteer*, *privateer*, *pulpiteer* (Hergesheimer MB 111), and *sonneteer*, *-eer* (but only after *t*) has acquired a contemptuous meaning, thus in the modern words *crotcheteer*, *patrioteer* (not in NED; Am. NP 1920), *profiteer* (Lloyd George, Speech 1917, quoted in *Language* 388; also Bennett PL 183), and *racketeer* 'one who practises racketeering, i. e. blackmail' (orig. Am.).

15.5₃. There are a few verbs in *-eer*, too. Most of them are secondary, derived from substantives, e. g. *electioneer* (the sb is rare (Wells A 147); note also *electioneerer* derived from the vb), *engineer*, *foreigneer* (nonce-word? Smedley F 2.231), *pamphleteer* and *profiteer* (15.5₂, esp. in the gerund), *pioneer*, and *volunteer*; *commandeer* is from S. African Dutch (NED from 1881); *domineer* (NED from 1588) also seems to have been borrowed through Dutch.

-lier

15.5₄. The suffix *-lier* [-ˈliə] is from *chandelier* (from Fr.), in which *l* belongs to the stem, by metanalysis. Two words only: *gaselier* and *electrolier*.

Nexus-Substantives

-ure

15.6₁. *-ure* [-juə, -ə]. From F *-ure* < Lat. *-ura*, in many words of F or Lat. origin. In Lat. it primarily denoted action or process. Later it came to mean also result of the action, and in some cases a collective body.

The existence in some cases of a corresponding verb as in *closure—close*, *pressure—press*, *investiture—invest*, gave rise to native new-formations, mainly from words of Lat. origin, as *composure*, *exposure*, *vomiture* and a few others, but also in a very few cases from native words, as in *clefture* and *raisure* (both obsolete), and *wafture* (Lamb E (World's Class.) 94).

In *pleasure* and *treasure* the French endings *-ir* (OF *plesir, plaisir*) and *-or* (OF *tresor*) have been replaced by *-ure*. Note the change of consonant in PE pronunciation: *close* [-z] : *closure* [-ȝuə, -ȝə]; *press* [-s] : *pressure* [-ʃ(u)ə]; *please* [pliˑz] : *pleasure* [pleȝ(u)ə].

-our, -or

15.6₂. *-our, -or* [-ə] in nexus-words is from OF *-our* (ModF *-eur*), Lat. *-or*. The spelling *-our* is still the rule in British English in *colour, fervour, honour, labour*, etc., but in the 17th and 18th c. the spelling of more and more words was conformed to Latin; and now *-or* is the established spelling in e. g. *error, horror*.

In America *-or* is used in a great many words spelt with *-our* in British English, see vol I 9.72.

As *candour* is to *candid*, so is *pallor* to *pallid*. But the suffix cannot be called a living one in PE.

-red

15.6₃. *-red*, from OE *rǣden* 'condition'. Only a few words have survived: *hatred, gossipred* 'spiritual affinity' (obs.), 'small-talk', *kindred* (often apprehended as an adj on account of the ending *-ed*).

-ery, -ry

15.7₁. *-ery, -ry (-try)* [-əri, -ri (-tri)], from F *-erie*, of double origin: (1) common Romanic *-aria*, corresponding to F words in *-ier;* (2) to OF *-ere, -eor* (ModF *-eur*), from Lat. *-ator+-ie*. But *-erie* in F came to be considered as an independent formative that might be added to verbal stems direct. The existence of E action nouns in *-er(e)* facilitated the adoption of this suffix in English.

For a full treatment see F. Gadde, On the History and Use of the Suffixes *-ery (-ry), -age* and *-ment* in English. Lund and Cambr. 1910.

Strictly speaking many of the early formations in
-*ery* should be considered derivatives from agent nouns
in -*er* with the suffix -*y*, but from its first appearance
in English -*ery* was also an independent suffix which
it was possible to add direct to verbal stems. Derivatives
with -*ery* hence were, and still are, possible, from sbs,
vbs, and adjs, the latter being comparatively rare.

15.7₂. The old formations *gentlery* (remarkable by
being derived from an adjective), *dairy*, *husbandry*, and
reavery 'robbery', and probably also *Englishry*, *Danishry*,
Irishry, *Welshry* originate from Anglo-Fr.

Early new-formations are *harlotry*, *riotry*, *nouricery*
'nursery', *japery*, *devilry*, *yeomanry*, and *cookery*. "From
the beginning of the 15th c. the suffix is a living formative in English" (Gadde 31).

Most of the words with this suffix are trisyllables
with stress on the first syllable (cf vol I 5.61 and 5.63),
at any rate the suffix is always unstressed.

In ModE the suffix occurs in two main forms, -*ery*
and -*ry*, the former being added to monosyllables ending in a consonant, e. g. *cookery*, *fishery*, the latter
being added to words of more than one syllable (without end-stress) ending in *d*, *t*, *l*, *n*, or *sh*, or to roots
ending in a (stressed) vowel or diphthong, e. g. *heraldry*,
gallantry, *devilry*, *yeomanry*, *Englishry*, *Jewry*, and
avowry.

With *jewel*, both spellings of the suffix may be used:
jewelry and *jewellery*.

15.7₃. Though -(*e*)*ry* cannot compete with -*ment*, -*age*,
and -*ness* with regard to popularity, it is still used
rather freely in nonce-formations, even from phrases:
Galsw TL 54 the "flapping *cockatoory*" of some English-
women | Ridge Mord Em'ly [vg] 233 get up to any
dodgery-fraudery business, and I'll foller you, my gel |
Shaw TT 12 golden exceptions of *idle richery* and its
leaden rule of anxious poverty | Greig Priscian's Head

22 [Amr] This pedantry, this *schoolmarmery* | Locke
FS 94 she kept a *tame-cattery* of adoring young men.

15.7₄. In a few cases we find the ending *-try* instead
of *-ry*, chiefly on the analogy of sbs in *-t+-ry*, e. g.
artistry, gallantry, infantry, peasantry, etc. The only
living form with *-try* as an independent suffix seems to
be *deviltry* (Kipling S 49, Maugham Pl 4.165). For some
obsolete forms see Gadde 48.

15.7₅. Semantically the words in *-(e)ry* fall into 4
groups:

(1) quality or behaviour a) Fr: *adultery, bravery,
chivalry, gallantry, sorcery, treachery*, etc., b) Native:
beggary, bribery, cuckoldry, daredevilry, devilry (from
1375), *drudgery, heathenry* (from 1577, Kingsley H 297),
pageantry, parrotry (Galsw WM 313), *tomfoolery, wizardry*
etc.

(2) occupation, rank, condition a) Fr: *ancestry,
brewery, butchery, chancellery, embroidery, forestry, sav-
agery*, etc. b) Native: *artistry, chemistry, cookery, co-
partnery* (Mitford OV 18), *fishery, housewifery, outlawry,
slavery*, etc.

(3) place or product of an action. a) Fr: *armoury,
artillery, chancery, cutlery, embroidery, jewellery, laundry,
nunnery, poetry, pottery, poultry, surgery*, etc. b) Native:
*bakery, colliery, fishery, forgery, millinery, pastry, rookery,
swannery, turkery* (irregular from *turkey*), etc.

(4) collectivity. a) Fr: *gentry, imagery, infantry,
ministry*, etc. b) Native: *balladry, blackguardry, citizenry,
crockery, peasantry, yeomanry*, etc.

These classes cannot, of course, be strictly separated.

-teria

15.7₆. A by-form of *-ry* is the recent Amr *-teria*. It
originates from *cafeteria*, a Spanish word used at first
in California and which has proved exceedingly productive. Since about 1900, when the word seems to

have made its first appearance in American English,
a large number of shops and businesses of various
kinds have been called by a name ending in *-teria*.
Mencken AL⁴ 176 f. enumerates some 30 such names,
among which are *basketeria, bobateria* (where hair is
bobbed), *chocolateria* (with haplographic *-te-* for *-tete-*),
casketeria 'an undertaker's shop', *drugteria, drygoodsteria,*
fruiteria, groceteria, with the variants *grocerteria* and
groceryteria, millinteria, mototeria 'a groceteria on wheels',
resteteria 'rest-room', *shoeteria, sodateria*, and *wrecketeria*
'bone-yard for old motor-cars'.—'The accent in *cafeteria*
is sometimes on the penult, but the custom now seems
to be establishing itself of stressing the antepenult"
(Krapp ELA 1.143).

-ary

15.8₁. *-ary* [-əri], adj and sb: generally from L *-arius,*
-arium. These ordinarily became E *-er, -ier*, or *-ar*,
see *-er*. In later French loans both forms became *-aire*,
AF and ME *-arie*, later *-arye*, now *-ary*, which is the
ordinary modern representative of L *-arius, -arium*,
and F *-aire*.

According to NED more than 300 words in *-ary*
exist in English.

From Early ModE the suffix has been used as an
independent formative, thus e. g. in *dignitary, unitary,*
votary; fragmentary, parliamentary; functionary, tradi-
tionary, visionary, etc.

-ary means '(person or thing) pertaining to'. Some
words are used primarily or exclusively as adjs: *arbitrary,*
elementary, hereditary, etc, others primarily or exclusively as sbs, e. g. *actuary, adversary, antiquary, secretary,*
but others may be used equally well as both: *mercenary,*
ordinary, voluntary, etc.

Some words are derived from *-arium*, meaning 'thing
connected with, place for', e. g. *diary, dictionary,*
glossary, granary, salary, vocabulary.

In a few cases -*ary* is from L -*aris* (cf -*ar*). This in later F loans became -*aire*, hence E -*ary*, as in *exemplary*, *military*, *salutary*.

-ory

15.8₂. -*ory* [-əri] occurring in substantives and in words primarily used as adjs, is of different origin.

As a substantival suffix it originates from ONorm., F and AF -*orie* (OF -*oire*), from L -*oria* (as in *victoria;* often ultimately from Greek, as in *categoria*) or from -*orium* (as in *oratorium*), neuter form of the adj suffix -*orius*, a form retained in some learned words, e. g. *auditorium*, *crematorium*.

From ME times a great many sbs have been borrowed into English, thus from orig. -*oria: category, history memory, victory*. From -*orium* (most of them denoting a place): *depository, dormitory, laboratory* [læbərətəri], but BBC recommends [ləˈbɔrətəri], *purgatory, territory*, etc.

Oratory 'small chapel' is from L *oratorium*, but = 'the art of an orator' from *orator*+-*y*. Thus also *rectory* 'the seat of a rector' from *rector*+-*y*. But otherwise this substantival -*ory* has not been used as an independent formative in English.

15.8₃. As an adjectival suffix -*ory* is ultimately from the compound L adj ending -*or-ius*, -*a*, -*um*, as added to L participial stems in -*t* and -*s*, and adjs in -*ory* have been borrowed from ME times, e. g. *amatory, ambulatory, circulatory, illusory, obligatory, salutatory, satisfactory, transitory*.

Some of the words from -*orius* are frequently used as sbs, e. g. *accessory* (esp. in the plural), *monitory*.

English new-formations have been formed from orig. Latin participial stems (generally verbs in -*ate* and -*ute*), as in *compulsory, contributory, ejaculatory, migratory, statutory, vibratory*, and *vindicatory*.

On stress and parallel forms in *-ary* and *-ory* such as *accessary* : *accessory*, see vol I 9.77.

-ard, -art

15.9₁. *-ard* [-əd], *-art* [-ət, -a·t] belongs to the small number of suffixes which were originally independent words. It is a development of Gothonic *-hard*, *-hart* 'hardy', especially occurring in personal names, e. g. G. *Bernhard*, Eng. *Bernard*, OE *Rīchart* > F and E *Richard*, OHG *Regin-hart* > G. *Reinhardt* = F *Renart*, which from the tale of *Reynard the Fox* became the ordinary F word for fox: *renard*.

This became an independent suffix in French at an early date, generally with a depreciatory sense. English forms adopted from OF are: *bastard*, *coward* (OF *coart* from *coe*, L *cauda* 'tail'), *mustard*, *Spaniard*, *standard* (OF *estendard*, from L *extend*-; also influence from E *stand* vb), and some words of obscure origin, e.g. *galliard*. Later loans are *poniard* (NED 16th c.), *Savoyard* (1687), and the modern words *communard* (NED 1874), on the analogy of which has been coined *dynamitard* (1882; Shaw D 63 | Henderson Shaw 108).

15.9₂. The suffix has been productive from ME. It has been added to verbs, as in *blinkard* (sb and adj; Carlyle FR 272 in a most blinkard, bespectacled generation), *dotard* (adj in Ch D 291), *laggard*, *sluggard* (AV Prov 6.6 Goe to the ant, thou sluggard; adj in Keats), *stinkard* (Dekker G 9.49), or to sbs, adjs or ptcs: *costard*, *dastard* (prob. from *dased* 'dazed'), *drunkard*, *dullard*, *wizard* (from *wys, wis* 'wise'), nearly all with a pejorative sense. *Izzard*, esp. in the phrase *from A to izzard*, is a variant of *zed*.

At a certain period *-ard*, *-art* was considered as a by-form of the *-er* of agent nouns, thus *loller* (e. g. Ch B 1173 and 1177) alongside of *lollard* (from MDu.), in early ModE and mod. vg we find *scholard* for *scholar*,

and early ModE *vizard* (Puttenham 48 and Earle Micro-
cosmographie 30 vizzard) for *vizer, vizar* 'vizor'. Cf also
gizzard from OF *g(u)iser.*

Some words are of more or less obscure origin, thus
U. S. *blizzard* (NED 1834; and on the analogy of this
U. S. slang *sizzard* 'a heat wave', Weseen 394), *bollard*
(nautical), *haggard, niggard,* and *tankard.*

Custard seems to be a perverted form of obs. *crustade,*
from French. *Steward* is from OE *stīg-weard* 'house-
ward'.

Obs. *cockard* has become *cockade* with substitution of
the suffix *-ade,* cf 24.2₂.

In earlier times we find both *-d* and *-t,* the former
now being the established form except in *braggart;* in
the 19th c. the form *laggart* may occasionally be found.

-(e)rel

15.9₃. *-(e)rel* [-(ə)rəl] originates from OF *-erel(le)*
(ModF *-ereau*). From ME times it is found in formations
from native roots, e. g. in the diminutives (denoting
young animals) *cockerel* (from *cock*), *hoggerel,* and
pickerel (from *pike*), or from verbal roots (these with a
depreciatory sense), e. g. *dotterel* (from *dote*), *mongrel*
(apparently from the root *meng-, mong-* 'mix', cf *among*),
and *wastrel* (from *waste*). The suffix has long ago ceased
to be used in forming new derivatives.

-trix

15.9₄. This is a learned feminine suffix, mainly used
in law-terms, corresponding to masculines in *-tor.*
Examples are:

arbitratrix (from *arbitrator,* but *arbitress* from *arbiter*),
executrix, inheritrix (Sh H5 I. 2.51, also *inheritress*),
mediatrix, prosecutrix, testatrix.

Among forms not especially legal Knutson, Gender
of Words Denoting Living Beings p. 40, quotes:

admonitrix, directrix, liberatrix, and *victrix* (not so common as *victress*).

On *-stress* see 15.1₁.

Chapter XVI

The Ordinary s-Ending

16.1₁. The ending here termed 'the ordinary s-ending', has three forms according to the final sound of the word to which it is added:

[iz] after one of the sibilants [z, s, ʒ, ʃ], as in *noses* [nouziz]. *adzes* [ædziz]. *horses* [hɔ·siz]. *fox's* [fɔksiz]. *changes* [tʃein(d)ʒiz]. *villages* [vilidʒiz]. *dishes* [diʃiz]. *churches* [tʃə·tʃiz].

[z] voiced, after voiced non-sibilants, as in *cabs* [kæbz]. *rides* [raidz]. *bags* [bægz]. *lambs* [læmz]. *man's* [mænz]. *rings* [riŋz]. *proves* [pru·vz]. *bathes* [beiðz]. *falls* [fɔ·lz]. *pears* [pɛ·əz]. *pities* [pitiz]. *virtues* [və·tju·z]. *mamma's* [məˈma·z]. *boys* [boiz].

[s] voiceless, after voiceless non-sibilants, as in *caps* [kæps]. *rights* [raits]. *backs* [bæks]. *proofs* [pru·fs]. *baths* [ba·þs] (vb).

16.1₂. This ordinary s-ending has the following functions. It forms:

(1) The plural of substantives, as in *princes, kings, dukes, somebodies;* on plurals formed in other ways see vol II 2.21.

(2) The genitive singular of substantives and some pronouns, as in *prince's, king's, duke's, somebody's* (substantive and pronoun primary), *his, its, whose;* this ending is the only one in ModE; in OE we had a variety of endings; in ME we find unchanged genitives in some words, *fader, heven, lady, doughter;* there are some unchanged genitives in present dialects.

(3) the genitive plural of substantives, as in *princes', kings', dukes', somebodies'* (sb);

(4) the primary form of some possessive pronouns, such as *hers, ours, theirs;*

(5) some adverbs, such as *nowadays, towards, thereabouts;*

(6) the third person singular of the present of most verbs, as in *kisses, goes, sticks;* see on this Ch. III;

((7) *'s* may stand for *is, has, does;* cf also *let's = let us;* but such abbreviations fall outside our Morphology.)

((8) *-s-* as a formative element in verbs, found in a number of OE vbs in *-sian,* survives in one example: *cleanse.*)

We shall now first offer some formal remarks and then pass in review these various functions.

Spelling

16.1₃. In ME the *e* before *s* denoted a real vowel, as it still does after a sibilant. But after it had become mute, an apostrophe came to be used, at first irregularly and without any regard to case-function, whether a syllable was added in pronunciation or not (*Thomas's, Edward's*), the apostrophe simply taking the place of the *e,* which might also be written (just as now in *stabb'd = stabbed*). Thus in Shakespeare we find *earth's* as a gen sg and *prey's* as a nom pl, but such forms are quite exceptional, the ordinary spelling at that time being *Monarkes, hearts* etc. in the gen sg, *lookes, things* etc. in the pl. Similarly there is often no apostrophe in *heres, theres,* etc.: Sh Ro 196 hees [= he is] some other where | ib 1764 whose there [= who is there].

The apostrophe in the common case of the pl was formerly often used in *genius's* (e. g. Swift P 47), now *geniuses,* and may still be used in some unfamiliar plurals; in Sh Tw II. 5.96 the spelling "her very *C's,* her *U's,* and her *T's*" is kept unchanged in modern editions; we have such plurals of unfamiliar proper

names as *Hrolf's* (Carlyle H 29); in the Spectator, no.
80, Steele speaks of the manner in which people use
"their *who's* and their *whiches*". Thus also *pro's and
con's* (Sterne 71), *the why's and wherefore's* (also without the apostrophe), with hearty *ha-ha's* (Carlyle R
1.94), the *ay's* and *no's* of Parliament (also *ayes, noes*),
8's and *9's,+'s* and ÷*'s*, and other cases in which words
not properly substantives are treated as such. Thus
also abbreviations: *M.P.'s, M.A.'s*. On *fly's* cf below.

The spelling *ha's* for *has*, frequent in the sixteenth cent., is
probably due to the notion that the *v* of *have* is left out in
this form.

When the use of the apostrophe became regulated,
before the genitival *s* towards the end of the seven-
teenth century and after the *s* in the ordinary gen pl
towards the end of the eighteenth century, the present
distinction was established between three forms identical
in sound and previously written indiscriminately *kings,
ladies:*

gen sg *king's*   pl *kings*   gen pl *kings'*
       lady's   *ladies*   *ladies'*

One of the reasons for this use of the apostrophe as a
sign of the genitive case was the popular supposition
that *the kings castle* was an abbreviation of *the king
his castle;* cf below, 17.9. See on the wavering use of
the apostrophe S. A. Leonard, The Doctrine of Correctness in English Usage 1700—1800. (Madison 1929)
p. 196, 234.

The apostrophe is not used in the primary possessive
pronouns; Lowth, *Introd. to E. Grammar* 1762, prescribes
the spellings *her's, our's, your's, their's*, which now are
by no means rare in letters, though not often found in
printed books. The genitive of *who* (OE *hwæs*, the
vowel refashioned after the nom., the final consonant
made to conform with the other genitives, i. e. with

[z] instead of [s]) is now spelt *whose*, though occasionally we find *who's*: Hardy F 45 Who's farm | Caine M 272 Isn't that his voice? Who's, dear? | id C 284 Who's child is this?

While the present usage with regard to the apostrophe may in a few cases prevent an ambiguity inherent in the spoken form, it should not be forgotten that in other cases it creates difficulties, thus especially in the genitival compounds: is *a hornet's nest* or *a hornets' nest* the correct form? (See details vol II 7.4).

16.1₄. In the plural and in the third person singular we have the following orthographical changes:

-y after a consonant is changed into *-ies*: *lady* : *ladies; armies, (soliloquies), he marries*. In proper names we have generally the spelling *-ys* : *Marys, Pollys, Henrys*. Austen M 224 the Gregorys | Meredith H 246 Carrys [pet-name for Caroline]. In Thack H we find both *Hoggarties* and *Hoggartys*. An artificial distinction is often made between *flies* (insects; also in the vb) and *flys* (Hardy W 135) or *fly's* (carriages).

After a vowel *y* is kept unchanged: *days, valleys, boys, guys, he buys*. Up to the beginning of the 19th c. *-ies* was very often written in the plural of words in *-ey*: *vallies*, now *valleys; monies* (Wordsw P 3.37, Mrs Browning A 71), now *moneys* (thus in the same books 5.471; 73).

16.1₅. After *-o, -es* is written in the most familiar words : *heroes, negroes, cargoes, potatoes, echoes; he goes, does* (on the vowel sound see 3.1). (In some short words we have the spelling *-oe* already in the kernel : *doe, roe;* see vol I 4.96). But a great number of words in *-o* take no *-e-* before the *-s;* thus when a vowel precedes the *-o*, as in *folios, cameos, cuckoos; he woos* (rarely *wooes*); in abbreviations, such as *photos, pianos, dynamos* (abbr. of *photograph, pianoforte, dynamo-electric*); in proper names, such as *Neros, Romeos, Michael Angelos, Ariostos, Basutos;* in words felt to be foreign, chiefly of

Italian and Latin origin: *cantos, grottos, lazarettos, solos, virtuosos* (or *virtuosi;* in Swift T *virtuoso's*), *sopranos, quartos, embryos, ratios; albinos.* We find, however, a good deal of uncertainty: *volcano(e)s, banjos* and *banjoes* (Kipl.), *mementos* (Thack N 326) and *mementoes* (James S 38), *porticos* and *porticoes* (Thack S 137, Macaulay E 4.84), *innuendoes* more often than *innuendos.* (Cf Fowler MEU 396), *domino(e)s, peccadillo(e)s.*

16.1₆. *-s* and *-z* are doubled after a stressed vowel, though not consistently: *gasses* sometimes found for *gases, busses* for *buses; quizzes* pl of *quiz.* After a weak vowel, however, only one *-s* or *-z* is written: *omnibuses, canvases* (pl of *canvas*, the fabric, e. g. Kipling L 147; but *he canvasses* from *canvass*, 'solicit votes; discuss'), *aliases* (e. g. Stevenson D 208), *geniuses* (in the 18th c. *genius's*, e. g. Fielding 3.413); *topazes.* (See Fowler MEU 562).

As a variant spelling of *-cks* in the pl *x* is found in *pox* = 'pocks', and according to the NED *sox* has been adopted in the hosiery trade as a convenient shortening of *socks.* Thus in Wells Kipps (q NED). He would have considered himself the laughing stock of Wood Street if he had chanced to spell *socks* in any way but 'sox'.—A similar spelling in the gen. is seen in *coxcomb* for 'cock's comb'.

From the purely orthographical point of view, *horses* and *grottos* are inflected in the same way, and differently from *foxes* and *heroes*, which have added *-es;* but phonetically *horses* and *foxes* go together with their [iz] added, while *grottos* and *heroes* belong to another group, adding [z].

In the French word *corps p* and *s* are mute [kɔ·(ə)]; in the spoken language the pl is regular [kɔ·(ə)z], but in the written language the pl is like the sg *corps.* A distinction was formerly pretty often kept up between *pease* 'collectively' and *peas* 'individually'; the *s* here originally formed part of the kernel, see vol II 5.63.

Similarly in *chamois*, [ʃæmwa·], *patois*, [pætwa·],
rendezvous [ra·ndeivu—also with other pronunciations]
the final *-s* is mute in the sg and pronounced [-z] in
the pl.

Sounds

16.1₇. The ME ending was *-es;* /s/ became voiced if it
followed a weak vowel (vol I 6.61 and *Linguistica*
346 ff). Afterwards the vowel disappeared (vol I 6.16),
except between sibilants (vol I 6.17); /z/ after voiceless
became voiceless. Where the vowel had disappeared before the voicing of /s/, we still have [s], see vol I 6.61
and below. On Shakespearian isolated instances of
sounded *e* see vol I 6.16; on dialectal [iz] after [st] in
the South see vol I 6.17.—In some vulgar forms a [t]
has been dropped after [s], and the ending then is [iz]:
GE S 83 ghos'es | Caine M 181 texes ('texts') | ib 359
breakfas'es (Bennett P 243 (vg) gues's). But Miss Kaye
Smith GA 45 has *fistses* as a Sussex form. On dialectal
forms [bi·stəzəz], etc., see Wright EDG § 378.

In some cases the final consonant of the kernel disappears in rapid pronunciation before the *s*, thus

[d] between [n] and [z]: *hands* [hænz], *friends* [frenz],
stands [stænz], *thousands* [þauzənz]; and between [l]
and [z]: *fields* [fi·lz].—Is Shakespeare's rime (Ven. 677)
downes : hounds an early instance of this pronunciation?

[þ] between a consonant and [s]: *months* [mʌns] or
[mʌns·], which Thackeray in one of his Ballads rimes
with *once. sevenths* [sevns(·)], *sixths* [siks·] and similarly
in other fractions.

The vowel sound is changed before the *-s* in two
verbs: *say* [sei] : *says* [sez] (vol I 11.35).—*do* [du·] :
does [dʌz] (vol I 11.64, above 3.1).

Princess generally in British English has end-stress,
but may change into ['prinses] before a proper name,
but the pl always has end-stress. In U. S. the stress
is on the first syllable according to R. M. Pierce, who
looks upon end-stress as 'improper'.

The final consonant of the kernel is in some instances
voiced, see next paragraph.

Voiceless and Voiced Consonants

16.2₁. As a spirant became voiceless at the end of a
word, while in the interior the voiced sound was retained (vol I 2.541, etc.), we have many words with
[-f, -þ, -s] in the sg and [-vz, -ðz, -ziz] in the pl. (Cf
Linguistica p. 374, where some ME and early ModE
forms are given, which I have not repeated here).

[-f, -vz]

The original alternation (OE. see vol I 2.541) is best
kept up after a long vowel or diphthong or -*l*-, but in
some of the words we have more or less radical analogical disturbances:

belief, pl -*fs*; formerly sg -*ve*, pl -*ves*; cf above 12.2₃.
calf, pl *calves*.

delf, pl *delves* and the new pl *delfs* are now local
forms; in StE we have a sg *delve* (pl *delves*) either from
the old pl or formed on the verb.

elf, pl *elves* (e. g. Meredith E 350), rarely *elfs* (Dryden);
I have found also a sg *elve* in a poem by G. Darley.

half, pl generally *halves*; but sometimes *halfs* = 'terms
at school', see Davies, *Suppl. Gloss.*: there are usually
three halfs in the year (!).

hoof; the old pl *hooves* (Marlowe H 2.143 *houes*, rime
loues; BJo P 1.2.284 *hooves*) is still found, especially in
poetry (Tennyson Lady of Shalott; Morris E 54; Kipling
B 170, 178; Stevenson V 265; Phillips P 115; A. Lang;
Gosse F 246; Tarkington Pl 539). But *hoofs* is the
ordinary form (already Marlowe *hoofes* T 79, 1243; Sh
hoofes R2 III. 2.7, H4A I. 1.8, H5 I. Prol 27; Wordsw
P 2.137, 9.449, 10.603; Scott A 1.160, 314; Di D 802;
id N 782; Morris E 44; Tennyson later poems; Kipling;
Stevenson; Ruskin; Meredith; Doyle; Hope, etc.).

knife, pl *knives*.

leaf, pl *leaves*. Note *ash-leafs* = 'ash-leaf potatoes' (vol II 8.9₁).

life, pl *lives;* but More U 284 lyffes (though in other places *liues, lyues*); NP 1911 "still-lifes".

loaf, pl *loaves*.

loof 'palm of the hand', pl *looves* (see especially EDD) and *loofs;* also sg *loove*. The word is found in Sc. and northern dial. only.

oaf, pl *oaves* or usually *oafs*.

roof, pl *roofs* (Marlowe T 1500 rooffes; Sh Tim IV. 3.145 roofes); but I have heard [ru·vz] in England, and it is found in U. S., too (Mencken).

self, pl generally *selves; selfs* occurs in philosophical writings = 'egos' (Sayce, Introd. Sc. Lang. 2.291); also in the signification 'a flower or blossom of a uniform colour' (Annandale).

sheaf, pl *sheaves;* but in Caine C 131 sheafs of play-bills, also Clutton Brock in NP 1920.

shelf, pl *shelves*.

staff, original pl *staves* (on the vowel sound, see below); in the sense 'sticks' we have this pl in Caxton R 86; Sh H 5 IV. 2.46 torch-staues; Scott Iv 137 quarter-staves; Di Do 150 men with scarves and staves; Caine E 130 cowherds carrying long staves; Barrie W 27; Zangwill G 184 staves, sticks, and umbrellas. In the sense 'body of men' we have now *staff*, pl *staffs*. In the sense 'piece of a cask' we have now a new sg *stave* formed from the pl and now to be considered a separate word; thus also in the sense 'stanza, part of a piece of music' (Di, A Christmas Carol; Stevenson V 266 Pan trolls out a stave of ecstasy; Caine C 335 Won't our nightingale come down and give us a stave?) The compounds *flagstaff* and *distaff* now have always pl *-ffs* (Caxton R 95 distaues; Sh Wint I. 2.37 distaffes); *broomstaff* has *-ffs* or *-ves*, but Lowell uses *broomstave* in the sg.

thief, pl *thieves*.

wife, pl *wives*. Curiously enough Fulg 84 has *wyffes*, *wiffes* (but in the gen 40 *wyues*). The compound *house-wife* (cf *hussy* in vol I) has generally the pl *-ves*, but Kyd HP 1338 and Swift J 80 huswifes. In a different sense Austen S 270 the huswifes [= needle-cases] she gave us.

wolf, pl *wolves*.

16.2₂. In two of the words ending in [f] that have the corresponding voiced consonant in the pl, the vowel sound of the kernel is changed in the pl: *cliff* [klif], *cleves* [kli·vz] (see 16.2₃); *staff* [sta·f], *staves* [steivz]. This is due to the quantitative difference between a closed and an open syllable; see vol I 4.2, and on the vowel sound in *staff* vol I 10.67.

16.2₃. After a short vowel or *r* the influence of analogy on the original alternation of [f] in the sg, [vz] in the pl is much more pronounced than in the words just mentioned; thus in the following list there is not one word in [f] that has a form in [vz] as its only possible pl.

cliff, pl now always *cliffs;* the old pl *cleves* is rare; a new sg *cle(e)ve* has been formed. (On the vowel sound, see 16.2₂)

scarf (origin and history uncertain): according to the NED *scarfs* is the original pl, and *scarves* dates only from the beginning of the 18th c.; but Ben Jonson has *scarves* (Merm. ed. 3.208, 209) as well as *scarfes* (P III. 4.344). I have found *scarfs* in Sh (Cor II. 1.280; Alls II. 3.213 scarffes; III. 5.89 scarfes), Scott, Byron, GE (A 217, M 1.54), Dickens (N 219), Brontë, Thack, Kingsley, Tennyson, Hawthorne; and *scarves* in many recent authors: Dickens (Do 150), Caine, Mrs Ward, Black, Kipling, Stevenson, Walter Pater; in London commercial use *scarves* appears, according to NED, to have become universal.

sheriff, pl *-ffs*, now universal; Wharton 1655 has *sherif*, pl *sherives;* the ME form had /v/ also in the sg:

sher(r)eve, OE *scir-gerefa*. Lediard 1725 writes *f*, but pronounces [v] even in the sg.

turf; pl *turfs* (Defoe R 78) and *turves* (Wharton, Gram. 1655, *turvs;* Kipling, Masefield, Hewlett, Hardy).

wharf; the pl *-fs* is as old as Sh (Ant II. 2.218 wharfes) and is more common now than *wharves*, though I find the latter form pretty often (Di, GE, Thack, Tennyson, Ruskin, Doyle, Wells, in U. S. Longfellow, Whitman, Holmes, Hawthorne).

On dialectal [fs] in *calf*, etc., see Wright EDG § 378.

16.2₄. Words in which [-f] is of late origin generally have [-fs].

Thus [-fs] is the only plural of words in which [-f] originates in /x/: *choughs, coughs, laughs, roughs, sloughs, troughs.—Dwarfs* (ME *dwerghes*) goes with the other words in *rf*.

16.2₅. Words from the French have [-fs] in the pl: *briefs* (but Pegge, Anecd. 293 *brieves*), *chiefs, fiefs, fifes, gulfs, rebuffs, safes* (a modern sb from the adj), *strifes*. Thus also *griefs* (but BJo P has *grieves* (I. 3.63, II. 2.59) as well as *griefes* (II. 2.63); and in a few places Sh quartos have *grieues, greeues* for *griefs* (Franz 182)); *kerchiefs* (but Caxton R 64 kerchieuis); *mastiff* (a blend between F *mastin* and *mestif*) has now *-ffs*, but Camden (quoted Ordish, Sh's London 227) has *mastives;* Peele D 428 *mastiues; mischief* had formerly a rare pl *mischieues* (Ascham S 78, Bale 3 Lawes 1156 *myscheues;* but early quotations for *-fs* are found in LondE 97); *proofs* (Sh Wint V. 2.34 proofes, though the sb had originally *-ve* as the vb); *waifs* has supplanted the old *wayues*, cf OF *waif*, pl *waives*.

The only French word with *-f*, pl *-ves* is *beef, beeves* (e.g. Swift G 59, Tennyson 363, Thack N 147, Twain M 168); and here also *beefs* is found. Sh had both forms. Fowler (MEU) distinguishes *beeves* 'oxen' and *beefs* 'kinds of beef'. Dan. Jones gives as an alternative pronunciation of *handkerchief* [-iˑf] with pl [-iˑfs, -iˑvz].

Bluff, cuff, rebuff, reef have [-fs] only.

Words from other languages have pl in [-fs]: *paragraphs, monographs, markgrafs* (Carlyle R 2.334).

Scotch in some words has -*v* in the sg: *neive, caave, staave, scheive* (Murray, Dial. 122). In the standard *nerve* (Ch *nerfe*) the *v* is doubtless due to the Latin form, while *f* is from the French.

[-þ, -ðz].

16.3₁. The alternation is still found (after a long vowel or diphthong) in *bath* [baˑþ] : *baths* [baˑðz], *mouth* [mauþ] : *mouths* [mauðz], *oath* : *oaths* [ouðz], *path* : *paths* [paˑðz], *sheath* : *sheaths* [ʃiˑðz] (these were mentioned by Elphinston 1787 2.93; but the earliest mention of the alternation was made by Wallis 1653, see my EK 207). Thus also *wreath* : *wreaths* [riˑðz]. According to G. R. Carpenter, Princ. of E. Grammar 1898, some plurals, e. g. *paths*, may be pronounced either [ðz] or [þs]; [þs] may be American in *paths*. The American R. M. Pierce has [ðz] in *baths, mouths, paths, wreaths*, and prefers [ðz] to [þs] in *oaths*, but inversely in *sheaths*.

In *laths, truths, youths* both [ðz] and [þs] are heard, in England as in America; Fowler MEU 631 gives also *baths, sheaths, wreaths* as vacillating. *Moths* according to Sweet and other English scholars is [mɔþs], but others pronounce [mɔˑðz] with a long vowel and voiced ending (the latter form of the pl must be an analogical formation, seeing that the OE form of the word is *moþþe*); Pierce gives [mɔˑðz, mɔˑþs]. *Faiths* is always [feiþs], and *heaths* [hiˑþs].

Sc. has [þs] in *mouths, truths* (Murray, Dial. 129).

16.3₂. After a short vowel, and after a consonant [þs] is the rule, thus also after the long vowel resulting from the absorption of /r/ into the preceding short vowel: *Smiths* [smiþs], *piths* [piþs], *myths* [miþs], sometimes [maiþs], *breaths* [breþs], *deaths* [deþs], *mammoths* [mæməþs], *months* [mʌnþs, mʌns·], *healths* [helþs], *sevenths* [sevənþs], *births* [bə·þs], *girths* [gə·þs]. Still [ha·ðz] is sometimes heard for *hearths*, but the usual pronunciation is [ha·þs]; and *earths* according to Jones has [ðz] as well as [þs] (on [þ] in this word (< OE *eorðe*) see vol I 6.92).

Some of these words are not very frequent in the plural.

The original pl of *cloth* [kləþ, klɔ·þ] (see vol I 10.75, 10.81) is *clothes* with now a different vowel [klouðz]; in this [ð] was lost [klouz] (vol I 7.76); this form, which occurs in rime in Dryden : *knows*, and jocularly in Thack B 200 *close : hose*, is differentiated from *cloth*, as seen e. g. Macdonald F 236 they had not the cloth with which to make their own clothes | Mackenzie S 1.10 a fender on which hung perpetually various cloths and clothes. In the 18th c. a frequent spelling was *cloaths* (c. g. Swift T 37, cf ib 40 cloth; Defoe R 144 the sca-mens cloaths .. some neckcloths, but ib 325 neck-cloaths). In the pronunciation [-ðz] is now often re-introduced from the spelling. A new pl is formed *cloths* (table-cloths, neck-cloths, etc.; Di N 49 the helpers [waiters], who stood with the cloths over their arms), pronounced [klɔ·ðz, klɔ·þs, kləþs], the last form esp. in compounds and in the signification 'kinds of cloth'.

with or *withe* is variously pronounced [wið, wiþ, waið, waiþ], pl [wiðz, wiþs, waiðz].

In the pl of fractions *-ths* is always pronounced voicelessly: *five sevenths*, etc.

The rare plurals *growths*, *faiths* have [þs]. On dialectal [þs] see Wright EDG § 378.

[-s, -ziz]

16.4. In standard English this alternation is now only found in *house* [haus], pl *houses* [hauziz] (the pl in *-es* is as old as AR 296; OE had *hūs*). The pl of the proper

name *Woodhouse* is pronounced [-siz]. Sc dialects have
[hu·səz], Wright EDG § 376. In all other words in [-s]
the consonant remains unvoiced in the pl, e. g. *glasses*
[gla·siz].

Hart 1569 gives *uses* sb pl with medial /z/, which I do not
find mentioned elsewhere. NED thinks it probable that the
17th c. had sg *device* [-s], pl *devises* [-ziz]. Nowadays *faces,
places, prices* with [-ziz] are said to be very common colloquially in the Midlands and elsewhere.

Voice-Alternation in the Genitive

16.51. The same alternation between [f, þ, s] and
[v, ð, z] that is found in the pl, also occurred in the
genitive sg; but the power of analogy, which was here
stronger because the genitive ending was felt to be a
looser addition than the pl ending (see Progress p.
312 ff.), has now introduced the voiceless sound with
scarcely any exception. (Examples from Chaucer,
Malory, etc., see my *Linguistica* 375).

wife : the gen sg, which was always *wyues* in Ch
(e. g. B 1631, 3102; E 599, 1133, 1170, 1181, 1239;
MP 17.20) and Caxton, is also regularly *wiues* in Sh
('corrected' in modern editions), (also *huswiues, mid-
wiues* (Wint IV. 4.272)), e. g. H4B II. 2.89 the ale-
wiues petticoat, but the new form is also met with in
Sh, Wint V. 1.167 my arriual, and my wifes, in safetie.
BJo, Peele *wiues*. AV has *wiues*, e. g. Tobit III, Matth.
8.14; this form is found in Mi PR 2.134 and was the
only one recognized by the grammarians Bullokar 1580,
Cooper 1685, Maittaire 1712); it lived on till the end
of the 18th c.; Walker 1791 § 378: we often hear of a
wives jointure ... for *a wife's jointure;* this is the last
trace of the old form I know of. The new form in [-f]
is found as early as More U 300, Heywood P 1044
wyfes.

life: Sh R2 II. 1.15 my liues counsell, R3 IV. 4.351,

Mcb II 4.29, but ib III. 2.23 lifes fitfull feuer, thus also
Dekker F 1146; Gil 1621 has *ljfs* as gen sg. The form
in [-f-] (*life's*) has prevailed.

staff: Sh Tw V. 292 at the staues end.

wolf: Gamelyn 700 wolues-heed. No later example of
gen sg *wulues* is known to me than Caxton R 76, but ib
53, 96, 106 *wulfis;* and Sh Tro II. 1.11 Thou bitch-
wolfes-sonne.

Knife: Sh Tit V. 3.63, Ado II. 3.264 a kniues point;
BJo A 2.59 on a kniues point; thus also 1681 (NED
s. v. *bolus*), but Wharton 1655 has *knif's* as a gen sg.

Calf: Sh has *calues*, e. g. John III. 1.129 ff., Ado
V. 1.155 a calues head, Hml V. 1.124 *calues-skinnes*
(or *calue-skinnes, calue-skins*), Err IV. 3.18 *calues-skin;*
Cy II. 3.34 *calues-guts;* but Tp II. 2.115 *moone-calfes*.
In compounds both *calf's-* and *calues-* are still used,
cf NED *calf's-foot calues-foot, calf-skin calfs-skin
calves-skin, calf's-snout calves'-snout*, Goldsm Stoops to
Conquer II. 2 a calue's tongue [in the Globe ed. *calf's*],
in all of which the gen pl has of course been a con-
comitant reason for the *v*-form. Walker 1791: we often
hear of *a calves head*, for *a calf's head*. Cf Alford Q § 35
[*calves'-head*] as describing a dish made of a single
calf's-head, is hardly defensible on any rules of propriety [he thus does not know the historical reason];
but it is universally used in preference to *calf's-head*.
Di Do 37 and Stevenson T 99 have *calf's-head*.

Self is rarely used in the gen; I know no instance of
selve's. Sh R3 IV. 4.421, Err. II. 2.125, Sonn. 13.7 has
selfes.

It will be seen that the voiced genitives have greater
power of survival in fixed compounds (wive's-jointure |
staves-end | knives-point | calves-head), which is quite
natural because the compound words are learnt as
wholes, whereas other combinations are freely formed
on the spur of the moment.

16.5₂. Though we must suppose that Chaucer had

[ð] in the gen G 502 the bathes hete, I know no ModE examples of [ðz] in the gen of *th*-words. Ellis (p. 1165) expressly says that he pronounces *path's* [paˑþs], and that is probably universal.

House's is always [hausiz].

Irregular [s] in the Plural

16.6₁. An irregular [s] instead of [z] after a vowel or a voiced consonant is due to the fact that the late ME change [s] > [z] took place only after a weak syllable, as in the regular ending *-es* found in the pl, gen sg, and gen pl of most substantives, but no change took place if, for some reason, the *-s* followed a strong syllable. (Cf vol I 6.12 and 6.61 and *Linguistica* 361).

In some French plurals the *s* remained unvoiced, because there never was a weak *e* before the *-s;* thus *invoice, quince,* and some others, which are now used as sg (Cf vol II 5.71). The only one of them which can still be regarded as a pl is *dice,* the pl of *die.* Its pl with one syllable is frequent in ME, e. g. Ch A 4386 dys (riming with *prentis*).—In the sense 'cube for gambling' the sg *die* is seen in the phrase: the die is cast, e. g. Di DC 246 the die is cast—all is over;—but is otherwise rare: Thack N 531 over the wine-cup and the die | Meredith T 83 cast the die for love | Galsw WM 90 No word to her till he had thrown the die.—The original pl *dice* is often used as a sg in this sense; cf vol II 5.71₁.—The sg *die* is now used in the sense 'stamp for coining' e. g. Haggard S 292 she was stamped and carven on our hearts, and no other woman or interest could ever raze that splendid die;—or 'the cubical portion of a pedestal, between the base and the cornice' (NED). The word is practically dissociated from the old pl, and has formed a regular pl *dies.* (In the sense 'cube for gambling' I have found one instance of the regular pl: Keats 4.159 the Fates ... threw the dies which of them should be drowned).

16.6₂. In the pl of a few native sbs the *e* of the ending had early disappeared, hence the retention of the unvoiced *-s; truce, bodice*, which, however, have come to be considered sg (cf vol II 5.712). Only in *pence* do we still find the irregular [s] as mark of the pl. In most cases this pl of *penny* is used when the value is indicated: *three halfpence* = 1½ d. When individual coins are meant, the regular pl is used, e. g. a shilling in pennies | Galsw M 138 He turned the honest pennies. The old pl used in this sense is seen in Wordsw 134 shillings, pence, And halfpennies. The compound *halfpenny* has the pl *halfpence* as well as *halfpennies* when the coins are meant: Sh Ado II 3.147 she tore the letter into a thousand halfpence | Bacon Ess (q NED) the late new halfe-pence, which though the silver were good, yet the peeces were small | Swift J 496 coining halfpence and farthings | Shaw M 142 children whine for halfpence || GE M 152 St George who slew the dragon on the half-pennies. In U. S. only *pennies* Mencken AL 178).

On the pronunciation [-pəns] in *twopence*, etc., see vol I 9.52, on the use of the forms *penny* and *pence* in compounds see vol II 7.12 and 7.23, 8.93; on the (double) plural *sixpences*, etc., vol II 5.171.

An irregular unvoiced gen is found in *foolscap* [fu·lskæp] when used about 'paper size'; but in the sense 'cap' the regular genitival ending is used: [fu·lz-].

16.6₃. In a number of adverbs the *e* of the ending disappeared early, so that the *-s* came to follow a strong syllable and remained unvoiced: *hence, thence, whence, else, once, twice, thrice, since*. Cp the regular development of the ending in the sb *hens, ells, ones, sins* < late ME *hennes*, etc. in which the weak vowel was preserved till after the voicing of the consonant.

-s instead of -ses. Plural

16.7₁. The retention of the weak vowel in *-ses* as in *glasses*, etc, is a kind of reaction against the general

tendency to drop it, due in the first place to the want
of distinctiveness, as the two numbers would otherwise
be identical. But we see pretty often that the tendency
to drop the vowel has prevailed, the result being that
we have no plural ending (haplology vol I 7.8). This
coincides with the old pl form in some cases, in which
-*ses* is an analogical formation, thus in *horse* (See vol II
3.71) and in many French words.

On words from Lat. in -*es* unchanged in the pl see
vol II 2.66 *series, species,* etc; to the rare *specieses*
mentioned there we may add *serieses* of men (Bosw
2.69).

16.7₂. French *cas* sg and pl; hence E pl *caas* (Ch A
323); thus also in Ch *pas* (B 306), *vers* (MP 3.463) and
others. This was retained in *ambs-ace* (OF *ambes as*),
see NED. In the occasional Elizabethan plurals *sense,
corpse, voice, juice* we may see survivals of this F pl.
Examples: Sh Mcb V. 1.29 their sense are shut (but
V. 2.23 *senses*); cf Oth IV. 3.95, Sonn. 112.8, probably
also Meas I. 4.59, II. 2.169, Merch V. 136 | *corpse*
(spelt *corpes* fol.) H4A I. 1.43, H4B I. 1.192 | Cor III.
1.119 Why shall the people giue One that speakes thus,
their *voyce*? Ile giue my reasons, More worthier then
their *voyces*. They know the corne (in both places pl
and only one syllable) | Bacon A 38 *iuyce.*

16.7₃. But we find pl without -*es* also in cases in
which F had -*ses* (-*ces*), and in such a native word as
mightiness; these are clear instances of E haplology:
Sh Merch IV. 1.255 *balance* | Cor III. 3.122 as the dead
carkasses [2 syll.] of vnburied men | Cor V. 1.54 These
pipes, and these *conueyances* [3 syll.] of our blood |
H6B III. 2.21 *euidence* (cf R3 I. 4.188 Q are, F is) |
Ant II. 5.104 the *marchandize* Are all too deere for me;
thus also Bacon A 3.20 and other places, Ml J 85,
1540 (pl?), Bunyan P 121 at this fair are all such mer-
chandize sold | Sh H5 V. 2.28 *mightinesse* pl; thus also
Greene F 16.69 | Tp I. 2.338 *place* pl | Tp I. 2.173

princesse pl, also As I. 2.176 | Bale T 567 *sentence* pl.—
A 19th c. instance is Shelley 456 (Epips. 100) The
crimson *pulse* of living morning quiver. Cf also *allspice*
for *allspices*. See on *-ses* without vowel Abbott § 471,
Ellis EEP III. 940, König Vers 16; cf also NED s. v.
bolus, cf *hose*, vol II 3.11.

16.7₄. This may lead to the metanalysis seen in *alms*,
riches: the *s* of the kernel is taken as the pl ending.
(vol II 5.62).

A further step in this development is seen in the
back-formations *asset*, *eave*, *pea*, etc., in which the *s* of
the original kernel, being taken as the pl ending, has
been subtracted to form a new singular.—See vol II
5.631.

Words in *-ese* show similar formations. Formerly
they had pl in *-eses: the Chineses*. But now the form
in *-ese* is used as a pl, and vulgarly a new sg is deducted,
e. g. *a Chinee, a Portuguee*, etc. (vol II 5.632).

The reverse of this development is seen in *a gallows*,
a pincers etc., where the pl ending has come to be
mistakenly apprehended as part of the kernel.— New
plurals in *-ses* are found in vg speech and dial. Thus
Kaye Smith GA 45 fistses (Sussex).—See vol II 5.7.

Genitive Singular

16.8₁. The assimilation is much more common in the
gen sg than in the pl common case, at any rate in early
ModE; cf already Ch F 272 Venus children, HF 175
Eneas wyf, etc.

Examples are particularly frequent in classical names:
Bale T 436 Venus syckenes | ib 510 Moyses yearde |
ib 518 saynt Thomas lottes | Marlowe J 1238 by Mathias
meanes | Sh Ven 180 by Venus side | ib 1172 Adonis
breath | Tp III. 3.23 Phoenix throne | ib IV. 1.117
Ceres blessing | Cor I. 1.244 Tullus face | ib I. 1.277
Cominius honours | ib I. 3.93 in Vlisses absence, etc. But

As III. 4.9 Something browner then Iudasses [colour]:
Marrie his kisses are Iudasses owne children.

In other names: Roister 35 mistresse Custance house |
Sh R3 I. 4.191 poore Clarence death, ib III. 1.144, IV.
2.44 | Ro II. 4.193 Frier Lawrence cell (thus often) |
R3 III. 4.95 poore Hastings wretched head | H4A II.
1.2 Charles wain.

16.8₂. Outside proper names the same gen is also
frequent: Roister 35 our mistresse husbande | Sh Ro
II. 1.24 his mistresse circle | ib 28 in his mistris name
(very frequent; but As III. 2.92 my new mistrisses
brother) | Marlowe J 263 his Highnesse sonne | Sh Mcb I.
4.6 your highnesse pardon (ib I. 4.23, I. 6.27, etc.) |
R3 IV. 4.254 thy kindnesse date | As II. 2.10 the Prin-
cesse gentlewoman | ib III. 2.4 thy huntresse name |
ib III. 2.144 at euerie sentence end | Tp II. 1.133 mo
widdowes in them of this businesse making | AV Is.
11.8 on the cockatrice denne (cf in the margin: or,
adders; thus felt as gen).

The shortened genitive is rare after other sibilants
than *s:* [Sh] Edw3 II. 1.260 in violating mariage sacred
law. It is also rare after monosyllables: Sh H6B IV.
3.14 at my horse heeles; this may be a compound, cf
John II. 1.289 on's horsebacke, and on the other hand
H6A I. 4.108, Tro V. 8.21, V. 10.4, Lr III. 6.20, where
the gen is *horses.* The full gen is found in Ro III. 3.7
the princes doome | LLL V. 2.354 your houses guest |
Tp IV. 1.98 Marses hot minions.

Pope has *Cynthus', Lewis', mistress', Nilus', Par-
nassus' ... Thames'.* On the other hand he has three
times *Thames's*, once *Pegasus's*, and also *Pythagoras's*
(Concordance, p. V).

16.8₃. In recent usage the apostrophe alone is often
written instead of *'s*, especially in classical names:
Thack P 2.239 the great Railroad Crœsus' wife | Ward
D 1.171 in Jesus' ear | Beaconsfield L 43 Mrs. Giles' party
| Murray Trans. Philol. Soc. 1877. 564 Mr. Sweet, who

has done Heicules' share in contributing papers at our meetings.

Outside proper names it is now rare: [Wordsworth P 2.275 the chamois' sinews—the *s* is mute in the nom.] | Thack P 2.252 what in goodness' name | Bridges E 153 the goddess' mind | Carlyle S 189 a Sonnet to his mistress' eyebrows (thus often in imitation of Sh. As II. 7.149).

Very often the full genitive is written, e. g. Swift T 82 Hercules's oxen | Mrs. Browning A 38 by Keats's soul | Keats 2.152 Oceanus's lore, Enceladus's face (but 2.63 St. Agnes' Eve; 68 Agnes' dreams, etc.).

16.8₄. In the spoken language the full form is nearly always used: *St. James's Square* [sn ˈdʒeimziz skwɛ·ə]. *Chambers's Journal* [tʃeimbəziz dʒəˈnəl]. *Lewis's teas*, etc. Thus also pretty generally in reading forms like *Evans' garden* [evənziz ga·dn], though some prefer the shorter form in reading. Always *Pears' soap* [pɛ·əz soup], and I suppose *Hercules' share* [ˈhəˈkjuli·z ʃɛ·ə].

Genitive Plural

16.8₅. The old gen pl in -*a* (-*ena*) disappeared in the ME period; and already in the *Ancrene Riwle* we find, besides survivals of the old forms, as in *monne* 154, 160, 162, and *Ancrene* (never *Ancren:* the usual name of the book *Ancren Riwle* is a blunder on Morton's part), the analogical formation in -*s: monnes* 108, 156, 190 (thus without the mutation, which is proper to the nom. and acc. pl only), *huses* 62, *Giwes* (Jews') 114, 404, *frendes* 180. In Chaucer we have only forms corresponding to the modern flexion, that is -*es* added to plurals formed without -*s*, and no additional ending in plurals formed with *s*. As Ten Brink in his Chaucer Grammar does not treat the subject, I may add some references: *mennes* C 115, G 687, MP 3.976. *wommennes* B 4446. *folkes* HF 1322, 1720. *quenes* MP 3.58. *kinges* ib. *hertes* MP 5.128. *woundes* ib. *Jewes* B 1749, 2054, C 475.

wintres B 577. *ladyes* B 2085. *foxes* B 3223. *wyves* B 3483.
lordes C 73, 76. *soules* C 916, G 37. *lyves* G 56. *seintes*
G 186, 372. *bodies* G 854. *halwes* G 1244. *sterres* HF
997. *partriches* ib 1392. *yeres* MP 5.67.

16.8₆. These forms (in which *e* was still pronounced)
show that the origin of the ModE gen pl is the old
gen pl in -*a* (which in ME became *e*) + the ending *s*
from the gen sg, which was added analogically for the
sake of greater distinctiveness. The *s'* in *kings'* thus is
not to be considered a haplological pronunciation of
-*ses*, though some of the early grammarians look upon
it as an abbreviation: Bullokar Æsop 225 writes the
gen pl *ravenzz* and *crowzz* with his two *z*-letters, which
do not denote two different sounds, but are purely
grammatical signs, one for the plural and the other for
the genitive.—Wallis 1653 writes *"the Lord's* [sic]
House, the House of Lords .. pro the Lords's House",
with the remark "duo *s* in unum coincidunt." Lane,
Key to the Art of Letters 1700 p. 27: *"Es* Possessive
is often omitted for easiness of pronunciation as ...
the Horses bridles, for *the Horsesses bridles."*

In dialects and in vg speech the ending -*ses* is found:
Franklin 152 (vg) before gentlefolkses doors | GE M 1.10
other folks's children; thus also 1.293, 1.325, 2.7 | id
A 251 gentlefolks's servants; ib 403; all in dialect |
London schoolboy, in Orig. English 25: I wish my head
was same as other boyses. Cf Murray D 164 the bairns's
cleose, the færmers's kye, the doags's lugs; Elworthy,
Somers. 155 voaksez (not other words, cf GE).

16.8₇. In PE the gen pl is distinct from the gen sg
and from the common case pl in mutation words
(*men's*, *women's*) and words in -*en* (*children's*, *oxen's*, the
latter for instance in Tennyson the 7 oxen's low); it is
distinct from the gen sg, but not from the common
case pl, in *wives'*, etc. But in the great majority of
words the three forms are now identical; and that leads
to the disuse of the gen pl, which is now comparatively

rare: in the two first volumes of Thackeray's P (Tauchn.
ed.), 658 pages, I counted only 13 such instances of the
gen pl, apart from such groups as are really compounds
(*the ladies' maids*, etc.) and 14 instances of indications
of time and measure (his three hours' reading, at some
miles' distance, etc.).

For fashion sake

16.8₈. The *s* of the genitive is often haplologically
omitted before a word beginning with *s*. Some ME
examples are found in Zupitza's Guy of Warwick p.
503: the emperowre sone | the sowdon sone; Zupitza
does not give the obvious explanation. Early ModE examples are:

Malory 130 Arthurs sword bote not lyke Accolon
swerd | Sh Ro I. 1.129 from this city side (Q citie side) |
ib V. 3.186 from this church-yard side (Q church-yards
side).

This is particularly frequent before *sake:* Latimer
(Specimens 21.165) for the lyuinge sake | Marlowe J 204
for fashion-sake | Sh H4 I. 2.174 for recreation sake | ib
II. 1.78 for sport sake .. for their owne credit sake |
ib V. 1.65, R3 II. 2.147, As III. 2.271, Tw III. 4.326 |
Massinger N IV. 1.192 for health sake | Mi S 1629 for
intermission sake | Osborne 4 for God sake | Spect 32
for rhime sake | Swift T 62 for brevity sake | Trollope
O 32 for fashion sake | Darwin L 209 for brevity sake.

There is a special reason for the omission of *'s* in
words ending in a sibilant (cf above 16.8₁ ff.):

Sh LLL IV. 1.36 for praise sake | Cor II. 3.34 for
conscience sake | Mi PL 11.514 for his Maker's image
sake | Di T 2.153 for gracious' sake | Carlyle S 66 for
cleanliness sake | Pattison Mi 16 for knowledge sake |
Ward D 2.27 for peace' sake | Hardy L 96 for politeness
sake | Ru T 173 for clearness' sake | Maugham PV 244
for face' sake. Cf the alternation in Carlyle R 1.181
for cheapness sake and health's sake. As will be seen,

the apostrophe is written by some, but not by all
authors.

The full genitive is sometimes written: Sh LLL IV.
1.32 for fames sake | Tw III. 3.34 for traffiques sake |
generally in Milton | Trollope D 1.261 for his con-
science's sake | Ward M 40 for appearance's sake |
Stevenson JH 23 for old sake's sake as they say |
Hewlett Q 75 for peace's sake I came hither. Thus
sometimes after the gerund: "when we read for reading's
sake", instead of the more usual "for the sake of reading".

-*ses* > -*s* in Verbs

16.8₉. If in the third person sg of the verbs we find
fewer examples of the haplology -*ses* > -*s* than in the
substantives, the reason no doubt is the existence of
the ending -*eth*, which was especially frequent after
sibilants in ElE (see 3.6).

We find, however, *please* in some cases in which we
might expect *pleases:*

Sh Ado II. 1.56 it is my cosens dutie to say, as it
please you | ib II. 3.37 her haire shal be of what colour
it please God | Hml III. 2.76 to sound what stop she
please | Tw V. 1.119 Even what it please my lord |
Selden Table Talk 17 the King may give them to whom
he please | Ward M 457 let science play what havoc
it please with outward forms | Hewlett Q 12 you will
only hear what she please to tell you.

This, however, might be explained as an encroach-
ment on the part of the subjunctive, due to the frequent
occurrence of such phrases as *if it please you, and't
please you.* In the following instances we have probably
either a subjunctive, or else an infinitive with *will it*
or *may it* omitted by prosiopesis (Cf Sh Wiv I. 1.1275
Wil't please your worship to come in):

Sh LLL V. 2.311 Please it your Maiestie Commaunde
me any seruice to her thither? | (also Ado I. 1.160,
Mcb III. 4.44, Gent I. 2.7, I. 3.73, etc.) | Ford 131

Please you to give me freedom? | ib 164 please you
visit her.

Suffice one example is now taken to be a subjunctive;
but it might be the indicative developed from -*ces*, cf
Ch C 103 Suffyseth oon ensample.

Is *chance* < *chances* in the obsolete *how chance*? Marl-
owe J 123 How chance you came not? | Sh Err I. 2.42
How chance thou art return'd so soone (other examples
Sh-lex., Abbott § 37) | BJo 1.99 how chance that you
were of Cob's? | Swift J 61 How chance you did not see
that.—Cf Sh Hml II. 2.343 How chances it they trauaile?
See also *chance* as an adv.

On *list* in Sh for *lists, listeth, listest* see above 2.4.

Genitival *s* in Compounds

16.9₁. As already remarked (8.1) it is really impossible
to draw a sharp line between loose combinations and
compounds. But the following must certainly be considered compounds.

Genitival compounds have been called "weak compounds" and dealt with very ably by N. Bergstein,
A Study of Compound Substantives in English (Uppsala 1911), p. 101 ff. He speaks at some length of OE
and ME; this I have generally left aside in the following treatment, which is based on my own collections.

Sweet NEG § 2003 draws attention to the difference
in stress between ˈðæt ˌbutʃəz ˈʃɔp (= the shop of that
butcher) and -ðæt ˈbutʃəz ˈʃɔp (*butcher's shop* a compound qualified by *that*).

The general analytic formula is 1^2-1, but it should
be remembered that 1^2 is equivalent to 2, these compounds are therefore on a line with other compounds
like *bedroom* 2-1. Cf AnalSy 6.3.

Such compounds are especially frequent with names
of human beings; very often a possessive notion is
implied. The difference between these and compounds
with the common case is clearly seen in *a baker's boy*

(but *a schoolboy*), *a lady's maid* (but *chambermaid*),
a clergyman's dress (but *night dress*), *a bachelor's gown*
(but *silk gown*), *a shepherd's dog* (but *sheep dog*), *Queen's
College* (but *Trinity College*), etc.

In some cases the distinction between common case
compounds and genitival compounds is not obvious:

Bates Poacher 258 Lizzie dressed him ... in sailor-
suits of blue and white and a blue sailor's cap.

A difficulty is created by the coincidence, in the
spoken language, of the gen sg and pl with the common
case pl, apart from a few irregular plurals. Though of
course the meaning in most cases leaves us in no doubt,
some compounds allow of double interpretation. The
spelling *girls' school* is probably correct, but strictly
girl's school is defensible. Similarly with *oarsman* (16.9₄)
and many other compounds. On the difference between
gen sg and gen pl compounds (*a printer's error* | *two
printers' errors*) see vol II 7.41.

The pl of *a lady's maid* is written *ladies' maids*.

The gen in the compound must logically be a pl in
cases like *a lovers' quarrel*.

16.9₂. Further examples of genitives of names of
human beings:

Thack P 2.75 all sorts of millinery and goldsmith's
ware | Hardy W 234 you are in man's clothes | Galsw
FS 575 he had never fancied himself a woman's man
(= 'lady's man, gallant') | Stopford Brooke, ELit
124 it [Pilgr's Progr] is a people's book | Fletcher in
BDS 407 the Doctor of Divinity's hat which bishops
always wear | Christie LE 86 she was child's play to
manipulate | Sitwell M 29 a chaplain, who always
suffered from curate's-voice, an occupational disease
comparable to housemaid's knee | Moore EW 319 she
had accomplished her woman's work—she had brought
him up to man's estate.

Here we may place Sh As III. 2.4 thy [Diana's]
huntresse name, as *huntresse* = *huntress's* (cf 16.8₂).

An example of the spreading of genitival composition is furnished by *bridesmaid*. This form dates only from the 19th century; the earlier form *bridemaid* is instanced in the NED from 1552.

16.9₃. Compounds with animal names are very irregular; often one and the same compound is found in both forms: *dog('s)-grass, crow('s)-bill*. Sometimes usage favours one of the forms, but it is hardly possible to find any guiding principle other than the vague one of general euphony: *bull's eye, hartshorn | horse-hair, fox-brush | cat's tail, dog's tail, horse-tail, foxtail, dovetail | bird's nest, birdcage | beeswax, bee-bread | ratsbane, rat-poison*.

Further examples:

Sh R3 V. 2.23 True hope is swift, and flyes with swallowes wings | LLL V. 2.332 whales-bone | AV Matt 7.15 Beware of false prophets which come to you in sheepes clothing | Lowell St 58 wolves in sheep's clothing and certain other animals in lions' skin | Swift 3.341 a piece of ass's flesh | Keats 2.42 Quick cat's-paws on the generous stray-away | Carlyle FR 418 at a snail's pace | Di Do 186 a mouse's hole (generally mouse-hole) | ib 233 the horse's cough | Thack V 213 making sheep's eyes at a half-caste girl | Trollope DC 1.203 like spiders' webs | dogs' ears alongside of dog-ears | Kipling L 222 fear of fire in the chambers and a louse's death in red flames | Mackenzie S 1.48 a woman with ... little pig's eyes | Galsw M 74 a yellow, crow's-footed face.

Note the vacillation between the two forms in Walton A 94 cow dung, or hogs dung, ... horse dung.

16.9₄. With names of things stem composition is far the more common, but *s*-forms exist. By the side of *hair-breadth* we have *hair's breadth;* similarly with other indications of measure: *hand('s) breadth, stone('s) cast;* always *keep at arm's length*. We say a *shilling's worth*, but a *pennyworth; a death's blow* (Scott Iv 265).

The gen of *ship* and synonyms is frequent in compounds: Di Do 21 the Ships' [!] Instrument-maker | Doyle S 5.252 half an ounce of strong ship's tobacco | Priestley F 193 in true ship's passenger style | Harris Shaw 62 Walter, being an Atlantic liner's surgeon, was not in port often enough. Cf. vol. VII 9.5₃.

Cf however ship-biscuit, -builder, -chandler, -owner, -wright, etc. | Wilde L 52 Peter the Great's residence in this country as a ship carpenter [not onboard ship!].

It is curious how many compounds with *man* as the last part have a genitival form (cp Bergsten 114):

backwoodsman, beadsman (*s* only from 16th c.), *bondsman, craftsman, gownsman, headsman, huntsman, kinsman, landsman* (as contrasted with *sailor*), *plainsman* 'man of the plains' (from 1881), *privateersman* (e. g. Franklin 281), *salesman, sidesman, spokesman, sportsman, statesman, steersman, townsman* (Maclaren A 55, cf ib countryman), *tradesman, oarsman*.

Similar forms are *saleswoman* || *towns-people* || *tradesman, trades-people, trades-folk* (Gissing B 319), *trades-unions, trades-associations* (both McCarthy 2.391), *trades-organization* (ib 392).

Bergsten 117 gives a list of compounds of common case +*man*.

The rule was once given me in England by a professor that it should be *on a winter day*, but with an adj *on a cold winter's day*. This rule is sometimes observed e. g. Byron (T) 5.217 A fair summer's twilight | ib 249 The close and sultry summer's day | ib 2.362 And some long winter's night | Thack V 347 of black winter's mornings | Stevenson MB 206 a fine summer's night | Shaw C 148 the monotony of the long summer's day.

But compounds with the common case are now used most frequently, even with an adj: Macaulay W 9 On one bright summer day | Thack P 91 in a calm golden summer evening | ib the pleasant summer air | Stevenson JH 14 about three o'clock of a black winter morning

| Meredith E 454 I am brighter on a dull winter after-
noon.

And we also find the gen without an adj: Hamerton
F 2.221 to get up at five o'clock on a winter's morning
| Keats 195 on a summer's day.

In ME *someres day*, etc., seems to be prevalent without
an adj; cf Sh A Winter's Tale, and Sonn 13, 18 | VA
23 A summers day will seem an hour but short.

16.9₅. The gen may be preceded by an adj, which
qualifies the whole compound (cf vol II 12 with appendix):

Ch A 624 a somnour . . . That hadde a fyr-reed cherub-
innes face | Sh Ro I. 4.59 long spinners legs | Swift
P 183 thou art a right woman's man | Defoe Rox 183
an honest, substantial weaver's wife | Austen M 52 that
is a complete brother's letter | Brontë V 455 the gar-
ments were genuine nun's garments | Mrs Browning
A 30 he wrapped his little daughter in his large Man's
doublet | Di D 46 a certain gloomy, arrogant, devil's
humour that was in them both | Thack V 371 his first
Speaker's dinner | Ritchie M 17 her manners were true
grandmother's manners | Meredith R 296 those soft
watchful woman's eyes | Mackenzie C 373 an excep-
tionally tall grandfather's clock | Stevenson T 205 a
haggard, old man's smile | Locke HB 265 a sort of peace
—a rotten politician's peace | Walpole Cp 141 his
sharp actor's face | Maugham MS 260 His body was
shaped like a huge duck's egg | NP 1927 her married
life has become an elaborate fool's paradise || Maxwell
S 255 thoroughly enjoying this carpenter's job || King
O 116 a wire squirrel's cage (*wire* ≠ an adj).

Analytic formulas: those soft watchful women's eyes
$2221(1^2$-1); his sharp actor's face $1^2 21(1^2$-1).

Some writers mark off this adj by means of a comma
(cf vol II 13.32):

Ward E 379 His absent, seer's eyes | Galsw D 204
his thin, horseman's legs | Bennett LR 373 he hated

his white, invalid's hand | Sitwell M 82 it seemed that his pointed, boar's teeth had grown still longer.

Note the double gen in Thack H 66 the poor clergyman's widow's son (*poor* qualifying *clergyman's widow's son*): 21(1²1²-1).

16.9₆. But the adj may also be placed after the gen: Collins M 29 I could see no more of his boy's rosy cheeks than of his boy's trim little jacket | Crofts Ch 90 concealed by the painter's blue overall which she wore | Locke CA 226 he had lost his bear's shambling gait.

Note the two adjs in Doyle S 1.59 grey shepherd's check trousers | Locke HB 72 Baltazar sat down to his usual hour's mental relaxation; the latter is 1²1 (21(1²21)).

It is different when the gen is qualified by a preposed adj which qualifies the gen only:

Locke CA 27 drinking his French peasant's breakfast bowl of black coffee | ib 46 for all his big dog's docility | ib 66 with an old warrior's artlessness; this is 1(21)²-1.

16.9₇. Particularly interesting are those cases in which the genitival compound is preceded by a gen or a possessive pronoun: the owner is, so to speak, expressed doubly, but the syntactic relation between the two genitives is different; the first gen (possessive) qualifies the whole: Swift J 8 Steele will lose his Gazetteer's place = 'his place as a Gazetteer': 1²1(1²-1).

Similar examples: Ch T 2.921 A nightingale ... sang ... in his briddes wyse, a lay Of love | Goldsm 630 What the plague do you send me of your fool's errand for? | Brontë P 197 Pelet's bachelor's life had been passed in proper French style | Di OT 19 The master, in his cook's uniform | id D 389 Mrs Micawber, keeping Mr Micawber straight by her woman's wisdom | Doyle M 65 she knew, with her woman's instinct | Trollope O 276 when your man's work was done | Meredith

T 95 his man's vanity | Walpole RH 172 her large, grave, questioning eyes, her child's face [note the difference from the face of her child] | Swinburne L 136 you will forgive my preacher's tone | Wells TB 1.84 my mother's white-panelled housekeeper's room | Walpole RH 58 I have been driven into the East by my collector's passions | Locke HB 167 in the gracious fullness of her woman's beauty | ib 205 in her Sister's uniform she looked very demure (also 212) | Sitwell M 15 chipping away at some fossil with his geologist's hammer.

The gen is a group-genitive in Locke HB 177 her woman of the world's sound sense.

16.9₈. It should be remarked that combinations with the indefinite article before a gen generally must be considered compounds: Sh As IV. 3.26 | Thack P 1.225 he was as gloomy as a death's head at parties | Mc Kenna Sb 231 it was treated with a scholar's judgment and knowledge and a philosopher's insight: with something, too, of a prophet's fervour.—Other examples are given in the preceding paragraphs.

Chapter XVII

Group Formations, with *s*-Ending

Group Genitives

17.1. We shall here deal with the phenomenon that the genitive ending is added to a whole group of words instead of to the word that might, perhaps, logically be expected to be in the genitive case, as in "the King of England's power", "somebody else's hat", cf Progr § 216 ff. = ChE 114 ff., where the whole subject is discussed at greater length and supplementary quotations may be found.

This chapter is placed here with the ordinary *s*-ending
though it includes remarks on pronouns which do not form
their genitive in this way (17.4₄, 17.6); the excuse is the impossibility of separating things belonging closely together.

Secondary and Primary

17.1₁. In a group consisting of an article, (or) an adj,
and a sb each element was originally put in the genitive;
but as early as the thirteenth century the modern construction came up of inflecting the sb only, thus often
in AR and still more frequently in Orrm.

AR 82 þes deofles bearn | ib 402 of reades monnes
blod | Orrm D 274 naness kinness schaffte || AR 314
þuruh þen abbodes gropunge | ib 388 on mihti kinges
luue | Orrm 2.331 þatt te birrþ flen þe defless hird |
ib 2.338 þatt laþe wifess faderr wass.

The latter construction is always used in ModE when
the adj is placed before its noun, but in ElE we sometimes
find the genitive mark affixed to a sb followed by an
adj: Marlowe J 242 you will needs haue ten years
tribute past [= the tr. of ten years past]. In Sh John
II. 1.65 With them a bastard of the kings deceast
[= a b. of the deceased king's] is taken from the old
play (Next them, the bastard of the kings deceast),
but the later folios change it into ... *the king deceased*,
evidently no longer understanding the construction.

The genitival *s* is regularly added to an adj when it
follows its sb: Davys Dream [Emerson ME Reader
232.17] for god almiȝtties drede | Steele F 101 the heir
apparent's eldest son | Kipling B 168 God Almighty's
storm | Holmes A 96 falling of the old-gentleman-
opposite's lower jaw | NP 1904 The Postmaster Gen-
eral's illness | NP 1913 the President-elect's views |
King Henry the Fourth's reign.

This genitive can, however, be used only in such
fixed groups as those instanced. It is not possible to
say, for instance, "the women present's opinion."

Words in Apposition

17.1₂. Two or more sbs in apposition originally had the genitive ending affixed to each word; they were frequently separated by the governing word, as in A. S. Chron. E. 853 Æðelwulfes dohtor West Seaxna cininges. In ME the same word-order is extremely common, but often it is only the sb before the governing word that is put in the genitive, while the common case is used in the other(s); in ModE this construction is getting rarer again, *of* being used to avoid it:

Sh H4A II 4.114 I am not yet of Percies mind, the *Hotspurre* of the North, *he* that killes me some sixe or seauen dozen of Scots | id Oth II 2.1 It is Othello's pleasure, our noble and valiant general | Eastw 455 your learned counsailes wife, The lawyer, Maister Bramble | Arnold P 1.191 Doubtless thou fearest to meet Balder's voice, Thy brother, whom through folly thou didst slay | Thack N 517 Mr. Honeyman's sister, the preacher, you know || Bennett W 1.230 it was the force of Cyril's will, Cyril the theoretic cypher, that took them.

In ME the governing word is sometimes found after the whole apposition-group; this word-order has become the rule, especially when the group consists of a title and a proper name; the genitive mark is added to the last word of the group only:

Orrm 2.334 ure Laferrd Christess bird | Caxton B 13 of the quene his modres owne brestis | Roister 67 For my friende Goodlucks sake | Marlowe T 1168 By Mahomet my kinsmans sepulcher | Sterne 41 to Dr. Slop the man-midwife's house | Thack P 1.18 Miss Hunkle, of Lilybank, old Hunkle the Attorney's daughter | Galsw FS 282 He rose from the perusal of Waterbuck, Q. C.'s opinion.

We may place here also Galsw SS 128 Whose [nose] was it? A man called MacGown's.

The genitive mark is rarely added to each part:

Bacon (quot. by Bøgholm) in the Queen's my excellent Mistress's time | Thack (quot. by Poutsma) his chaplain's, Mr. Sampson's careless life.

Cf also Bennett W 2.183 to the door of Allman's shop, the ironmonger's.

17.1₃. When the governing word is not expressed, the *s*-ending is added to the first sb if the word in apposition forms part of a long combination: Swift J 27 at Mr. Delaval's, the Envoy for Portugal | Thack N 54 I was there in the old woman's time, and Mr. Newcome's, the father of these young men | Bennett Cd 9 he slipped into Shillitoe's, the young tailor who had recently set up || Hunt A 123 he took me out with him to Nunn's the bookseller's in Great Queen Street.— Otherwise the ending is mostly added to both sbs or to the whole group, and the latter is the only form used now, when the group consists of a title + a proper name. But formerly the genitive ending might be added to the first part of such groups: Sh H5 I 2.105 Inuoke his warlike spirit, and your great vnckles, Edward the Black Prince | Swift J 120 I went to Bateman's the bookseller | Tennyson L 3.12 we started for their private tutor's, Mr. Paul, at Bailey Gate | Beaconsfield L 16 Villas like my cousin's, the Duke of Luton || Brett Young PC 23 she had tremulously entered Milton's the mantle-makers || Defoe M 297 at my friend's the Quaker's | Merrick C 226 would you tell us where Gaudy's the greengrocer's is? || Austen M 5 she may have a bed at her cousin the saddler's.

17.1₄. The group-genitive is also possible in such cases as the following, where the first word is a pronoun:

GE S 97 you youngsters' business | Di P 335 Which of you gentlemen's name's Snodgrass.

But the construction is usually evaded as in Sh Cor III. 3.100 the power of us the tribunes.

The genitive *you all's* is unknown in England, but

with regard to the southern American states, where
you all is used as a plural of *you* (cf vol II 2.88), C.
Alphonso Smith writes (*The Kit-Kat*, Jan. 1920):
"the use of possessive *we all's*—I have never heard
they all's—is confined to the illiterate, while the possessive of *you all*, which is *you all's* or *yo all's* is employed in social circles that have never used and never
heard *we all's*. Many persons, however, use *you all* who
yet stickle at either form of the possessive."

17.1₅. As the genitive of *we two*, etc., we may find
the possessive pronoun followed by the uninflected
numeral, which in some of the cases notionally qualifies
the sb instead of the pronoun:

Sh Cy V. 5.388 your three motiues [= the m. of
you three] Ado II. 1.396 I, with your two helpes |
Alls I. 3.117 Fortune had put such difference betwixt
their two estates | Wordsw 135 I will relate to thee
some little part of our two histories | Stevenson D 310
there is but one point in common to your two positions.

In earlier times a double flexion was found:
Ch A 586 hir aller cappe | id R 6947 our alder dede | Malory
98 To our bothes destruction | Bullokar Æsop 90 our twooz
chanc' (Differently in Lond E 120 thorough her both consent).—
On the construction when *both* or *all* precedes the pronoun,
see 17.6.

As the subject of the action expressed by a gerund
is sometimes expressed by a genitive or a possessive
pronoun (I insist on your coming) and sometimes by
a common case (I insist on all coming) (see vol V
Chs 8 and 9), a possibility arises of combining these two
expressions.

Sheridan 56 The confusion that might arise from our
both addressing the same lady | Fielding T 3.71 It
cannot be wondered at that their retiring all to sleep
at so unusual an hour should excite his curiosity |
Beaconsfield L 435 I fancy the famous luncheons at

Crecy House will always go on, and be a popular mode
of their all meeting. Cf vol V 9.5₆.

Finally some quotations showing how the difficulty
of the genitive of *we all*, etc. is avoided:

Ch G 192 Iesu Crist, herde of us alle | Greene F 10.25
To avoid displeasure of you both | Trollope D 1.254
For the happiness of them all | Thack P 2.215 The
happiest fortnight in the lives of both of them | Swin-
burne L 263 give Frank my best love and excuses in
the name of us all ‖ Mulock H 2.209 You must let me
go ... anywhere—out of their sight—those two.

Prepositional Groups

17.2₁. A group of two sbs connected by a preposition
was originally not felt as an inseparable unit; consequently, in the genitive, the group was separated by
the governing word; this was the universal practice up
to the end of the fifteenth century, and the construction
is resorted to even in more recent times when the
ordinary construction would present special difficulties:
Ch E 1170 For the wyues loue of Bathe | Malory 45 the
dukes wyf of Tyntagail | Sh LLL II 209 What's her
name in the cap? | id H4A III 2.119 The Archbishops
grace of York (= the Archbishop of York's grace =
his Grace the Archbishop of York) | Milton SA 372 For
honour's sake of former deeds. | Browning 1.431 The
Duke (with the statue's face in the square) [= with
the face of the statue in the square].

17.2₂. But as early as Chaucer we find *s* added to
the whole group, and from the Elizabethan period this
may be considered settled. While Ben Jonson in his
grammar mentions "for the Dukes men of Mysia" as
existing beside "the Duke of Mysias men" (is this
merely conservatism?), the only form mentioned in
Wallis's Gramm. Linguæ Anglicanæ 1683 p. 81 is The

King of Spain's Court.—Some examples of this modern construction with *of:*

Kemp NDW 22 on a publique stage, in a merry hoast of an innes part | Marlowe E 1293 My lord of Pembrokes men (also T 645, 3298) | Sh R3 I. 4.131 The Duke of Glousters purse | AV Luke 19.29 for the kingdome of Gods sake | Swift 3.116 to any village or person of quality's house | Defoe Rox 16 my fool of a brother's whole house of children | Sterne 89 the master of the inn, and the master of the inn's wife | Carlyle H 87 The man of business's faculty | Thack P 1.20 Mrs Wapshot, as a doctor of divinity's lady | ib 1.164 The member of Parliament's lady | GE L 2.190 a quarter of an hour's chat with her | Ru Sel 1.133 In some quarter of a mile's walk | Brontë V 298 the man of the world's respectability | Pinero M 36 Three-quarters of an hour's journey.

Sometimes, but very rarely, an ambiguity may arise from the construction, as in the puzzle:

The son of Pharaoh's daughter was the daughter of Pharaoh's son.

The word governed by *of* may be in the pl:

GE A 207 in plenty of people's hearing | Mrs. Marshall, Life of Mary Shelley 1.277 her love, like a woman's, —perhaps even more than most women's—was exclusive; Shelley's, like a man's,—like many of the best of men's—inclusive | Merrick MG 106 What does nine out of ten men's success do for anyone || Austen E 145 the Master of the Ceremonies' ball | Di H 121 his (and the Board of Directors') view of a railway accident | Thack N 221 at no very great distance from either of his brothers' town houses | GE Mm 95 after a couple of miles's [N.B.] riding | Christina Rossetti,Verses: Lo, the King of Kings' daughter, a high princess | Doyle St 88 I endeavoured to get a couple of hours' sleep | Mason 3G 305 the cellars where Mary Queen of Scots' Secretaries were put to the rack | id Ch 247 Major

Scott Carruthers would have dearly loved to have wrung that pedantical patron of the arts' abominable neck | NP 1923 The League of Nations' sub-committee of 1921.

Finally, an example with the group-genitive as primary: Carlyle R 1.270 Laplace's face, perfectly smooth, as a healthy man of fifty's, bespoke intelligence.

17.2₃. With other prepositions it is not so frequent to have groups that belong so closely together, cf, however, *my son-in-law's property*, etc.

This type offers the possibility of distinguishing the gen sg, common case pl and gen pl, *son-in-law's, sons-in-law, sons-in-law's*, but the last-mentioned form is probably never used.

Other examples: for God in Heaven's sake | Thack E 1.345 the Commander-in-Chief's levees | Locke BV 112 It isn't the Man in the Moon's fault || Ru P 1.136 affectionate to my father and acknowledging a sort of ward-to-guardian's duty to him | NP 1913 the Financial Secretary to the Treasury's action was a piece of disgraceful trickery || Philips L 33 a man-about-town's chambers | Galsw Rubein 28 a man-about-town's life || Di N 457 a case in the day before yesterday's paper | Ridge G 231 Use mine [handkerchief]. It's only the day before yesterday's.

But in dialects it is used with other prepositions as well; Murray gives as Scottish (Murray D 166): the man-wui-the-quheyte-cuot's horse; and Elworthy quotes from Somersetshire (Gramm. of the Dial. of W. Som. 157): Jan Sneok uwt tu Langvurdz duungkee 'John Snook out of Langford's donkey' | Mr. Buurj tu Shoalder u Muutuns paig 'Mr. Bridge of the Shoulder of Mutton's pig'.

Word with Adverb Added

17.3. The *s* is tacked on to the end of the whole group: Sheridan 283 at your service—or anybody else's |

Di M 372 Everybody else's rights are my wrongs | Thack V 244 On a day when everybody else's countenance wore the appearance of the deepest anxiety | Ru F 188 to change her for somebody else's wife. If you like somebody else's better than yours | Shaw P 216 dressed in somebody else's very second best | Galsw MP 241 his own unhappy home, not someone else's | Ibsen Master Builder [transl. by Gosse and Archer] 51 Yes, who else's daughter should I be?

Instead of the last mentioned form, some people would perhaps prefer *whose else*, especially when the sb is understood, as in Goldsmith 675 my only daughter, my Kate; whose else should she be?

It is unusual to attach the genitive ending to both pronoun and adv, as in the following quotations:

Di X 59 "Don't drop that oil upon the blankets, now". "His blankets?" asked Joe. "Whose else's do you think?" | Meredith H 481 on somebody's else's ground | Sketchley, Cleopatra's Needle 27 (vg) As if it it was easy for any one to find their own needle, let alone any one's else's.

The same construction might be expected for the genitive of *whoever*, as in

Mrs. Parr, Peter Trotman: The lovely creatures in my imagination took the form of the Matilda, Julia, Fanny, or whoever's image at that moment filled my breast.

But the form seems to be avoided; it is more natural to say *whose ever* or *whosescever*, and if the governing sb separates the pronoun and the adv, the ending is, of course, attached to the pronoun, as in Sh R3 IV. 4.224 whose hand soeuer. See vol III 3.6$_6$.

A group-genitive is possible with sbs like *looker-on* (where *on* belongs really to the verb *look*):

Hardy F 92 Every looker-on's inside shook | you've got the chucker out's place | this is the whipper-in's chair.

Coordinate Words

17.4₁. When one word should properly govern two
or more genitives, connected by *and* or some other
conjunction, it was the usual word-order in OE to place
the governing word after the first of the genitives; this
construction may still be used, especially when two
distinct objects are denoted, while it is rare if the same
object is meant, as in the last example below:

Sh H6A I. 2.75 against Gods peace and the Kings
[set phrase] | Thack P 1.16 Little Arthur's figure and
his mother's | ib 217 Affecting Miss Costigan's honour
and his own | Ward D 3.65 in spite of her friendship
and Ancrum's | Brett Young PC 243 They all drank
Clare's health and Ralph's.

17.4₂. As the same word-order was seen above (17.1₂)
to cause the dropping of the genitive ending in the last
word of an apposition-group, we cannot wonder at
finding here again the common case instead of the
genitive of the last part of the group:

Marlowe J 278 How, my Lord! my mony? Thine and
the rest [= that of the rest] | Sh LLL V. 2.514 'Tis
some policie To haue one shew worse then the kings
and his companie | BJo 3.169 if you had lived in King
Ethelred's time or Edward the Confessor | Trollope D
1.82 It is simply self-protection then? | His own and
his class [i. e. protection of himself and of his class] ||
Lamb E 2.V a two years' and a half existence || Meredith
H 78 Better if we had run a little ahead of your minute,
perhaps—and the rest of you.

Cf the similar phenomenon of leaving out the *s*-ending
in cases like the following; the construction is rather
frequent in ME and ElE (cf Schmidt, Sh Lex. 1423):

Ch A 3935 As piled as an ape was his skulle | Sh Cor
I 6.27 I know the sound of Marcius' tongue from every
meaner man | Austen P 421 to enjoy his conversation
as an agreeable and sensible young man | Di D 341

she put her hand—its touch was like no other hand—
upon my arm | Thack N 37 his delivery is grander and
more impressive than any divine now in England.

17.4₃. When the governing word is placed after all
the genitives, the *s*-ending is usually added to each
of them, if the governing word refers to each separately,
as in *Tom's and his brother's children*, while the group-
genitive is used, if the words form some sort of unit,
as in *Beaumont and Fletcher's plays; An hour and a
half's talk; In a year or two's time*. But the rule does
not always hold good.

Sh R2 II 3.62 your loue and labours recompense |
BJo 1.19 in Adam and Eve's kitchen | Bacon A 2.9
after an houre and a halfs sayling | Sterne 28 after an
hour and a half's silence | Fielding 1.507 you will break
both master and mistress' necks | Sterne M 1.169 my
father and my uncle Toby's discourse | Goldsm V 1.192
Dryden and Row's manner, Sir, are quite out of fashion |
Austen P 176 in the course of Jane and Elizabeth's
correspondence with her | Darwin L I 144 The difference
he felt between a quarter of an hour and ten minutes'
work | Galsw Frat 33 this one did not do in anybody's
presence, much less one's wife and daughter's || Locke
HB 95 Baltazar listened to Pillivant, the nurse and the
doctor's story || Sh Cor V 3.130 Nor childe nor womans
face | Defoe R 272 in a week or a fortnight's time |
Austen S 142 Such a thought would never enter either
Sir John or Lady Middleton's head | Shaw 1.151 the
test of a man or woman's breeding is how they be-
have in a quarrel | Wells T 62 in a minute or so's
time.

There is no conjunction in By 215 And Otway, Radcliffe, Schiller, Shakespeare's art.

If two persons have the same family name, there is
no difficulty in using the group-genitive:

Mr. and Mrs. Brown's compliments | both James and
John Stuart Mill's works.

If one and the same person is meant, the group-
genitive is the rule, but exceptions are found:

Defoe P 106 I took my friend and physician's advice |
Chesterton F 18 The shop was a popular greengrocer
and fruiterer's | Flaherty The Informer 130 He owned
a small tobacconist and newsvendor's shop || Di P 359
before a small stationer's and print seller's window.

17.4₄. With personal pronouns no exact parallel to
the last-mentioned construction is possible. No difficulty
arises in such combinations as the following, as *his* has
only that form:

Franklin 176 his and his companions' guns would
not go off | Tennyson L 1.176 His and my great-uncle |
Ruskin T 59 his and your adversary | Holmes A 250
he read to his and our friend the Poet.

But with those possessive pronouns that distinguish a
primary and a secondary form, the choice is difficult,
and we find different ways of getting out of the difficulty.—In this place we shall mention only those instances in which the pronoun precedes *and:*

(a) Sh Cor V. 6.4 in theirs and in the common cares |
Mi SA 808 mine and love's prisoner | Browning (T) 3.36
Mine and her souls | Cowper L 1.376 the present state
of mine and Mrs. Unwin's health | Thack E 2.144 He
was intended to represent yours and her very humble
servant || Walpole ST 164 Hamilton, a fellow club-
man of mine and of Wilbraham's.

(b) Carlyle H 4 Our and all men's sole duty | GE L
4.18 I received your and your husband's valued letters |
ib 167 I had heard of your and the professor's well-be-
ing | Crofts Ch [p. ?] he exactly covered your and the
manager's description.

(c) Caxton R 79 alle ye that ben of my kynne and
reynarts | Goldsm 630 you are her friend and mine |
Quincey 83 both on his own account and mine | Collins
W 558 by her consent and mine | Caine P 40 ruin her
own life and mine | Myers M 107 in the fifteen mi-

nutes between his arrival and Nilsson's I learned nothing.

(d) Thack P 2,103 Trifle with your own and others' hearts.

(e) Thack P 2.229 becomes one of your name and my own.

(f) Di DC 444 a polite wish for his happiness and the lady's | Ward El 135 the burden of his life and Aunt Pattie's | Maugham FPS 37 he made himself very funny at her expense and at Gerry's | Bennett Acc 130 Can he be my son and Elaine's? | Rose Macaulay P 186 Kindly let my affairs and Jane's alone.

(g) Thack V 372 For the expenses of herself and her little boy | Ward R 2.297 the shortest way to the pockets of you and me | Hardy T 411 for the sake of me and my husband.

(h) Bosw 2.158 on his own account, your's, and that of Mr. and Mrs. Thrale | Doyle in NP 1899 my life and that of my wife have been made miserable | Hope M 70 I rely on her account and that of the Colonel.

Cf also vol II 16.25 and 16.29 and below 17.6$_4$.

Clause

17.5. Finally, the group-genitive is rather common in colloquial language when a relative clause forms part of the group:

Cambridge Trifles 140 It [a brick] went into the man who keeps below me's saucepan | Stockton R 206 The man who kep' the house's wife.—In dialects the phenomenon is widely spread (Murray D 166; Darlington E.D.S. XXI 55; Elworthy Gr 15, Wright EDG § 388), and according to Mencken (AL 315) it is the usual construction in vg Amr: that umbrella is the young lady I go with's.

Cf Mr. What's his name's stupid remark | Di D 609 they took some of the trouble out of you-know-who's head.

The construction has points of contact with the
anacoluthia found, for instances in AV Ierem. 31.30
euery man that eateth the sowre grape, his teeth shall
be set on edge.—Cf below 17.9.

Difficulties with Pronouns

17.6₁. If the last word of a group corresponding to
those dealt with above is a personal pronoun, a difficulty
arises from the fact that we have possessive pronouns
instead of an *s*-genitive. Very often *both, all,* etc. may
be taken as belonging to the following sb rather than
to the pronoun:

Ch MP 5.618 I have herd al youre opinion | Caxton
R 35 he shal wynne bothe their good willes and loues |
Sh Hml III. 1.42 to both our Honors | ib III. 2.91 we
will bouth our iudgements ioyne | Cor IV. 6.35 all our
lamentation | Wint V. 3.147 Both your pardons | Ford
115 By both our loues I dare | Mi PL 6.170 As both
their deeds compared this day shall prove | Swift P 38
I have laboured both their characters with my utmost
ability | Shelley PW 2.68 For both our wretched sakes |
Austen M 326 for both your sakes | D 569 the gentle
cheerfulness of Agnes went to all their hearts | id
M 400 For all our sakes | Thack V 258 Both their hus-
bands were safe | ib 507 Both their lives | Collins W 58
for both our sakes | ib 76 For my own sake and for all
our sakes | Stevenson T 283 It went to all our hearts |
Ward E 11 it is the most monstrous folly on all our
parts | Philips L 66 it was for both our advantages |
Shaw 1.90 I beg both your pardons | id 2.126 I beg
all your pardons | Masterman WL 164 I shall want
all your help.

A different construction is seen in Wycherley Plain
Dealer 110 for your two sakes | Brontë (quot. by Pouts-
ma) all through our two lives.

17.6₂. As *both* and *all* were thus often felt to belong
to the sb, this might by attraction be put in the pl:

Sh All's I 3.169 you are my mother, Madam; would
you were (So that my Lord your sonne were not my
brother) indeed my mother, or were you both our
mothers | Swift P 163 one brimmer to all your healths |
Sterne 30 for all our sakes | Lamb E 1.127 a sister
died in both our infancies | Williams N 126 It was
both your faults, I suppose.

In the following quotations *both* and *all* undoubtedly
qualify the pronouns:

Sh John IV 2.102 to all our sorrows | Swift J 310
Dr. Swift is all our favourite | Priestley F 116 Ah [= I]
pay both our expenses | Maugham Pl 2.114 I think
she's been pulling both our legs successfully.

But the construction is generally avoided in such
cases.

17.6₃. What is the genitive of *some of them, one of
us*, etc.? A group-genitive is found in dialects (Sc. Is
this ony of you's?), and in colloquial E we find, though
rarely, expressions like these: Hardy L 214 one of 'em's
features | Tarkington MA 19 two hired men and one
of 'em's family | This must be some of you's.

Generally the *of*-construction is used to avoid the
difficulty ("the features of one of them"), but we also
find instances like the following, in which the poss.
pron. is used where the genitive belongs properly to
the whole combination. Note that in most, though not
in all cases it does not affect the meaning much whether
the adj is taken as referring to the pronoun or to the
sb, and that the latter sometimes takes the pl form
even where the sg might be expected:

Malory 79 I maye not graunte neyther of her hedes |
Sh Tw III. 4.184 God haue mercie vpon one of our
soules [i. e. the soul of one of us] | ib IV. 1.32 I would
not be in some of your coats for two pence | H4B II.
4.16 They will put on two of our ierkins [i. e. the jerkins
of two of us] | Tro II. 2.111 if he knocke out either of
your braines | Ant I. 2.46 Mine, and most or our fortunes

| Cy II. 3.71 I know her women are about her: what If I do line one of their hands [= the hand(s) of one of them] | Drayton Love's Farewell: Be it not seen in either of our brows That we one jot of former love retain | Fielding 4.27 it might have fallen to any of your shares | Tennyson L [p?] you remember my asking you whether either of your grandmothers was dead | Thack P 862 a painful circumstance, which is attributable to none of our faults [i. e. to the fault of none of us] | Twain H 1.140 in neither of your lives | Stevenson C 29 For all of our sakes | Wells TM 18 it ran in most of our minds | Doyle St 141 Without meaning to hurt either of your feelings | Joyce Ir 62 she knocked one of their brains | Kennedy CN 98 She's one of their daughters | id R 20 [children:] It's my theatre. 'Tisn't. It's all of ours.

17.6₄. When a personal pronoun forms part of a group of words connected by *and*, no group-flexion is possible, but the possessive pronouns are always used; with the possessives that have different forms as primaries and secondaries there is some hesitation between the forms (17.4₄); the difficulty is often avoided by adding *own* to the possessive, by placing the governing word after the first part of the group, or by using the *of*-construction.

Hardy L 137 for the boys' and my sake, if not for your own | Hankin 2.141 the waste of my time and their's || Thack P 2.103 Trifle with your own and others' hearts || Marlowe J 969 For your sake and his owne | Thack P 2.229 As becomes one of your name and my own | Ward R 2.297 The shortest way to the pockets of you and me | Haggard She 132 the first care of Job and myself was to wash ourselves.

17.7. To understand the phenomenon which has occupied us in this chapter it is not enough to point out that the words put in the group-genitive are felt to be closely connected in meaning: this may account for some of the cases (Macmillan & Co.'s publications, etc.), but does not explain the difference between the genitive *the Queen of England's* and the plural *the Queens of England*.

The first condition of forming genitives of whole groups as if they were single words is that the way of forming the genitive has become practically uniform, viz. by the addition of *-s* instead of the variety of endings in OE (*-a, ra, -en, -e, -re*, etc.). This condition is fulfilled in Danish (Norwegian, Swedish) as well as in English, and we therefore find group-genitives there as well (see my paper in *Studier tilegnede Verner Dahlerup* 1934, p. 1 ff.).

We have seen also in the previous sections that the personal pronouns in which this condition is not fulfilled offer some difficulties in the formation of a group-genitive.

If now we ask why the genitive has been thus regularized (by analogy) to a much greater extent than the formation of the pl (where we find a great many irregular forms, *men, children, oxen, geese*, etc.), the reason must be a different function of the two endings: if we put a sg into the pl, the change affects this word only; its relation to the rest of the sentence remains the same. But if we put a word in the genitive case which was in the nominative, we change its syntactical relation completely, for the function of a genitive is that of closely connecting two words. This also implies a difference from OE conditions in which the genitive (in much the same way as in Latin) had several other functions.

But it is noteworthy that in OE when the genitive had this special function it nearly always preceded the noun, and this later became the invariable rule.

The result may be said to be: one particular function of the genitive, one fixed position, and one invariable ending (though with three phonetic variants [z, s, iz]).

This *s*-ending thus is a kind of interposition—and that
explains the frequency, nay in certain conditions, the
universality of the group-genitive.

The theory here developed is confirmed by the fact
that when the conditions indicated are not fulfilled,
we find the *s* attached to the word to which the genitive-
ending would belong in other languages. We saw this
already to some extent above in the section about
apposition. The following are other instances showing
the same thing when there is no governing sb and the
s consequently cannot be put as an 'interposition'.

(1) a sb with a postposed adjunct:

Churchill C 469 I'd sooner shake her hand than anybody's livin'.

(2) prepositional groups:

AV Exod. 9.4 there shall nothing die of all that is
the childrens of Israel | F. E. Schelling, Sh-Jahrbuch
1904 242 The rest of the book is the editor's in chief |
Hardy W 148 I would on your account if on anybody's
in existence.

(3) word followed by an adv:

Latroon, Eng. Rogue, 1665, 1.53 I should devote
myself to her service and nones else | Thack P 1.79
They were more in Pendennis's way than in anybody's
else | Twain M 236 The entire turmoil had been on
Lem's account and nobody's else.

(The group-genitive forms to some extent a parallel
to group-ordinals like the twenty-seventh).

Group-Plurals

17.8. The pl of word-groups show the same tendency
of adding the ending to the last part, though for the
reason stated above (17.7) it could not be carried
through to the same extent as with the genitive. The
subject was dealt with in vol II 2.3 (see also Appendix
to vol II, p. 486 ff.), and a short summary is, therefore,
all that is needed here.

Apposition: lady friends | fellow travellers—but men servants, women folk; gentlemen commoners alongside of gentleman commoners (here the phonetic difference is generally obliterated).

When a group consisting of a title + a proper name is used as a common name, the natural formation of the pl is to add the *s*-ending to the latter element: Sh Wiv I 1.2 twenty Sir John Falstaffs | ib IV 5.71 Three Doctor Faustasses | MacCarthy 2.651 hundreds of Mrs. Tullivers all over England | Hope C 178 a thousand Mr. Taylors. Cp Poutsma p. 146 Are there Mrs. Nicklebies—or, to speak more correctly, are there Mistresses Nickleby in France? (Thack).

On the use with *Miss* see vol II 2.38 and Appendix.

Christian name + surname: the pl inflexion is added to the latter, whether the group is used as a proper or a common name: *in the party there were two John Browns | Michael Angelos are not common in every generation.*

With compound titles there is some hesitation:

Lord Chancellors by the side of *Lords Chancellor* (even *Lords Chancellors*); see vol II 2.37.

postmaster-generals by the side of *postmasters-general; court-martials, courts-martial;* and other compounds with the adjs, after the French idiom, placed after the sbs; see II 2.41.

Always *handfuls, spoonfuls* etc., but in less familiar compounds with *ful(l)* the first part may be inflected, e. g. *bucketsfull* (or *bucketfuls*) *of tea.* See vol II 2.42.

Compounds of the base of vb + an adv (prep.) generally have *s* added to the whole word : *drawbacks, stowaways;* but inflexion of the first part is found: *locks-out* (*lock-outs* is the usual form); *takes-in* and *take-ins.* See vol II 2.43.

Some *and*-groups are inflected as a whole: *bread-and-butters, whisky-and-sodas.* Shaw StJ 46 everything that the Black and Tans did in Ireland [= British soldiers, from their uniform, cf *a black and tan* = a black-and-tan terrier]. But we also find plurals like *brandies and soda(s)*.—See vol II 2.57.

On *this (these) kind of things*, etc., see vol II 3.81.

Similarly *grown-ups; breakwaters; forgetmenots; ne'er-do-wells; at-homes; something elses.*—See II 2.44-9 and 2.58 for other examples of these types. Quotation word: hand-shakings and "How are you"s.

The group-plural is not used with compounds consisting of verbal substantives in -*er* or -*ing* + adv: *lookers-on; goings-on.*—See vol II 2.51-2.

Similarly in groups of sb + prep. + sb: *two maids-of-honour | three quarters of an hour | two Commanders-in-chief.* Still the tendency to treat such compounds as inseparable units makes itself felt in some cases: *will-o'-the wisps | slugabeds.* | Kaye Smith T 178 [I] reckon we won't want any more Sophia of Worchesters to open our shows.—See vol II 2.53.

Son-in-law in StE has the pl *sons-in law*, but such combinations have the pl ending added to the last part in some English dialects; and according to Mencken (AL 315) this is always the case in vg Amr: *two son-in-laws.*

The pl of *good-for-nothing* is *good-for-nothings;* the reason for this group-plural is obvious: *good* is an adj and *goods-for-nothing* would suggest a wrong idea.

His instead of Genitive-Ending

17.9₁. A genitive relation is sometimes expressed by a common case plus a possessive pronoun; the full treatment in Progr § 248 = ChE § 146 is here abbreviated. Similar constructions are found in many languages, I quote only one instance, Goethe: Ist doch keine menagerie So bunt wie *meiner Lili ihre!* In many cases they are due to anacoluthia: the reader or writer begins his sentence without thinking exactly of the proper grammatical construction of the word that first occurs to him, so that he is subsequently obliged to use a correcting pronoun, e. g. Ch MP 5.99 The wery hunter, sleping in his bed, To wode again his mynde goth anon | Sh R3 I. 4.217 Alas! for whose sake did I that ill deed? For Edward, for my brother, for his sake.

And with the possessive following immediately its antecedent: Sh Tp V. 1.268 This mishapen knave, his mother was a witch | Scott Lay of the Last Minstrel 1.7 But he, the chieftain of them all, His sword hangs rusting on the wall | Tennyson 616 The great tragedian, that had quenched herself In that assumption of the bridesmaid, she that loved me, our true Edith, her brain broke with over acting || Ch M 3.145 For sothly he that precheth to hem that liste not to heere his wordes, his sermoun hem anoyeth | RV Num. 17.5 It shall come to pass, that the man whom I shall choose, his rod shall bud (cf AV: ... that the man's rod whom I shall choose, shall blossom).

17.9₂. Not infrequently we find an (indirect) object followed by a possessive where a genitive would have been possible: Malory 110 Syr Tor alyghte and toke the dwarf his glayue | By 5.260 and there at all events secure My nephews and your sons their lives | Hughes T 1.5 there is enough of interest and beauty to last any reasonable man his life | Tennyson 322 Merlin ... had built the king his havens, ships, and halls.—*To ask a man his pardon* is nearly equivalent to asking a man's pardon.

17.9₃. Now in English this is strengthened by the fact that the ordinary genitive ending in its three forms coincided with a shortened form of *his*, see e. g. Sh Alls II. 2.10 Put off's cap, kiss his hand | Cor II. 2.160 May they perceiue's intent | ib II. 3.160 At's heart | ib 171 For's countrey | ib V. 3.159 To's mother | Meas I. 4.74 For's execution | Marlowe J 1651 on's nose.

In the Prayer Book we find "for Jesus Christ his sake": here the old syllabic ending of *Christes* remained unaltered after the *e* had generally become silent, on account of the accustomed rhythmic enunciation; a better way of spelling the word would therefore be *Christès* as in *blessèd*, etc.

Thus we find the explanation of the following cases: Ch LGW 2593 Mars his venim is adoun | Sh Hml II. 2.512 Neuer did the Cyclop hammers fall On Mars his armours | Tw III. 3.26 'Gainst the Count his gallies | H4B II. 4.308 Art not thou Poines his brother? | LLL V. 2.528 A man of God his making (folio: God's) | Thack P 2.6 [housekeeper:] In George the First his time | Gilbert 36 Seven years I wandered—Patagonia, China, Norway, Till at last I sank exhausted At a pastrycook his doorway.

To the popular feeling the two genitives were then identical, or nearly so: and as people could not take the fuller form as originating in the shorter one, they would naturally suppose the *s* to be a shortening of *his;* this is accordingly a view that we often find either adopted or contested in old writers (Hume, Maittaire, Addison, Enquire Within).

And thus we have the explanation of the famous "Bill Stumps his mark."

(The phenomenon has been treated by Mätzner 3.236; Fr. Koch 2.249; Abbott Sh-Gr. § 217; Storm EPh² 775; Einenkel, Streifzüge 109, and Paul's Grundriss 1.909; Kellner, Blanch. xxxvi, and Outl. § 308; Franz ESt 17.388, and Sh-Gr.³ § 332.).

Chapter XVIII

The Endings -*s* and -*st* in Particles

(Particles here include Adverbs, Prepositions and Conjunctions)

-*s*

18.1₁. This ending is generally supposed to derive from the genitive, but its origin is not altogether certain.

The addition of an -s in adverbs, or the use of this ending as a means of forming adverbs, is a widespread phenomenon within our family of languages—developed perhaps independently in each language.

It is seen in Gk *houtōs, hōs, tōs*, and probably in *ex*, variant of *ek*, and *eis* (<*ens*), variant of *en*.

In Lat: *cis, sus* for *subs* (e. g. *suscipio*), *ex, abs*, etc.

F: *sans* < *sine* | *jadis* < *jamdiu* | *tandis(que)* < *tamdiu* | *jusques* < *deusque* | *lors* (*lorsque, alors*) < *illa hora;* (the *s* seems here to be a pl ending, if anything) | *certes* (which has been borrowed into E).

Spanish: *antes, entonces, mientras*.

In the Gothonic languages this *s*-ending is quite common; thus in Gothic it is found in advs derived from nouns, e. g. *gistradagis* ('to-morrow'), as well as in cases where no corresponding noun is known, e. g. *suns* ('soon').

G has a considerable number of such advs: *vergebens, fluges, stracks, damals*, etc.

Dan: *i morges, betids, undervejs, nys, me(de)ns, ingensteds*, etc.; in vg Dan the adverbial *s* is added even more freely: *kuns, slets ikke*, etc.

In OE the ending is found in a number of advs formed from nouns, and there naturally considered as a genitive e. g.: *selfwilles* | *unwilles* | *his āgenes willes* | *wordes ond (oþþe) dǣde* | *ānes* ('once') | *elles* from *el-*, an adj which is only known in compounds in OE | *dæges*. In early OE *nihtes*, formed on the analogy of *dæges*, is only found together with this, but in late OE it is also found standing by itself.

But there are also OE advs in -s in many cases where no corresponding noun exists: *hidres, þædres* (besides *hider, þider*), *togenes him* (Chron A 911), *þwyres* (Oros 188.15), *þweores, -weardes* in *hāmweardes, tōweardes*, etc.

In ME this ending spread considerably. On the analogy of *anes* the forms *twie* and *þrie* (< OE *twiwa, þriwa*) became *twies, thries*.—We find *alwayes* besides *alway* (< *ealneweg*); Ch has *otherweyes*. These advs must be regarded as formations from the gen sg, not from the pl; cp in Juliana 12 *eisweis* (and ib 13 *eanis weis*).

Also *now-a-deyes* must be the gen sg, seeing that it is found at the time when the pl of *day* was still *dawes*.— *whiles* is found besides *while* (< OE *þā hwīle þe*); *hennes*, *thennes*, *whennes* besides *henne*, etc (< OE *heonan*, *þanon*, *hwanon*), Ch has both forms. We find *togidres*, *amonges* (both in Ch), and *sinnes;* but *sin* is found in Ch and Malory; *sith* for *since* is found in Marlowe J 2146. The form without the *-s* is still used in Sc meaning 'since' or 'ago', Scott A 1.72 sin' auld P. J.'s time | ib 1.191 as ye did a while sinsyne.

18.1₂. In ModE the *-s* has spread further, and has become established in a number of advs:

thereabouts, whereabouts, hereabout(s); in Sh these advs are found with and without the ending. Defoe Rox 82 she let him easily know whereabouts he rode | Goldsmith 673 Whereabouts do you think we are? | Austen M 341 whereabouts does the thrush lie? | Masefield S 312 Whereabouts do you live? | Di F 770 hereabouts. —When *whereabouts* is a primary, as in *I don't know his whereabouts*, the *-s* is felt to be the pl ending.

needs (now almost exclusively used before or after *must*); Ch often has the old form. Swift J 32 Sir A. F. would needs have me go to the tavern.

unawares; in Sh both with and without *-s*.

amidships, betimes, etc.

The form with the *-s* added also became established in the following words, which, however, are now archaic or obsolete:

anights: Sh As II 4.48 a night;—thus in F1, but the later folios have *a nights* | Marlowe J 798 you'le like it better far a nights than dayes | Lamb R 10 her cough was less troublesome a-nights.

Ch MP 3.1087 algate | ib 1171 algates | Sh Tw V 199 other gates.

Besides *while* we find a variant in *-s* in ModE, but the latter is passing out of use. (For *whilst* see 18.2₁).

Sh LLL IV 1.99 erewhile | id R3 I 2.32 Rest you,

whiles I lament King Henry's corse | id Meas IV 3.84
whiles | Ward F 185 I advise you to agree with him
quickly whiles you are in the way with him.

Similarly the variant in -*s* has become extinct in:
togethers (e. g. More U 29), *alives*, and others.

In vg E the -*s* is found in numerous cases where it
has not prevailed in StE: Stevenson T 129 *nows* and
thens | ib 228 *where's* they are | vg *nowheres* | Kipling
B 61 *somewheres* | Twain M 17 *anywheres*.

Thus also *everywheres, oftens, anyhows, somehows*, etc.

18.1₃. The adverbial -*s* has in many cases come to
be associated with the pl ending. Cf also Moon's remarks
(Eccles. Engl. 1886, 137) on the hesitation of the Revisers of the Old T. between *alway* and *always, afterward*
and *afterwards;* he concludes: The Revisers' notions of
singular and plural, though plural, are truly singular.

Some instances of advs that are felt as pls:

perhaps according to Skeat is *per* + pl of *hap;* Zupitza,
however, quotes *perhappous* from Lydgate.

oftentimes now always with the adv -*s* added, but
Ch has *ofte tyme* (B 1719) and *often-tyme* (MP 18.44).
Malory 134 oftyme, but 97 and 119 ofttymes.

sometime(s): the old form is found in Malory 148.3 some
tyme ... and some. The two forms are used indiscriminately in Sh Ro 967 where Q₁ has sometimes,
Q₂ sometime. Similarly Tp III 2.145 sometimes, 146
sometime in the same sense.—But now on account of
the association with the pl *sometimes* is only used in
the sense of 'at times', whereas *sometime* is used as an
adjunct in the sense of 'at one time', 'formerly'; e. g.
Zangwill G 197 his sometime prejudice. Still the form
in -*s* is found in the latter function in Mitford OV 50
the wife of our sometimes gardener.

always: Malory has *alwey* as well as *alweyes*. The AV
also has both forms.

out-of-doors: Ch has both forms with *at* (B 4567,
H 306). In Sh we also find both forms; Wint II 3.67

Hence with her, out o' dore | As III 1.15 push him out of dores.

on all fours: the earliest example in NED is from Defoe 1713.

early days: Sh has the form in -*s* in Troil IV 5.12.— Caine E 325 It is early days to call you by a dearer name.

now-a-days, betimes, mornings (= in the morning), *upstairs,* etc.

The use of an adverbial form in -*s* in phrases containing *way* has, no doubt, been strengthened partly by the mentioned association with the pl, partly by a confusion between these forms and adverbs in -*wise.* The confusion is seen in instances like the following:

Swift T 128 if I can have any ways contributed to the repose of mankind | Meredith R 165 I wish they'd let us ride our ponies strideways.—Cf also Murray D 226 the word *ways* [wez] = *wise, ways* is also used to give an adverbial force ...

See also vol VII sub Case.

In Sh the form in -*s* is frequent: Ro V 3.19 What cursed foot wanders this wayes to night (thus F, but Q has: this way) | Tp II 2.76 Come on your ways | Meas III 2.88 | Tw II 5.1.

Further examples: Malory 59 ye must other wayes than ye do | Fielding T 2.134 we have travelled a great ways out of your way | ib 3.146 that is a great ways off yet | ib 3.229 nothing any ways material to this history | Carlyle H 34 Skrymir went his ways | Kipling P 280 they fled from me everyways.

18.1₄. With some of the advs that exist both with and without the -*s* there is a distinction between the two forms as to function or meaning:

beside(s): of position both forms are found in Malory, with the ending as an adv in 111 here besydes, without the ending as a prep. in 121 besyde humber. Nowadays only the latter function of the word is found in this sense, and the shorter form is always used. This is

also the case in the phrase: beside oneself = mad; e. g.
Ward F 419 he was nearly beside himself.—Meaning
'over and above' *besides* is now the only form used,
whether as prep. or adv; but in Marlowe J we find
beside (2001) as an adv and *besides* (1997) as a prep.

sometime(s), see above, 18.1₃.

As to the adv *indoor(s)*, *out-(of-)door(s)* the same
tendency is observable of employing the shorter form
as an adjunct and the longer as a tertiary; still there
is a good deal of wavering.

Darwin L 1.113 Two peculiarities of his indoor dress |
ib 117 his only outdoor recreation | Sinclair R 269
indoor playgrounds for bad weather, and a big all-
outdoors romping ground | Darwin L 1.113 His usual
out-of-doors dress | Murray D 227 an out-of-doors
servant || Darwin L 1.113 he then went out of doors.

18.1₅. *-ward* [-wəd, (after unstressed syllable) -wɔ·d]
in adjs originates from OE *-weard*, primarily meaning
'having the direction of', corresponding to G *-wart*,
and ultimately related to Lat. *vertere*, *versus*.

In its two forms, without and with *s*, this ending
occurs chiefly after local advs.

toward as an adj meaning 'about to happen' is without
s: there is a case toward pronounced [touəd].—The prep.
is found with the *-s* in Ch HF 196 towardes, whereas
the AV and the Rev. Version have *toward* exclusively.
Sh has both forms. Stevenson HJ 100 The movement was
thus wholly toward the worse. In StE the prep. is now
towards, but in Amr the form without the -s is still
found in that function. The pronunciation used to be
most frequently [tɔ·(ə)d(z)], but of late years [təˈwɔ·d(z),
tuˈwɔ·d(z), twɔ·d(z)] has been gaining in favour, though
Fowler (MEU) seems to regard it as half-educated.

downward(s): as an adjunct without the -s: a downward movement, as a tertiary with hesitation between
the two forms.

forward(s): always *look forward to* and *from that*

day [*time*, etc] *forward*; otherwise both forms are
found, but Fowler (MEU) thinks there is a recent
tendency to displace *forwards*. According to him
afterward, once the prevalent form, is now obsolete in
British use, but survives in U. S. *Onward* is much commoner than -*s* except possibly in phrases of the type
"from the tenth century onwards" (ib).—The -*s*-form
is established in the phrase: backwards and forwards.
(Still I find in Hope R 300 Which is it to be? Backwards or forward).

The adverbs in -*ward* and -*wards* are so nearly synonymous
that it is impossible to give any hard and fast rule for their
use. "The choice between them is mostly determined by some
notion of euphony in the particular context; some persons
apparently have a fixed preference for the one or the other
form." (NED) "Where the meaning to be expressed includes
the notion of manner as well as direction of movement, -*wards*
is required, as in 'to walk backwards', 'to write backwards'.
In other instances the distinction seems to be that -*wards* is
used when the adv. is meant to express a definite direction in
contrast with other directions: thus we say 'it is moving *forwards* if it is moving at all' ... Hence -*wards* seems to have
an air of precision which has caused it to be avoided in poetical
use." (NED).

To the common derivatives from adverbs (preposi-
tions) *afterward*(*s*), *backward*(*s*), *downward*(*s*), *forward*(*s*),
inward(*s*), *onward*(*s*), *outward*(*s*) and *upward*(*s*), may be
added *elsewards* (Trollope A 298 these earthly sufferers
know that they are making their way heavenwards,—
and their oppressors elsewards), *hitherward* (Wallace
Reporter 233 it was hitherward that the crime reporter
made his way), *leftward*(*s*) (Carlyle R 2.340 Wordsworth
who was leftward on my side of the table | Bennett C
1.259 he peered as far as he could leftwards), *withinwards*
(Bertram Atkey in BDS 278 ... he said very silently
withinwards).

18.1₆. *Weard* (*ward*) was also used as an independent

sb = 'direction' after nouns preceded by *to*, from ME
also after pronouns and also preceded by *from*, e. g.
AS Chron. 1009 to scipan weard | Ch A 397 From
Bordeaux ward (frequent in Ch) | Malory 70 thow gost
to the deth ward | Caxton R 17 to the ryuer ward
(frequent in Caxton) | Sh Cor I. 6.32 to bedward |
Wint II. 1.64 to th' Nay-ward 'in the direction of No'.

With pronouns: Ch Boeth II p. 4.54 to thee-ward |
Caxton R 14 to you ward (frequent in Caxton) | AV
2 Cor 1.12 to you wards | Bunyan G 5 to you-ward.

Mrs Carlyle (NED) The eyes starting out of them
me-ward | Swinburne SbS 13 Thy vesture ... Hides
usward thine impenetrable sleep | ib 95 turn usward |
Caine C 82 staring me-wards | R. Brooke Poems 18
There grew Meward a sound of shaken boughs. This is
never found in colloquial speech.

18.17. The following are rare forms or words coined
for the nonce, some of them (after ||) derived from
place-names:

Thack V 512 to bedward (and 4 quotations in NED
1530—1834) | Trollope A 323 the world which is sup-
posed to have gone altogether shoddywards | Wells
PF 41 we were all ... moving luncheonward | id V 178
some great force drove life beautyward | ib 207 directed
doorward | Hughes T 2.20 he strolled college-wards |
Rose Macaulay T 268 Maurice's thoughts were not now
woman-ward | Freeman Th 1066 we resumed our pro-
gress riverwards | NP 1930 the aims of education
should be turned "starwards" | Sayers GN 414 Harriet
turned back with him marketwards | Mannin W 53
the Anthony Eden hat bobbed steadily stationwards ||
Shaw A 106 he ... dashes off Strandwards | Black F 71
the cab rolled away down Kensington-wards | Wells
Ma 2.250 now both their minds were Londonward |
Ridge Mord Em'ly 109 the train went Londonwards
(fairly common). It will be seen that both forms with
and without *-s* occur.

Some sb derivatives are well established, such as Godward (e. g. Swinburne T 87), heavenward, home-ward, landward, seaward, skyward, windward, world-ward (Wells H 379), southward (in nautical language pronounced [sʌðəd]), east-, west-, and northward.

-st

18.2₁. In practically all the words in question, *against, amongst, amidst, whilst,* etc. we find earlier forms in *-(e)s*, like those mentioned in 18.1. Murray explains *t* as due to form-association with the superlatives, but there is no semantic connexion to justify this assump-tion.

In some of the words *-st* may have developed from *-s þe* through the regular transition *þ > t* after *s*, thus *whilst* from *whiles þe (te)*, cf *lest* (Early ModE *least*, e. g. Spenser FQ I. 1.12) from *(þy) læsse þe*, but most cases are to be differently explained.

We have no doubt to do with a phonetic development as in Dan. *taxt* (cf E. *tax*), Sw. *eljest, medelst*, Germ. *papst* (cf E. *pope*), *obst, palast* (cf E. *palace*), etc., see vol I 7.64 and Linguistica 354-5, and cp. vol I 7.62.

18.2₂. A special case is *erst*. In OE we have *ærest* as a real superlative, 'first', from *ær* 'formerly'. ME *erest;* in Ch *erst* has the superlative sense only in the phrase *at erst* (e. g. B 1884 And than at erst he loked up-on me), and soon after Ch the superlative became obsolete. But in ME we also find *erst* = 'formerly, before', common in Ch even with *than* after it, e. g. A 1566 That shapen was my deeth erst than my sherte. Also with *er*, e. g. C 662 Longe erst er pryme rong of any belle. This *erst* is probably developed from *eres + t*. *Erst* survives into ModE: Caxton R 98 | Lyly E 97 | Marlowe T 1773, 2859, Jew 2090 | Greene F 3.65 | Sh frequent (see Sh-Lex) | Spenser FQ 5.11.16 | Mi SA 339 etc. Used by modern poets as an archaism, e. g. Arnold P 1.177.

18.2₃. In one case a differentiation has taken place: *again* adv, orig. 'against', thus still in Sc (*agin*), and vg (Shaw A 110 dont let him lay a charge agen me ...); *against* prep. and conjunction.

18.2₄. Other adverbs with -*st* with corresponding examples in -*s*: *alongst* (Stevenson C 269) | *amongst* (More A 60 etc. amonges) | *amidst* (Spenser FQ I. 1.36 amiddes); does the sb *midst* belong here, too? At any rate forms without *t* occur, e. g. More A 74 in the middes of the Ilande | Cooper Dict. s. v. Biton: in the mids of his glorie. But it may be a superlative, even though strictly speaking the notion 'mid' does not lend itself to comparison, cf Dan. *midterst*. Wordsw has (260): The types and symbols of Eternity, Of first, and last, and midst and without end—thus parallel to other superlatives | *betwixt* (Ch A 277 Bitwixe) | *whilst* (Spenser FQ I. 2.4 whiles; note that the subst *while* may occur with -*s*, too: Ford 161 a pretty whiles ago).

In vg speech -*t* is added to words in -*s* pretty frequently, thus from Barker Orig. Engl. 17 and 45 *nicet*, 147 *scarstly* | *wonst* (for *once;* Pegge Anecd 70-1) | *acrost* (Kipling Plain Tales 116 acrost the river | id Mandalay; 'crost the bay) | *chanst* ('chance'; Kipling Plain Tales 293 | Shaw P 266 chawnst) | even St. Pancrusst (St. Pancras; A. Sketchley, Cleopatra's Needle 77).

In Irish, too, the phenomenon is well-known according to Joyce Ir 97, who quotes *oncet* and *twiced*, cf also Kipl Plain Tales 158 [Mulvaney:] unbeknownst | Flaherty Informer 35 unknownst (already Di, quoted by Storm). —In the dial. of Lincolnshire occurs *alust* = always.

Chapter XIX

Other Endings with Sibilants

-*ess* I

19.1₁. This suffix offers a striking example of the way in which a suffix may spread. It originates from

Greek, in the classical language occurring in one word
only, viz. *basílissa* 'queen', from *basileús* 'king', of
obscure origin. Note the *-i-* in feminine endings (see
Linguistica 298).

From *basílissa*, the suffix *-issa* spread in late Gk to
other words, e. g. *diakónissa* and *prophetissa*, which
were adopted into Latin, and hence, with new formations
into the Romanic languages.

In French the ending *-esse* became the ordinary
feminine suffix (see Nyrop, Gramm. hist. II § 422 ff.),
and from here it was adopted into English, see A.
Knutson, The Gender of Words Denoting Living Beings
in English (Lund 1905).

Among French words adopted after the Conquest we
find *abbess*, *baroness*, *countess*, *duchess*, *hostess*, *princess*,
lioness, to mention only some of those that still survive.

The suffix soon came to be considered as an ordinary
English feminine suffix, and many new words were
coined, at first from French words only, but from the
14. cent. from English roots, too, e. g. *goddess* (from
1340), *herdess* (Ch T 1.653), *Jewess*, *frendess* (both in
Wyclif).

"By writers of the 16th and succeeding centuries
derivatives in *-ess* were formed very freely; many of
these are now obsolete or little used, the tendency of
modern usage being to treat the agent-nouns in *-er* and
the substantives indicating profession or occupation as
of common gender, unless there is some special reason
to the contrary." (NED)

In many cases French has no corresponding form in
-esse:

chiefess (Maugham TL 45, MS 260, Alt 146), *citizeness*
(Fr. *citoyenne*), thus in Mrs Stowe (NED) and Jerome
Three Men on the Bummel 147 (both with the two
words *citizen* and *citizeness* together), *Jewess*, *mayoress* (a
Fr. *mairesse* is now only jocular), *millionairess* (Zangwill

G 41, Galsw SS 246), *soueraignnesse* (Dekker F 101; obs.), *squiress* (NED from 1823, Meredith EH 394).

19.1₂. In many cases the suffix is simply added to the unchanged masculine form, e. g. *countess, heiress, hostess, lioness,* and, from English words: *goddess, quakeress, (shep)herdess,* and more or less obs. forms like *bakeress, breweress.*

On stress in *princess* see vol I 5.58.

19.1₃. But there are a good number of irregularities. Some of these are due to French rules of formation, e. g., *duke—duchess, emperor—empress, negro—negress.*

The discrepancy between *abbot* and *abbess* is due to the former being borrowed at an early stage from Romanic *abbed* (> OE *abbod*), *abbess* being a later regular French development of Lat. *abbatissa.*

19.1₄. With words in *-er, -or* there are several methods of derivation:

1) the stem is preserved unchanged: *archeress, bakeress, breweress, manageress, porteress* (Thack S 110; in NED examples of *portress*), *quakeress* (e. g. in Brontö J 171), *seeress, trooperess* (nonce-word: Galsw WM 152 lying to them like a trooperess), (*grand*) *Vizieress* (rare; NED 1884, Wells JP 96) || *authoress, inquisitoress* (Oppenheim Prod. Monte C 98; NED has *inquisitress* 1727—1897 and *inquisitrix* 1879), *prioress, tailoress, warriouresse* (Spenser FQ V. 7.27).

2) the vowel before *r* is elided:

a) *-e-* is dropped, e. g.:

arbitress (Swinburne L 146), *enchantress* and *dis-*(Carlyle SR 101), *foundress, huntress, jointress* (law term, from an obs. *jointer* 'joint holder'; first quotation in NED: Sh Hml I. 2.9), *laundress, offendresse* (Sh Alls I. 1.153; only quot. in NED), *paintress, waitress.*

b) *-o-* is dropped:

actress, ancestress (e. g. Galsw MW 70), *benefactress* (Shaw), *conductress, directress* (Defoe G 6), *doctress, editress, electress, executress, inheritress, instructress, pro-*

prietress, protectress (Sh Oth IV. 1.14), *sculptress,
tormentress* (Kingsley H 187), *traitress, translatress,
tutress* (Ruskin S 2.432; rare, generally *tutoress*).

3) loss of *-er, -or* through haplology:

adventuress (e. g. Thack V 382), *conqueress, fruiteress,
murderess, procuress* (e. g. Defoe M 128), *sorceress*.

Adulteress and *laundress* are derived from the earlier
forms *adulter* and *launder*.

4) *governess* (but Ch MP I. 141, II. 80 etc. govérn-
erésse).

19.1₅. The frequency of *-tress* (corresponding to *-tor*)
as seen in the above list has led to the use of *-tress* as
an independent suffix. Knutson, *l. c.* 37, mentions
hermitress, hostress (Wyclif), *poetress* (Spenser) and others
but most of them are obsolete.

To *marquis* (from OF *marchis* 'governor of the
marshes') corresponds *marchioness* (from late Lat.
marchionissa).

To the two forms *master* and *mister* corresponds
mistress with its two pronunciations [mistris] and
[misiz] and the shortened form *miss*.

Kipling K 255 has the strange form *necromanciss* from
necromancer.

Tyranness (e. g. Spenser FQ I. 5.46) corresponding
to *tyrant* with an excrescent *t*, OF *tiran*.

Votary forms *votaress*.

19.1₆. The frequent occurrence of nonce-words with
the suffix *-ess* shows that authors are well aware of
its existence and the need for it. On the other hand,
authors frequently offer a kind of apology by putting
it between inverted commas, or even apologize in words.

Among nonce-words may be mentioned: Thack V 41
cockneys and *cockneyesses; farmeresses* (Mitford OV 78
"May I be allowed that innovation in language?"),
giantesses (Chesterton Shaw 124), *philosopheress* (Huxley
L 2.333), Kipling P 137 [child speaking:] "Was your
nurse a—a *Romaness* too?", Browning (T) 5.396 a small

spanieless (if one may coin a word), Thack V 345 the
sweeperess at the crossing, *Swissess* (NED), *Turkess*
(Marlowe T 1261, 1317; only this in NED).

On the meaning of *-ess*-words as 'vocation-feminines',
'marriage-feminines', etc. see vol. VII ch. VI, Sex.

-ess II

19.2₁. Another suffix *-ess* represents Fr. *-esse* from
Lat. *-itia* in nexus-sbs. In former times the suffix was
used to some extent, thus we find in Spenser i. a.
feeblesse, gentlesse, humblesse, and *simplesse,* which are
now all obsolete and have been supplanted by forms
in *-ness* (*feebleness, gentleness*) or *-ity* (*humility, nobility,
simplicity*).

Nobless, used by Spenser and (once only) Sh, was
revived by Ruskin.

The ending has no formative power. The existing
forms are felt as having no connexion with the adjs:
largess, prowess and *duress.*

F *richesse,* ME *richésse* with stress shifting *riches*
[ritʃiz] was interpreted as a pl, see vol II 5.62.

-ice

19.2₂. *-ice* [-is] in sbs, mainly nexus-words, from Lat.
-itia (or *-itium*) through OF *-ice* (*-ise*).

Only in *cowardice, justice, notice* and *service* can this
ending be considered an Engl. derivative suffix.

-ness

19.3₁. This suffix, pron. [-nis] comes from OE *-nes(s),
-nis(s), -nys(s),* parallel to German *-niss,* Goth. *-nassus.*

In OE *-nes* is the suffix most usually attached to
adjs and past ptcs to form sbs expressing a state or
condition. A large number of these OE formations
survive, and it is now possible to add the suffix to any
adj or adjectival word.

19.3₂. Because of the characteristic 'English-ness' of

this suffix, comparatively few words from Romanic
adjs are in common use. In many cases these words
compete with other derivatives, most often in -(i)ty, e. g.

ableness (rare), cf *ability; capableness* (Bennett Helen
65)—*capability; impassableness* (London M 21)—*im-
passability; impossibleness* (North 245)—*impossibility;
persuadableness* (Austen M 254)—*persuasibility; ab-
normalness* (Benson D 165)—*abnormality; materialness*
(Ruskin T 171)—*materiality; cruelness* (rare)—*cruelty;
entireness* (Mitford OV 36, Carlyle E 124, 153)—*entirety;
humanness* (London M 233, AHuxley Little Mexican
277)—*humanity; immaculateness* (Galsw MP 83)—*im-
maculacy; silentness* (Shelley 71)—*silence; simpleness*
(Sh, e. g. Ado III. 1.70), now *simplicity; sincereness*
(Meredith E 294)—*sincerity; vainness* (rare)—*vanity.*

Cp. also *calmness* with *calm* (Bennett Cd 98 with
false calm he gave the paper to Ruth. Her calmness in
receiving it upset him).

Purists at various periods have had a special predilection for this ending, as also such modern authors
as D. H. Lawrence and Aldous Huxley, who have
coined or revived such words as *awareness, otherness,
aloneness, oneness, allness, togetherness, newness,* see O.
Vočadlo, Saxonismy v novější angličtině, Časopis pro
mod. fil. 21.3-4. (With a brief summary in English).

With *oldness* (Mulgan) cp. *age.*

Littleness (e. g. Browning 2.299, 308, 314, Wells Mr
Polly 185) is an equivalent of 'small size'.

19.3₃. From *busy* we have two words, now differentiated with regard to both spelling, pronunciation and
signification, cf vol I 3.138 and 9.91:

business [biznis] 'transactions, shop',
busyness [bizinis] 'being busy'.

Derivatives from comparatives and superlatives:
Carlyle F 3.111 I am growing better ... it is a kind of
road towards *betterness* | Kipling K 251 It is indeed all
finished. Mahbub snapped his fingers to show the

utterness of that end | Trollope D 94 that *nearestness*
and *dearestness*.

The following are derivatives from pronouns or
similar words:

nothingness (Shelley P 73, Carlyle SR 9, Galsw M
155, etc.), *oneness* (Meredith E 43 this gives us our
oneness, our isolation, our happiness), *sameness* (Jackson
Shaw 23).

And then there is the common phrase *much of a
muchness*.

19.3₄. Derivatives from second ptcs in *-ed* and adjs
in *-ed* are quite common:

accustomedness (Jerome Three on the Bummel 215),
ashamedness [əˈʃeimidnis], *contentedness* (Mitford OV 13),
devotedness (Carlyle E 161), *unexpectedness* (Skimpole
Shaw 133), *unprotectedness* (Mitford · OV 13), *wide-
awakedness* (Benson N 285) || *level-headedness* (Sherwood
Anderson Many Marriages 79), *selfcentredness* (Skimpole
Shaw 32).

Cf also *deadness* (Seeley E 203).

Formations from first ptcs also occur:

knowingness (GE M 1.60), *smilingness* (By Ch 3.16)
winningness (Kipling Plain Tales 44).

Words from ptcs with adv added: Lawrence LG 117
If he had seen the least sign of *coming-on-ness* in her,
he would have fluttered off in a great dither | Sayers
Bellona Club 25 general *fedupness* | Galsw D 224 her
quaint *grown-upness*.

19.3₅. Many *-ness*-words are formed from such words
and groups as *without being technically adjs* re-
semble them, especially if they can be used predicatively,
e. g. *aliveness* (Carpenter Art of Creation 111), *aloofness*
(Kipling S 120), *awareness* (frequent, also *unawareness*).

Further:

London V 111 such *fast and looseness* I never saw
[without hyphens] | Cabot P 178 her *hard-upness* last
night | Fletcher Dan. Quayne 103 he approached the

farmstead and ... recognised its *well-to-do-ness* of
appearance | Dickinson R 87 the *'worth-whileness'* of
life | Galsw MP 57 the family *matter-of-factness* | id
WM 139 his eternal *in-the-rightness* | Mitford OV 7 a
charming *in-and-outness* | Waugh W 18 airing his
man-of-the-world-ness.

Awayness (AHuxley Barren Leaves 108 the awayness
of it | Lawrence L 16 Something of the terrible far-
awayness of a child), *downrightness* (Ward M 80),
togetherness (AHuxley Eyeless in Gaza 61).

Phrases with vbs may take *-ness*, even though the
phrases could not naturally be used as predicatives:
Kipling L 106 *can't-get-at-ness* | Galsw WM 10 their
restlessness and practical *get-there-ness*.

A feeling that *-ness* can be attached to adjs only,
is probably responsible for the addition of *-ish* in Wells
H 9 that delightful *out-of-the-wayishness*. But *out-of-
the-way-ness* may also be found.

Out of the common are *wilderness* and *witness*. The
former, from OE *wildēor* 'wild beast', the latter is OE
witnes(s) from *wit*, vb, cf OHG *(gi)wiznessi;* from meaning 'attestation, testimony' it has come to mean 'person
giving evidence', etc.

As late as the 16th and 17th centuries we sometimes
find such spellings as *profaness* for *profaneness, proness*
for *proneness, clenesse* for *cleanness, brownesse* for
brownness, and especially *finesse* for *fineness*, e. g.
More U 150 fynesse | Walton A 89 finess,—if this is
not direct from Fr.

Here also belongs *forgiveness*, OE *forgifennes* from the
second ptc.

On *-ness* as supplanting *-ess* see 19.2.

-ize, -ise

19.4₁. The verbal suffix *-ize, -ise* [-aiz] is from Fr.
-iser. Late Latin *-isare*, Gk *-izein*. NED recommends
the spelling *-ize* in all Gk and modern words, cf Fowler

MEU sub *-ise* and *-ize*. Nexus-sbs are formed in *-ization*, *-isation*, agent-nouns in *-izer*, *-iser*. In some cases we have corresponding nexus-sbs in *-ism*, and agent-nouns in *-ist*, see 19.9.

Meanings: provide with, bring into, become, follow or have such a practice or feeling, impregnate with, etc.

19.4₂. The suffix is used to form vbs from adjs and sbs. It occurs in originally Gk words, such as *agonize*, *chrystallize*, *scandalize*, *symbolize*, in words from Latin, e. g. *civilize*, *patronize*, *realize*, and from French, c. g. *authorize*, *organize*, *mesmerize*. Sometimes it is difficult to decide whether a word is formed on Fr. or Engl. soil, e. g. *moralize*.

A great many derivatives formed from Engl. roots are in common use. The derivative generally preserves the stress of the word from which it is derived, see vol I 5.64, but on other points irregularities of derivation are not infrequent, thus we have several forms derived from words in *-ist* (or *-ism*) by subtracting this suffix and then adding *-ize*, e. g. *alchemize* (Tenn 619 and NED) from *alchemist*.

The nonce-words *darwinize* (Marett Anthropology 9 We are all Darwinians in a passive kind of way. But we need to darwinize actively ...) and *journalise* (Gissing B 144 and G 68) probably belong here. So also *bolshevise* (Maugham Pl 4.98 I was only going to bolshevise it [the car], so to speak).

Other irregularities in the relation between root and derivative are:

appetize (with *appetizer* or *-ser*, e. g. RBennett P 138) from *appetite*, *attitudinize* with *-n-* from L *aptitudinem*, *deputize* from *deputy* (Walpole C 57 deputise), *patronize* [pætrənaiz] from *patron* [peitrən], *sensitize* 'to prepare sensitive paper' from *sensitive* (e. g. Butler Essays 270, Egerton Kn 117), *stabilize* corresponding to *stable*, *tantalize* (with *tantaliser* 'tantalus, spirit-stand' Galsw FM 239) from *Tantalus*.

19.4₃. Derivatives in *-ize* may either be used transitively or intransitively or both, thus e. g. *materialize* means 1) make material, or 2) become material or real (e. g. Kaye Smith HA 48 Gervase's scheme of going into a workshop materialized more quickly than his family had expected).

Womanize in Meredith E 32 he womanized his language means 'make womanly', but the derivative *womanizer* (*womaniser*) as in Galsw WM 194, Philip Macdonald The Maze 93 means a 'person given to loose life'.

19.4₄. A great many occasional formations in *-ize* are found, e. g. Shaw F 24 they [i. e. gold-fields] should be internationalized, not *British-Imperialized* | Wells H 365 they had been *circularized* [= 'had had circulars sent to them'] | Galsw T 266 they [hat and shoes, etc.] *commonised* her | McKenna While I Remember 117 a *deracialized* Jew | Meredith E 80 *Londonizing* | Dowden Shelley 159 "*nakedize*", i. e. 'run about without clothes' | Butler Essays 306 a person "*ostrichising*" the evidence which he has to meet | Carpenter Ad 48 Hindus who come to London *outwesternise* us ... other westernising Hindus | James RH 435 He had been *pedestrianising* for six weeks | Wells H 268 a kind of *respectable-ization* of divorce | London War of Classes 268 *sailorizing* | Galsw TL 292 the *semi-bolshevized* imperialism (cf above Maugham) | Gissing B 350 I would *sonnetise* on this idea.

In U. S. there are a great many derivatives in *-ize*, see Mencken AL 192 f., where the author mentions "monstrosities" like *backwardize*, *fordize*, *belgiumize*, *respectablize*, *scenarioize*, *manhattanize*, and *cohanize*, adding "I suppose I could dredge up at least a hundred more."

-ish in Verbs

19.5₁. *-ish* [-iʃ] as a verbal suffix is developed from *-iss-* in the extended stem of F vbs in *-ir*, *-iss-*, as in *finir—finissant—finissent*, etc., and originates from Lat.

-isc- in inceptive vbs. The [ʃ]-sound comes from the
OF dialects of Normandy and Picardy, see J. M. Booker
in *Studies in Philology.* Univ. of North Carolina. 1912.

The majority of E vbs have developed regularly
from F -*iss*-verbs, and call for no detailed discussion
in this chapter: *abolish, banish, cherish, finish, furnish,
perish, polish,* etc.

19.5₂. In several other cases different verbal endings
have been changed into -*ish* by analogy, thus *admonish*
< OF *amonester* | *astonish* < ME *astonen, astunen* <
OF *esto(u)ner, estuner* | *diminish,* a mixture of *minish*
with the obs. *diminue* from F *diminuer* | *distinguish* <
ME *disting(u)en* < OF *distinguer* | *famish* < *fame* vb
from Lat. *fames* 'hunger' | *lavish* < *lavish* sb < OF
lavasse, lavage 'deluge of rain' | *minish* < OF *menusier,
menuisier* | *publish,* from OF *puplier,* later *publier,* was
adopted in the form *publy* (the NED from 1300 to
1500) | *vanquish* < OF *vencus* past pple and *venquis*
past tense of *veintre* (ModF *vaincre*).

19.5₃. In some cases the vb was adopted with end-
stress, e. g. *banish, finish, punish,* see vol I 5.56, but
now the invariable rule is to stress the syllable before -*ish*.

Note. Not all F verbs in -*iss*- developed to -*ish*-verbs in
English, thus we have *rejoice* from OF *rejoiss-* (only case with
non-palatal [s], cf vol I 2.743), *advertise* from OF *avertiss-* (perhaps
under the influence of *advertisement*), *chastise* from *chastiss-*,
amortize from *amortiss-* etc.

-ish, -sh (-ch) in Adjectives

19.6₁. The adjectival suffix -*ish*, -*sh* belongs to the
common Gothonic material.

The ordinary English form is -*ish*, but in a few old
forms the *i* has been elided. In Scottish the ordinary
form is -*is*, syncopated -*s*, -*ce*, see below on *mennisc*
and *Scottish, Scots.*

In a few cases the final consonant of the root becomes
voiced before the suffix, see Linguistica p. 376: *elvish*

(Meredith E 321, Wells N 364) from *elf*, though *elfish* is found, too, from 1542 according to NED; *thievish* from *thief;* Coleridge Anc. Mar. 275; *wolvish*, occurring from 1430, e. g. Bale Three L., Sh, BJo P V. 3.667 woolvish, is now obsolete, although Coleridge has it 1817; *wolfish* is quoted in NED from 1570; *wivish* and *wifish* are rare. *F* is found in *dwarfish* (Marlowe, Sh) and *selfish*.

In OE the ending was especially used in derivatives from national names, causing, if possible, *i*-mutation, thus *Brittisc, Denisc* (< **danisk*), *Englisc* (from *Engle, Angle*), *Frencisc* (from pl *Francan* 'the Franks'), *Grēcisc* (> *Greekish*, now archaic, still in Sh more common than *Greek*, Franz³ 128), *Scyttisc* (from *Scottas*, in OE meaning 'Irish'), and *Wielisc* (from *Wealas*, pl of *wealh* 'a foreigner', now *Welsh*, or, in the names of regiments, *Welch* (e. g. Graves Good-bye to All That 121)).

In ME the mutated forms developed from *Denisc*, as also those developed from the corresponding OE sb *Dene*, were supplanted by forms with *a*, probably under the influence of Danish *a*-forms. Mutated forms were preserved in Scotch till a late period in the now obs. *Dence, Dense.*

In *French* the mutated vowel was preserved, because the relationship with *Frank* was loosened. To this a new derivative *Frankish* was formed.

In late OE *Scyttisc* was supplanted by *Scottisc*, a new formation on *Scotta* 'Scot', later *Scottish*. In England a shortened form *Scotch* arose in the 16. c. (first in the compound *Scotchman*), and "the adjective did not become common in literature until the second half of the 17th century" (NED; first quotation 1606). Later *Scotch* was adopted into Sc. and was 'used regularly by Burns, and subsequently by Scott' (NED). In the Sc. dialects *Scottish* phonetically became *Scottis* (cf *Inglis*), later *Scots*, and nowadays the forms *Scottish*

and *Scots* are preferred by Scottish people; see the following quotations:

Macdonell E 13 ... a Scotch ...—Not Scotch. Scots.
Or Scottish.—Sorry—A Scottish Commander-in-Chief |
NJacob Lie 159 the Scottishmen—remember never to
say Scotch, Max, unless you speak of whisky.

During the ME and ModE periods other adjectival
derivatives from national names arose, such as *Cornish,
Flemish, Irish, Jewish, Jutish, Pictish, Polish, Spanish,
Swedish, Turkish,* etc.

Note. In some cases there is also a form in *-ic*, thus
Finnic used only as an adj, parallel to *Finnish* which
may be used as a sb as well, to designate the language
of the Finns. Similarly the adj *Gallic,* from Lat. *gallicus*
beside *Gaulish* from *Gaul,* adj and sb. *Icelandic* is the
ordinary form beside the rare *Icelandish. Romic* (coined
by Sweet 1877 for his phonetic alphabet) beside *Romish*
'Papistical'.

Other OE forms that have survived are *hǣðenisc*
'heathenish', *cīldisc, cierlisc* from *ceorl* 'man of low
degree' > *churlish.* (On *mennisc* 'human (being)', Low-
land Sc *mense* 'good manners, propriety of behaviour':
'Meat is good, but mense is better' see Skeat, Princ.
of Engl. Etym. 1.271).

19.6₂. After OE times the ending has been used more
and more, at first, as in OE, only to form adjs from
sbs with the meaning 'pertaining to, of the nature of';
boyish, dwarfish, elfish (see above), *feverish, girlish,
liverish* 'suffering from disease of the liver' (Hankin
2.17 a lean, liverish Anglo-Indian), *nightmarish* (Crofts
in BDS 367), *selfish, vixenish* (Ru 1.308), *wolfish* (*wolvish*
see above).

In a great many cases the derivative is derogatory.
(But sometimes the sb in itself represents something
objectionable, e. g. in *brutish, currish, devilish, foolish,
foppish, hellish, knavish, roguish, shrewish, sluttish,
snobbish, whorish*). Clear examples are:

babyish (Chesterton, etc.) | *barristerish* (Wells A 157) |
childish (as distinct from the colourless *childlike*, e. g.
in NP 1924 [songs for children] their only fault is a
tendency to be more childish than childlike; cf also
Browning 2.315 Genius has somewhat of the infantine:
But of the childish not a touch nor taint) | *doggish* |
goatish | *hoggish* | *mannish* 'masculine' (generally used
of women, though not in Barrie MO 130 politics were
in her opinion a mannish attribute to be tolerated;
distinct in colour from *manlike* and *manly*) | *missish*
'affected' (In NED from 1795, also Austen P 314) |
monkish | *mulish* (Cowper L 1.382 muleish) | *popish*
(see Bennett T 5 there were at least three Methodist
chapels to every church and the adjective 'popish' was
commonly used in preference to 'papal') | *selfish* |
womanish (as distinct from *womanly*).

19.6₃. The suffix is further used to modify adjs, here
meaning 'somewhat, rather, approaching the quality
of'. According to NED it was used "apparently first
with words of colour, e. g. *blueish* (a 1400), *greenish*
(first in Ch), *blackish* (a 1500) ... " Cf *purplish* (Sayers
HC 340), *ochreish* (Bennett HL 129, beside *ochreous*,
ochry). But later it was used with other adjs, especially
monosyllables.

These adjs belong to colloquial language, when the
speaker does not want to be too categorical. Some of
those exemplified are nonce-words:
baddish (Doyle S 420) | *baldish* (Maugham FPS 23) |
biggish (Sayers HC 209) | *carefulish* (Huxley L 1.491) |
cleverish (Swinburne L 58) | *coldish* (Jerome T 186) |
dearish (Priestley) | *dullish* (id) | *easyish* | *fastish* (Swin-
burne L 91) | *fine-ish* (Meredith EH 227) | *flattish*
(Priestley) | *genteelish* (Cowper L 1.198) | *goodish* (Sayers)
| *heavyish* (id) | *largish* (Galsw MW 146) | *littlish* (Sayers) |
longish (Wodehouse) | *more-ish* (Swift P 60 How do
you like this tea, Colonel?—Well enough, madam; but
methinks it is a little more-ish) | *newish* (Maxwell F 22

they all talked of new or newish books) | *oldish* (Priest-
ley) | *queerish* (Sayers) | *roughish* | *sharpish* | *slenderish*
(Fletcher) | *smallish* (Freeman) | *smartish* (NED from
1740) | *strongish* (Hope Ch 165) | *tallish* (Bennett LR
1 Tallish—but stoutish) | *thickish* (Freeman) | *tiredish*
(Priestley G 281) | *weakish* (Sayers) | *youngish*.

19.6₄. "In recent coll. and journalistic use, *-ish* has
become the favourite ending for forming adjectives for
the nonce (especially of a slighting or depreciatory
nature) on proper names of persons, places, or things,
and even on phrases" (NED). To the long list given by
the NED, the earliest of them dating from 1815, may
be added:

Priestley G [Tauchn.] 1.58 Mr. Truby in his Dickens-
ish little office | Lamb E 2.177 that pretty insipid half-
Madonna-ish chit of a lady | Wingfield-Stratford Victor-
ian Tragedy 8 their John Bullish complacency | Galsw
WM 237 Leonardoish || Quentin P 62 I felt a bit hang-
overish | Galsw MW 72 she's still honey-moonish |
Meredith EH 439 innuendoish | Galsw F 108 a loverish
fancy | Ertz Mme Claire 39 mother-in-lawish | Meredith
E 286 nincompoopish idealizations | Priestley A 191
Anything northish | Chesterton Shaw 194 Shaw's ideals
are . . . even, one might say, old-maidish | Kaye Smith
HA 180 silly . . . schoolgirlish . . . novel-reading-old-
maid-ish | Dreiser F 283 a light summery dress, very
smart and out-door-ish | Graves Goodbye to All That
61 We would . . . naturally refuse to be hearty and
public school-ish | Carlyle R 2.177 Mrs. Taylor, a very
will-o'-wispish irridescense of a creature [NB. from will-
o'-*the*-wisp] | [Lucas Rose and Rose 125 out-for-funnish-
ness | Di P 77 a touch-me-not-ishness in the walk].

Further may be mentioned U. S. slang *ittish* 'sexually
attractive'. *Stand-offish* is an established form, Mackenzie C 20 has: [she was] blooming stuck-up . . . her
reputation for stuck-uppishness. *Snappish* is an established derivative form *snap* vb. Finally *uppish* (Meredith

EH 184 don't be uppish about it—will you? | Shaw
D 175 | id uppishly | R.Bennett P 54 "uppishness").

19.6₅. A recent use of the ending is to modify points
of time, also as stated in figures. This usage, as suggested
by NED Suppl., may be after words like *earlyish*,
lateish (NED from 1611, Carlyle R 2.330 *latish*).

Examples with numerals are:

Maxwell HR 249 Then it won't matter if I am a
little late. Very well. Sixish. Till then goodbye | Priestley
AP [T] 1.117 And—er—eightish then, next Tuesday,
eh? | Bennett LR 320 The fat, little, thirtyish nurse |
Graves Goodbye 19 his eighteen-fortyish riding-boots.

Cf also Priestley G [T] 1.63 Can I descend upon you
some time to-morrow, dinner-ish? [i. e. about dinner-
time].

-esque

19.6₆. *-esque* [-ˈesk] is etymologically the same suffix as
adjectival *-ish*, but adopted through Romanic, medieval
Latin *-iscus*, which in Ital. became *-esco* > Fr. *-esque*.

Some words in *-esque* were adopted from French:
arabesque, *burlesque*, *grotesque*, *moresque* (Fr. *mor-*,
mauresque), *romanesque*. From Spanish came *picaresque*
(Sp. *picaresco*, from *picaro* 'a rogue'). The sense of the
suffix is 'in the manner or style of', and in Italian
"derivatives in *-esco* are formed *ad libitum* on names of
artists, and Fr. and Eng. writers have imitated this
practice" (NED), thus we have *Casanovesque* (AHuxley
BL 67), *Garboesque* (NP 1936), *Kiplingesque* (Archer
A 162), *Molièresque* (Henderson Shaw[1] 390), *Rembrandt-
esque* (Galsw MP 36), *Shawesque* (Henderson Shaw[1]
340), *Titianesque* (Chesterton), etc.

If the word from which the adj is derived ends in a
vowel, this is dropped (Casanov(a)esque), if semantic
reasons do not prevent this (Garboesque).

Picturesque is remodelled from Fr. *pittoresque* (Ital.
pittoresco) on the analogy of *picture*.

From *Monaco* we have *Monagasque* (Philips L 224).

Further the ending may be found in some nonce-words, mainly of a jocular character:

Locke GP 91 something of the exotic, Arabian Night-esque | Wells H 354 a neat bonnetesque straw hat | cigaresque (NED) | Henderson Shaw[1] 309 Cunninghame Graham, the hidalgesque and fantastic | Galsw Ca 222 his pipchinesque little old face.

-ous

19.7₁. *-ous* [-əs] from OF *-o(u)s*, developed from Lat. *-osu(m)*, parallel to ModFr. *-eux*. General sense 'full of'. On stress see vol I 5.65.

A great many direct loans from Fr. are not felt as direct derivatives, thus *anxious, dubious, hideous, odious, serious*.

Others are felt as E derivatives from sbs, e. g.

(ad)venturous, dangerous, desirous, famous, hazardous, joyous, marvellous, monstrous, mountainous, nervous, ruinous, venomous, villainous, virtuous.

19.7₂. In words derived from sbs in *-y* there are two spellings according as they are derived from an OF word in *-ie*, in which case they are spelt with *-ious*, or from OF *-té*, where the derivative has *-eous*, e. g.

envious—envy, furious, glorious, but *beauteous—beauty, bounteous, duteous, piteous*.

In one case Engl. has derivatives from both the Fr. and the Lat. form of a word, viz. *envious* 'feeling envy', and *invidious* 'exciting envy'.

Note also the following three related synonyms: Locke SJ 117 a *treacherous, traitorous* Macchiavelli | Carlyle FR 160 *Treasonous* to the public peace.

19.7₃. Derivatives from Engl. words:

(1) from words in *-r* (in some cases *e* before *r* is dropped): *murderous, murmurous, slaughterous* (Sh Mcb V. 5.14), *slumbrous* (Keats 1 vol. ed. 197), *thunderous* (ib

207), *wondrous* (from ME gen. *wonders, wondres*, then analogically with *-ous*).

(2) from other words: *burglarious* (Galsw Sw 280, *burglariously* Stevenson D 130), *flirtatious* (Lewis MA 67, id EG 122), *knowledgeous* (Ferber S 61, 307), *timous* (Sc, = 'timely'), *uproarious* (common).

19.7₄. Phonetic difference between the derivative and the word it is derived from:

(1) *v* in the derivative, *f* in the original word: *grievous—grief, mischievous—mischief*.

(2) Different vowels:

omen [oumən]—*ominous* [ɔminəs], *studious* [stju·diəs] —*study* [stʌdi], *zealous* [zeləs]—*zeal* [ziˑl].

(3) [ʃ] in the derivative, [s] in the orig. word because an *i* has been dropped in the sb, but preserved in the adj:

gracious [greiʃəs]—*grace* [greis], *spacious* [speiʃəs]— *space* [speis], *officious* [ɔ'fiʃəs]—*office* [ɔfis] (with shift of stress).

Similarly with loss of *u* in the sb:

contemptuous [kən'tem(p)tʃuəs]—*contempt* [kən'tem(p)t] *sensuous* [senʃuəs]—*sense* [sens].

(4) Shift of stress; in some cases with other changes, too:

advantage—advantageous, auspice(s)—auspicious, burglar—burglarious, calumny—calumnious, censor—censorious, ceremony—ceremonious, courage—courageous, fallacy—fallacious, ignominy—ignominious, labour—laborious, luxury—luxurious, malice—malicious, melody—melodious, moment—momentous, office—officious (see above 3), *outrage—outrageous, platitude—platitudinous, tempest—tempestuous, tumult—tumultuous, victory—victorious*.

19.7₅. Various irregularities:

tyrant—tyrannous, angle—angulous, fable—fabulous, scruple—scrupulous, number—numerous, tremble—tremulous, people—populous.

In a large number of cases the adj (generally a development from a Lat. word) corresponds to a sb with a suffix (or part of a suffix) not found in the adj, e. g. *-on* (in *-ion, -tion*):

oblivion—oblivious, religion—religious, suspicion—suspicious, caution—cautious, contradiction—contradictious (Galsw Tat 147), *disputation—disputatious* (Stevenson M 19 young men are disputatious; obviously felt as a derivative of *dispute*, also Galsw F 153), *ostentation—ostentatious, vexation—vexatious, fiction—fictitious* (with an extra syllable from Lat.).

Loss of *-y* in the sb:

analogy—analogous (with the shift [-dʒ- : -g-]), *blasphemy—blasphemous, calamity—calamitous, chivalry—chivalrous, infamy—infamous, iniquity—iniquitous.*

Or the adj may have another (Lat.) derivative ending before *-ous*, e. g. *platitude—platitudinous* (Wells N 343, Locke FS 248), *merit—meritorious, labour—laborious.*

Corresponding to *moment* there are two adjectives in *-ous: momentaneous,* corresponding to *moment* = 'point of time', and *momentous,* corresponding to *moment* = 'importance, weight'.

In slang or coll. language there are a good number of adjectives formed from other adjectives for the sake of emphasis by adding *-ous* or some fancy suffix ending in *-ous,* thus from *splendid* we get *splendidous* (BJo 3.41), *splendidious* (with shift of stress to the second syllable), *splendiferous* (Barrie TG 396), *splendacious* and *splendiculous* (both from Weseen Dict. of Amr. Slang p. 401), and from *grand* (Weseen 344-345) *grandacious, grandiferous,* and *grandilious.* In a great number of other fancy words the etymology of which in most cases is uncertain, and which are used as slang expressions for 'excellent, etc.' *-ous* or *-ious* is also very often used, see e. g. the chapter on general slang expressions in Weseen and Partridge, Slang p. 20.

19.7₆. In some cases we have now *-ous* developed

from another ending which became weakened and then
was interpreted as *-ous*, e. g.

courteous from OF *courteis* (More U 24 courteys),
theftuous (obs.) acc. to NED from ME *thiftwīs; righteous*
is generally interpreted as developed from *rihtwis*,
bounteous acc. to NED is originally *bontif* + *-ous*, later
transformed as if from *bounté* + *-ous;* similarly *plenteous*
from *plentif* + *-ous* (see Mandv 209 plentifous, ib 211
plenteevous).

Late OF *eu* in Engl. regularly developed into [iu,
ju·]. So we get in Engl. two parallel suffixes /-us/ >
[-əs] and /-ius/ > [-iəs], see further I 9.83. Examples:

(1) *hidous* (Ch, Mandv 24), supplanted by *hideous*,
pitous (Ch R 420)—*piteous*, *glorous* (Heywood P 901
vaynglorously)—*glorious*, *labourous* (Ch D 1428 lábor-
óus)—*laborious*.

(2) modern vulgar forms with *-ious, -jous:*

barbarious (Kipling B 45), *covetious* (Shaw C 234, see
also Fowler MEU sub *covetous*), *heinious* (heard by myself), *grievious, tremenjous* (Stoffel Int 186, 189), *trem-
enjis* (Thenks), *tremenjus* (Shaw A 182), *terrimenjious*
(Di F 734).

Note also *uproarious* (common).

In some cases *-ous* is probably to be interpreted as
an adaptation of Lat. nom. masc. *-us:*

anonymous, barbarous, conscious (no Fr. or Ital.
correspondent, earliest occurrence 1601 BJo, who
ridicules it), *conspicuous, continuous, credulous, decorous,
erroneous* (Fr. erroné), *facinorous* (BJo 3.109), *frivolous,
garrulous, notorious, previous, prosperous, ridiculous,
rufous* (e. g. Wells JP 137), *spurious, stupendous, superfluous, surreptitious, various*.

Note that the sb developed from Lat. *callus* 'hardened
skin' is spelt *callous*, e. g. Kaye Smith HA 46 pl callouses
| London M 24 a hand so calloused | Norris S 103, 260.

The objection of NED that *igne-ous*, answers also to
igne-a, igne-um, etc., does not seem very convincing.

-ous was even so firmly established that the Lat. ending *-is* was replaced by it, e. g., in *enormis—enormous, hilaris—hilarious, illustris—illustrious, scurrilis—scurrilous, tenuis—tenuous.*

19.7₇. In some cases we have *-acious* (apparently in adherence to the ending *-acity*) because the Lat. adj (in *-ax, -acem*) could not naturally be transferred to Engl., thus e. g.

audacious, capacious, efficacious, fallacious, loquacious, tenacious.

Here belong the analogous forms *flirtatious* (from *flirtation,* Zangwill G 42, Bennett T 55, etc.) and *gossipaceous* (Darwin L 1.375).

From Lat. adjs in *-ox* we similarly get Engl. adjs in *-ocious,* e. g. *atrocious, ferocious.*

-ose

19.7₈. *-ose* [-ˈous]. A more Lat. form of the suffix *-ous.* Some spellings in *-ose* from the 15. and 16. centuries are probably only graphic variants of *-ous,* e. g. *pompose, virtuose.* In other cases the adj is a direct loan from Lat. without any corresponding E word in *-ous* or F word in *-eux,* e. g. *morose* [moˈrous].

The only words rightly included in the theory of derivation in E are *jocose* [dʒo(u)ˈkous] from *joke* and (perhaps) *verbose,* though the relationship of the latter word with *verb* is hardly felt.

-ose is further used as a substantival suffix in some chemical names such as *cellulose* [seljulous], *glucose* [glukous], etc.

-oso occurs only in words borrowed direct from Italian, e. g. *virtuoso.*

-ese

19.8₁. The origin of *-ese* [- iˑz] is from Ital. *-ese* and OF *-eis* now *-ois, -ais* (as in *norrois, français*), both from Lat. *-ensem* 'belonging to, originating in (a place)'.

A word ending in -*a* drops this before adding -*ese*,
e. g. *China—Chinese, Genoa—Genoese, Malta—Maltese*,
etc. *Portuguese* is a direct loan from Port. *portuguez*.
Javanese is probably derived from *Javan* 'a native of
Java', or may be due to analogy with *Japanese*.

The suffix denotes first inhabitants of a country,
such as *Chinese, Maltese, Portuguese*, etc., or a town,
such as *Cantonese, Pekinese, Genevese* (rare for *Genevan*),
Viennese, especially of Italian towns, e. g. *Bolognese,
Cremonese, Genoese, Milanese, Veronese*.

19.8₂. These derivatives are mainly used as adjs,
both as secondaries (*the Chinese people*) and as primaries
in a pl sense to designate the whole population or a
representative group (e. g. the army) as distinct from
individuals (*the Chinese* v. *some Chinamen*). Many of
them, however, may also be used to designate individuals (*a Japanese, some Japanese*), see vol II 11.57.

Formerly (especially in the 16th cent.) pl forms in
-*eses* were in regular use, cf vol II 9.32, but now the
only pl form is -*ese*. In spoken language, especially
sailor's and vulgar language, singular forms in -*ee* may
be formed by subtraction of [s], which was conceived
as the plural -*s*, see vol II 5.632 and *Language* 173.

19.8₃. Words in -*ese* also denote the language in
question, a use of the adj as a primary.

In modern times the ending has been used to denote
also the style of certain mannered writers, e. g. *John-
sonese* (NED first quotation Macaulay 1843) | *Carlylese* |
Kiplingese (Wells TB 2.256).

This use is carried further to styles not especially
characteristic of one person, thus *journalese, telegraphese*
(both common), and nonce-words like *novelese* (Marshall
Sorry Sch 206) | Locke CA 177 the World to Come;
when I expect they'll all talk *Heavenese* | *Daily-Telegraph-
ese* (Stephen L 245) | NP 1917 worthless novels written
in *sentimentalese*.

The subject of Heinrich Straumann's book News-

paper Headlines (L 1935) is termed *headlinese* by the
author (passim).

From Weseen's Dict. of Amr. Slang I quote:
*Americanese, Bryanese, flapperese, Manhattanese, New
Yorkese,* and *Times Squarese.*

The form *parsonese* coined by Huxley (L 1.212 ignorant
parsonese superstitions) is abnormal by being used as a secondary and by its meaning 'characteristic of parsons'.

-est

19.9. The common superlative ending as in *greatest*
will be treated together with comparatives in *-er* in
Syntax, vol VII under the heading Comparison.

-ist

19.9₁. From Gk *-istēs* used especially to form agent
nouns as *agonistēs, sophistēs.* In Latin *-ista,* in words
from Gk, such as *evangelista, psalmista,* and native
words, such as *realista.* In F the ending became *-iste,*
and here, too, it was productive, as in *Bonapartiste,
royaliste.*

In E *-ist* occurs partly in words borrowed from these
languages, partly in new-formations.

In some cases it is impossible to decide whether
the word in question is from F or native E, e. g. (*bi-*)
cyclist (Fr. or Eng.), *pacifist* (the form *pacificist,* which
has been advocated as more correct has never been
much used).

On stress in words in *-ist* (and *-ism*) see vol I 5.66.

E, as distinct from F often preserves the final vowel
of the root-word, e. g.

celloist besides the commoner form *cellist* (= F.
celliste), *copyist* (F *copiste,* earlier Eng. also *copist*),
soloist (F *soliste*).

Further, *autoist* (Amr NP 1904), *banjoist* (Priestley),
canoist (U. S.).

But *pianist* without *o* from F *pianiste.* Cf also *theorist.*

19.9₂. Often a word is formed from foreign elements
on English soil, as in *ambitionist* (Carlyle E 292), *careerist*
(Wells N 461, Bennett), *co-religionist* (Chesterton),
hedonist (coined by Professor Wilson, see Quincey 218),
philologist (F *-logue*), *plagiarist, statist* (= 'statesman',
Sh), *suffragist, telephonist, tobacconist* ("with inserted *-n-*,
perh. suggested by such words as *Platonist,* with etymological *n.*" NED. Originally = 'smoker of tobacco'
(e. g. Dekker F 351), later = 'seller of tobacco').
Scientist, coined by Dr. Whewell in 1840, but as late
as 1874 violently attacked as "an ignoble Americanism."

In *Bolshevist -ist* has ousted the Russian ending *-ik.*

A great many words have been formed from an E
word + *-ist,* e. g. *Cocksurist* (Wells N 393), *faddist,
fightist* (NED), *landscapist* (coined by Ruskin), *walkist*
("as our American cousin calls him", Payn S 1), *wordist*
(Butler N 144).

Words from compounds and phrases, e. g. *black-and-
whitist* (Galsw TL 182), *free-knowledge-ist* (Kipling),
free-willist (James, Talks to Teachers 191), *red-tapist,
topsy-turvyist* (Henderson Shaw 312).

Many words in *-ist* are formed from personal names:
Brownist (follower of the Puritan Browne), *Calvinist,
Darwinist* (less frequent than *Darwinian*), *Kropotkinist*
(Henderson Shaw 108).

Special Amr forms are *behaviorist, columnist, electrag-
ist, manicurist,* etc., see Mencken AL⁴ 178.

In two cases we have double forms : *artist* [ˈaˑtist]
'one who practises one of the fine arts', and *artiste*
[aˑˈtiˑst] 'professional singer or dancer'; *pianist* [pjænist,
piənist] common sex, and *pianiste* [piəˈniˑst] 'female
piano-player' (as if *-e* was the Fr. feminine ending,
but both are from Fr. *pianiste*). Cf. I 8.33 and VII 5.3₂.

19.9₃. Words in *-ist* are

(1) agent nouns (often corresponding to verbs in *-ize*),
e. g. *colonist, theorist,* etc. *Analyst* (with *y* from *analysis,
analyze*) belongs to the same group;—or denote

(2) 'person occupied with', e. g. *artist, dentist, tobacconist; banjoist, cell(o)ist, violinist,* etc.

(3) adherent of system or creed, e. g. *Calvinist, Darwinist, fatalist, hedonist, pacifist,* etc.

Words in *-ist* may form groups with words from same root with *-ize* and (or) *-ism,* e. g. *baptist, baptize, baptism.*

From some *-ist* derivatives may be formed adjs in *-istic (artistic)* or *-istical* (cf 22.3), but others may be used unchanged as secondaries: the royalist party.

19.9₄. Derivatives from adjs are rare, except for adjs in *-al,* e. g.

Chesterton Shaw 238 aristocratic in politics or *clericalist* in religion [N.B. secondary] | *controversialist, sentimentalist* (both Priestley) | *transcendentalist* (Carlyle E 292).

In some cases *-ist* words may be said to have been derived from a sb through an *-al* adj, e. g. *anecdotalist* (Wells Cl 536) | *conversationalist.*

See Fowler's discussion of various *-ist* forms in MEU 300 f.

-ism

19.9₅. *-ism* [-izm] from Gk *-ismós,* L *-ismus,* F *-isme.* This suffix (with *-ist*) has been very productive in European languages.

From Latin and Romanic languages originate *individualism, egoism, altruism* (coined by Comte), *realism,* etc.

Other words are derived from foreign words on English soil, e. g. *Presbyterianism, ruffianism, cosmopolitanism* (Carlyle E 126; cf F *cosmopolitisme*), etc.

19.9₆. To this group belong a great many occasional formations:

attidudinarianism (Bennett T 29, 40), *governmentalism* (Franklin 234), modest egoisms, and flattering *illeisms* (Coleridge B 5), *literaryism* ('literary words in dial.

writings'), *militaryism* (Kidd S 196), a religion of
miserabilism (Caine E 569), the difference between ...
monism and *multimillionism* (Bullett, Innocence of
Chesterton 227), *reactionaryism* (Galsw P 8.46), the
religionism of the new school (Thack N 554).

Absenteeism is a clearly E formation, *defeatism* (e. g.
Galsw Sw 124) is an adjustment of F *défaitisme*.

But many words have also been formed from native
words: all *"bigstickism"* (NP 1906), *bigwigism* (GE Mm
158), *blackguardism* (Kipling), *blockheadism* (Ru S 2.195),
funnyism (Fox 1.84), *heathenism* (Bacon, Mi, Addison,
etc.), *jingoism, landlordism* (Jerome), *scoundrelism* (Mc
Carthy 2.23), *toadyism, truism, witticism* (coined by
Dryden from *witty* on the analogy of *criticism*).

Occasionally *-ism* words may be derived from phrases
or compounds: *Church-of-Englandism* (Carlyle E 264),
dog-in-the-mangerism (Galsw C 275), a noble *19th-
century-ism*, if you will admit such a word (Tennyson
L 1.272), *old-maidism* (Kipling DW 344), *public-schoolism*
(NP 1937), *spread-eagleism* (Jerome Idle Ideas 1905
142).

19.9₇. Words in *-ism* are either action nouns (verbal
nexus-words) corresponding to verbs in *-ize*, e. g.
baptism, or predicative nexus-words derived from
adjectives or substantives, e.g. *Americanism, parallelism,
barbarism, charlatanism*. These 'abstract nouns' then
may develop a concrete sense, e. g. *Americanism* 'phrase
or word characteristic of U. S.'.

Words in *-ism* generally stand for a system or doctrine or movement, e. g. *Protestantism, Presbyterianism;
Communism, Fascism, Nazism, Socialism; Expression-
ism, Symbolism, Cubism, Classicism, Romanticism;
Platonism, Positivism*, etc.

Words like *alcoholism, cocainism* denote 'a habitual
and excessive addiction to the drug, etc.'.

The suffix may have a derogatory sense as in *mannerism*, see, e. g. Watts-Dunton Poetry 24 the poet's style

is liable to degenerate at once into mere manner—after-wards to sink farther still into mannerism.

Egotism (with *t* perhaps from such words as *idiotism*) besides its sense of *egoism* or selfishness also may mean 'frequent use of the word I'; *wegotism* also occurs.

Criticism is both = F. *criticisme* (system) and = F. *critique* (one item).

The suffix is frequently used in derivatives from proper names such as *Byronism* (Carlyle E 295), *Calvin-ism, Darwinism, Johnsonism* (Carlyle E 185), to de-signate the doctrine or a feature characteristic of a person; also from persons in fiction, e. g. *Götzism* and *Werterism* (Carlyle E 322), *Don Juanism* (Henderson Shaw¹ 296), *Forsyteism* (Galsw IC 12), *euphuism, malapropism* ('ludicrous misuse of word', from Mrs Malaprop in Sheridan's *Rivals*), *quixotism*, the last three now belonging to the common word-stock.

A proof of the popularity of the suffix is the use of *ism* as an independent word meaning 'movement, system', etc., from which then new words have been derived such as *ismal, ismate* etc., see NED (*ist* has been similarly used (though rarely) = the follower of some ism).

On -*some* see 25.2₅, on -*age* 24.3,

Chapter XX

The Ending -n (-en)

20.1₁. The ending -*n* (-*en*) is used as a grammatical means in ModE in the following forms:

(1) plural of substantives: *oxen* (20.2)
(2) primary of a pronoun: *mine, none* (20.3)
(3) adjectives from substantives: *woollen* (20.4)
(4) second participle: *taken* (above, 5.7)
(5) derived causative or inchoative verbs from adjectives: *sharpen*, or substantives: *heighten* (20.5).

Our investigation will disclose some curious points of agreement, phonetic, morphological and syntactic, between these seemingly disparate uses.

In OE final -*n* was found in a great many words and played an important grammatical part, thus in most cases of the sg and in the nominative and accusative pl of weak sbs and weak (determined) adjs: *oxan, tungan, godan*, etc.; further in the pl forms in vbs (subjunctive in -*en*, prt ind. in -*on*): *binden, bunden, bundon*, in infs: *bindan*, and in the second ptc of strong vbs: *bunden*, and finally in some derivatives, feminines of sbs: *gyden*, some diminutives: *cycen*, and adjs from sbs: *gylden*.

The only survival of the feminine suffix is *vixen*, fem. of *fox* with the southern dialectal voicing of *f*, now disconnected from *fox* and meaning 'quarrelsome woman'.

Besides, non-final *n* was found in many endings, e. g. acc. masc. of adjs and pronouns: *godne, hiene;* gen pl: *gumena*, the inflected inf: (*to*) *bindanne*.

In late OE the number of final *n*'s was increased by the transition -*m* > -*n*, as in the dat pl *dagon* for older *dagum*. An early vacillation between the two endings is seen, e. g. in Oros. L 82 mid his ormætan menige = C 47 mid his ormætum menigeo, and Chron. 917 MS A on fullum fleame = MS D on fullan fleame.—It is curious that the old dat pl ending has kept -*m* in the adverb *whilom*, and still more curious that this has been transferred to *seldom*, OE *selden*, ME also *selde*(*n*), cf *seld-shown* Sh Cor II. 1.229, *seld-seen* in use till the 17th c.

20.1₂. On the loss of final -*n* see vol I 2.424 ff., which will here be supplemented by a treatment of those instances in which *n* acquires morphological significance.

The general tendency to drop final *n* is found as early as the oldest Northumbrian, where, e. g., the infinitive ends in -*a*. In ME the tendency was very strong in the southern dialects, but was nowhere carried through consistently, chiefly because *n* was preserved when a vowel followed either in the next word or in inflected forms of the same word.

. Isolated survivals of final *n* in verbal forms are found in archaic language in Spenser, in *killen* in Gower's speech in (Sh?) Per II 19; the sailor Ben in Congreve's Love f. Love 248: *sayn*.

The latter influence is absent in some particles in which the *n*-less forms have prevailed: OE *butan* > *but* | *abutan* > *about* | *wiþutan* > *without* | *abufan* > *above* | *biforan* > *before*. If in the last four *n* was kept longer than in *but*—Ch, e. g., has *withoute* and *withouten*, *aboute* and *abouten*, *above* and *aboven*, *bifore* and *biforn*—the cause must be the stronger stress.

-*n* was formerly dropped in *couz, cooz, coze*, frequent spellings in 17th c. for *cousin*, chiefly in address.

Fr. *hautein* becomes *haughty*, the ending being assimilated to adjs like *mighty* (doubtful, see 13.3₆).

OE *filmen* > ModE *film* (cf below on loss of -*en* after *m* in ptcs).

20.1₃. Some numerals developed double forms, OE *seofon* > AR *seoue* before a consonant, *seouen* before a vowel, *seouene* when absolute (as a primary); the last form has prevailed: *seven*. Similarly OE *nigon*, AR 22 nie lescuns ... alle niene, ModE *nine*. OE *twegen* > ME *tweye* and *twein*, the latter > ModE *twain*, chiefly used after the sb or as a primary, now archaic; but Swinburne uses it against the former rule: A 76 twain hounds | ib 83 thy twain brethren.

20.1₄. In some substantives we have double forms, the *n*-forms chiefly when something followed.

OE *æfen* > ME *eue* and *euen*, Ch pl only *evenes*, Sh still sometimes *even*, thus in the salutation *good even* (also *godden, gooden, God-dig-you-den, godgigoden*); Marlowe J 1339 this *euen*. AV often *eve, eventide*, in the plural never *eves* (often *evenings*, cf below). *Even* is

now obsolete, except in poetry; Sc. *e'en*, thus *yestreen;*
further in compounds: *eventide*, *-star*, *-song*. *Eve* in
actual use only in the meaning 'day (evening) before
a festival': Christmas eve, All-Hallow-eve, on the eve
of the New Year = new-year's eve, etc.

For 'the last part of the day' generally the extended
form *evening* has been usual from the 15th c.

OE *morȝen* (AR *morwen*, Ch *morwe(n)*) has been
similarly differentiated into *morrow* and *morn*. The
former was for a long time the usual word for 'the
first part of the day', thus clearly in Ch MP 21.9, and
in the salutation *Good morrow!*, frequent in Sh (also as
in R3 III. 2.35 Many good morrows to my noble Lord),
still (archaic) in Lamb R 8.

But with a natural transition found in many languages
(G *morgen*, Dan. *imorgen*, F *demain*, Ital. *domani*, Russ.
zavtra, etc.) it comes to mean 'the following morning,
or the following day', at first perhaps in *to-morrow*
(Ch E 955, etc., *to-morwe*), cf Ch B 1100 The morwe
cam, And Alla gan him dresse | Sh Ro II. 2.185 Parting
is such sweete sorrow, That I shall say good night,
till it be morrow.

To-morrow becomes such a fixed combination that it
is even possible to use it after *till* or *to* (vol III 1.21).

Morrow nowadays has completely lost the meaning
of 'morning' and means nothing but the following day:
Carlyle SR 57 Nowhere in Entepfuhl, on the morrow
or next day, did tidings transpire | Thack V 53 Rebecca
lay awake ... thinking of the morrow | Di M 367 made
an appointment with him for the morrow.

Pl: Byron (T) 4.341 After the bright course of a
few brief morrows,—Ay, day will rise.

The clearest sign that *morrow* comprises the whole
of the following day is found when a special indication
is added: Mi PL 4.662 Those have thir course to finish,
round the earth, By morrow eevning | ib 4.588 by
morrow dawning I shall know | Arnold P 1.158 with

to-morrow's dawn | Beaconsfield L 106 on the noon of
the morrow they were to depart | Di D 116 I left Salem
House upon the morrow afternoon.

But this makes it impossible to use the salutation
good morrow as of old, and Pegge, Anecdotes 1803 p.
303, has the curious remark that when the families of
his grandfathers met at breakfast they said *good morrow*
as much as to say "We meet together well to-day,
may we do the like to-morrow!" And later, "A good
morrow morning to you" is an evening compliment,
which I have heard made use of, as well as a morning one".

Morn in the meaning 'morning' was used frequently
by Sh though only poetically; it was the usual form
in Mi and has been preserved in the higher literary
style, as in Thack P 1.111 They walked in the summer
evenings: they met in the early morn | Tennyson 292
yestermorn | Ridge L 110 on her wedding morn (to
avoid -*ing* -*ing*),—artificially in Hewlett Q 46 he would
wed you the morn's morn if you would have him.

This form, too, for a time acquired the meaning 'the
next day'. Malory (e. g. p. 86) uses *to morowe* and *to
morne* in the same sense; further Marlowe J 647 He
said he wud attend me in the morne | Greene F 127
in the morn [= 'to-morrow morning'] | Sh Tp V. 1.306
In the morn [same sense] I'll bring you to your ship.

This is preserved in Sc. *the muorn, the muorn's muornin'*
(Murray Dial. 227, Black F 1.121), but in the South
of England it has died out; *morn* is not found in the
AV.—Note in literary style Coleridge 110 A sadder and
a wiser man He rose the morrow morn | Hawthorne
1.511 for him that has died to-day, his morrow will be
the resurrection morn.

In the ordinary sense the expanded form *morning*
(Ch *morwening*) has become the usual word; as a salutation *good morning* (Sh Meas IV. 3.116) did not finally
supplant *good morrow* till the end of the 18th c; cf
above Pegge.

20.1₅. OE *gaman* has been split up into the two forms *game*, the usual word, and *gammon* (e. g. in *back-gammon*).

From OE *man(n)* we have the two forms *man* (usual) and *me*, which in early ME was often used as a kind of indefinite pronoun (= F *on*) with the verb in the sg (thus not from the plural *men*, e. g. AR 4 al þet me euer deð; the pl of the vb is *doð*).

Luncheon (formerly *nuncheon*) and *lunch* (both from 16th c.) are used indiscriminately in Great Britain, the fuller form is somewhat more formal; always *luncheon basket*, -*table* (Shaw 2.243, 247; thus as an adjunct, cp. 20.4₂). In U. S. the forms have been differentiated: *luncheon* = 'the ordinary midday meal', *lunch* 'a light meal at any time' (= Brit. *snack*).

On *fount(ain)* and *mount(ain)* see below 21.3₁.

20.1₆. The existence side by side of two forms without any clear distinction in course of time led to an *en* being added to a form originally without *n*. This could only happen when the phonetic structure of the word was such that *n* came to form a new syllable. Examples are:

OE *oft*, ME *ofte:* from the 14th c. *often*, note *often-time(s)* | OE *eald*, ME (from 1200) *old: olden* from the beginning of 15th c.; in Sh only once Mcb III 4.75 i'th olden time; neither AV, Mi, nor Pope, but revived by Scott; chiefly in *olden days, times*, exceptionally as in By DJ 12.43 olden she was, cf ib 13.50 | *hid, hidden;* the treasure is hid, hidden treasures (cf 5.7₅) | OE *bedrida*: ModE *bedridden* (as if a ptc, see 5.7₅).

Here we may perhaps place U. S. *offen* = *off* as prep., frequent in Jack London (W 206, V 303, 525) and Hay B (182, 191), cf Mencken AL.[4] 471 with wrong explanation.

This excrescent nasal is especially frequent in the same rhythm as we have in *passenger, nightingale*, etc.;

on the intrusion of *n* here see vol I 2.429 and the literature quoted there.

Plural

20.2₁. In OE *-n* was characteristic not only of the
pl of *n*-stems, but of the oblique cases in the sg as
well. Later these latter were used without any ending
(on the analogy of the other classes of sbs) and *n* thus
became a sign of the pl and was in that function extended
to other sbs. On its use in early ME see R. Maack, Die
Flexion des engl. Substantivs von 1100 bis etwa 1250
(Hamburg 1889).

For some time it might even seem as if *-s* and *-n*
had an equal chance of being the universal sign of the
pl (AR *limes* and *limen, uorbisnes* and *uorbisnen, ʒetes*
and *ʒeten* 'gates' and many other *n*-pls; Ch *bees* and
been, etc.). But the tendency to drop final *n* made
this ending less distinctive of the pl than *s,* which
prevailed.

-n was kept in some specified cases, in *oxen* without
any hesitation, but otherwise with a good deal of
vacillation.

OE *eage,* pl *-an.* ME *eyen.* Spenser *eyen* in rime,
eyes otherwise. Sh *eyen* 11 times in rime, outside rime
only Lucr 1229 and in Gower's Prologue, Per III. 5;
otherwise always *eyes.* BJo Gr both forms, Wallis 1653
rarius cyen pro eyes. AV only *eyes.* Mi once *eyn* in
rime, otherwise *eyes,* Shelley *eyne* three times, ALang
Ban and AB 37 eyne (: : mine), archaic. Sc. *een* (Burns,
Scott). *Eyes* has now long been the only natural form.

OE *(ge)fa,* pl *-n;* AR 220 *uoan,* but throughout the
ModE period *foes,* though NED has one quotation *fone*
(Spenser).

20.2₂. After a sibilant *-n* was sometimes found as a
plural ending.

OE *hus,* pl *hus.* BJo Gr *houses* and *housen;* NED
some Elizabethan quotations for *housen.* Wallis 1653

rarius housen pro houses. -n still in some dialects |
hose, pl hosen (hözn) as a Somerset form in Gil Log.
Archaically Ru F 52 | pease, pl peasen (pëzn) as a Somer-
set form in Gil. Wallis 1653 nonnulli a pease, pl peasen,
at melius a pea pl peas (cf vol II 5.631) | In Dorset
according to Barnes Gr 19 cheesen, pleacen, vu'zen.

After vowels: tree, pl treen twice in Shelley in rime
as an artificial archaism.

Shoe, OE sc(e)oh, pl sc(e)os, but gen pl sceona "nach
art der n-stämme" (Sievers § 242 anm. 2). AR 362,
420 scheon. Ch B 1922 some MSS s(c)hoon, but Ellesm.
shoos. Sh once shoon in rime in Ophelia's song, which
was probably not written by Sh, also in Cade's language
2H6 IV. 2.195. AV only shoes. BJo Gr and Wallis
shoes and sho(o)en. Mi once (Com. 635) shoon. In Sc
shuin, written shoon in Scott A 1.164 and Barrie M 113;
on a new pl shuins, see Murray Dial., quoted vol II
5.793, Keats 4.203 shoon (: : noon).

On chicken as a plural of chick see vol II 5.791; the
-en was originally a diminutive ending (OE cycen, sg,
from coc).

Other n-pls are sistren (AR 50 and Ch a few times
sustren alongside of sustres); in vg Am. brethren and
sistren (Carpenter Gramm.), and the completely obsolete
doghtren (AR 54 douhtren, Ch doghtren alongside of
doghtres).

20.2₃. In some cases -n has been added to an original
pl (pl raised to the second power, cf vol II 5.79, 5.793):

OE cild, pl cildru > pl childer (still Hart 1569 p. 62;
dialectal in Phillpotts M 13), with -n children (as early
as AR 10) | OE cu, pl cy, retained in Sc. kye (Burns,
etc.). "In West Holderness, kye is used to denote
particular herds, kine being used for cows in general"
(q NED). With -n Malory 103 and Caxton R 78 kyen.—
Kine was for a long time the received pl, thus in Sh,
Bacon, AV (Pharaoh's lean kine, often mentioned, e. g.
Swift P 176), and Mi. Poetically in 19th c. Words-

worth P 8.21, Tennyson 73, Kipling J 1.203. The new
pl *cows* from the beginning of the 17th c.; still Dyche
Dict 1740 pl *cows* or *kine*.

OE *broðor*, pl generally *broðor* or *broðru*, very rarely
with mutation *broeþre* (Rushw. gl.), but this was continued in ME, Orrm *breþre*, Cursor M. *breþer*, and still
in Lancashire and Sc. *brether*. With -*n* added *brethren*
(oldest example 1175), which became the usual pl in
later ME and early ModE, the only form in AV. *Brothers*
is found in Layamon, but does not appear again till
ElE. Marlowe T 563 brothers = 567 brethren. Sh and
BJo (Gr) have both forms, seemingly without distinction, Gil Log. breðren aut breðern, but not *brothers*.
Mi *brothers* a few times in early poems, but in his later
poetry only *brethren*. Swift T 63, 65, 66 both forms
about sons of the same parents; in that sense still
sometimes in 19th c. (Macaulay, Tennyson, Thack
N 274, Swinburne A 49, 83, etc.).

Most 19th c. grammarians would establish the distinction that *brothers* is used of blood-relations, *brethren* of spiritually connected people; but the distinction
tends to be neglected, and *brothers* is very often used
in a figurative sense, e. g. Wordsworth P 9.227 a Republic ... we were brothers all | Tennyson 101 Men, my
brothers, men the workers | in Hall Caine C several times
of the members of the Brotherhood, a kind of monastic
organization | Archer A 133 every war is civil war, a
war between brothers, etc. Curious is Byron 723 Call
not thy brothers brethren!

On dialectal pl in -*n* see Wright EDG § 379, [fi·tn]
§ 383.

-*n* in Primaries

20.3. -*n* is kept in a few pronouns used as primaries
while the corresponding adjuncts have dropped it:
mine | *my*, *none* | *no*, cf vol II 16.2, 16.6. On the analogy
of these doublets we have the dial. and vg primary

forms *hisn*, *ourn*, *yourn*, *theirn* (vol II 16.26), also *thisn* U. S.

Adjectives (Adjuncts) in -*en*

20.4₁. OE had an adjective suffix -*en* (Gothonic -*īno*, cf Gk -*ino*-, Lat. -*īno*) used especially to indicate the material of which something is formed. The greater part of these OE-adjs have been lost (e. g. *ættren*, *yteren*, *cyperen*), but others survive, though with the same vowel as the corresponding sb, where OE had mutation: *gylden*, ME *gilden* has now become *golden*, *liþeren* > *leathern*. ME had *stonene* AR 378, *stanene* Juliana 76 = OE *stǣnen*, but this is lost.

In course of time a great many new formations have been added, but "It is only in a few cases (e. g. *wooden*, *woollen*, *earthen*, *wheaten*) that these words are still familiarly used in their literal sense. In s. w. dialects, however, the suffix is of common occurrence, being added without restriction to all sbs denoting material of which anything is composed, as in *glassen*, *steelen*, *tinnen*, *papern* etc." (NED).

Cf also Wright, Rustic Speech 145.

20.4₂. It is important to note that when -*n* disappears in these adjs the result is indistinguishable from the sb itself used as the first part of a compound. Two originally distinct modes of combining adjunct and primary have thus to some extent coalesced. The retention of -*n* in the adj may be due to the inflected forms.

We shall arrange the following adjs according to the final sound of the sb; cf the arrangement in 20.5.

It is worth remarking that when the -*en* form is used as an adjunctal form, *n* serves, as I have expressed it, as a kind of buffer-syllable between two words, cf 5.7 and 20.5.

p: hempen: Marlowe J 1708 his hempen tippet; figuratively ib 1702 an old hempen proverb. Cf *hemp seed*, etc. ‖ *aspen:* Marlowe T 661 a quivering aspen

leafe. But *aspen* is also now used as a by-form of the
sb itself || *b:* no examples.

t: oaten: Sh LL V. 2.913 oaten straws; archaic in
LMorris 224 some fair stripling's oaten melody. Cf
oatmeal, etc. || *wheaten:* Quincey 295 good wheaten-
bread | GE A 38 wheaten bread; Scott A 2.146 | Ward
E 37 flat wheaten cakes | Swinburne A 111 a wheaten
ear || (*guesten chamber, -hall;* archaic and rare, see
NED.)

d: golden obsolete of material: Sh golden rings, axe,
etc. | Lyly C 287 a golden mine (now *gold mine*) | (poet.)
Tennyson 561 She that holds the diamond necklace
dearer than the golden ring. Now figuratively: the
golden age (Sh Lucr 60, Tp II. 1.168, As I. 1.125;
common) | Quincey 298 a golden mean | Ward E 140
In the golden afternoon | golden wedding. But of
material: *gold watch, ring; the Gold Coast* || *leaden,*
chiefly figuratively: Brontë P 180 leaden sky | Di N
138 in the leaden light | id D 357 [it] oppressed me with
a leaden dread | id N 393 the minutes appeared to
move with leaden wings | HSpencer Man v. State:
There is no political alchemy by which you can get
golden conduct out of leaden instincts | Macaulay (q
NED) a leaden coffin. But: *lead colour, mine, works* ||
threaden, rare: Sh H5 III prol. 10 the threaden sails ||
wooden: wooden house (made of wood), but *wood-house,*
-box (containing w.) | Ward E 38 the wooden cup.

k: silken: In the old Sh-editions *silken thread* and
silk thread are used indiscriminately; *silken* both of
material and figuratively (silken dalliance H5 II Prol
2, often quoted, e. g. By T 5.212). Now usually *silk* of
material (*silk stockings,* etc.), *silken* figuratively (Lowell
Poems 1.155 Our silken bards), rarely of material
(Ward E 325 the elaborate silken thing). Note Zangwill
G 318 she moved with a rustle of silken skirts and
heaved an opulent black-silk bosom || *milken* †: Bacon
A 30.4 the Milken Way, now *milky* || *oaken:* GE SM

228 the oaken table | Merriman S 204 oaken panels |
Doyle S 6.208 .. oaken ceiling, oaken panelling ...
oak mantelpiece ... oaken chair | Whittier 436 the
oaken log | Galsw MP [T] 138 the oaken rug chest |
Chesterton Thursday [T] 278 large oaken stairs.—Now
generally *oak: oak forest, table, leaf,* etc.

g: no examples.

þ: earthen, OE rare *eorþen,* now with voiceless con-
sonant: Sh Ro V. 1.46 earthen pots | earthenware |
Caine E 351 the earthen [i. e. earth-coloured] cheeks
were rouged | Defoe R 143 earthen pots; but ib 141
earthern things, 142 an earthern pot | earth-nut, -worm.

s: brazen [breizn] from *brass,* [bra·s], of material:
Hawthorne S 160 that .. brazen-clasped volume |
Thack N 399 to the brazen notes of the orchestra.—
But generally figuratively = 'cheeky, impudent':
Zangwill G 87 the maddening music of brass instruments and brazen creatures. Note the vb *brazen*
it out.—Of material: *brass button, the three brass balls*
(pawnbrokers' sign) || *glazen* from *glass,* OE *glæsen:*
BJo 3.115 glazen-eyes. New formation *glassen* (NED);
glass used in *glass-case,* etc. || *waxen:* 1) made of wax:
in Sh *waxen tapers,* etc. Cf Quincey 132 wax-lights
... my tall waxen lights | Di N 648 waxen busts;
2) soft, penetrable: women's waxen hearts | a waxen
epitaph.—Figuratively: GE Mill 1.12 a waxen com-
plexion.—About material now always *wax: wax doll,
vesta, works* || *flaxen,* material: James S 68 a flaxen
wing.—Generally of colour: Di N 154 flaxen hair |
Ward E 648 flaxen-haired.

sh, ch: ashen[1] from *ash*(*es*), only figuratively = 'ash-
coloured, pale', quite modern, earliest example in NED
1808 Scott: the ashen hue of age; further: Swinburne
A 38 the ashen autumn days | Doyle S 1.179 his face
was of an ashen white | Caine E 145 Roma was ashen
pale.—Of material *ash: ash-bin, -heap, -like, -tray* ||
ashen[2] from ash-tree, NED. i. a. Tennyson || *beechen,*

OE *bēcen:* NED examples as late as the 19th c. (1878
B. Taylor: Under yonder beechen shade), but: "Now
superseded in common use by *beech* attrib." Keats
Ode to Night st. 1 In some melodious plot Of beechen
green **||** *birchen* formerly in a direct sense: Caxton R
41 Two birchen trees; now especially = 'pertaining to
the birch rod used in flogging': Fielding T 1.294 the
same birchen argument.—In a direct sense now *birch:
birch rod, birch tree*, etc. **||** *larchen:* Keats (q NED).
For *lunch, luncheon basket* see above 20.1₅.

l: woollen: Bennett W 1.15 the millinery and silken
half of the shop ... the woollen and shirting half |
woollen bag (made of woollen stuff), but *wool-bag* (containing wool), cf the *woolsack* (in the House of Lords);
also a *wool-merchant.*

r: leathern: Marlowe F 744 in an olde leatherne bag; in
the ed. of 1616: in a leather bag | Scott A 1.41 an ancient
leathern-covered easy chair | Di N 146 a small leathern
valise | Hawthorne S 160 the leathern-bound volume |
Ward E 37 leathern hat; ib 42.—Now *leather jacket* **||**
cedarn: NED: Mi Co, Coleridge, Mrs Browning, Tenny-
son. Also Shelley 159 cedarn mountains **||** *hairen:*
Butler Bees 159 a strong hairen bag **||** *silvern*, now
poet. or archaic: Carlyle E 201 Speech is silvern, Sil-
ence is golden | Spencer Facts 71 golden verse ...
silvern prose. But *silver watch, wedding.*

Special Cases

20.4₃. *Linen* was originally an adj from sb OE *lin*,
now nearly obs. *line* 'flax', but was so often used as a
sb 'cloth woven from flax' that when it is now found
in *linen garment*, etc., it is "apprehended chiefly as an
attributive use of the sb." (NED).

Linden, the adj from obs. *lind* 'lime', is now used
chiefly as a sb, and *linden-tree* is felt as parallel to *oak-
tree*, etc.

20.4₄. In the following cases two forms of a sb ending

originally in -*n* have been utilized the *n*-form being used especially as an adjunct before a sb.

OE *mægden* (a diminutive of *mægþ*), Orrm *maȝȝdenn*. Ch *mayde* and *mayden* without any difference.

But it is important to note that before flexional *s* in the gen and pl Ch always used the *n*-form: *maydens*, a distinction not noticed by ten Brink and Skeat, cf in the Nut-brown Maid (Spec. 3.97) *maide*, but *maydens* gen and pl. This is the first instance of what we shall find in other cases, the retention of *n* when something is added. In Malory, Marlowe and Sh *maid*(*e*) and *maiden* without distinction, e. g. Ro III. 2.135 But I a maide, die maiden widowed. In Marlowe and Sh inflected both *maids* and *maidens*. But already at that time there was a tendency to use the *n*-form adjunctively Ro II. 2.85 a maiden blush | LLL V. 2.351 by'my maiden honour | ib V. 2.789 in our maiden council | H6A II. 4.47 | John IV. 2.52 a maiden and an innocent hand | Tw V. 262 my maiden weeds, but ib V. 282 my maides garments, cf ib V. 280 thy womans weeds.

This differentiation has prevailed nowadays: maiden speech, assize | Di N 304 actresses always keep their maiden names | Trollope D 3.61 her maiden shame | Tennyson 564 the maiden fancies | Beaconsfield L 201 maiden aunts.

Note the adv in GE A 55 these two hopelessly-maiden sisters.

That it is felt as an adj is seen from the uninflected use in Maugham FPS 57 Elderly ladies, maiden and widowed, lived there.—Thus the curious thing has happened that -*en*, which originally was a diminutive sb suffix, now is rather felt as a totally different adj suffix.

Apart from this use *maiden* is more solemn, *maid* more everyday, thus = 'domestic servant'.

Note the derivatives *maidenly* and *maidenhead* or -*hood* (earlier also *maidhood*, Sh twice, meaning 'girlhood', different from the meaning 'virginity').

OE *lencten* (the time when days lengthen, cf G *lenz*), ME *le(i)nten, lente,* has become ModE *lent* as the usual sb, and *lenten,* used as an adjunct before a sb (thus three times in Sh) and now felt as a derived adj, e. g. in Swift J 416 I hate Lent ... I had a true Lenten dinner ... my Lenten porridge.

Iren (iron) dial. Elworthy, Somerset Wordb., quoted NED: *ire* iron ... *iron* is the adj form. Compare *Iron-Bar* with *Bar-ire.* But in StE *-n* is always preserved.

Derived Verbs in -en

20.5₁. The previous treatments of this suffix, in Sweet NEG § 1616, C. Palmgren in *Nord. tidsskr. f. filol.* 3. række 19,27 ff., J. Raith, *Die engl. nasalverben,* (Beitr. zur engl. philol., herausg. v. Max Förster, 1931), and Koziol § 588 (based on Raith) have been superseded by my own paper *The History of a Suffix* (in *Acta Linguistica* vol I (1939) 48 ff.), from which the following is an abridged extract.

We have seen in 20.1₆ that *-en* was in some cases added to a word without changing its meaning. This has also taken place with some verbs. (I leave out some obs. or dial. instances). Thus in: *fright* OE *fyrhtan,* now rare : *frighten* from 17th c. | *glass* vb from 16th c.; cf *glaze* from 14th c. (above 12.4₂) : *glassen, glazen* from 16th c. | ME *happe* : *happen* from 14th c. | *haste* obsolete vb : *hasten* from 16th c. | *heart,* OE *hiertan* : *hearten* from 16th c. | *height* vb from 16th c., † exc. Sc : *heighten* from 16th c. | *length* vb from 14th c. † : *lengthen* from 16th c. | *list* OE *hlystan* : *listen* from 13th c. (But there is an OE Northumbrian vb *lysna*) | *piece* vb from 14th c. : *piecen* from 19th c., local | *rid* vb from 13th c. : *ridden,* not in NED, but Wells War that will End War 78 a New Europe riddened of rankling oppressions | *shape* vb from 13th c. † : *shapen* from 16th c., rare | *strength* vb from 12th c. †: *strengthen* from 14th c. |

threat OE *þreatian*, now arch. or dial. : *threaten* from 13th c. | (*a*)*wake* : (*a*)*waken* see above 5.3₅.

20.5₂. Now there were in early ME a certain number of vbs differing from the corresponding adj by a final *e* only (Cf above 6.9). This *e* like other *e*'s was subsequently lost. When now an (*e*)*n* was added to such verbs—in the first place just as devoid of significative value as in *often*, etc.—it came to be looked upon as a derivative suffix and was assimilated to those few verbs that were originally formed by means of this suffix. *Harden* and other similar vbs were then apprehended as vbs belonging to the adj rather than to the existing vb *hard;* in many cases the verbs without -*n* went out of use, and then naturally -*en* was felt as a suffix added to an adj meaning 'to make', or 'to become, (hard, etc.)'. From having no meaning at all -*en* thus came to have a definite meaning. In this case we have thus really a linguistic creation *ex nihilo* (cf Language, p. 384 ff. "Secretion").

We shall now go through those cases in which we have first a vb formed without *n* from an adj and then an -*en*-form; the arrangement is according to the final sound of the adj as in 20.4₂.

20.5₃. -*p:*

damp vb from 16th c. : *dampen* from 17th c., now chiefly U. S. ‖ *deep* vb, OE *diepan;* in ModE very rare : *deepen* from 17th c. ‖ *ripe* vb, OE *ripian*, now rare : *ripen* from 16th c. ‖ *sharp* vb, † exc. dial. : *sharpen* from 15th c.

-*b:* no examples.

-*t: bright* vb, OE *beorhtian*, † : *brighten* from 16th c.—OE Lindisfarne: "God geberhtnade hine" has probably nothing directly to do with the ModE new-creation ‖ *fat* vb, OE *fættian* (fatted calf) : *fatten* from 16th c. ‖ *flat* vb from 17th c., now chiefly technical : *flatten* from 17th c. ‖ *light*[1] vb 'lessen the weight', OE *lihtan*, now comparatively rare exc. = *alight* : *lighten* from

14th c. || *light*[2] vb 'shine, kindle', OE *lihtan* : *lighten*
from 14th c. || *quiet* vb from 15th c., still common :
quieten from 19th c., rare || *short* vb, OE *sceortian*,
Sh, † : *shorten* from 16th c. || *smart* vb said to be used
in U. S. : *smarten* 19th c. || *stout* vb from 14th c., †
exc. in the phrase *stout it out*, now rare : *stouten* from
19th c. || *straight* vb from 14th c., † exc. Sc : *straighten*
from 16th c. || *strait* vb from 14th c., † : *straiten* from
16th c. (Swinburne A 110) || *sweet* vb, OE *swētan*,
now rare : *sweeten* from 16th c. || *tight* vb from 16th
c., † or dial. : *tighten* from 18th c. || *white* vb, OE
hwītian, now rare (whited sepulchres) : *whiten* from
14th c. In -*stn*- and -*ftn*- *t* tends to be mute, see vol I
7.734 and 5 || *chaste* vb from 13th c., † : *chasten* from
16th c. || *fast* vb, OE *fœstan*, † : *fasten, unfasten*. (As
Sweet has pointed out, OE *fœstnian* is not formed on
fœst, but on sb *fœsten*) || *moist* vb from 14th c., nearly
† : *moisten* from 16th c. || *soft* vb from 13th c. † : *soften*
from 14th c.

　　d: *bold* vb, OE *bealdian*, † (still Sh Lr V. 1.26, Defoe)
: *bolden* from 16th c., † (cf below *embolden*) || *broad*
vb from 13th c., † : *broaden* from 18th c. || *dead* vb,
OE *deadian*, † (Marlowe E 1472), but revived in U. S.
college slang 'to fail, or to cause one to fail to recite' :
deaden from 14th c. || *glad* vb, OE *gladian*, (Sh often,
Marlowe E 598, Otway 201), now poet. (Carlyle S 151) :
gladden from 14th c. || *hard* vb, OE *heardian*, ME *harde*,
† : *harden* from 13th c. || *mad* vb from 14th c., Sh R2
V. 5.61, now rare exc. U. S.; note "far from the madding
crowd" from Gray's Elegy : *madden* from 18th c. ||
mild vb, 14th to 17th c., † : *milden* from 17th c. ||
old vb, OE (e)*aldian*, † : *olden* from 19th c., rare (Thack
N 804) || *red* vb, OE *readian*, † : *redden* from 17th c. ||
sad vb from 14th c., † or dial. : *sadden* from 17th c. ||
wide vb from 14th c., † : *widen* from 17th c.

　　-*k:* *black* vb from 13th c. : *blacken* from 14th c. ||
brisk vb from 17th c. : *brisken* from 18th c. (NED

Suppl.) || *dark* vb from 14th c., †; used by Mrs Browning and W. Scott : *darken* from 14th c. || *like* vb from 15th c., rare (Sh) on account of the other vb *like* : *liken* from 14th c. || *meek* vb from 13th c., † : *meeken* from 14th c. || *quick* vb, OE *cwician*, † : *quicken* from 14th c. || *sick* vb from 12th c., Sh, † : *sicken* from 13th c. || *slack* vb from 16th c. : *slacken* from 16th c. Cf *slake*, OE *sleacian*, from the disyllabic forms of the adj : *slaken* from 14th c. † || *thick* vb, OE *þiccian*, † or rare : *thicken* from 15th c. || *weak* vb, OE *wǣcan* : *weaken* from 16th c. (An earlier ex. direct from Scandinavian).

-*g*: no examples.

20.5₄. -*ð*: *smooth* vb from 14th c. : *smoothen* from 17th c.

-*f*: *deaf* vb, rare (still Byron, Sh R2 II. 1.15 vndeafe) : *deafen* from 16th c. N.B. *deave* from 14th c., still Sc. || *rough* vb from 15th c. : *roughen* from 16th c. || *stiff* vb from 14th c., † : *stiffen* from 16th c.

-*v*: (*live* vb : *liven* rare, Galsworthy M 166 I saw her eyes liven again, cf *enliven* below.)

-*s*, -*z*: *close* vb [N.B. -z] from 13th c. : *closen* from 19th c., very rare; only one quotation in NED; add: Galsw FS 798 a slight stoop closened and corrected the expansion given to his face || *hoarse* vb (OE once ic hasige), † exc. with *up* (dial. and U. S.) : *hoarsen* from 18th c. || *less* vb from 13th c., † : *lessen* from 14th c. || *loose* vb from 13th c. : *loosen* from 14th c., not common till 1600 || *tense* vb from 17th c., rare : *tensen* not in NED, Wyld Hist. Study 332 the sound ... being gradually tensened to (ē) || *worse* vb, OE *wyrsian*; Mi PL 6.440 weapons ... May serve to better us and worse our foes : *worsen* from 15th c., rare in literature before 19th c.

Note that *lessen* and *worsen* are the only ones from comparatives, but then these are the only comparatives not ending in -*r*; and the positive forms (*little, evil*) are

on¹ account of the final sounds incapable of having *-n*
added to them.

-ʃ: *fresh* vb from 14th c., nearly † : *freshen* from
17th c. || *rich* vb from 14th c., † : *richen* from 14th c.;
cf below *enrich*.

-ʒ: *large* vb from 14th c. : *largen* from 19th c., rare;
cf below *enlarge*.

-l: *dull* vb from 14th c. : *dullen* nonce-word 19th c.,
also Spencer Autob. 1.178 || *pale* vb from 14th c. :
palen nonce-word 19th c.

20.5₅. In other cases no form in *-en* has been substituted for the one no longer in use (vb = adj): Beaumont
1.128 I'le *bloudy* my sword | *fond* on someone Sh Tw
II. 2.35 | *happy* 'make happy' Sh Sonn 11, cf R2
III. 1.10 vnhappied [= rendered unhappy] | BJo
3.162 you have very much *honested* my lodging with
your presence [= honoured] | Mi A 34 if we so *jealous*
over them | *malign* Sh Cor I. 1.177 | *pale* 'make pale'
Hml I. 5.90 | Tit I. 1.121 *patient* yourself.

There are no examples of *n*-vbs formed from adjs
in vowels (or diphthongs): *free, blue, low, slow, high,
sly, shy, new; narrow, yellow, steady, holy;* nor of such
disyllables as *able, noble;* nor of adjs in *m, n, ŋ, r: slim,
thin, brown, clean, long, strong; far, poor, near.* Note
the contrast in Kipling L 135 to see the smoke roll
outward, thin and thicken again | Hardy L 147 her hair
greyed and whitened | Quincey 295 to soften and refine
the feelings.

Verbs in *-en* are formed from words ending in the
same consonants after which we also find ptcs in *-n*
(above 5.7). There is, however, the difference that we
have many ptcs with *-n* after vowels, diphthongs, and
r, which do not admit of the formation of *n*-vbs: *seen,
known, born.* The explanation is simply that here we
have the retention of ME stressed monosyllables, exactly as *n* is kept in *mine, thine, one, none, own,* but in

the vbs something was added in a much later period,
and this something should form a second syllable.

From *high* we have, however, ME *heie*, Orrm ptc.
heȝhedd and with *n* 15th c. *hawnyn* or *heynyn* (Prompt.
Par.), † exc. dial. (see NED *hain*). From *dim* (vb from
14th c.) we find the exceptional *dimmen* as a nonce-
word in the 19th c.

Our rule accounts for the formation of *length(en)* and
strength(en): there are no vbs *long* or *longen* 'make or
become long', *strong* or *strongen*. On the analogy of
these we have the rare *depthen* (17th c.) and *breadthen*
(19th c.); no corresponding vbs without *-en*.

Adjs in *-l* generally have no vbs in *-en* (thus none
from *small, full, still*); the two named above are exceptional and late.

20.5₆. In favour of my view I may call attention to
the fact that at the time when the *n*-forms were comparatively new, the simple forms were preferred in the
inf and present, while the extended forms occurred
most frequently before the endings *-ed* and *-ing* (cp.
above *maid* : *maidens, broke* : *brokenly*). A. Schmidt
in his Sh-lex. noticed this with *threat* "used only in
verse and in the present time" [i. e. tense], while
threaten is the usual verb in all forms. We find in the
Sh-Concordance a corresponding number of occur-
rences for such vbs as *bold(en), dark(en), deaf(en),
hap(pen), haste(n), length(en), list(en), moist(en), ripe(n),
short(en), thick(en)*.

Compare with this the fact that though *oft* and *often*
are equally frequent, Sh has only the comparative
oftener (4), no *ofter*, also *oftentimes* (7), but *ofttimes*
only once.

The sound [n] here again is a 'buffer-syllable' between two words or elements.

A look into the Kyd-Concordance shows similar relations. This of course is no more than a tendency, but
it is clear that such a condition cannot be stable, and

in the following centuries we see that the *n*-forms become more and more frequent in the inf and prs, while
it is only a few of the short forms that are powerful
enough to survive (e. g. *black, fat, flat, slight, smoothe*);
some of the short forms survive only in archaic and
poetic literature (i. a. *fright, hap, haste*). But after say
1660 we find no new formations in which *-en* is added
to *verbs*, and the *n*-vbs (*brighten, shorten*, etc.) are
apprehended as directly derived from the *adjectives*.
Thus *broaden* does not come into existence till long
after the vb *broad* had ceased to be used. There has
never been a vb *coarse*, and a vb *coarsen* was formed
from the adj in the beginning of the 19th c., it is frequent in Shaw; similarly the rare *biggen, laten, louden*,
and *meeten* from the end of the 19th c.

20.5₇. In some of those cases in which both forms
are in use a more or less pronounced differentiation
has taken place. *Black* is only transitive and generally
means 'put black colour upon': *black boots; blacken* may
be used figuratively: *blacken a reputation*, and may be
intransitive. Cf, however, Galsw Sw 3 coal; it's blackened
our faces, and now it's going to black our eyes. *Loose*
= undo or set free (opposite to *bind*), *loosen* = make
looser (opposite to *tighten*). *Rough* is preferred if *up, in*,
or *out* is added, also in some special meanings, and in
rough it; roughen is the ordinary vb, transitive or intransitive = make or become rough. *Slack* similarly is
often used with advs like *up, off, out*, it also means 'be
slack or idle', and it trespasses on the territory of
slake; slacken is the ordinary word for 'become, or
make slack'. (This paragraph is to a great extent based
on Fowler MEU.)

20.5₈. The view here advanced gives a natural explanation of the chronological relations (long after the
ceasing of Scand. influence) as well as of the transitive
(causative) meaning attached to these vbs, while we
should have expected only an intransitive (inchoative)

meaning if the vbs were due to Scand. influence, as
maintained by Sweet. If now these vbs are used intransitively as well as transitively, this is a phenomenon
found in a great many other vbs as well, e. g. *get*, *hide*,
tire, *withdraw*, etc. I have counted 36 of the vbs with
which we are here concerned as used transitively either
exclusively or before the intransitive usage, as against
12 used either only intransitively or intransitively before the transitive usage, while in the rest both usages
seem to have arisen at about the same time.

20.5₉. It is curious to notice that instead of a final
en we have sometimes a prefixed *en* (*em* before a labial)
with the same effect of making an adjective into a vb.
This is due originally to French vbs taken over into
ME: *enfeeble* (F *enfeblir*), *enrich* (F *enrichir*), *ensure* (OF
enseurer), and probably also *enlarge* (F *élargir*), all of
them from the 14th c., *ennoble* (F *ennoblir*) from the
16th c.

On the analogy of these corresponding vbs were
made from English adjs—and it should be noted, from
adjs ending in sounds that do not admit of the *en*-ending:
embitter, *embrown* (e. g. Hardy R 3), *encalm* †, *endear*,
enfree †, *entame*, and others, all dating from the 16th
or 17th c. Here we may place also *enable* (from the 15th
c.) though *able* of course is originally a French word.

We may even have *en* both before and after the
English word, if the adj ends in one of the consonants
that admit of English vbs in -*en*:

embold (15th to 16th c.) † : *embolden* from 16th c. ||
embright (16th to 18th c.) † : *embrighten* from 17th c. ||
endark (14th to 17th c.) † : *endarken* from 16th c., † ||
enlight (14th to 18th c.; not a continuation of OE
inlihtan) † : *enlighten* from 16th c. || *enlive* (16th to
17th c.) † : *enliven* from 17th c.

These vbs with double *en* (which offer some difficulty
to Raith, p. 94) are a strong argument in favour of the
view that the vbs formed in -*en* were not originally

formed on adjs, but were extensions of existing vbs.—
It will be seen that all the vbs in this list with *en* in
the beginning alone have since disappeared, and only
some of them with both *en*'s have survived.

Chapter XXI

Other Suffixes Containing Nasals

-an, -ian, -ean

21.1₁. *-an* [-(ə)n], from the Latin adjectival suffix
-anus, was first borrowed through French in the form
-ain or *-en* (after *i*) in ME times (*Christian* had been
introduced with Christianity and is recorded from OE
in the form *cristen*, preserved in *Christendom*), but later
it was adjusted to the Latin spelling, which is now
used in all words adopted from the Romanic languages
or coined in English.

It is of very frequent occurrence in adjs derived from
place-names ending in a vowel (an *a* is dropped before
the suffix): *African, American, Australian, Eurasian*
(from *Europe* and *Asia*), *Amerindian* (American-
Indian), *Austrian, Russian, Crimean, Serbian, Indian,
Bornean* (from *Borneo* with *o* dropped), *Utopian, Laputan*
(in Swift *Laputian*); *Roman, Lancastrian* (from the Latin
form *Lancastria*), *Chilian, Chicagoan, Ohioan* (Mencken
AL⁴ 205), etc.

Note *Trojan* [troudʒən] from *Troy* [troi]. The word was
borrowed as *Troian* (Ch, etc. *Troyan*) with diphthongal *oi;*
after the introduction of the distinction between *i* and *j* the
word was spelt with *j*, and later the spelling-pronunciation
with [dʒ] developed.

The suffix is further added to personal names, e. g.
Lutheran, Mohammedan, Petrarchan (Bailey Mi 135,
but Saintsbury 781 *Petrarchian*), *Thackerayan* (Shaw),
and used as a sb or adj to denote '(person) following

the doctrines or style of—', in *Elizabethan* '(person)
belonging to the period of—'.

And it is added to adjs, to denote '(person) following
a system', e. g. *Anglican, Gallican*, etc. *Publican* (from
L or F) in NT means 'tax-gatherer', but is now popularly
used for 'owner of public-house'.

Finally, it is used in Zoology, added to names of
classes or orders, e. g. *molluscan, protozoan*, etc., first
as adj, but also as sb.

As adjs these words mean 'belonging to such and
such a place'. As a sb it generally denotes a person
from the place in question, or a language, or an adherent,
e. g. *Lutheran, republican*.

From E words in *-ey, -y* we have derivatives spelt
with *-eian: Bodleian, Rugbeian*.

21.1₂. Words in *-an* generally preserve the stress of
the radical. Exceptions are, e. g.

Elizabeth : *Elizabethan* [i'lizəbəþ ‚i‚lizə'bi·þən], ˈmoll-
usc : moˈlluscan, ˈsuburb : subˈurban.

Only in the zoological names is *-an* in regular use to
form new words. In other cases *-ian* or *-ean* is preferred,
see the following paragraphs.

21.1₃. *-ian* [-iən, -jən] is from L *-an* as added to
i-stems, e. g. *Ital-i-anus*. It came to be felt as the actual
suffix rather than the simple *-an*.

Guardian is from OF *guarden* and thus a doublet of
warden with *w* from another OF dialect.

We have here the same groups as of words in *-an*,
thus *-ian* is added to place-names: *Iranian, United
Statesian, Devonian, Lilliputian; Bristolian, Bostonian,
Parisian*, etc.

Derivatives from personal names abound: *Arthurian,
Carlylian, Chestertonian, Dickensian, Edwardian, Galsworthian, Georgian, Gladstonian, Goldsmithian, Malthus-
ian, Marxian, Pickwickian, Shakespearian* (better than
Shakespearean), *Spenserian*, etc. etc.

Note *Lancasterian* (schools, from Joseph Lancaster
† 1838), different from *Lancastrian* (from the town).

The suffix is further used in adjs denoting '(person)
following some doctrine or system', e. g. *Episcopalian*,
Presbyterian, etc.

And in Zoology, e. g. *mammalian*, *reptilian*, etc.

-ian may also be added to adjs, e. g. *perfectibilian*
(Campbell Shl 47 Was he [Peacock] no perfectibilian?),
precisian (BJo 1.54), *vulgarian*, etc., cf *-arian* (21.2).

And *-ian* and *-ean* may be used to facetious formations
such as *any-lengthian* (NED), *Big-Endian* (Swift),
butlerian (Tracy P 14 Brown [butler] explained, in the
best butlerian style), *Everybody-elseian* (Ruskin in
Collingwood R 159 dissatisfied with the Linnæan,
Jussieuan, and Everybody-elseian arrangement of
plants), *something-ean* (Di P 162 the four something-ean
singers).

Fowler in MEU insists on the distinction between
Olympian from *Olympus:* Olympian Zeus, etc., and
Olympic from *Olympia:* Olympic games.

Sound

21.1₄. The learned character of this suffix is clearly
shown in the fact that words in *-an*, *-ian* are frequently
derived from a Latinized form of the radical. Thus a
final *-ugh*, *-w*, and *-y* become *v* before *-ian* in

Borrovian (from Borough), *Bungavian* (Thack P 422
"This is one of Bungay's grand field-days," he said.—
"We are all Bungavians here."), *Cracovian*, *Harrovian*
[hæ'rouviən], *Marlovian*, *Shavian* [ʃeiviən] (Bernard
Shaw), *Varsovian* (Warsaw).

An *n* is added before *-ian* on the analogy of Latin
n-stems (i. a. in the oblique cases of the Lat. word),
e. g. *Brunonian* (from *Bruno*, Latinized form of *Brown*,
see NED), *Diabolonian* (from *diabolo;* Shaw Pur xx and
xxiv), *Panamanian*.

Swift (in Gulliver) has the arbitrary formation
Blefuscudian from *Blefuscu*.

Examples of derivation from earlier or Latinized
forms are:

Aberdonian (from Aberdeen), *Cantabrigian* (from L
Cantabrigia 'Cambridge'), *Carthusian* [ka·ˈþjuˑziən],
orig. about '(member) of the Carthusian order of monks',
now also '(member) of Charterhouse School', *Galwegian*
(coined on the analogy of *Norwegian*) and *Gallovidian*
'(native) of Galloway', *Wincastrian* (Sayers DC 91,
from Winchester), *Glasgowegian* and *Glaswegian* (Glas-
gow), *Norwegian* (from med. L. *Norvegia*, with *w* from
Norway), *Oxonian* (Oxford), *Salopian* (from *Salop*
'Shropshire', or Shrewsbury School.)

21.1₅. Words in *-ian* (cf vol I 5.62) are stressed on
the syllable immediately preceding the ending; hence
we often have a shift of stress from radical to derivative,
often with other phonetic changes, e. g.

history [histəri] : *historian* [hiˈstɔ·rien], *precise* [priˈsais]
: *precisian* [priˈsiʒən].

Thus also in derivatives from place-names:

Devon [devən] : *Devonian* [diˈvouniən], *Bristol* :
Bristolian, *Paris* : *Parisian* [pəˈrizjən, pəˈriʒ(i)ən],
Canada [kænədə] : *Canadian* [kəˈneidjən], *Brobdingnag* :
Brobdingˈnagian, *Grumbleˈtonian* (cf Linguistica 417), and
in derivatives from personal names:

ˈ*Arthur* : *Ar*ˈ*thurian* [a·ˈþjuəriən], ˈ*Byron* : *By*ˈ*ronian*,
ˈ*Cromwell* : *Crom*ˈ*wellian*, *Gladstone* [glædstən] : *Gladstonian* [glædˈstouniən], ˈ*Hegel* : *He*ˈ*gelian*, ˈ*Malthus* :
*Mal*ˈ*thusian* [mælˈþjuˑziən], ˈ*Pickwick* : *Pick*ˈ*wickian*,
ˈ*Pluto* : *Plu*ˈ*tonian*, ˈ*Spenser* : *Spen*ˈ*serian*, ˈ*Milton* :
*Mil*ˈ*tonian*, ˈ*Tennyson* : *Tenny*ˈ*sonian* (and others in
-on-ian),*Wordsworth* [wəˑdzwə·þ] : *Wordsworthian* [wəˑdz-
ˈwəˑðiən] (but NED: ˈ*Galsworthian*).

-ician

21.1₆. *-ian* is frequently added to sbs in *-ic* to form
sbs denoting 'person concerned with . . .', e. g. *arith-
metician, clinician, logician, magician, mathematician,
physician* (from *physic;* but *physicist* from *physics*),
politician, rhetorician, etc.

Note the sound: *logic* [lɔdȝik] : *logician* [lou|dȝiʃən],
and correspondingly with the others.

On the analogy of these forms *-ician* [-|iʃən] has
been used to form similar words which have no radical
in *-ic,* e. g. *algebrician* (from *algebra*), *geometrician* from
geometry), and *paradoxician* (Locke S 240 the airy
paradoxician). Or are they from adjs in *-ic*?

-ician has been especially fertile in U. S., cf Mencken
AL⁴ 78 ff.: *asphaltician, beautician* 'owner of beauty
parlor', *bootician* 'bootlegger', *cosmetician, dialogician,*
and *mortician* (Sinclair Oil 35 *-s*).

-ean

21.1₇. *-ean* (sometimes *-aean*) is a by-form of *-an* with
e from the stem retained.

Some words in *-ean* are stressed like derivatives in
-ian, i. e. on the syllable immediately preceding the
ending, e. g. *Archi|medean, Hyper|borean, Pro|methean,
ce|rulean, Medite|rranean.*

Thus also, with shift of stress from radical to derivative
Mephisto|phelean from *Mephi|stopheles, Shake|spearean*
(also *-ian*) from *Shakespeare.*

The ending here is [-iən].

But in many cases, "by the influence of the English
pronunciation of Latin" (Sweet NEG § 1738), the ending
takes the stress and becomes [-|iˑən], here, too, generally
with shift of stress from radical to derivative as in

|Epicure : Epicu|rean, |Europe : Euro|pean (cf vol I
5.61), *|Jacob* or *Ja|cobus : Jaco|bean, |Pericles : Peric|lean,
Py|thagoras : Pythago|rean.*

Herculean is given by Daniel Jones as [həˑkju(ˑ)ˈliˑən, həˑlkjuˑliən]. In earlier grammars and dictionaries only the latter form is given.

-arian

21.2₁. *-arian* [-ˈɛˑriən], for stress cp above 21.1₅. From the end of the 16th c. it became possible to coin sbs and adjs by adding *-an* to Latin adjectives in *-arius*, thus *disciplinarian* (1585), later *agrarian, antiquarian, librarian, proletarian, trinitarian, veterinarian*, etc.

Thus also learned derivatives from Latin numerals generally to denote 'person of that age', or (adj) 'of such a person', *octogenarian, centenarian; millenarian* 'of the millennium, believing in the millennium'.

Corresponding coinages from words in *-ary* are *necessarian, parlamentarian, sanitarian, sectarian*, etc.

21.2₂. On the analogy of these words *-arian* came to be used as an independent suffix, as in *latitudinarian*, on the pattern of which we have the later *attitudinarian, platitudinarian* (Zangwill G 230), *predestinarian, strictarian* (nonce-word; NED 1867), *tractarian*, and *vegetarian* (irreg. from *vegetable*), on the analogy of which are coined *fruitarian* (London Before Adam 197) and *nutarian* [nʌltɛˑəriən].

On the analogy of *trinitarian, unitarian*, etc., interpreted as derivatives of *trinity, unity*, etc., + *-arian*, we have several formations from words in *-(i)ty:*

authoritarian, brutalitarian (contrast to *humanitarian;* NED Suppl 1904), *egalitarian* (AHuxley), *equalitarian, futilitarian* (Weseen 338), *humanitarian, libertarian* (Bennett PL 81), *necessitarian, uniformitarian, universitarian*, etc.

Note facetious formations like *anythingarian* and *nothingarian* (McKenna S 244).

Words in *-arian* generally denote '(member) of a sect, (holder) of a certain doctrine, religious or otherwise'.

-ane

21.3₁. *-ane* [-ein], originally an orthographic variant of *-an*, has now been differentiated from *-an* in

germane [dʒəˈmein] 'relevant, pertinent', cf *German*, *humane* [hjuˈmein] 'compassionate', (of studies) 'refined', cf *human*, *urbane* [əˈˈbein] 'courteous, suave', cf *urban*.

An unconnected form is *mundane* [mʌndein].

A rare spelling: *-ain* in *riverain* (Tennyson L 4.229).— *Fountain* and *mountain* might be taken as E derivatives from *fount* and *mount* (The Sermon on the Mount, Mount Everest), but are loans from F *fontaine* and *montagne*. Some stationers advertize *fount-pens* instead of the usual *fountain-pen*.

-ana

21.3₂. *-ana* [-ˈeinə, -ˈaːnə], substantival suffix, is from L *-ana*, neut. pl of adjs in *-anus*, *-anum* in expressions like (*dicta*) *Vergiliana*, (cf *-an*, *-ane*), and has been used in English from the beginning of the 18th c. to denote (collections of) notable sayings of, or notes about some person, e. g. *Johnsoniana*, *Shakespeariana*, *Byroniana*, etc., thus always preceded by *-i-*. *Ana* may be used as a generic name of collections of such sayings, etc., literary gossip. It may take the plural *anas* or *ana's*, though the plural *ana* is the most usual.

-in, -ine

21.4. *-in*, *-ine* occurs in various functions, which will be treated separately.

1) as an adjectival ending, of Lat. (Gk) origin,

2) as a feminine ending of Lat. (Gk) or German origin,

3) with the forms *-in* and *-ine* differentiated in names of (esp. chemical) substances, of Lat. (Gk) origin.

21.4₁. *-in*, *-ine* [-ain, -in, (-i·n)], as an adjectival (or secondarily substantival) suffix, is from L *-īnus* or *-ĭnus* 'pertaining to, of the nature of' (cf Gk *-inos*). The two endings are not etymologically distinguished in English although two pronunciations occur: [-ain] and [-in].

In a few popular loanwords (cf vol I 4.84) Daniel Jones has [-in] as the only pronunciation, thus in *feminine*, *genuine*, and *sanguine*, but in other, especially learned, words [-ain] only, thus in *alpine*, *asinine*, *bovine*, *equine*, *Florentine*, *labyrinthine*, *Pauline* (adj from *St. Paul*). In some words in which Jones gives [-ain] only, SOD also has [-in], thus *crystalline*, *elephantine*, *leonine*. The tendency is towards pronouncing only [-ain] in all such words.

French end-stress and [i·] occurs in *marine*, cf also names of chemical substances below.

Most of the words in *-ine* are loanwords, but the ending has also been used, though not very frequently, as an independent formative in English, as in *amaranthine* (NED 1667 Milton), *culturine* (Lewis MS 96 though I might be affected and culturine), *riverine* (1860; Lawrence Seven Pillars 36), and *Sphingine* (AHuxley Barren Leaves 83 my most Sphingine smile).

21.4₂. The ending *-ine* as a feminine suffix, pronounced [-in], now occurs in very few modern British English words. In *heroine*, the only surviving word adopted through French, the suffix represents Fr. *-ine*, from Lat. *-ina*; in *landgravine, margravine* it represents German *-in*.

Examples of new-formations with this suffix in Am. English have been collected by Louise Pound in Am. Speech 3.368, among which are *actorine*, *chorine* 'chorus-girl', *doctorine*, and *knitterine*, to which may be added *dudine* (see ib 447) and *batherine* (Weseen 306). Cf Mencken AL⁴ 180 and vol. VII 5.4₂ (end).

21.4₃. *-in* [-in, (-iˑn)] and *-ine* [-iˑn, -in, -ain], forming names of (chemical) substances are etymologically identical with adjectival *-ine*. The two endings were formerly used indiscriminately, but now *-in* is generally used to denote neutral substances, such as *albumin, casein, fibrin,* etc. A few words belonging to this group, however, have *-ine* in popular use, and often in scientific use, two, thus *butterine* (now supplanted by *margarine,* except in U.S.), *gelatine, glycerine,* etc. *-ine* is used in names of alkaloids, and basic substances, e. g. *caffeine, cocaine, morphine, nicotine, quinine, strychnine,* and the names of the four elements *bromine, chlorine, fluorine,* and *iodine.*

Most of these words are loanwords, but a few have been coined on English soil, thus *butterine, bromine, chlorine* (coined by Davy, 1810), *fluorine,* and *iodine.*

Words in *-in* are generally pronounced [-in], but if a popular by-form in *-ine* exists, they may be pronounced [-iˑn] e. g. *paraffin* [pærəfin, -fiˑn], *gelatin(e)* [dʒelətin, (pop.) dʒeləˈtiˑn].

Most words in *-ine* have [-iˑn] as the only pronunciation, but some have [-in], besides, e. g. *chlorine, vitamin(e).*

Note *cocaine* [koˈkein], *bromine* [broumi(ˑ)n, -main], and *iodine* [aiodain, -diˑn].

-ina

21.4₄. *-ina* [-iˑnə], substantival, especially feminine, ending, is from *-īna,* in L *regīna,* extended in Ital. and Span. to form feminine titles and Christian names, as *czarina, Angelina, Christina, Georgina,* etc. It has also been used to form names of some musical instruments, such as *concertina, ocarina,* etc.

-een

21.5₁. *-een* [-iˑn], substantival suffix, has two distinct functions, and represents two etymologically different suffixes.

1) From F *-in, -ine*, L *-ĭnus, -ĭna*, adj suffix. This suffix was first borrowed in ModE times, as in *canteen, tureen*. An E derivative is *velveteen*, on the analogy of which we have *sateen*, an alteration of *satin*.

2) From the Irish diminutive suffix *-in*. It primarily occurs in Anglo-Irish, and has been added both to words of Irish origin, as in *colleen, dudeen, spalpeen*, and to English words as in *buckeen, girleen, jackeen* 'self-assertive, worthless fellow' (Henderson Table-Talk of G. B. S. 133), *poteen, squireen*.

Cf Joyce Ir 90.

-ern

21.5₂. *-ern* [-ən] occurs only in adjs derived from the names of points of the sky, *eastern, northern, southern, western*.

On the relationship of the ending to the corresponding IE endings, see NED.

-oon

21.5₃. *-oon* [-ˡuˑn] is found as a rendering of F *-on* in loans from the late 16th or early 17th c. (see vol I 8.36), such as *balloon, cartoon, doubloon, Octoroon* is an irregular formation on the pattern of *quadroon*. The only genuine native formation seems to be *spittoon*. But the ending, which has no definite meaning, can hardly be considered a real E suffix. In *mushroom* from F *mousseron* the final consonant has been assimilated to the initial.

-ant, -ent

21.6₁. Both suffixes, for adjs and sbs, originate from L active ptcs in *-ant(em), -ent(em)*, and mainly occur in words borrowed from L or through F. In F the ptc in all classes of vbs became *-ant*, the ME spelling of which was *-aunt*. In later times the spelling was generally re-adjusted as *-ant* or *-ent* to the L form, though without complete consistency, as seen in *assistant* (sb), but *persistent* (adj), *attendant* (sb), but *superintendent* (sb). The sound of *-ant* and *-ent* is the same: [-ənt].

A great many words were adopted which have no

connexion with E vbs, e. g. *arrogant, diligent, elegant, evident, present, violent* (adjs), *lieutenant, merchant, miscreant, torrent* (sbs), *patient* (adj & sb).

21.6₂. But we are in this volume more concerned with those words that are felt to be derived from existing E vbs, either as adjs or as agent-sbs, the former more adjectival than the corresponding forms in *-ing*, which are truly verbal in character. Complete conformity is found, e. g., in *defiant (defy), defendant, attendant, triumphant, assailant, servant, observant, assistant, absorbent,* but the sound is different in *errant* [erənt] : *err* [ə·], *apparent* [ə'pærənt, ə'pɛ·ərənt] : *appear* [ə'piə], *abundant* [ə'bʌndənt] : *abound* [ə'baund], *obedient* [o'bi·djənt] : *obey* [o'bei], *student* [stju·dənt] : *study* [stʌdi]. To vbs in *-ate* correspond forms in *-ant* : *radiant, stagnant, extravagant, congratulant, intoxicant, stimulant,* etc. Sometimes the stress is shifted: *protestant* ['prɔtistənt] : *protest* [pro'test], *president* ['prezidənt] : *preside* [pri'zaid] *excellent* ['eksələnt] : *excel* [ek'sel], *provident* ['prɔvidənt] : *provide* [pro'vaid], *ignorant* ['ignorənt] : *ignore* [ig'nɔ·ə]. To vbs in *-fy* we have *-ficant: sig'nificant* : 'signify.

Indignant is semantically out of the ordinary, hence the sb is *indignation*, not *-ance*.

-ant has rarely been used as an independent formative in English, as in *benignant* coined on the anology of *malignant.*

Note the tendency towards a differentiation between *dependant* sb and *dependent* adj, and *pendant* (in naut. language *pennant*) sb and *pendent* adj.

But the distinction made by Johnson between *descendant* sb and *descendent* adj is no longer valid.

Covenant sb is etymologically identical with *convenient* adj. And *serjeant, sergeant,* and *servant* are ultimately the same word.

Cormorant, peasant, pheasant, truant, tyrant and others do not belong here; the *t* is excrescent, see vol I 7.62.

-ance, -ence, -ancy, -ency

21.6₃. These four forms may be considered different
shapes of what is essentially one and the same suffix,
mainly used to form nexus-substantives corresponding to the just treated sbs and adjs in *-ant* and *-ent*.
The forms in *-nce* are from F *-nce* < L *-ntia*, the ME
spelling was generally *-aunce;* later we have the same
re-adjustment to L spellings as we saw in *-ant*, *-ent*,
also with the same inconsistency. The forms in *-cy* are
to be considered a subdivision under the suffix *-sy*, on
which see above 13.2₁. A good deal of vacillation
between *-nce* and *-ncy* (see 21.6₅) may partly be
attributed to the fact that the plurals *-nces* and *-ncies*
are identical in sound, e. g. *inadvertences = inadvert-
encies, impertinences = impertinencies*.

On stress see vol I 5.64.

Originally L words borrowed direct or through F, to
which we have no corresponding word in *-nt*, are, e. g.,
circumstance and *(in)temperance*.

Sometimes we have F alongside of L forms: *com-
plaisance* : *complacence*, *-cy*, *purveyance* : *providence;* cf
doublets like *ordinance* : *ordnance* : *ordonnance*.

-ance was used as an independent suffix in F to form
verbal nexus-words, many of which were borrowed into
E, too, e. g. *annoyance, defiance, entrance, grievance,
maintenance, nuisance, quittance, repentance, severance,*
and *sustenance*.

In many cases the F vb was adopted in E together
with its derivative in *-ance*, e. g. *appear* : *appearance,
abound* : *abundance*, (formerly also *aboundance*, Sh Sonn.,
1.7), *observe* : *observance, suffer* : *sufferance*. Hence
-ance, as in F, came to be used as an independent
suffix to form nouns of action, as in *avoidance, clearance* (Ru P 1.351 and wish the Dustman Oblivion good
clearance ['riddance'] of them), *dalliance, guidance,
joyance* (Spenser FQ I. 4.37 joyaunce | Tennyson 3), etc.

The ending was added even to native verbs, as in *abidance, forbearance, forbiddance, furtherance* (and obs. *fartherance*), *hindrance, riddance, utterance,* and the nonce-word *come-uppance* (Lewis B 359).

21.6₄. Among F formations in *-ence,* we may note *pertinence, prurience, recurrence.* Note the stress in *reference* [ˈrefərəns] from [riˈfəˑ].

21.6₅. Forms in *-ce* and in *-cy* were formerly often, and may to some extent still be, used indiscriminately. Thus *arrogance : -cy, compliance : -cy, exuberance : -cy; competence : -cy, (im)pertinence : -cy, inconvenience : -cy* and others. But in many cases one or the other form has become fixed, and sometimes a differentiation has taken place between two co-existing forms.

There is thus a clear tendency towards using the form in *-ance* to denote action, state, or quality, whereas *-ancy* denotes state or quality only (cf Fowler MEU: *-ce, -cy*). Thus in

arrogance 'presumption' : *arrogancy* 'state or quality of being arrogant' | *brilliance* 'sparkling brightness' : *brilliancy* 'quality of being brilliant' | *observance* 'action or practice of observing' : *observancy* 'quality of being observant' | *significance* 'importance' : *significancy* 'quality of being significant'.

Similarly with *-ence* and *-ency*:

consistence 'degree of density in liquids' : *consistency* 'quality or state of being consistent' | *excellence* 'great merit' : *excellency* 'title' | *dependence* 'depending, reliance' : *dependency* 'something subordinate, dependent state' | *emergence* 'emerging' : *emergency* 'crisis' | *frequence* 'frequent occurrence' : *frequency* 'fact or rate of frequent occurrence' | *permanence* 'duration' : *permanency* 'permanent occupation'.

Among words in which the forms in *-nce* have now prevailed to the exclusion of *-ncy* may be mentioned *abundance, exorbitance, ignorance, importance, pursuance* (with *issuance* in U. S.), *temperance, vigilance,* and

those from native words mentioned above (21.6₃);
further in *-ence: benevolence, consequence, correspondence, difference, eloquence, evidence, impudence, innocence,
insolence, intelligence, omnipotence, penitence, prudence,
vehemence,* and *violence.*

Among words in which the *-ncy* form is practically
the only one in active use may be mentioned *brilliancy,
buoyancy, constancy* (but *Constance* as a proper name),
infancy, irritancy, piquancy, pliancy, poignancy, riancy
(Carlyle SR 129)—and with *-ency: clemency, currency,
decency, efficiency, fluency, inconsistency, persistency,
regency, tendency, transparency.*

-ion (-sion, -tion, -ation)

21.7₁. Latin *-ion-em* was added to a participial stem.
It had primarily a passive import (being originally
added to the Latin 'passive' participle) and denoted
'state of being -ed'. In English words derived with
-ion are usually nouns of action or process (verbal nexus-
words).

On the place of the stress see vol I 5.62, on the sound
changes, by which [i] became [j] and [tion, sion] became
[tʃən, ʃən, ʒən] see ib 9.87, 12.22.

21.7₂. Sometimes the relation between the vb and
the sb is comparatively simple, e. g.

suggest : suggestion [-stʃən] | *except : exception* [-pʃən],
corrupt-ion | *select : selection* [-kʃən], *collect-ion, protect-
ion, correct-ion, restrict-ion, react-ion,* and other derivat-
ives from verbs in *-ct* | *assert : assertion* [-ʃən] | *contribute*
[kənˈtribjuˑt] : *contribution* (kɔntriˈbjuˑʃən), similarly
from *persecute, substitute.*

From *connect, reflect,* etc., the sb is variously spelt,
connexion and *connection,* etc., the former preferred by
classical scholars.

Cp also *opine* [oˈpain] : *opinion* [oˈpinjən].

(Popularly, *notion* may be taken as formed from
know).

21.7₃. But very often the change is more violent in consequence of L rules combined with E sound-development:

extend : *extension* [-ʃən], thus *expand, condescend, intend* | *revise* [-ˈvaiz] : *revision* [-ˈviʒən], thus *supervise* | *recognize* [rekəgnaiz] : *recognition* [rekəgˈniʃən] | *intervene* [-ˈviˑn] | *intervention* [-ˈvenʃən], thus *convene, supervene* | *permit* [-ˈmit] | *permission* [-ˈmiʃən], thus *remit, submit* | *exhibit* [igˈzibit] : *exhibition* [eksiˈbiʃən], thus *inhibit, edit* | *decide* [-ˈsaid] : *decision* [-ˈsiʒən], thus *persuade, divide, collide,* etc. | *describe* [-ˈskraib] : *description* [-ˈskripʃən], thus *con-, in-, subscribe* | *reduce* [-ˈdjuˑs] : *reduction* [-ˈdʌkʃən], thus *intro-, pro-, seduce* | *adhere* [-ˈhiə] : *adhesion* [-ˈhiˑʒən], thus *cohere* | *acquire* [əˈkwaiə] : *acquisition* [ækwiˈziʃən], thus *require* | *resume* [-ˈzjuˑm] : *resumption* [-ˈsʌm(p)ʃən], thus *con-, pre-, assume* | *redeem* [-ˈdiˑm] : *redemption* [-ˈdem(p)ʃən] | *move* [muˑv] : *motion* [mouʃən] | *solve* [sɔlv] : *solution* [səˈluˑʃən], thus *dis-, resolve, e-, revolve* | *impel* [-ˈpel] : *impulsion* [-ˈpʌlʃən], thus *compel.*

In a great many cases the derivative keeps rather close to the L pattern, whereas the vb often has a special F form, thus

abstain [əbsˈtein] : *abstention* [æbsˈtenʃən], thus *re-, sustain* | *conceive* [-ˈsiˑv] : *conception* [-ˈsepʃən], thus *de-, per-, receive* | *enjoin* [inˈdʒoin] : *injunction* [inˈdʒʌŋ(k)ʃən] | *destroy* [disˈtroi] : *destruction* [disˈtrʌkʃən] (but *instruct* : *instruction*) | (*appear* [əˈpiə] : *apparition* [æpəˈriʃən]).

Corresponding to *possession, discussion* the E vb has *ss* as against F *posséder, discuter.*

Note some verbs from F in *-ish* with corresponding sb in *-ition: abolish, admonish, demolish, nourish* [nʌriʃ] : *nutrition* [njuˑˈtriʃən], *punish* [pʌniʃ] : *punition* [pjuˈniʃən].

-ition is also found in *addition* from *add, composition* from *compose* and similarly *im-, suppose.* (The simple *pose* | *position* is semantically on a different footing).

Shortenings of the derivatives are seen in *declension*,
L *declination-em*, *coercion*, L *coercition-em*.

21.7₄. Some vbs have been coined in recent times
by back-formation from sbs in *-ion*, many of them
were originally Americanisms (cf EStn 70. 120): *electro-
cute* (NED Suppl. 1889) | *elocute* (not NED; Lewis
MS 47 Ella is our shark at elocuting | ib 121 you can
elocute as well as Ella) | *excurse* (NED 1748; Brynild-
sen has *excursh* as an Americanism) | *extradite* (NED
1864) | *intuite* (NED 1848; Times LS 31.5 1928 Trollope
knew (or 'intuited') very well the ecclesiastical types)
| *irrupt* (NED 1855, Farmer Americanisms) | *preempt*
(NED 1857; Lewis B 266) | *televise* (NED Suppl. 1927;
Times LS 24.8. 1933) | *vivisect* (NED 1864; Meredith,
Housman, Shaw). Cf also Galsw EC 175 It's no good
fashing yourself till something happens. The vb *suase*
is presupposed in Kipling S 169 We're strictly moral
suasers. — Cf. on *-ate* 24.8₂.

21.7₅. The majority of the sbs end in *-ation*, from the
participial form of Lat. *a*-vbs. Thus we have from vbs in

-ate : *-ation* : *adulteration*, *exaggeration*, *assimilation*,
etc.

-fy : *-fication* : *classification*, *amplification*, *simplification*, etc.

-ize (*-ise*) : *ization* (*-isation*) : *civilization*, *central-
ization*, *organization*, etc.

Besides the pronunciation [-ai'zeiʃən] with [ai] from
the vb, we have also [-i'zeiʃən]; cf vol I 5.62 and 9.87;
in Hay B 56 *organize-ation*, *combine-ation* are given as
vulgar forms (influenced by the less learned vb).

Narration might formerly (e. g. Austen S 344) be
used = *narrative*. Byron has both words in DJ 14.7
This narrative is not meant for narration. Cf *relation*
and *relative* that may both be used = 'person related
to some one'.

The ending *-ation* is also added to a certain number
of other verbs, e. g.

arrest : *arrestation* | *ruin* : *ruination* | *annex* : *annexation*
| *alter* : *alteration* | *quote* : *quotation*.

Note *resign* [ri'zain] : *resignation* [rezig'neiʃən].

-ation therefore becomes the only ending in formations
from native stems, which only make their appearance
at a late date. The two earliest recorded in NED are
flirtation (1718) and *starvation* (1778). Further:

backwardation (and obs. *backwardization*) | *bothera-
tion* (Scott in Lockhart L 577, Di T 2.26, Galsw F 164,
Maugham Alt 480, etc.) | *flotation* (Wells H 410, also
spelt *floatation*) | *Westernization* (Wells in NP 1914).

-ment

Cf F. Gadde, *On the History and Use of the Suffixes -ery
(-ry), -age and -ment.* Lund and Cambr. 1910.

21.8₁. The suffix *-ment* originates from F *-ment* <
L *-mentum*, which was added to verbal stems, generally
to denote the instrument, result, or product of an
action, later also the action itself. From Anglo-French
words in *-ment* were borrowed into English, the earliest
being *sacrament* (12th c.), but the ending did not come
to be considered as an E formative till the latter part
of the 13th c.

Among early F adoptions were such words as *ad-
vancement, amendment,* and *judgment;* the existence
in E of the corresponding vbs then gave rise to new
formations, and from the 16th c. formations both
from F and native roots abound, among them such
words as *acknowledgment, amazement,* and *atonement.*
Since then the suffix has been active, especially in the
19th and 20th centuries.

The pronunciation is generally [-mənt], on occasional
[-mint] see vol I 9.52.

Final *y* in the root-word is altered in spelling to *i*
before *-ment.*

On the sounds in *chastise* [tʃæs'taiz] : *chastisement*

[ˈtʃæstizmənt], the earliest of the native formations, corresponding to *advertise* [ˈædvətaiz] : *advertisement* [ədˈvəˑtizmənt], see vol I 5.64.

21.8₂. Formations from orig. F words in *-ish* are rather frequent, e. g. from Spenser *blandishment*, *blemishment*, *rauishment*, and *stablishment* (now *establishment*). Rose Macaulay K 108 revives the obsolete word *minishment*.

A favourite type of stem with this suffix seems to be disyllables with stress on the second syllable, thus the French adoptions *commandment, commencement, concealment, contentment* (Browning 2.298), *refreshment, sustainment* (Browning 2.306), and native formations like *concernment* (Sterne M 1.9), *convincement* (Mi A 46), *escapement, fulfilment* (from 1775), *recal(l)ment* (e. g. Browning 1.392), the nonce-words *tattooment* (Kipling L 122), *unfrockment* (Carpenter D 76).

Formations from verbs with the prefixes *en-* (*em-*) and *be-* are especially frequent, e. g.

enlightenment | *entoilment* (Browning) | *endowment* | *ennoblement* (Shaw) | *endearment* | *enjoyment* || *embroilment* (Browning) | *embodiment* | *embankment* || *bequeathment* (Browning 2.296) | *bereavement* | *bewilderment*.

There are a few formations from sbs:

basement | *devilment* | the nonce-word *motherment* (Locke A 120, or from the vb?) | *speechment* (Huxley L 1.113, another nonce-word) | *rabblement* (in the sense of 'mob', Spenser FQ 1.6.8, Bunyan P 133).

A small number of words are formed from adjs, such as

funniment, merriment (Spenser FQ 3.1.57, common), *oddment* (generally in the pl).

Spenser has *dreriment* (e. g. FQ 1.2.44), *hardiment* (e. g. 1.1.14), *iollyment* (e. g. 2.6.3, 4.11.12), *vnruliment* 'unruliness' (4.9.23), and *wariment* 'caution' (4.3.17).

We often find words the stems of which end in *-er*, *-ure* [-ə] or *-le* [-l], e. g.

betterment | *disfigurement* (Carlyle E 210) | *wonder-*

ment || *couplement* (Spenser FQ 4.3.52) | *dazzlement* |
disgruntlement | *puzzlement* | *scribblement* (Cowper L
1.317, 2.154).

21.8₃. Most of the words in -*ment* are nexus-words
and correspond rather closely to -*ing* of the gerund,
but in some cases they may have a passive import
('being -ed'), thus *fulfilment, refreshment, contentment,
degradement, astonishment, bewilderment, puzzlement*, etc.

But like other action-nouns words in -*ment* may (also)
denote the means or result of the action. A few examples:
abridgement (1) 'action', (2) 'compendium' | *achieve-
ment* | *advertisement* | *government* (1) 'governing', (2)
'persons governing' | *judgment* | *management* | *settlement* |
statement.

-ing

21.9₁. On the syntactical use of *ing* as a Gerund
and as First Participle see vol V Chs VIII (with bibliography), IX, XXII. Here we are exclusively concerned
with formal questions.

As other Gothonic languages OE had two forms for
the nexus-substantive, -*ung* and -*ing*, formed from
weak vbs, originally -*ung* from the second class, -*ing*
from the first: *hergung* 'plunder' (cf the preterit *hergode*),
hering 'praising' (cf the preterit *herede*). But in some
texts -*ing* and -*ung* alternate according to the vowel
of the ending (-*ingum*, but otherwise -*ung*). In early
ME, in AR -*unge* (with rarer -*ung*, -*unke*) is much more
frequent than -*inge*, but from that period -*ung* disappears pretty rapidly, and -*ing* becomes the regular
form.

From the late OE period substantives begin to be
formed from strong vbs as well as from weak ones,
e. g. (with earliest date in NED) *breaking* 975, *blowing*
1000, *bidding* 1175, *biting* 1175, *eating* 1175, *drinking*
1200, *choosing* 1200, *fighting* 1225, *beating* 1230, *bearing*
1250, *falling* 1300, etc.

From the 13th c we also find frequent formations
from French words: *spusing, riwlunge, serving, assail-
lynge, plainynge*, etc. Thus it has for many centuries
been possible to form them from any verb.

There are also a certain number of words in -*ing* seemingly
without any verb: *morning, evening* (20.1₄), *farthing. Shipping,
stabling, schooling* were probably formed from the sbs without
any regard to the existing vbs of the same form.

Ings are sometimes formed from particles and from
compounds and phrases, e. g. *inning(s)* | Maugham
Alt 1267 The tenant of their house in Dorset was leav-
ing and though there was another in the *offing* ... |
Quiller-Couch M 199 until her small boat had made
her offing | NP 1917 after all the *hitherings* and *thither-
ings* of the last ten days ‖ NP 1902 the best way of
week-ending | Carlyle S 192 a kind of infinite, unsuffer-
able, *Jew's-harping* and *scrannel-piping* | Shaw M 125
vowings and pledgings and *until-death-do-us-partings* and
the like.

21.9₂. The first participle was originally distinct
from the sb by having the consonants -*nd:* oldest
-*ændi*, -*indi*, rarely -*onde*, the regular OE form being
-*ende*. In early ME we had most often -*inde* in the
South, -*ende* in the Midlands, and -*and* in the North.
But pretty soon the form in -*ing(e)* begins to be used
for the ptc.

The development of the nexus-sb may also have to
some extent been influenced by the old inflected infinitive in -*nne*.

The latest treatment of the intricate relation between
the *nd* and the *ng*-forms (after van Langenhove and
others) is in F. Mossé, *Hist. de la forme périphrastique*,
Paris 1938, vol 2 p. 77 ff., with comprehensive stat-
istics.—For the continuation in Sc dialects of the
forms in -*nd* (-*n*) see Ellis EEP 5.753, Dixon and Grant
§ 54 and Wright's EDG.

From late ME it looks as if the substantival form
-*ing* [-iŋ] had prevailed for the ptc as well, at any rate
in StE. But as a matter of fact the sound [-in] is very
common indeed, see for the earlier period Mossé, p. 89 f.
and for PE dialects EDG § 274 "Final unstressed ŋ
has generally become *n* in all the dialects, *evenin*(*g*),
farthin(*g*), *mornin*(*g*), *sendin*(*g*), and similarly in all
present participles and verbal nouns in -*ing*." Cf especially the many quotations in vol I 13.1, where the same
pronunciation is mentioned as used by educated people,
not only aristocrats and "horsy" people.—But note
inverse forms like *kitching*, *capting* for *captain*, etc.;
early sporadic examples like *lyning* for *linen*, etc.
Wyld, Coll. 290, Mossé 91. Cf also *tiding* from Scand.
tiðindi and the place-names collected by Mossé and
Ekwall, Engl. Pl. Names in *ing* (Lund 1923).

In this case the distinction between [n] and [ŋ],
which in other cases are independent phonemes and
serve to keep apart words like *sin* and *sing*, *ran* and
rang, etc., is thus in weak syllables made irrelevant.

The phonetic confusion of *n*(*d*)- and *ng*-forms was
furthered by the syntactic relations, on which see vol V.

21.9₃. With regard to form the following points should
be noticed:

The long vowel [ə·] from the verbs is found, e. g.
in *erring*, *concurring* [ə·riŋ, kənˈkə·riŋ] as against the
regular development in *error*, *concurrence* [erə, kən-
kʌrəns].

The number of syllables is often reduced in familiar
words when *ing* is added to words ending in syllabic
[n, l]; while *lessening*, *thickening*, *tightening*, *threatening*,
reasoning, *tickling* and others may have three or two
syllables, *troubling*, *settling* and others generally have
only two. The same vacillation is found with *entering*,
wandering, etc. between [əriŋ] and [riŋ]. *Being*, *lying*
and similar forms in Sh and other poets are sometimes
disyllabic. A difference may be made between *lightning*

'electric discharge' [laitniŋ] and *lightening* 'the act of
shedding light upon, or making less heavy' [laitn-iŋ].

In spelling consonants are doubled after short vowels:
sitting, hopping, bidding, begging, winning, swimming,
kidnapping (*concurring* though the sound now is long);
travelling (in U. S. *traveling*), but *galloping*.

Mute *e* is dropped in *having, saving, leaving, striking,*
biting, hoping, hiding, coming, facing, seizing, fertil-
izing (*-ising*), *managing*, etc.

(But kept in *ageing, singeing* (e. g. GE Mm 240);
dyeing from *dye* 'colouring' is kept apart in the spelling
from *dying* from *die* 'cease to live').

Note the spelling *ski-ing.*

On *-ling* see below 23.5—6.

Chapter XXII

L-Suffixes

Adjectival -*al*

22.1₁. The ending -*al* [-(ə)l] is found in adjs and
sbs. Here we shall first speak of the adj-ending, from
L -*alis*. Words in -*al* were borrowed into E either direct
from L or through F, or both.

In OF -*al*- became -*el*, which is also found in Early Eng.,
e. g. *mortel*, but in most cases this was later refashioned after
Latin, as -*al*. It was preserved in such sbs as *channel, charnel*
(-*house*), *hostel*, and *minstrel* (cf. *ministerial*)). But it cannot
be considered an E suffix.

Many words in -*al* have been borrowed isolatedly, without
their roots existing in English, e. g. *capital, equal, estival,*
moral, mortal, real, rival, rural, social, etc. From the English
point of view such words are not derived.

The first loanwords in -*al* are found before 1000,
cardinal sb is recorded from 1125, *capital* from 1225
(AR), and *special* from 1225, but many of the words

in actual use are first recorded from the first half of
the 14th c. The latter half of the 14th c. offers especially
many new words. From about 1400 *-al* was felt as en
independent suffix, and it became possible to coin new
words in *-al*, e. g. *influential, national, occasional,
commercial, confidential, educational, suicidal* (these
from the 16th—18th c.); *abnormal, abysmal, basal,
cultural, featural* (Galsw WM 138 every kind of featural
disharmony), *pubertal* (Ellis M 37; NED one quotation,
1897), *scribal, secretarial, sensational, spatial* (and many
others from the 19th c.).

Some Adjs in *-al* are from Greek roots, as in *baptis-
mal, colossal, patriarchal, skeletal* (from *skeleton*), but
only exceptionally from native roots; *tidal* (NED from
1807), *spinsterial* (Quentin P 21 suffering from a sort
of spinsterial hang-over; NED from 1849), to which
may be added from Carlyle: *buddal* and *meadowal*.

Some late derivatives, the spelling and pronunciation
of which are now very English, *coastal, creedal*, and
nounal, are condemned by Fowler as 'spurious hybrids'
(MEU). He adds *racial*, which, though both *race* and
racial occur in F., cannot be traced back to any Latin
root.

Tombal recorded once (NED 1900) offers some difficulty of pronunciation, and is given in NED both as
[tɔmbəl] and [tu·mbəl].

22.1₂. As regards form, some adjs simply add *-al* to
the unchanged sb. Thus a great many from sbs in *-ion*
(*-tion*), *-sion: additional, educational, examinational*
(Gissing B 19 trophies from examinational prowess;
NED from 1826), *fictional* (Bennett A x; NED from
1843), *functional, improvisational* (Collingwood R 48),
occasional, provisional, and *rational*.

In spelling a mute *e* is dropped: *base : basal, scribe :
scribal, suicidal, tidal, universal, conjectural*, and others
in *-ural*.

Vocalic *r* (*-er, -re*) [ə] becomes consonantal before the

suffix: *centre* [sentə] : *central* [sentrəl], *nature* [neitʃə] : *natural* [nætʃrəl], etc.

Words in *-y* generally alter *y* to *i*, as in *industry* : *industrial*, etc., with stress-shifting, see below, but in some cases *-y* is dropped before the ending: *navy* : *naval*, *puberty* : *pubertal* (rare).

The sound is altered in accordance with vol I 4.71: *nation* [neiʃən] : *national* [næʃənəl], *nature* [neitʃə] : *natural* [nætʃ(ə)rəl], but we have analogical length in some words enumerated ib, *occasional, conversational*, etc.

The stress is often shifted. To substantives in *-ment* [-mənt] with stress on the first syllables correspond adjectives in *-mental* [-ˈmentl] (cf vol I 5.62) : deˈpartment : departˈmental, experiˈmental, and many others.

Further ˈaccident : acciˈdental, *horizon* [hoˈraizn] : *horizontal* [horiˈzontl] with *t* from the Latin (Gk) root ─and many words in *-ual, -ial, -eal* in the following paragraphs.

A special case is conˈgressional (NED from 1691), which now functions as a derivative from ˈcongress, especially with reference to the Congress of U. S. A.

A pronunciation of *spiritual* with stress on the second syllable seems to have existed, see vol I 5.62; Burns 1.31 Seize your sp'ritual guns, now [ˈspiritjuəl, -tʃuəl].

Archival is given by NED as [ˈaˑkivəl], by Jones as [aˑˈkaivəl].

22.1₃. In many words in *-al* the suffix has protected a fuller form of the L stem than the corresponding sb. Thus we get

1) adjs in *-ual*, in which the sounds [tj, dj, sj, zj] often become [tʃ, dʒ, ʃ, ʒ], e. g. *act* : *actual* [æktjuəl, -tʃuəl] and analogically *factual* though the Latin stem has no *u*, *effect* : *effectual*, *rite* [rait] : *ritual* [ritjuəl] (generally sb), *spirit* : *spiritual*, *grade* [greid] : *gradual* [grædjuəl, -dʒuəl]; *sense* : *sensual* [sensjuəl, -ʃuəl], *sex* :

sexual [seksjuəl, -ʃuel], *case* [keis] : *casual* [kæʒuəl],
use [juˑs] : *usual* [juˑʒuəl].

With change of stress ˡconvent : conˡventual, ˡintellect :
inteˡllectual.

2) adjs in *-ial* : *aerial* [ˡɛəriel] better than [eiˡiəriəl],
beast : *bestial;* the *i* entails some changes in the consonant: *part* [paˑt] : *partial* [paˑʃəl], *race* [reis] : *racial*
[reiʃəl], *space* : *spatial* sometimes written *spacial*.

The stress is often changed: ˡadverb : adˡverbial, thus
also proˡverbial.

The adj is nearer to the Latin stem than the sb:
ˡmatter : maˡterial; ˡempire : imˡperial.

Stress-shifting is especially frequent in adjs corresponding to sbs or adjs in *-or* and *-ar(y)*, thus *authorial*
(NED from 1796, from *author;* other rarer forms are
autorial (Poe) and *auctorial*, cf vol I 7.241), *candidatorial*
(Shaw J 73 beaming candidatorially; not in NED),
conspiratorial, editorial, gubernatorial (NED from 1734;
esp. U. S.), *pictorial, professorial, senatorial, tonsorial*
(esp. U. S.), *actuarial, factuarial* (Wells Ma 2.30 the
Factuarial Estimate of Values; not in NED), *secretarial*.

Cf also the irregular *reportorial* from *reporter* (cf
editorial).—From ˡmanager we have manaˡgerial.

Combined changes of stress and consonant are found,
e. g., in ˡpresident : presiˡdential [-ʃəl], ˡartifice : artiˡficial
[-ʃəl], and in many adjs in *-tial* corresponding to sbs
in *-ce (-nce)*, e. g. *essential, influential, confidential*, etc.

3) *-eal*: *corporeal, funereal, marmoreal, purpureal*
from L stems in *-eus*.

4) *crime* [kraim] : *criminal* [kriminəl].

In a few cases we have distinct forms from the same
root, e. g.

regal : *royal* (F.) | *legal* : *leal* (the land of the leal)
and *loyal* (F.) | *special* and *especial* (both from L through
F.) | *diurnal* : *journal* (formerly also adjectival, e. g.
Spenser FQ I. 11.31 their iournall labours) | *funereal*

(L *funereus* + *-al*), *funebrial* (L *funebris* + *-al*) : *funeral* (OF), all from L *funus*.

22.1₄. With regard to meaning the general rule is that an adjective in *-al* = 'of the nature of', 'belonging to'. There are, however, a few exceptions, thus *additional* does not mean 'belonging to addition', but 'added', 'extra'. *Accident* often means 'mishap', but *accidental* means 'happening by chance' without any connotation of 'misfortune', *pictorial*, though from L *pictor* 'painter', relates to 'picture'.

Many of the words in *-al* coined in England are formed from L adjs by adding *-al*, such as *corporeal* (L *corpore-us* + *-al*), *perpetual* (L *perpetu-us* ..), *supernal* (L *supern-us* ..), etc. On the originally Greek words in *-ic*, *-ac* see below. A third Greek ending found with or without *-al* in Eng., is *-oid*, as used in scientific language. When the word in *-oid* is a sb, the corresponding adj is formed in *-oidal*, e. g. *alkaloid* : *alkaloidal*, *rhomboid* : *rhomboidal* etc.

The limited number of native adj suffixes, and the fact that adjs have a wider and more abstract, sometimes learned, application than the corresponding sbs explain the frequent occurrence of adjs of L origin. Hence such pairs as *mouth* : *oral*, *nose* : *nasal*, *hand* : *manual*, *back* : *dorsal*, *son* : *filial*, *the Middle Ages* : *medieval*, etc. (GS § 131).

Substantives in *-al*

22.2₁. *-al* [-(ə)l] in sbs is from Lat. *-alis*, *-al*, *-ales*, or *-alia*. A great many of such words were adopted into E either direct or through F; *-alia* became in OF *-aille* (fem. sing.) with pl *-ailles*, adopted in ME as *-aylle*, *-aille*, later *-aile*, *-al*, as *sponsalia*, OF *espousailles*, ME *spousaille*, *spousailes*, etc.

Many sbs come from adjs, such as *cardinal*, *principal*, *academicals*, *regimentals*, *moral*, *oval*, *signal*, etc. When used as sbs, the adjs in *-al* often have a special, generally concrete, sense, thus *aerial* 'aerial wire', *editorial* 'leading article', *journal* (now completely differentiated from *diurnal* 'belonging to the day'), *manual* 'hand-book', *natural* 'half-witted person', *pictorial* 'illustrated paper', *ritual* 'order of performing religious service', *terminal* 'screw at end of battery', etc.

Some are used only as plurals, e. g. *annals* (cf the adj *annual*), *nuptials*.

The old loan *moral* [mɔrəl] and the modern *morale* (also sometimes written *moral*, but in italics) [mɔ'ra·l] are differentiated, *moral* meaning 'moral teaching of a story, etc., moral principle', *morale* 'moral condition, esp. of troops'.

22.2₂. Many words in -*al* are nexus-sbs, meaning 'the act of -ing or the state of being -ed'; thus from Romanic end-stressed verbs; e. g. besides those in the list below:

acquittal (with gemination after the short vowel), *avowal, denial, dismissal, survival*, and a great many in *re-*, e. g. *recital, refusal, rehearsal, removal, renewal, reprisal, requital, retiral* (Bradley Shakspearean Trag. 50 a regular alternative of smaller advances and retirals), *revival*.

In many cases we have two derivatives from the same root. Thus, see the following pairs, in which it will be noted that the form in -*ion* always is practically identical with its L parallel, whereas the -*al* form in some cases shows by its form that it has been coined in England. In some cases the form in *al* is very rare and the sense may be different.

accusal (By DJ 12.34) : *accusation* | *approval* : *approbation* | *committal* : *commission* |

dis-		dis-		
inter-		inter-		
pro-	posal :	pro-	position	
sup-		sup-		
trans-		trans-		

renewal : *renovation* | *reversal* : *reversion* | *revisal* : *revision*
| *suppressal* : *suppression* | *transmittal* : *transmission*.

22.2₃. On the analogy of these it becomes possible to
form nexus-substantives in *-al* from native end-stressed
verbs, e. g.

bestowal (NED 1773 and 1867 only) | *betrayal* (NED
from 1816) | *betrothal* (NED from 1844) | *overthrowal*
(not in NED; Locke HB 257 the ultimate object of
this gathering was the overthrowal of the government) |
upheaval (from 1838) | *withdrawal* (from 1824).

Thus also *carousal* (from 1765; *carouse* from G. *gar
aus*).

Where *-al* is added to a vowel or diphthong, the vowel
of the suffix may be dropped in pronunciation, e. g.
betrayal [biˈtrei(ə)l], *renewal* [riˈnju(·)əl, -ˈnju·l], *trial*
[trai(ə)l], *withdrawal* [wiðˈdrɔ·(ə)l].

22.2₄. In two cases *-al* has a different origin:

Bridal is from OE *brȳd-ealo* 'bride-ale', but is now
felt as a simplex; it is mainly used in compounds
and conceived as an adjective (vol II 13.72).

Burial is from OE *byrgels* 'burying place, tomb', later
'funeral', with *-s* being interpreted as a pl sign and
dropped in late ME (vol II 5.631).

-ic, -ical

22.3₁. *-ic(al)* [-ik, -ik(ə)l] is from L *-icus* (often through
Fr. *-ique*) forming adjs from Latin roots, as *civicus* from
civis 'citizen', *domesticus* from *domus* 'house', etc., or—
more frequently—representing Gk *-ikós* as in *comicus*,
criticus, *poeticus*, *stoicus*, etc.

Among the first loans of words in *-ic* into English
is *clerk*, from Late Latin *clericus*, OE *cleric*, *clerec*, *clerc*.
Later the word was borrowed again in the form *cleric*
(now archaic; first quoted in NED 1621) and *clerical*
(NED 1592).

Later, especially from the late ME period, a great

many words in -ic were borrowed, very often with the
addition of -al if in adjectival use.

22.3₂. With regard to form the following points should
be noticed.

On stress see vol I 5.66. It should be emphasized
that the forms in -ical now all stress the syllable preceding -ic, which is not true of the forms in -ic.

It should further be noted that most of the words
in -ic stressed on the antepenultimate (*catholic*, etc.) are
especially frequently used as sbs. Adjs, because of the
frequent parallels in -ical, prefer stress on the syllable
before -ic, hence *arith|metic* (Jones) and *ar|senic* as adjs.

The tendency towards regularity of stress is seen
in the pronunciation of *climacteric*, given in NED as
[klaimæk|terik, klai|mækterik], in Jones inversely, cf
Fowler MEU.

We have shifting of stress in many word-pairs, e. g.
*|Byron : By|ronic, |Milton : Mil|tonic, |Iceland : Ice-
|landic, |metal : me|tallic, |hobbyhorse : hobby|horsical,
|nonsense : non|sensical*, etc.

Further *|artist : ar|tistic, |cholera : chole|raic, |economy :
eco|nomic(al), ge|ography : geo|graphical, |history : his|tor-
ical, |method : me|thodical, phi|lology : philo|logical,
|symbol : sym|bolical, |system : syste|matic*, etc.

The vowel of the syllable before -ic(al) is generally
short: *systematic, typical*, etc., cf vol I 4.75. There are,
however, some exceptions, namely words with a vowel
immediately before -ic, e. g. *heroic* [hi|rouik], *prosaic*
[prou|zeiik], *Romaic* [rou|meiik], and some disyllabic
words with long *u* (cf vol I 4.73), e. g. *cubic* [kju·bik],
music [mju·zik], and *rubric* [ru·brik]; *scenic* may have
analogical [i·] alongside of [senik].

22.3₃. The relation between sb and derived adj is
simple enough in cases like *chivalry* [ʃivəlri] : *chivalric*
[ʃivəlrik], stress retained, *dropsy : dropsical, economy :
economic(al)*, and the others just mentioned.

In spelling an *e* is left out: *climate* : *climatic, Philistine* : *Philistinic* (Jerome Idle Ideas 190), *Quixote* : *quixotic, theatre* : *theatric(al)*, etc.

But some words in *-ic(al)* show another form of the radical than the corresponding subst., thus *apathy* : *apathetic, energy* : *energetic, sympathy* : *sympathetic, theory* : *theoretic(al)* ‖ *analysis* : *analytic(al), ellipsis* : *elliptical, emphasis* : *emphatic, hypothesis* : *hypothetical, paralysis* : *paralytic, synopsis* : *synoptic, synthesis* : *synthetic*.

In many words we have the ending *-atic(al)*:

aroma : *aromatic, Asia* : *Asiatic, dogma* : *dogmatic, drama* : *dramatic, grammar* : *grammatical, lymph* : *lymphatic, opera* : *operatic, schism* : *schismatic, system* : *systematic*.

On the analogy of these we have *judgmatic* (Galsw MW 112, 207; Mason Ch 171 -ical). *Hanseatic* is from Med. Lat. *Hanseaticus*.

Further irregularities: *climax* : *climactic*, rare *climax-ical, devil* : *diabolic, giant* : *gigantic, opium* : *opiumonic* (Collier Engl 347; not in NED), *tyrant* : *tyrannical*.

22.3₄. Substantives in *-ic*. Some words were thus used as early as Greek.

1) To denote persons: *classic, cleric, critic, cynic, heretic, mechanic, sceptic, stoic*.

2) To denote branches of knowledge, arts or practice. The sg form is found in *arithmetic, logic, magic, music,* and *rhetoric*. But from 1600 onward the plural form *-ics* "has been the accepted form with names of sciences as *acoustics, conics, dynamics, ethics, linguistics, meta-physics, optics,* or matters of practice, as *æsthetics, athletics, economics, georgics, gymnastics, politics, tact-ics*." (NED). See vol II 5.775 on the construction of these forms as sg and pl.

Here also belong such names of styles or metres as *Anacreontics, iambics, Sapphics*.

22.3₅. Adjectives. In late Latin the suffix *-alis* was

very frequently added to words in *-ic-us* (see *-al* 22.1),
and in English *-ical* became a very popular ending.
Adverbs from adjectives in *-ic* now end in *-ically* except
in *franticly, heroicly* and *publicly* (NED). *Politicly* corresponded to *politic* (22.8₄), whereas *political*, of course,
has *politically*. This use of *-ically* as an adverbial suffix
is probably the chief reason for the popularity of the
ending *-ical* in English (as against Lat. and Fr.). And
it seems that in the cases where forms in *-ic* and *-ical*
with the same root have been semantically differentiated (below 22.3₇), the latter is the one which would
most naturally be used as an adverb, e. g. *economically,
comically, historically, prophetically, tragically.* Cf also
the fact that adjectives of locality, nationality and
language, e. g. *Baltic, Arabic, Teutonic,* and those of
chemical and other technical nomenclature which have
usually no form in *-al*, generally do not form any
adverb either.

Here especially belong words derived from personal
names, such as *Byronic, Homeric,* and *Miltonic,* and
adjs referring to localities, nationalities and languages,
e. g. *Atlantic, Baltic, Arabic, Asiatic, Celtic, Cymric,
Gaelic, Gothic, Hanseatic, Icelandic, Lettic, Nordic,* etc.

Likewise scientific terms e. g. *carbonic, dactylic,
felspathic, ferric, megalithic, oxalic, pelagic, Prussic.*

Elphinston (Principles of E. Gr. 1765 1.323) already
noticed this popularity of *-ical*. He writes: "*ic* is a
foreign, and *ical* a domestic termination. The former
therefore is used upon solemn, the latter on familiar
occasions; as *seraph seraphic* or *seraphical, microscope
microscopic* or *microscopical.* Where the subject then is
naturally solemn, the solemn ending prevails; and where
familiar, the familiar. So we say almost only *majestic,
miltonic,* from *majesty, Milton,* &c. and *whimsical,
finical,* from *whimsy, fine,* &c."

If we compare the combinations a *critic* : a *critical
remark* : *critically*, we see that the syllabic [l] plays a

similar role as a 'buffer-sound' between the stopped
consonant and what follows as we have seen with [n],
e. g. in *drunk* : *a drunken soldier*, *drunkenly* or in *maid* :
maiden speech : *maidenly*, cf 5.7, 20.4₄, 20.5₆.

22.3₆. Adj forms in *-ic* only; *barbaric, catholic, characteristic, civic, despotic, domestic, dramatic, enclitic,
frantic, gigantic, idiotic, laconic, lunatic, metallic, operatic,
organic, patriotic, phonetic, photographic, prehistoric,
public, satanic, systematic, telephonic*, and perhaps a
few more.

In some of these by-forms in *-ical* are found occasionally: Scott Iv 259 the *idiotical* folly.

Forms in *-ical* only. These are virtually obligatory
whenever there is a subst. in *-ic* or *-ics* in use, e. g.
arithmetical (Jones also has *arith|metic*), *arsenical* (chem.
ar|senic), *classical* (note, however, Morley Human
Being 166 her range extending from classic curiosa of
the trade to the best modern novels; also *neo-classic*
(Wells Par 226)), *clerical* (Pattison Mi 152 Dr. Johnson,
more clerical than any cleric), *critical, cynical* (Walpole
OL 62 she was something of a cynic, and her marriage
... made her ... yet more cynical | Maugham FPS
54 What an odious cynic you are.—If it's cynical to
look truth in the face ... then certainly I'm a cynic
and odious if you like), *heretical, logical, magical* (rarely
magic: Wells T 13 the magic shop | id Cl 26 a sort of
magic crystal), *mechanical* (formerly also *mechanic*, Defoe;
as sb formerly also *mechanical:* Sh Mids III. 2.9 rude
mechanicals), *musical* (but Sh Hml III. 1.164 his musicke
vowes), *physical* (in Defoe R 181 it means 'curative'),
rhetorical (Walker L 266 If the style is rhetorical, the
rhetoric is of the best sort), *sceptical* (NP 1920 Mr.
Santayana is a Latin sceptic—one could hardly be more
sceptical than he is), *stoical* (Brontë V 283 Though
stoical, I was not quite a stoic | Galsw in NP 1918 we
have evolved a fresh species of stoic, even more stoical
than were the old Stoics).

Corresponding to *-ics:*

classical, hysterical, mathematical (but Dreiser F 103
like some axiomatic, mathematic law ... It also was
axiomatic, mathematic; as a sb we find *mathematicals* in
Cooper's Dict. 1584), *mechanical, political,* cf above
(but Sh Tw II. 5.174 reade politicke authours), *rhetorical,
statistical, tactical, theatrical.*

Other forms in *-ical,* in which *-ic* is not usual:

Botanical (*botanic* still in names of institutions founded
many years ago), *chemical, farcical, identical* (*identic*
'now a mere archaism except in the language of diplomacy (*identic note, declaration, action,* &c.).' Fowler MEU),
lexical, methodical, nonsensical (Swinburne L 87 this
nonsensical business), *practical* (formerly also *practic:*
Sh H5 I. 1.51 | Bunyan P 108), *surgical, whimsical,
zoological.*

22.3₇. Both Forms, in *-ic* and in *-ical* in use.

There is often a more or less distinct semantic difference between the two forms.

Mr. Ian Maxwell writes to me: "My impression is
that the forms in *ic* may indicate either the quality or
the category of a thing, but that those in *ical* always,
or almost always, indicate the quality only ... One
might speak of "a tragical speech" (emphasising its
manner), but scarcely of "a tragical theme", which
has no manner until it is embodied ... I dare say
this is no more than a tendency, but I think it exists.
One would speak of "a great philosophic advance"
(= advance in philosophy), where the *-ical* form would
be unnatural to say the least; but "Don't be so philosophical" if one were poking fun at someone's metaphysical
talk or air."

A definite semantic distinction is made in the following cases:

comic 'of or belonging to comedy' : *comical* 'laugh-
able' (The comic papers | Fielding T 4.102 nothing can
be imagined more comic, nor yet more tragical than

this scene | Di X 48 he is a comical old fellow | Doyle
S 2.258 you cannot imagine how comical he was | Hardy
T [p. ?] his unsteadiness produced a comical effect ...
and, like most comical effects, not quite so comic after
all | Maugham Alt 1482 the large red face of a comic
actor. But in Doyle B 150 Her bulky figure ... might
have been comic were it not for the intensity of feeling
upon her face—and in Morley Human Being 164 He
was so comic—one would have expected *comical*) | *econ-
omic* 'relating to political economy' : *economical* 'saving,
thrifty' | *electric*, in many set phrases, e. g. *electric arc,
battery, charge, circuit, light, resistance, spark* (Bennett
GS 156 the electric cars) : *electrical*—the ordinary
word | *historic* 'noted or celebrated in history' (of
much historic interest | on that historic spot | Chesterton
Shaw 205 Historic Christianity has always believed in
the valour of St. Michael riding in front of the Church
Militant | ib 160 all this side of historic and domestic
traditions | ib 164 all historic common sense | Times
Lit. Suppl 1931 Dr. Strachan ... draws a distinction
between the historic and the historical Jesus, to which we
are reconciled only because it verbally symbolizes about
the right amount of difference that should exist between
the human Jesus and the Christ of faith. "The historical
Jesus is the Jesus who comes to us through the medium
of faith ..."); practically always *pre-historic* : *historical*
'dealing with history, treating of history, as *a historical
treatise or writer;* based upon history, as *a historical
play, novel,* etc., representing history, as *a historical
painting*' (SOD) | *politic* 'characterized by policy;
scheming, crafty'; always in the phrase *the body politic* :
political 'belonging to politics, engaged in civil admin-
istration; public, civil' | *theatric* 'suggestive of the
theatre, stagy' (Wilde In 126 theatric presentation |
Collingwood R 273 theatric display) : *theatrical* 'pertaining to or connected with the theatre, artificial, showy,
spectacular'. But Tennyson apparently uses the two

forms for stylistic variation in L 3.188 this might be
modern theatrical art, but is entirely opposed to the
canons of true literary dramatic art: and that the
theatric and the dramatic were always being mistaken
the one for the other.

Arsenic is used in chemistry only, otherwise *arsenical*
(Collins Engl 348 the Manchester arsenical beer episode).

NED gives *syntactical* as the usual form, but Sir
Allen Mawer writes to me: "I certainly prefer *syntactic*
to *syntactical* and I think my preference accords with
general usage in the present day."

In some cases no distinction seems to be made:
anarchic(al) (Shaw Getting Married (T) 260 a gay, dis-
orderly, anarchic spoilt child | ib 11 disastrous anarch-
ical action), *artistic(al)*, *authentic(al)*, *dogmatic(al)*, *egot-
istic(al)*, *emetic(al)*, *epic(al)*, *fantastic(al)*, *iambic(al)*,
linguistic(al), *oratoric(al)*, *parsonic(al)*, (Brontë V 40 and
J 504 *-ic;* Galsw MW 69 and Christie 3A *-ical*), *pneum-
atic(al)*, *prophetic(al)*, *rustic(al)*, *synthetic(al)*, and *trop-
ic(al)* (Roosevelt Am. Ideals 283 upon tropic aboriginal
races, and the tropical lands ...).

22.3s. Adjs in *-ic* and *-ical* are chiefly found with
Gk or Lat. roots, but there are also a few roots of
different origin, e. g. *aldermanic* (Shaw D 240), *drudg-
ical, dryasdustic(al)*, and *gigmanic(ally)* (these three from
Carlyle), *fistic(al)* (Di F 397 heated by verbal or fistic
altercation), *freemasonical* (Galsw TL 145), *hobbyhors-
ical* (Sterne M 1.69, Tennyson L 2.264), *mushroomic*
(Meredith R 107), *lackadaisical* (Meredith E 360), *quizzi-
cal* (Barrie M 133, Galsw MW 267), *spleenical* (Keats
4.187), *whimsical; common-sensical* (Locke W 149).

In some cases *-ic(al)* has ousted other suffixes, e. g.
historial, storial (Ch, Wyclif, etc.; last quot. in NED
1649) replaced by *historic(al)*. In popular language
rheumatism has been replaced by *rheumatics* (e. g. Di
P 365 | Meredith E 255 | Hope Z 234). Similarly *hysterics*
in colloquial language for *hysteria*, though there may be

a semantic difference, *hysterics* meaning 'a fit of hysteria')

In other cases two endings compete, e. g. *barbaric*
(Bennett T 15) with *barbarous; melancholic* (Congreve
144) has nearly given way to *melancholy* in ordinary
use, and *centric(al)* (Scott Iv 159 at York, or some
other centrical place) is much rarer than *central*.

"In Chemistry, the suffix *-ic* is specifically employed
to form names of oxygen acids and other compounds
having a higher degree of oxidation than those whose
names end in *-ous*." (NED).

-ique

22.3₉. A few words in *-ique* [- li·k] have been borrowed
from Fr. in modern times, thus *antique* (cf *antic*),
critique (cf *critic*), *physique* (cf *physic*), and *unique*. The
pairs have also been semantically differentiated. See
vol I 2.326 and 8.33.

-ac(al), -iac(al)

22.4. *-ac(al)* [-æk(l)] is from the Gk adjectival suffix
-akos (Lat. *-acus*, F *-aque*), on *-al* see 22.1. It is added
only to roots in *i-* (*ia*). Loanwords are found from ME,
e. g. *ammoniac, aphrodisiac, cardiac, demoniac, elegiac,
hypocondriac, maniac, paradisiac, simoniac, Syriac,* and
zodiac.

Most of these and the following words in *-ac* have
by-forms in *-acal*, cf *-ic* : *-ical*. In one or two cases
only *-acal* is used.

Words coined on English soil are *aphasiac* (Gk root;
Wells PF 85), *insomniac* (Lat. root; Mannin W 154),
dandiacal (coined by Carlyle SR III Ch. 10 headline),
and some derivatives with *maniac*, e. g. *Anglomaniac,
bibliomaniac, horsemaniac* (nonce-word; Ruskin S 51 a
bibliomaniac. But you never call any one a horsemaniac;
—pun on *horseman*), *kleptomaniac, megalomaniac,* and
monomaniac.

Before *-ac i* is generally pronounced [i] or [j] : *demoniac* [diˈmouniæk, -njæk]. Exception: *elegiac* [eliˈdʒaiǝk]. Before *-acal i* is pronounced [ai] : *demoniacal* [dimǝˈnaiǝkǝl].

On stress see vol I 5.66.

-le, -el, -l, -il.

22.5. The suffix *-le, -el, -l* (*-il*) [-l] occurs in
1) some sbs of English origin,
2) some sbs of French (Latin) origin, in a small number of which *-le* is excrescent,
3) a few adjs of native origin, and
4) a large number of vbs of native origin.

The suffix is from a different source in all these groups, which will therefore be treated separately in what follows.

-le, -el in Substantives

22.5₁. *-le, -el,* from OE *-l, -el, -le, -ela,* etc., occurring in diminutives or names of tools, instruments and other appliances, e. g. *bramble* (connected with *broom;* on *-b-* see vol I 2.11), *ladle, scuttle, shuttle, spindle,* has been little used as an independent formative in English. *Bristle, cobble* 'rounded stone', and *whittle* 'knife' are only recorded from ME in NED, *nozzle* (from *nose*) from 1608 only and *dottle* 'plug of tobacco' from 1825.

22.5₂. A number of sbs borrowed from F (L) also end in *-le, -el,* thus *angle, bottle, candle, castle, cattle, chapel, funnel, travel, tunnel,* the ending of which was never used as an independent formative in E. In this *-le, -el* various Latin endings have been merged.

On the analogy of such words as *manciple* (OF, from L *mancipium*) and *participle* (a by-form of OF *participe,* from L *participium*), *-le* was added to a few words in AF or E, thus *chronicle* (from 1303, AF *cronicle,* OF *cronique* (found also in Ch B 4398 and later, now obs.)), *periwinkle* (plant name; OE *peruince* from L *pervinca;*

with *l* from 16th c.), *principle* (from 1380; OF *principe*), and *syllable* (from 1384, AF *sillable*, OF *sillabe*). Note that this *-le* is only added after stops.

-le in Adjectives

22.5₃. *-le* in adjs is from OE *-el*, *-ol*, or *-ul*. *Fickle*, *idle*, *little*, and *nimble* (*evil* belongs to the same group) are recorded from OE. The only word first recorded in later E seems to be *brittle*, ME *britul*, related to OE *breotan* 'break'.

-le, -l in Verbs

22.5₄. *-le*, *-l* [-l] in vbs is from ME *-len*, OE *-lian*, like corresponding forms in other Gothonic languages used to form frequentative vbs or vbs with a diminutive sense (as in OE *handlian* > *handle*, related to *hand;* *steartlian* > *startle*, cf *start; twinclian* > *twinkle*, cf *twink; wræstlian* > *wrestle*, cf *wrest*).

New-formations of a more or less echoic character are frequent in all periods, e. g. *crackle* (from *crack;* Rogers Wine of Fury 197 the crack of the shot ... The crackle of the gun was stopped as peremptorily as it had broken out) | *crinkle* (from OE *crincan*) | *dartle* (from *dart;* NED from 1855 Browning) | *dazzle* (from earlier *dase* > *daze*) | *drawl* (from *draw*) | *dribble* (from *drib*, related to *drip, drop*) | *drizzle* (from OE *drēosan* 'fall') | *fondle* (*fond*) | *frizzle* 'fry' (*frizz*) | *gruntle* (*grunt*) | *hurtle* (? from *hurt*) | *joggle* (*jog*) | *mewl* (*mew*) | *mumble* (from *mum* interj) | *noddle* (*nod*) | *quibble* (? from obs. *quib* < Lat. *quibus*) | *sipple* (*sip*) | *snarl* (from obs. *snar*) | *sniffle* (*sniff*) | *snuggle* (*snug*) | *sparkle* (*spark*) | *tinkle* (*tink*) | *tootle* (*toot*) | *trample* (*tramp*) | *tumble* (from OE *tumbian*).

In some cases we have shortening of the vowel in the derivative: *dwindle* [dwindl] from *dwine* [dwain] (now Sc. dial. or arch.), *prattle* [prætl] from *prate* [preit], and *waddle* [wɔdl] from *wade* [weid].

Besides these native words there are a great many
l-verbs adopted from other languages, esp. Dutch and
Low German, e. g. *drivel* (? from LG; ultimately related
to *drive*) | *foozle* (G dial. *fuseln* 'work badly') | *hobble*
(Du.) | *niggle* (from Scand.) | *ogle* (from LG, related to
HG *auge* 'eye') | *scrabble* (Du.) | *scribble* (med. Lat.
scribillare, dim. f. L. *scribere;* Byron L 110 I shall
post-scribble this half sheet) | *shuffle* (? from LG;
related to *shove*) | *snuffle* (from Du.) | *sprinkle* (? Du.) |
wiggle (? (M)LG) | *wrangle* (? LG).

Between the following pairs we have a relationship,
though the *l*-form may not be derived direct from the
shorter form:

chuckle : *chuck, dangle* : *ding* 'ring with a metallic
sound', *fizzle* (earlier form) : *fizz, grapple* : *grip, grope,
prickle* : *prick, straddle* : *stride.*

But the etymologies of many *l*-verbs are more or
less obscure, and we may have to do with arbitrary
echoic formations, e. g. in *boggle, bogle, bungle, footle,
fribble, gurgle, jingle, nibble, puzzle, rumble, ruffle, rustle,
scramble, scuttle, squiggle* (Sayers HC 192 as a sb),
squizzle, straggle, threddle (Kipling P 81 he took the
stern-oar, and threddled the longship through the sea),
tickle, twiddle, twizzle (Sayers HC 409 they looked up
the paper thing that twizzles round in the till).

The echoic character of the suffix is seen *i.a.* in its
occurrence in reduplicative forms such as *argle-bargle,
fiddle-faddle, little-tattle*, etc., cf 10.3, and *hubble-bubble,
jiggle-joggle, razzle-dazzle*, etc. (10.4).

Darkle, grovel, and *sidle* are back-formations from the
adverbs *darkling, grovel(l)ing, sideling* interpreted as
ptcs, cf *-ling* adv. 23.6.

-il, -ile

22.5₅. *-il* [-l, -il], and *-ile*, generally [-ail], are from the L
adj suffixes *-ilis* and *-ilis*. *-ilis* in OF became *-le*, cf the
Eng. loanwords *able* (L *habilis*), *frail* (L *fragilis*), *gentle*

(L *gentilis*), and *humble* (L *humilis*); *-ilis* became OF
-il masc., *-ile* fem., and in some early Eng. loans *-il*
[-l] or [-il] is preserved, thus *civil, fossil, utensil.* But
later loans, borrowed direct from L, or through F,
have all *-ile,* as in *agile, edile, exile, gentile* (Latinized
form corresponding to *gentle*), *hostile, mercantile* (from
Ital.), and many others.

In all such words the pronunciation of the suffix is
given by Daniel Jones as [-ail]. *Fragile* (Latinized loan
corresponding to *frail*) is given by Jones as [frædʒail,
(rarely) -dʒil], *mobile* as [moubail, -biˑl, -bil], and *volatile* as [vɔlətail], but in *sal volatile* as [voˈlætəli].
On pronunciation cf also vol I 4.84.

All these, however, must from an E point of view be
considered un-derived root-words, with the exception,
perhaps, of *infantile.* Derivatives with *-ile* on E soil
are rare. The only ones, perhaps, are *insectile* (NED
1615), *protractile* (1828; Jones: [-ail]), *refractile* (1847),
and *vibratile* (1826); NED has [-il, -ail].

-ble

22.61. *-ble* (*-able* [-əbl], *-ible* [-ibl] or [-əbl] (Jones has
only [-əbl]), *-uble* [-jubl]).

This suffix was adopted through F from L *-bilem* as
used to form active and passive adjs from verbal stems
(often stems of past ptcs). In borrowed words we find
i (very frequent) and *u* (comparatively rare) before
-ble. In F a great many words in *-ble* had an *a* before
the suffix, from stems in *a* (L inf *-are*), and there and
in E *-able* came to be the only productive form.

OF derivatives in *-ble* were adopted at an early date,
thus *feeble, noble,* but the ending cannot there have
been felt as a formative. From about 1300 an ever increasing number of words in *-able* (*-ible*) appear, among
them *determinable, reasonable, honourable, impossible*
(*in-*), etc. Chaucer has a large number, e. g. *accordable,*

agreeable, charitable, convertible, deceivable, fusible, movable, sensible, serviceable, many of them connected with other existing words.

From the latter half of the 14th c. *-able* was treated as a living suffix, mainly because of form-association with the adj *able,* and was used to form adjs from E stems. At the same time the meaning of the suffix began to develop in the direction of 'able'. Such early hybrids are: *unknowable* (Ch), *understandable* (Wyclif), *seeable, unseeable, unfillable, unspeakable, unstirrable.* From the 15th c. there are *unthinkable, knowable, hearable,* obs. *behovable, eatable* and *biteable* (the latter rare; besides one example in NED I have noted Wells Fm 107), *speakable* and *teachable.* Among formations from the 16th c. are *saleable* and *unsaleable, unclimbable, workable, unforgivable, breakable, readable, utterable* and *unutterable,* and *wearable.*

Shakespeare seems to have coined three words only within this group, viz. *answerable, laughable,* and *unmatchable,* see Franz³ § 124 (p. 131). Cotgrave (1611) shows a certain predilection for forms in *-able.* The following words are first quoted from Cotgrave in NED: *burnable* (rare, cf *combustible*), *climbable, drinkable, let(t)able, liveable, rideable, uneatable, unendable, woundable* (rare, cf *vulnerable*).

22.6₂. As to the spelling of words in *-able* derived from verbs in *-e,* Fowler (MEU: Mute *e*) gives the following "only satisfactory" rule: "if the suffix begins with a vowel the mute *e* is dropped. ... The chief exception ... is that *e* remains even before a vowel when the soft sound of *c* or *g* is to be made possible ..."

But the following list, which might easily be lengthened, shows that this rule is by no means observed: *likeable* (Trollope D 2-53), *liveable-with* (Benson B 5), *tuneable* (Keats 191), *unforgiveable* (Tennyson L 1.254), *unsaleable* (Chesterton Shaw 223), *unsettleable* (Spencer A 311; here perhaps *e* because of the syllabic *l*).

Even deviations from the exception may be found in
ModE, as in Carlyle SR 31 *peacably*, 46 *peacable*.

The "Authors' and Printers' Dictionary" made an
artificial distinction between *movable* (in ordinary use)
and *moveable* (law term), a distinction, however, that
is not recognized by NED, and *moveable* is even in the
Oxf. Concise Dict. Preface, together with others written
with *e*, branded as a monstrosity.

A final consonant after a single vowel in stressed
syllable is doubled before *-able: forgettable, lettable,
regrettable, clubbable,* obs. *reférrable* and *reférrible* (now
réferable), etc.

Final *y* after a consonant is changed into *i* before
-able: pitiable, reliable, variable, etc.

Romanic words with three or more syllables are
according to the general rule ordinarily stressed on the
last syllable but two, but in some cases the stress has
been shifted on the analogy of the root-word, or two
pronunciations are allowable. For details see vol I 5.66,
cf on analogical influences PG p. 23. Other phonetic
questions are discussed in vol I 4.66, 4.71, 9.211 (with
reference to 9.14), and 12.23.

22.6₃. In ModE it is possible to form adjs in *-able*
from practically any verb. The list of new-formations
with *-able* in Schmeding, *Wortbildung bei Carlyle*,
comprises nearly a hundred words, many of which are
now commonly used. Other late formations are: Ru Sel
1.95 *untraversable* hills | Tennyson L 2.228 Had I been
a *piquable* man I should have been piqued | Wells Am
95 *ownable* things | id V 283 *confessible* | Angell I 51
the *loanable* value of money.

It is even possible to add the suffix to verbal phrases.
The earliest example of such formations I have noted
is Ben Jonson's nonce-word *un-in-one-breath-utterable*.
The words *come-at-able* and *get-at-able* with their negatives have been adopted into colloquial standard language
as in Elphinston, Propriety ascertained (1787) 1.84

Widhout dhis happy power, poor Inglish, in her vulgar
dress, must remain *uncomattabel* | Congreve 127 un-
comeatable (and Defoe M 60, both older than the
earliest in NED) || Southey (1799, NED) *get-at-able* |
R.Bennett P 144 *ungetatable* (Cf also Cambr Trifles 138
the ... most *getoutable* part of the day). NED has some
nonce-words of the same type sub *Un-* 7 b (b) (all from
1840 on): *uncomoverable* | *un-do-without-able* | *undryup-
able* (ink) | *un-keep-off-able* (flies) | *unrelyuponable* | *un-
talkaboutable* | *unwipeupable* (blood).

In some cases the particle in question (an adverb or
a preposition) is put after *-able* with or without a hyphen,
e. g. Mrs. Braddon (NED 1873) the most *un-get-on-able-
with* girl | Tennyson L 3.83 thinking of you as no longer
the comeatable, *runupableto, smokeablewith* J. S. of old |
NP 1892 enough to make the house *unliveable in* for
a month | Shaw Ibsen 41 the husband being fairly
good-natured and *livable-with* | Benson D 2.121 she is
unspeakable to | Jerome Novel Notes (T) 19 *unlivable in* |
Williams N 249 Pamela—gentle, yet somehow *un-
trifleable-with*.

To avoid such clumsy forms the particle is very often
simply left out, if there can be no doubt of the particle
understood, e. g. *unaccountable* ('that cannot be accounted for'; Mi (1643 NED), Behn 309, Congreve 230,
Spect 172, Defoe, Swift, Goldsm, Quincey, Austen, Di,
etc. etc.), *indispensable, laughable* (Sh Merch I. 1.56,
further in Drydon, Carlyle, Thack, etc.), *dependable*
(from Pope (NED 1735), frequent), *livable* (Ferber S
264 the place looked more than livable,—lived in; cf
Stevenson V 123 the Liveableness of Life).

Further *available, disposable, objectionable*, etc.

In the following examples, in which there is a complement after the particle, the latter actually belongs to
the vb from which the adj is derived: Bunyan P 91
inclinable to go (also Lamb E 2.195) | Stevenson B
189 a countenance of great command and dignity,

answerable to the richness of his attire and arms |
Shaw P 254 *accountable* for what she did.

On this background it is curious to see how *reliable* was as
late as in 1889 branded as "an indefensible solecism ... useless
... bastard ... nonsensical," etc.

The suffix -*able* lends itself especially to negative
formations. Several such words with *un-* are quoted in
NED from much earlier dates than the corresponding
positive ones.

Here may also be mentioned the "absurd names
(*inexpressibles, inexplicables* (Di Sketches), *indescrib-
ables, unmentionables, unwhisperables,* ...) which were
used to avoid the simple word *trousers,* at which no
one takes offence nowadays" (GS § 257).

22.6₄. In L and F we had words in -*able* (-*ible*) derived
even from sbs, thus L *amicabilem* (Eng. *amicable*) from
amicus 'friend', OF *paisible* (ME *peisible,* ModE *peace-
able*) from *pais* 'peace'. Further there were in some
cases in E a sb of the same form as the vb from which
the adj was derived, as in *comfortable, honourable,* etc.,
and this led to the possibility of deriving adjs in -*able*
from sbs, thus at any rate in the following: *actionable,*
obs. *conscionable* (from *conscion,* the obs. popular
singular of *conscien-ce,* cf *unconscionable*), *leisurable,*
marriageable, merchantable (Holmes A 32), *objectionable*
(common), *personable* (Late ME, Hewlett Q 159),
proportionable (Late ME, Goldsm V 2.37 proportion-
ably), *saleable* (from 1530, Mi A 35 unsalable, Chesterton
Shaw 223), *serviceable* (More U 281, Marlowe F 151),
sizable (Page J 90 a sizable house), *treasonable* (from
1375).

But in some cases it cannot be definitively decided
whether the word is derived from a sb or a vb, thus
clubbable (coined by Johnson; Galsw WM 102), *com-
panionable* (which has supplanted *compan(i)able*), *know-
ledgeable* (NED derives some uses from vb, some from

sb), *marketable* (Sh Tp V. 1.267, Shaw), *meritable* (*un-meritable* used twice by Sh), *palatable, pleasurable, profitable, razorable* (Sh Tp II. 1.250 till new-borne chinnes Be rough and razor-able), *seasonable* (Stevenson JH 63).

It is even possible to form adjs from groups of adj + sb as in *common-sensible* (NED from 1851; but found in Byron Corresp. 2.145) and *small-talkable* (Collins W 28). Of course the existence of *sensible* and *talkable* have facilitated these formations.

Some words in *-able* (*-ible*) are frequently used as sbs, especially in the pl, thus the negative euphemistic words for 'trousers' mentioned above 22.6₃. Others are *breakables* (Wells TB 1.72 among these breakables; not in NED as a sb), *combustibles, comestibles, drinkables, potables, valuables,* and some in the following list.

22.6₅. Often we have two words more or less synonymous, one originally Latin (generally in *-ible*) and the other formed from an E root with *-able.* The originally L word is the official word belonging to the literary language, whereas the native word often is colloquial. In some cases the latter has not been generally accepted, but is of rare occurrence. Perhaps in most cases there has been a semantic differentiation of the two words. Examples:

audible—hearable (much rarer) | *combustible—burnable* (very rare) | *dirigible* (also used as a sb of airship) *—steerable* (rare) | *edible—eatable* (both also as sb) | (*in*)-*habitable—livable*(-*in*) (distinctly colloquial, see examples above 22.6₃) | *intelligible—understandable* | *legible* 'that can be read'—*readable* (1) 'legible', (2) 'worth reading' | *portable* 'convenient for carrying'—*bearable* 'tolerable' | *potable* (mainly facet.)—*drinkable* | *responsible—answerable* (1) 'responsible', (2) 'capable of being answered', (3) 'corresponding' | *risible* (1) 'inclined to laugh', (2) 'of laughter', e. g. risible faculties, (3) 'laughable'—*laughable* 'exciting laughter, worth laughing at' |

visible—seeable (rare, though one of the earliest native formations) | *vulnerable—woundable* (very rare).

With native formations *-able* is simply added to the basic form of the vb (or sb) (on some unimportant orthographical changes see above), but with words originally Latin, there may be a discrepancy between the form of the simple vb and the corresponding adj in *-ble*, thus a group of L words were taken over into English in the form of the past ptc, whereas the adj was derived from the infinitival stem. Hence we have such pairs as:

abominate : *abominable*, further *calculable, demonstrable, educable* (Ellis M 362); *elect* : *eligible, neglect* : *negligible.*

In other cases it is the other way about, with adj from participial stem and vb from inf stem, as in

comprehend : *comprehensible*, similarly *reprehensible, defensible, divisible, extensible, permissible.*

Many vbs underwent considerable phonetic changes during their development from L through F and early E. Hence pairs like the following:

damn [dæm]—*damnable* [dæmnəbl] | *despise—despicable* (Benson A 181 she did not despise him for being despicable) | *destroy—destructible* (McKenna M 15 undestroyed and indestructible) | *explain—explicable* | *perceive—perceptible* | *receive—receptible* (Defoe G 110) | *practise—practicable.*

All these divergencies in connexion with the development of *-able* as an independent formative have created a great variation in the formation and adoption of forms, thus we have doublets like *divisible* : *dividable, explicable* : *explainable* (Myers M 11), *extensible* : *extendible, perceptible* : *perceivable, persuasible* : *persuadable, producible* (Carlyle E 241) : *productible* (rare) : *produceable, soluble* : *solvable.*

In other words the divergence is merely orthographic, as *-ible* is often pronounced [-əbl]. Thus we find both

spellings in *(in)accessible, advisible, ascendible, depend-
ible, discussible, forcible, negligible*.

22.6₆. Fowler MEU: *-able, -ible*, writes: "The suffix
-able is a living one, & may be appended to any transitive verb to make an adjective with the sense *able*, or
liable, or *allowed*, or *worthy*, or *requiring*, or *bound*, *to
be -ed*." Thus he recognizes only passive senses of new
adjs in *-able*, and this no doubt is in accordance with
the most frequent usage. But a small number of words
preserve an active sense, mainly derived from intransitive vbs, thus

agreeable, assistable 'helpful' (Fox 1.286; not in NED),
*comfortable, (un)suitable, (dis)creditable, durable, fav-
ourable, forcible, perishable, risible* (cf Scott OM 57
risibility), *(un)shrinkable, (un)suitable*.

Many words may further be used both in an active
and a passive sense. Sh sometimes uses words with an
active sense, which could now be used only passively,
e. g.

contemptible 'contemptuous, scornful' (Ado II. 3.187,
but = 'despicable' H6A 1. 2.75), *deceivable* 'deceptive'
(R2 II. 3.84, Tw IV. 3.21), *defensible* 'able to make
defence' (H4B II. 3.38), *disputeable* 'disputatious' (As
II. 5.36). *Questionable* is also used in a special sense in
Sh, thus 'inviting questions' (Hml I. 4.43), and *un-
questionable* 'averse to conversation' (As III. 2.393).

Similarly Mi PL 9.563 *speakable* 'able to speak'.

Accountable for is = *responsible for*, thus active, but
unaccountable has a passive sense, see above 22,6₃.

Answerable very rarely means 'that can be answered'
(passive), but generally 'who must answer' (= 'responsible, liable to be called to account'), also 'that answers'
(responds to demands, needs, purposes), 'corresponding
in amount to' (Swift 3.235 the success has not been
answerable) | *changeable* NED: (1) 'that may change',
(2) 'liable to be changed (by others)' | *honourable* (1)
'worthy of being honoured', (2) 'accompanied with

honour, showing or doing honour', (3) 'honest' | *variable*
'that can be, or is, varied', *invariable* 'unchangeable,
or unchanging', also 'from which you may not vary',
as *an invariable rule*.

Insensible both an active and a passive sense, but
sensible generally in the special meaning 'of good sense'.

Note the two prepositions in Swinburne Study of
Sh 235 Another test, no less unmistakeable by the
student and no less indiscernible to the sciolist.

-*ly* in Adjectives

22.7₁. -*ly* [-li] as an adjectival suffix is a development
of ME -*lik* (Northern), -*liche* (Southern), OE -*līc* (with
parallels in the other Gothonic languages) from the sb
līc 'appearance, form, body'. The weakened forms -*li*,
-*ly*, which seem to be due chiefly to Scand. influence,
occur as early as the 13th c., and before the 15th c.
had become universal.

When appended to sbs the most common meaning
is now that of 'having the qualities appropriate to or
characteristic of'. During all periods of English the
suffix has been very much used.

Originally the ending was added to words of native
origin only, e. g. OE *eorþlic* > *earthly*, *freondlic* >
friendly, etc., but from rather an early stage it was
added to F words as well, e. g. *princely*, *scholarly*, etc.

22.7₂. In some cases we have formations both in -*ly*
and -*like* (cf 23.1), e. g.

brotherly—*brotherlike;* thus also *sisterly*, -*like*, and
kingly, -*like*. Besides *villainly* Sh has *villainlike* (Lr V.
3.98 villain-like he lies); *gentlemanly* perhaps mainly
about inner qualities, -*like* about appearance, dress,
etc. (but we have only *ladylike*); *manly* 'possessing the
virtues proper to a man as distinguished from a woman
or child; courageous, frank, etc.', also used of a woman;
manlike (1) same meaning, (2) 'resembling a human

being', e. g. manlike apes; *godly* generally 'pious', *godlike* 'resembling God'.

Homely primarily means 'belonging to home, domestic' (rarely 'familiar'), further 'simple, plain, unpolished', finally 'plain, ugly', thus especially in U. S. see Horwill, Dict. of Amr. Usage 168, and cf Rev. of Reviews Dec. 1905 595 Copenhagen is a homely city— homely not being used in the American sense, but as signifying a city homelike and habitable.

22.7₃. -*ly* is freely added to words denoting persons, especially relatives or holders of a trade or profession, e. g. *auntly* (Wells Br 200 to promote her to Auntly rank), *niecely* (AHuxley Barren Leaves 240), *wifely* (Galsw MP 73), *manly, womanly, beggarly, clerkly* (Smart Shakesp. 51 neatly written in a clerkly hand), *musicianly* (Kennedy CN 22), *rascally* (Skimpole Shaw 108).

Words in -*ly* often have a laudatory sense, e. g. *lovely, womanly* (though it is used by Sh in a depreciatory sense, too (= 'womanish'), e. g. Mcb IV. 2.77), *masterly* 'excellent', *scholarly*.

It can also be added to compounds, e. g. in a *fellow-creaturely* way (Shaw D 1), she grew *elder-sisterly* (Bennett C 2.176). Cf. vol. II 12.312.

Formations from words denoting material and immaterial things are not so frequent, e. g. *lively, lovely, leisurely, heavenly, earthly, worldly;* the latter two, on the analogy of the biblical phrase *of the earth, earthy* (13.3₃) are used by Locke HB 247 She's of the earth earthly, of the world worldly; cf Di T 1.168 brazen eccelesiastics, of the worst world worldly.

-*ly* is further used to form adjs denoting periodic recurrence, e. g. *hourly* (Fielding T 4.70 I lived in hourly horrors on her account), *daily, weekly, monthly, quarterly, yearly. Daily, weekly, monthly, quarterly* are also used as sbs to denote newspapers and periodicals.

22.7₄. Added to adjectival stems -*ly* generally denotes an approximation to the sense of the radical, as a weakening or a tendency, thus

sick 'affected by some disease'—*sickly* 'habitually indisposed' (in Sh *sick* is mainly used predicatively, *sickly* as an adjunct) | *kind*—*kindly* (the latter slightly weaker than the former, and only used as an adjunct, e. g. McCarthy 2.472 there were many excellent landlords, humane and kindly men—men, too, who saw the wisdom of being humane and kind | Walpole Cp 300 They were true, kindly people, and now they were more kind to her than ever) | *poor*—*poorly* 'unwell, in delicate health' (adv?) | *low*—*lowly* 'humble' | *clean* 'free from dirt'—*cleanly* 'clean in person or habits'; on the sound see below 22.7₅.

An interesting pair are *deadly* and *deathly*. An obs. sense of *deadly* is 'mortal, subject to death', now it means 'causing death': *a deadly blow, deadly poison, deadly sin, a deadly foe;* thus also as an adv (Sh Ado V. 1.178 if shee did not hate him deadlie, shee would loue him dearely), *deadly pale, deadly faint, deadly tired* (e. g. Galsw C 147). *Deathly* used in the same sense, but also (rarer) in *a deathly stillness*, etc.; also as an adv (Galsw C 66 deathly white | Williamson S 85 deathly pale).

22.7₅. Note the difference between radical and derivative in *clean* [kliˑn]—*cleanly* [klenli] | *one* [wʌn]—*only* [ounli] (adj and adv) | *sour* [sauə]—*surly* [səˑli].

-*ly* in Adverbs

22.8₁. -*ly* [-li] as an adverbial suffix originates from OE -*lice*, from -*līk* (= adjectival -*ly*) + the adverbial suffix ō. Thus it only belonged to advs corresponding to adjs in -*līc* (-*ly*), and the adverbial element was -*e*, which disappeared in ME. But as early as in OE the suffix was added to other adjs to form advs, -*ly* becoming the real indication of the adverbial function, and later was used to an ever increasing degree.

22.8₂. The addition of *-ly* involves a loss of syllabic [l], written *le*, after a consonant (cf vol I 7.84 and 9.67): *able* [eibl]—*ably* [eibli], thus also *doubly*, *idly*, *nobly*, *peaceably* and all in *-ably*, *simply*, and *terribly* [teribli, -əbli], thus all in *-ibly*.

NED states that examples of the uncontracted forms (e. g. *doublely*) are found as late as the 17th c.

Sh has Err IV. 4.132 *idlely* (two syllables) | John V. 1.72 (in $F_{1,2}$) *idlely*, ($F_{3,4}$) *idely* (also two syll.) | H4B II. 2.32 *idlely* (prose), ib II. 4.391 *idly* (verse).

From *supple* NED has one example of *supply* (generally avoided in writing, because it might be read as *supply* sb and vb), the ordinary, though rare, form is *supplely*.

22.8₃. If the word ends in *-ll*, only *-y* is added, and in the compounds with *-ful* and words in *-le* the full ending *-ly* is added. Examples:

chill [tʃil]—*chilly* [tʃili] (rare) | *dull* [dʌl]—*dully* [dʌli] (Dan. Jones also [dʌlli]) | (*evil* [i·vl, i·vil]—*evilly* [i·vili]; Walpole DW 314 he had never known London so evilly perceptive) | *ill* [il]—*illy* [ili] (Amr; Dreiser AT 2.57 illy-dressed) | *shrill* [ʃril]—*shrilly* [ʃrili] (Galsw TL 183) | *still* [stil]—*stilly* [stili] (Sh H5 IV Prol. 5, Stevenson D 190) | *tranquil* [træŋkwil]—*tranquilly* [træŋkwili] (Gissing B 223).

"In southern Eng. [words of this type are] commonly pronounced with a single *l*, but in Scotland often with double or long *l*" (NED).

After a long vowel or a diphthong we have [-lli]: *cool* [ku·l]—*coolly* [ku·lli] (Gay BP 19 cooly,—representing the pronunciation [ku·li]?) | *foul* [faul]—*foully* [faulli], Jones also [fauli]; Sh H4A I. 3.154 (Fol.) *fouly*, Mcb III. 1.3 (Fol.) *fowly* | *genteel* [dʒenˈti·l]—*genteelly* [-ˈti·lli] (Jones, Gay BP 147 genteely) | *male* [meil]—*malely* [meilli] (not in Jones, Miss Broughton q NED: many horses, malely and femalely saddled, Golding SD 31 arrogantly malely possessive) | *pale* [peil]—*palely*

[peilli] | *small* [smɔ·l]—*smally* [smə·lli] (obs.; common
1525—1650, e. g. More U) | *sole* [soul]—*solely* [soulli]
(Sh Alls I. 1.112 *solie*) | *stale* [steil]—*stalely* [steilli]
(Jones) | *vile* [vail]—*vilely* [vailli] (Jones) | *whole* [houl]
—*wholly* (with loss of *e*) [houlli], Jones also [houli], cf
More U 27 *holye*).

From adjs in *-ile* adverbs are generally avoided,
though *fertilely* is not rare; *servilely* [sə·vailli] (Jones,
Carlyle E 202; but Eastw 443 *servily*); *facilely* is rare;
versatilely is hardly ever used; instead of *juvenilely* we
say *youthfully*.

22.8₄. *Publicly* is the only adverb formed by simply
adding *-ly* to the adj in *-ic*. The following forms are
now obsolete or archaic: *heroicly* (Mi SA 1710), *politicly*
(Sh, Pope), *mysticly* (Morris E 109). The other words
in *-ic* all form their adverbs from the by-forms in
-ical, e. g.

comic(al)—*comically* [kɔmikl-li], *phonetically*, *politically*, *tragically*, *tyrannically*.

Thus even in cases where such by-forms are very
rarely used: *domestically*, *phlegmatically*, *rustically*,
terrifically.

Thus also with words in *-ac*: *hypocondriacally* (Quincey
183).

Corresponding to *melancholy* we have both *melan-
cholically* from obs. *melancholical*, and *melancholily*
(*melancholicly* from the now rare *melancholic* is obs.).

22.8₅. Note the difference in pronunciation, whereas
the spelling follows the general rule (two *l*'s):

(1) (from Sweet's Elementarbuch) [ri|spektfl—ri-
|spektfəli] | [wʌndəfl—wʌndəfəli]. In the adjs Dan.
Jones has facultative [u].

(2) *radical* [rædikl]—*radically* [rædikəli]. Dan. Jones
has facultative [ə] in both words. *mortal* [mɔ·tl]—*mort-
ally* [mɔ·təli] or [-tlli].

(3) *ordinary* [ɔ·din(ə)ri]—*ordinarily* [ɔ·dinærili]. Dan.

Jones does not acknowledge this difference; cp. the Amr. pronunciation of -*ary* vol I. 5.63 and 9.77.

(4) Adverbs in -*edly* from participles are generally pronounced [-idli] (cf 4.2₂) on the analogy of adjs in -*ed* (*naked, wretched, learned,* etc.), thus

assuredly [əˈʃuəridli], *confusedly* [kənˈfjuˑzidli], *fixedly* [fiksidli], *hurriedly* [hʌridli], etc.

But *good-naturedly* [ˈgudˈneitʃədli].

Fowler MEU, in a long article: -*edly*, gives a list of allowable words of this type, and only recognizes new-formations ending in [-idli] or [ədli] (of the types *animatedly, composedly, hurriedly, good-naturedly,* etc.).

(5) A medial vowel in a trisyllabic adj may be dropped in the adv because of the relatively stronger stress on the ending:

continual [kənˈtinjuəl]—*continually* [kənˈtinj(u)əli] | *usual* [juˑʒuəl]—*usually* [juˑʒ(u)əli] | *easy* [iˑzi]—*easily* [iˑzlli], Sweet has [izli] alongside of [izili], Jones has the latter only.

Miss Soames 54 has *annual* [ænjuəl] or [ænjwəl], but *annually* only [ænjwəli]; *conspicuous* [kənˈspikjuəs] or [-kjwəs], but *conspicuously* only [-kwəsli].

(6) Final [-it] in adjs in -*ate* is weakened to [-ət] in the adv, see Sweet Elementarbuch:

unfortunate [ʌnˈfɔˑtʃənit]—*unfortunately* [ʌnˈfɔˑtʃonət-li] | *separate* [sepərit]—*separately* [seprətli]. See also Jones EPhon. p. 70 note.

The adv *cleanly* is [kliˑnli], different from the adj spelt in the same way (22.7₅).

22.8₆. Merely orthographical changes:

(a) *e* is omitted after *u: true—truly, due—duly;* after *l* only in *wholly.*

(b) *y* is changed into *i: happy—happily.* Thus always in weak syllables, but not always in strong syllables; thus we have both *drily* and *dryly, slily* and *slyly, shily* and *shyly.*

From *gay* we have *gaily*, *gayly* is oldfashioned and Amr according to Sweet NEG § 1500.

22.9₁. Different meanings of adj and adv:

bare—barely 'scarcely' | *brief—briefly* (1) 'in a short space of time'; in ElE also 'a short time ago', e. g. Sh Cor I. 6.16 briefly we heard their drums, (2) 'in a few words' | *fondly* has to some extent preserved the old meaning of *fond* 'foolish' | *hard—hardly* (1) 'in a hard manner' (Thack P 716 Lady Clavering's daughter had been hardly treated | Hope Q 249 he spoke to her hardly and coldly | Shaw J 104 she looks at him hardly | Maugham Pl 4.283 Don't feel hardly towards me, Charlie), (2) 'scarcely'; note the position before the verb: he hardly works (at all) | *latter—latterly* 'of late, ultimately' | *near—near* 'close to' (adv of place), *nearly* (1) 'closely' (adv of place), (2) 'almost' (adv of degree) | *present* 'now existing, being in the place in question'— *presently* 'soon, shortly', formerly 'immediately' (and *present* adj 'immediate', e. g. Sh Wint III. 3.4 the skies ... threaten present blusters), thus Sh R2 III. 1.3, 2.179, Hml II. 2.620, III. 2.392, etc., Abbott Sh-Gramm. § 59, BJo I. 1 and frequently, still common in Irish-English according to Joyce Ir 307 | *short—shortly* 'soon'.

22.9₂. Advs in *-ly* are sometimes formally identical with the adjs, thus in the following words derived from sbs:

(1) denoting spaces of time: *hourly, daily, nightly* (he played nightly at the theatre), *weekly, monthly, quarterly, yearly;* cf also *early, leisurely, momently* (Tennyson 74, Twain M 198, Stevenson B 78), *instantly, minutely* 'every minute' (Sh Mcb V. 2.18; otherwise avoided because of the adj *minute*).

(2) others: *homely* (More U 25 a cloke caste homely about hys shoulders), *bodily* (Tennyson L 3.41 how much better he felt spiritually, mentally, and bodily),

only (with change in meaning), *fairly* (Keats 181 shadows haunting fairily the brain).

In this group *only* would seem to be the only established form. The adverbial use of adjs in *-ly* is generally avoided through circumscriptions such as *in a lively manner* | *in a masterly way*, etc. Cf also the use of forms in *-like* as advs mentioned below 23.1₁, where formerly *fatherly, motherly, friendly* (frequent in Sh), *godly, orderly*, etc. might be used.

22.9₃. Forms in *-lily* are rare. Daniel Jones has *jollily, sillily* and *surlily*, Concise Oxf. Dict. has further *lovelily* (rare) and *livelily*. I have noted: More U 77 and Sh Mcb V. 1.58 *holily* | Fielding T 3.52 and Ridge Mord Em'ly 151 *surlily* | Otway 197 and Byron 4.341 *lovelily* | Browning (Everyman ed.) 470 *sillily* | Kipling MOP 206 *livelily*.

It should be noted that all these advs are from disyllabic adjs.

Fitzedward Hall says (ModEngl. 188) *Holily, jollily, lowlily, sillily,* and the like, we barely endure; we have given up *idlely* (it was of frequent occurrence down to 1650); and we will have nothing to do with the equally regular *dailily, hourlily, monthlily, weeklily, yearlily,* and a great number of similar formations. In preference to using them, we make the adverbs the same as the adjectives.

Special cases

22.9₄. *Accordingly* is the common adverbial form, except before *to* and *as*, where *according* is used. Still I have noted Quincey 362 accordingly as they had or had not an adviser like myself | Hawthorne 1.507 accordingly as he may happen to have leisure.

Likely is now mainly used as an adj, both as an adjunct (a likely story) and predicatively (*he is likely to die soon;* formerly *he is like to ...*). Formerly it was fre-

quent as an adv too (thus London W 38), now in StE
generally only in *very likely, most likely*.

In some cases advs have been formed from sbs,
thus the obs. forms *angerly* (Sh, Bunyan) and *hungerly* (Sh Tim I. 1.262, Oth III. 4.105; note, however,
that Sh also has *hungerly* as an adj Shr III. 2.177).
Other forms are *averagely* (Cambr St 96 they were
averagely riled), *cheerly* (Shelley 57 The lamplight
through the rafters cheerly spread), *machinely* (Kipling
B 70 gentleman ... machinely crammed), *masterly*
(NED from 1394—1887, but rare), *namely*.

From prepositions at least two advs have been
formed, *inly* and *overly*. Examples:

Gray Ode III. 67 That inly gnaws the secret heart
| Shelley 154 he is wise, whose wounds do only bleed
Inly for self | Stevenson C 199 I fear I am not overly
welcome | Kipling K 405 making him overly truthful.

22.9₅. In some cases advs in *-ly* are avoided:

futurely was formerly used, but is now obsolete |
difficultly is rare. Fitzedward Hall (ModEngl. 189) has
some 30 quotations from i. a. Otway, Addison, Fielding,
Johnson, and Goldsmith. Nowadays *with difficulty* is
used instead | *fitly* is rare, but is used by i. a. Sh, Mi,
Shelley, and Swinburne. Perhaps now only poet. | *bigly*
is rare, too; mainly used in the transferred sense of
'haughtily' | *naïvely*, though used by Pope, Ruskin,
Leslie Stephen, etc., was branded as a 'horrid hybrid'
by Strachey (see GS, note to § 106).

As an adv corresponding to *content* we use *contentedly*
from the synonym *contented*.

Corresponding to *off(-)hand*, which may be used also
as an adv, we may use *offhandedly* (e. g. Shaw 1.110).

Adjs in *a-* used only predicatively, such as *afraid,
alive, aloof, asleep*, generally do not take *-ly*, still I
have found *aloofly* (Mackenzie S 1.421 he said aloofly,
Bennett T 509; not in NED).

Colour-adjs rarely take *-ly*. I have noted only two

examples: By DJ 14.87 *bluely* | King O 194 her straight, *whitely* powdered nose.

22.9₆. With the superlative *-ly* is avoided except in *mostly*, *lastly* (and *firstly*). *Most* as an adv originally denoted both frequency of occurrence and degree (the latter sense NED 1300—1734). *Mostly* is quoted in NED from 1594 to denote frequency of occurrence, 1691—1768 to denote degree, but since then the two forms have been differentiated so that *mostly* now only means 'for the most part', and *most* denotes the highest, or a very high, degree.

Lastly is now only 'used to indicate the last point or conclusion of a discourse or the like' (NED), as e. g. Fielding 3.537 first ... and secondly ... and lastly.

A related use is seen in *firstly*, *secondly*, etc, to denote place in a series. *Firstly* is not used so often as *secondly*, *thirdly*, etc, perhaps because originally a superlative. Often *first* is used even if closely followed by *secondly*, etc.

I have noted *firstly* in Di D 157, 371, id L 585, Butler W 166, Wells V 159.

In the beginning of the 19th century *firstly* was considered a neologism, and treated as such by some authors, e. g. Quincey 323 first (for I detest your ridiculous and most pedantic neologism of *firstly*) ... secondly ... thirdly; but NED has quotations from 1532 on. (*In the first place* is often used as a substitute.)

Half-ly (said by a child) occurs in Galsw M 37 half-ly dead.

22.9₇. Two consecutive advs in *-ly*, the former determining the latter, are generally avoided, instead a prepositional phrase is used. Thus, e. g. *with complete regularity* instead of *completely regularly*, see further vol II 12.25.

Exceptions may be found: Merriman S 137 I shall do it horribly badly.

But if the former adv is a sentence-adv the construction is allowable:

it was probably hardly necessary to state this |
Wilde L 33 she was simply perfectly proportioned.

22.9s. A kind of group-advs is seen in *matter-of-factly*
(e. g. Myers M 183, AHuxley Barren Leaves 41), *arm-in-
armly* (HWalpole, q NED *arm*), *thought-outly* (Wells
Br 306 doing it as directly and thought-outly as you
can).

Note also combinations of the type *more than usually*,
in which *-ly* modifies the whole phrase:

Thack N 232 Barnes was more than usually bitter |
McKenna SS 172 I had passed a more than ordinarily
hideous night.

Usual only takes *-ly* before an adjective: he spoke
more than usual. Cf Sh As I. 3:117 Because that
I am *more than common tall*.

With two co-ordinate advs (often connected by *and*)
-ly is sometimes added to the last word only.

Caxton R 94 fowle and dishonestly (ib 96) | Sh Lr
V. 3.144 safe and nicely | Tw V. 135 apt and willingly |
H4A V. 2.12 sad or merrily | LLL V. 2.841 true and
faithfully.

In recent E the construction is exceedingly rare:

Di N 729 He knocked—gently at first—then loud and
vigorously | Ward D 1.51 she began again, slow and
feebly.—But *loud* and *slow* are in themselves advs.

Sh in some cases adds *-ly* to the first adv only, and
we get constructions that cannot be called group-
advs:

R2 I. 3.3 sprightfully and bold | R3 III. 4.50 His
grace looks cheerfully and smooth | Oth III. 4.72 speak
so startingly and rash | Meas V. 36 And she will speake
most bitterly and strange.—Most strange; but yet
most truely will I speake. Here perhaps also belongs
Cor V. 3.188 most dangerously ... if not most mortal
to him.

Cf Abbott Sh-Gr. § 397, who calls attention to the fact that in all these cases of 'ellipsis' the word without *-ly* is a monosyllable. Cf also Sh-Lex. p. 1419.

Chapter XXIII

L-Suffixes Continued

-like

23.1₁. Adjs and advs in *-like* [-laik] are originally compounds with *like*, adj or adv, as second component. The oldest forms quoted by NED date from the 15th c. Gradually *-like* came to be felt as an independent suffix, which may now be added to any sb and is frequently added to adjs.

Adjs from sbs mean 'similar to—, characteristic of—, befitting—', e. g. *godlike, gardenlike, snakelike*, etc.

'In formations intended as nonce-words, or not generally current, the hyphen is ordinarily used' (NED). 'Nouns in *-l* require the hyphen' (Fowler MEU), e. g. *flail-like, owl-like, rebel-like*.

In a few cases it may be used to form adjs from adjs, e. g. *humanlike, suchlike* (e. g. Defoe Pl 76), meaning 'having the appearance of being—'.

Further, it forms advs from sbs, often corresponding to adjs in *-ly*, cf 22.9₂.₃.

According to NED advs from sbs are 'now employed only to characterize the subject of the sentence, not, as formerly, to indicate the manner of an action', but in a sentence as the following quoted to illustrate this, the word in *-like* may just as well be conceived as an adj: Mr. Justice Rivers, Brutus-like, was constrained in justice to condemn.

23.1₂. This *-like* is very much used in coll. and vg language to modify the whole of one's statement, a word or phrase, modestly indicating that one's choice

of words was not, perhaps, quite felicitous. It is generally used by inferiors addressing superiors. I have no
examples from before Dickens. Cf my *Linguistic Self-
Criticism* in *S. P. E. Tract* No. 48 p. 278 f. In Danish
preposed *ligesom* may be used in a similar way.

In the following examples (-)*like* modifies a word (sb or
adj) or a phrase, and it is not always easy to decide which:

Di D 123 they got to be more timid, and more fright-
ened-like, of late | id F 566 You have had a faint like,
or a fit | ib 32 in revenge-like | Thack V 287 They say
she was out of her mind like for six weeks | Collins
W 406 He seemed not so much sorry, as scared and
dazed like, by what had happened | Haggard She 240
Job, he said to me, solemn like | Stevenson T 144
Would that be respectful like, from me to you, squire? |
Hope Ch 16 it mostly comes round to me, being a
centre, like | Mackenzie C 325 She got worse all of a
sudden like | Bennett T 354 I feel we sh'd both be
better for a change like | Walpole C 461 Your mother
seemed in a hurry like | Wells T 91 I was a good useful
sort of chap like | ib 92 I was regular scared like.

Also after an adv (with or without -*ly*):

Ridge L 292 you are going on peacable and calm
like | Bennett T 36 we just mentioned it quietly like
to a few friends | Wells T 56 to put it different like |
ib 81 jumping on him suddenly-like.

And even after a vb (no examples in NED):

Shaw A 135 I brought it to her just to oblige you
like | Wells T 39 she asked him many questions, 'laugh-
ing like' all the time | ib 40 she choked like | ib 40 she
stood smiling like | Bennett HL 52 he hasn't passed
his examinations like ... he has that Mr. Karkeek to
cover him like.

-ful

23.2₁. -*ful* [-fl (-ful)], adjectival suffix, is originally
identical with the adj *full*. Corresponding forms are

used in the same way in connected languages, as in
G -voll, Dan. -fuld.

In OE it is added practically to sbs only, see the
following words, which have been in use from OE times:
aweful, baleful, careful, shameful, sinful, and *wonderful*.

From ME times on the ending has been added to
both native and foreign sbs, as in the following words
first recorded in ME: *doubtful, fruitful, graceful, helpful,
lifeful* (note *lifull, lyfull* with haplography Spenser
FQ VI. 11.45 and id Epithalamion 118), *merciful*, and
many others.

23.2₂. From ME times the sb from which a word in
-*ful* was derived in many cases was identical in form
with a vb. Hence it became possible and natural to
form adjs in -*ful* directly from vbs, the suffix then
meaning 'apt to—, able to—', as in *assistful, bashful*
(from the obs. vb *bash* < *abash*), *dareful* (Sh), *forgetful*
(ME; Spenser), *fretful, mournful, neglectful, refreshful*
(Keats), *resentful*, and *weariful*.

In some cases -*ful* has also been added to adjs, thus
in the rare *darkful* (OE, NED), and words recorded
from ME such as *direful, gladful, grateful* (obs. *grate*
from L *gratus*), and *tristful* (Lamb E 4). Here the ending
means 'full of the quality denoted by the adj.'

23.2₃. In sense -*ful* often corresponds to the foreign
-*able*, which may be the reason why many poets often
favour the former. Thus Tennyson has 30 words in
-*ful* according to Dyboski 377 f.

The words derived from sbs may be arranged in the
following three chief semantic groups:

1) Full of e. g. *beautiful, changeful, cheerful, deceitful, pushful* 'full of 'push'', *respectful*, etc.

2) Fraught with, or causing or exciting ... as in
aweful, delightful, dreadful, wonderful, etc.

Many words belong to both of these groups, thus
distressful, fearful, hateful, hopeful, and *pitiful*.

3) Full to ..., as in *brimful* and the obsolescent *topful*.

But a great many words fall outside these groups, thus *artful, faithful, fanciful, lawful* 'according to law, permitted by law', *masterful, needful* 'necessary' (funds, etc.), *useful,* and *wilful.*

The origin of the suffix is generally no more considered by speakers, hence the weakening to [-fl]. In the words belonging in group 3 above, the connexion with *full* is still distinctly felt, and we have the pronunciation [-ful] in words belonging here, and often the spelling *-full.* Cf further vol I 9.65.

-less

23.3₁. *-less* [-lis], adjectival suffix, is from OE *leas* 'devoid (of), free from', which was used both as an independent word and as a privative suffix added to sbs. From ME times the latter function only has survived.

The following words in *-less* have been in use from OE times: *lifeless, lightless, mindless, restless,* and *shameless.* And the following among others from ME: *breathless, faithless, fearless, fruitless, guileless, homeless, joyless, needless, reasonless* (Mi SA 812), *tongueless,* etc.

Later formations are legion. This ending seems very popular with many poets, thus Byron, Keats, Shelley, Browning. Dyboski 379 ff. quotes more than 50 words in *-less* from Tennyson.

23.3₂. On the analogy of words in which the first component was formally identical with a verb, e. g. *countless, numberless,* the ending came to be added also to vbs, meaning 'not to be -ed, un—able'. Examples are: *dauntless, drainless, exhaustless* (By Ch 4.2), *fadeless, fathomless, imagineless* (Francis Thompson), *opposeless* (Sh), *plumbless* (AHuxley), *quenchless* (Shelley 498, By Ch 3.42), *resistless* (Marlowe Jew III. 5), *staunchless* (Sh Mcb IV. 3.78, Shelley 238), *tameless* (very common), *teachless* (Shelley 209), *thinkless* (London M 268), *tireless* (common), and *utterless* (Keats).

The suffix is not ordinarily added to adjs. *Sapidless* (Lamb E 1.171) is 'badly formed' (NED).

23.3₃. *-less* is the negative counterpart of *-ful*, cf Negation 146, and often two semantically equivalent words compete, one in *un—ful*, and another in *-less:*

uneventful (more common) : *eventless, unfaithful* : *faithless, ungraceful* : *graceless, unmerciful* : *merciless.*

But *unlawful* is different from *lawless.*

In other cases *-less* competes with *un-* (*in-*) *-able* (*-ible*), cf Dyboski 381. Thus in

changeless : *unchangeable* | *countless* : *uncountable* | *doubtless* : *indubitable* | *fathomless* : *unfathomable* | *limitless* : *illimitable* | *numberless* : *innumerable* | *profitless* : *unprofitable,* etc.

In words derived from vbs *-less* often has the meaning 'unable to be -ed', e. g.

exhaustless : *inexhaustible* | *quenchless* : *unquenchable* | *resistless* : *irresistible* | *tameless* : *untameable,* etc.

23.3₄. In early texts we may find haplography in words in *-less* derived from sbs in *-l* or *-le*, thus, according to Fitzedward Hall M 189 Ben Jonson has, in verse, *example for exampleless;* Beaumont and Fletcher *paralleles for parallelless.* Spenser Virgils Gnat 431 has *rulesse* for *rule-less* 'lawless'.

In PE words derived from sbs in *-l* or *-ll* are generally spelt with a hyphen, as in Galsw D 259 will-less | Rose Macaulay I Would be Private 268 sail-less.

-let

23.4₁. *-let* [-lit] (but [-let] may be heard). The earliest words in *-let* are F adoptions, such as *hamlet* (NED from 1330), *chaplet* (1375), *mantelet* (1386), *gauntlet* (1420), *bracelet* (1438), *frontlet* (1478), and *crosslet* (1538). The suffix originates from *-ette* added to F words with the diminutive ending -(e)*l*. By metanalysis of such words as *crosslet* and *frontlet*, -*let* easily came to be felt as the ending, and from *crosslet*, *mantlet* and perhaps some of the other F words in which the suffix had a diminutive sense, this became the usual meaning in English. A third factor of importance for the development may have been the existence of *lyte*, the obsolete by-form of *little* with the *i* characteristic of diminutives and other words denoting something small, see *Linguistica* 283 ff. It seems that /e/ had developed into [i] already in the 14th c., see vol I 9.111.

The number of new words formed with -*let* in earlier periods seems to be comparatively limited, but from the beginning of the 19th c. an abundance of words in -*let* crop up, especially words denoting things.

23.4₂. Established forms in -*let* denoting human beings, such as *kinglet* (NED from 1603) and *princelet* (from 1682) are few. Schmeding's list of words in -*let* from Carlyle includes 15 forms in all, 4 of them denoting human beings, *Byronlet*, *mayorlet*, *queenlet*, and *squirelet*.

Words denoting animals are rare:

birdlet (NED 1867) | *crablet* (NED from 1841) | *deerlet* (Kipling J 2.50) | *dragonlet* (nonce-word; Macdonell E 30 Donald presented himself nervously at the dragonlet's den) | *fishlet* (from 1886) | *starlet* 'a star-fish' (from 1854) | *troutlet*.

Words in -*let* denoting things (in a wide sense) naturally fall into three groups: (1) general, (2) ornaments, and (3) scientific, especially from botany and zoology, denoting small organs.

Among names of ornaments or articles of dress, sometimes not especially diminutive, we may note:

Lubbock, Orig. of Civ. (1875) 55 The savage also wears necklaces and rings, *bracelets* and *anklets*, *armlets* and *leglets*—even, if I may say so, *bodylets* | Locke GP 45 a *necklet* of fur.

The rare word *crownlet* (in NED Scott and Carlyle
only) has the diminutive sense.

Among the words especially used by naturalists are
*bladelet, bonelet, budlet, conelet, featherlet, finlet, fruitlet,
hooflet, hornlet,* and *leaflet,* nearly all of them coined in
the 19th c.

Words denoting things, but falling outside the two
groups just treated, are numerous.

Some are frequently used, such as *booklet* (19th c.),
flatlet (Bentley TI 215), *ringlet* 'lock of hair' (from
1667; = 'small ring' rare), *runlet* 'small stream' (from
1755), *streamlet* (from 1552), *townlet* (from 1552), and
wavelet (from 1810).

Others are very rare, e. g. *cloudlet* (from 1788; Thack
N 472), *droplet* (Sh Tim V 4.76, and NED two later
quotations), *notelet* (from 1824), *speechlet* (from 1881).

Nonce-words are *flasklet* (1862 Trollope), *heartlet*
(1826), *houselet* (1802), *playlet* (1911 Zangwill), *shoplet*
(Butler Er 59), *textlet* (Carlyle SR 48), *squeaklet* (id E
170; and some 8 others from Carlyle, see Schmeding),
and *valleylet* (1866).

According to Weseen, *Dict. of Am. Slang,* the suffix
-let seems to be a very popular diminutive formative in
America. I shall quote only a few: *adlet* = advertisement-
let, *baglet, boomlet, buslet, catlet, churchlet, cowlet, dinglet*
'thingumbob', *doglet.*

23.4₃. Words like *circlet* (Fr. *cerclet: cercle* + *-et*),
eaglet (Fr. *aiglette:* OF *aigle* + *-et*), *tablet* (OF *tablete:
table* + *-ete*) are now probably felt as *-let* derivatives.

In some cases we have now forms in *-let,* where
earlier times knew diminutives in *-et* only, thus *brooket*
(1538—1610) : *brooklet* (from 1813) | *chainet* (1623 only) :
chainlet (from 1805) | *flasket* (from 1460) : *flasklet*
(1862 nonce-word) | *fishet* (Lamb 1823 nonce-word) :
fishlet (from 1886).

Here perhaps belongs *riveret* (Drayton) as compared
with *rivulet* interpreted as *river-let.*

-ling

23.5₁. *-ling* [-liŋ] forming sbs is a Common Gothonic
formative. It can (and could from OE times) be added
to sb, adj, vb and (rarely) adverbial stems, and in OE
only formed sbs with the sense of 'person or thing
connected with ...', e. g. *hȳrling* 'hireling', *geongling*
'youngling, youth', *deorling* 'darling', *underling* 'subordinate person'.

In ME and ModE the suffix was freely used; the
diminutive sense (symbolical value of *i*!) probably
originates from ON, where the suffix was used especially
to denote the young of animals, e. g. *ketling-r* (cf *kitling*,
e. g. BJo 3.133; now only dial.). Thus also in E *codling*
(NED 1314), *gosling* (15th c.; earliest form *gesling* from
ON), *duckling* (from 1440), and cf *sapling* (from 1415)
and *seedling* (1660) about young plants.

23.5₂. Sbs in *-ling* denoting persons very frequently
have a contemptuous ring, which, of course, may
already be inherent in the primary word. Thus, *change-
ling* (1555), *courtling*, *groundling*, *princeling* (1618),
professorling (Wells T 2; only quot. in NED), *starveling*
(1546), *swineling* (Bird Rival Captains (1937) 30; not
in NED), *underling* (1175), *weakling* (1526), *wiseling*
'wiseacre' (from 1633, now rare), *worldling*, and *worm-
ling*.

But others are merely diminutives, perhaps with a
slightly hypocoristic nuance in some cases, e. g.
manling (NED: two old examples only, but Kipling
has it, too), *nurseling*, *suckling*, and *weanling*.

Words for things are rare; *bookling* (Southey L 79,
also in Carlyle), *eyeling* (Carlyle; not in NED), *hireling*
('hired motor-car'; Maugham Alt 293 private cars and
hirelings).

Finally a few nonce-words: *antling* (1879), *beastling*
(1872), *daughterling* (Brontë V 269), *Edithling* (Southey
L 94), *giantling* (1871), *giftling* (1860 Thack).

-ling(s), *-long* in Adverbs

23.6. *-ling(s)* [-liŋ(z)] from Gothonic *-ling(es)* was in OE added to sbs to form advs of direction, e. g. *bæcling* 'back'. Later formations are *grovelling*, *headling(s)*, *sideling(s)* (on the back-formations *grovel* and *sidle* see 22.5₄), and, from adjs, to denote condition or situation, *blindling(s)*, *darkling(s)*, *flatling(s)*, *mostlings*, and a few others.

Most of these are now obs. or arch. except in dialects. *-long* [-lɔŋ] seems to have been transferred from *endlong*, ON *endlangr* 'from end to end' to some of the earlier formations in *-ling*, so that we have now *headlong*, *sidelong*. Neither of these endings are now living formatives.

Chapter XXIV

Suffixes Containing Dentals

24.1. For the flexional ending *-ed* in verbs with its three phonetic values [-d, -t, -id] I refer to 4.3 above; on the cases in which we have *-t* after a voiced sound see 4.3₂, 4.5 and 4.6.

-ed in Adjectives

24.1₁. *-ed* [-id, -d] to form adjs from sbs is an old Gothonic suffix, OE *-ede*, as in *hringede* 'ringed', *sūrēagede* 'sour-eyed, blear-eyed', OSax. *-ôdi*, meaning 'provided with', and ultimately related to *-ed* in weak verbs.—In OE and ME these words also occurred with the participial prefix *ge-*, *y-*, *i-*, e. g. OE *gegymmod* 'set with gems' | Ch A 3738 He felt a thing al rough and long *y-herd* 'haired', etc.

In *anhungered* (Caxton R 91 sore an hongryd and a colde | AV Matth 25 35 I was an hungred) and *a-hungered* (Keats Hyperion 2.163 *a-hunger'd*) *a-* or *an-* is explained

as a substitution for *of-* (OE *ofhyngrod*), cf *athirst* and
the early confusion of *on* and *of* (still in vg). The following forms then are analogous formations after *ahungered:*
Swift J 173 I was *a-dreamed* last night that I ate ripe
cherries | Fielding T 4.291 (vg) when I was *a hoped* to
have nothing more to do.

Pronunciation

24.1₂. In most adjs -*ed* has the same three sounds as
the flexional -*ed*, e. g. *moneyed* [ˈmʌnid], *long-legged*
[ˈlɔŋˈlegd], *self-willed* [ˈselfˈwild], *bad-tempered* [ˈbæd-
ˈtempəd], *old-fashioned* [ˈouldˈfæʃənd]; *hunchbacked*
[ˈhʌntʃˈbækt], *pimplefaced* [ˈpimplˈfeist]; *landed* [ˈlæn-
did], *talented* [ˈtæləntid].

The vowel in -*ed* is often pronounced in poetry, e. g.
Wordsw 229 a claspèd book | Shelley 30 and 583 many-
voicèd | 279 Over its wheelèd clouds | 614 Many domèd
Padua | 680 pearlèd. Thus also often in recent poetry.

In some words there is vacillation:

Aged, according to NED [ˈeidʒid] in the sense (1) 'of
advanced age', (2) 'belonging to old age', as *aged wrink-
les;* but [eidʒd] in the sense (3) 'at or of the age of',
e. g. *a lady aged 50.* In *middle-aged* always [-eidʒd] |
crisped, NED [krispt] or [krispid] | *crooked*, Daniel
Jones: 'not straight' [krukid], 'having a crook' [krukt] |
hooked, NED [hukt, hukid], Jones only [hukt] | *horned*,
NED and Jones: [hɔ·nid, hɔ·nd], Jones: -*horned* [-hɔ·nd]
| *winged*, Jones: [wiŋd] and [wiŋid] (but -*winged* only
[wiŋd]). In poetry the fuller form is frequent, thus
Wordsw 177 and 196 | Shelley common, also in com-
pounds, e. g. 614 thought-wingèd | 616 morning-wingèd |
674 spirit-wingèd, etc. | Keats (Oxf. 1921) 14 Or as
the winged cap Mercury | 29 And the broad winged sea-
gull never at rest (as a second component generally
spelt -*wing'd*).

In some cases the root is changed when the suffix
is added.

Thus the vowel is shortened in *dry-*, *roughshod* [-ʃɔd] from *shoe;* cf above the vb.

Fricatives are in some cases changed from voiceless to voiced, see *Linguistica* 378 f. Thus in *-lived*, but an earlier form is *long-lifed*, *-lif't*. As to the vowel, the usual pronunciation seems to be [-livd] (thus Professors Mawer, Moore Smith, D. Jones s. v. *short-lived*), but H. W. Fowler says that the right pronunciation is [-laivd] "the words being from *life* and not from *live*". But in *high-lived* and *low-lived* (both in Goldsmith) one would say [-laivd], as also in "some *hundred-wived* kinglet" (Kingsley H 239).

From *leaf* we have both *-leafed* and *-leaved:* Rice Imperial City 102 his loose-leafed notebook ‖ Browning 2.135 a million-leaved mimosa | Brontë P 137 single-leaved devoirs.

Both *hoofed* (Kipling J 2.98 sharp-hoofed) and *hooved* are found.

Scarf : *scarved:* D. H. Lawrence in Anthol. of Mod. Verse 135 black-scarved faces of women-folk.

In *-mouthed* the sound is uncertain: Jones *foul-mouthed* [ˈfaulˈmauðd], but Furnival Sh's Life 131 writes *foul-moutht*, which must stand for [-mauþt], and NED *deep-mouthed* and *wide-mouthed* [-ðd, -þt].

The pronunciation of *toothed* is given by NED as [tuˑþt], thus also Wyld *sabre-toothed* [-tuˑþt]; but Jones has both [tuˑðd] and [tuˑþt].

Well-breathed, SOD [-ðd, -þt], cf. 12.3₂.

Spelling

24.1₃. The ordinary spelling after a consonant is *-ed*, though the earlier spelling *-'d* is often found in poetry.

We have the ordinary doubling of consonant after a single stressed vowel, e. g. *crabbed*, *dogged*, *hatted*, *starred*, etc. Also after unstressed vowel + *l*, e. g. *gravelled*, *laurelled*, *jewelled*, *olive-sandalled* (Shelley 616), etc.

y after a consonant becomes *i*, e. g. *ivied* (Shelley
30), *propertied*, *feeble-bodied*, etc., but is generally retained after a vowel. Always after *a: rayed*, but with
-ey the first vowel may be dropped in spelling, e. g.
honey : *honied* (By Ch 1.3), or *honeyed*, *money* : *monied*
or *moneyed*.

Derivatives from words ending in double vowels are
generally written with an apostrophe: *knock-knee'd*,
pedigree'd. Thus also as a rule with words ending in
"unEnglish vowel terminations", e. g. *idea'd*, *mou-
stachio'd*, cf Fowler MEU: *-ed* & *-d*.

24.1₄. As added to a simple sb this *-ed* has been a
living formative throughout all periods. Among innumerable examples a few may find place here: *caftaned*
(Scott Iv 300 the turban'd and caftan'd damsel),
creepered (Galsw MP 107 creepered trellis), *jacketed*
(Carlyle SR 44), *minded* (More U 26, Sh Tp V. 1.126
Were I so minded | Kingsley H 128 He was half minded
once to escape), *petticoated*, *poppied* (Keats), *propertied*,
spectacled (Keats), *talented* (often objected to in the
19th c.), *verandahed*.

Several words in Ru 1.228 broad-breasted; level-
browed like the horizon;—thighed and shouldered like
the billows;—footed like the stealing foam.

With some words *-ed* has the sense 'having the ways
or character of' instead of 'provided with', e. g. *bigoted*,
crabbed, *cupped* 'cup-shaped' (as in Keats: the little
cupped flowers), *dogged*.

Sh Cor I. 1.266 to be commanded 'entrusted with or possessed of command' may be interpreted as the participle, thus
with exactly the opposite meaning.

24.1₅. In the majority of instances the sb from which
an adj in *-ed* is formed is accompanied by an adjunct,
and as remarked in vol II 15.34 ff, we may have a
choice between two expressions, e. g. *moderate sized*
and *moderately sized;* in the former we have a derivative

from a composite expression (*blue-eyed* = *blue-eye* + *-d*),
in the latter a derivative from the simple sb, and an
adverb is used because the derivative is an adjective.
In vol II full lists are given, the first of which I shall
here supplement by a few characteristic quotations:
soft-bedded (Carlyle SR 132) | *lidless-eyed* (Keats 73) |
a *twinkling-eyed*, pimple-faced man (Di D) | Shaw D 1
a *wide-open-eyed* youth | Di D 132 *back-handed* knock |
fearless-hearted (Shelley 118) | *-looked* (obs.; Defoe M 151
wholesome-looked | Fielding 5.558 *ill-looked;* from the
pl vg GE S 124 *queer-looksed;* ib 168 more *pleasanter-
looksed*) | *feeble-minded and bodied* (with the adj referring
to two words; Carpenter P 75) | *great-moneyed* (Thack
N 50) | *different-shaped* (Christie LE 141) | *bad-tasted*
(Stevenson T 250) | *sole-thoughted* (Keats 181) | *sweet-
voiced* (Shaw J 200).

The adjunct before the sb may be another *-ed* form,
adjective or participle, as in Swift J 17 he is a *rawboned-
faced* fellow | Carlyle E 193 its scot-and-lot paying,
beef-and-ale loving, *cocked-hatted*, pot-bellied Landlord |
Di N 439 the four Miss Kenwigses gathered round
Nicholas, *opened eyed and mouthed*.

The adjunct before the sb may also be an adjectival
pronoun: Beresford G 66 the consideration of *what
coloured* hair would go with the green of the overall |
Rose Macaulay T 249 [toy] For *what aged* child is it? |
Di F 815 green bottles, blue bottles, and *other coloured*
bottles. *Same* + *-ed* is pretty frequent: Crofts St 269
typed ... with the same coloured ribbon and spacing |
Cabot P 241 the *same shaped* room (also Mannin W 26).

Compounds with an adj as first element have normally level-stress, e. g. ¦*absent-*¦*minded*, ¦*good-*¦*natured*,
¦*kind-*¦*hearted*, but if preceded or followed by a stressed
syllable, one of the two stresses may be weakened
under the influence of sentence-stress: He is ¦very
¦good-¦natured | a ¦good-¦natured ¦man. *Long-tailed* is
always [ˈlɔŋteild] because it is always attributive

(Jones EPhon 126). "There is an exceptional case in which single stress is used, namely when the compound adjective is practically synonymous with its first element," e. g. ꞌoval-shaped (ib).

24.1₆. The loose connexion between the elements in such combinations is shown (beside the stress) by the fact that the indefinite article is sometimes placed between the two components (cf vol II 15.18): Sh Gent IV. 4.196 such a colour'd perrywig | John IV. 2.27 so new a fashion'd robe | Tp IV. 1.123 so rare a wondred father [i. e. a father possessed of so rare wonders] | Mi PL 3.643 wings he wore of many a coloured plume | Butler H 1.3.330 Pigmalion ... That cut his mistress out of stone Had not so hard a hearted one | Osborne 137 as well an humord Younge Person | Swinburne T 38 so sweet a spirited thing | Meredith H 4 [vg?] he was as kind a hearted man as ever breathed.

The adjective may also be separated from the -ed-form by an adv, as in Maugham Pl 2.14 I was not at the time *quick enough witted* to profit by it more; cf AR 136 hu swete he was iheorted.

24.1₇. The adjunct preposed to the sb is often a sb (see on the adjectival character of the first part in a compound vol II ch XIII. Examples (written with or without hyphens): *horn-rimmed* glasses | Sh Mcb V. 3.15 Thou *Lilly-liuer'd* Boy | As IV. 3.25 a *freestone colourd* hand | Tp IV. 1.152 The *cloud-capp'd* towers | Keats 208 *tiger-passion'd*, *lion-thoughted* | Tennyson 235 *citadel-crown'd* (see further Dyboski 422 f.) | Carlyle E 172 a cleanly, *shovel-hatted* look | Di T 1.171 powdered, *gold-laced*, pumped, and *white-silk stockinged* | Trollope D 255 a very *self-willed* lady | Meredith T 51 *gold instead of snow crested* | id Selected Poems 55 *stripe-shadowed* | ib 150 *Iron-capped* and *iron-heeled* | Doyle Sh 1.168 *slate-roofed* | Wells T 6 the *life-sized* model | Galsw MW 68 the *yew-treed* garden | ib 78 Men, *silk-hatted* or plus-foured | Drinkwater Poems 1908-14 37

Strong-armed, sure-footed, *iron-willed* | ib 105 Laughing
and *rainbow-aureoled* | Brooke Selected Poems 7 *mist-
garlanded* | Morley Human Being 174 the *fire-escaped*
vista of 114th Street.

24.1₈. The adj before the *-ed*-form is very often in
the comparative or the superlative, e. g. Ch B 4059
the *faireste hewed* | Sh Gent II. 3.6 the *sourest-natured*
dog | R3 III. 5.33 the *covert'st sheltered* traitor | Mids
III. 2.415 *lighter-heel'd* | H4B II. 4.415 *truer-hearted* |
Cæs I. 3.122 *noblest-minded* | Cymb I. 6.165 *truest
manner'd* | ib IV. 2.398 the *prettiest-dazied* [i. e. daisied]
plot | Mi PL 3.691 *sharpest-sighted* | Walton A 142 and
150 the *longest lived* | Defoe M 141 her *lowest-rated*
customer | Swift J 159 The walks there are *finer grav-
elled* than the Mall | Fielding 1.457 the *finest legg'd*
woman | id T 1.262 *quicker-sighted* | By DJ 3.41 the
mildest manner'd man | Austen E 43 *coarser featured*
| id P 273 *prettier-coloured* | Di D 113 *harder-hearted* |
ib 282 Mr. Omer, *shorter-winded* than of yore | id Do
117 a *newer-fashioned* child | id N 321 the *sweetest-
tempered, kindest-hearted* creature | Thack V 248 a
stronger minded woman | Carlyle FR 30 *lightest-hearted* |
Kingsley H 394 the ancestors of *"bluest-blooded"* Castilian
nobles | Collins W 238 the *highest-couraged* thing |
Lowell W 128 the *fastest-footed* | Swinburne A 76 Ancæus,
mightiest thewed | Doyle S 1.142 the *largest landed* pro-
prietor | Stevenson B 361 the *softest-hearted* simpleton |
Wells T 98 the *bigger-sized* people | NP 1904 *thinner-
skinned* | Shaw D 261 the *lowest-priced* article | Phill-
potts GR 34 *milder-mannered* | Galsw FCh 171 *flatter-
cheeked*.

Thus even with irregular comparison: Sh Shrew IV.
3.100 *better-fashion'd* | Swift J 348 the silliest, *best-
natured* wretch | Lamb E 1.146 finding her a little
better humoured | Austen P 210 a *better sized* room |
Di Sk 107 *better-hearted* | ib 150 one of the *best-hearted*
men | Thack N 717 the finest girl in England, and the

best-plucked one | Barrie MO 50 the Dr. says this
morning that he is *better hoped* now || Sh Err IV. 2.20
ill-fac'd, *worse bodied* | Osborne 34 the *worst natured*
person (also Fielding T 1.285).

Note Kingsley H 7 the wisest, *eldest-hearted and headed*
of them—with *eldest* referring to two following adjectives.
Cf. vol. VII 10.5₂.

This use of the superlative has been facetiously transferred
to a substantive as first component in Di M 1.45 the simplest,
hardest-working, *childest-hearted* man.

Sometimes we have the periphrastic comparative or
superlative, even with adjs of irregular comparison:
more good-natured (Goldsm 670), most good-natured
(Thack V 292), *more far-sighted*, always *more* before
old-fashioned, which is felt as an indivisible form.
Further Macaulay E 4.109 the fiercest and *most high-
minded* of the Roman Pontiffs | Bennett ECh 126 these
two stout, thick-necked, red-faced old men grew stouter
and *thicker-necked and more red-faced*.

The comparative or superlative ending is rarely added
to the second component: Sh H4B II. 4.77 the *foule-
mouth'dst* rogue in England | London V 208 the mildest,
good-naturedest man | Caine M 125 [vg] they're are
tender-hearteder than us.

Finally, we may in facetious or vulgar language
find both components in the superlative form: Fielding
T 1.222 one of the *sweetest temperedest, best naturedest*
men | Di Do 42 [vg] *best-temperedst*.

24.1₉. In vol II 15.352 a number of examples of adv
+ -ed adjs were given. To these I shall here add some
of a somewhat different character: *down-hearted* |
undersized | Shaw IW 338 *super-incomed* neighbour.

But *upended* is a ptc of the vb *up-end*.

24.1₁₀. The first part of a compound in -*ed* is in rare
cases a vb, as in *knock-knee'd* (common), *totter-knee'd*

(nonce-word; Meredith Selected Poems 75), *crack-brained,
crack-headed, draggle-tailed, scatter-brained.*

As verbal stems do not usually function as adjuncts,
I venture the guess that it here stands instead of a
ptc, *knocked* or *knocking,* etc.

An extraordinary formation is seen in Gay BP 162 an old
out-of-fashion'd philosopher—coined on the analogy of *old-
fashioned.*

24.1₁₁. In some cases we have old formations without
an ending competing with forms in *-ed.*

Barefoot, OE *bærfōt* adj and adv, AR 420 gon ...
baruot | Puttenham 49 played barefoote vpon the
floore | Scott Iv 84 a barefoot Palmer | Di T 2.70 bare-
foot and barelegged | Ru C 100 they will go anywhere
barefoot. Similarly *hot-foot:* Kipling J [p. ?] He [Shere
Khan] crossed the ranges last night with Tabaqui, hot-
foot on thy trail | Vachell H 106 the laughter sent
him hot-foot to Scaife himself | ib 152 to run, hot foot |
dry-foot (q Poutsma 206). Cf. vol. VII 8.7₆.

Barefooted (NED from 1530) is now more common
than the short form. Both forms are found together
Thack N 132 he always walked barefoot ... bare-
headed and barefooted | ib 133 the barefooted business.

With numerals always *-ed:* More U 284 fourefooted
beastes. And cf Keats 220 the unfooted sea.

Barehead is recorded in NED from 1320, now very
rare, NED one quot. from the 19th c. (1854). I have
further noted Carpenter Ad 92 barehead and bare-
foot | Hewlett Q 200 the admiral stands barehead in
the raw drizzle (but id F 41 go barefooted and bare-
headed; the latter in NED from 1530, now common).

Hard-heart, OE *heard-heort,* Ælfric 1.108 þa heard-
heortan Iudei (q Sweet), NED further 1475, 1616,
1895. *Hard-hearted* from 1205. OE also *hatheort* 'hot-
hearted, angry'.

Off-hand, adj and adv, from 1694 (Mackenzie C 125

you treated him so off-hand), besides *off-handed* and *off-handedly*.

24.1₁₂. In some cases it is impossible to decide whether the *-ed*-form is a derived adj from a sb or a ptc from a formally identical vb, cf the examples starred in vol II 15.34 ff. Such words are *bearded* (Shaw C 103), *crowned, cultured, hatted and feathered* (Mitford OV 3), *ringed*.

Buskin: the NED has many quotations with 'buskined' 1590-1877; as a nonce-verb 1795 | *butter:* a butteryd loof 1496, vb 1528 | *cap:* capped 1370, vb 'provide with a cap' 1483.

Words in *-ed* with the negative prefix *un-* are frequent, e. g. *unbearded, unlettered, unrivalled, unskilled,* and occasional formations like Shelley 278 the *unpavilioned* sky | Meredith Selected Poems 93 Idly the flax-wheel spun *unridered* | Drinkwater Poems 1908-14 31 In *uncompassioned* woe | Brooke Selected Poems 36 *unmemoried* | ib 67 the keen *unpassioned* beauty of a great machine.

Here, too, it may be difficult to decide whether we have to do with a ptc or an adj derived from a sb, cf e. g. *unfeathered, unbiassed, unlabelled, unlicensed,* etc.

But it is possible, and even probable, that adjs in *-ed* from sbs have contributed to the facility with which in E vbs can be formed from sbs without any change (above Ch VI).

24.1₁₃. We always say *ill-, well-behaved* instead of **-behavioured* (Fielding 7.260 They are very pretty behaved), *ill-, well-disposed* for **-dispositioned*. These may be considered second ptcs in an active sense, somewhat like *fair-spoken* (Tennyson 322), *smooth-* and *well-spoken* for **-speeched* (as referring to persons), etc.

The ending *-ed* has in a few cases been added to adjs, generally without apparently causing any semantic differentiation: *wicked,* ME *wicked, wikked,* from *wicke,* *wikke*, perhaps adjectival use of OE *wicca* 'wizard', *new-fangled* (Sh LLL I. 106), from ME *newefangel*, from *newe* + *-fangel*, OE **fangol* 'inclined to take', on the analogy of which has been coined *old-fangled* (NED from 1842).

Outside the subject dealt with in this chapter fall some adjs in *-ed* [-id]: *crabbed, dogged* (which does not mean 'provided with dogs'), *naked, wretched*.

-ad, -ade (-cade)

24.2₁. *-ad* [-əd] is from Gk *-áda* (nom. *-ás*) in some words generally borrowed through F, thus in collective numerals like *monad, dyad, triad* (and *decade*, with *-e* from French retained), *myriad*, etc., on the analogy of which E *milliad* '1000 years' has been coined ('badly from L. *mille*'). Further in names of poems, such as the *Iliad*, after which Pope's *Dunciad* and others.

In *ballad* and *salad* from F forms in *-ade* the *e* was dropped.

24.2₂. *-ade* [-ˡeid], substantival suffix, is from F *-ade*, L *-ata*, fem. sg ptc of verbs in *-are*, or from Sp. or Pg. *-ado*, the corresponding masc. form. Formations in E are few: *blockade, orangeade, lemonade, gingerade, pineappleade* (Mackenzie S 1.130).

Some of these words are action nouns (*blockade, cannonade, fusillade, tirade*), some others denote person or body concerned in an action or process (*ambassade, cavalcade, comrade*), and others again products of various kinds (*lemonade, marmalade, arcade, colonnade, pomade*).

Decade is of different origin, see *-ad*, and hence pronounced differently: [dekəd, dekeid].

In *cockade* the ending has been substituted for *-ard*, as in F *cocarde*, from *coq* 'cock', see *-ard*, 15.9₂.

24.2₃. On the analogy of *cavalcade* we have *aerocade, autocade, camelcade*, and *motorcade* (Mencken 179).

-age

24.3₁. *-age* [-idȝ] originates from F. *-age* < Lat.
-aticum, which was used for abstract sbs of appurtenance
and collectives. The Lat. suffix in Medieval Lat. was
remodelled into *-agium* after F. *-age*, and both Latin
forms are found on Eng. soil in ME times. See for many
details F. Gadde, On the History and Use of the Suffixes *-ery* (*-ry*), *-age* and *-ment* in English (Lund & Cambr.
1910). The first loanwords in *-age* date from the former
half of the 13th c. "The suffix can hardly be called a
living formative in English before the fifteenth century"
(Gadde 56), but from now on to the present day *-age*
is very much used to form sbs of the following semantic
groups, each group comprising (a) adopted formations,
and (b) native formations.

24.3₂. 1) Nexus-words derived from nouns and a few
vbs and denoting state or condition:

(a) *bondage* (from 1330) | *vassalage* || *marriage* 'married
life' | *dotage*.

(b) *orphanage* | *pupilage* || *shortage* (e. g. Jackson S
114; this, and one or two rare formations quoted by
Gadde, are the only derivatives from adjs) || *linkage*.

2) Nexus-words derived from vbs and expressing process or function, in some cases also result of an action,
etc.:

(a) *arbitrage* | *agiotage* | *coinage* (action and result) |
marriage 'wedding' | *passage* | *usage*.

(b) *breakage* | *chattage* (recent; e. g. Allingham P 98) |
cleavage | *drainage* | *flowerage* (Carlyle) | *shrinkage* |
stoppage | *storage* | *stowage* | *tillage* | *tutelage* | *waftage*
(Gissing R 36) | *wreckage* (Carlyle 1837).

3) A related group are nexus-words derived from
sbs and denoting the activity or function characteristic of or relating to the thing or person designated by
the sb.

(a) *brigandage* | *carnage* (from Lat. *carnaticum*) |

language (ultimately from Lat. *lingua* 'tongue', cf
Butler E 195 ideas expressed by *eyeage* or by *tonguage*
... written words are *handage, inkage* and *paperage*) |
voyage (ME and OF *viage* < Lat. *viaticus* from *via*).

(b) *brokerage* 'business of a broker' | *cooperage* |
leverage 'action of a lever' | *oarage* 'rowing' | *porterage*
'carriage of luggage etc. by a porter' | *tankage* 'storage
in tanks' | *vicarage* 'office of a vicar' (rare in this sense).

From the groups of derivatives with an abstract
sense various other groups have developed, such as

4) Words (mainly derived from sbs) denoting tax or
charge. A great many words from this group, (often
legal), are now obsolete

(a) *arrearage* | *demurrage*.

(b) *cartage* | *cellarage* 'charge made for storage in
a cellar' | *keelage* | *mileage* 'allowance for expenses, etc.
reckoned by miles travelled' | *porterage* 'money paid to
a porter' | *postage* | *quayage* 'quay dues' | *tankage* 'pay
for storage in tanks' | *wharfage* = quayage.

5) Collectives from names of things:

(a) *baggage* | *cordage* | *foliage* | *fruitage* (Tennyson
23) | *garbage* (? < OF *garbe* 'sheaf, bundle') | *plumage*.

(b) *acreage* | *cellarage* | *inheritage* | *leafage* (AHuxley
Mortal Coils 213) | *luggage* | *oarage* 'set of oars' | *package* |
verbiage | *wrappage* (Carlyle H 7 a wrappage of tradi-
tions).

6) Collectives from personal names:

(a) *baronage*.

(b) *baronetage* | *companionage* | *knightage* | *peerage*
(those—with *baronage*—may also mean a list of baro-
nets etc. as in the book-title Debrett's Peerage, Baronet-
age, Knightage and Companionage) | *clientage* | *matron-
age* | *vagabondage*.

7) Derivatives from substantives, denoting places:

(a) *cottage* | *hermitage* | *village*.

(b) *anchorage* | *harbourage* | *orphanage* | *quayage* |
vicarage 'residence of a vicar'.

24.3₃. A great number of *-age* words are used in two or more senses, e. g.

breakage 1) act of breaking, 2) article broken, 3) the actual area of breaking | *brokerage* 1) broker's business, 2) broker's commission | *steerage* 1) process of steering, 2) manner in which a vessel answers to the helm, 3) part of a ship | *tankage* 1) storage in tanks, 2) pay for this, 3) cubic capacity of tank, 4) kind of fertilizer.

24.3₄. A good number of derivatives in *-age*, however, could hardly be classed in these groups, such as a few for concrete objects, e. g. *carriage* 'vehicle', *visage* 'face', etc. Or *personage* designating a 'person of importance' (e. g. Churchill C 457 with him was—well, another person. Nay, personage would perhaps be the better word), or the various meanings of *percentage*, etc.

24.3₅. In the native formations *-age* is simply added to the root-word, with gemination of the final consonant of the root according to the general rules. The only irregular formation is *jettage* from *jetty*.

24.3₆. In some words *-age* does not originate from Lat. *-aticum* (*-aticus*). *Image* is from Lat. *imago, cartilage* from *cartilago; vintage* is *vindage, vendage* from OF *vendenge* 'gathering of grapes'.

In *saussage* and *cabbage* [dʒ] is from [tʃ], see vol I 6.8 and *Linguistica* 372; there also on the double-forms *skirmish* and *scrimmage* (also *scrummage*), and *rubbish* and *rubbage*.

24.3₇. In early loanwords from F the stress was on the suffix (see e. g. rime and rhythm in Chaucer). On the phonetic development see vol I 2.731-2 and 9.141.

But in two recent loans we have stressed or half-stressed [-aˑʒ]: *camouflage* and *sabotage;* note that both are used also as vbs, see above 6.6.

-th, -eth

24.4. This suffix is used

1) in verbs, to form the third sing. pres. indicative:

see above Ch III.

2) to form ordinals, see $24.4_1\text{-}4_4$.

3) in nexus-substantives, see 24.4_5 ff.

Ordinals

24.4₁. From OE times, more especially towards the
end of the ME period, there has been a tendency towards a levelling of the formal differences between
cardinals and ordinals, the latter being thus more and
more regularly formed by adding *th* to the cardinal.

a) Levelling in the root of the numeral. In OE *n*
was generally dropped before *th* (*þ*, *ð*): Thus as late as
the AR: seoueþe, nieþe, etc.

But in Ch we find *n* on the analogy of the cardinals:
tenthe (e. g. HF 63), and during the whole ModE period
n occurs regularly except in the word *tithe*.

In Sh *tithe* occurs twice as a numeral, though both
cases are doubtful: Alls I. 3.89 and Tro II. 2.19 | AV
Numbers 18.26 a tenth part of the tithe—shows the
ordinary modern usage, *tithe* being the name of a special
tax. The latter meaning already in Ch.

In modern literary language *tithe* = 'tenth part'
may be found, e. g. Lamb E 34 a tythe part | Poe S 35
one tithe of the horror | Kipling L 192 this won't be
a tithe so difficult | Wells Mr Polly 157 a tithe of the
pleasure.

Only one of the old deviations is preserved, viz.
-fth in *fifth* and *twelfth*, the consonant-group causing a
shortening of the vowel in *fifth*, the pronunciation of
which is given by Hart (1569) as [feivþ].

Besides *twelfth* (e. g. Malory 42 on twelfth day) we
find in early ModE *twelfe* in the combinations *twelfe
day* (Sh Tw II. 3.90) and *twelfe night* (thus as the title
of Sh.'s play in the folio; Manningham's diary (1601)
has the spelling *Twelue night*, quoted in Wright's ed.
p. VI). This is simply an elision of the medial consonant
in the group, cf Sh As IV 1.46 the thousand part of a

minute. Similarly *f* is often elided in *twelfth:* [twelþ],
and *d* in e. g. *thousandth* (Gil 71 thouzanth), in earlier
times also in *hundredth* (Gil ib).

24.4₂. b) Levelling in the suffix. In OE an original
þ ordinarily developed into *t* after voiceless fricatives
([f þ s x]), so we have OE *fifta, sixta, twelfta. Fift* and
sixt were the rule as late as the latter part of the 17th
cent., thus in Sh and Mi. Gil (1621) has: *fift, sixt*, but
twelfth, Butler Bees (1634) *fift, sixt*.

As early as Malory we find analogical forms in *th*
(122 fyfthe), but these forms obviously were long in
gaining general currency in speaking, for as late as
1765 Schade laid down the rule that *th* was pronounced
t in *twelfth* and *fifth*.

After *t* an original þ also ordinarily develops into *t*
(merged into the final sound of the stem), thus in *eight*,
common in ME, and still found in Sh, e. g. Mcb IV.
1.119. Hart has [aehtþ], Butler Bees (1634) [eitþ],
Milton (PL 9.67) has the new form *eighth* (which would
be more adequately written *eightth*), but Rehearsal 63
Harry the Eight.

Instead of the expected *-tith* cardinals in *-ty* form
ordinals in *-tieth*. Formerly *-tith* was the only form,
see vol I 9.811. Jones Pron. Dict. sub *twenty* gives only
[-iiþ, -jiþ], but Moore Smith tells me: I don't believe we
say [-iiþ]. I think the first *i* here tends to make *-eth*
rather [-əþ].

24.4₃. The fancy numeral *um(p)teen* may also take
-th, e. g. Galsw WM 229 I can lie to the umteenth
when there's no harm in it. Similarly Meredith (in NED)
in the eighty-somethingth year of his age | the how-
manyeth time | NP 1913 my three-thousand-and-oddth
word. And in mathematical parlance we may, of course,
add the suffix to a letter, e. g. the nth power.

The suffix is further added to regular substantival
numerals: *hundredth, thousandth, millionth*. For 601 the

ordinal in AV Gen 8.13 curiously is *the sixe hundredth and one;* now it is *six hundred and first.*

Dozenth is quoted by the NED from Swift and Cobden. NED also has 1840 Every half-dozenth window,—and *fourscorth* = 'eightieth' from 1571 to 1713.

24.4₄. Ordinals from *third* on may be used as denominators of fractions, either alone, in which case they take *-s* in the plural, or in combination with *part,* as in Greig P 19 a two-thousandth part of them.

The curious form *secondth* with *-th* added to the ordinal corresponding to *two* occurs in Shaw M 8 just the thirty-secondth of an inch too wide open. *Second* could not be used in a fraction (½ = a half), so the author must necessarily add *-th.*

Nexus-Substantives

24.4₅. *-th,* developed from OE *-uþ, -þ,* see Sweet NEG 1599, is used to form nexus-substantives (abstract nouns) from adjs and a few vbs.

The only usual forms that may be termed regular from a ModE point of view are *growth* (from 1557) from *grow, sloth* from *slow* (with a slight orthographical irregularity; the OE form was *slǽwþ,* ME *sleuth*), *tilth* from *till, truth* from *true,* and *warmth* from *warm* (*wealth* from *well*).

There are very few formations from recent centuries: *blowth,* now practically obs. except dial. Lowell says 198 With us a single blossom is a *blow,* while *blowth* means the blossoming in general. A farmer would say that there was a good blowth on his fruit-trees | *coolth* (rare, except dial.), Philips L 174, Kipling Plain Tales 137, K 329, Weseen 322 | *illth* is a coinage of Ruskin's (Ru 2.328) from *ill* on the analogy of *well—wealth,* and in his usage meaning 'ill-being' (Weseen 354 translates it 'illness, sickness, disease'. Is the word used in U. S. in this sense?). The word has been used later by O. Lodge (1886) and Shaw (1889) (NED) |

spilth seems coined by Sh (Tim II. 2.169) and has been revived in the 19th c., though not much used.

Grimth (nonce-word?, Sayers DC 72 Even H. was a little moved from his usual grimth.)—Fowler MEU 650 quotes *greenth*, *gloomth*, and *blueth*, all coined by Horace Walpole.

Youth is hardly now felt as derived from *young*.

24.4₆. Irregularities are caused by

(1) Shortening and subsequent alteration of vowel: *deep—depth*, *wide—width* (a literary formation of the 17th c. (NED: Drayton 1627). Johnson 1755 calls it 'a low word'), *dear—dearth*, *steal—stealth;* *mirth* is hardly now felt as derived from *merry*.

(2) *I*-mutation: *strong—strength, long—length, broad—breadth; whole—health* and *foul—filth* are no longer felt as etymologically belonging together.

24.4₇. (3) Consonant shift: *þ > t*, as in the ordinal suffix (24.4₂), thus *height* from OE *hiehþu*. From the 13th c. we find the form in *-t*, which soon becomes prevalent, though forms in *th* occur sporadically as late as the 19th c., often spelt *highth*, thus always in Milton; Bunyan G 36 quoting Rom. 8.38 has *heighth*, Swift both *heighth* and *height* | Defoe R 2.351 heighth | Di D 808 [Mr. Peggotty] heighth | NED examples from the 19th c. 1809, 1849, 1850.

Joyce Ir 97 quotes *heighth, sighth*, and *drooth* (i. e. *drouth, drought*) as common Ir. forms. *Drouth* is the ordinary Scottish form, but is also used (besides the ordinary Eng. *drought*) by English poets (Tennyson, Browning, Swinburne) see NED.

See further under *-t* 24.5.

-t in Nexus-Substantives

24.5. The suffix *-t* in nexus-sbs is

(1) a variant of the above-mentioned *-th* with the

sound changed as in 24.4₇. Examples: *height* (see above),
theft (OE *þeofþ*), *drought* (from *dry*);

(2) OE *-t*, e. g. *flight* (from *flee* or *fly*), *might* (from
may in the old sense 'have power'), *drift* (from *drive*),
gift (from *give*), *shrift* (from *shrive*), *thrift* (from *thrive*),
thought (from *think*);

(3) in a few cases OF *-te: deceit* (from *deceive*), *receipt*
(from *receive*), *ascent* (from *ascend*), *descent* (from *descend*), *pursuit* (from *pursue*), *conquest* (from *conquer*,
note the different sound).

This is not a living, productive suffix in ModE.

-et, -ette

24.6₁. *-et* [-it] in substantives is from OF *-et* (masc.),
-ete (fem.). Many words in *-et* were borrowed from F
into ME and early ModE, such as *banneret, billet,
bullet, floweret* (refashioned from OF *florete*), *plummet,
pocket, puppet* (ME *poppet*), *riveret, sonnet, tablet, turret,*
etc.—Later loans generally have *-ette*.

In English *-et* has been used as an independent
formative with a diminutive sense from the 16th c.
Examples of derivatives are: *cellaret* (NED from 1806),
freshet (NED 1596; 'stream of fresh water', U. S. 'flood,
inundation', *nugget* (1852; perhaps from dial. *nug* 'lump,
block'), *owlet* (NED 1542), *pearlet* (NED 1847, cf *pearl-
let*), *singlet* (NED 1746; from *single* after the analogy
of *doublet;* Priestley F 267 fellow dressed in a dirty
singlet), *smilet* (Sh Lr IV. 3.21), *squiret* (NED 1838),
and *swimmeret* (NED 1840; 'swimming-foot').

There are also a few adjectives in *-et: dulcet, russet,*
and *violet* (and cf *brunette*), all from French.

24.6₂. *-ette* [-ˈet], substantival suffix, is etymologically
identical with *-et*, see above, and occurs in loans (from
17th c. on) from French, such as *chemisette, cigarette,
maison(n)ette* (NED 1818; Sayers Unn. D. 197 a flat,
or rather maisonette, in a small house which had been
divided to make two establishments), *statuette*, etc.

After 1800 a great many words in -*ette* have been
coined on English soil, e. g., with a diminutive sense,
balconette, blousette (U.S., Weseen 309), *essayette, kitchen-
ette* (common), *leaderette* (Chesterton Flying Inn [T] 93),
sermonette, storyette (Galsw T 83), *trouserette* (Galsw MW
79), *waggonette* (Chesterton B 186).

24.6₃. In recent times the suffix has further been
used as a feminine ending, as in *suffragette* (irreg. from
suffrage sb; used as a vb Wells V 134 her straight hair
was out demonstrating and suffragetting), *typette* 'girl
typist' (NP 1927), *undergraduette* (NED 1920; Plunket
Greene E 112 | Sayers GN 77), *usherette* 'girl usher at
a cinema' (NP 1936, Mencken AL⁴). Cf. vol. VII 5.3₂.

This function of the suffix seems to be especially
popular in U. S. Mencken AL⁴ has *conductorette, farmer-
ette*, and *officerette*, and Weseen a great many words,
e. g. *chauffeurette, devilette, freshette* 'first year college
girl', *lemonette* 'girl regarded as a poor companion'.

24.6₄. Finally, it has been used to form commercial
names of materials, as in *Brusselette* (kind of carpet),
flannelette (Freeman Certain Thorndyke 39), *leatherette*,
etc.

Stockinette (Lawrence L 221 | Rose Macaulay T 30
in a crimson stockinette jersey), also *stockingette* (Galsw
TL 194), according to NED is probably from an earlier
stocking-net.

24.6₅. In some cases we have forms both in -*et* [-it]
(rarely [-'et] in late loans, as in *cellaret*, also *cellarette*,
both [seleˈret]), and -*ette* [-'et] borrowed at different
times and in some cases with different senses, e. g.

    *aglet : aiguilette, banneret : bannerette, basnet, bassinet :
bassinette, pantalet*, -*ette* (irregularly from *pantaloon*).

-ite

24.7₁. -*ite* [-ait], substantival and adjectival suffix,
is from Gk -*ites* through L -*ita*, F -*ite*. It is found in

loanwords from ME times on, to denote '(person)
belonging to, (person) from a certain place, follower
of a teacher or doctrine, etc.', as in (*Anti-*)*Semite*,
Israelite, *Canaanite*, *Jesuite*, etc., and a great many
native formations, such as *Jacobite* (NED 1611) and
the following, all coined after 1800.

(1) from personal and place-names: *Bradlaughite*
(Chesterton), *Browningite* (and *anti-Browningite*, id),
Buchmanite (AHuxley EG 13), (*Henry*) *Georgeite* (Hen-
derson Shaw 107, 154), *Hitlerite* (Sayers GN 64 Hitlerite
Berlin), *Ibsenite* (Chesterton), *Kiplingite* (id), *Main
Streetite* (Lewis MS 242), *Marxite* (Henderson Shaw 164;
rare for *Marxist*), *Nietzscheite* (Chesterton), *Pittite*
(from William Pitt), *Wagnerite* (Shaw, title The Perfect
Wagnerite), *Whistlerite* (Chesterton).

(2) from common names: *beachite* 'person frequent-
ing bathing beaches' (Weseen 306), *cityite* (Weseen 319),
panelite (Bennett ECh 52, i. e. patient 'on the panel'),
pittite 'person occupying seat in pit of theatre' (Gissing
B 62), *ruggerite* (rugger football), *Rule of Thumbite*
(Wells Br 16), *socialite* 'socially prominent person'
(Weseen 399 | NP 1936 and 1938), *suburbanite* (Mannin
CI 72), *summerite* 'summer guest at a hotel' (Lewis
B 285), *turfite* 'person interested in horse-racing' (Caine
C 377), etc.

24.7₂. -*ite* is much used in scientific language to
denote species of minerals, e. g. *anthracite*, *chlorite*,
Epsomite (and others from proper names); names of
fossils, such as *ammonite*, *dendrite*, *lignite*, *trilobite*, etc.,
and certain salts, e. g. *nitrite*, *sulphite*, and some explos-
ives, e. g. *cordite* (native, from *cord*) and *dynamite*
(coined by Alfred Nobel). Further artificial products
such as *ebonite* = *vulcanite*.

Note *Yperite* (from *Ypres* in Belgium), orig. French
military slang for 'mustard gas'.

Another -*ite*, from Latin participles in -*itus*, as in *appetite*,
contrite, *recondite*, has not been productive in English (except

for *drinkitite* 'thirst', a facetious coinage on the analogy of *appetite*, perhaps with allusion to *tight* 'intoxicated').

-itis

24.7₃. *-itis* [-aitis], from Gk *-itis*, denotes certain, esp. inflammatory, diseases, e. g. *appendicitis, arthritis, bronchitis, gastritis, rhachitis, tonsilitis,* etc.

In recent English, especially in U. S., it has been used in facetious formations (mainly nonce-words), such as *walkeritis* (NP 1911), *Kiplingitis, pageantitis* (Rose Macaulay T 246) || Mencken AL 179 *motoritis, golfitis, radioitis, Americanitis,* and in a footnote such forms as *headlinitis, crosswordpuzzleitis, let-George-do-it-itis,* etc. | Weseen at least twenty words of this kind.

The suffix may even be used as an independent word.

-ate

24.8₁. *-ate* (*-at*) [-it] as a substantival suffix is of different origin and function.

1) From L *-ātus,* in nouns of state or office, F. *-at,* ME *-at,* later E *-ate,* except in some recent F loanwords and their analogues. Loanwords are *consulate, episcopate, magistrate, pastorate, pontificate, principate, triumvirate, vicariate* (from Latin), and *noviciate* (from F, also written *novitiate*), *marquisate,* also spelt *marquessate.*

On the analogy of these *-ate* has been used in English to form words like *aldermanate, cardinalate, electorate,* and *emirate* (Lawrence Seven Pillars 49), denoting 'office of—, body of -s'.—From *professor* we have *professorate* and *professoriate.* Fowler MEU s. v. would make an artificial differentiation: *-rate* the office of professor, & *-riate* the body of professors.—*Proletariat* is a late loan from French (NED 1853), which generally preserves the F spelling in *-at.* As a counterpart of this word we have *salariat* (from F; Keynes in NP 34 the salaried class [has come] into power. Not yet a

Proletariat. But a Salariat, assuredly) and *proprietariat*
(Shaw IW 223).

-ate

24.8₂. *-ate* [-eit] as a verb-forming suffix, from the
Latin participial ending *-atus*, cf above 4.2 *-ed* in vbs,
had developed its function as an ordinary verbal ending about 1300. From the 15th c. it has been used as an
independent formative, though practically to form vbs
from foreign (L and F) roots only. The list of analogical
formations in Ole Reuter's paper (in Soc. Scient. Fennica.
Comm. Hum. Litt. VI) p. 146 ff. includes about 500
vbs; more than half, however, are now obsolete.

Some of these are formed from L forms not otherwise
occurring in E, such as *exculpate, granulate, rejuvenate,
tintinnabulate,* etc.

A few are from Greek elements, e. g. *dehydrate,
diagnosticate,* and many are from F: (a)*meliorate, decapi-
tate, facilitate, orientate, tolerate,* etc.

Many are formed from E words of L origin, such as
activate, capacitate, exteriorate, formulate, hyphenate
(note the Am. phrases *hyphenated Americans* about
immigrated Americans, as in *Irish-Americans*), *mission-
ate* (U. S.), *opinionate, orchestrate, sensate, tambourinate*
(Mackenzie S 1.47), *vaccinate.*

Many verbs in *-ate* are back-formations, generally
from sbs in *-ation, -ator,* e. g. *aviate, cavitate, commentate,
demarcate, gradate, legislate, negate* (Beswick OD 22),
obligate (U.S., Dreiser AT 1.186), *orate* (Kipling P 176 the
little green man orated like Cicero; common i U.S.;
direct from L in NED 1600) *profiterate* (NED 1873; Wells
457), *reparate, sanitate, spectate,* and *valuate.*

Finally the suffix is used in some facetious slangy
formations, many of which are portmanteau words
formed from Latin elements. Reuter p. 143 enumerates
some twenty such words, among them *absquatulate*
'decamp' (L. *ab-* + ?), *bibulate* 'drink', *confusticate*

(from *fusty*), *flustrate* (*fluster*), *gallivate* (*gallivant?*), *quituate* ('leave college before graduating'), *smothercate*, *stuffocate* (*stuffy* + *suffocate*), *tit(t)ivate* (*tidy* + *cultivate?* common).

A great many such formations also occur in Weseen, many of them given in the participle only: *atticquated* 'outmoded' (*attic* + *antiquated*), *busticate* 'break, go bankrupt' (from *bust* = *burst*), *frolicate*, *infanticipate* 'anticipate the coming of an infant', *obfusticated* and (*s*)*pifflicated* (fanciful) 'intoxicated'.

-ty

24.9₁. The various forms *-ity*, *-ety*, *-ty* [-iti, -ti] ultimately originate from L *-tatem*, with or without a preceding *i* or *e*.

The original sense of the suffix was that of state or condition, and derivatives were, and still are, formed from sbs, adjs (even comparatives, e. g. *inferiority*, *majority*), and in a few cases from pronouns as in *quiddity* (scholastic Lat.), *quoddity*, and the recent *egoity*, *ipseity* (Logan Pearsall Smith).

24.9₂. In French there was a double development: (1) *-itat(em)* > *-ité*, which in ME became *-ite(e)*, ModE *-ity*, which is now practically the only active form; (2) popular F *-eté*, *-té* (*-tet*), thus OF *sauveté* > E *safety*, OF *bontet* > E *bounty*, and OF *plentet* > E *plenty*. The latter development gave rise to an ending *-ty*, and with that there was a possibility of development of such double forms as *personalty* : *personality*, *specialty* : *speciality*, *squirealty* ('all the squires', Ru P 1.293) : *squireality* (Sterne M 1.44).

But otherwise *-ty* occurs only in F loanwords.

24.9₃. F adoptions occur already in Early ME, thus AR has *autorite* and *cherte* 'charity' and others, *enmity* appears about 1300. Chaucer has a good number of words in *-itee*, e. g. *auctoritee*, *curiositee*, *dignitee*, *diversitee*, *superfluitee*, *universitee*, etc. But during the Late

ME and ModE periods many new formations arise on E soil, especially in the later period.

Among formations from the last two centuries may be mentioned:

accountability, biblicality (Carlyle), *catholicity, comicality* (Di F 902), *conviviality, eventuality, excitability, gloriosity* (Locke CA 155), *historicity* (Bennett T 277), *identity, motority* (on shop sign 1906), *omnivoracity* (Locke CA 229), *quizzicality, sentimentality, totality.*

The ending is practically confined to form derivatives from words of F and L origin. NED gives a list of adjectival suffixes which particularly often take *-ity*, among them *-al-*, *-ar-*, and *-bil-* (*-abil-*, *-ibil-*). The ending *-bility* (*-ability*, *-ibility*) has become so frequent as to attain almost to the rank of an independent suffix.

Formations from native roots are not very frequent, and seem to have been coined from about 1700 only, thus *oddity* (Steele NED), *betweenity* (NED 1760, Mitford OV 49), *fairity* (Shaw A 134 vg). NED further gives such playful forms as *coxcombity, cuppeity, threadbarity, womanity* (after *humanity*), etc.

Semantically *-ity* is the Romanic (L) counterpart of *-ness*, i. e. it generally denotes state or condition. On its use as compared with *-ness*, see Fowler (MEU s. v. *-ty* & *-ness*), who writes i. a.: "Of the *-ty* words that exist, a very large majority are for all purposes commoner and better than the corresponding *-ness* words, usage and not anti-Latinism being the right arbiter."

24.9₄. Often a more Latin(ized) derivative form corresponds to a radical in originally F form:

double : duplicity, noble : nobility, simple : simplicity, sober : sobriety.

24.9₅. All words in *-ity* (*-ety*) are now stressed on the third last syllable, cf vol I 5.61 and 5.63, and this generally causes an alteration in stress between radical and derivative, and at the same time a more or less marked difference in the quality of the vowels, e. g.

Christian ['kristʃən] : *Christianity* [kristi'æniti] | *equal*
['i·kwəl] : *equality* [i(·)'kwɔliti] | *equanimous* [i(·)'kwæni-
məs] : *equanimity* [i·kwə'nimiti] | *national* ['næʃənəl] :
nationality [næʃə'næliti] | *superior* [sju(·)'piəriə] : *super-
iority* [sju(·)piəri'ɔriti], etc.

Shift of vowel also occurs in such trisyllabic words
as *chaste* [tʃeist] : *chastity* [tʃæstiti] and *sane* [sein] :
sanity [sæniti].

24.9₆. In derivatives from words in *-(i)ous* this suffix
is dropped before *-ity* (*-ety*) is added (and there is vocalic
change):

atrocious : *atrocity* | *audacious* : *audacity* | *congruous* :
congruity | *conspicuous* : *conspicuity* | *dubious* : *dubiety* |
notorious : *notoriety* | *pious* : *piety* | *precocious* : *precocity* |
superfluous : *superfluity* | *various* : *variety*.

Various other differences from words in *-ity* (*-ety*)
and the corresponding adjectives or substantives may
occur, thus *hospitality* corresponds to *hospitable*, *enmity*
to *enemy*, *speciality* [speʃi'æliti] (with the first *i* pronounced) to *special* ['speʃəl]. *Nicety* from OF *niceté*
(NED) is now pronounced as if derived from *nice* +
-ity. *Ingenuity* is used as nexus-word from *ingenious*,
and has lost its semantic connexion with *ingenuous*.
Laity [leiiti] from *lay* [lei] is pronounced as if two
syllables were added. *Benign* [bi'nain] but *benignity*
[bi'nigniti].

From *proper* there are two derivatives: *property* (F
type), and *propriety* (L type).

From *mayor* the derivative *mayoralty* is formed, to
sheriff corresponds *shrievalty*, derived from the obs.
form *shrieve*.

24.9₇. Adjs in *-ic(al)* form sbs in *icity* [-'isiti] and
-icality [-i'kæliti], e. g. *atomicity,, domesticity, technical-
ity, theatricality* (Carlyle H 43), and agent nouns in
-ician [-'iʃən], e. g. *geometrician, rhetorician.*

-tude.

24.9₈. The suffix *-tude* for nexus-sbs is ultimately from L *-tudinem* through F *-tude*. Most of the words are loans, e. g. *altitude, amplitude, attitude, exactitude, longitude, magnitude, solitude, torpitude,* many of them of a decidedly learned character. Some are perhaps coined on E soil, such as *finitude* (from *finite,* from 1644), and *infinitude* (Milton 1641; Carlyle H 120); a word not in NED is *correctitude* (Housman J 24; after the usual *rectitude*).

Chapter XXV.

Final Batch of Suffixes.

-fy.

25.1₁. *-fy* [-fai], verbal suffix, is from F *-fier,* from L *-ficare,* which in MedL sometimes also represents Classical L *-facere,* as in *liquefy* from *liquefacere.* In both cases the suffix has the meaning 'make' or 'make into'. In words from orig. *-ficare* we have always *i* before the suffix, thus in the following early loanwords: *certify, clarify, deify, glorify, justify, pacify, purify, sanctify, signify,* and *testify;* whereas in words from *-facere* we may have the vowel *e,* though the real sound may be the same, before *-fy,* as in *putrefy, rubefy, stupefy* (formerly also *stupify,* perhaps with allusion to *stupid,* thus Thack V 309); *satisfy* falls outside this rule.

A few loanwords are coined in French, thus *codify* (NED 1800), *mystify* (NED 1814; Fitzedward Hall M 129 quotes Southey 1816: a word which seems now to be naturalized), *personify* and *solidify* (NED 1799).

A good number of verbs in *-fy* have been coined on English soil, thus from L (Gk) roots *electrify, intensify, objectify* (London M 23), and *typify.*

25.1₂. Most of the following E coinages have a colloquial, often a facetious, character. It is preferably words in [i] that take the ending, and in the small number of words coined from monosyllables an *i* is inserted before the suffix. Examples:

argufy (very colloquial; Bennett, Shaw, etc.) | *beautify* | *cockneyfy* (esp. in the second ptc; earliest example Byron L 26.4.1821 | Galsw MW 168) | *countrify* (ptc: Galsw IC 4) | *dandify* | *divorcified* (jocular pun on *diversified*, Weseen 328) | *foozlified* 'intoxicated' (sailor's slang, Brynildsen) | *Frenchify* (Galsw, Chesterton) | *funkify* (Brynildsen) | *happify* (NED from 1612, "Now unusual"; but according to Mencken it is used in U. S.) | *ladyfy* or *ladify* (Eastw 479) | *nazify* (Weseen 370) | *negrofy* (Franklin 159) | *preachify* (on the analogy of *speechify*, though there is no subst. *preach;* Thack V 71) | *speechify* | *stiltify* (Byron L 217) | *Sundayfied* (Wells, Locke) | *talkify* (jocularly after *speechify*, Weseen 408) | *tipsify* (Thack V 4, Stevenson B 197) | *Toryfy* or *Torify* (first quotation in NED 1763: the whiggified Tories, the torified Whigs) | *townify* (Fowler below) | *uglify* | *whiskify* (Thack P 56) | *yankeefy* (Fowler below) | *youthify* (Am.) 'make young'.

"The spelling of the jocular compounds in which a verb in *-fy* hardly exists is unsettled (*countrified* or *countryfied* &c.). It seems best to use *-i-* when the noun or adjective does not provide a convenient connecting syllable, but when it does, not to alter it; so *cockneyfied*, *countryfied*, *dandyfied*, *Frenchified*, *ladyfied*, *townified*, *yankeefied*." (Fowler MEU 179).

The following seem to be nonce-words:

citified (Churchill C 34) | *clothified* (Fielding 5.434; only quot. in NED) | *funnified* (Mackenzie C 172) | *once-upon-a-timeyfied* (Jerome) | *Shelleyfy* (Wells V 327) | *Swiftify* and *Popify* (Byron Correspondence 1.49).

In accordance with their origin words in *-fy* are generally transitive, but some of them may be used intransitively, too, cf vol III 16.5₄, thus e. g. *intensify*

(Rogers Wine of Fury 187), *liquefy, mollify* (Butler Er), *putrefy, solidify,* and *vivify* (Southey L 57).

On stress see vol I 5.63.

-fication.

25.1₃. *-fication* [-fiˈkeiʃən], substantival suffix, is from F *-fication,* L *-ficationem,* in action-nouns from the vbs in *-ficare.* It sometimes represents *-faction,* which is the correct form in words derived from orig. *-facere,* cf *-fy.*

Loanwords are *clarification, edification, justification, mystification, pacification, purification, signification, simplification,* and *versification.*

Many words have been coined on English soil, even from native roots. Examples: *beautification, dandification, electrification, intensification, minification* (Mackenzie PR 47), *nazification, personification, prettification* (Prokosch A 62), *speechification, typification, uglification* (Shelley 442).

It is worth noting that *-fication* is an independent formative which need not necessarily be based on a word in *-fy.* Thus *jollification* (NED 1798) is recorded earlier than *jollify* (NED 1824), and Wells Cl 691 has "slumification", but there does not seem to be any corresponding vb. According to NED several scientific terms are derived with *-fication* without any corresponding vb.

Cf *-tion* 21.7.

-ive.

25.2₁. *-ive* [-iv], adjectival suffix, is from F *-if,* fem. *-ive,* from L *-ivus, -iva, (-ivum).* In Latin the suffix was added to participial stems, as in *act-ivus, pass-ivus, demonstrat-ivus,* etc., which in French developed into *actif* m., *active* fem., etc. In ME many words were taken from French in the masc. form, see e. g. Ch HF 847 *conservatif* | ib 146 *fugitif,* etc., but later these were readjusted to *-ive* on the pattern of L and through

the voicing of spirants in weak position, vol I 6.52 and
Linguistica, p. 358. (Exceptions are poet. and archaic
caitiff 'base, coward(ly)', etym. = *captive*, and *plaintiff*,
etym. = *plaintive*.)

On *-if* > *-y* (as in *jollif* > *jolly*) see 13.3₈ and vol
I 2.534.

A great many of these words end in *-ative*, 25.2₄.
Words borrowed from F and L (often through F)
are *attentive, deceptive* (Swinnerton S 271 she found
her unmanageable. Polly was deceptive. Not deceitful,
but deceptive. She seemed a child to be easily moulded.
She was, in fact, stubborn), *definitive, elective, furtive,
inventive, native, pensive, progressive, sensitive*, and
votive. Many of these have no connexion with other
E words.

25.2₂. Words coined in E from L stems are *aggressive,
allusive, assertive, competitive, conductive* (used in physics; cf *conducive*), *consumptive, elusive, impressive,
preventive* (cf *preventative*), *selective* (Wells Time Machine
50 selective breeding), and *submissive*.

Some adjs in *-ive* are derived directly from the base
of vbs, especially those ending in *-s* and *-t*, thus resembling L participles), e. g.

accusive 'accusatory, self-accusing' (OHenry C 16 and
104; not in NED), *adoptive, appointive* (Archer A 116
many offices which had been elective were made appointive), *caressive, connective* (cf obs. or rare *connexive*),
contrastive (Maxwell EG), *influencive* (Coleridge B 46),
purposive (NED 1855), *restive* and *secretive* [ˈsiˈkritiv]
or [siˈkriˈtiv].

As in L a few words are derived from sbs, e. g. *massive*.
Many words are used as substantives, e. g. *adjective,
substantive, expletive, locomotive*.

This suffix practically occurs in words of L origin
only, or in words formed from Latin roots. Note, however, Am. *stick-to-it-ivenes* (Edison in NP 1911 Genius
is hard work, stick-to-itiveness, and common-sense |

Lewis MS 199 | Weseen 403 also has *Stick-at-ive-ness*
and *Sticktivity*).

Costive does not belong here; it is from OF *costivé*, from
L *constipatus*.

The meaning of the suffix is 'tending to—, having
the character or quality of—, given to—'. *Restive*
'stubborn' is often, as it were, in meaning a derivative
of *resist*.

25.2₃. In many cases there is a difference between
the adj and the corresponding vb, either because the
latter has been adopted through French, or because
the two words have been derived from different verbal
stems, or both, e. g.

allude [ə'ljuˑd] : *allusive* [ə'ljuˑsiv] | *compete* [kəm'piˑt] :
competitive [kəm'petitiv] | *comprehend* [kɔmpri'hend] :
comprehensive [kɔmpri'hensiv] | *compel* [kəm'pel] :
compulsive [kəm'pʌlsiv] | *deceive* [di'siˑv] : *deceptive*
[di'septiv] | *decide* [di'said] : *decisive* [di'saisiv] | *permit*
[pə'mit] : *permissive* [pə'misiv] | *produce* [prə'djuˑs] :
productive [prə'dʌktiv] | *receive* [ri'siˑv] : *receptive*
[ri'septiv] | *restrain* [ri'strein] : *restrictive* [ri'striktiv] |
subvert [səb'vəˑt] : *subversive* [səb'vəˑsiv].

Note *attend* [ə'tend] : *attentive* [ə'tentiv], *retain*
[ri tein] : *retentive* [ri'tentiv].

On stress see further vol I 5.65.

From some adjs in *-ive* we have some nexus-words
in *-ivity* (*sensitivity*), others have only *-iveness*.

-ative.

25.2₄. *-ative* [-ətiv], is from F *-atif*, fem. *-ative*, L
-ativus, etc., i. e. the suffix *-ivus* (see *-ive*) appended
to *-at-*, participial stem of verbs in *-are*. In L only a
limited number of such adjs existed, but in F and E
a good number have been coined, in English especially
from verbs in *-ate*.

Words borrowed from L are *accusative* (sb in gram-

mar; now rare in the adjectival use 'accusatory'),
affirmative, contemplative, demonstrative, derivative, imaginative, relative, and *significative.*

English coinages are *opinionative* (Swift 3.266 and
271) and *preventative* (Ridge G 181, cf *preventive*).

On the analogy of pairs of the type *imagine : imaginative* was coined the word *talkative*, which again leads
to *speakative* (Am., Weseen 400) and *writative* (Pope
Letter, quot. Bladin 18: Increase of years makes one
more talkative, but less writative). Cf also Wilkins:
unwalkative cripple.

A few words in *-ative* have been coined directly from
substantives in *-ty* with no corresponding verbs in
-ate, e. g. *authoritative, qualitative, quantitative.*

Many words in *-ative* are chiefly used as sbs, e. g.
derivative, indicative, and other grammatical terms.

-some

25.2₅. *-some* [-səm], OE *-sum,* related to German
and Sw. *-sam,* Da. *-som,* and meaning 'like, having the
quality of'. It is used to form adjs from sbs and adjs,
(rarely) from vbs.

The suffix has been productive during all periods,
though comparatively little used. Few OE words
have survived into ModE, *longsome, lovesome* (Morris
E 121 her sweet lovesome lord), *winsome* (OE *wyn*
'joy'), all more or less archaic.

From the ME period we have *fulsome, wholesome*
(13th c.), *gamesome, gladsome* (Spenser, Gray, etc.),
loathsome, and *noisome* (from obs. *noy* < *annoy* sb;
Sh Cymb I. 5.26 noysome; those four from the 14th c.),
handsome (orig. 'easy to handle'), *irksome,* and *wearisome* (15th c.).

From the modern period we have *awesome, burdensome* (*burthensome*), *darksome* (Spenser), *heartsome* (chiefly Sc.), *quarrelsome* (Sh three times), *tiresome, toilsome,*
and *troublesome* (all from the 16th c.), *gaysome* (Ford;

now rare), *furthersome* (NED: 17th c., revived by Carlyle, e. g. FR 83), *humoursome, lonesome,* and *venture-
some* (from 17th c.), *fearsome* (18th c.; now frequent),
and finally *bothersome* (AHuxley) and *shuddersome*
(Locke; both from the 19th c.).—Nonce-words: *chuckle-
some* (NP 1934) and *jumpsome* (Kipling Just So Stories
40), see also NED: *-some.*

The word to which the suffix is added is generally
unaltered, but *lissom* is contracted from *lithesome.* In
the case of *noisome* and *winsome* the roots are now
obsolete.

Fulsome is sometimes pronounced [fʌlsəm] instead
of [fulsəm].

25.2₆. In connexion with a numeral *-some* represents
OE *sum* 'some' as used after a numeral in the gen. pl, e. g.
Beowulf 207 fiftēna sum 'as one of fifteen'. The modern
expressions *twosome* (Sc.), *foursome* are especially used
for a game for two, etc.

-fold

25.2₇. The adjectival suffix *-fold* [-fould], is an old
Gothonic ending, ME *-fald, -fold,* OE *-feald,* HG *-falt,*
ON *-faldr,* Goth. *-falþs,* and is cognate with the vb
fold. It is added to numerals (as in *two-fold, three-fold,
ten-fold, thousand-fold*) and *many* (*manifold;* also occasionally to other adjs denoting an indefinite number)
with a sense of 'multiplied or folded by—, plaited by—
strands' (*a three-fold cord*), often used vaguely, as in
I shall repay you a thousand-fold. (Note the substantival
use).

Derivatives in *-fold* now practically belong to educated speech only, and have largely been supplanted
by orig. Latin words in *-ble, -ple,* as *double, treble,
quadruple,* etc.

-proof

25.2₈. The suffix *-proof* [-pruˑf], from the adj *proof,*
is used to form words meaning 'impenetrable by the

thing denoted by the first component'. Several of these
formations are more or less established forms, e. g.
bomb-proof, *bullet-proof*, *burglar-proof* (Sayers), *fire-
proof*, *fool-proof* (Shaw in NP 1914), *kissproof* (about
rouge), *rain-proof*, *sound-proof*, *water-proof*, and *weather-
proof*.

Nonce-formations with *-proof* are pretty frequent,
see NED

-ety

25.2₉. *-ety*, *-ity* [-iti] occurs in a few popular American
adjectives as a by-form of adjectival *-y*, and has probably arisen from metanalysis of words in which *-et-*
belongs to the root, such as *rickety*, *snippety*, cf *per-
nickety* of unknown origin. Examples: *blankety*, eufem-
istic for 'bloody', from *blank* (Mencken AL⁴ 316),
uppity 'fashionable, haughty' from *up*, and some from
Weseen, Dict. of Am. Slang, 308 *biggety* 'proud, vain',
itchety 'uneasy', *scratchety* 'inclined to scratch',. and
topplety 'top heavy, likely to topple'.

-hood, -head

25.3₁. The suffix *-hood* [-hud], *-head* [-hed], ME
-hod(e), *-hood(e)* < OE *-hād* parallel to OSax. *-hêd*,
OHG *-heit*. Originally OE *hād* was a distinct sb, meaning
'state or condition or dignity', but it has now become
a mere suffix. On the development of the vowel see
vol I 3.522, 4.42, and 11.67.

-hood is added primarily to names of persons in their
relations to (1) family, (2) age, (3) married state, and
(4) less frequently, social position:

(1) *brotherhood, fatherhood, motherhood, parenthood*, and
sisterhood (Sh R2 I. 2.9 brotherhood). *Brotherhood* and
sisterhood besides their primary sense may also be
collectives for associations for a certain purpose, cf
also in a transferred sense: Sherwood Anderson Windy

McPherson's Son 315 the scarlet sisterhood, ib 112 the red sisterhood.

(2) *babyhood* (Browning 2.307, Galsw TL 47), *boyhood* (common), *cubhood* 'boyhood' (nonce-word, Jerome), *girlhood* (id), *Hebehood* 'youth' (nonce-word, id), *hobbledehoyhood* (Fowler MEU 427), *womanhood* (Sherwood Anderson Winesburg Ohio 213 she emerged from girlhood into womanhood), *youthhood* (Carlyle E 212, id FR 255).

(3) *bachelorhood, spinsterhood, widowhood, wifehood* (Tennyson 6).

(4) *priesthood* (Carlyle E 208), *waitresshood* (Hemingway).

Outside these groups -*hood* occurs in a few noncewords: Dickinson S (1915) 154 In universal *Anthood* there are no ants | Carlyle E 187 a kind of *beast-godhood* | NP 1912 *nationhood*.

Few derivations from adjs have survived: *falsehood, likelihood, hardihood*.

25.3₂. -*head*, by-form of -*hood*, on its origin see NED. The earliest forms recorded are derived from adjs, such as *boldhede, falshede*, but the suffix was soon applied to sbs as well. In the ModE period -*hood* got the upper hand (More U 275 *falshed* in second ed. (p. 147) altered to *falshod*), and the only surviving forms are *godhead* 'divine nature, deity' as distinct from *godhood* 'state of being a god', and *maidenhead* 'virginity', as distinct from *maidenhood* 'maiden age'.

The few surviving derivatives from adjs have all -*hood*. Tennyson's *lowlihead* (p. 6) is an archaism.

-ship

25.3₃. OE -*scipe* is a development of Old Gothonic *skapi-z from **skap-* 'create', and is parallel to Dan. -*skab*, Sw. -*skap* and German -*schaft*.

The form -*ship* [-ʃip] is added to adjs and second participles to denote state or condition. This type was common in OE and ME, but the only survivals now in common use are *hardship* and *worship* (from OE *weorþscipe*, properly 'worth-ship'). Shaw has coined the form *softship* as an antonym of *hardship* (D 171).

The commonest living formations with *-ship* are from names of persons, e. g.

acquaintanceship | *authorship* (Carlyle E 234) | *church-manship* (NP 1907) | *citizenship* | *goodfellowship* (Sherwood Anderson) | *friendship* | *generalship* (in a figurative sense, Kipling S 99) | *guardianship* (Galsw MP 122) | *membership* (1) 'the state of being a member' (2) 'all the members'.

As a subdivision of this group may be mentioned words denoting dignity, etc., e. g.

attaché-ship (Kipling Many Inventions 24) | *Attorney-Generalship* (Macaulay 3.52) | *Deanship* (Galsw MW 144) | *head-mistress-ship* | *judgeship* | *kingship* (rare, Carlyle FR 6) | *prefectship* (Kipling S 139) | *secretary-ship* (Jackson S 106).

"In the case of *fellowship, scholarship, postmaster-ship* and the like, the compound has come to denote not only the office or position itself but the emoluments, etc., pertaining to it." (NED).

Another subdivision are the honorific designations *ladyship, lordship*, and *worship* with preposed possessive pronoun, and on the analogy of these, mock titles may be formed, as in *His Jewship* used by D. L. Lawrence to designate a certain publisher (Letter of 22.8.1912). Thus also Ford 211 One word with your old *bawdship*.

Such titles are rarely used in the plural, as in Caine C 151 their three ladyships ..., or with an adj between pron. and sb as ib her stout ladyship.

Formerly *-ship* might also be added to names of inanimate things, but only two words of this type are still in common use, *courtship* (first in Sh), and *township* (from OE).

Finally a few nonce-words: Scott A 1.248 her youthful arts of *sempstress-ship* | Southey L 336 [a cat's] *tomship* | Carlyle E 182 His devout *Discipleship* seemed nothing more than a mean *Spanielship* | ib 223 *Mœcenasship* | Ruskin F 51 *sonship* | id 1.236 *dogship*.

-scape

25.3₄. The form *-scape* was originally found in one word only, *landscape,* which on account of the sound [sk] cannot be a direct continuation of OE *landsceap.* It was introduced as a technical term of painting from Dutch *landschap* ab. 1600. From this word the suffix has in modern times, especially in painters' and art reviewers' language, been transferred to names of other kinds of scenery, thus *cloudscape* (Wells PF 20) | *earth-scape* (used by aviators) | *house-scape* (Chesterton Di 161) | *machinery-scape* (Bentley T 58) | *mindscape* ('mental view'; Weseen 367) | *moonscape* (Morley) | *parkscape* (OHenry B 51) | *roadscape* (Weseen 387) | *seascape* (Bennett, Chesterton) | *skyscape* (Galsw WM 171) | *waterscape* (Brynildsen).

-dom

25.3₅. *-dom* [-dəm], from OE *-dōm,* parallel to German *-tum.* This was originally an independent word, denoting setting, statute, judgment. In OE the suffix was added to sbs and adjs, as in *biscopdōm, freodōm, wīsdōm,* and it has been freely used during the later periods to form words denoting 'state, dignity or sphere', or a collective body.

The following words all belong to ModStE:

bachelordom (Shaw A 192 *old-bachelordom*) | *boredom* | *Christendom* (collective) | *dukedom* 'dignity or territory of a duke' | *officialdom* 'body of officials', (in unfavourable sense) 'red-tapism' (Wells A 253, Galsw Sw 6) | *puzzledom* (Locke BV 201) | *swelldom* (Thack N 521) |

thralldom | *topsy-turvydom* 'confusion' (Chesterton) | *villadom* (Wells A 58, etc.).

25.3₆. The suffix lends itself very freely to the formation of nonce-words as in the following (*filmdom* and *stardom* may, however, be on the threshold of being accepted into StE):

bourgeoisdom (Carpenter LC 44) | *butlerdom* (Galsw FCh 105) | *Christmasdom* (Walpole OL 111 no other tree in all C.) | *demirepdom* (Carlyle F 3; *-dom* is a favourite suffix of Carlyle's) | *draperdom* (Gissing B 137) | *fagdom* (Kipling S 224) | *filmdom* (NP 1934) | *Forsytedom* (Galsw MP 196) | *Grocerdom and Grazierdom* (Carlyle E 149) | *motordom* (Locke W 84) | *newspaperdom* (Sims) | *noodledom* (Browning) | *parsondom* (Huxley L 1.212) | *ruffiandom* (Gissing B 201) | *snobdom* (Russell Soc Reconstr 115) | *stardom* (NP 1936) | *Tsardom* (Macdonell E 79).

-kin

25.4₁. The suffix *-kin* [-kin] originates from Flemish and Dutch forms like *-kijn*, *-ken*, cognate with G. *-chen*. It is first recorded in E about 1300 in personal (pet) names such as *Janekin*, *Watekin*, and *Wilekin*, and in the 14th c. such names were rather popular, but about 1400 they seem to have mostly passed out of use as Christian names. Many of them, however, are still used in surnames, either with the addition of *-son*, as *Dickinson*, *Wilkinson*, or in the elliptical genitive forms in *-s*, *Jenkins*, *Dickens*, *Wilkins*, etc.

Very few common names in *-kin* appear before 1400, and on the whole the suffix has not been very much used in England. A good number obviously have come from Dutch, e. g. *cannikin*, *catkin*, *firkin*, *kilderkin*, *manikin*, and *minikin*. *Pumpkin* and *tamkin* are from earlier *pumpion* and *tampion*, and a few forms are known from oaths, such as *bodykin*, *lakin* (for *ladykin*), and *pittikin*. *Lambkin* is "the only one which has obtained real currency" (from 1579; NED), but many words are of more or less obscure origin, e. g. *bumpkin, griskin, jerkin,* and *pipkin.*

The suffix was a great favourite with Carlyle, no doubt under the influence of German (*-chen*). Schmeding quotes 34 words from him, and "we can, at least in jocular speech, add *-kin* to almost any noun to form a diminutive" (Bradley M 138).

-ock

25.4₂. The suffix *-ock* [-ək] is from OE *-uc.* It was originally a diminutive ending, as still in *bittock* (dial.) 'little bit' and *hillock,* but in other words this sense has been lost, e. g. in *bullock, buttock,* and *mullock.* The ending is no longer a living one in StE, but is pretty frequent in Northern dialects (Scotch), see Hewitt Key in Trans. of Philol. Soc. 1856 p. 223 ff.

-ton

25.4₃. The suffix *-ton* [-t(ə)n] for persons (especially foolish) I take to originate from place-names used as surnames, such as *Middleton, Milton, Newton,* etc., in the same way as *Rudesby* and other town-names (Sh) have been used as nicknames, cf *Cunningham* in Grose.

Examples are *simpleton* (often in Swift J), with its variant *sinkerton* (ib 437), *idleton, pinkerton* (dial.), *singleton* (NED from 1876, but Defoe has Captain Singleton 1720), *skimmington, boozington* (Australia), see more at length *Linguistica* 417-18. Cf also *Grumbletonian* = grumbler: there is hardly a town Grumbleton in existence.

-cide

25.5₁. *-(i)cide* [-(i)said], substantival suffix, is used partly in agent-nouns from F *-cide,* L *-cida,* partly in nexus-sbs, from F *-cide,* L *-cidium.* Loanwords are *homicide, parricide, matricide, fratricide, suicide,* etc.

On the analogy of these has been coined *liberticide*
[li'bə'tisaid] (Shelley 524), as well as a few jocular
forms like *canicide*, and *girlicide*.

-archy

25.5₂. *-archy* [-a·ki], substantival suffix, from Gk
-arkhia 'rule', as in *hierarchy*, *monarchy*, etc. An English
derivative is *squirearchy*.

Chapter XXVI

Prefixes

Negative and Related Prefixes

26.1. English has three important negative prefixes,
un-, *in-* with its variants according to the following
sound, *il-*, *im-*, and *ir-*, and *an-* or *a-*. All these, the
first native, the second from Latin (often through
French), and the third Greek, go back to the same
Aryan (Indo-Eoropean) form *ən-*, related to the negative adverb *ne*.

All three forms are also used as prefixes with a different value, *un-* as privative (see 26.4), *in-* from the preposition (see 27.4) and *a-* as a native prefix (see 27.3).

Negative *un-*

26.1₁. Negative *un-* has in all periods been attached
to innumerable words.

With regard to stress the general principle of value-
stressing and the strong negative force of the prefix *un-*,
which is usually felt as an independent semantic unit,
lead in most cases to even stress on the two elements
of the word. Thus when the word following *un-* begins
with a strong stress: *'un'just*, *'un'truthful*, *'un'musical*,
'un'aided, *'un'cultured*, *'un'erring*, *'un'licensed*, etc.

Even stress is also the rule when the word begins

with a weak syllable before a strong one: ˈunaˈbashed, ˈunconˈtested, ˈunimˈportant, ˈunproˈductive, ˈunreˈpentant. Here, however, un may sometimes take secondary stress: ˌunaˈdulterated, ˌundeˈfinable. If the word has secondary stress on the second syllable, un has full stress: ˈunconˌventioˈnality, ˈundeˌnomiˈnational, ˈuninˌtelligiˈbility. Thus also with words that have secondary stress on the first and full stress on a later syllable: ˈunˌcompliˈmentary, ˈunˌsentiˈmental, ˈunˌsympaˈthetic.

Exceptional weak stress is found in some of the most common words, unˈcommon, unˈusual, unˈhappy, unˈfortunate, unˈkind, unˈnatural, unˈnecessary, unˈpleasant, unˈfeigned, unˈstinted, unˈutterable. Further in those words in which un- is added to a word which is not used in itself or not used in that sense: unˈcanny, unˈgainly, unˈwieldy, unˈmeaning, unˈprincipled, unˈdoubted (doubted not being used as an adjunct); unacˈcountably (though the adj is ˈunacˈcountable).

These rules are based on the transcriptions in D. Jones's Pron. Dictionary, cf the same author's Engl. Phonetics, p. 230 f. The indications in Wyld's Universal Dict. deviate on some points. As with sentence stress generally, much depends on individual fancy for the moment. Thus in contrasts, ˈhappy, not ˈunˈhappy; not quite ˈunˈnecessary, etc.

26.1₂. It is important to note that the proper sphere of this prefix is with adjs and advbs. It is found frequently with sbs, but practically only such as are derived from adjs, e. g. unkindness, untruth, unwisdom. *Unemployment*, which came up in the 1860's, really stands for **unemployedment*. It means of course the state of things when people cannot find work. Cf also the rare *unproportion*, from *proportionate* (Kinglake E 178 the wide unproportion between his slender company, and the boundless plain of sand). *Unfriend* (frequent in Sc.) also smacks of *friendly;* it is found in Kipling K 202 and Hewlett Q 30. *Unsuccess* (Saintsbury) re-

Not OE rule

minds one of *unsuccessful*. *Unthinker* (Carlyle FR 107
Thinkers and unthinkers) is a nonce-word.

Un- is not used with vbs (cf privative *un-* 26.4)
except with the adjectival participles: *unabridged, un-
finished; undying, unwilling*, etc.

Not all adjs admit of having this prefix, and it is
not always easy to assign a reason why one adj can
take the prefix and another cannot. Still, the same
general rule obtains in English as in other languages,
that most adjs with *un-* have a depreciatory sense: we
have *undue, unkind, unworthy*, etc., but it is not possible
to form similar adjectives from *foolish, naughty, ugly*,
or *wicked*.

Nor is it felt as natural to negative adjs denoting
large size; *un-* is never prefixed to words like *great,
large, huge*, and *vast*. A formation like *untremendous*
(Keats) is exceptional.

Un- may be prefixed to participial groups: *uncalled-
for, uncared-for, unwished-for, undreamed-of, unheard-of,
unthought-of, unspoken to* (Trollope W 80), etc.

To the same category may be referred Bennett W
2.235 that the time was out of joint and life *unworth
living* | Whitney Or. Studies 1.286 were a generation
of infants to grow up *untaught to speak* || BJo 1.25
you have very rare, and *un-in-one-breath-utterable* skill.

Awkwardly, with *un-* added twice in a phrase, in Dreiser
F 164 this rather *un-happy go un-lucky* scribbling world.

26.1₃. The modification in sense brought about by
the addition of the prefix is generally that of a simple
negative: *unworthy* = 'not worthy', etc. Formula
$3^n\text{-}2$. Thus especially with words in *-able, (-ible)*, and
ptcs, e. g. *unabsorbable, unadaptable, unanalysable,
unsusceptible; unabbreviated, unadapted, unadulterated;
unavailing*, and *unbefitting*. The two terms are thus
contradictory. But very often the prefix produces a
"contrary" term or at any rate what approaches one:

unjust generally implies the opposite of *just; unwise* means more than *not wise* and approaches *foolish, unhappy* is not far from *miserable*, etc. Still, in most cases we have only approximation, and *unbeautiful* (which is not very common, but is used, for instance, by Carlyle FR 1.118, Swinburne L 187, Zangwill, Galsw Sw 305) is not so strong as *ugly* or *hideous*. Sometimes the use of the negative is restricted: *unwell* refers only to health, and we could not speak of a book as unwell printed (for *badly*). *Unfair* is only used in the moral sense, not of outward looks.

Instead of prefixing *un-* to adjs in *-ful* it is usual to substitute *-less*, thus *careless, hopeless, thoughtless, useless* corresponding to *careful, hopeful, thoughtful, useful;* but *unfaithful* and *unmerciful* are used by the side of *faithless, merciless; unlawful* does not mean the same as *lawless; uneventful* and *unsuccessful* are preferred to *eventless* and *successless; unbeautiful* is used, but there is no *beautiless*.

26.1₄. In a great many cases, *un-* was formerly used, either alone or concurrently with *in-*, where now the latter is exclusively used. Examples are: *unactive* (Sh Cor I. 1.102, Mi e. g. PL 4.621), *uncapable* (Sh Merch IV. 1.5, Oth IV. 2.235, Defoe G 84, Swift 3.271 and 318, Spectator 166), *unconstant* (Lyly C 313, Sh e. g. Shrew IV. 2.14), *uncredible* (More U 33 and 175), *uncurable* (ib 223, Sh H6B III. 1.286 and V. 2.86), *undecent* (Lyly C 308), *undocile* (Defoe G 84), *unhonest* (More U 146), *unmeasurable* (Sh Wiv II. 1.109, Tim IV. 3.178), *unnoble* (Lyly C 292, Sh Ant III. 11.50, Beaumont 1.95), *unnumerable* (More U 51), *unperfectness* (Sh Oth II. 3.298), *unperfect* (AV Ps 139.16), *unplausible* (Mi A 54), *unpossible* (common in 16th c. and beginning of 17th c., e. g. Ascham, Gascoigne, Webbe, Lyly, Sh, Arden of Feversham, AV Luke 1.37, and Goldsm 650 (vg)), *unproper* (Sh Oth IV. 1.69), *unsatiable* (More U 53), *unsatiate* (Sh R3 III. 5.87), *unsufferable* (Defoe

R 2.153), *unsufficient* (More U 96), *untractable* (Defoe
G 84), and *unvulnerable* (Sh Cor V. 3.73). Cf Franz
§ 79, McKnight EW 172.

Many similar *un*-words, are still in use in dialects,
see EDD, and Wright, *Rustic Speech* p. 31.

Words in which *in*- was formerly used, while *un*- is
now recognized: *incertain* (Sh, e. g. Meas III. 1.127,
Alls III. 1.15), *incharitable* (Sh Tp I. 1.44), *infortunate*
(Kyd 36, Sh John II. 1.178, H6B IV. 9.18), *ingrateful*
(Sh, e. g. Tw V. 1.80, Lr II. 4.165, Mi S 282), *insubstantial*
(Sh Tp V. 1.155).

26.1₅. Pretty often *un*- is preferred before the shorter
word, and *in*- before the longer word derived from it,
which is generally also of a more learned nature; thus
we have

unable : *inability* | *unequal* : *inequality* | *unquiet* :
inquietude | *unjust* : *injustice*.

Note, however, Shaw Major Barbara 263 I cannot
bear to hear you doing yourself such an unjustice,
and Barbara such an injustice. Cf Austen P 239 some
excuse for *incivility* if I was *uncivil*.

Un- is preferred where the word has a distinctly
native ending, as in

unanimated : *inanimate* | *unceasing* : *incessant* |
undiscriminating : *indiscriminate* | *undigested* : *indigest-
ible* | *ungrateful* : *ingrate* (arch.), and *ingratitude* | *un-
lettered* : *illiterate* | *unlimited* : *illimitable*.

Cf further the following examples with such forms in
un- and *in*- together: By Cain I. 1 all the unnumber'd
and innumerable multitudes | Page J 175 Their faces
undistinguished and indistinguishable in the crowd |
Swinburne Sh 212 the fragments we possess of Shake-
speare's uncompleted work are incomplete | Gissing G
90 unmitigated and immitigable | McKenna M 15 un-
destroyed and indestructible | Bennett P 85 they re-
mained uncured because they were incurable | NP 1917
after an unexplained, but not inexplicable delay.

26.1₆. It should also be noted that while most of the *in-*words are settled once for all, and have to be learned by children as wholes, there is always a possibility of forming new words on the spur of the moment with the prefix *un-*.

Hence the difference between *unavoidable* from the existing verb *avoid*, and *inevitable;* there is no Engl. verb *evite.* (Both words are used together for emphasis in Bennett P 106 Inevitably, unavoidably, he was the new rich). *Unexplainable* (Myers M 11), but *inexplicable.*

Similarly *undestroyable* (cf *destroy*) and *indestructible.*

Uncertainty is supported by *certain; incertitude* is an isolated loanword.

In *irresponsible* : *unresponsive, inexpressible* : *unexpressive* the two prefixes serve to keep words apart which are otherwise easily confused. Thus *unpractical* is recommended by Fowler instead of *impractical* (used e. g. Mannin CI 165 His wife, Essie, declares him hopelessly impractical), which is often confused with the established form *impracticable.*

26.1₇. While *immoral* means the opposite of *moral*, i. e. what is contrary to (the received ideas of) morality, the necessity is sometimes felt of a term implying 'having nothing to do with morality, standing outside the sphere of morality'; this is sometimes expressed by *amoral* (thus by the late ethnologist A. H Keane), but perhaps more frequently by *unmoral.* Examples: Stevenson (NED) There is a vast deal in life and letters both, which is not immoral, but simply a-moral ‖ NP 1909 children are naturally neither moral nor immoral, but merely unmoral | NP 1923 the best and wittiest plays of the [Restoration] time are not immoral, but unmoral | Hope King's M 185 heights of unmoral serenity | OHenry C 66 Not much of a town … No sidewalks to speak of, no amusements. Rather unmoral | Maugham TL 96 he does not know what remorse is. He is completely unmoral.

Both *unfrequent* and *infrequent* are in use, and seem to be equally common. The former I have noted among others in Trollope, Lytton, Thack, Stevenson, H. Bradley, the latter in Galsw, Bertrand Russell, Sinclair Lewis, Mencken (AL³ 38), and Curme. Fowler MEU 263 recommends *in-*.

Unelegant and *unfirm* are rarer than *inelegant* and *infirm*.

The distinction now made between *human* and *humane* is recent (cf 21.3₁); *inhuman* has the meaning corresponding to *humane*, while the negative of *human* is expressed by *non-human* or *unhuman*, the latter in Stevenson MB 166 *he was so unaffectedly unhuman that he did not recognise the human intention of that teaching* | Walpole ST 100 *hills ... all the more friendly and intimate because they were not unhuman giants* [like the Swiss mountains].

Insane has the contrary meaning of (mentally) *sane*, *unsane* (Saintsbury Short Hist. of Eng. Lit. 768) only denotes the absence of sanity.

Inartistic means 'outraging the canons of art', *unartistic* 'not concerned with art'.

Insanitary 'implies danger' (Fowler 681), *unsanitary* 'has and needs no provisions for sanitation' (ib).

Inartificial 'unskilful, rude', *unartificial* 'artless, natural'.

As *irreligious* is very often used as the opposite of *religious*, Carlyle in one passage avoids the word, in speaking of University College, London, "it will be unreligious, secretly antireligious all the same, said Irving to me" (R 1.293).

Corresponding to *apt* we have the L and F *inept* with change of vowel and of meaning ('foolish') and the E formation *unapt;* the corresponding substantives are *ineptitude* and *unaptness* or the less common *inaptitude* (NED and Shaw Ibsen 10 *women ... their inapti-*

tude for reasoning—in Shaw evidently with a sly
innuendo of the other word).

Inutterable was in use in the 17th c. (Mi, etc.), but
has been superseded by *unutterable;* it has been revived,
however, in one instance by Tennyson, no doubt to
avoid two successive words beginning with *un-*: Tennyson 383 killed with inutterable unkindliness. Also used
by Abercrombie in Georgian Poetry 15.

Words beginning with *in-* or *im-* do not admit of
the prefix *in-*; hence *un-* even in long and learned
words like *unimportant, unintelligible, unintentional,
uninterrupted,* etc. *Unimmortal* (Mi PL 10.611) is rare.
Note also *disingenious* (e. g. Shelley L 729).

26.1₈. It is sometimes felt as an inconvenience that
the negative *in-* is identical in form with the prefixed
use of the Latin preposition *in.* The verb *inhabit* contains the latter; but *inhabitable* is sometimes used with
negative import, thus in Mandv 161 and Sh R2 I. 1.65
Euen to the frozen ridges of the Alpes, or any other
ground inhabitable.—The ambiguity of this form leads
to the use of two forms with *un-*, a rarer one as in Defoe
R 156 the *unhabitable* part of the world (but the form
inhabited is used ib 188 in the positive sense) | Sayers
GN 300 There are no seas innavigable nor lands unhabitable,—and the more usual *uninhabitable,* which is
found in Sh Tp II. 1.37 and has now practically prevailed. The corresponding positive adj ('what can be
inhabited') is *habitable.* Ambiguities are also found in
other similar adjs, as seen by definitions in dictionaries:
investigable (1) that may be investigated, (2) incapable
of being investigated; *infusible* (1) that may be infused
or poured in, (2) incapable of being fused or melted;
similarly with *invertible, importable* (now only 'capable
of being imported', but formerly also 'unbearable'),
and *improvable* (formerly 'incapable of being proved',
now 'capable of being improved'). *Inexistence* means

(1) the condition of existing in something, and (2), rarely, the condition of not existing. Cf GS § 140 for a few more examples.

26.1₉. In some instances we find *un-* alternating with some other prefix in related words:

unfortunate : *misfortune* | *unsatisfactory* : *dissatisfaction* | *uncomfortable* : *discomfort.*

E. g. Lawrence L 91 March was not so much afraid as uncomfortable ... She felt discomfort and gloom | Mason Ch 73 He was being made uncomfortable, and he disliked discomfort.

Negative *in-*

26.2₁. According to Latin sound-laws *in-* became *il-* before *l*, *im* before the labials *b*, *p*, and *m*, and *ir-* before *r*. This differentiation is seen not only in loanwords, but also in new-formations on English soil. In former times forms like *inpossible*, etc., were sometimes used, but they have now all been adjusted according to the above rules.

Before *gn-* the *n* of the prefix was dropped in Latin, as seen in the loanwords *ignoble, ignominious,* and *ignorant.* No words of this type have been coined on English soil.

The relation of *in-* to *un-* has been discussed in 26.1₄—1₇, the conflict between two senses of *in-* in 26.1₈.

This prefix occurs in loanwords from ME on. Many of these have been borrowed from or through French. Loanwords are: *inaudible, incapacity, incest, incorrect, incredible, indifferent, individual, inelegant, innumerable; illegal, illicit; imbecile, immature, immediate, impatience, improper, impudence; irrational, irrefutable,* and *irreverence.*

In some loanwords with stress on the prefix only, the first vowel (or both) of the radical has (have) been shortened:

impious [impiəs] : *pious* [paiəs] | *impotent* [impotənt] :

potent [poutənt] | *infinite* [infinit] : *finite* [fainait] | *infamous* [infəməs] : *famous* [feiməs].

26.2₂. New-formations with negative *in-* (and its by-forms) occur from late ME, most of them from adjs, but also many from sbs, chiefly predicative nexus-words. There are also a few vbs in *in-*, most of which have been derived from adjs in *in-*.

New-formations are: *inability, inaptitude, inexactitude; imperception; irrecognition; inaccurate, inattentive, inconceivable, invaluable; illegible, illoyal; immeasurable, impecunious, impracticable; irrealizable, irredeemable* (and many others in *irre-*).

26.2₃. Most words with negative *in-* are stressed according to the rules discussed in vol I 5.59 and 5.61 ff., thus in many words the prefix is unstressed, or has secondary stress, but most of these may be pronounced with equal stress, especially if the speaker wants to emphasize the negative character of the word.

Always full stress on the prefix occurs in some loan-words, e. g. *'ignorance, -nt, 'impious, 'impotence, -nt, 'impudence, -nt, 'incest, 'infamous, 'infamy, 'injury, 'innocence, -nt, 'insolence, -nt,*—and some long words in *-bility* coined on E soil, such as *'inadmissi'bility.*

If the first syllable of the radical has full stress, the prefix is generally unstressed, but the word may be pronounced with equal stress, e. g. *in'definite, ir'regular,* or (secondarily) *'in'definite, 'ir'regular.*

In some words the prefix is always unstressed, among them such common words as *ig'nore, im'mediate, im'mense, im'patience, -nt, im'possible, in'cessant, in'congruous, in'difference, -nt, in'dignant, in'numerable,* and *in'visible.*

With unstressed first syllable of the radical (often another prefix), *in-* (etc.) has generally secondary stress, but most words of this type may also have equal stress, e. g. *,ille'galily, ,imper'turbable, ,inde'scribable, ,inex-'haustible, ,irre'deemable,* —or *'ille'galily,* etc.

26.2₄. *Infamous* has been separated from *famous* as in sound (cf above), so in sense; the negative of *famous* is now rather *obscure* or *unknown* (*to fame*).

Other examples, in which the word with the prefix has been separated in sense from the simplex, are *different* : *indifferent*, *pertinent* : *impertinent*. *Immaterial* often is not = 'not material' (spiritual), but = 'unimportant' (what does not matter).

Invaluable means 'priceless, very valuable' while the negative of *valuable* is *worthless*.

Note the curious fact that *dependent* takes the preposition *on*, but *independent* requires *of*.

Negative *an-*, *a-*.

26.2₅. *a-* [æ-, ə-], *an-* [æn-, ən-] before a vowel and *h*, from Gk, occurs in loanwords from OE on, e. g. *amorphous*, *anarchy*, *aneroid*, *anharmonic*, *anodyne*, *anonymous*, *apathy*, *asymmetry*, *atheism*, and *atom*. But in many words, like *amazon* and *asylum* it is not felt as a negative prefix.

Some learned words have been coined with *a-*, *an-* on English soil, generally from Gk roots, but also occasionally from L roots, e. g. *agnostic* (coined by T. Huxley), *anaesthetic*, *amoral* (cf 26.1₇), *asexual* (Gissing B 267 the truly emancipated woman is almost asexual; the latter two from L roots), and some very rare words.

In some words the prefix is stressed, in others unstressed, the rules of stress generally being according to vol I 5.61 ff.

n-.

26.3₁. In a certain number of pronouns and particles *n-* is found as the shortened form of the original negative adv *ne: neither, never, no, none, nor, not, nought*. Cf also the obsolete *nill* (= ne-will), preserved in *willy-nilly*.

no-

26.3₂. The pronoun *no* is sometimes used as a kind of negative prefix. In vol II 16.79 examples are given of *no-education, no-thoroughfare, no-ball*, etc. Cf also Carlyle FR 57 with such *no-faculty* as he has | ib 199 The Constitution which will suit that? Alas, too clearly, a *No-Constitution*, an Anarchy | NP 1917 there can be no settlement which is not a world-settlement. Even the *no-settlement* which a stalemate would involve would be an *unsettlement* of the whole world. (The latter with privative *un-*). Cf also the adv *nowhere*.

non-

26.3₃. *non-* [nɔn-] is from F *non-*, L *non* 'not', and occurs in loanwords from ME times, such as *nonage, nonchalant, non-claim, non-pareil*, and *non-payment*. From the 14th c. it has been used as an independent E prefix.

It is frequently prefixed to sbs, mainly nexus-words and agent-nouns, especially in those cases where no formations in *un-* or *in-* are available. A number of nexus-words belong to legal language, e. g. *non-ability, non-acceptance* (of a draft), *non-access, non-alienation, non-appearance, non-feasance, non-joinder, non-suit*, and *non-user*. Other nexus-words are *non-attendance, non-contagion, nonconformity, non-delivery, non-obedience*, and *non-resistance*.

Among agent-nouns may be mentioned *non-abstainer, non-combatant, non-belligerent, nonconformist, non-malignant*, and *non-partisan. Non-* is rarely added to other sbs, as in *non-ego, non-member*, and *non-metal* (Jeans Mysterious Universe 19 the metals and non-metals).

A special type of derivatives with *non-* are mainly used as adjuncts (exceptionally as predicatives), thus some from sbs, e. g. *non-church, non-jury, non-party, non-union*, and some from verbal stems, e. g. *non-return*

(valve), *non-skid* (tyre), *non-stop* (flight, train, etc.;
in war-slang used about a long range shell passing high
overhead, Frazer & Gibbons).

Non- is frequently prefixed to adjs, as in *non-acid,
non-adult, non-combustible, non-descript, non-effective,
non-electric, non-Episcopal, non-essential, non-Euclidian,
non-existent, non-natural* (Wells A 303), *non-ruminant,
non-sensitive, non-understandable* (London F 199 this
tangled, nonunderstandable conflict), and *non-viable*
(Macdonald F 309).

It is rarely added to vbs except in the participle,
e. g. *non-established* (church), *non-manufacturing, non-
marrying, non-participating,* and *non-provided.*

By far the largest number of words in *non-* are derived
from words of L or F origin, but the prefix *may* be prefixed to native words, e. g. *non-fulfilment, non-living*
(Jeans Mysterious Universe 29), *non-slaveholder, -holding,
non-smoker, non-talker,* and *non-understandable* (quoted
above).

26.3₄. *Non-* simply denotes the absence of the notion
inherent in the radical, and thus is different from the
other negative prefixes, *dis-, in-,* and *un-,* in which
there is generally also some characterizing element, cf
e. g. v. Draat Rhythm 15 "Non-rhythmical", which is
widely different from "un-rhythmical" | NP 1924
Mysticism is not irrational, but it is non-rational,—and
non-appearance : *disappearance* | *non-natural* : *un-
natural* | *non-moral* : *immoral* (26.1₇).

26.3₅. *Non-* is nearly always stressed and pronounced
with [ɔ], note, however, the early loanword *nonage*
[nounidʒ] or [nɔnidʒ] and *nonentity* [nɔˈnentiti]. In
words coined on English soil the radical is not materially
changed in the derivative.

Privative **un-**.

26.4₁. *un* [ʌn-] privative prefix, is from OE *ond-,
and-,* parallel to Gk *anti-* and G *ent-.* Already in OE it

was liable to lose *d* before a consonant. In *answer* it
is no longer felt as a prefix; and in *dread* the only thing
left of the prefix is *d*: OE *ondrœdan*, cf G *entraten*,
was felt as containing the prep. *on*, and when that was
subtracted, *drœdan* remained (Pogatscher, Anglia Beibl.
14.182).

In other instances the prefix remained living, but the
vowel was changed into *u* through influence from the
negative *un-* (cf *unless*, ME *on lesse* (*that*), where also
the negative notion caused confusion with *un-*). Thus
the old *onbindan, ontiegan* became *unbindan, untigan* in
Ælfric, ModE *unbind, untie*.

26.4₂. With regard to stress the rule formerly often
given that negative *un-* had strong and privative *un-*
weak stress does not agree with Dan. Jones's notations.
According to him nearly all vbs with privative *un-* are
generally pronounced with equal stress, e. g. 'un'balance,
'un'button, 'un'do, 'un'fix, un'lock, 'un'man, 'un'pack,
and 'un'wrap. But they may also be pronounced without any stress on the prefix. In a few words he gives
unstressed prefix as the primary possibility, though
pronunciation with stress on *un-* occurs, e. g. un'bosom,
un'cover, un'fit, un'hinge, and un'veil,—or 'un'bosom,
etc.

In un'burden and un'ravel the prefix is always unstressed.

26.4₃. Privative *un-* is prefixed to vbs and derivatives
from vbs, giving the derivative a contrary sense to the
simple word. *Un-*vbs are generally, though not always,
used transitively. Examples are: *unbar, unbeget* (Dryden
5.193 [he] wishes, he could unbeget these rebel sons),
*unbend, unbind, unblindfold, unbridle, unclothe, uncoil,
uncover, undeceive, un-dismiss* (Bennett LR 346 you
tell him from me to un-dismiss), *undo, unfasten, unhinge,
unlace, unload, unpack, unravel, unsay, unsheathe, unteach* (e. g. By Correspondence 2.34 In ten years I could
unteach myself even to your language), and *unwish*

(By 582 do not poison all My peace left, by unwishing
that thou wert a father).

Formula: *he unpacks his suit-case* S 3-V O.

Many words with privative *un-* are coined from sbs
or from vbs (= sbs)—it is not always possible to decide
which. The sense is 'deprive of, separate from'. Examples
are: *unbirdlime* (Coleridge, Letter 1800 I shall have
my wings unbirdlimed), *unbonnet* (Meredith E 358),
uncloak, uncrown, unflower, ungirdle, unglove, unroof,
and *unsex*.

A vb with privative *un-* (often a formation for the
nonce) is frequently used in connexion with the simple
vb, e. g. Defoe P 25 they were, as it were, alarmed,
and unalarmed again | Shaw StJ 102 I was burned,
all the same. Can they unburn me? | Mi PL 5.895 Then
who created thee lamenting learne, When who can un-
create thee thou shalt know | Browning 266 and, my
lesson learned ... I can't unlearn ten minutes after-
ward | Carlyle S 82 it makes and unmakes whole worlds |
Wells TB 263 [divorce] that's how one gets unmarried.
It's easier to marry than to unmarry | Dryden 5.392
to say or to unsay (common, e. g. Galsw MP 174) |
Bennett P 165 You're quite a decent sort of child, only
you've been spoilt. I'll unspoil you | Sh John III. 1.245
Vnsweare faith sworne | Lytton K 190 It is easy to
tell a fib, but it is very difficult to untell it | Sh VA
908 she treads the path that she vntreads againe.

Cf Brock K 25 I hate unswallowing an idea you know,
once I've absorbed it.

26.4₄. Another group of vbs coined from sbs mean
'release or drive from, take out of', e. g. *unbed, unearth,
unhandkerchief* (Twain M 190 [she] unhandkershiefs one
eye), *unhorse, unleash,* and *unspell*.

Finally, there is a (smaller) group of vbs coined
from sbs denoting human beings, the derivative meaning 'deprive of the position or qualities of', as in *un-
bishop, unfellow* (Mrs. Browning A 170 death quite un-

fellows us), *unking, unlord, unman* (common), *unpriest,*
and *unqueen.*

Outside these groups we have *unloose* (Sh, AV and
others), in which *un-* merely intensifies the negative
meaning inherent in *loose(n).*

While infs and other purely verbal forms can only be
privatives, participles with *un-* may be either negatives
or privatives, the written form at any rate being identical in both cases. Thus *uncovered* may mean 'not
covered' and 'deprived of cover', *unlocked* 'not locked'
and 'opened'; similarly *undressed, unwrapped, unhar-
nessed, unloaded, unpacked,* etc.

Sometimes it may be doubtful which of the prefixes
we have: Wells V 124 those *unsexed* intellectuals | Darwin
L 1.333 [an anonymous book] has been by some attributed to me—at which I ought to be much flattered
and *unflattered.* Cf also Swinburne's bold unidiomatic
formation SbS 83 Love or *unlove* me, *Unknow* me or
know, I am that which unloves me and loves.

From the priv. vb *un'dress* we have the sb 'undress'
'plain clothes' (not uniform), e. g. Scott A 1.298 in
military undress.

dis-

26.5₁. *dis-* [dis-] is from L *dis-,* related to Gk *dis,*
and connected with *duo* 'two', the original sense being
'in two, two-ways'. It occurs in loanwords from ME
on (here often written *dys-*), in some cases representing
F *des-,* the F form developed from *dis-,* which has been
preserved in a few words, e. g. *descant, despatch* (also
dispatch), and *dessert,* cf vol I 9.13.

Note the spelling *dispirited* (with elision of one *s*).

26.5₂. Stress: The general rule is for *dis-* to be unstressed, thus before a strong stress: *dis'arm, dis'bar,
dis'burse, dis'cern, dis'charge, dis'close, dis'cover(y), dis-
'comfort, dis'credit(able), dis'cuss, dis'dain, dis'grace, dis-
'guise, dis'gust, dis'like, dis'miss, dis'pose (-sal), dis-*

ǀpute, disǀreputable, disǀsolve, disǀtinguish, disǀtrust, disǀturb, etc.

But if the word after dis- begins with a weak syllable, dis- generally has half or even full stress: ǀdisaǀbuse, ǀdisadǀvantage, ǀdisapǀprove (-val), ǀdiscomǀposure, ǀdisinǀfectant, ǀdisoǀbey, ǀdisoǀbedient, ǀdisproǀportionate, ǀdisreǀspectful. Thus words in -ion: ǀdispoǀsition, ǀdisserǀtation, etc.

Half or full stress may also fall on the prefix to bring out a contrast, thus often in ǀdisǀharmony, ǀdisǀloyal, ǀdisǀmount, ǀdisǀtaste, ǀdisǀuse; dislike is generally disǀlike, but we speak of a man's ǀlikes and ǀdislikes.

A few words have stress only on the first syllable, e. g. ǀdissolute, ǀdissonance, ǀdistance, and ǀdistrict, but in most of these dis- can hardly be felt as a prefix.

In a few cases the sb has fore-stress and the verb end-stress, cf vol I 5.7₃: discard, discord, discount. This, however, is not always carried through strictly. Disdain, dislike, dispute, distrust and also the longer discomfort are sbs and vbs without any change of stress.

In vol I 6.64 and in Linguistica, p, 365 f. is treated the development in some cases of unstressed [dis-] to [diz-] before a voiced sound in stressed syllable. Daniel Jones gives the following words with [z] only: disaster (and disastrous), disease, (dismal of different origin), and dissolve (with dissolvability and dissolvent), and the following with both [s] (as primary pronunciation) and [z]: disability, disable, disarm, disarmament, discern, disdain, dishonest(y), dishonour(able), disorder, disorganization, -ize. In all other cases Jones has [dis-].

26.5₃. Among the large number of loanwords with dis- are the sbs disadvantage, disaster, discomfort, discount, discourse, disgrace, disgust, dispensation, disposition, disruption; — the adjs disagreeable, discontinuous, dishevelled, dishonest, dissolute, and distributive,— and the vbs disappoint, dismiss, disperse, displease, dissect, dissuade, and distribute. In many old loans,

such as *discuss(ion)*, *distress*, *district*, *distinct*, *dispute*,
etc., *dis-* cannot be called a prefix from the English
point of view.

As a living prefix with privative force *dis-* has been
used from early ModE. It has been added especially
to roots of L (F) origin, but also in many cases to native
roots. It occurs mainly in vbs and words with some
inherent verbal idea (especially action nouns and
deverbative adjs).

In new-coined sbs the prefix expresses the opposite
of or the absence of the notion denoted by the radical,
e. g. *disconnexion*, *disharmony*, *disillusion*, *disproof*,
disrepute, *distaste*, *distrust*, *disunion*, and *disuse*.

New-formations in *dis-* from native roots are chiefly
vbs, e. g. *disbar*, *disbelieve*, *disbench*, *disburden*, *disfrock*,
disgruntled, *dishearten*, *dislike*, *disown*, *disroot*, and *disseat*.
The sb *dislike* is from the vb.

Prefixed to adjs *dis-* has a negative force, though
it is generally stronger than *un-* (*in-*). It generally
does not only, as in *dispassionate*, *disproportionate*, and
dissimilar denote absence of the quality, but also the
opposite quality, as in *disadvantageous*, *discourteous*,
discreditable, *disharmonious*, *dishonourable*, *disreputable*,
and *dissymmetrical*.

Verbs in *dis-* are coined

(1) from sbs, meaning 'rid of, deprive of', e. g. *dis-
branch*, *disbud*, *disfrock*, and *dispirit* (esp. in the ptc,
dispirited), or 'turn out of—', as in *disbar*, *disbench*,
disbosom, and others;

(2) (rarely) from adjs, the vb meaning 'undo or
reverse the quality', as in *disable* and a few rare formations, and

(3) from vbs, in the sense of undoing or reversing
the action, e. g. *disaffirm*, *disarrange*, *disbelieve*, *dis-
connect*, *disenthrall*, *disestablish*, *disinfect*, *disinherit*, *dislike*, *disown*, *disqualify*, *disregard*, *dissatisfy*, and *dis-*

trust. In *disannul* and *dissever* the prefix has strengthening force or is pleonastic.

26.5₄. *Discover* has been specialized and differentiated from *uncover*, which is used in a material sense only.

A difference is made between *dis-* and *un-* in Amr NP 1916 The entrance of a fresh and powerful neutral [U. S.], honestly disinterested but not uninterested— the former referring to egoism, the latter to more ideal motives.

As with *in-* (cf 26.1₈) we sometimes have a drawback arising from the ambiguity of the prefix. *Dissociable* may be either the negative of *sociable* ('unsociable'), or derived from *dissociate* ('separable'); in the former case NED will pronounce double [s], while Daniel Jones has single [s] in both, but pronounces the ending in the former [-ʃəbl], in the latter [-ʃiəbl] or [-ʃjəbl].

de-

26.5₅. *de-* [di-, ˈdiˑ-], verbal prefix, from Lat. *de-* (or exceptionally from F *des-* < Lat. *dis-*, as in *defy*), occurs in a large number of vbs with their derivatives borrowed from L, often through F, e. g. *declare*, *denote*, *depend*, *designate*, etc.

From ME it has been used as an active English formative with a privative force:

(1) to form vbs with their derivatives, its sense being that of undoing the action of the simple vb, mostly words of a learned, at any rate foreign, character, ending in *-ate* and *-ize*, e. g. *decapsulate*, *decelerate* (after *accelerate*), *de-oxygenate*, *decarbonize*, *dematerialize*, *denaturalize*, *deodorize*, *devulcanize*, and from native or naturalized verbs, as in *debamboozle* (Mencken[4] 194), *debunk*, *defreeze*, *demote* (U. S., 'reduce to lower rank or class'), etc., and

(2) to form vbs from sbs, its meaning then being 'remove from, turn out of', e. g. *debadge*, *debag*, *debus*,

decode, decontrol, dejelly (Mencken[4] 194), *delouse, deplane* 'descend from an aeroplane', *detrain*, etc., most of them comparatively rare. Note the recent Amr *debunk* 'remove the nonsense from, put down'.

26.5₆. When *de-* is followed by a vowel, the hyphen is generally used, e. g. *de-acidify.*

In loanwords in which *de-* is no longer felt as an independent prefix and semantic unit, it is pronounced [di-] when unstressed, e. g. *define* [di'fain], ['de-] or [ˌde-] when stressed, e. g. *definite* ['definit], *definition* [ˌdefi'niʃən]. In words in which *de-* has its privative force, the pronunciation is [di·-], ['di·-] or [ˌdi·-], e. g. *decarbonize* [di·'ka·bənaiz], *depopulation* ['di·ˌpɔpju'leiʃən], *deformation* [ˌdi·fɔ·'meiʃən].

mis-

26.6₁. *mis-* [mis-], negative prefix, is represented in all Gothonic languages (OE, ON, OSax., OFris. *mis-*, OHG *missa-, missi-, misse-*, Goth. *missa-*). In English it has been frequently used as a prefix of native words, from early ME also added to words of foreign origin. "The most prolific period for the formation of *mis-* compounds was the 17th c." (NED), but it is still an active formative, always felt as a relatively independent unit, and therefore not subject to the same voicing of *s* as in *dis-*.

In Chaucer *mis-* might be used nearly as a word in itself, practically as an adj or adv, e. g. HF 1975 Of good or mis governement | G 999 But to correcten that is mis I mente || A 3139 if that I misspeke or seye | B 3112 That shal he finde, that hir misdooth or seith.

26.6₂. Sbs, with a few exceptions (e. g. *mis'fortune, mis'giving(s), mis'prision, mis'take*) are stressed on the prefix, thus also vbs in which the (two) first syllables of the rootword are unstressed, e. g. ˈmisaˈpply, ˈmisˌappreˈhend, ˈmisbeˈhave, ˈmisbeˈlieve, ˈmisconˈduct, ˈmis-

con'strue, 'mis|repre|sent, etc. But some vbs in which the
first syllable of the radical is stressed, have unstressed
prefix, e. g. *mis'carry, mis'lay, mis'lead, mis'take;* no
fixed rule can be given; many words of the same type
have stress on the prefix, e. g. *'mis'count, 'mis'deal,
'mis'govern, 'mis|judge, 'mis'read,* etc.

26.6₃. The chief sense of the prefix is 'wrong(ly),
mistaken(ly), bad(ly), ill-'. Hence it is primarily combined with vbs and secondarily with substantival,
adjectival and participial derivatives of vbs. It is
very rarely prefixed to sbs or adjs in which there is no
verbal element, such as *misqualities* (Carlyle FR 2.128).

Vbs in *mis-: misbehave, miscarry* (intransitive, whereas
carry is mostly transitive, cf vol III 16.1₈), *misconstrue,
misguide, misjudge, mislay, misplace, misquote, mis-
understand, misuse.*

Gerunds and participles: *misdoing, misgivings; mis-
begotten, misshapen* (note the *n*-form), etc.

Sbs: *misbelief, miscarriage, misdeed, misdemeanour,
misfit, misrule, misfortune* (here not added to a verbal
derivative, cf the synonym *mishap*).

26.6₄. *Mis-* also in some cases has a purely negative
sense, thus corresponding to negative *un-* or *dis-*, often
semantically identical with words in *dis-*. Examples
are *misbelieve = disbelieve* (with corresponding sbs),
misknow 'not know', *mislike = dislike, mistrust = distrust* (the former perhaps with a playful connotation),
miscredit 'disbelieve', *misthrive,* etc. Kipling B 49 I
misremember what occurred (= forget?).

Several obsolete or archaic words in *mis-*, especially from
early ModE, have been supplanted by forms in *dis-*, e. g.
misaffected, misarray (Scott), *miscomfort, misorderly* (Ascham).

26.6₅. In the following words *mis-* represents OF
mes- from L *minus: misadventure, mischance, mischief,
miscontent, miscreant, misease, misnomer, misprision,*
and *misprize.*

In the words in which this *mis-* is felt as an independent prefix, it is semantically identical with the Gothonic *mis-*.

mal-

26.6₆. *mal-* [mæl-], pejorative prefix, is from F *mal-*, prefixed use of the adv *mal*, Lat. *male*. It occurs in a number of French loanwords, sbs, adjs, and vbs, e. g. *malversation; maladroit, malcontent; maltreat,*—and from the 16th c. it has been productive on Eng. soil in the sense of 'wrong, ill, badly'. It has especially been prefixed to verbal nexus-words, e. g. *maladaptation, maladministration, malassimilation, malconduct, malformation, malodour,* and *malpractice,* rarely to adjs, as in *malodorous,* and vbs (and ptcs), as in *maladminister, malconceived,* and *malformed.*

Some words have been adopted with the Latin form *male-*, e. g. *malediction, malefic,* and *malevolence,* but only the French form has been productive on Eng. soil.

In new-formations *mal-* has generally full stress, as in ˈmaladˈjustment, ˈmalnuˈtrition, and ˈmalˈpractice.

anti-

26.7₁. *anti-* [ˈænti-] (in some loanwords [ænˈti-]), substantival and adjectival prefix, is from Gk (L) *anti-* 'against', and is found in loanwords from ME times, e. g. *Antichrist, antipode* (both ME), *antipathy, antipope, antistrophe, antithesis* (ModE).

Added to sbs *anti-* has various related meanings.

(1) 'rival': *anti-god, antipope,*

(2) 'opposing': *anti-chorus, anti-league,*

(3) 'the reverse of': *anticlimax, anticyclone.*

Added to adjs (frequently used as sbs), the prefix means 'opposed to': *anticatholic, anticeremonial, anti-Jacobin, anti-revolutionary,* and *anti-social.*

A large subdivision of this group is formed by words

with the sense 'counteracting a definite disease', e. g.
*antibilious, antifebrile, antihysteric, antiparalytic, anti-
pestilential*, etc.

The prefix further occurs in various other scientific
formations, e. g. *antichlore, antihelix*, and *antimeta-
bole*.

It is also used to denote opponents of some idea or
movement, etc., e. g. *anti-trinitarian, anti-militarist,
anti-protectionist, anti-tobacconist, anti-vaccinator* (Shaw
GM 257), and to denote a counter-movement, e. g.
anti-feminism, anti-Freudism, anti-Masonry (Farmer
Americanisms), *anti-Semitism, anti-squandermania* (Bennett P 120), and *anti-vivisectionism*.

26.7₂. Some words are coined by prefixing *anti-* with
prepositional force (= 'against') to a sb. These derivatives are generally used as adjuncts, occasionally as predicatives, e. g. *anti-aircraft, anti-church, anti-corn-law,
anti-tank* (gun), *anti-trade* (wind), *anti-Whig, anti-woman* (NP 1912 an anti-woman movement), and the
following established forms from U. S.: *anti-Bank,
anti-caucus, anti-negro*, and *anti-Union*. The formula
in such cases is p-1 or p-2 respectively.

contra-

26.7₃. *contra-* [kɔntrə-], general prefix, from L *contra*,
'against, in opposition to' (thus etymologically identical
with *counter-*, see 26.7₄), occurs in a number of loans
from Latin, e. g. *contradiction* and *contradictory* (both
ME), *contrapose* and *contraposition, contravene* and
contravention, and from Italian (Spanish), e. g. *contra-
band, contrabass, contralto, contrapuntal*, and *contra-
stimulant*.

The number of formations on English soil is small.
Examples are: *contra-account, contraception, contradistinction, contra-entry, contralateral*, and *contrana-
tural*.

counter-

26.7₄. *counter-* [kauntə-], substantival, adjectival, and verbal prefix, is from ME and AF *countre-*, F *contre-*, from L *contra-* 'against, in return', and occurs in a large number of loanwords, e. g. *counterfeit, countermand, counterpoise,* and *counterpoison*.

In vbs coined in English the prefix generally means 'against, in the opposite direction or sense'. Examples are *counteract, countercheck, countermarch, counterprove, countersecure,* all coined from French roots, and *countermake, counter-say, counterweigh, counterwork,* from native roots.

Similarly the prefix is used to coin sbs from sbs, especially nexus-words, but also from other sbs, the prefix here generally denoting correspondence.

Examples: *counter-advice, counter-attraction, counter-intrigue, counter-reformation, counter-stratagem,*—and from native words: *counterblast, -blow, -bond, -deed, -nut* ('lock-nut'), *-weight,* etc.

Adjs are rare except in terms from heraldry (see NED). Examples: *counter-coloured, counter-couchant, counter-courant, counter-passant,* and *counter-salient*.

In most derivatives *counter-* is a secondary in relation to the main word (*counter-revolution* would be symbolized 2-1 (X), cf AnalSynt Ch 6), but in a few cases the prefix has a prepositional force, and governs the main word as its regimen (Symbol: p-1). Examples are *counter-clockwise* (adj and adv), the loanword *counterpoison, counter-spell,* and *counter-taste*.

26.7₅. Vbs in *counter-* and their derivatives generally have the main stress on the root, whereas there is a tendency towards main stress on the prefix in sbs (especially in loanwords), otherwise sbs have equal stress. Examples:

counteract [ˌkauntəˈrækt] : *counteraction* = 'counteracting' [ˌkauntəˈrækʃən], but = 'action by way of

reply' [ˈkauntəˈrækʃən] | *counterbalance* vb [ˌkauntə-
ˈbæləns], sb [ˈkauntəˌbæləns] | *countermand* vb [ˌkauntə-
ˈmaˑnd], sb [ˈkauntəˈmaˑnd] | *countersign* vb as sb or
[ˈkauntəˈsain], sb [ˈkauntəsain].

Formula for *he counteracts the order:* S p*-V O*.

gain-

26.7₆. Corresponding to the foreign prefixes here
treated we have two native prefixes, the role of which,
however, is very insignificant indeed, *gain-* and *with-*.

Gain-, an aphetic form of *again* in the obsolete sense
now expressed by the expanded form *against*, is found
in the vb *gainsay*, while the words *gainstand* and
gainstrive 'resist' are obsolete.

with-

26.7₇. *With-*, originally *wiðer*, cf G *wider*, 'against',
was found in some OE vbs like *wiðcweðan*, *wiðsprecan*
'gainsay'; in ME we have *withdragen*, *withdrawen*,
which is continued in ModE *withdraw*. Further examples
are the vbs *withhold*, *withsay*, *withstand*, and the dialectal *withcall*, *withtake*.

In the particles *within*, *without* the prefix has hardly
any meaning. *Withal* is a variant of *with* in its modern
meaning.

ex-

26.8₁. *ex-* [ˈeks-, ikˈs-, igˈz-], *ef-* [(ˈ)ef-, iˈf-], *e-* [eˑ-,
i(ˑ)-] is from Latin *ex-*, *ef-*, *e-*, from the prep. *ex* 'out
of' (rarely from Gk, see below). The L rules for the
form of the prefix according to the following sound have
not always been observed in modern formations.

Loanwords of the various types have been increasingly frequent from ME times. Examples are: *example,
exercise, experience; exact; examine, effect, effort; efface;
education, event; elect, erect, evacuate,* etc. In most of
these there can be no English feeling for the value of
the prefix.

Some words borrowed in ME with the OF form of the prefix, *es-* (i. a. *essample* 'example', preserved in the aphetic form *sample*) were later latinized. On a false analogy of these we have now *exchequer*, from OF *eschequier*, MedL *scaccarium*.

26.8₂. In their original sense of 'out of' *ex-* and *e-* (rarely *ef-*) have been used as independent prefixes in connexion with words of L (Gk) origin. Most of these new-formations have a distinctly learned (technical) character. Examples: *excurvation; exannulate, exculpate; ˉepalpate*, and *evittate*.

26.8₃. As in other European languages *ex-* (generally with a hyphen) has been used from ME times in the sense of 'former, quondam' 'who has been' (perfect tense), 'who is no longer'. It may be added to practically any word denoting office or occupation. Examples: *ex-king, ex-emperor, ex-mayor, ex-secretary, ex-fisherman,* etc. Formula 2(3)-1.

It may also be added to word-groups as in Graves Engl. Ballads 29 *ex-sailing-ship men* | O'Brien Lord Russell 214 Mr. O'Donnell, an *ex-Irish M. P.* [= an Irish ex-M. P.] | Mencken AL⁴ 274 *ex-United States Senator, ex-Federal Trade Commissioner* | NED: an *ex-flogging Secretary of War* | *an ex-Liberal ex-Lord Chancellor*.

On the pronunciation and stress of *ex-* see vol I 5.59, 6.7, 9.13.

The Gk prep. *ex* occurs in some loanwords in the form *ex-* before vowels and *ec-* before consonants, e. g. *exegesis, eccentric, ecstasy,* and *eczema*.

A few scientific terms have been coined on English soil with both forms of the prefix.

Chapter XXVII

Prepositional Prefixes

27.1. In this chapter are collected those prefixes that owe their origin to prepositions. Some such pre-

fixes were already treated in the preceding chapter,
where attention was called to the difference between
these prefixes as real prepositions followed by their
regimen, and the same without a regimen, thus used
'adverbially' (or in some cases adjunctally).

There can be no fixed boundary between words derived by means of a prefix and compounds with a particle as their first element. These were dealt with in
Ch IX, see 9.4 (sbs), 9.6₂ (adjs) and 9.7₂ (vbs). Some of
the examples there given might equally well have been
placed in this chapter.

On account of the composite character of the English
vocabulary we often meet with two, three or even
four synonymous prefixes (native and foreign).

We take first a few prepositions that are as it were
counterparts of those placed last in Ch. 26 (*for* as contrasted with *against*). Then follow local and temporal
prepositions in their natural order according to their
significations, and finally a few prepositions which cannot
be arranged in this way.

for-

27.1₁. *for-* [fə-, fo-, fɔ·-], verbal prefix, is from OE
for, fær-, related to German *ver-*, Goth. *fair, fra, faur*.
Its original sense was 'forward, forth', and formerly it
was used as an active formative in various senses and
functions, see Leif J. Wilhelmsen, The Verbal Prefixes
for- and *fore-* in English (Avh. utg. av Det norske
videnskaps-akademi 1938. Oslo 1939). It now occurs
only in a comparatively small number of vbs and their
derivatives, the most common of which are the following (see Fowler in MEU): *forbear* (the sb *forbear* ought
to be spelt *forebear*, see Fowler s. v.), *forbid, fordo*
(mostly in the participle), *forfend, forgather, forget,
forgive, forgo* 'relinquish', *forlorn, forpined, forsake, for-
spent, forswear, forwearied*, and *forworn*. It is difficult to
assign any definite meaning to this prefix, but it has

been placed here on account of the general meaning of
the preposition.

According to Fowler *for-* should always be pronounced
[fə-], but in many of the words Dan. Jones also gives
the pronunciation [fo-, fɔ·-].—The prefix passed out of
use as living formative in the 16th c.

On *fore* see below 27.8₁.

pro-

27.1₂. *pro-* is from Latin adv and prep. *pro.* Many
loanwords, often borrowed through F, occur from ME
times, e. g. *process, product, profit, protest; profound;
procure, pronounce, protect,* etc. But such words were
taken over as wholes with no feeling for the prefix as
such. The pronunciation is often [prə-], but [prɔ-] if
stressed.

As an independent formative *pro-* [prou] is used in
various senses.

Thus with the sense 'instead of, acting as deputy of'
in sbs like *pro-cathedral, pro-Chancellor, pro-proctor,
pro-rector, pro-lunch.*

It can further, in the sense 'for, in favour of', be
added to any sb and adj, the derivative being often
used as an adjunct, and generally written with a hyphen,
e. g. *pro-Boer* (Rose Macaulay T 172 Pro-Boer. The
Latin word "pro" has been found always very useful
and insulting), *pro-Bolshevik, pro-German, pro-reforma-
tion, pro-tariff reform, pro-clerical,* etc., cf vol II
14.66.

Subdivisions are derivatives from agent nouns (*pro-
flogger*), and nexus-words in *-ism* (*pro-Boerism*). Note
also nonce-words like *pró-smash* (Wells JP 520 I'm
pro-smash. We have to smash), *pro-us* (Rose Macaulay
T 175 I'm not a pro-Boer at all. I'm pro-us).

27.1₃. The etymologically corresponding Gk prefix
occurs in a number of loanwords; the meaning 'before'
(in time, order, etc.), is no more felt in words like

problem, program(me), prophet, but rather more in *proclitic, prologue, propædeutic* and a few more.

As a living formative this *pro-* has a learned character and is chiefly used in scientific terminology, e.g. *procephalic, prognathous, prosternum,* and *prothalamium* (coined by Spenser, 1597).

super-

27.2₁. *super-* [s(j)u(˙)pə-], from L *super-* 'above', occurs in a large number of loanwords from ME on, e. g. *superabundance, superadd, supercilious, supererogation, superfluous, superhuman, superlative, superscription, supersede, superstition (-ous), supervene,* and *supervision.*

From about 1600 it has been used on English soil in the sense 'above, beyond, to excess' to form new sbs, adjs, and vbs, mainly from Latin roots, e. g. *superstructure; superconscious* (parallel to *subconscious*), *superexcellent* (GE S 142), *supernormal, supersane* (Dine B 211), *supersensual, superterrestrial; supercharged, supercivilize* (Shaw Ms 41), *superordinate.*

On the use of *super-* in the U. S. Mencken writes AL⁴ 464: The use of the adjectival prefix *super-* tends to be confined to the more sophisticated classes; the plain people seldom use it.

The prefix is frequently used in scientific terminology, thus in the following mathematical terms, *superbipartial, superbitertial,* etc., the chemical terms *superacid, superphosphate,* and *supersaturate;* in anatomy, e. g. *supercarpal, superglottal,* and *supersacral.*

In a few cases *super-* has been prefixed to a word of native origin (or a naturalized loanword), e. g. *supercooling, superdreadnought, superfatted* (soap), *superheat* (vb), *superman* (Bernard Shaw's translation of Nietzsche's *übermensch*), *super-people* (Locke GP 197; on the analogy of *superman*), *super-salt, super-show* (NP 1939), *super-silly* (King OF 209).

27.2₂. *Super-* has stress on the first syllable except in the loanwords *su|perfluous* and *su|perlative.*

Secondary stress on the first syllable of the prefix occurs especially in loanwords with full stress on the first syllable of the radical, e. g. ₁super₁annuate, ₁super-₁ficial, ₁super₁fluity, ₁super₁numerary, ₁super₁scription, ₁super₁stition, ₁super₁vene, and ₁super₁vision.

Some vbs have ˌsuper-, thus ˌsuper₁add, ˌsuper₁pose, ˌsuper(₁)scribe, and ˌsupervise (also ₁super₁vise), and a number of words, esp. late formations, in which the prefix is clearly felt as a semantic unit have initial full stress, too, e. g. ˌsuper₁bus ('large bus'), ˌsuper₁fine, ˌsuper₁glottal, ˌsuper₁normal, ˌsuper₁submarine, and ˌsuper-₁tonic.

sur-

27.2₃. *sur-* [sə·-, sə·r-], from OF *sur-*, developed from L *super-*, occurs in loanwords from ME, e. g. the sbs *surcharge, surface, surfeit, surplice, surtax,* and *sur-veillance,* and the vbs *surcease, surpass,* and *survive. Surround* is felt and spelt as if derived from *round*, but is etymologically from F *sur-onder* from *onde* (L *unda*).

New-formations, not very common, occur from early ModE, e. g. the sbs *surmaster*, title of the second master of St. Paul's school in London, *surrebutter, surrejoinder, surroyal,* the adj *surangular,* and the vb *surfuse,* all from words of F (L) origin. *Surname* is a translation of AF and OF *surnum, surnom.*

With regard to stress the tendency is towards stress on the prefix in sbs and on (some syllable of) the root-word in vbs, cf vol I 5.73 f., e. g. the sbs, ˌsurbase, ˌsurcoat, ˌsurface, ˌsurfeit, ˌsurname, ˌsurplus, and ˌsurtax, and the vbs sur₁charge, sur₁mise (also ˌsur-), sur₁mount, sur₁pass, sur₁prise, sur₁render, sur₁round, sur₁tax, sur₁vey, and sur₁vive.

Vacillation in some sbs (the most common form

given first): *sur|charge* and *|surcharge*, *|surmise* and
sur|mise, *|surtout* and *sur|tout*, *|survey* and *sur|vey*.

hyper-

27.2₄. *hyper-* [haipə-, hai|pəˑ-], from Gk *hyper* 'over
(much), beyond, excessively', occurs in loanwords
(sometimes borrowed through F or L) from ME times,
e. g. *hyperbola, -e, -ic, hyperborean, hypermeter*, and
hypertrophy.

New-formations chiefly belong to scientific language,
e. g. *hyperdeterminant, hypergamy, hypermetamorphosis*,
and *hyperoxidation*, but formations of a general character
occur, e. g. *hypercritical, hyper-Turk* (Kinglake E 9
such hyper-Turk looking fellows).

In most words with *hyper-* the prefix has full or
secondary stress on the first syllable. Some words of
four syllables follow the rule of stress on the antepen-
ultimate discussed in vol I 5.6, e. g. *hy|perbola, -e,
hy|pergamy, hy|permeter, hy|perthesis, hy|pertrophy.*

On compounds with the native *over-* corresponding
to the foreign *super-, sur-, hyper-* see 9.4₂, 9.6₂, 9.7₂
and 9.7₃.

a-

27.3₁. *a-* [ə-] represents several prefixes of native and
foreign origin, but is only a living prefix as a development of the OE preposition and prefix *on*, and the
Greek prefix *a-* (see 26.2₅).

The OE preposition *on* was frequently weakened to
o or *a* before consonants, and may be found as an independent preposition in the form *a* as late as Swift,
see vol I 2.424.

Most OE phrases with *on* + a sb survive as *a*-derivat-
ives, among them *abed, afloat, aground, alive, aloft,
asleep,* and *away*.

A great number of derivatives were formed in ME,

both from loanwords and native roots, but few survive,
e. g. *across, afire, apart, aside, aslant.*

Among surviving forms from those coined in early
ModE (many are obs.) are *abreast, adrift, aflame, agate,
ahead, astern, astride, a-tiptoe, atop.*

Derivatives are still formed from *a-* $+$ sb. Late
ModE forms of this type are *abeam, adream, aheap,
apoop, astir, awing,* cf the full treatment in 7.5₁.

A subdivision consists of words in *a-* $+$ gerund, as
areading, etc, see on this and its relation to the first
participle vol IV 12.2(1) ff. and vol V 8.2₅, 9.9, and
22.3₅ ff.

A- has also been prefixed to adjs, as in *amid* (from
OE), *awry* (from ME), *aweary* (from Early ModE), and
adead (1879).

Derivatives from numerals such as *atwo* (from OE
on tu, on twa), *a first, atween* (equal to and formed on
the analogy of *between,* cf *afore : before, among* : obs.
bimong), *a thre* ('athree'), *a seven,* etc. (all from ME),
are now obs., archaic, or dialectal, see Carl Palmgren,
A Chronological List of English Formations of the
Types *alive, aloud, aglow.* Norrköping 1923 (p. 19), cf
id, A Study on the History of English Words Formed
by the Prefix *a- < on (in).* Ibid. 1924.

In ModE, after the formal coalescence of many sbs
and vbs, it has become possible to form *a*-derivatives
from verbal stems (*ablaze, ablush, adangle,* etc.) see 7.5₁.

Many *a*-forms from advs are still in use, thus *about*
(OE *on-hutan, abutan*), *above* (late OE *abufan*), *again*
(OE *ongean, ongen, agen*), *asunder* (OE *on sundran*),
abroad (ME *a brod(e), o(n) brode*), *afar* (ME *a fer, on
fer*), *aloud* (ME *a loud, on lowde*), etc. Some such forms
are used as prepositions.

Note the differentiation between *again* adv and its
derivative *against* (on *-st* see 18.2₃) prep. and conj.

27.3₂. We have often aphesis of *a-*, see vol I 9.95,
NED *a-*, below 29.8₁ and E. Slettengren, Contributions

to the Study of Aphæretic Words in English. Lund 1912,
esp. p. 76 ff. and 81 ff. In many cases we have still
forms with and without *a-* without any semantic or
functional, but with a stylistic differentiation, e. g.
'bout : *about*, *'bove* : *above*, *'gainst* : *against*, *'mid* : *amid*,
'mong(st) : *among(st)*, *'tween* : *atween*, the aphetic forms
being archaic, vg, or dialectal.

The following pairs have been differentiated in some
way:

back 'to the rear' : *aback* (naut.) 'backwards', as in
take aback (also used figuratively) || *like* adj (and sb)
and prep : *alike* adv and predicative adj (Byron DJ
5.99 all clad alike; like Juan, too) || *live*, adj as an
adjunct : *alive*, pred. adj (a live wire; he is alive) ||
loud, adj and adv (always *laugh out loud*) : *aloud*, adv
(always *read aloud*) || *dead* and *weary*, adj : *adead* and
aweary, prd adj only.

On the original preposition *on* in compounds see 9.4₃,
to which add *onset* and *oncome*.

27.3₃. In many cases *a-* is of different (native or foreign)
origin. OE prefixes (or words developed into prefixes) preserved
to ModE in established forms, but obsolete as independent
formatives, are:

(1) OE *a-* (exceptionally *ar-*), corresponding to Goth. *us-*,
ur-, OHG *ar-*, *ir-*, *ur-*, ModG *er-*, as in *abide*, *arise*, *awake*,

(2) the OE prep. *of* > ME *a-*, as in *adown* > *down*, *afresh*,
ahungered (Keats 2.148 a-hunger'd | Locke GP 175 as though
she had asked him why he desired food when a-hungered),
anew, *athirst*,

(3) OE *and-* > ME *a-*, as in *along* (cf. *answer*, with *n* preserved),

(4) the OE prep. *æt* (now *at*) > ME *a-*, as in *adoors;* also in
ado, with the Scand. use of *at* like *to* before an infinitive (cf
Bale T 800 what was there a do?),

(5) OE *ge-* > ME *a-* (for *i-*, *y-*), as in *afford*, *adone*. See further
NED.

epi-

27.3₄. *epi-* [ˈepi-, eˈpi-] (before unaspirated vowel *ep-*
[ep-] and before an aspirate *eph-* [ef-]), from Gk *epi-*

'upon, at', etc. The prefix occurs in a number of loanwords borrowed through F and L, or direct from Gk.
Epistle was borrowed in OE, from ME we have the
loanwords *epicycle, epitaph*, etc.; later loans are *epicene,
epidemic, epidermis, epigastrium, epiglottis, epigram,
epilepsy, Epiphany, episcopacy* (and others from this
root), *episode, epithet, epitome*, and a great many others.

In ModE the prefix has mainly been used in scientific
language (biology, anatomy, botany, etc.), as in the
sbs *epicalyx* and *epiphenomenon*, and the adjs *epibasal,
epicerebral, epicranial, epigynous*, etc.

The monosyllabic forms of the prefix occur in a few
loanwords, e. g. *eparch, epenthesis, ephemera*, and *ephor*.
Formations on English soil are rare: *epaxial, ephydriad*.

Words in *epi-* generally follow the rules of stress
discussed in vol I 5.61 ff., i. e. trisyllabic words are
stressed on the first syllable, e. g. *epicene, epilogue,
epitaph*. Words of four syllables have in some words
the main stress on the last syllable but one, with
secondary stress on the first syllable (cf vol I 5.66),
e. g. |epi|cyclic, |epi|demic, |epi|dermal, |epi|glottis,
|epi|sodic. In others the second syllable is stressed, e. g.
e|pigrapher, e|pilogize, E|piphany, e|piscopal, e|pitome.

in- (il-, im-, ir-)

27.4₁. *in-* [in-] is from Lat. *in-*, prefixed use of the
adv and prep. *in*. According to Lat sound-laws *in-* became *il-* before *l, im-* before labials, and *ir-* before *r*
(like the negative *in-*, see 26.2), a differentiation preserved in loanwords and also observed in the formation
of new words on English soil. In OF the vowel of the
prefix became *e* in early loanwords, while in learned
and later loans *i* was preserved. Many words in *en-*
(*em-*) were borrowed into English and this form of the
prefix also became productive in English, see 27.4₄,
but in most words *en-* was re-Latinized to *in-*.

Loanwords now spelt with *i-* occur from ME, e. g.

the sbs *illusion, illustration, impetus, importance, inclination, infection, information,* and *inscription,* the adjs
illustrative, imperial, impulsive, instant, and *intelligent,*
and the vbs *illustrate, immigrate, impair, impel, include, infect, inform, inscribe,* and *invite.*

27.4₂. Some loanwords have full stress on the prefix,
thus a number of trisyllables according to the rule
discussed in vol I 5.61 ff., e. g. *illustrate, immigrant,
implement, incidence, indicate, intellect,* and *intimate.*

Some disyllabic loanwords also have stress on the
first syllable, e. g. *impost, impulse, incense,* and *instant.*

Stress in some cases is used to distinguish between
substantives and verbs in *in- (im-),* see the examples
in vol I 5.73.

Some words, thus some in *-tion* have a rhythmic
secondary stress on the prefix (cf vol I 9.87), e. g.
immolation, inclination, intuition; further e. g. *importun-
ity* and *incandescence.*

But by far the greatest number of words in *in-* have
no stress on the prefix, thus disyllables (cf vol I 5.59)
like *imbibe, impair, impound, incite, include, induce,
intend* and *intent, invite,*—and words of more than two
syllables (cf vol I 5.61 ff.) like *illuminate, imperative,
impoverish, incipient, inhibit, intoxicate, inviolate, ir
radicate,* and *irruption.*

Most of the new-coined words are vbs. There are also
a small number of sbs, chiefly verbal nexus-words, and
some adjs containing.a verbal element.

Some are derived from vbs, e. g. *immingle, impenetrate,
impersonify, incapsulate, infiltrate, innervate, inoscul-
ate,* and *inure.* Others from sbs, e. g. *impanel, imperil,
impocket, inspirit, instate.*

New-formed sbs are *impersonification,* and *innerva-
tion.* Adjs: *incarmined* and *induplicate.*

27.4₃. From late ME the prefix has been used as an independent formative on English soil, but as it is identical
in form and related in sense to the *native preposition*

in as used in compounds, it is not always possible to tell whether in a word in *in-* we have the L prefix or the E preposition. It seems natural to consider words coined from L roots as derived with the L *in-*, and words coined from native roots as compounds with the native *in*.

Especially the period immediately before and after 1600 was rich in new-formations with *in-*, but most of these words are rare or obsolete. A comparatively small number of new-formations are now in use.

Cf 9.4 and 9.7 compounds with native *in*. The examples there given might be supplemented with the following sbs: *income, indraught, ingrowth, inroad,* adjs (ptcs) *inborn, inbred,* vbs *inbreathe, inburst* (rare), *ingather,* the following chiefly in the ing-form, *inbreeding, indwelling, inflowing. In* has prepositional force in *inurn,* cp. with foreign vbs *incarcerate, incorporate.*

On the negative *in-* see 26.2.

en- (em-)

27.4₄. *en-* [en-, in-], *em-* [em-, im-], is from the French form of L *in-, im-*. In OF and ME the prefix in some cases developed into *am-, an-, a-,* as in *ambush, anoint,* and *appraise,* but on English soil it has been productive in the form *en- (in-), em- (im-)* only. The spelling *em-* occurs before *b, p,* and (occasionally) *m*. In many cases *in-, im-* have been substituted for *en-, em-* and inversely, see the discussion of this alternation in some twenty words in Fowler MEU 136-37, e. g. *embed, enclose, entrench, ingrain(ed), inquire, inquiry*. In a few cases the vb has *e* and the corresponding sb *i: encrust : incrustation, endorse : indorsation, enjoin : injunction*. Occasionally a semantic or stylistic differentiation has taken place, e. g. in *endorse* (commercial, general) : *indorse* (legal), *ensure* (general) : *insure* (financial), *enure* (legal) : *inure* (general).

See further vol I 9.13.

Loanwords (from ME on) are *embalm, embark, embellish, encourage, encroach, engage, enlarge, enrich, entomb, envelop*, and *envisage*. From ME *en-* has been used as an independent prefix, mainly added to words of native or French origin.

It forms vbs from sbs, the primary meanings of the derivatives being (1) 'enclose in, put into or on', e. g. *embed, embox, encage, encamp, encase, encloud, encradle, endanger, enface, engulf, enmesh, enshrine, ensnare, enthrone*, and *entrench;* (2) 'put what is denoted by the substantive into or on', e. g. *encrown* and *enjewel;* (3) 'make into—', e. g. *enflesh, enslave*, and *enthral*.

Further from adjs, the derivative meaning 'give the quality', e. g. *embitter, embrown, enable*, and *endear*. A subdivision of this group are the vbs in *-en*, e. g. *embolden, embrighten, engladden*, and *enwiden*, cf 20.5₉.

Finally *en-* may be prefixed to vbs, the prefix meaning 'within, into, on, against', or having merely intensive force. Examples are *emblazon, enclose, enclothe, engild, enkindle, entwine, enwrap*, and *enwreathe*.

En- is always unstressed, cf vol I 5.59.

intra-

27.4₅. *intra-* [intrə-] is from the L preposition *intra* 'within', and occurs practically only in modern scientific terms, especially from the sphere of biology, e. g. *intracranial, intramolecular, intramundane, intra-ocular, intra-organismal* (Thomson Spencer 190 differences between intra-organismal and interorganismal struggle), *intravenous*, see long list in NED. Rarely in sbs, as *intraselection*.

intro-

27.4₆. *intro-* [introu-] from the Latin adverb *intrō* 'to the inside', is added to vbs and verbal derivatives, and occurs in loanwords, such as *introduce, -duction, intromission, introspection*, and *introversion*, and a

number of vbs and verbal derivatives coined on English
soil, most of them rare words, e. g. *intro-active, intro-
ceptive, introflexion, introsuction,* and *introtraction.*

by-

27.5₁. The prefix *by-* is simply the E preposition,
used as prefix from OE times, chiefly in sbs. I copy
the list given in Fowler's MEU with the spellings preferred by that authority.

*by-blow, by-election, by-end, bygone, by-lane, by-name,
by-pass, bypast, by-path, by-play, by-product, by-road,
bystander, by-street, by-way, by-word, by-work.* In philology
we have *by-form.* The meaning is 'found by the side
of, accessory'.

By-law or *bye-law* does not contain the prep., but the Scand.
by 'town'.

On the phonetically and semantically weakened form
be- see 28.1.

circum-

27.5₂. *circum-* [ˈsəˑkəm-, səˈkʌm-] is from the L adv
and prep. *circum* 'round, round about', and occurs in
loanwords from ME times, as *circumcise, circumference,
circumscribe, -script* (Ch T 5.1865 Uncircumscript, and
al mayst circumscryve), *circumspect,* and *circumstance*
(all ME); later loans are *circumflect, -flex, circumlocu-
tion, circumnavigate, circumvent,* and *-vention.*

A number of derivatives with *circum-* have been
coined on English soil, thus from verbal stems, the
prefix meaning 'round, about', *circumambient, circum-
gyrate, circummure,* and *circumundulate.* Further from
adjs derived from sbs, e. g. *circumlittoral, circumoral,
circumpolar,* and *circumterraneous.* The prefix here means
'round, surrounding'.

Circum- is rarely prefixed to native roots. The only
established form seems to be the jocular mock-Latin

formation *circumbendibus*. NED quotes some nonce-
words, e. g. *circumbeamed, circumflowing, circumstanding,*
and *circum-walk*.

In the loanword *circumference* and a few others the
stress is on the second syllable of the prefix (cf vol I
5.61 ff.), in all other words, both loanwords and native
formations, the prefix has the stress on the first syllable,
but in some words this stress is secondary in relation
to a stress in the root-word, thus in the sbs in -*ion*,
e. g. ˌcircumˈcision, ˌcircumloˈcution, ˌcircumˈscription,
ˌcircumˈvention, etc.; also in words of four syllables like
ˌcircumˈpolar. Some trisyllables have main stress on
the first syllable, bute note ˌcircumˈvent.

peri-

27.5₃. *peri-* [peri-, pəˈri-], from Gk adv and prep. *peri*
'round (about), around, about', occurs in loanwords
from late ME on, e. g. *pericarp, perimeter, period,
peripathetic, periphery, periphrastic,* and *peristyle*. New-
formations, all of a learned character, belong to the
modern period only, e. g. *periaster, pericentral, periderm,*
and *periscope*.

Stress according to the rules given in vol I 5.61 ff.

inter-

27.5₄. *inter-* [intə-, (inˈtə·-)], from the prep. *inter*
'between', but often, in the case of early loanwords,
borrowed in the form *enter-* from F *entre-,* occurs in a
great number of loanwords from ME times on, e. g.
*interdict, interlude, interval, interview; intercalary, inter-
mediate, interrogative; interfuse, interject, interlace, interline, interpret, interrupt, intersperse,* and *intervene*.

Inter- has been used as an independent formative
on English soil from ME times and has been prefixed
to both foreign and native roots.

As prefixed to some sbs it means primarily 'reciprocal,
mutual' and functions as a secondary in relation to the

sb, thus in *intercommunion, interconnexion, interdepen-
dence, intermarriage,* and (from native roots) *inter-
growth, interleaf, interlink,* and *interplay.*

In connexion with some other sbs the prefix stands
in prepositional relation to the radical, thus especially
in derivatives used as secondaries ("pre-adjuncts"):
interstate affairs | *inter-island* steamer | *inter-school*
contests | Kinglake E 125 in short *inter-whiff* sentences,
—see further vol II 14.66.

Similarly in adjs derived from sbs, the prefix governing the sb implied in the radical as its regimen. This
seems to be the largest group of *inter*-derivatives.
Examples (all from foreign roots): *interalveolar, intercolonial, intercontinental, interdental, interglacial, inter-
molecular, international, interoceanic, interstellar,* and
intervocalic.

Adjs derived from vbs (Latin ptcs, etc.) in which
the prefix functions as a tertiary (= 'mutually'), e. g.
intercomparable, interdependent, and *interrepellent,* are
less frequent.

In vbs, finally, the prefix functions as a tertiary. Here,
especially, there are many derivatives from native
words. Examples: *interact, interconnect, interpenetrate*
(from foreign roots), *interbed, interbreed, interflow, interknit, interleave, interlink, interlock, intermarry, intermingle, intertangle, intertwist, interweave* (especially the
ptc *interwoven*), and *interwreathe* (from native roots).

Most vbs in *inter-* are generally used transitively, but
as a natural consequence of the sense of reciprocity
which the prefix often has, some verbs are, either always
or occasionally, used intransitively, e. g. *interact, interbreed* (Wells A 221 they interbreed and fight), *intercede,
intercommunicate* (Wells A 138), *intermarry, intersect*
(Froude C 1.153 Irving's history intersects with that
of Carlyle), and *interweave* (Wells Br 137 with it there
interwove still subtler elements | id V 178 the thought
of beauty interwove with the biological work).

27.5₅. In some loanwords the second syllable of the prefix has full or secondary stress: inˈtercalary (also ˌinterˈcalary), inˈtercalate, inˌtercaˈlation, inˈterpellate, inˌterpelˈlation, inˈterpolate, inˌterpoˈlation, inˌterpoˈsition, inˌterpret, inˌterpreˈtation, inˈterrogate, inˌterroˈgation, and inˈterstice. In all other words transcribed by Daniel Jones this syllable is unstressed.

The largest group of words in *inter-* have secondary stress on the first syllable of the prefix and full stress on (some syllable of) the second element. For the words marked with an asterisk in the following list, Jones gives equal stress as a secondary possibility. Here especially belong verbs with a monosyllabic second element. Examples: *intercede, interfere, *interfuse, interject, *interknit, interlace, *interleave, *interline, *interlink, *interlock, *intermeddle, *intermingle, intermit, *intermix, interpose, interrupt, intersect, intersperse, *intertwine, *intertwist, intervene,* and **interweave.* Further: **interaction, intercession, *interdental, interjection, *interlocution, *intermarriage, intermediate, *international, *interracial, interrogative, *intertribal, *intervocalic,* etc.

A few verbs have equal stress as the primary possibility, as *interblend, interbreed,* and *intermarry,* but these may also have secondary stress on the prefix.

But a number of sbs and adjs have generally equal stress, e. g. *interplay, interrelation, interspace; intercolonial, interglacial, interoceanic,* and *interstellar.*

Finally some sbs are generally stressed on the first syllable only, e. g. *intercourse, interest, interleaf, interloper, interlude,* and *interval.*

Some sbs and vbs are distinguished by means of stress only, cf vol I 5.74:

ˈinteract sb—ˌinterˈact vb ‖ ˈinterˈchange (also ˈinterchange) sb—ˌinterˈchange vb ‖ ˈintercept sb—ˌinterˈcept vb ‖ ˈinterdict sb—ˌinterˈdict vb ‖ (ˈinterview both sb and vb).

cis-

27.6₁. *cis-* [sis-] from the L prep. *cis* 'on this side of'
as in the loanwords *cisalpine, cismontane*, and *cisrhenan*
'on the French side of the Rhine'. Among the rare
formations on English soil are *cisatlantic, cispontine* 'on
the northern side of the Thames bridges' (in London),
and in a temporal sense *cis-Elizabethan*.

trans-

27.6₂. *trans-* [træns-, tra·ns-, trəns-] is from Lat.
trans 'across, beyond, over'.

In certain cases the prefix in Latin was shortened to *tra-*
as seen in the English loanwords *tradition, traject* (and related
words), *tramontane, traverse,* and *travesty*. But only the full
form *trans-* has been productive on English soil.

This occurs in loanwords from ME, e. g. the sbs
transaction, transcript, transformation, transit, transla-
tion, transport, and *transposition,* the adjs *transalpine,*
transcendent, transitive, transparent, and *transverse,* and
the vbs *transact, transcribe, transfer, translate, transmit,*
transpire, and *transport.*

New-formations with *trans-* occur from early ModE.
It is used in prepositional relation to the sb (implied
in the adj) to which it is added, in the meaning 'beyond,
surpassing, transcending' as in *trans-border, trans-fron-*
tier, trans-continental, translunary, transoceanic and
transpontine. Subdivisions are adjectival scientific terms,
in which the prefix means 'through, across', e. g. *trans-*
frontal, transocular, and *transpalatine,* and geographical
terms in which the prefix means 'situated beyond or on
the other side of' as in *Transatlantic, Transvaal,* or
'passing across' as in *Trans-African, Trans-Siberian.*

Further it is used as a tertiary in the meaning 'beyond,
surpassing' in adjs, e. g. *transhuman, transnormal,* and

transsubjective, and in various senses to form vbs, e. g. *transfashion*, *transilluminate*, *transprose*, and the fanciful formation *transmogrify*.

Formations from native roots are rare; note, however, *transmake* and *tranship*.

Before a root beginning with *s* the prefix is generally written *tran-*, see examples above.

27.63. The vowel of *trans-* in most cases is given by Daniel Jones as [æ] with [a·] as secondary possibility, in a few words [a·] as primary vowel and [æ] as secondary, e. g. *transitive*, *translate*, *translation*. In a few words the vowel may also be pronounced [ə]: *transact*, *transaction*, *translate*, and *translation*. Cf vol I 6.64 and 10.554.

The *s* of the prefix according to the sound-development discussed in vol I 6.511 ff., see especially 6.64, shows a tendency towards becoming voiced before a voiced sound in a stressed syllable, as e. g. in *transact*, *transliterate*, *translucence*, *transmit*, and *transversal*, but in many words Daniel Jones gives [-s-] as secondary or primary possibility.

Before a voiceless sound in a stressed syllable *s* is normally voiceless.

In geographical names and terms, in which the prefix is always stressed, the *s* is practically always voiced whether the following sound is voiced or not, e. g. *Transbaikalia*, *-caspian*, *-continental*, *-pontine*. But this is not observed by everybody.

In most other words in *trans-* the prefix is unstressed, see further vol I 5.59 (disyllables) and 5.73 (nouns and verbs distinguished by means of stress).

preter-

27.64. *preter-*, *præter-* [ˈpri·tə-] (except in the loanword *preterit* [ˈpretərit]) is from the L prep. and adv *præter* 'past, beyond; besides'. It occurs in loanwords from ME, e. g. *pretermission*, *preternatural*, and in a

small number of words coined on English soil, e. g.
preterhuman (coined by Shelley), *preterlegal*, and some
nonce-words, such as *præter-christian, præter-determin-
edly, preteressential,* and *prætersensual.*

extra-

27.6₅. *Extra-* [ekstrə-], from the L prep. *extra* 'outside',
is found in many loanwords, among the earliest of
which are *extraordinary* and *extravagant* (ME). In ModE
it has been extensively used, chiefly in adjs before
foreign words, e. g. *extra-artistic, -christian, -corporeal,
-cutaneous, -European, -judicial, -logical, -national,
-professional, -territorial;* rarely before native adjs:
extrared. It is very rare before sbs: *extrados* (F *dos*
'back') and in vbs: *extravasate* 'force out fluids'; *extra-
vagate* is much rarer than the adj *extravagant.*

The first syllable has generally strong stress, and
extra tends to be apprehended as a separate word
(adj) as in *extra charge,* (adv before an adj:) *extra strong,
extra-special,* (sb:) something for which an extra-charge
is made. The usual pronunciation of *extraordinary*
is [ik׀strɔ·din(ə)ri].

ultra-

27.6₆. *ultra-* [ʌltrə-] is from the L prep. *ultra* 'beyond'.
As a prefix it is used extensively in the modern period,
chiefly in adjs (often used as sbs) in the meaning 'going
or lying beyond', as in *ultra-human, -microscopic,
-natural, -terrene, -terrestrial, -territorial;* note the colour-
names *ultra-red, ultra-violet.* It often has the meaning
'in an excessive degree': *ultra-affected, -fashionable,* and
in speaking of political and other parties: *ultra-con-
servative, -liberal, -revolutionaire;* hence such sbs as
Ultra-Calvinist, -pietist, -dandyism, -royalism.

Ul- has strong or at any rate half-strong stress.
Hyphens are often used.

through-, thorough-

27.6₇. *Through-* and *thorough-*, two suffixes from the OE prep. *þurh*, are found in comparatively few formations, before *-going* in both forms. An obs. adj is *throughold* 'very old' (NED 1639). Among sbs we may mention *thoroughbass*, *thoroughbrace* (U. S.), *thoroughfare* (common from ME times), *thoroughlight* (obs.), *thoroughpin* and *thoroughwort;* among adjs *thoroughripe* and the ptc *thouroughbred;* among vbs *thoroughbore*, *thoroughdry* and *thoroughdrain*.

In none of these we have the prefix with prepositional force.

sub-

27.7₁. *sub* [ˈsʌb-, səb-] is from the L prep. *sub* 'under'.

According to Latin sound-laws the final consonant in certain cases was assimilated to the following sound or dropped. All these assimilated forms occur in English loanwords: *suc-* (succeed), *suf-* (suffer, suffix), *sug-* (suggest), *sum-* (summon), *sup-* (supply, suppose), *sur-* (surreptitious), *sus-* (suspend), and *su-* (suspect), but only the primary form *sub-* has been productive on English soil, hence only words with this form of the prefix will be considered in what follows.

Loanwords occur from ME, thus the sbs *subaudition*, *subdean*, *subject*, *subjunctive*, *subscription*, *subsidy*, *substance*, *substantive*, and *suburb*, the adjs *subacid*, *subalpine*, *subfusc*, *sublime*, *subsequent*, *subterranean*, and *suburban*, and the vbs *subdue*, *subjoin*, *submerge*, *submit*, *subscribe*, *subside*, *subsume*, and *subtract*.

From early ModE the prefix has been used to form new words.

It is used with prepositional force in relation to the sb implied in an adj, partly with the meaning 'under, below' as in *subaerial*, *subaqueous*, *subcelestial*, *submarine* (also used as a sb), and *subsolar*, and especially in terms from anatomy, e. g. *subaxillary*, *subcranial*, *subepidermal*, and *subocular*,—partly with the meaning 'next below,

close to', as in *subarctic, subdorsal, sublateral, submontane,*
and *subtropic.*

Further, it is used in a secondary function with sbs,
here meaning 'subordinate, subsidiary' as in *sub-abbot,
sub-editor* (with the back-formation *sub-edit*), *sub-head*
(and *sub-heading*), *sublibrarian, sub-prefect, subsizar,*
and *sub-type,* meaning 'existing, occurring below', as
in *sub-arch, sub-crossing, sub-current, sub-railway, sub-
soil, substructure,* and *subway* (the last word with
different meanings in British and American English),
or denoting a division or branch of something, as in
*sub-atom, subclass, subcommittee, subdialect, subfamily,
subgenus, subkingdom, sub-office, suborder, subvariety,* and
many others.

Next, it is used in a tertiary function, to denote a
further action, thus in vbs like *sub-classify, sub-colonize,
sub-contract, sublet,* and *sub-rent,* in verbal nexus-words
like *sub-articulation* and *sub-classification,* and in agent-
nouns like *sub-purchaser.*

Finally, it is used as a tertiary with the meaning
'incompletely, imperfectly, partially', as in the adjs
(and advs) *subaudible, subconscious(ly), sub-defiantly*
(Butler ER 150), *sub-savage* (Robinson Mind in the
Making 65 man's pristine sub-savage ignorance), and
subtypical,—and especially in technical terms like *sub-
acrid, subfossil, subcylindrical, subacute* and *subchronic.*

Sub- is chiefly used in new-formations with roots of
L and F origin. Still, it has been pretty frequently
used to form words from roots of native origin, many
of which have become established forms. Examples:

Sbs: *subgrin* (Lewis MS 114), *subhead(ing), subkingdom, subman* (as contrasted with *superman*), *subshaft,*
and *subway.*

Adjs: *substony,* and formations for the nonce like
sub-angry (Wells N 313), *sub-golden* (Galsw SS 2 a sub-
golden hue), and *sub-wealthy* (Butler Er 227).

Vbs: *sub-blush, sublet,* and *sub-understand.*

Some loanwords have kept their original stress
(generally on the second syllable), cf for some of them
vol I 5.59 (and for the quality of the vowel ib 9.224),
but a great many loanwords have stress on the prefix,
and so have all new-formations.

hypo-

27.7₂. *hypo-* [haipo-, hai‖pɔ-, (in some loanwords
‖hipo-, hi‖pɔ-)], before a vowel *hyp-* [haip-, hip-], from
the Gk prep. and adv *hypo* 'under', occurs in loanwords
from ME times, e. g. *hypocondria(c), hypocorism, -ristic,
hypocrisy, -crite, hypostasis, hypotenuse*, and *hypothesis*.

It occurs in a great number of new-formations, sbs
and adjs, from scientific terminology, e. g. *hypoblast,
hypobromite, hypocycloid, hypophosphate; hypobranchial,
hypochlorous*, and *hyponitrous*.

infra-

27.7₃. *infra-* [infrə-], from the L adv and prep. *infra*
'below, underneath', occurs in a good number of adjs
(and ptcs), and a few sbs, mainly borrowed or coined
in recent times. Most of them are formed from (orig.) L
or Gk roots, and belong to scientific terminology (esp.
that of anatomy), such as *infracephalic, infracostal,
inframaxillary, infrarenal*, and *infraspinal*, but formations of a more general application occur, e. g. *infra-
bestial, infrahuman* (James T 23), *inframontane, infra-
natural, infra-ordinary, infraposed*, and *infraposition*.

In most derivatives the prefix has prepositional force,
meaning 'below or lower than', but in one or two words,
in accordance with MedL usage, it means 'within', as
in *inframercurial, infraterritorial*, and in *infraposed,
infraposition* it has adverbial force, meaning 'below,
under-'.

The only derivative from a native root quoted in
NED is *infra-red*.

On the use of the native preposition corresponding to *sub, hypo,* and *infra: under* see 9.4_2, 9.6_2, 9.7_2, 9.7_3.

fore-

27.8₁. *fore-* [fɔ·-, ˈfɔ·-] is from the OE adv and prep. *fore*. It has been an active formative through all stages of English, though it is now, according to NED, affected and archaic. It may be considered the prefixal equivalent of the preposition 'before', both applying to place and time, e. g.

(1) (place) *foregoer, forerunner,* and some obs. or arch. words, e. g. *foregird, forelie;* further *forecourt, forefinger, forefoot, foreground, foreland, foreleg, forelock, foreman (-woman), foreword,*

(2) (time) *forearm* 'arm beforehand', *forebode, -boding, forecast, foreordain, foresee, foreshadow, foretaste, foretell forewarn.* In this function the orig. L prefix *pre-* is now preferred, see 27.8_2. Further *forefather, forethought, foretime, foretoken.*

A subdivision consists of words in which *fore-* denotes the front part of something, e. g. *forearm, forehead, foreshore.*

Another subdivision is formed by some nautical terms, in which *fore-* means 'near or towards the stem of the ship', as in *fore-cabin, forecastle, foremast, foresheets,* or 'connected with the foremast', as in *foresail, foretop, foreyard.*

In these sbs *fore-* is syntactically a secondary. Differently in *forenoon,* where *fore* is a prep. with *noon* as its regimen.

Fore- is stressed in sbs (ˈforecast), unstressed in verbs (foreˈcast); cf vol I 5.72 and above 11.9.

Note the pronunciations *forehead* [fɔrid, fɔred] and *forecastle* [fouksl], cf vol I index. Sailors' pronunciation of *foresail* is [fɔ·sl].

pre-

27.8₂. *pre-* [pri-, ׀pre-, ׀pri·-], from L *præ* 'before, in
front, in advance', occurs from ME in a great many
loanwords, frequently borrowed through French, e. g.
sbs (mainly action and agent nouns) like *preamble,
precaution, precept, precipice, precursor, predicament,
preface, prejudice, prelude, preoccupation, preparation,
preposition, presage,* and *presence,* adjs like *precise, pre-
mature, preparatory, preposterous, present,* and *previous,*
and vbs like *precede, precipitate, predestine, predict,
prefer, prepare, prescribe, preserve, preside, prevaricate,*
and *prevent.*

From early ModE *pre-* has been used as an independent prefix, mainly added to words of Latin origin,
though also to native roots.

Prefixed to sbs, it means 'previous, preceding', as in
*pre-apprehension, preconception, pre-contract, predesigna-
tion, predisposition, pre-engagement, pre-existence,* and
pre-option.

It is often used to form adjs, e. g. *pre-Christian, pre-
exilian, -ic, pre-glacial, pre-historic, pre-Islamic, pre-natal,
preprandial, pre-revolutionary,* and *prescientific.*

Pre- with a̤ sb as its regimen is often found in words
used only as adjuncts (rarely as predicatives), e. g. *pre-
Conquest, pre-election, pre-Raphael, pre-war,* etc.

A great many vbs have been coined with *pre-* in a
temporal sense, e. g. *prearrange, preconceive, preconsider,
pre-date, predefine, predispose, pre-engage, pre-establish,
pre-exist, premeditate, pre-ordain,* and *prepossess.*

New-formations from sbs with *pre-* in a local sense
are rare outside scientific terminology (anatomy, zoology), e. g. sbs like *precava, presternum, premaxilla.*
Adjectival formations are commoner, e. g. *preaxial,
precentral, prefrontal, prevertebral,* etc.

Most derivatives with *pre-* are from roots of L or F
origin, but *pre-* may also be prefixed to native roots,

as in *pre-knowledge, pre-name; pre-war; pre-cool, pre-doom* (Tennyson 407 Predoom'd her as unworthy), *pre-warn; pre-mixing* (of gas and air, etc); cf also from vol II 14.66 *pre-railroad, pre-board school days, pre-smoking days*. We may even find NP 1922 the pre-'14 period.

27.8₃. In loanwords the tendency is towards the following pronunciations of *pre-:*

If the prefix is unstressed, and is no longer felt as a semantic unit, it is pronounced [pri-] or (in a few words) [prə-], e. g. *precaution, precipitate, pretence; precise, preparatory, preposterous; predict, prefer, prepare, prescribe, prevent* (= 'hinder'; but = 'go before' generally [pri·ˈvent]).

But some loanwords with unstressed prefix vacillate between [i·] and [i], e. g. *preamble, precursor; preeminent; precede, predestine*.

In loanwords with full or secondary stress on the prefix this is generally pronounced [ˈpre-], e. g. *preface, prejudice, prelude, preparation, preposition, present*. Some words, however, have [i·]: *prefect, prefix* (sb), *premonition, pretext; previous*.

Most words coined on English soil, especially recent derivatives, in which the prefix is still felt as a semantic unit, have stress on the prefix, and the vowel is [i·], e. g. *preadmission, pre-existence, pre-history; pre-exilian, preprandial; prearrange, premeditate* (also with [i]), *prepossess*, etc.

In vol I 5.73, in the list of sbs and vbs with different stress there were a few words with *pre-*. It may not be amiss to give here the pronunciation of these according to Daniel Jones (ed. of 1939):

preface sb and vb [prefis] ‖ *prefix* sb [ˈpri·fiks], vb [pri·ˈfiks] (or as sb) ‖ *prelude* sb and vb [ˈprelju·d] ‖ *premise* sb [ˈpremis], vb [priˈmaiz] (or as sb) ‖ *presage* sb [presidʒ], vb as sb or [priˈseidʒ] ‖ *present* sb and adj [preznt], vb [priˈzent, prə-].

ante-

27.8₄. *ante-* [ænti-] from the L adv and prep. *ante* 'before', occurs in loanwords from ME times, as in *antecedent, antechamber, antefix, antelucan, antepenultimate, ante-temple.*

From about 1600 *ante-* has been used as an independent prefix with the primary meaning of 'before' in place, time, or order. Thus in a local sense it is added to sbs, the derivative usually denoting a smaller introductory building, room, etc., as *ante-cavern, antechapel, antecloset, anteporch, anteportico, ante-stomach,* etc; similarly with adjs, mostly of a learned character, such as *ante-cœcal, ante-palatal, ante-pectoral.*

It means 'previous' in time or order in sbs like *antedate* (from which the vb), *ante-marriage* (Hope Q 274; also quoted vol II 14.66), *ante-taste,* etc. In adjs temporal *ante-* means 'existing or occurring before', as in *ante-Christian, antediluvian, antehistoric, ante-humous* (on the analogy of *posthumous,* cf sub *post-*), *antenatal, anteprandial.*

The prefix has also been added to native roots as in *ante-garden, ante-hall, ante-room; ante-dawn, ante-spring, ante-war.*

In some cases there are corresponding and generally commoner forms in *pre-,* thus with *-natal, -war, -historic, -classical, -human, -prandial.*

The loanwords *antecede, antecedence, antecedent* are stressed on the third syllable, all other words in *ante-* are stressed on the prefix.

post-

27.8₅. *post-* [poust-], from the L adv and prep *post* 'after, behind', occurs from early ME in loanwords borrowed direct or through F, e. g. *postpone, postposition,* and *postscript.*

It has been pretty frequently used to form derivatives

from words of L or F origin, referring to time or order, as in the sbs *post-date, post-existence,* and *post-issue,* in adjs like *post-classical, post-Darwinian, postdiluvian, postglacial, postmundane, postnatal,* and *postprandial,* and in vbs like *post-date, postfix.*

In some words mainly used as pre-adjuncts (exceptionally as predicatives) *post* retains its prepositional force, e. g. *post-Easter, post-election, post-lunch* (Bennett P 135 post-lunch coffee was merging into afternoon tea), *post-war* (period).

Post- refers to place (= 'behind') especially in words belonging to the terminology of anatomy and zoology, e. g. sbs like *post-abdomen, postcava, postfrons,* and adjs like *postaxial, postcentral,* and *post-palatal.*

Post- is always stressed and pronounced with [ou] except in *posthumous* [pɔstjuməs], which is actually from the Latin *postumus* 'last', but has been popularly interpreted as derived from *humus* 'earth' or *humare* 'bury'. In some words *t* may be dropped in interconsonantal position, e. g. in *post-graduate, post-mortem,* always in *postscript* [pous(s)kript].

mid-

27.9₁. *mid-* as a prefix, from the OE prep. *mid* 'with' was found in a certain number of sbs in OE, but they are all of them extinct. In ModE we have only one, *midwife.*

On a different prefix *mid-* 'middle' see vol II 12.55.

co-

27.9₂. *co-* [ko(u)-, ˈkou-] is from Latin *co-,* a prefixed form of the prep. *cum* 'with', as used before vowels, *h, gn,* and *n.* It occurs in loanwords from ME times, e. g. *coadjutor, coalesce, cooperate, coopt, cognate, cohere,* and as a living prefix has been used from ME, too, though without the phonetic limitations as in L: it

may be prefixed to L and native words beginning
with any sound.

It is prefixed to

(1) vbs, adding the sense 'together, jointly, equally',
e. g. *co-adjust, co-assist, co-assume, co-exist, co-extend,
co-twist* (Tennyson 320 New things and old co-twisted).
See list of nonce-words in NED,

(2) adjs (with derived advs), adding the sense 'together, mutually', etc., e. g. *co-adjacent, co-agent, coaxial*
(math.), *co-educational* (U. S.), *co-essential, co-eternal,
co-existent, co-extensive, co-polar* (math.), and *co-tidal*.
Here, too, NED has a list of nonce-words,

(3) nouns, thus to nexus-substantives, adding the
sense 'joint, mutual', e. g. *co-adaptation, co-agency, co-
effect, co-establishment, co-existence, co-insurance*, etc.

Further to agent-nouns and semantically related
words, adding the sense 'fellow-, joint', as in *co-brother*
(F *confrère*), *co-director, co-favourite, co-formulator* (Clodd,
Pioneers of Evolution 68), *co-godfather* (Tennyson L
2.114 a friend of mine, co-godfather to Dickens's child
with me), *co-inmate* (Brontë V 430), *co-labourer, co-
martyr, co-mate* (Tennyson 533), *co-owner, co-partner,
co-regent, co-sovereign, co-tenant*, etc.

A subdivision of (3) is formed by legal terms, such as
co-defendant, co-executor, co-heir, etc.

(4) Finally, *co-* is used in some mathematical terms
in the sense 'of the complement, complement of', e. g.
co-altitude, co-declination, co-latitude, etc.

The popularity of *co-* as compared with the related
forms *col-, com-, con-, cor-*, has given rise to some by-
forms of words with these prefixes, e. g. *co-centric,
co-natural, co-numerary, co-relation, co-rival, co-tempor-
ary, co-terminous; co-join, co-mingle*.

Words in *co-* are generally written with the hyphen,
though some established forms are frequently written
without the hyphen, e. g. *coadjutor, cooperate*, see MEU.

We may here mention the recent half-facetious use of L *cum*, though it is not strictly a prefix (not in NED with Suppl.): Priestley F 144 a lavatory-cum-smoke-room | ib 183 drawing-room-cum-writing-room |˙Porlock X v. Rex 151 the smartest dance-cum-supper places | ib 174 A first-class number one mystery-cum-counter jumper | Quentin P 47 the weekly formal dance-cum-bridge party.

syn-

27.9₃. *syn-* [sin-] is through L from Gk *syn-* 'with', which by assimilation developed to *syl-* before *l*, to *sym-* before labials, and was shortened to *sy-* before *s* + consonant and before *z*.

It occurs in loanwords from ME, e. g. *synagogue, synchronism, synonym, syntax, synthesis; symbol, symmetry, symphony, symposium, symptom; syllable, syllogism; system; syzygy.*

New words are formed with *sym-* and *syn-* only, all of them scientific terms, as *synchronology, syngamete, syntype; synclinal; sympatric, symmedian.*

In disyllables the prefix is stressed, in words of more than two syllables the (want of) stress on the prefix is rhythmically determined by the stress on the radical (cf vol I 5.61 ff.), e. g. *sym'bolic, sym'metric, syn'onymous, sym'posium, syn'thetic; ₁sympa'thetic, ₁sympto'matic.*

meta-

27.9₄. *meta-* [metə-], before a vowel *met-* [met-], thus also before *h, meth-* being pronounced [meþ-], is from the Gk prep. *meta* 'with, after'.

It occurs in loanwords from ME, e. g. *metabolic, metamorphosis, metaphysics,* and *metathesis.*

New-formations mainly belong to scientific and technical terminology, e. g. *metachromatic, metacyclic, metalbumin, metanalysis,* and *metaphosphate.*

On the mistaken analogy of *metaphysics* the prefix

has been added to names of sciences to denote 'higher' sciences, as in *metageometry*, *metamathematics*, *metaphysiology*, and *metapolitics*.

para-

27.9₅. *para-* [pærə-, pəⁱræ-], before a vowel or *h* generally *par-* [paˑ-, pəⁱr-], the Gk prep *para* 'beside', occurs in loanwords borrowed direct or through L or F from ME on, e. g. *parable*, *parabola*, *paradigm*, *paradox*, *paregoric*, *parenthesis*, *paragraph*, *parhelion*, *parallel*, *paralytic*, *parody*, and *parasite*.

New-formations on English soil are e. g. *paracentric*, *parachronism*, *paragenesis*, *paramagnetic*, and *paravane*.

Most words are stressed according to the rules given in vol I 5.61 ff.

In *parasol* we have not the prep., but It. *para* 'shelter (against)'; *paramount* and *paramour* are from F *par* + words beginning with *a-*.

Chapter XXVIII

Prefixes Concluded

First we take such prefixes as originate in particles.

be-

28.1₁. *be-* [bi-] is from OE *be-*, unstressed form of the particle *bi* (ModE *by*); cf G and Scand. *be-*. In ME *bi-* was the ordinary spelling, but in ModE *be-* has become the established form.

In early times the prefix was used in its original meaning 'about, at, near' to form prepositions and advs, as *before*, *behind*, *beneath*, *beside*, *between*, *beyond*. But its main function now is that of forming vbs.

The original sense 'about, around', figuratively 'thoroughly', is found in some old-established (and some obsolete) vbs derived from vbs, e. g. *bedabble*,

*bedaub, bedeck, begird, beslaver, beslobber, besmear, be-
smirch, bespatter, besprinkle, bethumb.* Vbs are no longer
coined with *be-* in this sense.

From the meaning 'around' etc., there is a natural
development to an intensive sense, 'thoroughly, too
much, ridiculously', as in *becalm, bedine* (Tennyson
L 2.21 I have been be-dined usque ad nauseam; not in
NED), *befit, beguile, belaud, bemuse, berate* (obs., exc. in
U. S.), *beseech.* Cf Börje Brilioth, Intensiva och iterativa
verb, bildade genom affix i engelskan. Nord. tidskr. f.
filol. 3. r. 20. 109.

28.1₂. *Be-* has further been used to form transitive
vbs from intransitives, as if adding a prepositional
meaning to them, e. g. *becrawl, bedrivel, beglare* (Di F
683 the person glared at . . . the beglared one), *bemoan,
bemock, bespeak, bestraddle, bestride, bewail,* and *bewrite.*

A use of *be-* now archaic is that of forming denominative vbs, the sbs or adjs being "taken as complements
of the predicate meaning to make" (NED), e. g. (from
adj) *bedim, befoul, belate* (especially in the second ptc),
belittle; (from sb) *bedevil, befool, bejesuit* (Mi A 54 who
has so bejesuited us . . . ; also Carlyle).

A subdivision of this group are words meaning 'to
style or dub', e. g. *be-David* (Stevenson K 80 I had
never been so be-Davided ['called David', his real
name] since I came on board), *beknave, berascal, berogue*
(Fielding (q Bladin 128) She beknaved, berascalled,
berogued the unhappy hero).

A privative sense of *be-* is found in the long-established
behead, and some obsolete words like *besleeve (a bishop).*

28.1₃. *Be-* is frequent in adjs in *-ed,* meaning 'provided
with' (a garment or similar object), and generally con-
ferring an element of depreciation or ridicule. This is
the commonest modern use of *be-.* Examples: *bebooted,
begemmed, bediamonded, bemedalled, be-nightmared* (Keats
194), *beribanded* (Carlyle SR 66), *bespectacled, bewigged.*

Finally, *be-* is used to form vbs from sbs with the

meaning 'cover, affect, or treat in some way', e. g.
becloud, bedew, beflea (Lowell 312 one of those bores,
Who beflead with bad verses poor Louis Quatorze),
beflower (Caine E 456 gold beflowerings), *beglamour*
(Shaw D 155 beglamouring the human imagination),
begrime, bemire, benight, betroth. In some of these vbs,
too, there is an element of intensity or excess.

ana-

28.1₄. *ana-* [ænə-], before a vowel *an-* [æn-], from
the Gk adv *ana* 'up, back, again, anew', occurs in loanwords from early ModE on, e. g. *anabaptist, anachron-
ism, anacoluthia, anagram, analogy, analysis, anapœst,
anatomy*, and *aneurysm*.

Some words of a learned character have been coined
on English soil, mainly in recent times, e. g. *anacathartic,
anacrotism, anamorphism, anaseismic*, and *anatopism*.

re-

28.2₁. *re-* [re-, rə-, ri-, ˌriˑ-] represents Latin *re-* 'back,
again', and occurs in a great many loanwords borrowed
from about 1200 on, often through F. Most of these
are vbs or deverbatives, e. g. *receive, rejoice, remember,
respond, restrain, restrict; recruit, renaissance, respect,
review; reciprocal, recondite, relative*, and *reverent*.

From late ME, especially after 1600, the prefix has
been productive in English, chiefly in the sense of
'again' (repetition of an action or reversion to a former
state), as in *readjust(ment), reanimate, reappear(ance),
re-arrange(ment), reassume, re-attain* (Arnold Poems 113),
recommence, re-distil, re-edit, remarry, remodel (Pater
R 204), *remould* (ib 218), *retranslate*, and *revisit* (Pater
R 206). In the new-formation *reassure* the original
sense of the prefix has been lost.

28.2₂. *Re-* is not only, as in the above examples,
prefixed to words of L or F origin, but also to native

words, e. g. *reawake* (Morley Human Being 178), *re-become* (AHuxley Barren Leaves 273), *re-birth* (Ward M 10, Wells A 71, Shaw Ms 6), *reborn* (Ward M 406), *rebuild, re-do* (Linklater J 163 His fingers undid and re-did the single button in his coat), *refasten, regild, rekindle, reknit* (Ward M 235), *remake* (Morley M 1.201), *reread* (Ward M 424), *re-sale* (Bennett W 2.198), *re-sell* (Stevenson K 13 [T]), and *retake* (of a film, sb). Dyboski 391-2 quotes from Tennyson the following formations from native roots: *relive, resmooth, remade, re-makes, retake, reseated, regather, rebuilt, resold, reborn, requicken'd, re-arise.*

A group of derivatives are formed from sbs or vbs from nouns. These words mean 'provide anew with or again turn into', e. g. *recoal, recoat, recolour, re-engine, reface, re-father* (Tennyson 206 My father stoop'd, re-father'd o'er my wounds), *rehouse, re-ink, relabel, remast, repaper, resole, restock, retype*, etc. Further from vbs derived with a suffix (especially *-ize* and *-ate*), e. g. *rebarbarize, rehumanize, reinvigorate, repaganize, repopulate.*

28.2₃. The general rules for pronunciation of words in *re-* are as follows (cf vol I 9.13):

In loanwords the prefix, when stressed (with full or secondary stress) is pronounced [re-], e. g. in *reference, remedy, reminiscence; refutable, reticent, reverential; recommend, reconcile*, and *represent.*

When unstressed (thus in the great majority of loanwords), it is pronounced [ri-], as in *receipt, religion, renown; remote, repugnant; rebuke, reply*, etc.

In words coined on English soil the prefix is pronounced [ˈriˑ-], as in *re-apply, rediscover, refashion, re-open, re-write*, etc.

But there are many overlappings, thus some loanwords with stressed *re-* according to Jones have [riˑ-], e. g. *recantation, recapitulation, recrudesce(nce)* (also

[ˌre-]), *reflex* (sb and adj), *reflux, regress* (sb), *rehabilitate,
-tation, rejuvenesce(ence), relaxation, repass, repercussion,
retardation,* and *retraction.*

And some loanwords are always or occasionally pronounced with unstressed [iˑ], e. g. *react(ion), rebound*
(sb and vb), *recede, reclaim, repay, replete,* and *repletion.*

On the other hand some vbs and deverbative sbs
coined on English soil have (or may have) short unstressed [ri-], thus *recall, re-echo, refine, rejuvenate, re-
mind, renew, replace* (Jones: [riˑˈpleis] or secondarily
[riˈpleis]), and *requite* [riˈkwait, rəˈkwait].

It should be noted that in the above-mentioned
loanwords with stressed [riˑ-] the prefix has preserved
its independence and to the linguistic instinct is generally felt as identical with *re-* in the English formations.
In the native verbs with unstressed [ri-] the prefix
generally has the sense of 'back' (not 'again'), or it is
no longer felt as independent.

28.2₄. Often a new derivative with *re-* [ˈriˑ-] 'again,
anew' has been coined from a simple English loanword
where a corresponding loanword with [ˈre-] or [ri-] in
a different sense already existed. Such new-formations
are generally written with a hyphen to keep them apart
from the early forms, e. g. (the old loans placed first):

react [riˈækt] : *react* [ˈriˑˈækt] 'act again' ‖ *rebound*
[riˈbaund] 'spring back' : *rebound* [ˈriˑˈbaund] ptc of
rebind ‖ *recoil* [riˈkoil] 'shrink back' : *recoil* [ˈriˑˈkoil]
'coil again' ‖ *recollect* [ˌrekəˈlekt] 'remember' (Jones
also [ˈriˑkəˈlekt] in the sense 'regain one's composure') :
recollect [ˈriˑkəˈlekt] ‖ *recount* [riˈkaunt] 'tell' : *recount*
[ˈriˑˈkaunt] 'count again' ‖ *recover* [riˈkʌvə] 'get back' :
recover [ˈriˑˈkʌvə] 'cover again' ‖ *recreate* [ˈrekrieit]
'refresh' : *re(-)create* [ˈriˑkriˈeit] 'create anew' (Wilde
P 29 I hope to be able to recreate my creative faculty |
Collingwood R 277 man re-creating himself) ‖ *recreation*
[ˌrekriˈeiʃən] : *recreation* [ˈriˑkriˈeiʃən] ‖ *redouble* [riˈdʌbl]
(also [riˑˈdʌbl]) 'intensify' : *redouble* [ˈriˑˈdʌbl] 'double

again' || *redress* [ri·ǀdres] 'make amends for' : *redress* [ǀri·ǀdres] 'dress again' || *refôrm* [ri·ǀfɔ·m] 'make or become better' : *re-form* [ǀri·ǀfɔ·m] 'form again' (By DJ 3.59 Our little selves re-form'd in finer clay; frequent) || *rejoin* [ri·ǀdʒoin] 'answer' : *re-join* [ǀri·dʒoin] 'join again' || *remark* [ri·ǀma·k] 'observe' : *re-mark* [ǀri·ǀma·k] 'mark again' || *repay* [ǀri·ǀpei, ri·ǀpei, ǀri·ǀpei] 'pay back' : *re-pay* [ǀri·ǀpei] 'pay a second time' || *resign* [ri·ǀzain] 'give up' : *re-sign* [ǀri·ǀsain] 'sign again' || *resolution* [ˌrezəǀlu·ʃən] 'determination, etc.' : *re-solution* [ǀri·səǀlu·-ʃən] (Poe 173 the faculty of re-solution) || *resolve* [ri·ǀzɔlv] 'determine' : *re-solve* [ǀri·ǀsɔlv] 'solve again' || *resound* [ri·ǀzaund] 'echo, etc.' : *re-sound* [ǀri·ǀsaund] 'sound again'.

For voiced *s* in old loans, unvoiced *s* in new-formations see vol I 6.66.

28.2₅. In the list of sbs and vbs spelt alike but with different stress given in vol I 5.73 there are a number of word-pairs in *re-*. I shall here give a new list of such pairs in *re-* with pronunciation according to Daniel Jones:

rebate sb [ǀri·beit, ri·ǀbeit]—vb [ri·ǀbeit]
rebel [rebl]—[ri·ǀbel, rəǀbel]
record [rekɔ·d]—[ri·ǀkɔ·d, rəǀkɔ·d]
refuse [refju·s]—[ri·ǀfju·z, rəǀfju·z]
regress [ri·gres]—[ri·ǀgres]
reprint [ǀri·ǀprint]—[ǀri·ǀprint, ri·ǀprint]
retail [ǀri·teil, ri·ǀteil]—[ri·ǀteil, ri·ǀteil, ǀri·teil].

28.2₆. Derivatives in *re-* from words in *e-* have usually the hyphen, e. g. *re-echo*, *re-enter*, thus also often before other vowels, as *re-armament*, *re-iterate*, *re-organize*. Further the hyphen is used if the writer wants to point out that *re-* is here an independent prefix, perhaps coined for the occasion, e. g. *re-christen*, *re-group*, *re-label*, especially if there is another word (loanword) otherwise spelt in the same way, but with a different sense and pronunciation, e. g. *re-cover*, see above 28.2₄.

Finally the hyphen is frequently used if the derivative is contrasted with the simple word, e. g. *do and re-do, discussion* and *re-discussion,* etc.

retro-

28.2₇. *retro-* [retrou-, ri·trou- (-trə-)], from the L adv *retro* 'backwards, back', occurs in loanwords (sbs, adjs, vbs) from the 14th c. on, e. g. *retroact, retrocede, retroflex, retrograde, retrospect(ion),* and *retroversion,* and especially in the 19th and 20th c. has been used to form new words, practically only from L roots, e. g. *retrodate* (vb), *retroform* (vb), *retroject* (vb), *retro-operative, retroposition, retroseer* (N.B. nonce-word coined from native root), *retro-vaccination,* and *retrovision.* In these words the prefix has the meaning 'backwards, back'. In some scientific terms, mainly from the sphere of anatomy and pathology, the prefix has the meaning 'behind' (an organ), e. g. *retrolingual, retropharyngeal, retroperitoneal,* and *retrosternal.*

This prefix is always stressed (with primary or secondary stress) on the first syllable. For *retroflex* or *retrograde* Daniel Jones gives only the pronunciation [retrou-] or [retrə-], in all other words he gives [ri·-] as secondary possibility.

28.3. Finally we take prefixes not originating from particles, but from more or less full words, and first those referring to number and quantity. Corresponding to the native *half,* which enters into several compounds, e. g. *halfway, halfpay, halfmoon,* etc., we have no less than three foreign prefixes, *demi-, semi-,* and *hemi-.*

demi-

28.3₁. *demi-* [ᵈdemi-] from F *demi-,* prefixed use of *demi,* from L *dīmidium* 'half', occurs in loanwords borrowed from ME on, such as *demi-lance, demilune, demimonde, demi-season.*

From the 15th c. it has been used as an independent
prefix, mainly in substantival terms from official and
social life, thus in many heraldic and military terms,
and some musical ones, also in names of costume and
fabrics, stuffs, etc., e. g. *demi-bastion, demi-bombard,
demi-brigade, demi-cuirass* (military), *demi-angel, demi-
figure, demi-lion, demi-virgin* (heraldic), *demisemiquaver
demi(semi)tone* (musical), *demi-circle.*

There are few formations from native roots, note,
however, *demi-bath,* translating F *demi-bain,* and *demi-
god,* translating L *demideus,* and some heraldic terms,
e. g. *demi-belt, -horse, -man, -ship,* and *-wyvern.*

semi-

28.3₂. *semi-* [semi-] is from Lat. *semi-* 'half'. It occurs
in a comparatively small number of loanwords adopted
from ME on, e. g. *Semi-Arian, semibreve, semi-chorus,
semicircle, semicircular, semilunar,* and *Semi-Pelagian.*

It has been frequently used as an independent prefix from early ModE, mainly in derivatives from sbs
and adjs of L and F origin, as the following words,
which are in general use: *semi-form, semi-opacity; semi-
barbarian, semi-divine, semi-nude, semi-official, semi-
opaque, semi-savage,* and *semi-transparent.*

The prefix has been used to form nonce-words especially from the beginning of the 19th c., see long lists
in NED.

Advs in *-ly* prefixed with *semi-* occur, too, e. g.
semi-adjectively and *semi-consciously.* Further a few
participles, e. g. *semi-attached* and *semi-detached.*

Vbs in *semi-* are comparatively rare. Examples are
semi-close, semi-conceal (NED, nonce-word), and *semi-flex.*

According to Horwill Mod. Am. Usage 277 *semi-*
"is in much more frequent use in Am. than in Eng."
He quotes *semi-annual* (for *half-yearly*), *semi-centennial,
semi-national, semi-open-air* (used as an adjunct), *semi-
wild, semi-panic,* and *semi-occasionally.*

Besides these new-formations of a general kind we have a great number of words of a technical and scientific character, e. g. *semi-quaver* (and *semidemisemiquaver*); *semi-axis*, *semi-ellipse*, *seminvariant* (with elision of *i*, also *semi-invariant*), *semi-parabola; semifloret; semi-deponent*, *semi-vowel; semi-conjugate*, *semicubical; semi-oval*, *semi-palmate*, and *semi-vitreous*.

Semi- has been prefixed to words of native origin, too, e. g. in *semi-ape*, *semi-clasp*, *semi-darkness*, *semigod* (transl. of L *semideus*), *semi-hard* (steel), *semi-light*, *semi-mild* (steel), *semi-monthly*, *semi-smile*, *semi-weekly*, and *semi-white* (glass; or = 'half-caste').

This prefix has always initial stress.

hemi-

28.3₃. *hemi-* [hemi-] is from Greek *hēmi-* 'half-' (parallel to L *semi-*), and occurs in loanwords (occasionally borrowed through F) from ME times. Loanwords are *hemicycle*, *hemipter*, *hemisphere*, and *hemistich*.— New formations are such technical or scientific terms as *hemibranch*, *hemicarp*, *hemidemisemiquaver*, *hemidome*, *hemiprism*, *hemisymmetry*, and *hemisystematic*.

uni-, un-

28.4₁. *uni-* [juˑni-], before a vowel *un-* [juˑn-], from the L numeral *unus* 'one', occurs in loanwords from ME on, e. g. *unanimous*, *unicorn*, *uniform*, *unify*, *unisexual*, *unison*, *universe* (*-sal*), *university*, and *univocal*.

A large number of adjs and a few sbs, nearly all belonging to scientific terminology have been coined in ModE, all from L or Gk roots. Examples are: *unicursal*, *unilateral*, *uniplanar*, *unipolar*, *univalent*, and *univalve*.

mono-, mon-

28.4₂. *mono-* [mɔnou-, mɔnə-] (before a vowel sometimes *mon-* [mɔn-]), from Gk *mónos* 'alone, only, single', occurs in a number of loanwords such as *monarch*, *monochord*, *monochrome*, *monocle*, *monogram*, *monograph*, *monologue*, *monomania*, and *monophthong*, and in some words coined on English soil, mainly scientific terms derived from Gk and L stems. In terms from chemistry it denotes the presence of one atom of the element denoted by the stem.

Examples of new-formations are: *monocalcic*, *monocarbon*, *monochloride*, *monogyny* (1876, coined by Spencer), *monomark*, *monoplane*, *mono-rail*, *monorganic*, *mono-sentence* (Keats 4.7 a few mono-sentences), and *monoxide*.

bi-

28.5₁. *bi-* [bai-, bi-] represents L *bi-* from *bis* 'twice', and occurs in English in F and L loanwords from ME times, e. g. *bigamy* (ME), *bipedal* (ME), *biscuit* (ME), *biceps*, *bicycle*, *biennial* (cf *annual*), *biform*, *bifurcate*, *bilingual*, *bimetallic*, *binominal*, *bipartite*, *biped*.

From the 16th c. *bi-* has been productive and prefixed to sbs, adjs, and advs.

The largest group of new-formations is that of adjs, which may be subdivided as follows.

(1) The prefix adds the sense 'having two, doubly, in two ways, on both sides', as in *bicameral*, *bicaudal*, *bilabial*, *bilateral*, *bipolar*, *biramous* 'with two branches' (1877, coined by Huxley), and *bisexual*.

(2) Words denoting time. Most of these are coined from native forms in *-ly*, and some of them are used as sbs with the meaning 'periodical publication', and those in *-ly* may also be used as adverbs. Examples: *biannual* (cf the loanword *biennial*), *bi-monthly*, *bi-quarterly*, *bi-weekly*, *bi-yearly*. On account of their ambiguity (two-weekly and half-weekly) Fowler MEU condemns these words.

(3) In some words from the terminology of botany and zoology, *bi-* means 'twice over', e. g. *bicrenate*, *bipinnate*, *biserrate*.

(4) In terms from chemistry (both sbs and adjs) *bi*-has the sense 'having two equivalents of—', as in *biacid, bicarbide, bicarbonate, bichloride, bivalent*, etc.

Sbs in *bi*- are not very numerous. Examples are: *bilocation, bimillenary, bi-millionaire, bi-segment*, and *bi-venter*.

In words coined from native roots (thus those in *-ly*) the hyphen is generally used.

Bi- is pronounced [bai-] except in a few loanwords: *bigamist, bigamy, biparous, bipedal* (also [bai-]), and *biscuit*.

Sbs are generally stressed on the prefix, in most adjs the prefix is unstressed. Sbs with unstressed prefix are *bimetallism, bimillenary, bimodulus*, and others originally adjs. Adjs with full or secondary stress on *bi*- are e. g. *bicentennial, bifocal, biparous, bipedal, biquadratic*, and those derived from native roots (in *-ly*).

From the corresponding native prefix, OE *twi*- the only word surviving is *twilight*.

poly-

28.5₂. *poly*- [pɔli-, pɔ‖li-], from *polýs, polý* 'much' (pl *polloi* 'many'), occurs in loanwords from late ME on, e. g. *polyandry, polychrome, polygamy, polyglot, polygon, polyhistor, polyhedron, polytechnic*, and *polytheism*.

Sbs and adjs have been coined on English soil from early ModE, e. g. *polygeny, polygyny, polysyllable; polyatomic*, and *polygenic*.

Most words in *poly*- have full or secondary stress on the first syllable, but in a few cases the second syllable, being the third last syllable of the word carries the main stress, e. g. *po‖lygamous, po‖lygenous, po‖lyphony* (also ‖*polyphony*), and *po‖lytomy* (cf vol I 5.61 ff.).

pan-

28.5₃. *pan*- [pæn-], from Gk *pan*-, combining form of *pas, pan* 'all', occurs in loanwords borrowed direct from

Gk or through L or F, e. g. *pancreas, pandects, panegyric, panoply, pantheon,* and in a great number of words coined on E soil. The commonest use of the prefix is in words for nationality, religion, or related ideas, The three largest groups are adjs, nexus-words in *-ism,* and agent-nouns in *-ist.*

Examples: *Pan-American, -ism, -ist, Pan-Anglican, Pan-Buddhist, Pan-Celtic, Pan-German, Pan-Islamism,* and *Panslavism, -ist..*

Other formations: *pandemonium* (coined by Milton: PL 1.756), *pangenesis* (coined by Darwin), *panharmonic, panorama, pantechnic(on),* and *pantheist* with *pantheism.*

panto-

28.5₄. *panto-* [pæntə-], before a vowel *pant-* [pænt-], from the same Gk word as the preceding prefix, occurs in loanwords from early ModE, *pantometer, pantomime,* etc. New-formations are *pantisocracy, pantology,* and *pantoscope.*

proto-

28.6₁. *proto-* [proutə-], before a vowel generally *prot-* [prout-, prɔt-], from Gk *prōtos* 'first', occurs in loanwords from late ME on, e. g. *protocol, protomartyr, protonotary, protoplasm, protopope* (from Russ.), *prototype,* and *protozoon* (*-zoa*).

New-formations in *proto-* are not much used in general language. Among the examples quoted in NED, most of them nonce-words, are *proto-apostate, proto-architect, proto-bishop, proto-deacon, protogod* (N.B. from a native root), *protohistoric,* and *proto-rebel.* In these words the prefix means 'arch, chief, first, or primitive'.

But in scientific language the prefix is of frequent occurrence, thus to denominate primitive tribes or languages, etc., e. g. *proto-Arabic, proto-Celtic, proto-Greek,* and *proto-Semitic.* Further *proto-* is used to form terms of zoology, biology, crystallography, etc. Here, too, it generally means 'primitive'. Examples are *pro-tembryonic*, *protoblast*, *protocerebral*, *protodome*, *proto-morph(ic)*, *protopyramid*, *protosystematic*, etc.

Finally, it is used in various special senses to form terms of chemistry, e. g. *protoxide*, *protochloride*, *prot-iodide*, and *protosulphide*.

This prefix has initial stress.

neo-

28.6₂. *neo-* [ni(·)ou-], from Gk *néos* 'new', occurs in a number of loanwords, e. g. *neolithic*, *neologism*, and *neophyte*. As an independent prefix it is added to words denoting a doctrine or practice; it further occurs in derived adjs and sbs meaning 'pertaining or adherent to such new doctrine, etc.'. Examples: *neo-Catholic*, *neo-classic(al)*, *neo-classicism*, *neo-Darwinian*, *neo-Lamarck-ian* (Spencer F 92), *neo-Ignatius* and *neo-Sandow* (AHuxley EG 326), *neo-Kantian* (ib 192), *neo-Platonic*, *-ism*, *-ist*.

In geological terms forms in *neo-* mean '(belonging to) a later part of a period', e. g. *neo-Cambrian*, *neo-Devonian*, and *neolithic*. Finally, students of modern forms of plants, animals, etc. may be designated with a noun in *neo*, as *neo-botanist*, *neo-zoologist*, etc.

palæo- (paleo-)

28.6₃. *palæo-* (The spelling *paleo-* esp. common in U.S.) [ˈpælio-, pælioˈ-, pæliˈɔ-], from Gk *palaios* 'old', oc-curs in a number af loanwords, *palæography*, *palæo-litlc*, *palæontology*. It has been used to form sbs and adjs of a learned character, often corresponding to words coined with *neo-*, e. g. *palæobotany*, *-ist*, *palæo-type*, *-typography*, *palæozoic*, *palæozoology*.

pseudo-

28.6₄. *pseudo-* [(p)sjuˑdo-] (before a vowel generally *pseud-* [(p)sjuˑd-]) is from the stem of Gk *pseudés* 'false'; it occurs in loanwords from late ME, e. g. *Pseudo-Christ*, *pseudograph*, *pseudology*, and *pseudonym*, and has been used on E soil to form some learned words, mainly from Gk and L roots, e. g. *pseudannual*, *pseudo-carp*, *pseudo-catholic*, *pseudo-classicism*, *pseudembryo(nic)*, *pseudo-philosopher*, *pseudo-reduction*, and *pseudo-velocity*. It is rarely added to native roots as in *pseudo-heart* and *pseudo-nipple*.

In combination with more common words, as in *pseudo-catholic*, *pseudo-Gothic*, etc, the hyphen is gener-ally used, whereas it is generally left out in strictly scientific terms, e. g. *pseudoquadratic*, *pseudospherical*, and *pseudopregnancy*.

It is used as an independent sb in Mannin CI 106 someone in whom was no trace of the pseudo or third rate.

auto-

28.6₅. *auto-* [ɔ·to(u)-] (*aut-* [ɔ·t-], *auth-* [ɔ·þ-] before a vowel in some loanwords), is from Gk *autos* 'self'. Loanwords are found in English from the modern period only, e. g. *autarch(y)*, *authentic*, *autobiography*, *autocracy*, *automatic*, *autonomy*, and *autopsy*.

Formations on English soil are mainly of a more or less learned character, e. g. *auto-infection*, *autology*, *autometry*, and *autotype*.

Words like *autobus*, *autocar*, and *auto-coach* are compounds with *auto* as an elliptical form of *automobile*.

vice-

28.7. *vice-* [vais-] is from the L prep. *vice* 'in place of' from the sb *vix*, *vicis* 'change'. In OF it was shortened to *vi-*, *vis-*, and the earliest E loanwords (from late ME) were adopted with the forms *vis-* (*viz-*) or *vi-* (*vy-*). The short spelling (and pronunciation) is preserved in *viscount* [vaikaunt]. In all other words the L spell-ing and the pronunciation with *-s* have been restored.

Loanwords are *vice-admiral*, *vice-chancellor*, *vice-consul*, *viceroy*. New-formations occur from early ModE,
e. g. *vice-governor*, *vice-manager*, *vice-president*, *vice-rector*, *vice-regent*, and from native or naturalized roots
vice-chairman, *vice-dean*, *vice-god*, *vice-king*, *vice-sheriff*,
and *vice-warden*.

As occasion arises the prefix may be used to form
new words from any word denoting holder of some
office, e. g. (from the long list in NED) *vice-abbot*, *vice-Apollo*, *vice-butler*, *vice-husband*.

Corresponding to *viscount* and *viceroy* have been
coined the adjectives *vice-comital* and *vice-regal*.

According to Daniel Jones words in *vice-* as a rule have
double stress. The prefix is always stressed.

arch-

28.8₁. *arch-* [aˑtʃ-] is from OF *arche*, from Gk
arkhos 'chief'. It occurs in loanwords from OE times,
archbishop (OE *ærce-*, *erce*, *arce-*), *archdeacon* (OE *arce-*,
erce-), *archduke*, *archpriest*.

New-formations from Latin roots are *arch-enemy*, *arch-heretic*, *arch-traitor*, *arch-villain*, *arch-versifier* (Goldwin
Smith, Cowper 3 the arch-versifier Pope), etc. From
native roots *arch-fiend*, *arch-foe*, *arch-knave*, and *arch-liar*.

The meaning of the prefix is 'pre-eminent, chief,
superior, worst', and it is mainly added to words de-noting persons, but also to other words, such as *arch-diocese*, *archduchy*, *archdukedom*, *archheresy*.

To some of these sbs corresponding adjs have been
formed, e. g. *archbishoply*, *archducal*.

archi-

28.8₂. *archi-* [aˑki-] is a by-form of *arch-* and occurs
in the same senses in loanwords like *archimandrite*,
archipelago (from Ital.), *archiphoneme* (coined by
Trubetzkoy), *architect*, and in some new-formations, as
the sbs *archiepiscopacy*, *archiepiscopate*, *archigony*, and

adjectives like *architectural*. Occasionally we have an
adjective in *archi-* corresponding to a substantive in *arch-*,
e.g. *archideaconal* : *archdeacon, archiepiscopal* : *archbishop*.

Note the pronunciation with [k], which is also found
in the old loan *archangel* [a·keindʒəl].

Final Remarks on Prefixes

28.9. On surveying the whole field of prefixes I am
struck by the numerous instances of what in a recent
book I have termed *Efficiency in linguistic change*. If
we look through the older prefixes and their uses, we
see innumerable irregularities in form, in stress, in
pronunciation generally, and especially in meaning, the
modification in sense brought about by the addition of
the prefix being generally so vague that it cannot be
strictly defined. On the other hand those prefixes that
have been extremely popular in new-formations during
the last century or two have one invariable form with
regard to sound and stress, and each of them has one
easily defined meaning.

Compare thus the following examples, the new ones
placed before, and the old ones after the double-stroke:

co-worker ‖ *collide, conceive, compare, corrupt.*

ex-king ‖ *examine, example, excess, (edition, effect).*

prehistory ‖ *precise, prefer, preference, prejudice.*

pro-German ‖ *process, produce;* cf the native *forget,
forgive.*

re-write, re-sign ‖ *refer, reference, refuse, resign, resignation.*

superman, superstructure ‖ *superfluous, superstition.*

Chapter XXIX

Shortenings

29.1. After considering those cases in which a kernel
has been used unchanged, with internal change, and

with additions either in the form of suffixes or of prefixes, our task is now to consider those cases in which
a kernel is shortened in some way or other. The result
cannot be considered an incomplete kernel, for to the
speaker the expression of his thought is just as complete
as if he had used a full kernel or a kernel + a suffix
or a prefix: the outcome is rather to be considered a
new kernel, even if from a historical point of view it
can or must be looked upon as a shortened kernel.
These shorter words are called clipped words, elliptical
words, or curtailments: I have ventured to coin the
name *stump-words* (Dan. *stumpeord*, rendered in the
German translation of my *Language* as *stutzwörter*).

Literature. Karl Sundén, *Ellipt. Words in Modern English*.
Uppsala 1904 (after a valuable introduction on ellipsis in
word-structure and sentence-structure Sundén gives a full
treatment of shortenings of proper names; the continuation
promised in the preface never appeared).—H. Bradley, *The
Making of English* p. 147 ff.—Elisabeth Wittmann, *Clipped
Words* (Dial. Notes IV. 2. 1914: a wealth of material, but
badly arranged, i. a. according to number of syllables in the
original words, which is quite irrelevant).—Koziol pp. 218—
229 with numerous references to further literature on the
subject.—I myself have touched on the subject in various
places, to begin with *Subtraktionsdannelser* in *Festskrift til
Vilhelm Thomsen* 1894, in *Language* (= Die Sprache) VII § 7
and IX § 7, in *Monosyllabism* (*Linguistica* p. 387), and in
Efficiency in Ling. Change 3.5.

Beginning Kept
Clipped Compounds

29.2₁. First we take those cases in which the beginning is retained. This is the natural way of shortening
words for everybody who already knows the full word,
whether the shortening is done intentionally or by inadvertence.

Here we have different categories according to what
is left out. First we shall consider those words in which

the omitted part is a full word of independent meaning.
This is found in clipped compounds. I have dealt with
the subject first in vol II 8.9 and then above in 8.9₃
and 8.9₄: the analytic formula is 2-1⁰: an incomplete
compound in which the final part which is really the
semantically important (primary) part is left out. The
ellipsis is thus parallel to what takes place when *hard* is used
for *hard labour* (as a punishment), or *general* for *general
servant*, or *the Underground* for *the Underground railway:*
when the speaker has pronounced the secondary he
feels that he is sufficiently understood and therefore
leaves out the primary as superfluous for the moment.
(The phenomenon also resembles that found in bahuvrihi compounds, above 8.6 *red-coat* = *red-coat soldier*).

29.2₂. I may be pardoned for here adding still more
examples to those given in 8.9, my excuse being that
some of my slips had been mislaid when I wrote that
paragraph.

Alarum = alarum clock (the usual form, but Brontë
I 263 an alarm to call her up early) | *Billingsgate* = B.
language (common) | *briar* = b. pipe (e. g. Walpole
SC 10) | *coster* = coster-monger | *fag* = fag-end of
cigarette, hence also 'cheap cigarette' | *foots* = foot-
lights (theatrical slang) | *Ford* = F. car | *the frogs* =
frog-eaters, i. e. the French (Lynch, Isles of Illusion
311) | *gooseberry* = g. wine (Goldsm V 1.45) | *gran* =
grandfather (Galsw IC 168) | *hot-house* = h.-h. flower
(Bennett LM 137) | *house-warming* = h.-w. party
(Wells Ma 2.113) | *lunch* = l. room (common U. S.,
an all-night lunch) | *the Marshalsea* = the M. prison
(often mentioned in Dickens's times) | *the Mays* = the
May examination (Benson B 3) | *meerschaum* = m.
pipe (Doyle M 92) | *mid* = midshipman | *penalty* =
p. kick | *pinny* = pinafore | *Salvation* = S. Army
(a S. chorus, Caine C 162, 170) | *shower* = sh. bath
(Maugham Alt 238) | *sleuth* = s. hound (Galsw WM
195, 199) | *speak* = speakeasy (U. S., Hammett Th

96, 199) | *stage* obs. = stage-coach (e. g. Southey L
103) | *stock* = s. gilliflower | *Stop Press* = s. p. news
in the paper (Galsw FM 89, id IC 102) | *strawberry*
= s. ice (Zangwill G 66 "... another ice." "We haven't
got any more strawberries") | *string* = s. instrument
(NP 1924 an orchestra composed of a piano and a
few strings) | *tram* = t. car | *the Tate* = the T. Gallery
(Galsw WM 24) | *Worcester* = W. sauce (Jerome T
17).

Train is often left out in indications like Benson
D 67 telegraph to him to come by the eight-twenty |
Maugham HB 386 We'll go over by the eleven o'clock |
id Pl 2.238 They want to catch the four something
back to London | Lewis B 313 he leaves town on the
midnight.

Here also belong (with added [i]) *movie(s)* = moving
picture(s), *talkies* (for a short time *speakies*). Cf. 13.4₆.

This kind of shortening is frequent with articles of
garment: *patent-leather* = p.-l. shoe | *shovel* = (bishop's)
shovel-hat (Thack N 296) | *swallow-tail* = s.-t. coat
(Thack N 88) | *tails* = tail-coat (Maugham Pl 4.302 |
tam = *tam-o'-shanter* = tam-o'-shanter cap.

With the hypocoristic *-y* or *-ie* (above 13.4₆) we have
nightie for night gown or night shirt, *undies* = under-
wear, and *hanky* = handkerchief.

Dance is left out in *a two-step* (e. g. Norris S 241);
note the pl in Locke W 276 he could dance one-steps
and two-steps with the best | Wells JP 444 this Christmas
party was pervaded with One Steps and Two Steps.

The last element of an adj-compound is left out:
Cowper L 2.380 I have built one sommer-house ...
and am building another *spick and span*, as they say
(new, nowadays very common) | Maugham Alt 267
they had taken his English clothes off him and he was
stark (naked, also Buchanan J 83).

Snapshot is short for s. picture, but it may be further
shortened into *snap:* Mannin Conf 58 I have a collec-

tion of snapshots of himself and Charmian London ...
and a collection of snaps ...

Similarly *vacuum-cleaner* becomes first *vacuum* (Golding SD 290 the electric vacuum) and then *vac* (as a
vb in Pritchard Ess. Mod. E. 125).

Short words expanded by means of *-y* are *bookie* for
bookmaker, *cabby* for cabman, *middy* for midshipman.

Other examples above 13.4$_6$, examples with *-o* 13.8$_1$
with *-er* 14.2$_8$.

In some consciously coined compound terms one part only
of one of the elements is used. Ethnologists and geographers
will speak of *Amer*(ican)*indians*, *Eur*(ope)*asia* and *Eur*(ope)-
africa. In London the railway from Baker Street to Waterloo
Station is called the *Bakerloo*. In U. S. *Prohiblican* at one time
stood for Prohibitionist and Republican. Many chemical
names of substances are formed in this way, e. g. the international *chloroform* from chlorine + formic. So are many trade-
names, e. g. *Nabisco* from *Na*(tional) *Bis*(cuit) *Co*(mpany). Cf
also *cable*(tele)*gram*.

Back-Formations

29.3. Next we have to consider those clippings in
which what is left out has no independent value as a
word, but is a sense-modifying element. This is the
case with back-formations proper, or what in 1894 I
termed *subtraction-forms* (but El. Wittmann uses the
term = any shortening in which the end is retained).
Examples are found in various parts of this book,
listed under each of the suffixes subtracted, see Index
sub Back-formation.

The characteristic trait of back-formation in contrast to other shortenings is that it always presupposes
an analysis of the word different from the original or
historical way of building it up, a re-interpretation, a
'metanalysis'. Thus when *pease* becomes *pea*, or *Chinese*,
Chinee, the *s* is, contrary to etymology, taken to be
the plural ending. When the vb *housekeep* is formed,

the reason is that *housekeeper*, which is an ordinary
compound of *house* and *keeper*, is metanalyzed as
formed by the addition of the suffix *-er* to a composite
vb. (Or it may be from the gerund *housekeeping* being
similarly misdivided). Similarly with *-er* in *butcher*, etc.
(see 14.3₉). From *poetaster* we sometimes have a vb
poetast. From *motor* is formed the vb *mote* 'go by motor'.
In *cad* from *caddy* and *pup* from *puppy* the ending *-y*
has been subtracted as if the hypocoristic *-y*, though
it came from totally different F endings (see 13.4₉).
Note also *hon* from *honey* as a pet-name for one's
wife (Lewis B 25) and *beaut* for *beauty* (Plunket
Greene E 82 She's a beaut.). Consequently shortenings of this category differ from the other categories
in that they otten lead to a new word belonging to
another word-class than the original word. Thus the
occasional vbs *luminesce*, *reminisce*, *retice* and *reluct*
from forms in *-ent*, *-ant*, and *enthuse* from *enthusiasm*
(EStn 70.120 f.).

Main Class of Stump-Words

29.4₁. The last, and by far the most numerous class
of shortenings comprises those in which what is left
out has no significance at all to the speaker of the
moment, whatever it may have meant when the word
was originally framed. In such cases the curtailment is
simply an instance of 'aposiopesis', or more popularly
a stop-short or pull-up sentence parallel to "Well, I
never!" or similar exclamations. Thus in "Half a *mo*!"
(Doyle S 1153, Bennett LR 160, Maugham Pl 3.332,
Crofts C 29) | *sec* (Kipling S 62 Wait a sec). These
short forms can hardly be used in other cases, one does
not say: "a few mos after his departure", etc. Yet I
find Bennett ECh 24 only for ten secs | ib 46 I couldn't
come a see quicker.

Stump-words of this class very often have a slangy
character and therefore, at any rate when they first

crop up, are objected to by purists. This is seen in
Swift's ironic remark (PC 17): "The only Invention of
late Years, which hath any way contributed towards
Politeness in Discourse, is that of abbreviating or re-
ducing Words of many Syllables into one, by lopping
off the rest. This Refinement, having begun about the
Time of the Revolution ... I observe, to my great
Satisfaction that it makes daily Advancements, and I
hope in Time will raise our Language to the utmost
Perfection." On p. 32 he returns to the subject and
mentions among "Abbreviations exquisitely refined ...
Pozz for *Positive, Mobb* for *Mobile, Phizz* for *Physiog-
nomy, Rep* for *Reputation, Plenipo* for *Plenipotentiary,
Incog* for *Incognito, Hyppo* or *Hippo* for *Hypocondriacks,
Bam* for *Bamboozle,* and *Bamboozle* for God knows
what."

29.4₂. But, like other slang words, such abbreviations
may in some cases in course of time lose their slangy
character and be more or less accepted into the standard language, often without any feeling of anything
being left out. Thus we have, e. g., *brig* for brigantine,
cab for cabriolet (now differentiated in meaning), *navvy*
for navigator (labourer in canals, on railways, etc.), *fad*
from fadaise, *miss* from mistress, missis (formerly
often = 'kept woman', now = 'unmarried woman'),
hock from hockamore (G *Hochheimer*), *pram* from per-
ambulator, *Jap* from Japanese. In *bike* for bicycle a
consonant group [skl] has been simplified.

A combination of this and the first class of shortenings is found in *canter* for Canterbury trot, *pub* for
public house, *zoo* for Zoological Gardens (spelling-pronunciation!).

29.4₃. Like other slang elements stump-words originate
preferably in small more or less narrowly circum-
scribed sets of people who are in constant communication
with each other. Therefore they will often content
themselves with a mere hint, understanding what is

only half-expressed (On s'entend à demi-mot). Among
such sets we must first consider the narrow family
circle. Here we find numerous abbreviations of Christian
names ('given names, first names'), in which the initial
sounds stand for the whole, e. g. *Al* = Albert or Alfred,
Ben(jamin), *Cis* = Cecil, *Con* = Constance (Goldsm
656), *Deb*(orah), *Ed*(ward), *Fred*(erick), *Gil*(bert), *Nick*
= Nicholas (*Old Nick* = the devil), *Percy* = Percival,
Phil(ip), *Rob*(ert), *Sam*(uel), *Sue* = Susan(na), *Tim*(othy),
Tom = Thomas, *Val*(entine), *Vi*(olet), *Viv*(ian), *Will*-
(iam). The short form of *Diana* is generally spelt *Di*,
but *Dye* in Gay BP 70; *Di* as the name of a dog =
Diogenes (Di Do 158).

In *Abe* for Abraham and *Gabe* for Gabriel it has
been found necessary in writing to add -*e* to avoid
misreading [æb, gæb].

These, with many others, are given with scores of
quotations from old and recent authors, in Sundén's
book together with many forms with the pet ending
-*y*, -*ie*, e. g. *Emmy* for Emilia, Emmeline, *Henny* for
Henrietta, *Susie* for Susan(na), etc., cf *good old Viccy*
= Queen Victoria (Galsw IC 294). Note that names are
shortened in this way with practically no regard to
the place of the stress in the prototype.

29.4₄. Regular shortenings of this kind offer no difficulties. But what about the numerous irregularities?
Sundén is at great pains to classify them and to find
explanations (pp. 172—194). But he does not at all
take into consideration what to my mind is the chief
source, viz. the speech habits of small children. He
seems to look upon all such ellipses as due to formation
(and conscious formation) by grown-up people. But
much is certainly due to the faulty apperception and
imitation of sounds in children. Children in all countries
are fond of repeating the same sound (assimilation
at a distance) and say, e. g. [gɔgi] for *doggie* (*Language*
p. 109). This explains *Bob* for Rob(ert), *Mem* for Em(ily,

etc), *Lell* for Ellen, *Bab* for Barbara, and probably
Pip for Philip (Kennedy R 53). The difficulty of many
children in pronouncing *r* accounts for perversions like
Biddy for Bridget, *Fanny* for Frances, *Meg* for Margaret
(from 15th c.), *Hetta* for Henrietta, and the substitu-
tion of *l* for *r* in *Dol* for Dorothy, *Hal* for Harry, Henry,
Mal for Mary, *Sal* for Sarah. *D* is substituted for *r* in
Dick for Rick, short for Ricard, the old form of Richard.

The addition of initial *n* in *Ned*, *Noll*, *Nam* or *Namby*
for *Ambrose* has long ago been explained by Ch. P. G.
Scott from a misdivision of *Mine Ed* as *My/Ned*, etc.,
just as *Nuncle* (Sh, etc.) for uncle. (Cf, however, Sundén,
p. 218).

But how is *t* in *Ted* for Edward and Edmund to be
explained? From *that Ed* as in *t'other*? And the comparatively frequent *p*'s in *Peg* for *Meg* = Margaret, *Poll* for
Moll, which stands for Mary? It is possible that they
originated in reduplicative forms with *p* in the second
member (above 10.4 *Georgie-Porgie*, etc.): *Meg-Peg*, etc.

With regard to a very small residue of stump-names
we may possibly have recourse to the explanation
given by Sundén under the name *Pseudo-ellipsis*, p.
141 ff.: a pet-name is not really a shortening of a longer
name, but an existing, at first totally distinct short
name that is substituted for a name of similar sound,
thus OE *Hicca* produced *Hick*, which was taken as a
pet-name instead of shortening *Richard (Ricard)*. The
explanation should not be urged too much.

29.45. Family names (surnames) may be shortened
in the same way, the beginning only being kept.
Dr. Johnson was not the only one who "had a way
of contracting the names of his friends, as Beauclere,
Beau; Boswell, *Bozzy:* Langton, *Lanky;* Murphy, *Mur;*
Sheridan, *Sherry;* and Goldsmith, *Goldy*, which Goldsmith resented" (Bosw 1.486). Swift has J 160 the *Vans*
= the Vanhomrighs, Cowper L often the *Trocks* = the
Trockmortons, ib 2.65 *Kitch* = Kitchener; Macaulay is

called *Mac* in Tennyson L 1.115, Fitzgerald, *Fitz* ib
1.211. Thackeray constantly says *Pen* for Arthur
Pendennis, *Cos* for Costigan, *Fo* for Foker, *Pop* for
Popjoy, old *Col* for Colchicum. In the beginning of the
last century Napoleon Bonaparte was generally called
Nap or *Boney;* later we have such shortened names of
public characters as *Dizzy* for Disraeli, *Pam* for Palmer-
ston, *Labby* for Labouchere, etc.

29.4₆. Place-names are not often abridged; Oxford
students speak of the *Char* = Cherwell; we might also
mention the *Cri*(terion, theatre and restaurant in London), the *Pav*(illion, the *Troc*(adero) and the *Vic*(toria
Theatre, ibd); from U. S. I have *Chi*(cago, Dreiser AT
1.172), *Frisco* = San Francisco, *Okey City* (= Oklahoma,
Wilder H 55), *Philly* = Philadelphia (Hammett Th 70).
See further Mencken AL⁴ 542-43. The E names of
shires *Hunts* = Huntingdonshire and *Hants* = Hamp-
shire (note *nt*) are probably due to abbreviations in
writing, cf the established abbreviations of the states
in U. S. *Cal*(ifornia), *Ill*(inois), *Ky* = Kentucky,
etc; also *Ave*(nue).

29.5₁. Here I give a great many examples of *common
names*, distributed according to the class of people
that will use them. I star those which (probably) owe
their origin to written abbreviation, but some of the
others should, perhaps, have had a star too.

Universities, Colleges, Schools.—U. = University
(Lewis B 88, 89; also Ferber S 227) | **Univ.* = Univers-
ity College, Oxford (McKenna SS 103) | **coll.* = college
(Kipling S 131) | *Tech* = Technological Institute (e. g.
Boston Tech, Dine B 37; Carnegie Tech, NP 1936) |
**commem.* = commemoration (Oxf) | *con* = construe |
dic(tionary) | *exam*(ination; only in technical use, not
e. g., in "the policeman's examination of the house") |
hols. = holidays (common) | *matric(ulation) | *mods* =
Moderations (Oxf) | *prep*(aration; Sheriff J (Novel) 6,
22, Kipling S. 28; as a vb Hemingway Sun Also 4 the

military school where he prepped for Princeton) |
priv(ilege; Harrow) | *pun*(ishment) | *rep*(etition, Macken-
zie S 1.190) | *trips* = Tripos (Cambr) | *tu.* = tuition
(Kipling S 166 He's up to his eyes with extra-tu.) |
vac(ation).

arith(metic; Mackenzie S 1.103) | *calc*(ulus) | *chem-*
(istry) | *gym*(nastics) | *logs* = logarithms (Dine B 110
struggling with your logs and antilogs) | *math*(s) =
mathematics (Dine B 115 math; Freeman CT 81 maths)
| *Pol Econ* = Political Economy | *Psyk* = Psycho-
logy | *prop*(osition, in mathematics) | *Greek *Test*(ament;
Mackenzie S 1.224) | *trig*(onometry).

ag(ricultural student) | *barb*(arian; U.S., not belong-
ing to a fraternity, Lewis MA 21) | *co-ed* = 'girl or
woman student at co-educational institution' (NED
Suppl; Lewis MS 3, Ferber S 241) | *deac*(on) | *doc*(tor,
common also for physician) | *frat*(ernity; U. S., Ferber
S 236) | *grad*(uate; *undergrad*) | *opt*(imus 'top boy') |
pess(imus 'boy at the bottom of the class') | *plebe*(ian
'freshman' U. S.) | *prof*(essor) | *res*(ident teacher, living
in college) | *Rug*(by boy, Brett Young PC 661) | *soph-*
(omore; U. S.).

digs = diggings (McKenna SS 84) | *dorm*(itory;
Sherriff J (Novel) 23) | *gym*(nasium; Kipling S 17 Said
to me in the Gym last night ...) | *lab*(oratory, com-
mon) | *lav*(atory, Mackenzie S 1.99) | *libe* = library |
quad(rangle) | *rec*(reation ground).

29.5₂. *Law, etc.—admors* = administrators (Brynild-
sen) | *con*(vict; Hammett Th 239 ex-con) | *crim. con.*
= criminal conversation | *pen*(itentiary) | *pro*(fessional;
detective McKenna Ninety 131, criminal common) |
pro and con(tra); the contrast best brought out by two
monosyllables | *Super*(intendent; common) | *sus*(pend-
atur) *per col*(lum).

29.5₃. *The Medical World.—consump*(tive; Galsw Frat
127 [young doctor:] loafers, drunkards, consumps) |
dill = delirium tremens | *dip*(hteria) | *doc*(tor) | *hip* or

hyp = hypocondria | *hydro*(pathic establishment) |
hypo(dermic syringe; Lewis B 363, Cronin C 241, etc) |
medic(al student; U. S., Lewis MS 28, id MA passim) |
san(atorium; ONeill Straw 166) | *temp*(erature, ib 144) |
vet(eran; Hemingway Have and Have Not 198) | *vet*-
(erinary surgeon, Rose Macaulay T 285 vetting or
farming, ib 301 why a vet?—also as a vb = 'subject to
medical treatment', e.g. Wells OH 526, Christie ABC 9).

29.5₄. *Theatres, etc.*—*cine* = *cinema*(tograph, Galsw
EC 852 until cine-cameras are installed in bedrooms) |
mike = microphone | *panto*(mime, Mackenzie C 215,
369) | *pop*(ular concert) | *pro*(fessional actor, Merrick
MG 3) | *prom*(enade concert or dance) | *props* = (1)
stage properties, (2) property man | *rep* = répertoire
(Priestley G 283 Each member of the troupe prided
himself or herself on having a large répertoire, known
always as a "rep") | *sink* = synchronize the moving
picture and the sound record (Paget Babel 90) | *strad*-
(ivarius) | *supe* (U. S.) = *super*(numerary (actor),
Jerome Idle Ideas 191) | *uke* = ukulele (Mencken AL⁴
585 tickle a uke).

29.5₅. *Army and Navy.*—*Adj* = adjutant (Mottram
EM 141) | *cap*(tain) | *loot* = lieutenant (Mencken AL⁴
169) | *non-com.* = non-commissioned officer (Kipling
MI 273) | *sub*(altern) | *conshy* (Beresford R 101), *conchy,
conchie* (Salt, Seventy Years Am. Sav. 225) = con-
scientious objector || *tar*(paulin) 'old sailor' || *demob*(ilize,
esp. in the second ptc, thus Galsw TL 86, Kaye Smith
HA 9, Brett Young PC 794) | *ammo* = ammunition,
and other words in *-o* see 13.8₁.

29.5₆. *Journalists and Printers.*—**ad*(vertisement; according to Mencken AL⁴ 170 used in compounds such
as *ad-writer, want-ad, display-ad, ad-rate* and *ad-man;*
Priestley G 325 has the form *adverts*) | **caps* = capital
letters | **mag*(azine) | **par*(agraph) | **quotes* = quota-
tion-marks | *steno* or *stenog*(rapher, Lewis B 41 a good

stenog; also used as a vb, OHenry B 92 to stenog) |
typo(grapher).

29.5₇. *Sports.*—*champ*(ion, U. S., Quentin P 26 ex-
champ) | *prelim*(inary fight (at a boxing-match), U. S.) |
pro(fessional player, golfer, etc, Mackenzie S 1.408,
NJacob Lie 179) | *pug*(ilist) | *scrum*(mage, in Rugby
football) | *tote* = totalisator. Cf *footer*, *soccer*, *rugger*
above 14.2₈.

29.5₈. *Money.*—**consols* = consolidated securities |
divvy = dividend or divide (Frankau Dance 218 And
now, old son, what about divvying up the swag?) |
exes = expenses (Merrick MG 233, etc) | *mon*(ey, U. S.
only?, not in Partridge) | *sal*(ary) | *sov*(ereign) | *spec*-
(ulation, Kipling S 138) | *thou*(sand, Galsw IC 15, etc) |
tick(et) 'credit'.

Outside the Above Categories

29.6₁. *Persons.*—*Aussies* = Australians (Lawrence
Kang. 27) | *bach*(elor, Lewis MS 115, also as a vb,
e. g. Maugham Pl 2.257 a couple of Englishmen who
were baching) | *Bolshy* = Bolshevist (Galsw P 11.7,
ib 56 I believe things are really going Bolshy, Lawrence
Kang. 1), also *Bolo* in army slang, cf -o 13.8₁ | *con-man*
= confidence man (Hart BT 87) | *coz.* = cousin, also
'friend, nephew', found in Sh, Marlowe Massacre at
Paris 983 sweet Cuz; Ford 143 my worthy coz, i. e.
nephew; now obs. | *cuss* 'fellow' from customer | *demirep*-
(utable, already in Swift, Fielding) | *demo*(crat; Galsw
WM 3 in days that knew not Demos) | *fan*(atic, especi-
ally used in compounds: *football fan*, *film fan*, *a film
star's fan mail*) | **gent*(leman, Storm EPh 571 NED
from 1564, now vg and rare) | *guv* 'father, employer'
from governor | *hub*(by) = husband | *Lib-Labs* =
Liberal Labour (members) | *mutt*(onhead, U.S., Mencken
AL⁴ 169) | *plenipo*(tentiary, old, 18th c.) | *plute* =
plutocrat (U. S.) | *rads* = radicals | *rebs* = rebels

(Churchill C 271) | *simp*(leton, Lewis MS 389, Wallace Green Archer 273) | *wiz*(ard, Lewis MS 24, id B 271, Tracy 163) | *Yank*(ee, Galsw MW 16).

29.6₂. Names of *animals* are rarely shortened: *chimp*-(anzee, Lewis MA 449) | *croc*(odile) | *hippo*(potamus) | *rhino*(ceros).—Two kinds of dogs: *Peke* = Pekinese (Galsw SS 5, id WM 176) | *pom* = Pomeranian dog (Rose Macaulay T 138, Maugham Pl 2.322).

29.6₃. *Things, etc.—Eatables and drinkables, etc:* *choc*(olate, only of lumps for eating, not of the drink, Shaw G 108), also *chokky* (Wells JP 115) | *cig*(arette, common) | *coke* = cocaine | *grog*(ram, cf. Language 308) | *sham* = champagne (Wells Kipps 673) | *strawbs* = strawberries | *veg*(e)s = vegetables.

Words in -o: *auto*(mobile, esp. U. S., not frequent in Brit. E except in compounds: *autobus, taxi-autos*) | *chromo*(lithograph, Locke W 6) | *curio*(osity) | *dynamo*-(-electric machine) | *electro*(type, Freeman Th 708) | *lino*(leum, Bentley O 217 lino-covered stairs) | *loco*-(motive) | *photo*(graph) | *piano*(forte). Cf. 13.8₁.

Cami(sole; Rose Macaulay K 86 cami-knickers,— with double shortening) | *daff*(odil, Sayers NT 65) | *flex*(ible wire, not in NED; Bennett LM 120) | *gas*(oline, U. S.) | *mack* = mackintosh (Sherriff F 152) | *mag*(neto, Sayers HC 385) | *mem*(o) = memorandum | *pam* 'knave of clubs' from *pamphile* | *pants* = pantaloons | *pic*(ture, Kipling L 77) | *roddy* = rhododendron | *sharry* = charabanc; written *sharrer* Sayers NT 106 | *specs* = spectacles | *sub* = subsidy or subsistence (Priestley G 247, 275), also subscription (Mackenzie S 836) and as a vb, esp. *sub up* 'subscribe' (Bird R 11, 275) | *tarmac*-(adam, *tarmac roads*) | *turps* = turpentine (Sayers GN 124) | *zep* = Zeppelin.

Note the writing *the L* = *the El* = elevated railway (U. S.).

29.6₄. *Abstracts.—bunk* = bunkum, buncombe 'non-sense' (orig. U. S., cf Language 409) | *cert*(ainty, com-

mon) | *circs* = circumstances (Galsw, Wells, Ridge, etc) |
confab(ulation, Keats 4.137) | *congrats* = congratula-
tions (By Corresp 292, etc) | *diff*(erence) | *i*(dea, Lewis
B 145) | *intro*(duction, Pennell L 51, Priestley G 515) |
pash = passion (Sayers UD 83, Christie 3A 39, orig. U.S.) |
posish = position (Mackenzie C 203, a dancer speaking) |
rep(utation, Swift (above), Lewis B 72; see *demirep*
above 29.6$_1$).

29.6₅. *Adjectives* are not often abbreviated, the most
usual is *comfy* = comfortable (Galsw F 451, Master-
man WL 147). I have further noted: *awk*(ward, Galsw
Sw 25) | *co-op*(erative, Lawrence SL 90) | *imposs*(ible,
Galsw WM 69, Bennett L 151) | *incog* (NED from
1700) | *pi*(ous, chiefly in schools, AHuxley EG 63).

29.6₆. *Verbs.*—Abbreviated vbs are rare, except those
formed from shortened nouns, e. g. *zep*(pelin, Locke
H 83 So you've been Zepped). Note Mannin W 20
Miss Graham's hair is what is known as '*permed*' (=
permanent-waved) | *tot up* 'sum up' from *total*.

Middle Retained

29.7. Very few words are shortened in the way that
both beginning and end are left out and only a middle
part is kept. I suspect that *taters* (*taties*) for potatoes
and *tec* for detective have arisen from a rapid pronunciation in which the first vowel was syncopated
(*p'tatoes, d'tective*), and a similar explanation applies to
Liz (*Lizzy*) for Elizabeth and probably to *Milly* or
Meely for Amelia. Among proper names we have the
rare *Fy* for Seraphima and *Tave* for Octavia. Outside
proper names we have *flu* from influenza (where neither
the beginning nor the end would be likely as stump-
words; *flu* is found, e. g. Mackenzie PR 251, Lawrence
L 101, Lewis MS 431). *Polly* for apollinaris is due to
association with the familiar feminine name.

What Koziol § 674 calls *Ausfall von mittelsilben* (*fancy* for phantasy, *frenzy* for phrenesie, etc.) does not belong in this chapter: the phenomenon is purely phonetic, see vol I 9.91.

End Retained

29.8₁. As already remarked the natural way of shortening words for those who are familiar with the full word is to keep the beginning. If, therefore, the end is retained, we must look for a special explanation.

First we have some instances of back-formation. The prefix *a-* has been subtracted in (*a*)*back*, etc, see above 27.3₂ and vol II 14.1 (esp. 14.18; on *alone* and *alive* see also ib the preceding sections).

See Slettengren, *Aphæretic Words* and Western in *A Gramm. Miscellany to O.J.*, p. 133 ff.

Even apart from the metanalysis implied in back-formation many unstressed initial syllables tend to disappear; pretty often both forms still exist; in others only the short form has subsisted. Examples: *amend* > *mend* | *attend* > *tend* | *apprentice* > *prentice* | *apply* > *ply* | *appeal* > *peal* | *affray* > *fray* | *avantgarde* > *vanguard*.

Further:

defend > *fend, defence* > *fence, despite* > *spite* || *espy* > *spy* | *esquire* > *squire* || *envy* > *vie* || *example* > *sample* || *disport* > *sport* | *distain* > *stain*.

In all these cases a differentiation has taken place, the short word meaning something different from the long one, see Bradley M 151 f. Similarly *story* as the more familiar word is now different from *history* as the more dignified word.

A weak prefix has also been dropped in *drawing-room* from *withdrawing-room*, the old form still (as an archaism?) in Galsw Ca 685. Dekker G 45 and BJo 2.568 have *withdrawing-chamber*.

Cf also such forms as '*cause* = *because,* '*cept* = *except,*

'stead of = *instead of*, etc, which may be heard in rapid
slovenly speech.

In compounds the end-member is rarely used alone,
as in the occasional *leg* for *blackleg* (Sundén 37). The
'house for *workhouse* (Galsw Ca 214) is a euphemism.

29.8₂. In some cases it is obvious why the shortening
has gone this way; *telephone* could only be made into
phone, as *tele* might stand for *telegraph;* similarly *concertina* becomes *teena,* and we have *skeeto, skeeter* for
mosquito.

But why *bus* < *omnibus, coon* < *racoon, davy* <
affidavit, loo < *lanterloo, van* < *caravan* (altered sense),
and *wig* from the old *periwig* = *peruke?*

At Shrewsbury the boys say *strue* for *construe* (also
as a sb; at other schools *con,* see above 29.5₁.), at Amr
universities *scope* may be heard for *microscope. The
'Varsity* is common for *the University* in England.

When soldiers say *'tion* (*'shun*) for *Attention!* (Barrie
Echoes 55) it is the last syllable of a forcibly shouted
command that is isolated.

29.8₃. Some of the above-mentioned examples may
in the first instance be due to small children's imperfect
imitation of the full form. It is a fact mentioned by
students of children's language that small children often
will repeat the fag-end of a long string of syllables which
they have only partially understood; see my *Language*
108: *tash* for *moustache, nanas* and *jamas* for *bananas*
and *pyjamas.* Many Danish examples of children's
repetition of the end of a sentence or a word are given
in my book on children's speech (the latest edition
Sproget 1941 p. 25 f., 144 f.). El. Wittmann mentions
(p. 117) children's shortenings, like *beel* for *automobile;*
curiously enough this form coincides with the Scandinavian word *bil,* which resulted from the Danish
newspaper *Politiken's* inquiry as to the best short expression for *automobil.*

At any rate we have here the obvious explanation

of the frequency of pet-forms of Christian names in
which the end only is preserved, such as *Bella* or *Belle* for
Isabella, *Belle* for Christabel or Isabel, *Bert* or *Bertie*
for Albert, Herbert, or Hubert, *Cora* for Glencora,
Dolf for Adolf or Rudolf, *Drew* for Andrew, *Duke* for
Marmaduke, *Etta* for Henrietta, *Gar* for Edgar, *Lena*
for Carolina, *Lottie* for Charlotte, *Milly* for Emily,
Nestie for Ernest, *Nora* for Eleanor(a), *Rona* or *Rone*
for Verona, *Sandy* for Alexander, *Tiny* for Clementina,
Tony for Anthony, *Tory* for Victoria, and *Val* for
Percival.

Irregularities in renderings of the end of a name are
here (as above 29.4₄) to be explained from small
children's mispronunciation, thus *Bet* (*Betty*) or *Bess* or
Betsy, also *Tetty* or *Tetsy* for Elizabeth: [þ] is a difficult
sound, *Mun* for Edmund, *Netta* for Henrietta, and *Totty*
for Charlotte.

It is worth noting that surnames are not shortened
in this way.

General Remarks

29.8₄. In this account of the various shortenings I
have intentionally refrained from dividing them into
those made consciously or intentionally and those made
by inadvertence: the two categories cannot always in
this domain be kept apart. But many of the clipped
words are whimsical, jocular, or even consciously
humorous.

Stress, of course, plays some role in deciding what to
leave out and what to retain, but on the whole its
role is here surprisingly small. Both in the first, greater,
class, in which the beginning, and in the last, smaller
one, in which the end is kept, we find numerous examples
of stressed syllables omitted and unstressed ones retained.

The curtailments considered in this chapter have
parallels in other languages, but are probably nowhere

quite so numerous as in PE and in fact constitute one
of the most characteristic traits in the development of
the English language in its recent stage. And it is in
accordance with my often expressed view on linguistic
development in general if I end here by saying that
these shortenings *on the whole* have made and are making
for progress in linguistic efficiency: the short crisp,
energetic forms are easier to handle than the original
long and cumbersome ones, in which much was really
superfluous for the purpose of being understood by
others.

Appendix to Chapter XXIX
Alphabetic Shortenings

29.9₁. In connexion with shortenings we shall here
consider the use of initial letters (read as in reading
the alphabet) standing for whole words. Some of these
are old-established, such as the names of some dignit-
aries: *M. P.* [em piˑ] = Member of Parliament, *K. C.*
or *Q. C.* = King's Counsel or Queen's Counsel, *M. A.*
= master of arts, *B. A.* = bachelor of arts, *D. D.*
= Doctor of Divinity, *LL. D.* = legum doctor, *P. M.*
= Prime Minister (Bennett LR). Further the time-
indications *a. m.* = ante meridiem, *p. m.* = post
meridiem (N.B. Latin!). And names of business-firms
or societies: *A. B. C.* = Aerated Bread Company,
Y. M. C. A. = Young Men's Christian Association
(abbreviated *the Y* [wai]); *P. & O.* = Peninsula (i. e.
Spain and Portugal) and Orient (Shipping Company,
cf Waugh BM 218 shipped to Southampton by the first
P. & O.; the steamers of this company are said to be
called *piano boats*); *A. A.* = Automobile Association
(hence an *A. A. man* a road mender); *O. U. D. S.* =
Oxford Union Dramatic Society; *G. P. O.* = General
Post Office, and others. A long list in Mencken AL⁴
208 ff. Cf also *W. C.* = water closet.

The initials *U. S.* (*U. S. Am.*) = the United States
(of America) has been facetiously interpreted as *Uncle
Sam.*—*O. K.* which is frequently said in England as
well as in U. S., is variously interpreted, see Mencken
AL⁴.

L. s. d. = money (libra, shilling, solidus, denarius).

We must mention also the facetious *p. d. q.* = pretty
damn quick; what the *bee aitch* are they all about?
(Galsw Sw 51; = *B. H.* = bloody hell); *n. g.* = no
good; *on the q. t.* = on the quiet.

29.9₂. Sometimes the initials are read together as
regular words. This became the fashion during the first
world war, when the pronunciation *Dora* [dɔ·rə] of the
unpopular *D*efence *O*f *R*ealm *A*ct became popular,
and similarly *Waac* [wa·k] = *W*omen's *A*rmy *A*ux-
iliary *C*orps, *Wrens* [renz] = *W*omen's *R*oyal *N*avy
*S*ervice; *Anzac* [ænzæk] = *A*ustralian-*N*ew *Z*ealand
*A*rmy *C*orps. Whether similar words have come into
existence during the second world war I am cut off
from knowing.

G. O. M. = the *G*rand *O*ld *M*an (Gladstone) was
read as [gɔm] and used as a nickname for a stubborn
Conservative.

Cf *Yipsel* = Y[oung] P[eople's] S[ocialist] L[eague]
(Alphonso Smith, *New Words* 212).

LIST OF VERBS TREATED IN CHS. IV & V.

General Index

For verbs treated in Chs. IV and V see list on pp. 553—555.

A.

a- + sb or vb 7.5₁, negative 26.2₅, from *on*, etc. 27.3₁-₃.

Ablaut 11.2.

-*able* 22.6, spelling 22.6₂, added to verbal phrases 22.6₃, synonymous with -*ible* 22.6₅.

abode : *abide* 11.2₁.

about face! 7.6₅.

-*ac(al)* 22.4.

accordingly 22.9₃.

ache 12.5₂.

-*ad* 24.2₁.

-*ade* 24.2₂.

Adjective before genitive-compounds 16.9₅, with -*n*, as adjunct 20.4. Cf. Compounds.

Adjuncts 5.5₁, 5.7₂, verbal stems as, 7.3₄.

Adverb in -*ly* 22.8-9, from ptc. 4.2₂, 5.7₂.

advice : *advise* 12.4₃.

after in compounds 9.4₂.

-*age* 24.3.

Agent-substantives, = vbs 7.1₂, in -*er*, -*or*, -*our* 14.1, in -*ant*, -*ent* 21.6.

-*aire* 14.1₂, 15.4₃.

-*al*, in adjs 22.1, -*ual*, -*ial*,

-*eal* 22.1₃, in sbs 22.2, nexus-sb 22.2₂-₃.

all in compounds 9.5₂.

Alphabetic shortenings 29.9₁.

Amerindians 29.2₂.

amoral 26.1₇.

an- 26.2₅.

-*an* 21.1.

ana- 28.1₄.

-*ana* 21.3₂.

-*ance*, -*ancy* 21.6₃-₅.

ancestor 14.1₄.

-*ancy* 21.6₃-₅.

-*ane* 21.3₁.

-*ant* 21.6₁-₂.

ante- 27.8₄.

anti- 26.7₁-₂.

Aphesis 27.3, 29.8₁.

Apophony chs. IV, V, 11.2.

Apostrophe in genitive 16.1₃, 16.8.

apple-John 8.3.

Apposition, group-genitive 17.1₂-₅.

Appositional compounds 8.2₁, 8.5.

-*ar* in agent-sbs 14.1₄, in sbs & adjs 15.4₁.

arch- 28.8₁.

archi- 28.8₂.

archie 13.4₄.
-archy 25.5₂.
-ard 15.9₁₋₂.
argument sb > vb > sb 7.4₁.
-arian 21.2.
-art 15.9₁₋₂.
-ary 15.8₁.
ashen 20.4₂.
-ate in vb and adj 4.4₃, substantival derivative 24.8₁, verbal derivative 24.8₂.
-ation 21.7.
-ative 25.2₄.
auto- 28.6₅.

B.

Bab 29.4₄.
baby 13.4₅.
bachelor 14.1₄.
Back-formations 29.3, 29.8₁; in sbs = vbs 6.8₂, 6.8₅, 7.5₁; from words in *-y* 13.4₉, from words in *-ese* 13.6₅, *roam* 14.3₂, type *housekeep* 14.3₉, from words in *-s* 16.7₄, in *-ate* 24.8₂.
Bahuvrihi-compounds 8.2₁, 8.6.
Bakerloo 29.2₂.
band (bond) : *bind* 11.2₁.
bare : *barely* 22.9₁.
batch : *bake* 12.5₁.
bath : *bathe* 12.3₁.
be- 28.1₁₋₃.
beacon : *beckon* 11.6.
beano 13.8₁.
bedridden 5.7₅, 20.1₆.
beechen 20.4₂.
beef : *beeves* 16.2₅.
behave 4.8₁.
-behaved 24.1₁₃.

behaviour 14.5₂.
behoof : *behove* 12.2₁.
belief : *believe* 12.2₃, 11.3₇.
beside(s) 18.1₄.
bespoke 5.3₅.
Bess 29.8₃.
Bet, Betsy, Betty 29.8₃.
between in compounds 9.4₂.
bi- 28.5₁.
Biddy 29.4₄.
billy 13.4₄.
birchen 20.4₂.
bit : *bite* 11.2₁.
black(en) 20.5₇.
-ble 22.6, synonyms in *-able* and *-ible* 22.6₅.
bleak 11.3₅, *bleak* : *bleach* 12.5₃.
blind adj > vb > sb 7.4₃, vb 11.2₃.
blood : *bleed* 11.5₁.
Bob, bobby 29.4₄, 13.4₄.
bolt sb > vb > sb 7.4₁.
bonnie 13.3₆.
bookie 13.4₆.
boot : *beet* 11.5₁.
bowyer 14.5₁.
brass : *braze* 12.4₁.
brazen 20.4₂.
brazier 14.5₁.
breach : *break* 12.5₁.
breath : *breathe* 12.3₂.
breathy 13.3₅.
brekker 14.2₃.
brethren 11.1₂, 20.2₃.
bridal 22.2₄.
bridle sb & vb 11.6.
brief : *briefly* 22.9₁.
broad adj & vb 11.3₅; *broaden* 20.5₃.
brolly 13.4₆.
brood : *breed* 11.5₁.